Integrated Marketing Communications

Integrated Marketing Communications

FOURTH EDITION **STRATEGIC PLANNING PERSPECTIVES** KEITH J. TUCKWELL

St. Lawrence College

Pearson Canada
Toronto

Vice-President, Editorial Director: Gary Bennett
Editor-in-Chief: Michelle Sartor
Acquisitions Editor: Deana Sigut
Marketing Manager: Leigh-Anne Graham
Developmental Editor: Madhu Ranadive
Project Manager: Richard di Santo
Production Editor: Munesh Kumar, Aptara®, Inc.
Copy Editor: Carolyn Zapf
Proofreader: Susan Bindernagel
Compositor: Aptara®, Inc.
Photo Researcher: Heather Jackson
Permissions Researcher: Heather Jackson
Art Director: Zena Denchik
Cover and Interior Designer: Anthony Leung
Cover Image: Fotolia

Credits and acknowledgments for material borrowed from other sources and reproduced, with permission, in this textbook appear on the appropriate page within the text.

10 9 8 7 6 5 4 3   [EBM]

Library and Archives Canada Cataloguing in Publication

Tuckwell, Keith J. (Keith John), 1950-, author
   Integrated marketing communications : strategic planning
perspectives/Keith J. Tuckwell, St. Lawrence College.—Fourth edition.
Includes bibliographical references and index.
ISBN 978-0-13-315787-1 (pbk.)
   1. Communication in marketing—Textbooks. I. Title.
HF5415.123.T82 2013   658.8'02   C2013-906142-8

ISBN 978-0-13-315787-1

PEARSON

To Esther...and our children, Marnie, Graham, and Gordon

Brief Contents

Contents

PART 2   PLANNING FOR INTEGRATED MEDIA   97

Preface

Teachers face many challenges in the classroom. It is difficult to get students to read a textbook; multicultural classrooms present language problems; and it is often hard to cover course material in the time allotted. This textbook is designed to conquer these problems. My primary goal is to present essential elements of integrated marketing communications in a clear, concise, and informative manner. Many students who have read previous editions comment that this book is an "enjoyable" book to read!

Keeping content current in such a rapidly changing environment is a constant challenge. The impact of new technologies makes it difficult for educators and practitioners to keep pace. The shift to digital communications is occurring rapidly, and it is presenting both challenges and opportunities for advertisers and their marketing communications agencies. Striking the right balance among the communications options is the primary task of the marketing communications agencies responsible for making recommendations to their clients. In such a rapidly changing environment, teachers and students must recognize that presenting the latest information in a textbook is difficult. I have done my very best to ensure that the content in this book is as up to date as possible. The core content and the strategic planning principles included here reflect contemporary practice.

From a teaching perspective, textbook readability has always been an issue with me. Readability is a primary strength of *Integrated Marketing Communications: Strategic Planning Perspectives*. The book is written in a straightforward, easy-to-understand manner and is full of examples and illustrations that students will quickly identify with. If you accept the notion that being familiar with something makes it easier to understand and apply, then your students will be better equipped to develop a marketing communications plan once they have read this book.

Most courses in marketing communications are one semester (14 to 15 weeks) in length with only 45 to 60 course hours available for teaching. You will find the format of this textbook ideal for such a course. The **primary strength** of this book is that it is truly a marketing communications book. It is not an advertising book with additional chapters devoted to integrated marketing communications (IMC) content. This book offers balance across the various components of marketing communications. Current users of the book have identified **other strengths,** which are:

- It is the only Canadian IMC book available, and features a Canadian perspective on media and marketing communications practice instead of an American one.

- There is an emphasis on strategic planning, with a separate chapter devoted to the subject as well as discussion throughout the text. The concept of "integration" is stressed and demonstrated continually.

- The lead-in chapter on branding is a natural starting point for marketing communications planning, since all plans start with a sound understanding of the brand.

- There is ample discussion of recent trends and issues facing the industry, identifying the challenges faced by practitioners.

- It is the only text on the market offering an illustration of a strategic plan, which demonstrates how an organization applies planning principles and concepts.
- Material is presented in an "easy-to-understand" writing style—practical, friendly, and student-oriented.

The textbook includes four parts and 12 core chapters that cover all aspects of integrated marketing communications. A common planning model is presented in relevant chapters that binds the various components of marketing communications together. Each chapter includes at least two **IMC Highlight boxes** that show how organizations apply marketing communications concepts. Approximately 70 percent of these boxes are new.

Appendix 1 offers information about how to plan and buy media time, and is an ideal supplement to all media-related chapters. **Appendix 2** presents an integrated marketing communications plan, something you will not find in any other textbook.

Some of the key issues and trends addressed in this edition of the text include:

- The integration of long-term strategic plans (all primary forms of media and marketing communications) with short-term tactical plans (experiential, event, and public relations tactics).
- The shift in control of brands and marketing communications from the marketer to the customer, a process referred to as brand democratization.
- The constantly changing consumers' media habits, which create a dynamic situation that presents new challenges and opportunities for reaching target markets.
- The impact of new technologies, which are changing the communications playing field and producing new opportunities for reaching consumers more directly through mobile devices, social media, and video games.
- The influence of database management techniques and customer relationship management programs on the direction of marketing communications strategies, moving them away from macro-based (mass appeal or traditional forms of targeting) toward micro-based (individual targeting).
- The expanding role of experiential marketing, public relations, mobile communications, and social media communications, and the presentation of new insights into this trend.

Organization of the Text

The book is divided into four essential parts.

PART 1: UNDERSTANDING INTEGRATED MARKETING COMMUNICATIONS

This section presents an overview of essential inputs that a manager would consider when developing a marketing communications plan. The content included in Chapter 1, Integrated Marketing Communications: An Overview, introduces the various components of the marketing communications mix and summarizes the essential concepts dealing with consumer behaviour and organizational behaviour. The chapter also discusses many of the ethical issues associated with the practice of marketing communications, content added for this edition.

Chapter 2, Strategic Planning Principles, shifts the focus to strategic planning. Relationships are drawn between plans and planning at various levels of an organization and how they are integrated. The structure and content of a marketing plan and a marketing communications plan are examined in order to show how plans work together to resolve marketing problems.

Chapter 3, Branding Strategy, introduces the concept of branding and branding strategy. Discussion about branding is strategically located in the textbook to precede detailed coverage of the components of the marketing communications mix. Branding strategies and brand positioning strategies are the foundation upon which marketing communications strategies are devised.

PART 2: PLANNING FOR INTEGRATED MEDIA

This section examines planning considerations for all primary media choices. Chapter 4, Advertising Planning: Creative, introduces the communications process and the various planning concepts that are considered when briefing an agency about message requirements. The role of strategies and tactics—and the distinctions between them and creative objectives—is considered. Chapter 5, Advertising Planning: Broadcast, Print, and Out-of-Home Media, presents the media planning process and stresses the importance of creating an effective yet efficient media plan. The various strategic decisions that apply to using broadcast, print, and out-of-home media alternatives are presented in detail.

Chapter 6, Planning for Direct Response Communications, introduces the rapidly expanding field of direct response communications. Since direct response relies on database management techniques, there is considerable emphasis on customer relationship management practices and the key role played by individualized marketing communications strategies in fostering solid customer relationships.

Chapter 7, Planning for Online and Interactive Communications, examines the expanding role of web-based communications, mobile communications, and social media communications in the marketing communications mix. The chapter offers expanded coverage of all forms of interactive communications.

PART 3: PLANNING FOR INTEGRATED MARKETING

Because organizations look for synergy, the objective is to integrate related marketing and marketing communications practices with the media strategies already presented in the book. Chapter 8, Sales Promotion, introduces the various sales promotion alternatives that are frequently employed in integrated marketing communications plans. The roles of consumer promotions and trade promotions are examined in detail. Chapter 9, Public Relations, examines the role of public relations in communications. The content focuses on the various strategies and tactics that are available, planning procedures, and measurement techniques.

Chapter 10, Experiential Marketing, Events, and Sponsorships, examines the expanding role of experiential marketing, event marketing, and sponsorships in contemporary marketing. It introduces the criteria for participating in events, and the steps and procedures for planning an event. Chapter 11, Personal Selling, covers the role of personal selling in a variety of business settings. Personal selling adds a human component to the integrated marketing communications mix, and for this reason plays a very important role in establishing and building solid customer relationships.

PART 4: MEASURING PLAN PERFORMANCE

This section examines the role of various research procedures for evaluating the effectiveness of marketing communications programs. Chapter 12, Evaluating Marketing Communications Programs, introduces some fundamental methodologies for collecting and analyzing primary research data, and distinguishes between qualitative and quantitative data. The role and influence of collecting and interpreting information on the development of marketing communications strategies are considered.

Additional Content

Each chapter includes at least two **IMC Highlight boxes.** These short inserts reflect important aspects of marketing communications planning or provide actual illustrations of how organizations apply marketing communications concepts. Among the featured organizations and brands are familiar names such as McDonald's, Scotiabank, Hyundai, Red Bull, BMW, Mountain Equipment Co-op, Nissan, Durex, Canadian Tire, Mark's, and Maple Leaf Foods.

Appendix 1, Media Buying Principles and Media Information Resources, is a supplement that provides additional media details and shows students some fundamental procedures for estimating costs and buying media time and space in a variety of media and other components of the marketing communications mix. Students can quickly refer to media-buying information in this specific section of the book. Review questions will challenge the students to understand and apply rate card information.

Appendix 2, Integrated Marketing Communications Plan: Mr. Sub, provides an example of a marketing communications plan so that students can quickly see the relationship between various planning principles such as objectives, strategies, and execution, and between the various components of the marketing communications mix with respect to how each contributes to achieving objectives. No other textbook offers an illustrative marketing communications plan.

Pedagogy

Learning Objectives. Each chapter starts with a list of learning objectives directly related to the key concepts contained in the chapter.

Advertisements, Figures, and Charts. Throughout each chapter, key concepts and applications are illustrated with strong visual material. Sample advertisements and other forms of marketing communications augment the Canadian perspective and demonstrate key aspects of marketing communications strategy and execution.

Key Terms. Key terms are highlighted in boldface in the text and in colour in page margins, where they are accompanied by definitions. Students also have quick access to key terms and definitions in the glossary at the end of the book.

Chapter Summaries. The summary at the end of each chapter reinforces major points and concepts.

Review Questions, and Discussion and Application Questions. Both sets of questions allow students to review material and apply concepts learned in the chapter.

Appendix 1, Media Buying Principles and Media Information Resources. The essentials of buying media time and space in various media outlets are covered in this section. Review questions that test students' understanding of and ability to apply rate card information are included.

Appendix 2, Integrated Marketing Communications Plan: Mr. Sub. This plan shows how various elements of marketing communications combine to form an integrated marketing communications plan. A variety of charts and figures are included to show how media and marketing communications budget allocations are presented in a plan.

Glossary. A glossary of all key terms and definitions appears at the end of the textbook.

Supplements

INSTRUCTOR'S RESOURCE MANUAL

The Instructor's Resource Manual includes learning objectives, chapter highlights that can act as lecture outlines, additional illustrations of key concepts that can be built into lectures, and answers to review and discussion questions.

MYTEST

MyTest from Pearson Education Canada is a powerful assessment generation program that helps instructors easily create and print quizzes, tests, exams, as well as homework or practice handouts. Questions and tests can all be authored online, allowing instructors ultimate flexibility and the ability to efficiently manage assessments at anytime, from anywhere. The MyTest for Integrated Marketing Communications, Fourth Edition contains over 1000 questions in multiple choice, true/false, short answer and essay formats.

POWERPOINT® SLIDES

A complete set of slides that are specifically designed or culled from the textbook is available electronically. Full-colour versions of ads, photos, and figures from the textbook, found in the Image Library, can be inserted into your presentations.

IMAGE LIBRARY

The Image Library contains various full-colour images from the textbook such as photos, ads, and figures. Instructors can integrate these images in their own presentations.

COURSESMART FOR INSTRUCTORS

CourseSmart goes beyond traditional expectations—providing instant, online access to the textbooks and course materials you need at a lower cost for students. And even as students save money, you can save time and hassle with a digital eTextbook that allows you to search for the most relevant content at the very moment you need it. Whether it's evaluating textbooks or creating lecture notes to help students with difficult concepts, CourseSmart can make life a little easier. See how when you visit www.coursesmart. com/instructors.

COURSESMART FOR STUDENTS

CourseSmart goes beyond traditional expectations—providing instant, online access to the textbooks and course materials you need at an average savings of 60%. With instant access from any computer and the ability to search your text, you'll find the content you need quickly, no matter where you are. And with online tools like highlighting and note-taking, you can save time and study efficiently. See all the benefits at www.coursesmart. com/students.

TECHNOLOGY SPECIALISTS

Pearson's Technology Specialists work with faculty and campus course designers to ensure that Pearson technology products, assessment tools, and online course materials are tailored to meet your specific needs. This highly qualified team is dedicated to helping schools take full advantage of a wide range of educational resources, by assisting in the integration of a variety of instructional materials and media formats. Your local Pearson Education sales representative can provide you with more details on this service program.

PEARSON CUSTOM LIBRARY

For enrollments of at least 25 students, you can create your own textbook by choosing the chapters that best suit your own course needs. To begin building your custom text, visit www.pearsoncustomlibrary.com. You may also work with a dedicated Pearson Custom editor to create your ideal text—publishing your own original content or mixing and matching Pearson content. Contact your local Pearson representative to get started.

Acknowledgments

Many organizations and individuals have contributed to the development of this book. I would like to sincerely thank the following organizations for their cooperation and contribution:

AP Images
BBM Analytics
BMO Bank of Montreal
Boston Pizza
Canadian Breast Cancer Foundation
Canadian Curling Association
Canadian Geographic Enterprises
Canadian Tire Corporation, Limited
Capstone Communications Group
CBC
CBC (CBHT) Halifax
CBS Outdoor Canada
Chris Woods
Chrysler Group
Colgate-Palmolive Company
Cornerstone Group of Companies
CP Images
Dick Hemingway

Diesel
Fotolia
General Motors
GetStock.com
Getty Images
Golf Canada
Grocery Gateway
Gunter Marx Stock Photos
Harry Rosen Inc.
The Old Mill Inn & Spa
Honda
Hyundai Auto Canada Corp.
ING Direct
JM Intimode Canada Inc.
Keystone Press Agency
Matt Forsythe/Push.ca
Mazda Canada Inc.
MEC
Mercedes-Benz Canada
Molson Coors Canada
Nestlé Canada Inc.
Newscom
Nova Scotia Community College

NWT Tourism
PepsiCo Beverages Canada
PepsiCo Canada ULC
Philips Electronics Ltd.
Purolator, Inc.
Red Bull Content Pool
Royal Bank of Canada
Scotiabank
Scott P. Anderson Photography
Sears Canada Inc.
Shoppers Drug Mart
Staples, Inc.
Statistics Canada
Subaru Canada, Inc.
Suzuki Canada Inc.
Thane International, Inc.
The Globe & Mail
The TDL Marks Corporation
Toronto Sportsmen's Show
United Way Halifax
VIA Rail Canada Inc.
Walmart Canada

From Pearson Canada Inc., I would like to thank Deana Sigut, Madhu Ranadive, and Richard di Santo. Special thanks to Heather Jackson for her hard work on securing permissions. I would also thank copy editor Carolyn Zapf, proofreader Susan Bindernagel, and production editor Munesh Kumar for their diligent work on this project.

As always, a very special thank you to my wife, Esther, for her patience, understanding, and support.

Keith J. Tuckwell
2013

Understanding Integrated Marketing Communications

Part 1 focuses on several introductory issues that are associated with the development of integrated marketing communications programs.

Chapter 1 introduces the components of the integrated marketing communications mix and the factors that encourage their use. The latter part of the chapter introduces the reader to a variety of ethical issues that confront marketing communications practitioners.

Chapter 2 introduces the student to essential strategic planning principles while drawing relationships between planning at various levels of an organization. The various inputs for marketing and marketing communications planning are presented along with the content of typical marketing and marketing communications plans. The intent is to show how integrated planning provides solutions to marketing problems.

Chapter 3 concentrates on issues related to branding strategy. Marketing communications strategies are the primary vehicle for building the image of a brand or company. Since brand positioning is the focal point of most marketing communications strategies, the role that positioning strategy statements play in the development of communications campaigns is examined in detail. The role and influence of packaging and product design strategies and their impact on brand image are also examined.

Integrated Marketing Communications: An Overview

Learning Objectives

After studying this chapter, you will be able to

1. Appreciate the role of integrated marketing communications planning in business today

2. Identify the components of the integrated marketing communications mix

3. Identify the conditions that have led to the emergence of integrated marketing communications

4. Explain how consumer behaviour and organizational buying behaviour influence marketing communications

5. Identify basic ethical issues confronting marketing communications practice

6. Describe the role that laws and regulations play in guiding marketing communications in Canada

Organizations today are searching for complete solutions to their communications needs and are calling upon experts in various marketing communications areas to get the job done. The challenge for organizations today is to successfully combine various communications disciplines into an effective marketing communications strategy and plan. This often requires specialists from various external agencies to collaborate on projects—that too is a challenge for organizations to coordinate.

The environment that businesses operate in today continues to change at a very rapid pace. The influence of technology alone has forced business organizations to examine how they deliver messages to their target markets. Generally speaking, there has been a movement toward targeted media and away from mass media. People's media habits have changed. The average consumer relies less on newspapers and television, and more on computers and telephones for receiving news and commercial messages. Consequently, marketing organizations are experimenting with new communications concepts such as *branded content* and *product seeding* to create a "buzz" for new products. They are also placing more ads on the Internet and are looking at ways to deliver advertising messages via social media outlets like Facebook, Twitter, YouTube, and Pinterest. Their objective is to deliver messages where their customers are.

The nature of marketing communications planning has changed dramatically. No longer do companies rely on disjointed strategies from a variety of sources, even though those sources are experts at what they do. The overall goal of communications now is to deliver the same message through a variety of media in order to have a synergistic impact on the target. Furthermore, the development of message strategy is now in the hands of fewer external suppliers. Many traditional advertising agencies have evolved into full-fledged marketing communications agencies and offer services in areas such as public relations, sales promotion, and direct response and online communications. The range of services and the level of specialization that agencies provide are much greater than before. In effect, these agencies are changing with their clients' needs and are providing integrated marketing communications solutions.

The Integrated Marketing Communications Mix

Integrated marketing communications involves the coordination of all forms of marketing communications in a unified program that maximizes the impact on consumers and other types of customers. It embraces many unique yet complementary forms of communication: media advertising (a focus on message strategies and media strategies

integrated marketing communications
The coordination of all marketing communications in a unified program that maximizes the impact on the intended target audience.

in a mass media environment); direct response communications (communications that encourage immediate action); digital communications (including online, social media, mobile, and video game communications); sales promotion (both consumer and trade promotions); public relations; experiential marketing; and personal selling (see Figure 1.1). The growth of social media is a factor that an organization must consider. Simply having a presence on Facebook and Twitter isn't good enough. An effective and well-planned social media strategy must be integrated into the communications mix.

Effective communications integration also considers the role of packaging and its impact on consumers at point of purchase, and the role that all employees of an organization play in communicating a positive attitude about a company to its various publics. Any customer touch-point is part of integrated marketing communications.

How an organization plans and manages the various components of the mix is important. An organization rarely employs all components at one time, but rather selects and uses those components that are deemed appropriate for the situation at hand. Clients look for a "total solutions" communications approach to resolve their business problems. As a result, they are seeking comprehensively planned, seamless campaigns from their communications agencies. Integration of message strategy, regardless of the medium, is crucial to generating maximum impact on the target audience.

Let's start the discussion about integrated marketing communications by clearly explaining the fundamental nature of each form of marketing communications. Refer to Figure 1.1 for a visual image of the marketing communications mix.

ADVERTISING

advertising
A paid-for media-delivered message by an identified sponsor designed to stimulate a positive response from a target audience.

Advertising is the placement of persuasive messages in time or space purchased in any of the mass media by organizations that seek to inform and persuade members of a target market about their products, services, organization, or ideas. In the context of the integrated marketing communications mix, good advertising (advertising that has an impact on the audience) will influence the behaviour of that audience—that is its primary function. Once a positive attitude toward a specific product or company is created in the customer's mind, that customer may be motivated to purchase the product or look favourably upon it.

FIGURE
1.1

The Integrated Marketing Communications Mix

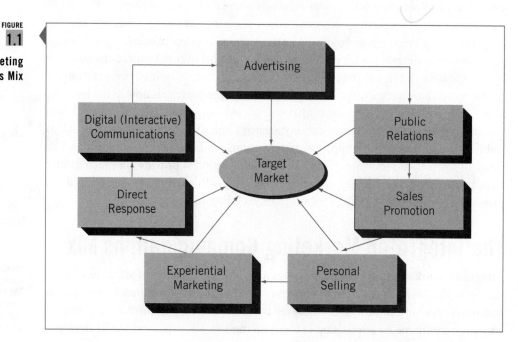

Advertising can be either product oriented or promotion oriented. **Product advertising** provides information and helps build an image for the product, whether it's a brand or a company, by presenting the features, attributes, and benefits of the product in a persuasive manner. An ad for Kellogg's Special K stresses essential benefits that consumers are looking for—nutritious food that tastes good. Special K has always advertised that it should be part of a healthy eating regimen. As can be seen in Figure 1.2, the ad for Kellogg's Special K emphasizes the benefits of fibre and whole grain ingredients—compelling reasons for buying the product.

Promotional advertising is designed to accomplish a specific task—usually to communicate a specific offer in order to elicit some type of immediate response from the customer. Including a coupon or contest promotion with a print advertisement, for example, is a form of promotional advertising. The content of the ad presents the features and primary benefit to help build the image, and the coupon provides an incentive for customers to buy. Automobile manufacturers, for example, are well known for their rebate programs and low-cost financing programs, both of which are advertised heavily to attract customers. Packaged goods manufacturers use coupons and other incentives to encourage more immediate action by consumers. Offering a promotion incentive could be the entire focus of an integrated marketing communications campaign.

product advertising
Advertising that provides information about a branded product to help build its image in the minds of customers.

promotional advertising
Advertising that communicates a specific offer to encourage an immediate response from the target audience.

FIGURE
1.2

A Benefit-oriented Advertisement for Kellogg's Special K

Source: John Raoux/AP Images.

DIRECT RESPONSE COMMUNICATIONS

direct response communications
The delivery of a message to a target audience of one; the message can be distributed by direct mail, direct response television, or telemarketing.

Direct response communications involves the delivery of a message to a target audience of one. As the term implies, "direct" means direct from the marketing company to a specific user or prospective user of a company's product. Direct mail is a common form of direct response communications. Other forms of direct response include direct response television (DRTV), telemarketing, and mobile communications. This segment of the communications industry is growing at a much faster pace than traditional forms of advertising. Time-pressed consumers, for example, find the convenience of direct response appealing. They can learn of a product's benefit and actually buy it, if they so desire, all in one stage.

Figure 1.3 shows the content of a direct mail leaflet for the Subaru Legacy. This attractive leaflet effectively displays the design of the automobile and offers an incentive (a $500 gift card) to encourage prospects to lease the automobile. More details about the incentive are available from a quick response (QR) code. Subaru also does a lot of television and print advertising to generate awareness and interest in the brand, another example of effective integration.

DIGITAL (INTERACTIVE) COMMUNICATIONS

digital (interactive) communications
The placement of an advertising message on a website, or an ad delivered by email or through mobile communications devices.

In an integrated marketing communications context, **digital (interactive) communications** are commercial messages for an organization placed on the Internet, a cell phone, or other personal electronic device. Technology is changing so rapidly that there is little

FIGURE
1.3

A Direct Mail Leaflet Encouraging Consumers to Lease a Subaru Legacy

Source: Courtesy of Subaru Canada, Inc.

doubt that communication by way of electronic devices will be the future of marketing communications. In fact, investment in online communications by Canadian advertisers is growing at a pace much faster than any other form of advertising. In 2010 (latest year available), investment in online advertising in Canada was $2.2 billion, ranking it second behind television advertising (3.4 billion).[1]

"The growth of online advertising in Canada speaks volumes about the importance of the medium to marketers in terms of its ability to reach, target, engage, and dialogue with consumers," says Paula Gignac, former president, IAB Canada.[2] Currently, the Internet is the number one medium among Canadians 18 to 34 years old in terms of time spent with a medium. This age group spends 25 hours a week online, compared to 22 hours a week with television.[3]

The new emphasis that business organizations place on **customer relationship management (CRM)**, combined with their ability to manage internal databases, is forcing them to move toward direct response and interactive communications. At present, organizations communicate through their own websites and through various forms of online advertising such as search advertising, display ads, and video ads. The addition of advertising on social media sites will play an increasing role in the communications mix in the future.

customer relationship management (CRM)
A process that enables an organization to develop an ongoing relationship with valued customers; the organization captures and uses information about its customers to its advantage in developing the relationship.

SALES PROMOTION

Sales promotion involves special incentives to stimulate an immediate reaction from consumers and distributors. An organization's promotion expenditures tend to be divided between consumers and distributors. Strategies that include coupons, free samples, contests, and cash refunds are classified as consumer promotions. The direct mail campaign shown in Figure 1.3 is a good example of how sales promotions are integrated with media advertising. Offering price discounts to distributors for purchasing goods in large quantities or for performing some kind of marketing or merchandising task on behalf of a marketing organization is classified as a trade promotion.

sales promotion
An activity that provides incentives to bring about immediate response from customers, distributors, and an organization's sales force.

The marketing organization is constantly challenged on how to divide the sales promotion budget between consumers and trade customers. Regardless of how the budget is allocated, it is imperative that consumer promotion strategies be aligned effectively with consumer advertising programs (to pull the product through the channel of distribution) and that trade promotions be aligned effectively with personal selling programs (to push the product through the channel of distribution). In business, it is the integration of various marketing communications programs that pays off for the organization.

PUBLIC RELATIONS

Public relations communications are primarily directed toward gaining public understanding and acceptance. Public relations (PR) messages influence the attitudes and opinions of interest groups about an organization. Consequently, progressive-minded marketing organizations fully appreciate the role that public relations campaigns can play in generating positive attitudes toward products.

public relations
A form of communications designed to gain public understanding and acceptance.

Public relations involve placing messages in the media that require no payment. In effect, they can generate "free" exposure. For example, a company issues a press release announcing a new product. The release includes all the virtues of the product, where it will be available, and how it will be advertised. Stories about the new product will appear on television newscasts and in newspaper and magazine articles. Such exposure offers a legitimacy that advertising does not have. To demonstrate, Hollywood movie producers rely heavily on public relations to generate publicity for new movie releases—this helps create the necessary hype they desire.

Public relations also play a major role when a company finds itself in a crisis. Senior managers of an organization must be prepared to deal with the media and to issue effective communications when unpleasant circumstances arise. Financial guru Warren Buffet once said, "It takes 20 years to build a reputation and 5 minutes to ruin it."[4] To illustrate, Toyota, a company built on quality, faced a crisis in 2010 when it had to recall over 4 million vehicles in North America due to sticky gas pedals. Key executives, including the global CEO, were on the hot seat. Toyota's public relations plan included a two-week halt in sales of its cars and full-page ads in major daily newspapers announcing to the public the actions it was taking. In spite of their PR effort, Toyota suffered a 15 percent decline in sales that year.

Traditional public relations are changing rapidly due to the popularity of social media. Communications tools such as Facebook and Twitter get regular people communicating information (positive and negative) about products and companies. Consequently, company-sourced social media communications are now part of an effective public relations strategy.

EXPERIENTIAL MARKETING

experiential marketing
A form of marketing that creates an emotional connection with the consumer in personally relevant and memorable ways.

Experiential marketing is a blend of marketing communications disciplines that engage people with a brand in a more personal way. For example, Kraft Canada promotes Kraft Peanut Butter with its "Spread the Feeling" advertising and experiential marketing campaign. The "Spread the Feeling" idea came from an insight that suggested consumers experience warm feelings when they eat and enjoy Kraft Peanut Butter. The "Hug" events are designed to recreate that warm home feeling for consumers across Canada. During each event, Kraft donates one jar of peanut butter to a local food bank for every hug given to the Kraft peanut butter mascot bears.[5] This promotion engages consumers with the brand.

Event marketing and sponsorships fall under the umbrella of experiential marketing. A well-planned event will engage consumers with a brand experience; once involved, they may perceive the brand in a more positive light. The experience could be anything from attending an event where a sponsor's product is freely distributed to devising a specific branded event that becomes the focal point of an entire integrated marketing communications campaign. The Coors Light Maxim Golf Experience weekend (Molson Coors) is an example; the event is the core experience but interest in the event is generated through television, print, and online advertising, and in the social media. **Event marketing**, therefore, involves planning, organizing, and marketing an event, whether it is an event for a company or a brand.

event marketing
The process, planned by a sponsoring organization, of integrating a variety of communications elements behind a single event theme.

sponsorship
The act of financially supporting an event in return for certain advertising rights and privileges.

Sponsorship simply means that a company provides money to an event in return for specified marketing privileges, granted because the company is associated with the event. Rogers, for example, is involved in event marketing as the title sponsor of the men's and women's Rogers Cup, a major tennis championship held annually in Toronto and Montreal. Rogers defrays the cost of holding such events by selling sponsorships to other companies. Those companies have advertising and on-site signage privileges at the event and can use the event logo to help market their product to the public.

Marketers are attracted to events because they reach their target market directly and improve brand awareness when associated with the right event. At events, people expect to see branded content; they are generally more receptive to brand messages and therefore more engaged with the experience. Scotiabank has significantly increased its sponsorship spending and has associated its brand with the National Hockey League (NHL) and the NHLPA (players' association). Scotiabank believes such a

FIGURE
1.4   **Scotiabank Is Very Active in Sports Marketing Sponsorships**

Source: Francis Vachon/CP Images.

partnership will raise its profile with consumers more efficiently than traditional advertising, where competition among major banks is intense. Scotiabank Place is home of the Ottawa Senators. See the image in Figure 1.4.

PERSONAL SELLING

As the term implies, **personal selling** involves the delivery of a personalized message from a seller to a buyer. The message presents the features, attributes, and benefits of a product or service. Personal selling is important in many situations, whether the seller is a car salesperson in a Toyota showroom, a store clerk in Best Buy, or the Pepsi-Cola sales representative presenting a new product to a buyer at the head office of Loblaws.

Compelling advertising campaigns for new automobiles encourage consumers to visit dealer showrooms. That money could go to waste if a salesperson at a dealership is unprepared to handle customer inquiries effectively. Equally, if Unilever's Dove brand is launching a new line of skin care products with a big advertising campaign and the salesperson does not successfully sell the new product to head office buyers at major chains like Shoppers Drug Mart, Rexall Drugs, Loblaws, and others, Unilever could face a significant setback. No amount of advertising will help sell the product—it simply will not be available in these stores. The job of the sales representative is to secure distribution of the product in a timely manner. The availability of the product in stores must

personal selling
Face-to-face communication involving the presentation of features and benefits of a product or service to a buyer; the objective is to make a sale.

Coffee Battle Heats Up

When you need a quick coffee where do you go? Perhaps you go to Tim Hortons or Starbucks, since those brands dominate the coffee market in Canada. McDonald's wants a piece of the action and has devised an effective marketing communications strategy to entice consumers of these more popular brands to make trial purchases of its coffee.

McDonald's does serve great-tasting coffee. The challenge, however, was to convince the Canadian public. Canadians perceive McDonald's to be a fast-food restaurant, known more for burgers and fries than anything else. The objective of the marketing communications campaign was to alter customers' perceptions about McDonald's coffee and to initiate trial purchases.

The campaign's key element was a two-week promotion offering a free cup of coffee—no purchase necessary—whenever breakfast was served. The premise of the campaign was clear: Get the coffee into as many hands as possible while encouraging the consumer to buy breakfast. A fully integrated communications campaign that included television commercials, outdoor ads, social media communications, public relations, and in-store signs supported the promotion. One of the more interesting, attention-grabbing components of the campaign was the placement of five steaming McDonald's coffee cups in high-traffic commuter locations (see image below).

Initial results were excellent. More than 6.1 million coffees were served during the promotion period, and 72 percent of the people who received the free coffee also bought a food item. Increased sales occurred on breakfast items where sales were previously flat or declining.

McDonald's has now run the free coffee promotion on several occasions. The impact on coffee sales during and after the promotion period has been significant. Further, McDonald's succeeded in altering consumers' perceptions about its product offerings. The boost in sales strongly suggests that people altered their routines and visited McDonald's for the coffee.

In a competitive market, attracting and retaining customers is a challenge. McDonald's free coffee promotions, supported with an effective media campaign, have proven to be a good way to meet that challenge.

Adapted from Kristin Laird, "McDonald's Serves Up Fresh, Free Coffee for All," *Marketing*, April 17, 2009, www.marketingmag.ca; Kristin Laird, "McDonald's Brings Back Coffee Giveaway," *Marketing*, February 24, 2010, www.marketingmag.ca.

Photo by Keith J. Tuckwell.

coincide with the scheduling of media advertising. If that is not the case, a lot of advertising money could be wasted.

In summary, contemporary organizations realize there are significant benefits to be achieved if all forms of marketing communications they choose to use are integrated successfully. Integration fosters a cooperative approach to communications planning, presents a unified message, and creates a higher level of impact on the target audience. For insight into how McDonald's used various marketing communications tools to increase its presence in the coffee market, read the IMC Highlight: **Coffee Battle Heats Up.**

Factors Encouraging Integrated Marketing Communications

Selecting the right combination of marketing communications alternatives to solve unique business problems is the key to success today. And that is a difficult challenge. Contemporary thinking suggests a cooperative approach to communications problem-solving and planning—an approach in which each communications alternative is an equal partner; an approach where there is media neutrality; an approach in which creative solutions are recommended to solve business problems. This way of thinking is the foundation on which integrated marketing communications strategies are built.

Several key issues and trends continue to affect marketing and marketing communications practice. Among these issues and trends are the following:

- Consumers' media habits are shifting toward digital media alternatives.
- The popularity of social media networks presents challenges and opportunities for organizations.
- Mobile communications are positioned to become the next "big thing" in marketing communications.
- The role of database marketing and direct forms of communications to reach individuals is expanding.
- The demand for efficiency and accountability in organizations is increasing.

MEDIA CONSUMPTION TRENDS AND THE SHIFT TO DIGITAL MEDIA

There is definitely a trend moving toward newer, electronic forms of communication and away from traditional forms of communication. Canadian consumers are spending less time with print and broadcast media each week and more time with the Internet (see Figure 1.5 for details). Readers of newspapers and magazines are migrating to online or tablet versions of their favourite read; television viewers are going "on demand" and are streaming their favourite shows to their computers or televisions at a time convenient for them. With so many Canadian households having access to high-speed Internet

FIGURE 1.5   Media Consumption in Canada: Time Spent with the Media

*The figures in the chart represent the average per capita weekly **time spent in hours** with each medium.*

Medium	Adults 18+	Adults 18–34	Adults 35–49	Adults 50+
Television	23.7	19.2	21.6	28.0
Radio	18.3	14.0	19.0	20.8
Internet	17.2	25.1	17.8	11.6
Newspaper	2.5	0.9	1.5	4.2
Magazine	0.8	0.4	0.5	1.1

Source: BBM Analytics, Spring 2011.

service, the demand for streaming of shows has skyrocketed. The streaming of video content presents new advertising opportunities.

With eyeballs shifting to digital formats, advertisers have to reconsider how and where they place their advertising dollars. As well, media outlets such as CTV, *The Globe and Mail*, *Chatelaine* magazine, and others have to encourage advertisers to move their dollars from their traditional format to their digital format or to place a portion of their budgets in both formats.

The fact that consumers multi-task when consuming the media poses other challenges for advertisers. Consumers will watch television while reading the newspaper, or they will view a downloaded television show online while talking on a cell phone. Grabbing a consumer's attention with an advertisement in such an environment is a challenge for those who create the message (creative planners) and those who plan the delivery of it (media planners). The situations described earlier in this section illustrate the need for a well-planned and integrated marketing communications strategy.

SOCIAL MEDIA PENETRATION AND POPULARITY

Data from Nielsen research reveal that "the reach of social networking and blogging venues is growing at twice the rate of other large drivers of Internet use such as portals, email, and search."[6] The most popular social networks include Facebook, MySpace, YouTube, LinkedIn, and Twitter. Just over 16 million Canadians are Facebook members (about 48 percent of the population), making Canada one of the most plugged-in countries in the world.[7] The sheer size of the Facebook audience seems overwhelming to many marketers, and they remain uncertain about the benefits that their investment in social media will generate.

Thus far, organizations have established a presence in the social media, but knowing how to use it effectively to generate revenue and build their business remains a work in progress. Companies are mainly using a "one size fits all" approach to social media communications. Everyone receives the same content in the same format: a brand page on Facebook or a Twitter feed.

Internally, there is an urgent need for a change in how an organization approaches social media. Presently, marketers have no tangible means for measuring the success of a social media campaign, at least in terms of metrics they are familiar with. However, once they adjust their thinking and see value in the dialogue-style of marketing present in social media, they will discover longer term benefits. Looking ahead, organizations have to step out of their comfort zone and begin developing social media campaigns that are strategically integrated with other forms of marketing communications. The tech-savvy generation of Canadians aged 18 to 34 is forcing such a change upon them.

MOBILE COMMUNICATIONS: THE NEXT BIG THING

Mobile communication devices are becoming a vital means for communicating information about goods and services, and conducting business transactions with customers. Currently, Canada has 24.5 million wireless subscribers and 5.7 million mobile broadband subscribers.[8] The potential reach to a target audience using mobile phones makes the medium an important component in the communications mix. Right now, mobile represents only 7.5 percent of a typical individual's media time, but it is growing at a faster rate than any other medium.[9]

With consumers' eyeballs shifting from the "big screen" (television) to the "small screen" (tablets and mobile devices), companies are reacting by experimenting with new media communications mixes to more effectively reach and have an impact on their target audiences. While all ages use cell phones, younger consumers spend much more time with their phones than older consumers. Younger consumers' mobile activities include using downloaded applications, emailing, and accessing social networks and blogs.

If the under-35 age group is a primary target, marketers have to give mobile communications due consideration. That group will carry their media behaviour forward as they age. Simply put, marketers must acknowledge mobile devices as an emerging platform for distributing advertising messages. With each passing year, mobiles will become a more prominent component of an integrated marketing communications strategy. For advertisers moving in this direction, there is one key benefit—they will have a personal link to consumers at any time, wherever they are.

There is no doubting the shift away from traditional media and toward digital media, social media, and mobile communications. Strategically thinking managers now realize that online and other forms of interactive communications are complementary to traditional media and, when used together, improve awareness levels and stimulate more action.

DATABASE MANAGEMENT TECHNIQUES AND CUSTOMER RELATIONSHIP MARKETING

Database management systems involve the continuous collection and analysis of information about customers. Companies that embrace database management can predict how likely the customer is to buy and then develop a message precisely designed to meet that customer's unique needs. Technological advances allow a company to zero in on extremely small segments of the population, often referred to as niches. The ultimate goal is to aim directly at the smallest segment—the individual. The database is the internal vehicle that facilitates implementation of customer relationship management programs.

database management system
A system that collects information about customers for analysis by managers to facilitate sound business decisions.

Business today is all about relationships—the relationships that an organization has with its customers, distributors, and suppliers. Customer relationship marketing may involve numerous companies working together to achieve common goals, or it may involve only one company trying to build a meaningful relationship with its consumers. Customer relationship management (CRM) programs are concerned with establishing, maintaining, and enhancing long-term relationships. These programs call for marketing and marketing communications programs that are designed to approach customer groups (targets) collectively and each customer individually, when applicable.

To demonstrate CRM, let's examine the marketing communications used by Shoppers Drug Mart. Shoppers Drug Mart has amassed information about its customer demographics and shopping patterns in order to identify items customers are "likely" to buy. Through its Optimum Rewards program, Shoppers has one of the largest customer databases in Canada, which provides a means to communicate information and offers directly to loyal customers. Consequently, Shoppers now spends much less on traditional media, such as television and weekly flyers (formerly a staple means of communication in its mix), and more on direct communications via mail and email. Shoppers also frequently sends loyal customers free samples of branded items in the mail that they

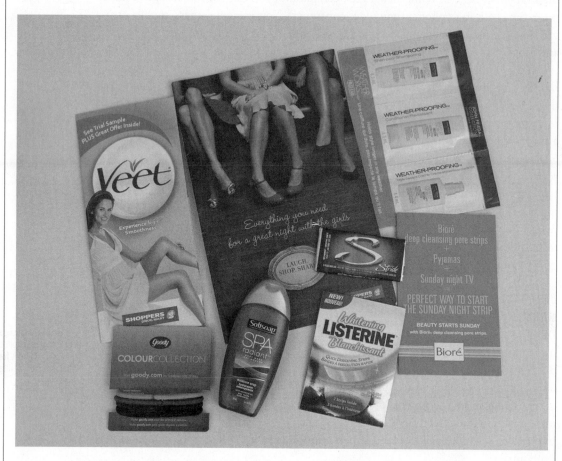

Source: Photo by Keith J. Tuckwell.

are likely to be interested in. An example of Shoppers' marketing communications appears in Figure 1.6.

In today's very competitive business environment, equal consideration must be given to attracting new customers and to retaining existing customers. Typically, the more traditional means of communications are used to pursue new customers, and non-traditional media, such as online communications, social networks, and loyalty programs, are used to retain and enhance the customer relationship.

THE DEMAND FOR EFFICIENCY AND ACCOUNTABILITY

Organizations now understand that scarce resources can be put to better use if the efforts of individual activities are coordinated. A coordinated effort encourages synergy, which in turn should have a stronger impact on the target audience. Managers today are under intense pressure to be more accountable for producing tangible results with their marketing communications investment. Therefore, efficient communications strategies are popular, as are strategies that can be measured easily in terms of return on investment.

Senior management likes the idea of tangible results. Such a demand is fuelling interest in digital communications because consumer responses to the communications can be tracked electronically and without cost. Similar measurements are not possible when traditional forms of communications are employed.

Toyota Canada was quick to recognize how integrated media and marketing strategies produce efficient communications. At Toyota, all communications departments now work together in one integrated group. "We combined all departments in order to ensure that we were speaking with a consistent voice and were sending out a consistent message all the time. It's given us an opportunity to think more 'out of the box' in terms of ideas. With all disciplines working together there are tremendous efficiencies," says Peter Renz, national director of public relations and advertising at Toyota Canada.[10]

Input for Marketing Communications Planning: Consumer Behaviour Essentials

A basic understanding of some important behavioural concepts is essential because such knowledge is applied directly in the development of marketing communications strategies. Knowledge in the areas of needs and motives, personality and self-concept, attitudes and perceptions, reference groups, and families is considered when an organization plans its marketing communications strategies.

Consumer behaviour is the study of how people buy, what they buy, when they buy, and why they buy. In the context of marketing and marketing communications, it is imperative that organizations understand what influences consumers' behaviour. Consequently, organizations invest considerable sums of money in marketing research to understand consumers better. Information is power, as the saying goes.

consumer behaviour
The combined acts carried out by individuals choosing and using goods and services, including the decision-making processes that determine these acts.

NEEDS AND MOTIVES

There is a direct link between needs and motives. Individuals have a **need** when they perceive the absence of something that is useful to them. A **motive** is a condition that prompts the individual to take action to satisfy the need. Consumers are motivated by friends and family members (word of mouth), or they can be influenced by what they see and read in the media, or by broadcast messages on radio and television. An appealing presentation of a product's features and benefits as they relate to a target's needs is often good enough to stimulate action—a purchase decision. For example, you might say to yourself, "I need (want) a fresh meat sandwich for lunch, so I'm going to a Subway restaurant. 'Subway…Think Fresh. Eat Fresh!'" That's the power of advertising!

need
The perception of the absence of something useful.

motive
A condition that prompts an individual to take action to satisfy a need.

Maslow's *hierarchy of needs* and *theory of motivation* have had a significant impact on marketing and marketing communications strategies. Maslow classified needs from lower level to higher level. His theory is based on two assumptions. First, when lower-level needs are satisfied, a person moves up to higher-level needs. Second, satisfied needs do not motivate; behaviour is influenced by needs yet to be satisfied.

Maslow states that individuals move through five levels of needs, as shown in Figure 1.7. Numerous advertising examples can be cited to show how needs theory is applied. For example, safety needs are used to motivate people to buy life insurance and retirement plans. A tagline such as "You're in good hands with Allstate" captures the message of protection and security.

FIGURE
1.7   **The Hierarchy of Needs**

Self-Actualization → Fulfillment, to realize potential

Esteem Needs → Recognition, achievement, status

Social Needs → Belonging, love from family and friends

Safety Needs → Security, protection, comfort

Physiological Needs → Hunger, thirst, sex, shelter

Source: Based on Maslow, A., Frager, R., Fadiman, J., *Motivation and Personality*, 3/E, © 1987.

Beauty and personal care products are famous for appealing to the social and esteem needs of both men and women. How a person's face and body look has an impact on social acceptance. The male grooming industry has exploded in recent years with brands like L'Oréal, Biotherm Homme, and Old Spice battling for market share. L'Oréal Men Expert, for example, uses popular male actors in its advertising. Hugh Laurie (the star of *House*, a popular TV series) extolls the merits of L'Oréal's anti-aging skin cream in television commercials and print ads. The inclusion of a celebrity does have an impact on the target market. As seen in Figure 1.8, Cadillac presents itself as a brand that will help satisfy the esteem needs of a car buyer—someone seeking prestige and status in their ride.

PERSONALITY AND SELF-CONCEPT

personality
A person's distinguishing psychological characteristics that lead to relatively consistent and enduring responses to the environment in which that person lives.

Personality refers to the individual's distinguishing psychological characteristics that lead to relatively consistent and enduring responses to the environment in which that person lives. Personality is influenced by self-perceptions, which in turn are influenced by family, reference groups, and culture. An understanding of that self-concept provides clues as to how to communicate with consumers. The self-concept goes beyond needs and focuses on our desires.

According to self-concept theory, the self has four components: real self, self-image, looking-glass self, and ideal self.[11]

1. **Real Self:** An objective evaluation of one's self. You as you really are.
2. **Self-Image:** How you see yourself. It may not be your real self, but a role you play with yourself.
3. **Looking-Glass Self:** How you think others see you. This can be quite different from how they actually see you.
4. **Ideal Self:** How you would like to be. It is what you aspire to.

FIGURE
1.8

A Luxury Car Brand like Cadillac Appeals to the Esteem Needs of an Upscale Group of Car Buyers

Source: General Motors LLC. Used by permission of GM Media Archives.

Based on these descriptions, the real self and self-image are less significant. In contrast, the looking-glass self and ideal self appear dynamic—they focus more on desires, the way in which we would like to be perceived. Consequently, many communications campaigns revolve around the looking-glass self and the ideal self. Marketing communicators know that consumers buy on emotion, so they present messages for goods and services that make consumers feel and look better. Marketers know that the next level of fulfillment is attractive to consumers.

As explained earlier, young males are buying grooming products to satisfy social and esteem needs. Such behaviour is influenced by the desire to achieve their ideal self—how they would like to be. It seems that physical imperfection can be a crippling disability! Brands such as Old Spice, Gillette, and Biotherm Homme have responded with a complete range of face scrubs, moisturizers, and cleansing products for men. Yes guys…it's all about image! See Figure 1.9 for an example.

Source: Dave Chang/Biotherm/Newscom.

ATTITUDES AND PERCEPTIONS

attitudes
An individual's feelings, favourable or unfavourable, toward an idea or object.

Attitudes are an individual's feelings, favourable or unfavourable, toward an idea or object. People form attitudes based on what they hear, read, and see about a product, as well as from the opinions of others they trust. Friends, for example, have a dramatic impact on the attitudes held by youth. Trendsetters and opinion leaders who embrace new products also help to shape consumer attitudes.

As a rule, organizations present their product in accordance with attitudes held strongly by their target audience. It makes little sense to go against the grain—many an organization has discovered it is very expensive to try to change an attitude. For example, if teens see themselves on the edge of what the rest of the world considers normal, they will be attracted to products where the advertising message pushes the boundaries. Apple, for example, has been successful with products like iTunes, iPhone, and iPad—its products are positioned as sleek and sexy, and relevant to the lifestyles of all ages.

Attitudes do change, and marketers must keep track of the changes. To demonstrate, the change toward a more health-conscious lifestyle has spawned many new products from food manufacturers. Consumers are demanding products that are easier on the waistline. Kellogg's Special K has always been positioned as a "good for you" product. There are now many new healthier lifestyle products in the Special K product line. See Figure 1.10 for details.

FIGURE
1.10

Special K Granola Bars Are a Good Fit for Canadians' Trend Toward Healthier Living

Source: PRNewsFoto/Kellogg Company/ AP Images.

Perception refers to the manner in which individuals receive and interpret messages. Given the prevailing model of human behaviour, it is safe to say that consumers accept messages that are in line with their needs, personality, self-concept, and attitudes, and ignore or reject messages that are not. Theory states that we are selective about the messages we receive and that there are three levels of selectivity:

perception
The manner in which individuals receive and interpret messages.

1. **Selective Exposure:** Our eyes and minds notice only information that interests us.
2. **Selective Perception:** We screen out messages that conflict with our attitudes.
3. **Selective Retention:** We remember only what we want to remember.

To demonstrate how perception works, consider a situation that Toyota recently faced. Toyota is a company built on a strong reputation for quality. Some years ago, Toyota surpassed General Motors and became the world's largest automobile company. The public believed in the company. That feeling changed in 2010 when Toyota suffered backlash from massive recalls, the result of sticky gas pedals and braking problems. While Toyota was dealing with the problems (see PR discussion earlier in the chapter), the public's perceptions of Toyota changed. In Canada, the company suffered a 20 percent decrease in sales. A common phrase applies here: "Perception is reality." And it is the perceptions held by consumers that advertisers must deal with.

In contrast, consumers will quickly tune in to messages for products and brands they are contemplating purchasing. As discussed earlier, consumers who are interested in healthier food products will tune in to advertising messages that include expressions such as "lighter," "less," "all natural," "no additives and preservatives," and so on. Relevant messages get noticed!

REFERENCE GROUPS

A **reference group**, or **peer group**, is a group of people with common interests that influence the attitudes and behaviour of its members. Reference groups include schoolmates, sports teams, fraternities and sororities, and hobby clubs. There is considerable pressure on members to conform to the standards of the group—a desire to "fit in." Take, for example, the mild hazing that occurs among rookies of a college or university sports team, or the rituals associated with joining a fraternity.

The influence of reference groups is quite strong among younger people. For example, teens share a desire to have the latest gadgets, shop at the trendiest stores, or have parts of their body pierced. It's all part of their social scene and their desire to satisfy social needs. They turn to their peers for information on what behaviour is desirable. With the right strategy, a marketer need only associate its brand with a certain situation and the target will become interested in the brand. Brands like Mountain Dew and Red Bull have carved out a significant niche with the youth market. Refer to the image in Figure 1.11.

reference group (peer group)
A group of people who share common interests that influence the attitudes and behaviour of its members.

FIGURE 1.11   Red Bull Effectively Connects with the Youth Market and Their Social Scene

Source: Sebastian Marko/Red Bull Content Pool.

Advertisers have to be very careful when approaching the youth market. Too much advertising and the target sees the practice for what it is: a disingenuous attempt to attract youth consumers without having a clue about their actual tastes.[12] Reaching youth works if the message is authentic. If a brand "goes underground" (the place where most pop culture originates) or uses some kind of viral marketing technique, such as a video on YouTube, it has a better chance of connecting with the youth target.

FAMILY INFLUENCES

Each member of a family has some influence on the behaviour of other family members and thus an influence on buying decisions. Perhaps the biggest influence on behaviour within families today relates to the *changing roles* and *responsibilities* of family members. Traditional attitudes, roles, and responsibilities are out—nothing is what it seems anymore.

Households are also different. There are same-sex households, lone-parent households, and dual-income (two-worker) households. In the dual-income household, much of the decision making is shared between partners. No longer can the maker of a household product assume the woman is the primary buyer, and a financial advisor cannot assume that the man makes all the investment decisions. In fact, men are handling grocery shopping more than ever before, either on their own or shared with a spouse. A research survey conducted by Yahoo among men aged 18 to 64 found that more than half now identify themselves as the primary grocery shoppers in their households, but only 24 percent feel advertising in packaged-goods categories speaks to them.[13] Marketing organizations such as Kraft, Nestlé, Procter & Gamble, and others should be paying attention to this kind of shift in household responsibility and adjust their advertising messages accordingly.

Companies that are in tune with these types of changes are **double targeting**—they are devising marketing strategies that reach both genders effectively. Financial companies, automobile manufacturers, and retailers recognize the role and influence of women in major buying decisions and are devising new campaigns that take advantage of such knowledge. Retailers like Mark's, Canadian Tire, Home Depot, and Best Buy are very active in this area. Each retailer has redesigned its store layout, created a better shopping environment, and implemented a new marketing communications strategy aimed directly at women. See the Mark's ad in Figure 1.12.

double targeting
Marketing strategies that reach both genders effectively.

Today's children (commonly referred to as Generation Y) have considerable influence on family buying decisions. They don't necessarily make requests, but parents actively seek their input on anything from clothing to cars to family vacations. "Their influence on family spending is that they essentially are co-purchasers," says Kelly Mooney, president of Resources Interactive.[14] Children are technologically savvy and are helping their parents research products and make online buying decisions—a real shift in power! Through Facebook, they access the opinions of their network of friends that they communicate with regularly.

Inputs for Marketing Communications Planning: Business and Organizational Buyer Behaviour

The buying process of organizations is very different from consumer buying. In a nutshell, organizations exhibit more rational behaviour than consumers—consumers do a lot of buying based on emotion. The **business-to-business (B2B) market** is managed by

business-to-business (B2B) market
A market of goods and services needed to produce a product or service, promote an idea, or operate a business.

FIGURE 1.12 Mark's Altered Its Marketing Communications Strategy to Appeal More Directly to Women

Source: Courtesy of Canadian Tire Corporation, Limited.

individuals in an organization responsible for purchasing goods and services needed to produce a product or service, or promote an idea. This market includes business and industry, governments, institutions, wholesalers and retailers, and professionals.

The business market has several characteristics that distinguish it from consumer markets. Business markets have fewer buyers, and those buyers tend to be concentrated in industrial areas in and near large cities. The buying criteria are very practical, with decisions based on the best buy according to predetermined requirements. There is usually a formal buying process for evaluating product and service alternatives. Business buying processes have changed dramatically because of advancing technology and the benefits derived from buying goods online.

The key issues that a business organization must address when marketing to other businesses are the criteria established by the buying organization. In most situations, those requirements are established in advance, and companies can compete with each other by submitting bids. The buyer customarily chooses the bid with the lowest price, assuming the criteria have been met. What are those requirements?

- **Quality:** Buyers want consistent quality on every order. What they buy could have a direct impact on the quality of goods they, in turn, produce and market.

- **Service:** Buyers want reputable suppliers who provide prompt service and believe that the initial order is simply the start of a business relationship.

- **Continuity of Supply:** Buyers want suppliers who can provide goods over the long term. A steady source of supply ensures consistent production scheduling.

- **Price:** Buyers evaluate price in conjunction with the other criteria. The lowest price is not always accepted. Potential long-term savings could outweigh an initial low price.

To ensure that the right buying decision is made, organizations employ a formal or informal approach. A formal approach involves a **buying committee**. The committee is made up of key representatives from various functional areas of the company, such as finance, marketing, manufacturing, purchasing, and so on. A committee takes a very rational approach when evaluating alternatives, and participants need to know that costly decisions are shared decisions.

A **buying centre** is an informal purchasing process with individuals in an organization involved in the purchasing process, but not necessarily having direct responsibility for the actual decision. These roles are summarized in Figure 1.13.

In terms of marketing or marketing communications, the seller must know who on the committee or within the buying centre has the most influence. It could be one person or several people. Once that is known, the best means of communicating can be determined. Based on the nature of business buying, it becomes clear that personal selling and direct forms of communications are vital components when trying to influence the decisions of business buyers.

INTEGRATION AND PARTNERING INFLUENCES B2B COMMUNICATIONS STRATEGIES

Business markets have embraced customer relationship management in an attempt to establish efficient business systems. CRM promotes the seamless transfer of information throughout the channels to ensure the efficient and continuous flow of goods. Forming partnerships with suppliers implies a long-term relationship. Therefore, to be part of a CRM system, the marketer must be more familiar than ever with the role the product

buying committee
A formal buying structure in an organization that brings together expertise from the various functional areas to share in the buying decision process.

buying centre
An informal purchasing process in which individuals in an organization perform particular roles but may not have direct responsibility for the actual decision.

FIGURE
1.13   The Buying Centre

Role	Description	Example
Users	Those in the organization who use the product directly.	If the product is a personal computer, any end-user in the organization.
Influencers	Those who define the product specifications.	An engineer.
Buyers	Those with the authority to buy.	A purchasing manager.
Deciders	Those with the power to finalize the purchase.	Where high-cost decisions are involved, the CEO may be the decider.
Gatekeepers	Those who control the flow of information to the members of the buying centre.	A purchasing manager may also fulfill the role of gatekeeper.

plays in the customer's operations. Collecting information about the customer and their operations is crucial.

The strategies employed to reach business customers are also evolving. Yet, in spite of all the technological advances and the direct nature of the buying and selling process, customers must still be made aware of the product alternatives that are available. Creating awareness is always the first step. Therefore, the need for print advertising directed at business customers will continue, along with the need for strong personal sales contacts. The inclusion of sales promotion programs to assist salespeople is also important. Event marketing in the form of trade show participation will help keep marketing organizations on a buyer's radar screen, and direct marketing techniques, such as direct mail and Internet-based communications, will become more of a priority. A website containing essential product information is indispensable in B2B marketing situations. The same tools are employed in consumer marketing; they are just given different priority.

Ethical Issues in Marketing Communications Practice

The way an organization communicates is always under review by the public and critics of the marketing communications industry. Rightly or wrongly, planned or unplanned, advertisers sometimes deliver messages that spark controversy. Many organizations tolerate the controversy as long as the campaign is delivering sales, while others bow to public pressure and remove offending messages. Some of the key issues that make the headlines are discussed in this section.

PRIVACY ISSUES IN AN ONLINE WORLD

An ongoing and rather hot issue revolves around the collection of information about people's behaviour when using the Internet. What do marketers know about people and how do they use this information? Consumers must recognize (many do) that every online activity is tracked and logged, and has potential value for marketers. For many people, this is a frightening thought, and it should be if the information is not used for legitimate purposes.

Data is king in marketing today, and marketers are good at collecting and interpreting data. Marketers have always done this, but in the age of technology the data is available in a fast and furious manner. The collection of online data provides marketers with an opportunity to devise unique advertising messages based on personal interests (as expressed by online surfing behaviour) that can be delivered directly to the individual's computer or mobile device.

So what do consumers fear? One recent survey found that 64 percent of respondents viewed targeted advertising as invasive, with 40 percent saying they would change their online behaviour if advertisers were collecting data. A survey by the Public Interest Advocacy Centre found that 75 percent of respondents were either "not very comfortable" or "not comfortable at all" with tracking-based advertising. In the social media world, 70 percent of Facebook users and 52 percent of Google users are "somewhat" or "very concerned" about their privacy.[15]

There are regulations in place to ensure consumers are aware of their rights with regard to how information is used. Various opt-in and opt-out clauses are found in agreements people sign when dealing with online organizations, but there is a fear that marketers disregard the regulations. Privacy law does exist in Canada through the *Personal Information Protection and Electronic Documents Act* (PIPEDA). The Act does not offer rules but does offer a list of guiding principles for businesses to follow. For example, an organization must obtain consent for the use or disclosure at the time of collection, and purposes for the collection of information must be limited and well defined, and stated in a clear and understandable manner. The degree to which organizations abide by these principles fuels the ongoing debate with consumers.

SEX IN ADVERTISING

A common complaint about advertising revolves around the use of sex to sell something. As an old saying goes: "Sex sells!" So what's the beef among members of contemporary Canadian society? Using sex appeal in an appropriate manner and for appropriate products seems natural, but gratuitous sex is something consumers shouldn't have to tolerate.

Is it pornography or simply provocative advertising? An American Apparel ad in downtown Toronto featuring a woman leaning forward in a provocative pose is the kind that can spark controversy. The behaviour of passersby showed the impact of the advertisement. It did get noticed and it did draw a reaction. The ad has raised the ire of feminists, who suggest it objectifies women. The company's reaction is quite different. "It is a bit disconcerting to see what feminism has evolved into," says Marsha Brady, a creative director at American Apparel. "When there's a group of people attempting to shame female creativity, female beauty, female pride under the auspices of protecting women, it's really, really scary."[16] Consider the ad for Diesel that appears in Figure 1.14. A sexual appeal technique certainly draws attention to the ad and the brand name. Diesel markets jeans, footwear, bags, and shades.

EXTREME ADVERTISING

The extent to which advertisers will go with their message in order to have an impact on their audience can sometimes be an issue. For example, the strategy of depicting dangerous or disturbing situations in advertising has come under much scrutiny in recent years. Automakers are under the gun for showing unsafe driving practices in ads. In some cases,

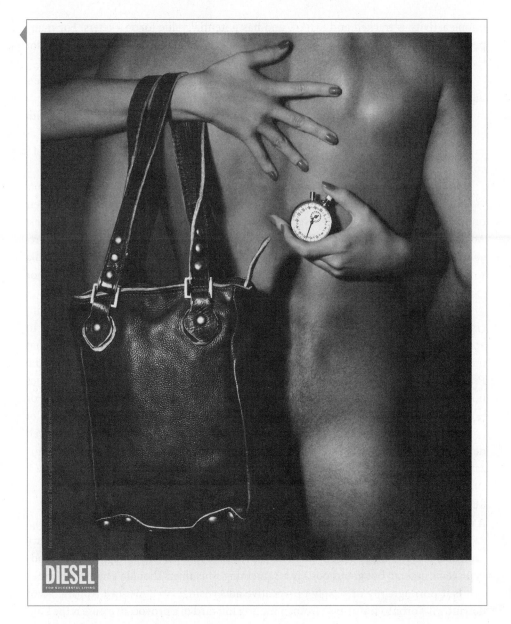

dangerous driving practices are glamorized. A Corvette spot entitled "A Boy's Dream" depicted an enraged driver racing wildly in the sports car. Many critics believe an ad like this helps encourage young people to get involved in risky activities such as street racing.

A more recent campaign for Toyota Matrix involved messaging of a "disturbing" nature. A series of individualized email messages were sent to a woman from a guy named Sebastian Bowler. The first message said, "Coming 2 Los Angeles. Gonna lay low at your place for a bit. Till it all blows over. Bringing Trigger." The second message referred to the recipient's home as a "nice place to hide out" and included a picture of Sebastian and his pit bull Trigger. At one point in the series of messages, the woman received an email from a motel manager demanding she pay for damages Sebastian had caused while staying there one night. The final email explained the entire thing was a virtual punking. It was, in fact, a campaign for the Toyota Matrix.[17]

Marketers want people to engage with their brands. Has Toyota taken the engagement principle too far? The recipient of the emails described above filed a lawsuit against

Toyota and the ad agency behind the campaign for intentional infliction of emotional distress, negligence, and false advertising. She feels the email messages were a form of "stalking." Perhaps that's taking things to the extreme, but how would you feel if you received those messages? Where's the message about the car?

MISLEADING ADVERTISING

Sometimes ads can mislead the public or simply misrepresent the brand. Sometimes the public misinterprets the advertiser's message and the campaign backfires. The control of misleading advertising is the responsibility of Advertising Standards Canada. (More information about its role in the advertising industry appears later in this chapter.) Some of the more interesting examples involve green marketing claims, targeting children, and cultural diversity.

EXAGGERATED GREEN CLAIMS   Given the rate at which organizations are making claims about how green they are and what they are doing to protect the environment, this category of misleading advertising is worthy of special attention. Manufacturers of bottled water, for example, claim they are offering a better product than the water that municipalities offer, forgetting that a large portion of the plastic bottles wind up in landfill sites, which ultimately harms the environment.

A recent survey about environmental claims shows that 75 percent of Canadians take into account the environmental impact of an organization's actions when they buy a product. As well, 75 percent of respondents firmly believe that most environmental claims are just marketing ploys. At present, phrases such as "green," "organic," or "low emissions" suggest all is good, but where's the proof?[18] Consumers want to ensure that companies are not getting away with "greenwashing," a term associated with the exploitation of environmental ideas to make a company look good.

TARGETING CHILDREN   Advertising messages directed at children often bypass parents. As a result, parents are concerned about the content of these messages, which have a powerful influence on the child's behaviour. Children may start demanding higher-priced "in" goods, while parents prefer to buy less expensive alternatives. In other words, at what age do children become "brand conscious"?

Companies such as McDonald's, Kellogg's, PepsiCo, and Nestlé, among many others, are frequently the target of critics who suggest the consumption of their products and the ads that encourage the consumption have contributed to the rise in childhood obesity. In fact, a panel appointed by the Chronic Disease Prevention Alliance of Canada called for a ban on all junk food advertising that targets children—a move the federal government has promised to consider. In the wake of the criticism, many food companies have committed to an industry-sponsored Children's Food and Beverage Advertising Initiative that encourages responsible marketing to children. Some companies are eliminating ads targeted to children altogether, while others are promising healthier products for children.[19]

CULTURAL DIVERSITY   Currently, Canada's foreign-born population represents 19.8 percent (one in five Canadians) of the total population and is expected to rise to as high as 23 percent by 2017.[20] The largest visible minorities are South Asians, Chinese, and black. These people tend to live in large cities. In Toronto, visible minorities comprise 43 percent of the population.

Given this data, advertisers are often criticized for not reflecting the diversity of Canada's population in commercial messages. Critics claim that advertising remains too

Smaller Target, Bigger Opportunity

The ethnic market is actually a big market in Canada. Statistics Canada reports that a vast majority of Canadians belonging to a visible minority group live in major cities. In Toronto they represent 63 percent of the population, in Vancouver 59 percent, and in Montreal 31 percent. Those numbers are significant! The largest visible minority group are people of South Asian descent, followed by Chinese, black, Filipino, and Latin American.

According to Emma Fox, senior vice-president of marketing at Walmart Canada, it is absolutely vital that her company pursue the ethnic market. "It's really important that we win our share of that market. It's a necessity because all the future market growth in terms of spending is coming from new population growth." She's right. The new Canadian population is growing at five times the rate of the overall population.

Walmart Canada has been a leader in ethnic marketing and marketing communications. The company is moving forward with a "store of the community" concept, which caters to local needs and tastes. Simply put, a store in the east end of a city may carry different merchandise than one in the west end. The location of various ethnic groups in a city will be a determining factor influencing what merchandise a store carries. Walmart uses one of its supercentres in Toronto as a laboratory for tailoring offerings to the large surrounding Asian population.

Scotiabank holds similar views and is pursuing niche markets that competitors may be neglecting. Scotiabank recently focused on the Hispanic market in Toronto and Montreal. According to Fabiola Sicard, director of Latin markets at Scotiabank, "They are a smaller market than other immigrant communities, they are fragmented geographically, and no significant research has been done on their needs." Despite this, the bank sees great opportunity, as the Hispanic population in Canada numbers over 600 000.

In Canada, the Hispanic community is highly educated—50 percent have at least a bachelor's degree and another 12 percent have a college diploma. Scotiabank sees Hispanic Canadians as a growth market for its StartRight bank accounts, which are tailored to the needs of newcomers.

In terms of marketing communications, Scotiabank stays away from mainstream media, preferring a more grassroots approach. The bank targets professional associations, street festivals, and blogs aimed at people living in Latin American countries who are mulling a move north. To reach recent arrivals, the bank gives seminars in Spanish—often as many as 150 people show up. Similar strategies are in place to reach the Filipino community. Scotiabank does not neglect the larger Chinese and South Asian communities, but the other banks are aggressively targeting them as well. Scotiabank is going into areas nobody else is targeting— a wise move on their part.

Source: Steve White/CP Images.

Adapted from Marina Strauss, "Walmart Aims to Cater to a More Diverse Palate," *The Globe and Mail*, April 17, 2012, p. B7 and Simon Houpt, "Unknown, Ignored and Invisible," *The Globe and Mail*, November 18, 2011, p. B7.

targeted on white consumers, and they may be right. Marketers must consider the size and profit potential of an ethnic marketing campaign. Multinational companies consider Canada to be a small market; to break down the market further and absorb the costs of a definitive marketing campaign for various ethnic groups may not be profitable.

Many advertisers are adopting multicultural marketing communications strategies and are including ethnic populations in their ads. Some of the leaders in ethnic-oriented advertising include Walmart, The Home Depot, McDonald's, Coca-Cola, and RBC Financial, among many others. These companies recognize the importance of appealing to the widest possible audience. It's only a matter of time before other organizations get on board.

For more insight into ethnic-oriented marketing communications, read the IMC Highlight: **Smaller Target, Bigger Opportunity**.

Laws and Regulations Governing Marketing Communications

The marketing communications industry in Canada is highly regulated. Regulation and control come from Advertising Standards Canada (ASC), which administers regulations based on codes of practice that are voluntarily established; and the Competition Bureau (a federal agency) through the *Competition Act,* which established laws and regulations for all marketing activity in Canada.

ADVERTISING STANDARDS CANADA

Advertising Standards Canada is the industry body committed to creating and maintaining community confidence in advertising. Its mission is to ensure the integrity and viability of advertising through industry self-regulation. ASC members include advertisers, agencies, media organizations, and suppliers to the advertising sector.

ASC operates two divisions. The Standards Division administers the industry's self-regulating code, the *Canadian Code of Advertising Standards*; handles complaints from consumers regarding advertising; and administers the industry's *Trade Dispute Procedure*. The Advertising Clearance Division previews advertisements in five categories, helping advertisers adhere to applicable legislation, regulatory codes, and industry standards.[21]

The *Canadian Code of Advertising Standards* (Code) is the principal instrument of self-regulation. The Code was developed to promote the professional practice of advertising and forms the basis upon which advertising is evaluated in response to consumer complaints. The Code is supplemented by other codes and guidelines, including gender portrayal guidelines, which are intended to help advertising practitioners develop positive images of women and men in their commercial messages. The Code also addresses concerns about advertising, including the accuracy and clarity of messages, disguised advertising techniques, price claims, bait and switch tactics, comparative advertising claims, unacceptable depictions, scientific claims, and advertising to children. Visit the ASC website at www.adstandards.com for more details.

Advertising Standards Canada rules against advertisers when necessary and makes suggestions for changes in message delivery. Copywriters and art directors are frustrated by such responses from the public or regulating bodies. It's no wonder there's so much dull advertising that simply blends together. Being cautioned to stay away from the creative edge is not good for the future of advertising. In the unregulated online world, user-generated content of a risky nature is quite common. The playing field doesn't seem as level as it once was.

COMPETITION BUREAU

The Competition Bureau is responsible for the administration and enforcement of the *Competition Act*, a law that governs business conduct and marketing practices in Canada. The *Competition Act* contains criminal and civil provisions to address false, misleading, and deceptive marketing practices. Among the practices that come under scrutiny are deceptive telemarketing, deceptive notices of winning prizes, and pyramid selling schemes. Other provisions prohibit representations not based on adequate and proper tests, misleading warranties and guarantees, false or misleading price representation, and untrue testimonials.

Organizations that violate these laws and regulations are subject to financial penalties and other actions. To demonstrate, the Competition Bureau determined that Bell Canada misled consumers about the prices it offered for its services. As an example, Bell's website had been advertising a bundle of home phone, Internet, and television services starting as low as $69.90 per month. However, it was impossible for customers to buy the bundle at that price. The lowest possible price, including mandatory fees, was $80.27 (15 percent higher). Mandatory fees were hidden from consumers in the fine-print disclaimers. Bell agreed to pay an administrative monetary penalty of $10 million, the maximum allowable under the *Competition Act*.[22]

For more insight into the Competition Bureau visit its website at www.competition-bureau.gc.ca.

SUMMARY

The rapid pace of change in business today has forced organizations to re-examine and change the way they communicate with customers. More than ever before, organizations are demanding integrated marketing strategies to help resolve marketing problems and to take advantage of new opportunities.

The integrated marketing communications mix is composed of seven unique yet complementary components: advertising, direct response communications, interactive communications, sales promotion, personal selling, public relations, and experiential marketing. The organization evaluates marketing situations and employs the components of the mix that will effectively and efficiently reach its target market.

Several key issues and trends have led to the emergence of integrated marketing communications. Among the key issues are consumers' changing media habits and their shift to digital media consumption; the popularity of social media networks, and the challenges and opportunities they present to organizations; the potential growth of mobile communications that lies ahead; the expanding role of database marketing and its impact on direct forms of marketing communications; and the greater demand for efficiency and accountability in organizations.

In the process of developing marketing communications strategies, an organization must understand and apply various consumer behaviour concepts. Among these concepts are needs and motives, personality and self-concept, attitudes and perceptions, reference groups, and family. Research into these factors provides clues about what forms of marketing communications to employ to deliver a more effective message.

Marketing communications strategies must also consider business buying behaviour. While consumers tend to be swayed by emotion, business buyers maintain a rational approach when making buying decisions. Business buying is based on predetermined criteria such as quality, service, continuity of supply, and price. Decisions are made formally by a buying committee or informally by a buying centre. Technology and relationship marketing practices have taken hold in B2B marketing. Companies must adapt to this way of doing business or perish. Tools such as personal selling, direct response communications, and interactive communications are effective in reaching business customers.

Marketing communications practitioners must contend with ethical issues when devising message strategies. Some of the more contentious issues today include consumers' concern for privacy in the online world, the use of sex in advertising, and the depiction of risky situations and use of disturbing messages in advertisements. Advertisers are also under the gun for making exaggerated green claims, targeting children with ads, and not portraying Canada's cultural diversity in advertising.

Regulation and control of the marketing communications industry is the jurisdiction of the federal government and Advertising Standards Canada. Laws and regulations are enforced by the Competition Bureau, and voluntary regulations are administered by Advertising Standards Canada.

KEY TERMS

advertising   4

attitudes   18

business-to-business (B2B) market   21

buying centre   23

buying committee   23

consumer behaviour   15

customer relationship management (CRM)   7

database management system   13

digital (interactive) communications   6

direct response communications   6

double targeting   21

event marketing   8

experiential marketing   8

integrated marketing communications   3

motive   15

need   15

peer group   20

perception   19

personal selling   9

personality   16

product advertising   5

promotional advertising   6

public relations   7

reference group   20

sales promotion   7

sponsorship   8

REVIEW QUESTIONS

1. Identify and briefly explain the components of the integrated marketing communications mix.
2. Explain the difference between product advertising and promotional advertising.
3. Briefly describe the key issues and trends that have led to the emergence of integrated marketing communications.
4. "An understanding of Maslow's hierarchy of needs and theory of motivation has a direct influence on advertising strategy." Explain.
5. According to the self-concept theory, the self has four components. Identify and briefly describe each component.
6. How important is assessing customer attitudes when developing an advertising campaign? Explain.
7. What role and influence do reference groups have when a consumer is deciding what products to buy?
8. Explain the term "double targeting" and provide a new example of a company or brand that is applying this concept.
9. What essential criteria do organizational buyers consider when making buying decisions?
10. What is the difference between a buying committee and a buying centre?
11. What roles do the Competition Bureau and Advertising Standards Canada play in the marketing communications industry?

DISCUSSION AND APPLICATION QUESTIONS

1. How significant will digital communications be in future marketing communications strategies? Will advertisers continue to shift their dollars to digital communications? Conduct some secondary research to offer new information that will justify your opinion.
2. Experiential marketing is growing in popularity. Will this trend continue and will this form of communications play a more dominant role in future marketing

communications strategies? Conduct some research on this topic and present an opinion on it.
3. "Relationship marketing practices will dramatically alter marketing communications strategies in the future." Is this statement true or false? Conduct some online secondary research and form an opinion on this statement.
4. Cite some examples and provide actual illustrations of companies or brands that use the following

consumer behaviour theories when developing communications strategies. Provide a description that relates the theory to the practice.

a) hierarchy of needs and theory of motivation

b) personality and self-concept

c) reference groups

d) family influences

5. From the following list of goods and services, identify what you think is the most important marketing communications tool for building and sustaining the brand. Provide some justification for your choices.

a) Coors Light

b) BMW automobiles

c) Shoppers Drug Mart

d) RBC Financial Group

6. Are advertising laws and regulations in Canada too conservative? Should riskier or more controversial advertising messages be allowed? Refer to the ethical issues section of the chapter for some background information before responding to this question.

ENDNOTES

1. Canadian Media Directors' Council *Media Digest*, 2011/12, p. 14.

2. Paula Gignac, "2007 Canadian Online Revenue Climbs to $1.2 Billion," press release, IAB Canada, July 3, 2008, www.newswire.ca/en/story/290659/2007-canadian-online-advertising-revenue-climbs-to-1-2-billion.

3. "Time Spent—Major Media," *TVB Canada Report*, 2011.

4. Angela Scardillo, "Old Spice Guys Lessons in Crisis Management," *Marketing*, August 30, 2010, p. 27.

5. Kristin Laird, "Kraft Hugs It Out Again," *Marketing*, July 25, 2011, www.marketingmag.ca/news/marketer-news/kraft-hugs-it-out-again-32800.

6. Brian Morrissey, "Nielsen: Social Nets Overtake E-mail," Adweek.com, March 9, 2009, www.adweek.com/news/technology/nielsen-social-nets-overtake-e-mail-98620.

7. Canadian Press, "Canadian Facebook Users Grow to 16 Million," *Marketing*, June 2, 2010, www.marketingmag.ca/news/media-news/canadian-facebook-users-grow-to-16-million-3009.

8. "Canada's Wireless Industry," Canadian Wireless Telecommunications Association, 2011, www.cwta.ca.

9. Lisa E. Phillips, "Trends in Consumers' Time Spent with the Media," *eMarketer*, December 28, 2010, www.emarketer.com/Article/Trends-Consumers-Time-Spent-with-Media/1008138.

10. Richard Rotman, "When Worlds Combine," *Marketing*, September 29, 2003, p.8.

11. John Douglas, George Field, and Lawrence Tarpay, *Human Behaviour in Marketing*, (Columbus, OH: Charles E. Merrill Publishing, 1987), p. 5.

12. Sam Grewal, "Manufactured Cool," *Toronto Star*, February 22, 2005, p. C4.

13. Jack Neff, "Marketers: Give Dads Their Due," *Marketing*, October 17, 2011, www.marketingmag.ca/news/marketer-news/marketers-give-dads-their-due-38065.

14. Jennifer Watters, "Young, with Tons of Purchasing Power," *Market Watch*, October 11, 2006, www.marketwatch.com/story/young-americans-a-giant-influence-on-buying-decisions-study.

15. Michelle Warren, "Too Much Information?" *Marketing*, November 28, 2011, p. 46.

16. Dakshana Bascaramurty, "American Apparel Is At It Again," *The Globe and Mail*, August 23, 2008, p. M3.

17. Simon Houpt, "Tormenting Your Target Market," *The Globe and Mail*, September 16, 2011, p. B8.

18. Richard Blackwell, "Eco-friendly? Canadians Want to See the Proof," *The Globe and Mail*, July 28, 2008, pp. B1, B3.

19. Megan Harman, "Sprouts with That?" *Canadian Business*, April 14, 2008, p. 23.

20. "Study: Canada's Visible Minority Population in 2017," Statistics Canada, www.statcan.gc.ca/daily-quotidien/050322/dq050322b-eng.htm.

21. Advertising Standards Canada, www.adstandards.com.

22. "Competition Bureau Reaches Agreement with Bell Canada Requiring Bell to Pay $10 Million for Misleading Advertising," Competition Bureau Canada, press release, June 28, 2011, www.competitionbureau.gc.ca/eic/site/cb-bc.nsf/eng/03388.html.

Strategic Planning Principles

Learning Objectives

After studying this chapter, you will be able to

1. Identify essential external trends and conditions that influence organizational planning

2. Describe the steps in the strategic planning process

3. Identify the distinctions and relationships among the various types of plans

4. Characterize the essential elements of a corporate plan

5. Outline the structure and content of a marketing plan

6. Outline the structure and content of a marketing communications plan

7. Show how integrated marketing planning provides solutions to marketing problems

All business planning is an integrated process that involves planning at three levels of an organization: corporate planning (planning conducted by senior executives), marketing planning (planning conducted by brand and marketing managers), and marketing communications planning (plans designed by communications specialists based on guidelines provided by brand and marketing managers). When a planning system works properly, each level of planning is linked to the other levels. Corporate plans provide guidance and direction for marketing plans, and marketing plans provide direction for marketing communications plans.

How plans are struck varies considerably from company to company. There is no perfect model to follow. Some organizations produce very detailed plans, while others take a more action-oriented approach. The common factor among all companies should be integration, meaning integrating one plan with another and integrating all the pieces of a plan together so that a consistent strategic direction is followed when the plans are implemented. This chapter presents a potential model for preparing strategic plans. Students should recognize that it can be altered to fit the specific needs of an organization.

Factors Influencing Strategic Planning

strategic planning (corporate strategy)
The process of determining objectives (setting goals) and identifying strategies (ways to achieve the goals) and tactics (specific action plans) to help achieve objectives.

objectives
Statements of what is to be accomplished in terms of sales, profit, market share, or other measures.

strategies
Statements that outline how the objectives will be achieved, such as the direction to be taken and the allocation of resources needed to proceed.

tactics (execution)
Action-oriented details that outline how a strategic plan will be implemented.

Strategic planning, or the **corporate strategy**, is the process of determining objectives (setting goals), and identifying strategies (ways to achieve the goals) and tactics (specific action plans) to help achieve objectives. Based on this definition, a strategic plan includes three common variables:

- **Objectives:** Statements of what is to be accomplished in terms of sales, profit, market share, or other measures.

- **Strategies:** Statements that outline how the objectives will be achieved, such as the direction to be taken and the allocation of resources needed to proceed.

- **Tactics (execution):** Action-oriented details, including precise details about the cost and timing of specific activities.

Strategic planning is a cyclical process in most organizations and typically occurs on an annual basis. A company's strategic plan is influenced by changes in the economy, among consumers, in technology, in laws and regulations governing business practices, in competitor activities, and in environmental issues. This section briefly discusses the nature and implications of these influences (see Figure 2.1).

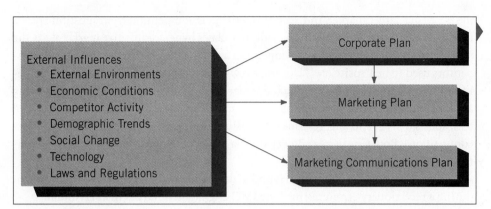

FIGURE
2.1

External Influences Affect All Levels of Planning in an Organization

ECONOMIC INFLUENCES

The general state of the economy has a direct impact on how aggressive or conservative a company is with its business plans. Should it be investing in marketing and marketing communications to expand its business, or should it conserve funds to protect profit margins? The general state of the economy is determined by growth rates in the gross domestic product, inflation rates, levels of employment, the value of the Canadian dollar in relation to foreign currencies, and income distribution among consumers. The relationship among these variables is dynamic. For example, and in very general terms, if the value of the gross domestic product has dropped for a few consecutive years, if levels of employment have been dropping, and if real income has been dropping marginally from year to year, the economy could be in recession. If consumers aren't spending, marketing organizations might adopt a conservative approach and control investment in marketing and marketing communications. In contrast, if an economy is expanding, employment is plentiful, and incomes are growing, it would be a time for an organization to invest more funds in marketing and marketing communications.

To demonstrate the connection between various economic variables and how they influence marketing, consider the impact of rising gasoline prices on the automobile industry. Consumers complain about rising prices, and many alter their buying behaviour because of them. When prices at the pumps rise significantly, demand for trucks goes down, and the demand for smaller, more economical vehicles goes up. Automobile companies have to be ready with the right products to meet consumer demand.

Smart marketing organizations find solutions to poor economic situations. Recession-weary consumers seeking a cheap meal have flocked to McDonald's in recent years. McDonald's value menu has been a hit with consumers. A step ahead of its competitors, MacDonald's is using the value menu as a good traffic builder. McDonald's knows that in better economic times, consumers will trade up to a higher price point on the menu.

COMPETITOR INFLUENCES

Assessing the activities of competitors is probably the most thoroughly analyzed aspect of marketing planning. Such analysis provides input into how one brand can differentiate itself from the others and perhaps stand out more in the eyes of consumers. Most Canadian markets are very competitive and described as being an **oligopoly** (a market with a few major brands) or as being **monopolistically competitive** (a market with all kinds of brands). In either case, the consumer has a choice of what brand to buy, and the effectiveness of the marketing and marketing communications strategies will influence the decision.

Competition comes in two forms: direct competition and indirect competition. **Direct competition** is competition from alternative products and services that satisfy

oligopoly
A market situation in which only a few brands control the market.

monopolistic competition
A market in which there are many competitors, each offering a unique marketing mix; consumers can assess these choices prior to making a buying decision.

direct competition
Competition from alternative products and services that satisfy the needs of a target market.

indirect competition
Competition from substitute products that offer the same benefit as another type of product.

the needs of a target market. **Indirect competition** is competition from substitute products that offer customers the same benefit. In today's hypercompetitive marketplace, the lines between direct and indirect competition are becoming blurred. Coca-Cola's competitors used to be Pepsi-Cola, 7Up, and a few other popular soft drinks (direct competition). Now consumers have a much broader choice and in the age of healthier living are looking seriously at beverage alternatives such as bottled waters, fruit juices, iced teas, sports drinks, and energy drinks as substitutes for carbonated soft drinks (indirect competition). Both Coca-Cola and Pepsi-Cola protect their position by offering alternatives in all beverage categories.

To see how another company, Hyundai, dealt with a very competitive environment during a recessionary economy, read the IMC Highlight: **Smart Is In at Hyundai.**

IMC HIGHLIGHT

Smart Is In at Hyundai

The recession of 2009 had an impact on many industries. The impact on the automobile industry was particularly harsh. Dealer lots were loaded with inventory, and cash incentives and discount financing were the name of the game. Despite the incentives, car and truck sales were dropping at the rate of 30 percent per month.

Automakers that had a stable of fuel-efficient cars took advantage of the situation, and nobody did it better than Hyundai. Hyundai enjoyed unit sales increases of over 24 percent a month, and market share rose from 4.9 percent to 7.3 percent. How did Hyundai do it? Good information obtained from a marketing research study long before the recession actually occurred determined that consumer spending was going to slow down.

In anticipation of the doom, Hyundai changed its marketing and marketing communications strategy. "We put together a plan to succeed in a down industry," says John Vernile, vice-president marketing. Hyundai introduced a "Smart is in" marketing communications campaign that was different from anything previously done. Hyundai recognized that people were falling behind financially and were concerned with keeping their heads above water.

Hyundai focused on the rational side of human behaviour and used the word "smart" to its advantage. "Smart" would be the new cool and would appeal to the thriftiness of consumers. One television commercial delivered the message by showing a young teen proud to be seen in mom's car when being dropped off at school (not the typical situation). Taglines such as "Smart on gas" and "Smart style" summarized the message in commercials and print ads.

The new communications strategy had an impact on middle-class Canadians. The sales and market share gains are directly attributed to the "smart" message that Hyundai delivered.

Courtesy of Hyundai Auto Canada Corp.

Adapted from Jeromy Lloyd, "Hyundai's Smart Moves," *Marketing*, September, 14, 2009, p. 25.

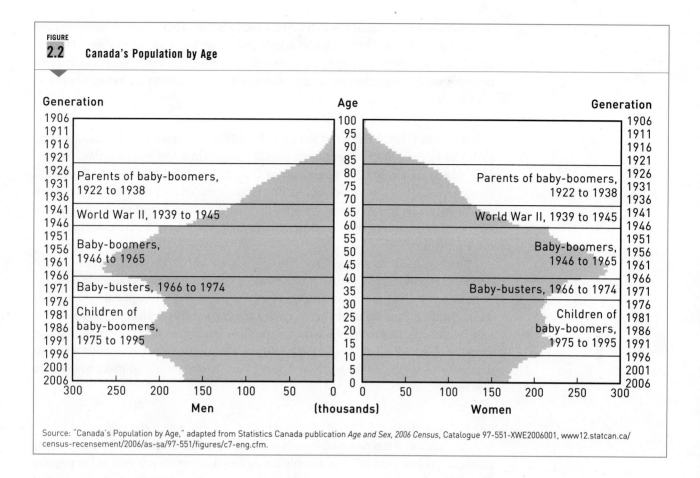

FIGURE 2.2   Canada's Population by Age

Generation | Age | Generation

Parents of baby-boomers, 1922 to 1938

World War II, 1939 to 1945

Baby-boomers, 1946 to 1965

Baby-busters, 1966 to 1974

Children of baby-boomers, 1975 to 1995

Men   (thousands)   Women

Source: "Canada's Population by Age," adapted from Statistics Canada publication *Age and Sex, 2006 Census*, Catalogue 97-551-XWE2006001, www12.statcan.ca/census-recensement/2006/as-sa/97-551/figures/c7-eng.cfm.

DEMOGRAPHIC INFLUENCES

For the purpose of devising a profile of potential customers, commonly referred to as a target market profile (see the discussion on this topic that appears later in this chapter), an organization must stay abreast of demographic and lifestyle trends occurring in Canada. This section highlights several of these trends.

THE POPULATION IS AGING   At the end of 2011, Canada's population was 34.5 million, and the annual growth rate is averaging about +1 percent a year. Within this framework, the population of Canada is aging. As Figure 2.2 shows, middle-aged Canadians (a group commonly called baby boomers) comprise the largest portion of the population. The baby boom generation (born between 1946 and 1965) were followed by a "baby bust" in the late 60s and early 70s; a mini-boom then occurred in the late 70s and early 80s. The latter group is commonly called Generation Y or Millennials (the computer/video generation). Generation Y, a tech-savvy group, is a primary target for marketers now and in the future.

Baby boomers will also be a primary target. It is estimated that by 2021 baby boomers will comprise 40 percent of the population. Further, many will be retiring, placing a burden on Canada's social programs and health care systems. Brands that focus on this target now will have to adjust their marketing strategies to stay in tune with the changing needs of older consumers. At the same time, these brands must attract younger consumers if they are to experience growth in sales. This poses a challenge for many existing and popular brands. A brand like Nike, for example, is popular with older customers, but Generation Y is well beyond such a brand. They are more interested in a brand like Sketchers, which presents a style and image more suited to them. The two generations are miles apart in age and attitude. For Nike to remain profitable, it needs to find a marketing communications strategy that will deliver cachet to the brand once again.

URBAN POPULATION   The trend toward urbanization continues in Canada. According to the 2011 Census, 80.3 percent of the population lives in urban areas. Further, six metropolitan areas account for 46 percent of Canada's population: Toronto, Montreal, Vancouver, Calgary, Ottawa-Gatineau, and Edmonton. The populations of Edmonton and Calgary have grown considerably in the past decade; much of the growth can be attributed to flourishing oil and oil-based industries, which have attracted workers from other provinces.[1]

Keeping track of where Canadians live is an important consideration when developing marketing strategies and marketing communications strategies. With the population so clustered, companies now devise plans that are regional in nature or dwell specifically on key urban areas. Such a trend also helps explain the popularity of regional brands. In Atlantic Canada, for example, Alexander Keith's beer is a leading brand of beer. A national brand like Molson Canadian or Labatt Blue must adapt its national strategy to suit the needs of Atlantic beer drinkers if it is to make headway in that region.

CHANGING HOUSEHOLD FORMATIONS   There was a time when the traditional family was described as a married couple with children. The father worked full time, and the mother stayed at home to raise the children (a family structure reflected in the popular TV drama about advertising called *Mad Men*). Trends such as the postponement of marriage, the pursuit of careers by women, increases in divorce rates, and same-sex partnerships are producing new households in Canada. Now, married couples comprise only 69 percent of households.[2]

Today, modern households are described as lone-parent families (either from divorce or the absence of a partner), same-sex families (openness and acceptance of gay and lesbian lifestyles), and blended families (families that bring together children from previous marriages).

Canadian households are also shrinking in size. Presently, the average size is 2.6, a reflection of the trends described above. Products and services must explore the unique opportunities these trends present. For example, companies in the packaged foods or household goods businesses must offer a variety of sizes to meet the needs of such household variation. As described in Chapter 1 (consumer behaviour section), they must also be aware of who is making the buying decisions or influencing the decisions. To present a brand improperly or in an old-fashioned manner could be harmful to the brand's development.

ETHNIC DIVERSITY   Canada is a culturally diverse country, a situation that presents unique challenges and opportunities for marketing organizations. The population is quickly changing from a predominantly European background to an Asian background. Existing within Canada are many diverse **subcultures**—subgroups within the larger cultural context that have distinctive lifestyles based on religious, racial, and geographical differences.

subcultures
Subgroups within the larger cultural context that have distinctive lifestyles based on religious, racial, and geographical differences.

Market	2006 (%)
Toronto	42.9
Montreal	16.5
Vancouver	41.7
Ottawa-Gatineau	16.0
Calgary	22.0
Edmonton	17.1
Winnipeg	15.0
Halifax	7.5

FIGURE
2.3

**Canada's Ethnic Population:
Key Urban Areas**

Source: "Canada's Ethnic Population: As Percentage of Each Market's Overall Population," adapted from Statistics Canada publication *Ethnic Origin and Visible Minorities, 2006 Census*, Catalogue 97-562-XWE2006001, www5.statcan.gc.ca/bsolc/olc-cel/olc-cel?lang=eng&catno=97-562-X2006001.

Canada's foreign-born population represents 19.8 percent of the population and is expected to rise to 23 percent by 2017.[3] Asian immigration has increased over the past two decades, and Asians now represent 58 percent of all immigrants.[4] Most Asian Canadians reside in the urban areas of southern Ontario, the Greater Vancouver area, and Montreal. Refer to Figure 2.3 for details about Canada's ethnic population in urban areas.

Companies that embrace ethnic marketing will profit the most in the future. The sheer size of this developing market and the fact that unique groups tend to cluster in urban areas make them a reachable target for Canadian brands. The key to an organization's success is to spend time learning more about the target—their customs, beliefs, mores, and so on—and then formulate appropriate communications strategies. Walmart is a leader in this area; the retailer adjusts its merchandising strategies to meet culture-based local market conditions and runs television ads featuring different ethnic groups.

SPENDING POWER AND WEALTH   How much people earn has an impact on their spending patterns. The trend in recent years is for Canadians' disposable income (after-tax income) to grow at a lower rate than the cost of basic necessities required in a household (food, shelter, car, clothing, household supplies, and so on). Canadians are working harder than ever, but there is less available for optional purchases such as vacations, sports, and recreational activities. Lower- and middle-income Canadians (the masses) are more cautious about how and on what they spend their money.

Another income trend in Canada is the concentration of wealth among upper-income groups. The old expression "the rich are getting richer and the poor are getting poorer" applies here. Census data from Statistics Canada verify a polarization of incomes at the upper and lower ends of the spectrum. The top one-fifth of Canadian families had an average after-tax income of $128 200 in 2005, while the lower fifth earned $22 800, a gap of $105 400.[5]

How people spend their disposable income varies with the state of the economy (as discussed earlier in the chapter). With the present economy only growing at a modest rate, consumers are more cautious about parting with their money. Therefore, marketers who stress value in their marketing strategies will be successful. To demonstrate, in the midst of the 2009 recession Walmart changed its slogan to "Save Money. Live Better." Walmart experienced monthly increases in sales, while competitors were losing business. Walmart always emphasizes price and value in its marketing communications.

SOCIAL INFLUENCES

Marketers and marketing communicators must also stay in touch with social change. For a variety of reasons, the lifestyles of Canadians are always changing, and generally speaking, Canadians are very concerned about the natural environment and what companies are doing to preserve and protect it.

LIFESTYLES   Two key issues prevail in terms of lifestyle: Canadians are living a very hectic lifestyle, and they are trying to live a healthier lifestyle. We are now a society that places greater emphasis on quality of life than on work, but we need to work to sustain the type of life we desire. For many Canadians the mythical "40-hour" work week doesn't exist. People choose to work longer hours to get ahead. Being pressed for time suggests a need for convenience. Is it any wonder that 50 percent of revenues at fast food restaurants like McDonald's, Wendy's, and KFC comes from the drive-through? It's all about satisfying the "on-the-go" consumer.

Canadians are also expressing more concern for health and welfare. Issues such as obesity and the aging process are causing consumers to make wiser choices. Marketers are responding to these demands by marketing healthier foods. Kraft Foods, one of the largest food companies, recently announced an "obesity initiative"—proposing healthful changes to its products and marketing strategies. Ultima Foods is also placing an emphasis on health with many of its new product offerings, including its highly successful IÖGO yogurt product lines. See the image in Figure 2.4.

NATURAL ENVIRONMENT   Today's consumers show serious concern for the natural environment and tend to favour companies that have a strong reputation for protecting our natural resources and for contributing to worthy causes. Essentially, companies with a strong social conscience stand to benefit now and in the future. Companies that are perceived to show only tokenism to such a serious issue can be quickly punished when consumers resist buying their products.

To demonstrate, Toyota and Honda are perceived by many to be leaders in automotive technology designed to protect the planet. Toyota's Prius model (a fuel-efficient hybrid) has been an overwhelming success in the marketplace, with demand so high that dealers have to form waiting lists for the cars. Refer to the illustration in Figure 2.5. As part of their marketing communications, Toyota communicates its green initiatives to the public.

TECHNOLOGY INFLUENCES

Several factors are combining to make an impact on how we learn about products and buy products. These factors include the availability of information through the Internet and our growing obsession with electronic devices such as smartphones and tablets. Canadians are a connected society; 80 percent of the population 16 and older (21.7 million people) use the Internet regularly. These people research products, view news and sports, and play video games, among many other activities.[6]

Canadians have also integrated social media such as Facebook, Twitter, and YouTube into their daily routines to the extent that ordinary people are producing video content for the brands they like, a phenomenon referred to as **consumer-generated content**. Once apprehensive about this practice, marketers seem to have embraced the idea of consumers actively engaging with their brands; some marketing organizations are running promotions to actively seek video content they may actually use.

consumer-generated content
Online content, often brand oriented, that is created by consumers for consumers.

FIGURE
2.4

Marketers Keep Pace with Changing Lifestyle Trends: In This Case Healthier Living

Source: Handout/Ultima Foods/ Newscom.

Advancing technologies are causing marketing organizations to re-examine their marketing communications mix. Given the shift in media consumption toward digital media and away from print and broadcast media, media planners are moving away from mass reach and frequency campaigns toward strategies that stress selective reach and engagement with the target audience. The Internet and social media will play a larger role in the communications mix in the future.

LEGAL AND REGULATORY INFLUENCES

Strategic plans are affected by new developments in the political and legal arenas. Most laws and regulations governing business practice are created by federal and provincial

FIGURE
2.5   The Toyota Prius Is Positioned as an Environmentally Friendly Vehicle

Source: Friso Gentsch/EPA/Newscom.

legislation. As well, many industries establish and abide by their own self-regulation policies and practices. In some cases, the self-regulation guidelines are more stringent. Industry Canada regulates Canadian businesses through the *Competition Act*. As discussed in Chapter 1, sometimes an organization disregards the law and finds itself in court for marketing issues related to exaggerated product claims or misleading advertising.

Advertisers should follow the *Canadian Code of Advertising Standards*. The Code contains regulations about gender portrayal, product claims, price claims, advertising involving product comparisons, and advertising to children. The Code is administered by Advertising Standards Canada, a group representing advertisers and advertising agencies.

Canadians are also protected by various privacy laws, the *Privacy Act*, and the *Personal Information Protection and Electronic Documents Act* (PIPEDA). The *Privacy Act* places limits on the collection, use, and disclosure of personal information and gives Canadians the right to access and correct any information about them held by government organizations. It also sets rules for how private organizations collect, use, and disclose personal information.

Self-regulation is an alternative to government regulation. The Canadian Marketing Association (CMA) has established policies and guidelines that all member organizations agree to follow. The CMA's *Code of Ethics and Standards of Practice* is a document covering issues such as protection of personal privacy, protecting the environment, and media-specific standards of practice. The CMA also established a Privacy Policy that identifies policies regarding the protection of information collected by CMA members. For more insight into CMA regulations and policies, visit its website at www. the-cma.org.

Strategic Planning Process

Organizations that develop strategic plans have their own unique ways of doing so. A fairly common approach to planning is to start the process at the top or senior level of the organization and work downward. In other words, the strategic plan, or corporate plan, devised by senior executives will influence the nature of the various brand marketing plans developed by middle managers, and the brand marketing plans will influence the nature of the marketing communications plan.

In the **corporate plan** developed by senior executives, most objectives are financial in nature and become the goals that must be shared by all of the company's divisions or products. Typically, the corporate plan is not an exhaustive document. Once the corporate plan has been struck, the various functional areas, including marketing, start their planning process. See Figure 2.6 for a visual illustration.

A **marketing plan** is developed for each one of a company's products and sets out the objectives for all brands. The plan determines how the various elements of the marketing mix will be employed so that they have the desired impact on the target market. The target market is identified through some combination of demographic, psychographic, and geographic variables, and a positioning strategy statement guides the development of the plan.

Once the role of marketing communications has been determined, specific plans are then developed for the various components of the marketing communications mix. At this stage, the goal is to develop a synergistic communications plan that will improve the well-being of the product or service. Decisions are made on what components of the marketing communications mix to employ—advertising, interactive communications including social media, direct response communications, sales promotions, public relations, and experiential marketing.

corporate plan
A strategic plan formulated at the executive level of an organization to guide the development of functional plans in the organization.

marketing plan
A short-term, specific plan of action that combines strategy and tactics.

The corporate plan provides guidance for the marketing plan, and the marketing plan provides guidance for the marketing communications plan. All plans are based on the same background information and any analysis stemming from that information.

FIGURE 2.6

Strategic Planning: Links Among Various Organizational Plans

The integration of all relevant components in a strategic plan will help achieve objectives. The saying "A chain is only as strong as its weakest link" appropriately describes the relationships among various components of the marketing communications mix. As in war, a unified attack has a better chance of success!

The corporate plan provides guidance for the marketing plan, and the marketing plan provides guidance for the marketing communications plan. All plans are based on the same background information and any analysis stemming from that information. Corporate plans are strategic in nature. Marketing plans and marketing communications plans are both strategic and tactical in nature.

The Corporate Plan

mission statement
A statement of an organization's purpose and operating philosophy; provides guidance and direction for the operations of the company.

The mission statement is the guiding light for all forms of strategic planning. A **mission statement** is a statement of an organization's purpose and an indicator of the operating philosophy the organization follows. A good mission statement is customer and marketing oriented, considers the competition, and looks to the long term. In other words, once a company establishes its mission, it must provide adequate time and resources to carry through with it. Mountain Equipment Co-op (MEC) uses different language to prepare and present their mission. They refer to it as Our MEC Charter. The charter sets out the organization's mission, values, vision, and core values. See Figure 2.7 for details.

corporate objective
A statement of a company's overall goal; used to evaluate the effectiveness or ineffectiveness of a company's strategic plan.

With the mission confirmed, executive attention turns to setting corporate objectives, determining strategic direction, and allocating resources. **Corporate objectives** are statements of a company's overall goals. These objectives are usually financial in nature and are used to evaluate the effectiveness or ineffectiveness of a company's strategic plan and the people who manage the organization. At the end of the year, actual financial results are compared to the objectives. The degree of success is there for all concerned to see. Here are a few examples of corporate objectives, both quantitative and qualitative:

- To increase company sales revenue from $50 000 000 to $60 000 000 in 20XX.

- To increase category market share (share in a market for all company brands) from 25 percent to 30 percent in 20XX.

- To increase return on investment from 10 percent to 15 percent in 20XX.

- To exhibit constructive social responsibility by investing in research and development to discover environmentally friendly new products.

The last objective on the list above is qualitative in nature. At the end of the year, however, the organization will evaluate in some way its investment in social responsibility programs. The first three objectives on the list are quantitative in nature. Objective statements like these have direct impact on the development of marketing objectives and strategies. All company brands must contribute to achieving the company's goals. It is the total of sales revenues for various brands that constitutes overall company sales revenue. For example, PepsiCo divides its brands into separate divisions: Pepsi-Cola soft drinks, Frito Lay salty snacks, Quaker food products, Tropicana juices, and Gatorade. In the Quaker division, the combined sales revenues and profits of brands such as Quaker Oats, Cap'n Crunch, Quaker Puffed Wheat, Quaker Chewy Granola Bars, and Aunt Jemima mixes and syrups contribute to the achievement of overall division objectives.

When an organization determines its corporate strategy, it considers several factors: marketing strength, degree of competition in current or new markets under consideration, financial resources, research and development capabilities, and management

Mountain Equipment Co-op's Charter: A Component of Its Strategic Plan

Our MEC Charter

The MEC Charter sets out our mission, values, vision, and core purpose. It's what guides us along the path to our future goals.

Why we're here

We inspire and enable everyone to lead active outdoor lifestyles. We do that by selling outdoor gear, clothing, and services. We match our members with gear that suits their needs. But we offer more than products. We offer passion. We love to share our expertise, experience, and enthusiasm.

Where we came from

We started small: a few young climbers in the mountains, who dreamed of outdoor gear that wouldn't let you down at prices that wouldn't break your budget.

Where we are

We've grown from a few members to millions. Our interests have grown too. Now we climb, ski, hike, run, paddle, and cycle. We've grown from a small business to a big one, yet we remain a different kind of business. We're a member-owned co-operative. We're not working to make big surpluses, just enough to sustain what we do.

What guides us as we go

Quality	We offer high-quality, high-performance products at very competitive prices.
Integrity	We listen carefully to one another. We deal in good faith. We are honest, fair, and ethical.
Co-operation	We understand the power of community and co-operative principles. We draw on the strength of people working together.
Creativity	We embrace original ideas and fresh ways of looking at the world. We draw on these to build and evolve our heritage.
Leadership	We lead by example. We seek to motivate other individuals and organizations to act for people and the planet.
Sustainability	We work to make and market our products sustainably. We strive to build and operate our facilities with minimum ecological impact.
Stewardship	We act to preserve and restore wild places. We do so actively, consistently, and generously.
Humanity	We work actively to ensure those who make our products are treated with respect.
Adventure	We believe in living life to the fullest, with a spirit of adventure, a thirst for challenge, and a desire to learn.

Where we want to go

We aspire to be the most viable, vibrant outdoor retail business in Canada. We want to bring about a future where Canadians of all ages, and especially our youth, play outdoors in self-propelled ways more often and in ever-increasing numbers; have access to a comprehensive, carefully nurtured network of parks, wilderness, and outdoor recreation areas; and have a connection to nature that is stronger than ever. We want MEC and our members to set examples that inspire other organizations and individuals towards environmental, social, and economic sustainability. In short, we want to leave the world better than we found it.

Courtesy: Mountain Equipment Co-op.

commitment to particular goals. It is common for a company to follow numerous strategic directions at the same time, largely due to the dynamic nature of the marketplace. To follow one direction and fail could have a negative long-term effect on the company.

To grow and be profitable, a company will give due consideration to a variety of strategic options. Among the options are a penetration strategy, an acquisition strategy, a new product development strategy, and a strategic alliance strategy. All these strategies imply a desire for growth. In some cases, a company may decide to get smaller. While that may seem odd, many companies find that too much expansion can have disastrous results on profits. Growing at the expense of profit doesn't make sense!

divestment strategy
Selling off divisions or product lines that no longer fit the strategic direction an organization is taking.

In such cases, a company may decide on a **divestment strategy** and sell off various divisions or products. Such a course may also have to do with how well a product or division of a company "fits" with the direction the company is heading in. In 2012, Procter & Gamble sold off Pringles, the fourth-largest brand of sweet and savoury snacks in the world, to Kellogg Co. Over a period of time, Procter & Gamble has been weaning itself of food products, preferring to increase its presence in personal care and household goods categories.

acquisition strategy
A plan of action for acquiring companies that represent attractive financial opportunities.

For Kellogg's the transaction was part of its **acquisition strategy**. Kellogg's bought a product of interest, a product that fit well with the direction the company was heading. For a price tag of $2.7 billion, Kellogg's became the second-largest snack company in the world (behind Pepsi-Co's Frito Lay division).[7]

penetration strategy
A plan of action for aggressive marketing of a company's existing products.

A **penetration strategy** involves aggressive marketing of a company's existing products. The goal is to build the business by taking customers from the competition or by expanding the entire market. Coca-Cola invests considerable sums of money into key brands such as Coca-Cola and Diet Coke to retain leadership in the soft drink category. Arch-rival PepsiCo invests considerable sums of money in Pepsi-Cola and Diet Pepsi to take market share away from Coca-Cola. It is a real marketing and marketing communications battle between the two companies! And that battle extends into other categories as well—Aquafina water (Pepsi-Cola) versus Dasani water (Coca-Cola) and Gatorade (Pepsi-Cola) versus Powerade (Coca-Cola)—though the latter battle is rather one-sided in favour of Gatorade.

new product development strategy
A marketing strategy that calls for significant investment in research and development to develop innovative products.

New products, the result of a **new product development strategy**, offer another option for growth-minded companies. New products create new revenue streams at a much greater rate than simply trying to expand existing products. Think of all the new products that have contributed to Apple's success: iPod, iTunes, iPhone, iPad, and so on. Apple is anything but a computer company these days!

Beer brand Alexander Keith's expanded beyond beer when it launched a new product in 2012: Alexander Keith's Original Cider. The new beverage appealed to both men and women, and consumers could experience both taste and refreshment all in one beverage. The marketing communications strategy aimed at adults 25 to 34 supported the "refreshing ritual" of serving Original Cider over ice and sharing it with friends.[8] Refer to the ad that appears in Figure 2.8.

strategic alliance
A relationship between two companies where the resources of those companies are combined in a marketing venture for the purpose of satisfying the customers they share.

Strategic alliances occur when separate companies with complementary strengths join forces to satisfy their shared customers. Alliances are now very popular among companies searching for ways to reduce costs or improve operating efficiency. A successful alliance between Target and Starbucks in the United States was introduced to Canada when Target opened its stores in 2013. The in-store Starbucks-licensed stores serve the usual customized beverages along with breakfast items and lunch sandwiches. Target Canada John Morioka, VP of merchandising said "It was a natural fit to expand its relationship with Starbucks to 'bring the true Target experience' to Canadian shoppers." Starbucks president Colin Moore said, "It represents another way we're able to create meaningful connections with both new and existing customers."[9]

FIGURE
2.8

Alexander Keith's Increases Sales Revenue by Launching Products into New Segments of the Alcohol-based Beverage Market

Source: Handout/Alexander Keith's/Newscom.

Marketing Planning

With the details of the corporate plan determined, the marketing department starts the process of marketing planning. **Marketing planning** involves analyzing, planning, implementing, and controlling marketing initiatives to satisfy target market needs and achieve organizational objectives. Marketing plans are short term in nature (one year), specific in scope (they involve precise actions for one product), and combine both strategy and tactics (they are action oriented). The marketing plan should also include a **contingency plan** to provide alternative courses of action in the event that new circumstances arise.

The marketing plan revolves around the customer, specifically the knowledge an organization has of its customers. An essential ingredient in the development of a marketing plan is a precise description of the target market. The **target market** is the group of persons for whom a firm creates and markets a product that specifically meets the needs and preferences of that group. A target market is described in terms of demographic, psychographic, geographic, and behaviour response characteristics.

marketing planning
The analysis, planning, implementing, and controlling of marketing initiatives to satisfy target market needs and achieve organizational objectives.

contingency plan
The identification of alternative courses of action that can be used to modify an original plan if and when new circumstances arise.

target market
The group of persons for whom a firm creates and markets a product.

DEMOGRAPHIC CHARACTERISTICS   Demographics describe a customer group in terms of age, gender, income, occupation, education, marital status, household formation, and ethnic background. Depending on the nature of the product, some characteristics may be more important than others. Some may not be important at all. Given the role changes among males and females in Canadian households, many brands and products that used to be gender-specific are rethinking their target market description.

PSYCHOGRAPHIC CHARACTERISTICS   Psychographics describe a customer group in terms of attitudes, interests, opinions, and activities. The focus is on the "lifestyle" of the members in the group. It is quite common in marketing and marketing communications to appeal to consumers based on their lifestyle or the lifestyle they would like to have. It's not so much what is said in a message but how it is said or portrayed visually. Psychographic knowledge can directly influence message and media strategy. For example, if the target market spends more time online and less time watching television than it used to, such knowledge will influence media selection strategy.

GEOGRAPHIC CHARACTERISTICS   Where a person lives (for example, a certain region of the country or large cities across the country) has an impact on marketing communications strategy. According to Statistics Canada, some 80 percent of the population lives in an urban area. More to the point, Canada's top three cities (and surrounding areas) comprise about one-third of the population. Marketers, therefore, have the option of marketing nationally, regionally, or in designated urban areas, all of which influences decisions on how to allocate a budget and what media to employ.

BEHAVIOUR RESPONSE   The behaviour of group members rounds out a target market description. For example, many products (suntan products, skis, flowers, and toys) are seasonal in nature, and consumers concentrate their purchases over short periods of time. Certain members may consume a product more quickly than others. Such users are described as "heavy users" and may have a slightly different profile than other users. Some members may also demonstrate more loyalty than others. Perhaps the profile of a truly loyal user is somewhat different from that of the average user. Can information about heavy users and loyal users be used to advantage? While usage and loyalty can never be taken for granted, it does give marketers an opportunity to develop strategies aimed at the less loyal users who could switch to competitive brands if enticed the right way. As is often said, "Knowledge is power!"

There is no perfect format for a marketing plan, although Figure 2.9 offers an illustration. Marketing plans vary considerably from one organization to another in length, detail, and content. This section will examine the content of a marketing plan, but readers must realize that the content of a plan is modified to suit the needs of each specific organization. Essentially, a marketing plan is divided into two major sections. The first section is a compilation of background information about the market, target market, competition, and product. The second section is the plan itself; it contains the objectives, strategies, and tactics for the product for the year ahead and provides specific details about how the budget is allocated and the timing of all activities.

MARKET BACKGROUND

The direction a marketing plan takes is directly influenced by internal conditions (strengths and weaknesses) and external conditions (opportunities and threats). The first step in planning is analysis. In marketing terms, such an analysis is referred to as a **SWOT analysis**. The acronym SWOT stands for strengths, weaknesses, opportunities, and threats.

SWOT analysis
An analysis procedure that involves an assessment of an organization's strengths, weaknesses, opportunities, and threats; strengths and weaknesses are internal variables, whereas opportunities and threats are external variables.

FIGURE
2.9   **An Illustration of a Marketing Plan Model**

MARKETING BACKGROUND	MARKETING PLAN	
External Influences • Economic trends • Social and demographic trends • Technology trends • Regulatory trends	**Positioning Strategy** • Positioning strategy statement	Corporate Plan
Market Analysis • Market size and growth • Regional market size and growth • Market segment analysis • Seasonal analysis	**Target Market Profile** • Demographic • Psychographic • Geographic **Marketing Objectives** • Sales volume • Market share • Profit • Other	Marketing Plan • Marketing Background (SWOT Analysis) • Marketing Plan
Competitor Analysis • Market share trends • Marketing strategy assessment	**Marketing Strategies** • Product • Price • Marketing communications • Distribution	Marketing Communications Plan
Target Market Analysis • Consumer data • Consumer behaviour	**Marketing Execution (Tactics)** • Product • Price • Marketing communications • Distribution • New products • Marketing research • Service • Partnerships and alliances	
Product (Brand) Analysis • Sales volume trends • Market share trends • Distribution • Marketing communications • New product activity		
SWOT Analysis* • Strengths • Weaknesses • Opportunities • Threats	**Budget and Financial Summary** • Budget allocations (by activity, by time of year) • Brand financial statement **Timeline or Calendar** • Activity schedule	

*Note: Including a SWOT analysis is optional. Some planners believe that the SWOT analysis occurs when the information is compiled in the preceding sections of the plan. Other planners believe that such information must be analyzed further to determine priorities. The latter is the intention of a SWOT analysis.

STRENGTHS AND WEAKNESSES   The internal capabilities and resources are reviewed to determine the relative condition of a brand and its capability to pursue new directions. The review considers a variety of controllable marketing factors and may extend to the areas of manufacturing, finance, human resources, and technology. Any limits on current strengths may justify developing new strengths.

OPPORTUNITIES AND THREATS   The manager reviews relevant external data that may affect the direction of the marketing plan. Such a review may include economic trends, demographic trends, social trends, legal and regulatory influences, competitive activity, and technology influences. Opportunities are prioritized, and threats are classified according to their seriousness and probability of occurrence. The absence of marketing action in either area could hinder the development of a brand.

A variety of information is collected and analyzed. The goals of a SWOT analysis are to capitalize on strengths while minimizing weaknesses and to take advantage of opportunities while fending off threats. Typically, a SWOT analysis should review the following information (refer to Figure 2.9 for an illustration of a marketing plan model).

EXTERNAL INFLUENCES

- **Economic Trends:** The current and predicted states of the economy are considered. Is the economy growing (recovery or prosperity) or is it sputtering (recession)? Appropriate statistical information is evaluated in this section of the plan.

- **Social and Demographic Trends:** Basic trends in age, income, household formation, immigration, migration, and lifestyles are evaluated to identify potential target markets. For example, the aging of Canada's population, the migration of the population to urban areas, or concern for the environment will be a factor influencing marketing strategies in the future.

- **Technology Trends:** The rapid pace of change and its impact on behaviour must be considered. Technology quickens the speed with which new products come to market and the way companies deliver messages about products to customers.

- **Regulatory Trends:** A company should always stay abreast of changes to any laws and regulations affecting the marketing of its products. For example, new privacy laws have been introduced in Canada to protect consumers and regulate companies engaged in e-marketing practices.

MARKET ANALYSIS

- **Market Size and Growth:** A review of trends over several years is considered for the purpose of making sales projections for the year ahead. Is the market growing or declining, and how fast?

- **Regional Markets:** Sales trends by region are analyzed to determine what areas need more or less attention in the year ahead. Some markets may be growing while others are not. A regional analysis helps determine priorities.

- **Market Segment Analysis:** There could be numerous product segments in a market. For example, in the hotel industry there are budget hotels, mid-priced hotels, and luxury hotels. Are all segments growing at the same rate, or are some segments doing better than others? Interpretive comments about the various segments should be included.

- **Seasonal Analysis:** Seasonal or cyclical trends over the course of a year are examined. For example, volume trends for beer and barbecue-related items would be much higher in the spring and summer seasons. The timing of proposed marketing activities needs to consider such trends.

TARGET MARKET ANALYSIS

- **Consumer Data:** The profile of primary users (and secondary users, if necessary) is reviewed for any changes during the past few years. The aging population and lifestyle changes could be affecting the profile of product users.

- **Consumer Behaviour:** The degree of customer loyalty to the market and products within a market is assessed. Are customers loyal to the brand or do they switch brands? Knowledge of such behaviour has a direct influence on advertising and promotion strategies. Should the plan attract new customers, prevent existing customers from departing, or do both?

PRODUCT (BRAND) ANALYSIS   An assessment of a brand's past performance is included in this section of the plan. An attempt is made to link past marketing activities to the performance of the brand. Have previous strategies been successful, and will changes be needed in the year ahead?

- **Sales Volume Trends:** Historical volume trends are plotted to forecast sales for the year ahead.
- **Market Share Trends:** Market share is a clear indicator of brand performance. Market share trends are examined nationally, regionally, and by key markets to determine areas of strengths and weaknesses. Is the brand's market share growing faster or slower than competitors' shares? Where are the priorities for improving market share?
- **Distribution:** The availability of the product nationally and regionally is reviewed. Regional availability will affect how much marketing support a brand will receive. Should the new plan focus on areas where distribution is high or low?
- **Marketing Communications:** Current activities are assessed to determine if strategies need to be retained or changed. A review of expenditures by medium, sales promotions, experiential marketing activities, and social media is necessary to assess the impact of such spending on brand performance.
- **New Product Activity:** Sales performance of recently implemented initiatives is evaluated. For example, the performance of new product formats, sizes, flavours, and so on is scrutinized to determine the impact of those factors on sales and market share.

COMPETITOR ANALYSIS   In order to plan effectively, a manager should know competitors' products as well as his or her own product. A review of marketing mix activities for key competitors provides essential input on how to revise marketing strategies. A brand must react to the actions of another brand or suffer the consequences of lack of action.

- **Market Share Trends:** It is common to plot and review the market share trends of all brands from year to year. Such analysis provides insight into what brands are moving forward and what brands are moving backward.
- **Marketing Strategy Assessment:** An attempt is made to link known marketing strategies to competitor brand performance. What is the nature of the competition's advertising, sales promotions, experiential marketing, and social media effort? Have they launched any new products or implemented any new distribution, pricing, or communications strategies? What changes are anticipated in the year ahead?

MARKETING PLAN

The market background analysis leads directly into the development of the action plan. The plan section clarifies the positioning strategy of the company's brands, establishes objectives for the year, determines how the various elements of the marketing mix will be employed, and outlines the investment and timing of all activities that are recommended.

POSITIONING STRATEGY   **Positioning** refers to the selling concept that motivates purchase or the image that marketers desire a brand to have in the minds of customers. The **positioning strategy statement** has a direct impact on the nature of the message that

positioning
The selling concept that motivates purchase or the image that marketers desire a brand to have in the minds of consumers.

positioning strategy statement
A summary of the character and personality of a brand and the benefits it offers customers.

must be communicated to consumers. To illustrate, consider the positioning statement that has guided Visa Canada recently:

> Visa gives you confidence that you are able to do anything.

The positioning statement clearly identifies where the company wants the product to be in the consumer's mind and guides the direction of the message that will ultimately be communicated to customers. Furthermore, it serves as the standard for considering what strategies to use and not use. For example, if a marketing communications agency presents a new creative strategy for the brand, the client will evaluate it against the positioning strategy statement to see whether the new creative idea fits with the strategy.

In the case of Visa, the benefits of having and using a Visa card are portrayed in ads that say: "More people go with Visa." This slogan aptly reflects Visa's positioning strategy and brand platform. 'Go' is the active word in the new slogan. It encourages consumers to take advantage of the superior value that Visa offers. Refer to the illustration in Figure 2.10.

TARGET MARKET PROFILE   At this stage, the manager identifies or targets a group of customers that represents the greatest profit potential. As discussed earlier in the chapter, a target market is defined in terms of similar needs and common characteristics based on demographic, psychographic, geographic, and behaviour response variables.

To demonstrate, the following profile might represent a target market for an upscale automobile or watch:

Age: 25 to 49 years old

Gender: Male or female

Income: $100 000+ annually

Occupation: Business managers, owners of companies, and professionals

Education: College or university graduate

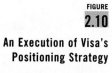

FIGURE 2.10

An Execution of Visa's Positioning Strategy

Source: Soe Than Win/AFP/ Getty Images/Newscom.

Location: Cities with 500 000+ population

Lifestyle: Risk takers who like to experiment with new products; adventure seekers interested in outdoor recreational pursuits; jet setters who travel extensively; and art lovers interested in the arts and entertainment

The advertisement that appears in Figure 2.11 shows how Mercedes-Benz appeals to the upscale target market described above.

MARKETING OBJECTIVES   **Marketing objectives** are statements that identify what a product will accomplish in a one-year period. Similar to corporate objectives, they tend to focus on financial measures, such as sales and profits, or other quantitative yardsticks. Objectives may also be qualitative in nature and include new product introductions, product line extensions, launching of new packaging, and so on. Here, the objective may be to simply get the new activity into the market at the planned time. Objectives do not always have to be measured in terms of dollars or market share.

marketing objective
A statement that identifies what a product will accomplish in a one-year period, usually expressed in terms of sales, market share, and profit.

FIGURE 2.11

Mercedes-Benz Targets an Upscale Market with Its M-Class

Source: Courtesy of Mercedes-Benz Canada Inc.

To illustrate how marketing objectives are written, let's assume you are the brand manager for Mountain Dew (a brand marketed by PepsiCo.). You are developing your objectives for the next year based on your present market share of 5 percent. Mountain Dew is the third most popular soft drink in Canada. The soft drink market in Canada is estimated to be worth $2 billion and is growing at the modest rate of +1 percent annually.

You might set out the marketing objectives for Mountain Dew for the year ahead like this:

- To increase market share from 5.0 percent to 5.2 percent (reflecting a desire to grow marginally in a very competitive market).

- To increase dollar sales from $100 000 000 to $105 000 000 (assumes +1 percent market growth and achievement of market share objective).

- To successfully introduce a new flavour (a product line extension) to extend Mountain Dew's presence in the market.

- To secure 75 percent distribution (in stores selling soft drinks) for the new flavour.

Objectives are written so they can be measured to facilitate evaluation at the end of the plan period. Were the objectives achieved or not? Was the plan too aggressive or not aggressive enough? It will depend on the dynamics of the marketplace over the next 12 months.

marketing strategy
A plan of action that shows how the various elements of the marketing mix will be used to satisfy a target market's needs.

MARKETING STRATEGIES   **Marketing strategies** are the master plans for achieving the objectives. The importance of having a good strategy must be emphasized. There is a saying that "Good strategy with weak execution can produce reasonable results." Likewise, another saying states, "Poor strategy with good execution produces terrible results." The reason these sayings have become so common is that they are true. The goal should be to have the right strategy and then simply to work on better execution as time goes on. Most professional hockey or football coaches would agree with this principle.

In the development of the marketing strategy, the role and contribution of each component of the marketing mix are identified. Priority may be given to certain components depending on the nature of the market. For example, the success of a brand of beer as measured by market share depends largely on the impact of advertising on the target market. In the transportation market, the product environment (a combination of product and additional services) is an important consideration among travellers. VIA Rail, for example, stresses the benefit of staying connected with Wi-Fi service on select rail cars and calls their railway "a more human way to travel." See the illustration in Figure 2.12.

The budget allocated to the product will be identified in the strategy section of the plan. There are various methods for arriving at a budget. Some methods estimate sales first and then base the marketing or marketing communications budget on sales. Other methods develop the budget first, a method based on the premise that investing in marketing communications creates sales, so the budget is not the outcome of sales. Regardless of the method used, the budget must be carefully calculated and defended when the plan is presented to senior level executives. See Figure 2.13 for details about budget methodologies.

MARKETING EXECUTION (TACTICS)   The tactics (execution) outlined in the plan are program details drawn directly from the strategy section of the plan. Such details will identify what programs are to be implemented, how much they will cost, what the timing will be, and who will be responsible for implementation. The unique action plan provides specific details regarding how the various elements of the marketing mix will be

FIGURE
2.12

VIA Rail's Differential Advantage Is a Promise of Staying Connected when Travelling

Source: Used by permission of VIA Rail Canada Inc.

used to achieve the marketing objectives. This section of the plan may also include a description of activities in areas such as marketing research, service programs, and potential partnerships and alliances.

Typically, only the key elements of various marketing communications plans (advertising, sales promotion, public relations, direct response, interactive communications, and so on) are included in the marketing plan. Specific and lengthier information about marketing communications strategies and tactics is presented in their respective plans or in a marketing communications plan.

BUDGET AND FINANCIAL SUMMARY   In order for a marketing plan to be improved, it is crucial to show the financial implications of the activities to be undertaken. Senior executives like to know how the company's money will be spent and how profitable the investment will be. Therefore, the budget section will itemize all activities and indicate the associated cost. Major areas such as media, consumer promotion, trade promotion, and marketing research are often subdivided into more specific activities.

FIGURE
2.13
FIGURE 2.13   Methods for Determining a Marketing Budget

Method	Procedure
Percentage of Sales	A predetermined percentage of forecasted sales is allocated to marketing or marketing communications.
Fixed Sum/Unit	A predetermined dollar amount per unit sold is allocated to marketing or marketing communications.
Industry Average	The average amount (current or forecasted) spent on marketing or marketing communications by all brands in a market is allocated to marketing.
Advertising Share/Market Share	Invest at a level to retain share (ad share equals market share); invest at a level to build market share (ad share is greater than market share).
Task (Objective)	Define the task, determine the activities to achieve the task, and associate a cost to the activities.

In many companies, the brand managers and marketing managers are responsible for bottom-line profitability for their brands. If so, a financial statement for the brand is included. Such a statement should provide some financial history for the previous year, current year, and a forecast for the plan year. Senior executives are interested in seeing progress in marketing terms and financial terms. The financial statement will include such measures as sales, market share, cost of goods sold, gross profit, marketing expenses, and net profit before taxes.

EVALUATION AND CONTROL   It is quite common for an organization to plan for semi-annual or quarterly reviews to assess its financial position. Marketing and marketing communications managers often fear such reviews, because it is a time when budgets are frequently given the axe. Nonetheless, evaluation of activities is essential because changes will likely be necessary while a plan is in midstream. **Marketing control** is the process of measuring and evaluating the results of marketing strategies and plans, and then taking corrective action to ensure the marketing objectives are attained.

The evaluation process also provides an opportunity to change marketing strategies if necessary. If financial obligations are not being achieved, then new strategies must be explored. Furthermore, it is an opportunity to review key financials, such as sales, costs, and profits, and to reforecast the figures for the balance of the year. If the original objectives are not achievable, they should be modified, as should the marketing activities and expenditures that support the product.

marketing control
The process of measuring and evaluating the results of marketing strategies and plans, and of taking corrective action to ensure marketing objectives are achieved.

Marketing Communications Planning

Since plans have to be struck well in advance of their implementation date, the marketing communications plan is developed simultaneously with the marketing plan so that its key components can be integrated into the marketing plan. The various components of marketing communications rely on the same input (background information, target market profiles, and positioning strategy statements) that are in the marketing plan. A marketing communications plan model is included in Figure 2.14.

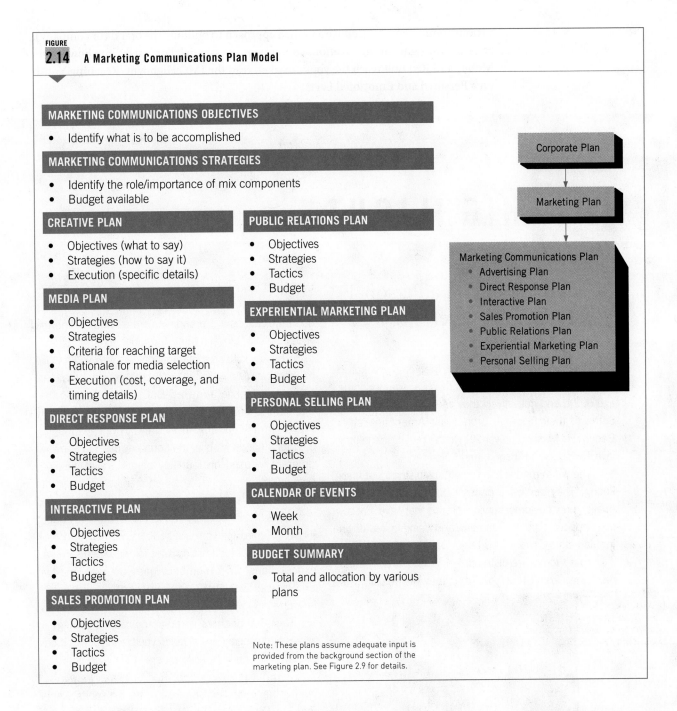

FIGURE 2.14   A Marketing Communications Plan Model

MARKETING COMMUNICATIONS OBJECTIVES

- Identify what is to be accomplished

MARKETING COMMUNICATIONS STRATEGIES

- Identify the role/importance of mix components
- Budget available

CREATIVE PLAN

- Objectives (what to say)
- Strategies (how to say it)
- Execution (specific details)

MEDIA PLAN

- Objectives
- Strategies
- Criteria for reaching target
- Rationale for media selection
- Execution (cost, coverage, and timing details)

DIRECT RESPONSE PLAN

- Objectives
- Strategies
- Tactics
- Budget

INTERACTIVE PLAN

- Objectives
- Strategies
- Tactics
- Budget

SALES PROMOTION PLAN

- Objectives
- Strategies
- Tactics
- Budget

PUBLIC RELATIONS PLAN

- Objectives
- Strategies
- Tactics
- Budget

EXPERIENTIAL MARKETING PLAN

- Objectives
- Strategies
- Tactics
- Budget

PERSONAL SELLING PLAN

- Objectives
- Strategies
- Tactics
- Budget

CALENDAR OF EVENTS

- Week
- Month

BUDGET SUMMARY

- Total and allocation by various plans

Corporate Plan

Marketing Plan

Marketing Communications Plan
- Advertising Plan
- Direct Response Plan
- Interactive Plan
- Sales Promotion Plan
- Public Relations Plan
- Experiential Marketing Plan
- Personal Selling Plan

Note: These plans assume adequate input is provided from the background section of the marketing plan. See Figure 2.9 for details.

A **marketing communications plan** is usually prepared by an outside organization. Depending on the nature of the plan, it could be an advertising agency, a public relations company, an experiential marketing agency, or any combination thereof. At some point, all the agencies working on the same plan must compare notes to ensure that their strategies are synchronized. Each aspect of the marketing communications plan has its own objectives, strategies, and tactical plans. In fact, it is crucial that the role and contribution of each component—advertising, sales promotion, public relations, direct response, interactive communications, experiential marketing, and personal selling—be identified.

The role of the marketing communications components will vary depending on the nature of the product and the target market. The key to success is the integration of the

marketing communications plan
A plan that identifies how the various elements of marketing communications will be integrated into a cohesive and coordinated plan.

various components to produce a unified approach to building the brand (or company). Selecting the right communications components is essential. For insight into how Virgin Mobile and Red Bull reach the youth market, read the IMC Highlight: **Reaching Youth on a Personal and Emotional Level**.

IMC HIGHLIGHT

Reaching Youth on a Personal and Emotional Level

Let's start with a few facts about the youth market in Canada. There are 10 million youth in Canada under the age of 24, and collectively they earn about $50 billion. Some of their favourite brands are American Eagle, Bench, H&M, and Forever 21. On the music scene they love Taylor Swift, Rihanna, and Cold Play.

The youth market has something to say about marketing. They don't like prices that are too high, poor quality, poor customer service, brands that have a negative impact on the environment, and being talked down to. Marketers beware! This target has a lot of power.

Youth today are distrustful of brands and companies; they aren't that loyal, and they are resistant to

Jörg Mitter/Red Bull Content Pool.

traditional marketing techniques. These characteristics call for a different form of marketing and marketing communications if a brand wants their loyalty. And the youth market is loyal if things are done right!

The key is to create emotional ties with youth while treating them as individuals rather than as a mass market. Virgin Mobile and Red Bull are two brands that understand youth and are communicating effectively with them. According to Andrew Bridge, managing director at Virgin Mobile, the company created a reward program focused on four key points: travel, fashion, entertainment, and music. Virgin members get benefits such as early access to concert or movie tickets, and discounts at retailers such as H&M and The Body Shop. Virgin listened to what subscribers wanted and took advantage of it. Redemption rates for these perks exceed expectations, and members pass on their positive experiences with Virgin to their friends—a means of boosting Virgin membership further.

Red Bull anchors its communications strategy in events and experiences to reach youth and youth subcultures. Its priorities lie with experiential-based activities. Yes, Red Bull does advertise "Red Bull gives you wings," but the brand focuses on music, arts, and sports events. Red Bull Crashed Ice Festival in Quebec City draws millions of people, while smaller events such as a movie festival for skiing enthusiasts may only draw a few hundred. Red Bull pursues subcultures that other brands neglect.

Youth will express their uniqueness through brands, so it is up to the brand to connect with them in an appropriate manner. Brands that reach and engage them on a more personal and emotional level will secure their loyalty.

Adapted from Megan Haynes, "Building Loyalty with Youth," *Strategy*, April 2012, pp. 26–27.

MARKETING COMMUNICATIONS OBJECTIVES

Marketing communications objectives are very diverse and could involve any of the following:

- Building awareness and interest in the product.

- Changing perceptions held by consumers about the product.

- Differentiating the product from others by presenting unique features and benefits.

- Attracting new target markets to the product.

- Engaging consumers with the brand or brand experience.

- Offering incentives to get people to buy the product.

- Creating goodwill and fostering a positive public image (usually for a company).

- Creating leads for follow-up at a later date.

- Motivating distributors to carry the product.

To demonstrate communications objectives, let's continue with the Mountain Dew example initially presented in the "Marketing Objectives" section. Mountain Dew is a firmly established and well-known brand, so awareness objectives are not relevant. However, here are some examples of other marketing communications objectives Mountain Dew might identify:

- To firmly position Mountain Dew as an "on-the-edge" brand in the minds of the primary target market.

- To achieve a brand preference score of 40 percent among primary buyers (12- to 19-year-old males).

- To achieve a trial purchase rate of 25 percent for the new flavour among members of the primary target market.

These objectives imply that marketing communications will be an integrated effort including activities beyond advertising. For certain, sales promotions (both consumer and trade) and interactive communications will be employed. There is also room for experiential marketing, as Mountain Dew likes to participate in extreme sports events. Such a marketing communications mix will help solidify the Mountain Dew brand image in the primary target's mind. Refer to the Mountain Dew image in Figure 2.15.

MARKETING COMMUNICATIONS STRATEGIES

The marketing communications strategy provides a basic outline of how the various components of the mix will be used. As indicated by the Mountain Dew example, all components may not be used, but those that are used are often ranked in terms of priority and what they are able to achieve.

This section of the strategy also identifies the budget allocated to marketing communications and how funds will be allocated to the various activities. What percentage of the budget will be allocated to advertising, to sales promotions, to experiential marketing, and so on?

ADVERTISING PLAN   The **advertising plan** is divided into two primary areas: creative (message) and media. The **creative plan** is concerned with what message will be communicated and how it will be communicated to the target market. The message usually

advertising plan
A plan that includes creative and media components.

creative plan
A plan that outlines the nature of the message to be communicated to the target audience; involves the development of creative objectives, creative strategies, and creative execution.

FIGURE 2.15   Mountain Dew Is an Active Participant in Experiential Marketing Activities

Source: Photo by Matt Forsythe/Push.ca.

media plan
A strategy that outlines the relevant details about how a client's budget will be spent; involves decisions about what media to use and how much money to invest in the media chosen to reach the target audience effectively and efficiently.

stresses the most important attribute of the product—that which is most important to the customer. Agencies draw on such techniques as humour, sex, emotions, and even facts to tempt us to buy something. To illustrate, consider the ad for JM that appears in Figure 2.16. A sexual appeal technique certainly draws attention to the ad and the brand name. JM markets underwear and swimwear. Complete details about creative planning are presented in Chapter 4.

The **media plan** involves strategic decisions about what media to use and how much money to invest in the media that are chosen. The overall goal of any media plan is efficiency: The plan must effectively reach the target audience at the lowest possible cost. Since a company invests considerable sums in media advertising, wise decisions about usage are critical. Other media decisions involve timing, what markets to advertise in, how much money to allocate to regional markets and to key markets (cities), how long the campaign should last, and so on. Developing a media plan is complicated and best left to media specialists. More details about media planning for mass media options are presented in Chapter 5.

DIRECT RESPONSE PLAN   Direct response communications have a significant advantage over traditional mass media advertising: The direct results of the investment can be determined. Because direct response techniques can be accurately measured for success or failure, they are attractive to companies that stress accountability in their operations.

FIGURE 2.16   A Sexual Appeal Technique Grabs the Reader's Attention Quickly

Source: Courtesy of JM Intimode Canada Inc. Photography by Jean-Claude Lussier. Model: Aleksandra Koska.

Advancing technology, database marketing practices, and customer relationship management programs have fostered interest in marketing and communicating directly to individuals. Now all forms of direct response are popular. More details about direct response communications are included in Chapter 6.

INTERACTIVE COMMUNICATIONS PLAN   The Internet is a fast-growing medium for placing advertising messages. What about a video on YouTube? If it goes viral, millions of views are a possibility, though that is the exception, not the rule. What about a brand page on Facebook? How about a Twitter feed? Engaging consumers in conversation with a brand is now an integral aspect of an interactive communications strategy. In the years ahead, the Internet and its advertising opportunities, social media networks, and mobile communications will become key components of a brand's marketing communications strategy. Interactive communications strategies are discussed in more detail in Chapter 7.

SALES PROMOTION PLAN   Sales promotions concentrate on reaching and influencing consumers, trade customers (distributors), and a company's sales force. Funds allocated to promotion strategies are traditionally divided between consumer promotions and trade promotions. Consumer promotions focus on objectives such as encouraging trial purchase, repeat purchase, or simply getting customers to buy a product in greater quantity. See Figure 2.17 for an illustration of a promotion incentive designed to achieve trial and repeat purchases.

Trade promotions are designed to encourage merchandising and marketing support among distributors. Getting a product listed and on the store shelves of major supermarkets, for example, requires offering financial incentives to retailers such as Safeway, Sobeys, Loblaws, Shoppers Drug Mart, and others. In Canada, prominent retailers have significant clout with manufacturers, and as a result, considerable sums are spent on trade promotions each year. Sales promotion planning is discussed in detail in Chapter 8.

PUBLIC RELATIONS PLAN   Public relations involve communicating with various groups beyond customers. For example, companies communicate with governments, prospective shareholders, the financial community, the media, and community groups.

FIGURE 2.17   Manufacturers Offer Incentives to Encourage Trial and Repeat Purchases

Source: Photo by Keith J. Tuckwell.

Typically, the goal of such communications is to enhance the company's public image. Public relations can be used to tell the public about the positive things a company is doing, for example, creating awareness of its environmental programs.

In a product sense, public relations play a role in generating interest in new products or spreading "news" about an existing product. Such communications are designed to secure media support for newsworthy information. The nature of public relations is such that written or broadcast news about a company or its products can be of more value. A third-party endorsement through public relations can have greater impact on consumers than advertising. Unlike advertising, public relations are an "unpaid" form of communications for the most part. For that reason alone, public relations' usefulness must be exploited. The role and impact of public relations are presented in detail in Chapter 9.

EXPERIENTIAL MARKETING   Engaging consumers in a brand experience is becoming a popular option for marketing and marketing communications managers. Participating in planned events hosted by others (say a sponsorship opportunity) or creating and implementing a unique branded event gets the target market more actively involved with a brand. Careful planning is needed if the organization is to achieve maximum value from the event. A variety of communications elements must be built into the plan to show how the event will be supported. All of this information is documented in the communications plan. Experiential marketing planning is presented in Chapter 10.

PERSONAL SELLING PLAN   Personal selling plays a key role in marketing, especially in business-to-business market situations. As indicated earlier, personal selling techniques create desire and action. The role of a sales representative is to present the benefits of products and show how they resolve a customer's problem. The sales representative is also responsible for presenting the marketing and merchandising support plans to distributors who resell the company's products. Trade customers must be made aware of all activities that will potentially influence sales. Personal selling is discussed in more detail in Chapter 11.

MEASURING AND EVALUATING MARKETING COMMUNICATIONS

The final step in the marketing and marketing communications planning process involves measurement and evaluation. It is essential that an organization monitor all programs to distinguish effective activities from ineffective activities. There's a famous expression about marketing planning and budgeting: "50 percent of my budget works and 50 percent doesn't work. But I don't know which is which." Yes, a lot of marketing decisions are made on instinct, but many more are based on hard and fast measurements.

In marketing communications, some activities are difficult to measure, and very often too much burden is placed on communications. It is such a visible aspect of marketing that it is convenient for senior managers to be critical of it. Each element of marketing communications should be accountable for what it can accomplish. If it is advertising, awareness scores can be measured; if sales promotion, the number of entries in a contest may be a useful measure; if social media, the number of views of a YouTube video may serve as evaluation. Each component can be measured and evaluated in unique and different ways. This topic is discussed in detail in Chapter 12.

SUMMARY

Strategic planning is an integrated process that involves developing plans at three different levels of an organization. The planning process is cyclical and is subject to constant change based on conditions in the marketplace. To stay on top of things, an organization monitors the economy, competitive activity, social and demographic changes, technology, and laws and regulations.

A marketing communications plan (its direction and content) is influenced by a marketing plan and a corporate plan. When one plan is complete, it provides direction to the next plan. Planning usually starts with the corporate plan, a document prepared by senior executives. Corporate planning starts with the development of a mission statement, followed by corporate objectives and strategies. When deciding upon a strategy, the organization evaluates its marketing strength, degree of competition, financial resources, research and development capabilities, and management expertise.

Marketing planning involves analyzing, planning, implementing, and controlling marketing initiatives. The plan revolves around the customer and includes a precise description of the target based on demographic, psychographic, and geographic characteristics; a sound position-ing strategy statement; and clearly worded objectives, strategies, and tactics.

The marketing communications plan identifies the various communications objectives for the year and the strategies that will be employed to achieve them. The plan is subdivided into specific areas, depending on which components of the mix will be employed. The advertising plan focuses on creative and media decisions. In the creative plan, objectives and strategies (what to say and how to say it) are identified. The media plan states the media objectives by identifying the target market, how often its members should be reached, and when they should be reached. The media strategies rationalize the use of media alternatives and provide detailed information about how the budget is allocated.

If the plan is an integrated plan, other components of the mix are included. Depending on the situation a brand or company faces, the plan could include sales promotion, public relations, experiential marketing, direct response communications, interactive communications, and personal selling. Objectives, strategies, and tactics for each are included in the plan. The goal is to have a unified plan—all forms of marketing communications delivering a unified message to a target market in a convincing manner.

KEY TERMS

acquisition strategy   46

advertising plan   59

consumer-generated content   40

contingency plan   47

corporate objective   44

corporate plan   43

corporate strategy   34

creative plan   59

direct competition   35

divestment strategy   46

execution   34

indirect competition   36

marketing communications plan   57

marketing control   56

marketing objective   53

marketing plan   43

marketing planning   47

marketing strategy   54

media plan   60

mission statement   44

monopolistic competition   35

new product development

strategy   46

objectives   34

oligopoly   35

penetration strategy   46

positioning   51

positioning strategy

statement   51

strategic alliance   46

strategic planning   34

strategies   34

subcultures   38

SWOT analysis   48

tactics (execution)   34

target market   47

REVIEW QUESTIONS

1. What are the external trends and conditions that should be considered when commencing a new planning cycle?
2. What are the key components of a corporate plan? What guidelines does the corporate plan provide to operational plans such as marketing and marketing communications?
3. What is a mission statement, and what role does it play in planning?

4. Identify and briefly explain the four variables or characteristics for describing a target market.

5. What role does a positioning strategy statement play in developing a marketing strategy?

6. "Marketing strategies are the master plans for achieving objectives." What does this statement mean?

7. What is the difference between marketing strategy and marketing execution?

8. What is meant by marketing control, and how does it influence marketing planning?

9. What are the essential decision areas for a creative plan and a media plan?

10. What is the relationship between the various components of an integrated marketing communications plan?

DISCUSSION AND APPLICATION QUESTIONS

1. "Marketing communications objectives are diverse by nature, but a good campaign must have a specific focus." What does this mean?

2. Evaluate the marketing situation for the following companies. What makes them unique, and what is their differential advantage(s) compared to their primary competitors? Develop a positioning strategy statement for each company based on your assessment of the situation.
   a) Canadian Tire
   b) Tim Hortons
   c) Roots
   d) Dairy Queen

3. Using a variety of online sources, conduct a market analysis for a branded product of your choosing. The market analysis should include the following information:
   a) market size and growth
   b) importance of regional markets
   c) market segment analysis (which segments are growing, declining, and so on)
   d) seasonal analysis

   What conclusions can you draw from your analysis?

4. Compare and contrast the marketing communications strategies of two competing brands (a brand leader and a brand challenger). Do these brands use all elements of the marketing communications mix or do they selectively use only certain elements? What conclusions can you draw based on your analysis of each brand? Some brands to consider might be
   a) Coca-Cola and Pepsi-Cola
   b) Nike and Adidas
   c) Dove soap and Olay soap
   d) Crest and Colgate toothpaste
   e) Canadian Tire and The Home Depot

5. Analyze the marketing communications strategies for an automobile (car or truck) of your choosing. Based on the images portrayed in any and all forms of marketing communications, describe in detail the target market that the automobile is pursuing and the positioning strategy of the brand. Provide a profile based on demographic, psychographic, and geographic characteristics. The IMC Highlight: **Smart Is In at Hyundai** will give you some insight into automobile advertising.

ENDNOTES

1. "The Canadian Population in 2011: Population Counts and Growth," Statistics Canada, www12.statcan.ca/census-recensement/2011/as-sa/98-310-x/98-310-x2011001-eng.cfm.

2. "Married Couples with Children, a Shrinking Group," The Globe and Mail, September 13, 2007, p. L1.

3. "Study: Canada's Visible Minority Population in 2017," Statistics Canada, www.statcan.gc.ca/daily-quotidien/050322/dq050322b-eng.htm.

4. Eve Lazarus, "The Cultural Connection," Marketing, August 29, 2005, p. 15.

5. "Income of Canadians," The Daily, May 3, 2007, Statistics Canada, www.statcan.gc.ca.

6. Canadian Internet Use Survey, 2009, Statistics Canada, www.statcan.gc.ca.

7. "Kellogg to Swallow P&G's Pringles for $2.7 billion," The Globe and Mail, February 16, 2012, p. B10.

8. Chris Powell, "Keith's Launches Ice Cider," Marketing, April 18, 2012, www.marketingmag.ca/news/marketer-news/alexander-keith's-ices-new-original-cider-product-50642.

9. Alicia Androich, "Target Canada Gets Its Roast On with Starbucks Coffee Canada," Marketing, February 15, 2012, www.marketingmag.ca/news/marketer-news/target-canada-gets-its-roast-on-with-starbucks-coffee-canada-46363.

Branding Strategy

Yoshikazu Tsuno/AFP/Getty Images

Learning Objectives

After studying this chapter, you will be able to

1. Describe the concept of branding and the role it plays in marketing communications and other business-building programs

2. Identify the various components of a brand

3. Describe the benefits of branding for organizations and consumers

4. Characterize the various stages of brand loyalty

5. Describe the role and importance of brand positioning and its relationship to marketing communications plans

6. Explain various brand positioning strategies commonly used in marketing communications

7. Describe the role and influence of packaging and product design in the brand-building process

Think of marketing and marketing communications as a loop. The loop starts somewhere and ends somewhere, but exactly where? Well, it starts with the brand and ends with the brand. Marketing and marketing communications programs create awareness for the brand (the start of the loop). All kinds of messages are sent to consumers through a variety of touch-points such as packaging, personal selling, events, promotions, news articles, advertising, and social media. Collectively, these messages heighten the interest and desire for the brand. While all this is happening, competing brands are doing the same thing. The goal for all brands is to get the consumer to buy their brand. The consumer is now standing in front of a store shelf looking at all the different brands. Which one does he or she buy? The customer takes action and places one brand in the shopping cart. Which one? The loop just closed.

What this loop principle suggests is that every form of communication is going to have some kind of impact. The impact of the message and its ability to stimulate action are determined by what a brand has to offer (for example, a compelling reason why someone should buy it) and the convincing way in which the message is delivered to potential customers. Essentially, the brand offering and the message communicated to consumers form the backbone of brand strategy and positioning strategy. This chapter provides insights into how brand strategy and positioning strategy are developed and shows the influence of marketing communications in developing a relationship between the customer and the brand.

Defining the Brand

Just what is a brand? A **brand** is a name, term, design, symbol, or any other feature that identifies one seller's good or service as distinct from those of other sellers. The legal term for brand is trademark. A brand may identify one item, a family of items, or all items of that seller.[1]

In today's hypercompetitive marketing environment, branding is a hot button. Marketing executives are busy trying to find or build their brand essence, brand architecture, or brand DNA. Maybe it's a little overdone! That said, brands and branding have been around for centuries; only recently has the concept worked its way into everyday conversation.

Marketing communications in any form have an impact on how customers perceive a brand. It seems that a brand is more than just a tangible product. It can embrace intangible

brand
An identifying mark, symbol, word or words, or combination of mark and words that separates one product from another product; can also be defined as the sum of all tangible and intangible characteristics that make a unique offer to customers.

67

characteristics as well. Customer perceptions of brands are largely based on the brand name and what it stands for. It is an image they hold of a brand over an extended period and that image is based on what they have learned about the brand. For example, a brand such as Rolex suggests a certain quality or status. A potential buyer does not have to question the quality of the watch; he or she is buying the image and reputation of the watch, created by marketing communications over a long period. A packaged goods brand like Cheerios cereal has a loyal customer following because it offers value beyond good taste—customers perceive Cheerios as a product that enhances their daily life (health) in some small way. Cheerios leads all adult cereal brands in brand loyalty rankings.[2] Refer to the image in Figure 3.1.

As indicated by the definition of a brand, there are elements beyond the name that contribute to a brand's image. These elements working together help differentiate one brand from the others that are available to customers. Let's take a closer look at the components of a brand.

brand name
That part of a brand that can be spoken.

The **brand name** is the part of the brand that can be spoken. It may consist of a word, letter, or group of words and letters. Nike, Gatorade, WD-40, Apple, Starbucks, and Google are all brand names. Brand names are usually presented with their own unique font style. For example, Coca-Cola appears in a stylized font on all bottles, cans, and other forms of marketing communications. The presentation of the name is consistent at all times.

FIGURE 3.1   **Packaging and Other Forms of Messaging Play a Role in Communicating a Brand's Intrinsic Value, a Factor that Encourages Brand Loyalty**

Source: Richard B. Levine/Newscom.

Some kind of symbol, referred to as a **brand logo**, also plays a key role in branding and creating an image. When marketing communications work effectively, consumers can quickly identify a brand logo or associate a logo with a brand. With Apple, it's an apple with a bite taken out of it. With Nike it's a swoosh. The swoosh is so well known that it can stand alone in advertisements and communicate a message about the brand. When this happens the trademark holder is a victim of its own success because the trademark loses its distinct nature. Such is the case for famous brands like Band-Aid, Kleenex, and Xerox—names which have become synonymous with their product categories.

The design of the product or package, along with a colour scheme, also plays a role in creating brand image. Coca-Cola has a unique bottle design and a red cap. Its canned beverage is red in color. In contrast, the dominant colour for Pepsi-Cola is blue. Brands protect their properties by trademark. A **trademark** is that part of a brand that is granted legal protection so that only the owner can use it. The symbol ™ designates trademark claims. The ® symbol is used when the trademark has not only been claimed, but registered with the government trademarks office. Trademarks can include the brand names and symbols described above. Coke®, Coca-Cola®, the unique style in which these names are printed, and the bottle design are registered trademarks of the Coca-Cola Company. For a selection of famous brand logos refer to Figure 3.2.

What to name a brand is a critical decision. Consequently, companies spend considerable amounts of time and money developing and testing brand names. When you think of it, virtually every marketing activity undertaken revolves around the brand name. It has to be distinctive and meaningful. It has to be the right name. What to name a product involves a creative decision and a strategic decision.

Brand names come in many different forms. They can be based on people (Calvin Klein, Tommy Hilfiger, and McDonald's), places (Air France and Air Canada), animals (Grey Goose vodka and Dove personal care products), inherent product meaning (Ticketmaster and Lean Cuisine), product attributes (Bounty paper towels and Fibre One cereal), or they can be completely made up to simply sound scientific or attractive (Telus in telecommunications and Classico in sauces).

Brands are more than just a tangible product. A company adds other dimensions that differentiate it in some way from other products designed to meet the same need.

brand logo
A symbol that plays a key role in branding and creating an image.

trademark
The part of a brand that is granted legal protection so that only the owner can use it.

FIGURE 3.2   A Selection of Famous Brand Logos

Sources: Ford Motor Company/AP Images; PRNewsFoto/PepsiCo/AP Images; Karen Bleier/AFP/Getty Images/Newscom; McDonald's/AP Images.

These differences may be rational and tangible, or they may be emotional or intangible entities related to what the brand represents. Through marketing communications, the "personality" of a brand evolves, and the combination of brand attributes (tangibles) and brand personality (intangibles) is what influences brand choices by consumers. The key for any brand is to be perceived as offering something unique. You could probably name at least 10 different brands of deodorant. Why does one person buy Gillette, another Mennen, another Right Guard, another Axe, and so on?

When it comes to branding, you would think that a company with the heritage that the Hudson's Bay Company possesses would be an expert. Surprisingly, and for a variety of reasons, Hudson's Bay recently completed a branding exercise that saw its corporate identity change. The company was marketing itself under the HBC acronym, but that said little about the company, and consumers were confused by it. There is a bank with a similar acronym (HSBC). The company redesigned its corporate logo to reflect its heritage and quality. The new logo is a modernized version of the company's original crest and features stripes in the colours of the original Hudson's Bay blanket—green, red, yellow, and blue. The cleaner, modern look of the branded name and logo is an attempt to stay relevant in today's competitive shopping environment.[3]

Brand Image and Reputation

Brands are more than physical products and services. Whenever and wherever a consumer is choosing between alternatives, brands play a role in the decision-making process. While brands provide customers with an assurance of quality, they also express a set of values that customers can identify with. The Coca-Cola brand is more than just a sweet-tasting soft drink; it carries a set of American values that strike a chord with consumers all over the world. Similarly, a brand like Virgin (Virgin Mobile, Virgin Atlantic Air, Virgin Radio, and so on) represents a youthful, rebellious attitude, much like that of Virgin's maverick founder, Richard Branson.[4]

Marketing communications play a key role in building a brand's image and reputation. A good reputation just doesn't happen—it is the end result of a consistent approach to marketing and marketing communications over an extended period. According to a 2012 reputation survey of Canadian brands, it is a dead heat between Jean Coutu and Tim Hortons (*Canadian Business* magazine survey) for reputation supremacy. Other brands on the top 10 list included WestJet, Shoppers Drug Mart, Bombardier, and Canadian Tire. Among international brands, Sony, Kellogg, and Colgate-Palmolive ranked as the top three brands.[5]

Canadian Tire is another brand with a solid reputation among Canadian consumers. Canadian Tire has withstood incredible competitive pressure from big American retailers like Home Depot and Walmart. It is an innovative company that experiments with new ways of providing value to its customers and as a result remains a leader in general merchandise and hardware retailing. For a list of the top brands in Canada by reputation, see Figure 3.3.

There are times and circumstances when an organization embarks on a rebranding strategy. Such was the case for McDonald's in 2011, when it spent $1 billion renovating all of its Canadian locations to make the restaurants look cozier. Gone were the old plastic furnishings, replaced with leather furniture, plasma televisions, and fireplaces. Exteriors also got a fresher, more modern look. McDonald's reacted to customer feedback, which indicated that people wanted to "hang out" more in restaurants, to take a

Accumulated scores for each brand are based on both good and bad options expressed about the brands by the respondents participating in the survey.

Company/Brand	Rank 2012	Rank 2011	Score 2012
Heinz	1	n/a	84.6
Google	2	1	84.5
Kellogg	3	3	82.6
Sony	4	2	79.0
Kraft	5	7	78.5
Tim Hortons	6	6	77.7
Campbell	7	n/a	77.6
Canadian Tire	8	5	76.2
Subway	9	10	75.5
Staples	10	4	75.3

FIGURE 3.3

Canada's Brand Leaders by Reputation

Source: Based on the 2012 *Marketing/Leger* Corporate Reputation Study, www.marketingmag.ca.

break from their hectic lifestyles, and perhaps enjoy some computer time while having a meal. It has worked. McDonald's enjoyed double-digit sales growth in an industry only growing about 3 percent a year.[6]

BRAND LOYALTY

Brand loyalty is defined as the degree of consumer attachment to a particular brand. Loyalty is influenced by such factors as marketing communications (what is said about a brand), family or peer pressure, friendship with a salesperson, and ultimately how satisfied a person is with the product. For example, someone intending to buy a new car might return to the same dealer and person he or she has bought from before. Satisfaction based on experience with that individual and product helps build loyalty.

Brand loyalty is measured in three distinct stages: brand recognition, brand preference, and brand insistence (see Figure 3.4).[7]

In the early stage of a brand's life, the marketing objective is to create **brand recognition**. It is imperative to communicate the brand name, the unique selling point, and what the product looks like (for example, the package if it is a consumer good, or the look and style if it is a shopping good, such as an automobile or appliance). A marketing communications campaign plays a key role here.

brand loyalty
The degree of attachment to a particular brand expressed by a consumer. There are three stages of brand loyalty: brand recognition, brand preference, and brand insistence.

brand recognition
Customer awareness of the brand name and package.

FIGURE 3.4   The Stages of Brand Loyalty

Brand Recognition
Consumer is aware of the name, benefit, and package.

Brand Preference
Brand is top of mind and considered a good alternative. Consumer will buy if available.

Brand Insistence
Consumer buys one brand only. If brand is not available, the purchase is postponed.

brand preference
The situation where a brand is perceived as an acceptable alternative by a customer and will be purchased if it is available.

When a brand achieves the status of **brand preference**, it is on a short list of brand alternatives that the consumer will consider buying. Such a position is good, because consumers only retain a select group of brand names in their minds for any product category. Furthermore, it is an indication that the message strategies and other marketing strategies are working; the customer knows something about the brand, has evaluated it in relation to his or her needs, and will purchase it if available when it is needed.

brand insistence
A situation where the consumer searches the market for the specific brand.

At the **brand insistence** stage, a consumer will search the market extensively for a particular brand. No alternatives are acceptable, and if the brand is not available the consumer will likely postpone the purchase until it is. Such an enviable position shows the type of bond that can develop between a brand and a consumer.

As suggested earlier, consumers want consistent quality from their brands. The famous Coca-Cola marketing debacle of 1985 confirms how brand insistence works. Coca-Cola made the decision to replace Coca-Cola with a new formula. When the change was implemented, the backlash from customers was so swift and strong that the company had to bring back the original formula under the name Coca-Cola Classic. Some 22 years later (in 2007), the Classic name was dropped, and Coca-Cola returned to its original brand name. Some critics insist that Coca-Cola is a brand that has gone beyond brand insistence. So strong is the bond with consumers, the product cannot be changed—ever.

Since one of the tasks of marketing is to keep customers loyal, smart companies plan and implement loyalty programs. Retailers such as Shoppers Drug Mart, Canadian Tire, Costco, and Choice Hotels, to name only a few, have their own rewards programs. More than 10 million people in Canada collect AIR MILES, a figure that represents about two-thirds of Canadian households. Sponsor members include Bank of Montreal, Shell Canada, Metro, Sobeys, and Rexall/PharmaPlus, among others.[8] Loyalty-oriented marketing programs are presented in Chapter 8.

Brand-insistent consumers often become advocates for the brand—they like the brand so much they will openly recommend it to others. As discussed in Chapter 1, a word-of-mouth network, particularly a social media environment, is a powerful communications tool that influences buying decisions. This phenomenon will be discussed further in Chapter 7.

For more insight into brand loyalty and how to achieve it, read the IMC Highlight: **Brand Loyalty: It's the Emotional Connection that Counts**.

BRAND EQUITY

brand equity
The value (monetary or otherwise) of a brand to its owners; influenced by brand name awareness, degree of customer loyalty, perceived quality, and the brand's association with a certain attribute.

Brand equity is a confusing term that has been historically defined in different ways for different purposes. For our purposes, **brand equity** is defined as the value a consumer derives from a brand over and above the value derived from the physical attributes. Equity is influenced by several variables: brand name awareness, the degree of loyalty expressed by customers, perceived quality, and the brand's association with a certain attribute. Canadian brands that consistently rated high based on this definition of equity include Canada Post, Canadian Tire, Tim Hortons, CBC, and Air Canada.

Brand equity can also be expressed in monetary terms. A brand is an asset of an organization, and therefore has some tangible financial value. On a global scale, brands such as Apple, Google, IBM, McDonald's, and Microsoft lead the way. Apple is presently the world's most valuable brand, estimated to be worth $185.0 billion.[9]

Brand Loyalty: It's the Emotional Connection that Counts

Some recent marketing research from the United States reveals that the core drivers of brand loyalty are emotional in nature rather than rational. The research produces a Customer Loyalty Engagement Index (CLEI) each year, and over the years emotional engagement factors have become more important. In the 2012 research, two specific components rose significantly: the brand's "values" and the consumer's brand "experience."

For the purposes of the research, brand value is defined as what a brand stands for or means to the consumer on an emotional level. Across 83 product categories studied, it became clear that consumer loyalty depends upon the degree to which a brand has established a clear core value proposition—something that

Source: Coca-Cola Co./AP Images.

goes beyond the tangible characteristics of the product. Typical rational characteristics such as quality and price will get people to knock the tires. For marketers, the challenge is to show how a brand enhances the consumer's daily life in some way.

To demonstrate, in the soft drink category the core drivers of loyalty are "refreshing taste" and "brand appropriate for entire family." On these criteria, Coca-Cola ranked first and Pepsi-Cola second. The research observed that Coca-Cola's "Open Happiness" brand positioning and tying its polar bear icon to social responsibility activities were emotionally connecting with consumers.

Among quick-serve restaurants, McDonald's and Subway tied for first place in the loyalty rankings. The top loyalty drivers in this category were "brand value" and "healthy choice." For certain, Subway's well-known slogan "Think fresh. Eat fresh," connects with consumers.

Among kids' cereals (your former favourites perhaps), Frosted Flakes and Lucky Charms lead the pack. In this category, loyalty used to be based on a good price/value proposition. The latest research shows that a brand family focus and taste are the leading drivers of loyalty.

Information of this nature, if known by brand marketers, will impact product and marketing communications decisions.

Adapted from Karlene Lukovitz, "Brand Experience, Values Increasingly Drive Loyalty," *Marketing Daily*, February 6, 2012. www.mediapost.com.

When Canadian brands are ranked on this basis, a different set of names emerge. Among the leaders are TD Bank, Thomson Reuters, RBC, BlackBerry, and Tim Hortons. A list of Canada's top 10 brands by brand equity appears in Figure 3.5.

Effective marketing and marketing communications strategies play a key role in building a brand's equity. Both Scotiabank and RBC Financial invest heavily in advertising media to build their respective images and to instill a feeling of trust among present customers and new customers. A sample of Scotiabank's advertising appears in Figure 3.6.

THE BENEFITS OF BRANDING

Based on the discussion of various branding issues in the preceding sections, it can be seen that consumers and organizations benefit from branding. Some of the benefits for consumers are as follows:

- Over time, the brand name suggests a certain level of quality. Consumers know what to expect; they trust and have confidence in the brand.

FIGURE

3.5

**Canada's Leading Brands
Ranked by Financial Value**

Source: Based on "Interbrand
Announces Canada's Most Valuable
Brands," press release, June 6, 2012,
www.newswire.ca.

Rank 2012	Brand	Industry	Value (C$ Billion)
1	TD Bank	Financial Services	9.7
2	Thomson Reuters	News/Communications	9.5
3	RBC	Financial Services	7.9
4	BlackBerry	Consumer Electronics	6.4
5	Scotiabank	Retail	3.9
6	Tim Hortons	Quick Serve Restaurant	3.4
7	Lululemon	Retail	3.2
8	Shoppers Drug Mart	Retail	3.1
9	Bell	Telecommunications	3.1
10	Rogers	Telecommunications	2.9

- There can be psychological rewards for possessing certain brands. For example, buying a brand new BMW automobile might suggest achievement to the owner. The automobile says something about the driver; it expresses his or her self-image.

- Brands distinguish competitive offerings, allowing consumers to make informed decisions based on what a brand stands for. Marketing communications play a key role in differentiating one brand from another.

Over time, a relationship develops between a consumer and the brand; it's like a bond. Consumers offer their trust and loyalty in return for consistent product quality from the brand. Essentially, a brand is a promise delivered to a consumer. Consumers place their trust in brands and make ongoing buying decisions based on that trust. Each year *Reader's Digest* commissions a research study conducted by Harris/Decima Research to determine the most trusted brands in various product categories. From the 2011 study, it was discovered that consumers want the facts and proof that a brand delivers; that transparency is essential for a brand to succeed; and that brands must be environmentally responsible to win Canadians' trust.[10]

So who are the most trusted brands in Canada? A survey by *Maclean's* magazine among Canadian consumers reveals that Jean Coutu, Tim Hortons, and Shoppers Drug Mart enjoy the strongest reputations. The survey measured consumers' attitudes toward companies based on, among other things, corporate citizenship, leadership, performance, and products and service.[11] Refer to Figure 3.7 for an extended list of Canada's most trusted brands.

Brands play a key role and offer numerous benefits to an organization as well. At the operational level, they help staff to plan production runs, maintain inventory counts, and facilitate order processing and delivery. In a marketing context, the key benefits are as follows:

unique selling point (USP)
The primary benefit of a product or
service that distinguishes it from its
competitors.

- A good brand name communicates the point of difference, or **unique selling point (USP)**, and highlights the distinctive value added. A name such as Lean Cuisine, for example, addresses two benefits: "Lean" communicates low calories and "cuisine" implies it tastes good.

It's not how much you make. It's how much you keep.

Investing outside a registered plan often comes with an unwelcome tax bill. **Scotia Corporate Class Funds** give you the freedom to adjust your investments as life changes, while keeping more of your wealth working for you.

Visit a branch today and ask a *Scotia®* advisor how **Scotia Corporate Class Funds** can work for you.

You're richer than you think:

Scotiabank®

scotiabank.com/corporateclass

® Registered trademarks of the Bank of Nova Scotia.
Scotiabank includes The Bank of Nova Scotia and its subsidiaries and affiliates, including Scotia Asset Management L.P., and Scotia Securities Inc. ScotiaFunds are available from Scotia Securities Inc. and from other dealers. ScotiaFunds are managed by Scotia Asset Management L.P. Commissions, trailing commissions, management fees and expenses may be associated with mutual fund investments. Please read the fund's simplified prospectus before investing. Mutual funds are not guaranteed or insured, their values change frequently and past performance may not be repeated.

FIGURE
3.6

Effective Marketing Communications Help Build a Brand's Image, Loyalty, and Equity

Source: Courtesy of Scotiabank.

- Branding (and the marketing communications that promote a brand) allows for the creation and development of an image. For example, Nike suggests an independent spirit, Visa provides freedom for people to follow their passions, and Coca-Cola inspires moments of happiness. For these brands, extensive advertising campaigns have instilled such images in the customer's mind.

- Satisfied customers will make repeat purchases and, marketers hope, remain loyal to the brand. Such loyalty stabilizes market share and provides for certain efficiencies in production and marketing. Reliable estimates of future sales facilitate internal brand planning.

In summary, branding decisions are important decisions. A brand name stands for much more than simply differentiating one brand from another. Decisions about brand

FIGURE
3.7   Canada's Most Trusted Brands

Rank	Category	Brand
1	Pharmacy	Jean Coutu
2	Quick Serve Restaurant	Tim Hortons
3	Pharmacy	Shoppers Drug Mart
4	Airline	WestJet
5	Technology	Research In Motion
6	Manufacturing	Bombardier
7	Communications	Yellow Pages
8	Convenience Stores	Alimentation Couche-Tard
9	Retail/Home Improvement	Canadian Tire
10	Manufacturing/Food	Saputo

Source: Canada's 10 Most Trusted Brands, *Maclean's*, August 14, 2012, www2.macleans.ca/2012/08/14/canadas-10-most-trusted-brands.

name, benefits offered, package design, and the desired image form the foundation for marketing and marketing communications strategies.

Building the Brand

Building a brand (building brand image and equity) is the responsibility of the brand manager (or category manager or marketing manager, depending on a company's organizational structure). A **brand manager** develops and implements the marketing plans for the brands he or she is responsible for. The process of building a brand involves four essential steps (see Figure 3.8 for a visual illustration):

1. Identify and establish brand values and positioning strategy.
2. Plan and implement brand marketing programs.
3. Measure and interpret brand performance.
4. Grow and sustain brand equity (managing a brand through its life cycle).

Since the concept of brand equity has already been discussed, the remaining discussion in this chapter will focus on brand values and positioning, and the development of marketing programs.

ESTABLISHING CORE VALUES AND BRAND POSITIONING

What does a brand stand for? The answer to that question will relate to the core values of a brand. **Core values** are the primary attributes and benefits a brand delivers to the customer. An **attribute** is a descriptive feature; a **benefit** is the value consumers attach to a brand attribute. For example, Dove tells women to focus on internal beauty and the

brand manager
An individual assigned responsibility for the development and implementation of marketing programs for a specific product or group of products.

core values
The primary attributes and benefits a brand delivers to the customer.

attribute
A descriptive feature of a product.

benefit
The value a customer attaches to a brand attribute.

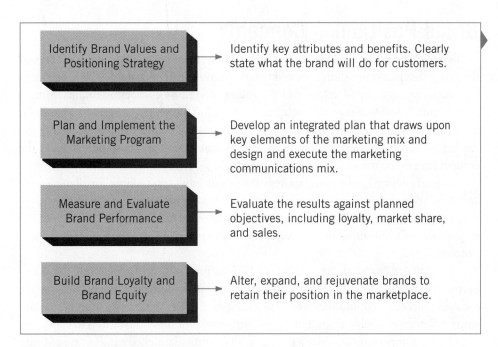

FIGURE
3.8

The Brand-building Process

health of their skin; everyone should be happy with who they are (a self-esteem message). Dove emphasizes an attitude more than the product itself.

The skin care category is large and very competitive. Brands have different means of communicating essentially the same message. They all offer the same proprietary benefit. Some brands focus on psychological benefits, while others focus on product-specific attributes. Each brand takes a different angle on how to communicate the key benefit. That's brand differentiation. As shown in Figure 3.9, Herbal Essences shampoo offers a complete range of products that meet the unique needs of consumers. For example, Touch Me Softly is a shampoo for a tousled look; Touchably Smooth makes hair silkier looking; and Long Term Relationship is for managing long hair. Herbal Essences effectively makes its case for resolving different skin care concerns consumers have.

FIGURE
3.9

Brands Differentiate by Focusing on Unique Attributes

Source: CNW Group/P&G Beauty/ Newscom.

Brand Positioning Concepts

As discussed in Chapter 2, **positioning** is the selling concept that motivates purchase, or the image that marketers desire a brand to have in the minds of customers. It is a strategy influenced by core brand values and the values offered by competing brands. Simply stated, each brand wants to differentiate itself from competitive offerings. Therefore, positioning involves designing and marketing a product to meet the needs of a target market and creating the appropriate appeals to make the product stand out from the competition in the minds of the target market.

A clearly defined positioning strategy statement provides guidance for all marketing and marketing communications strategies. The strategy statement provides a compelling reason why potential customers should buy the brand. Figure 3.10 illustrates the importance of positioning in the marketing and marketing communications planning process.

Typically, a brand sticks to a single-benefit positioning strategy, but for many brands and companies the competition is so intense that additional benefits become the focus of marketing communications. For example, Ruffles, the leading brand of potato chips, offers great-tasting chips, but it constantly looks for new innovations to stay a step ahead of its competitors. As shown in Figure 3.11, Ruffles launched a thicker ridged chip that will grip more dip in every scoop, an additional benefit since regular chips often break during the scoop. The image in the advertisement aptly portrays the benefit of the new product.

The positioning strategy statement should be clear, concise, and uncomplicated while addressing the target market's need and the primary benefit to be offered. Many experts adopt the 4D positioning rule when devising their strategy statement. A good positioning strategy must be *desirable* by consumers, *distinctive* from the competition,

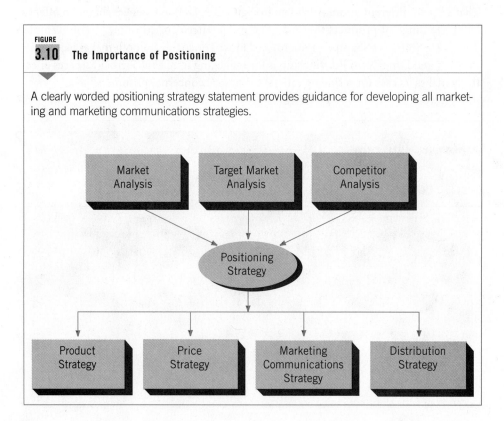

FIGURE
3.10   **The Importance of Positioning**

A clearly worded positioning strategy statement provides guidance for developing all marketing and marketing communications strategies.

FIGURE
3.11

An Ad that Communicates an Additional Benefit: A Thicker Chip Makes It Easier to Scoop Up Chip Dip

Source: Courtesy of PepsiCo Canada ULC.

Introducing NEW Ruffles Thick Cut Regular chips. They're thicker and have deeper ridges to grip more dip with every scoop.

Ruffles ridges grip dip.

deliverable by the company, and *durable* over time. Here is a potential positioning strategy statement for Apple branded products.[12]

> The core of Apple's brand is great innovation, beautiful design, and an ability to bring warmth and passion to those customers who may be completely averse to technical gadgetry, but need it nonetheless to survive in today's world.

One can start to see how such a statement is used as input for developing a marketing communications strategy. All consumer-directed communications for Apple focus on how simple Apple products are to use yet offer the absolute latest in technical innovation.

There are all kinds of ways a product can be positioned in the minds of customers. Let's discuss some of these positioning strategies.

PRODUCT DIFFERENTIATION

Here's what the product is! Here's what the product does! That's product differentiation—nothing could be more straightforward. When a **product differentiation strategy** is

product differentiation strategy
A plan of action for communicating meaningful attributes and benefits of a product to a target market.

employed, the product will communicate meaningful and valued differences to distinguish itself from competitive offerings. Such differences focus specifically on what the product may offer and refer to the form of the product (size, shape, or physical structure), performance quality (it lasts longer), durability (ability to withstand stress), reliability (it won't break down), or style (the look and appearance of the product or package). Glad food wrap products, for example, consistently differentiate on the basis of how a unique seal keeps things fresh.

As shown in Figure 3.12, Danone Activia is a brand that has always been positioned (differentiated from competing brands) as a "good for you" food product. The key benefit is clearly stated on the package and in ads for the product: Activia helps regulate your digestive system.

BRAND LEADERSHIP POSITIONING

leadership positioning
A marketing strategy in which a product presents itself as a preferred choice among customers.

As the name suggests, **leadership positioning** is a strategy often employed by brand leaders. Good marketing and marketing strategies from the past have helped such a product achieve an enviable position in the marketplace and in the minds of customers. These brands have high brand equity. The message such a brand delivers is designed to reinforce its lofty position. Probably the best example of leadership positioning is Coca-Cola. In most North American markets, Coca-Cola is the number one brand with a legion of loyal brand users. In advertising, Coca-Cola struts its stuff. The brand has used catchy phrases such as "Coke is it," "Can't beat the real thing," and "Always Coca-Cola" to communicate its leadership position. More recently the brand has used the phrase "Open happiness." The brand exists to "inspire moments of happiness" among its users.

Brand leaders have characteristics in common that give them an advantage over competing brands: They have greater consumer awareness, are readily available, and have significant marketing budgets to protect their position.

HEAD-ON POSITIONING (COMPARATIVE POSITIONING)

Head-on positioning involves a comparison of one brand with another. Typically, the brand doing the advertising presents itself as being better than another brand. The message focuses on an attribute that is important to the target market. To dramatize the claim of superiority or whatever the claim may be, it is common to demonstrate how both brands perform. For example, we often see popular brands of household products use head-on positioning strategies. Bounty, for example, shows how much water one of its towels can pick up, while a competing brand is shown to be incapable of picking up as much. The Bounty towel still looks partially dry; the competitor's looks saturated. Bounty is well positioned as "the quicker picker upper."

The "Pepsi Challenge" is now the classic example of effective head-on positioning. Originally, television commercials showed people trying both Pepsi and Coke in blind taste tests with Pepsi being the preferred choice—a hard-to-believe situation for those taking the taste test. In a recent television commercial, a Pepsi truck driver and a Coke truck driver are sitting at a diner counter. The Coke driver tries a sip of Pepsi, unaware that the Pepsi driver is taking his picture and uploading it to the Internet for the world to see. A fight ensues between the two. Pepsi effectively delivered its message in the commercial.

Challenger brands often adopt a head-on positioning strategy. Their mission is to instill "thought" leadership in the customer's mind. Such brands will spend considerable sums of money to deliver their message. Challengers must also be aware that a brand leader may retaliate, thus escalating the financial commitment required to maintain the challenge.

head-on positioning
A marketing strategy in which one product is presented as an equal or better alternative to a competing product.

INNOVATION POSITIONING

An innovation is a product, service, or idea that is perceived by consumers as new. **Innovation positioning** is a marketing strategy that stresses newness as a way to differentiate a brand from the competition. Innovation may imply that the company or brand is "leading-edge" in the market it competes in. Apple, for example, is well known for its easy-to-use yet technologically advanced products (think iPod, iTunes, iPhone, and iPad). It's not a coincidence that Apple is also the leader in all of these product or service categories.

In the razor and razor blade market, both Gillette Fusion and Schick Quattro duel with each other for innovation supremacy. Three blades, four blades, five blades—just how many blades are needed for a close shave? Now the focus has shifted to "thinner" blades that glide effortlessly through hair for incredible comfort—very convincing! Refer to the image in Figure 3.13.

innovation positioning
A marketing strategy that stresses newness (based on a commitment to research and development) as a means of differentiating a company or a brand from competing companies and brands.

PRICE (VALUE) POSITIONING

A **price positioning** strategy is based on the premise that consumers search for the best possible value given their economic circumstances. Some consumers search for low prices, others are willing to pay more for something perceived as offering good value, and still others don't even look at price. Some people shop for high-end goods and services, and expect to pay a lot for the products they buy.

price positioning
A marketing strategy based on the premise that consumers search for the best possible value given their economic circumstances.

FIGURE
3.13

A Technological Innovation Message Helps Position the Gillette Fusion ProGlide Razor in the Minds of Male Consumers

Source: Handout/MCT/Newscom.

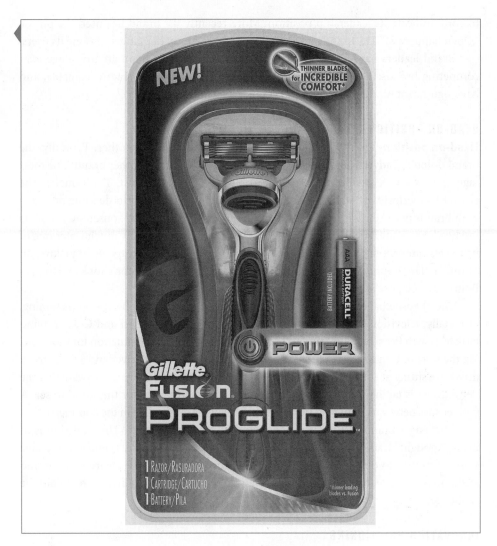

Walmart seems to have a lock on the low-price positioning strategy in the North American retail marketplace. The store's image is firmly entrenched in the consumer's mind from ads showing prices always being slashed to save people money. During the recession of 2008, Walmart shifted its price position somewhat when it began using the phrase "Save Money. Live Better." Their promise to consumers: Saving money on little things adds up and helps families live better. Refer to the image in Figure 3.14.

Another retailing example shows how high-price positioning is an effective strategy. In men's fashion, Harry Rosen (an upscale men's clothier) comes to mind. The Harry Rosen image has been carefully cultivated over time so that customers know exactly what to expect when they shop there. Harry Rosen keeps its edge on the competition by carrying many exclusive products and by moving to customer relationship marketing and pitching wares directly to individual customers in mailings and through special events. According to Larry Rosen, current CEO and son of the founder, "A man looks powerful, authoritative, confident, and professional in a suit. To get the right suit that man knows where to shop—Harry Rosen." Refer to the image in Figure 3.15.

FIGURE
3.14

Walmart's Price Proposition Is Firmly Entrenched in the Minds of North American Consumers

Source: Robyn Beck/AFP/Getty Images/ Newscom.

LIFESTYLE (IMAGE) POSITIONING

In very competitive markets where product attributes of so many brands are perceived to be equal by consumers, it is difficult to follow the positioning strategies outlined above. **Lifestyle positioning,** or **image positioning,** involves moving away from the tangible characteristics of the product toward the intangible characteristics (things that aren't there, for example). Products in categories such as beer, alcohol, perfume, automobiles, and travel frequently use this strategy, as do brands that wish to attract a youthful customer.

> **lifestyle (image) positioning**
> **A marketing strategy based on intangible characteristics associated with a lifestyle instead of tangible characteristics.**

The use of psychographic information allows companies to develop campaigns based on the lifestyle or desired lifestyle of the target market. Generally speaking, lifestyle

FIGURE
3.15

A High-price, High-quality Positioning Strategy Works for Harry Rosen

Source: Jesse Johnston/CP Images.

FIGURE
3.16

Lifestyle Imagery Positions Competing Brands in the Customer's Mind

Source: Jeep is a registered trademark of Chrysler Group LLC. Used with permission.

positioning involves using emotional appeal techniques such as love, fear, adventure, sex, and humour to influence the target. The automobile industry effectively uses lifestyle imagery to sell cars. It is common to see young, urban professionals driving a luxury car and see the rugged outdoors associated with SUVs. Refer to the image for the Jeep Cherokee in Figure 3.16.

REPOSITIONING

As a brand evolves and faces changes in the marketplace, an organization may decide to reposition the brand. For example, conditions in the economy may change, new competitors may enter the market, or consumers' preferences change. **Repositioning** is defined as changing the place a product occupies in the customer's mind, relative to competing products. When a positioning strategy is working, a company should avoid the temptation to change things. That old expression "If it ain't broke, don't fix it" applies here. That said, Hyundai had good reason to adopt a new positioning strategy. For details, read the IMC Highlight: **New Global Position for Hyundai**.

repositioning
Changing the place a product occupies in the customer's mind, relative to competing products.

New Global Position for Hyundai

When you're an automobile company operating on a global scale, you look for certain efficiencies when devising a marketing strategy. As you have learned, the foundation for a good marketing strategy is a solid positioning strategy—a strategy that fits with the marketplace you are operating in.

Hyundai recently moved to a "Modern Premium" global positioning strategy. Before defining what that means, let's first examine the situation in Canada to determine the need for the new position. Hyundai has been very successful in Canada. Market share doubled from 4 percent to 8 percent between 2004 and 2010. Since Hyundai markets smaller, economical cars, the brand was a good fit for middle-class buyers. So the

Courtesy of Hyundai Auto Canada Corp.

question is: Why change things? A lot of other car makers are losing market share.

According to John Vernile, vice-president marketing, "There's one area where people don't think positively about Hyundai, and that's around well-built and durable products." Hyundai wanted to change that impression. A new advertising campaign, supported by a much larger budget and featuring prominent television commercials (in prime time and on Hockey Night in Canada broadcasts), print ads, and out-of-home media, was launched in 2012. The objective of the campaign was to alter consumers' perceptions of Hyundai. Therefore, the message focused on the quality of important components of the automobiles.

To Hyundai, "Modern Premium" is an attempt to move the image more upscale but not to the luxury level. Hyundai realized that luxury is about exclusivity rather than quality, and that's not what Hyundai is about. According to Vernile, the new definition of premium is "good quality and performance that might be unexpected, but at an accessible price." Hyundai believes that this shift in positioning is a good fit for the target audience of 19- to 54-year-olds they are trying to reach.

Ironically, Hyundai dropped its online advertising when the new campaign was launched. Hyundai wasn't happy with the results of their past online advertising activities and decided to spend some time rethinking how to approach consumers with online communications.

Adapted from Jeremy Lloyd, "Hyundai Canada Adopts 'Modern Premium' Global Positioning," *Marketing*, January 18, 2012, www.marketingmag.ca.

PLANNING AND IMPLEMENTING MARKETING AND MARKETING COMMUNICATIONS PROGRAMS

To build brand loyalty and firmly position a brand requires effective marketing programs: activities that produce a strong and favourable association to a brand in a consumer's memory. It is an information transfer process that considers two essential factors. First, decisions must be made about how to employ various brand elements. These decisions involve brand names, trademarks, and characters. Second, appropriate marketing strategies must be developed to communicate the brand values and brand positioning strategy.

The most common brand elements are brand names, logos, symbols, characters, packaging, and slogans. The content of most advertising in any medium, from television to print to websites, usually includes these elements. Characters, whether they be paid actors employed in a commercial or something that an organization creates, help portray the personality of a brand. Think of the manager in A&W's television commercials or the actor who appeared in countless commercials for ING DIRECT bank—the guy who told you to "save your money." Fictitious characters such as Tony the Tiger (Frosted Flakes) and the Michelin Man (Michelin tires) also play key roles in brand advertising.

Slogans are also important in brand advertising, as they tend to summarize what a brand stands for—the brand's positioning strategy. When creating a slogan, creative planners attempt to suggest a key benefit and to reflect the brand's personality, while keeping the slogan short enough so that it is easy for consumers to remember.

Here are some famous slogans from the past:

Molson Canadian	"I Am Canadian"
Red Rose Tea	"Only in Canada? Pity."
Tim Hortons	"Always got time for Tim Hortons"
Budweiser	"The king of beers"
Campbell Soup	"M'm, M'm good"
M&M Candy	"Melts in your mouth, not in your hands"
KFC	"Finger-lickin' good"

Molson Canadian changed its slogan in recent years to "Made from Canada." The new slogan tapped into the brand's heritage and its association with hockey over an extended period. Refer to the ad in Figure 3.17.

FIGURE
3.17

Molson Canadian's Slogan "Made from Canada" Delivers a Strong Message About the Brand to Beer Drinkers

Source: Courtesy of Molson Coors Canada.

MADE FROM CANADA

This land gives us everything. It gives us amazing lakes, epic mountains and more square feet of awesomeness per person than anywhere else. It also gives us Canadian water, prairie barley and exactly what we need to brew one of the best tasting lagers in the world. So raise a glass to this land. We wouldn't be Canadian without it. Cheers.

Based on the numerous examples already cited in this chapter, it should be abundantly clear that marketing communications are the "voice" of a brand's (or company's) positioning strategy. Regardless of the medium selected, that voice must deliver a message with clarity and continuity. If the communications strategies are executed effectively and with sufficient financial support, the desired message and image should be planted in the customer's mind.

IMC HIGHLIGHT

Multi-faceted Campaign Repositions ING DIRECT

ING DIRECT is a successful online banking company. Much of its initial success is attributed to a well-known advertising campaign featuring a straight-talking Dutch actor by the name of Frederik de Groot. In television commercials, he encouraged consumers to "save your money" by banking online with ING DIRECT.

ING DIRECT determined the "Save your money" campaign had run its course. ING DIRECT wanted to move from being known as a bank with a high interest savings account to a bank offering a full range of products and services including RRSPs, GICs, mortgages, and a home equity line of credit. ING DIRECT's new

positioning strategy is "Forward banking," a strategy that reflects the evolution of its product offerings.

According to Andrew Zimakas, chief marketing officer, "We've been known as the bank that helps Canadians save their money since we launched (1997). It's an identity that served us well . . . but our offering has evolved significantly over the years." The new campaign will let consumers see ING DIRECT in a fresh way.

To communicate the new positioning to consumers, ING DIRECT takes a poke at traditional banks. One television commercial shows some hallmarks of bricks and mortar banks—pens attached to counters, velvet ropes, and next window please signs—being blown up in slow motion. The message: "It's time to stop banking in the past."

Since banking in Canada is dominated by traditional banks, ING DIRECT's objective was to be a game-changer, to be known as a brand that empowered its customers through a combination of technology and a human touch. ING DIRECT also adopted a café concept for its bricks and mortar locations. The CEO communicates with consumers about simple banking via Facebook and Twitter.

The repositioning was launched with a multimedia campaign featuring television, print, digital media, and out-of-home media. Social media communications complement the mainstream media strategy. ING DIRECT presently has 1.8 million customers in Canada.

ING ⚫ DIRECT
forward banking™

Courtesy of ING DIRECT.

Adapted from Chris Powell, "ING DIRECT Adopts New Positioning, Unveils New Marketing," *Marketing*, April 24, 2012, www.marketingmag.ca.

In terms of how the various elements of the marketing communications mix are employed, advertising should be viewed as an aerial attack on the audience it reaches. It is the most visible form of communications—a form of communications that creates awareness and interest in a brand. Advertising gets people talking about a brand. It creates hype. The other forms of marketing communications play more specific roles and should be viewed as the ground attack. Communications in the form of sales promotions, experiential marketing, and public relations generate buzz and create desire and action. They provide the stimulus that gets the wallet out of the pocket or purse. The Internet has become a useful vehicle for providing detailed information and for creating buzz. The use of social media such as Facebook and Twitter opens up new avenues for sanctioned and unsanctioned branded communications. Therefore, with all points of contact delivering a unified message, a brand begins to build momentum—the brand-building process has begun.

ING DIRECT's marketing communications strategy was effective in establishing a brand presence in Canada, but now ING DIRECT has decided to move in another direction. ING DIRECT is repositioning itself in the minds of consumers to show that it offers many more services in a more convenient manner than traditional banks. For more insight into ING DIRECT's brand-building strategies and the role played by marketing communications, read the IMC Highlight: **Multi-faceted Campaign Repositions ING DIRECT**.

Packaging and Brand Building

The package is what consumers look for when they are contemplating a purchase. For new products especially, the look of the package must be instilled in the customer's mind. For that reason, it is very common for the package to play a key role in introductory marketing communications programs. The product image that appears in Figure 3.18 demonstrates excellent package identification. Over time, consumers start associating specific colours with a brand, and they know exactly what they are looking for when trying to spot a brand on a cluttered store shelf. Coca-Cola, for example, is strongly associated with the colour red; Tide is associated with orange; and Sunlight is associated with yellow.

In today's competitive environment, packaging is playing a more significant role in differentiating one brand from another. Over the life cycle of a product, the packaging may change several times to spruce up the image of a brand. As well, a common package design across all product lines that make up a brand (that is, various sizes, shapes, and formats) helps maintain brand identity. As can be seen by the packages in Figure 3.18, Tide laundry detergent has a common look and colour scheme across various product formats.

A revolution is occurring in packaged goods marketing, as marketers see packages having a growing influence on purchase decisions amid ongoing media fragmentation. In-store is where a majority of decisions are made. It has been estimated that up to 70 percent of purchase decisions are made in-store (40 percent in supermarkets) by people navigating aisles, scanning shelves, and making spur-of-the-moment decisions.[13] As well, changes in media consumer lifestyles are now forcing a dramatic shift, making the package itself an increasingly important selling medium.

Given the way in which consumers scan merchandise on store shelves, it is clear that colour plays a key role in attracting people's attention. Many brands actually own a colour, at least in marketing terms, a concept known as brand blocking. For example, the colour red demands attention and is a sign of power. In the soft drink market, Coca-Cola

FIGURE
3.18

Consistent Brand Identification in Packaging Combined with an Effective Advertising Message Communicates the Benefit of Tide Laundry Detergent

Source: Photo by Dick Hemingway.

owns the colour red, and it is no coincidence that Coca-Cola is a dominant market leader. Colours are an emotional trigger and consequently are powerful marketing tools. Dark colours project richness and are common in the coffee aisle on brands such as Maxwell House and Nabob. When Unilever launched Dove Men+Care, it used a medium grey colour—a colour unique to the product category. Refer to the image in Figure 3.19.

The package is a very important touch-point with consumers. Familiarity with a package helps build trust between the consumer and the brand, so ultimately the package is a factor that can influence consumer loyalty. A good package serves four functions: It protects the product, it markets the product, it offers convenience to consumers, and it is environmentally friendly.

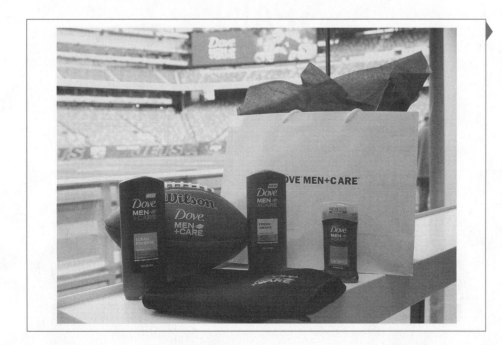

FIGURE
3.19

Dove Men+Care Uses Grey Packaging and White Lettering to Present a Consistent Image to Consumers

Source: Mark Von Holden/Invision for Dove Men/AP Images.

PROTECT THE PRODUCT

How much protection a product needs depends on how often it changes hands in the distribution process. For example, how long does it sit in a warehouse, how will it be transported, what kind of handling will it experience, and how much protection from exposure to heat, cold, light, and moisture will it need? Milk, for example, is traditionally packaged in bags and cartons, but the recent introduction of plastic containers in single-serving sizes has increased the shelf life of milk. In plastic containers, milk products are being positioned as "refreshing alternatives" to fruit juices, energy drinks, and soft drinks.

MARKET THE PRODUCT

In its marketing role, the package does the same thing an advertisement in any medium would do. The design and colour scheme should be coordinated so that the overall look of the package creates a good impression. The package should be attractive and eye-catching to grab the attention of consumers. It should contain useful information and tell consumers what the product's benefits are so they will have a reason to buy it. To demonstrate, refer to the image in Figure 3.20.

FIGURE
3.20

Colgate's Package Clearly Communicates the Key Benefit: It Helps Repair Enamel Damage

Source: Courtesy of Colgate-Palmolive Company.

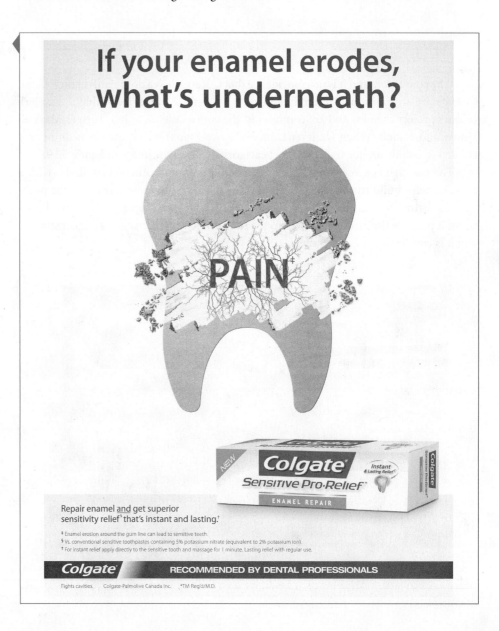

FIGURE
3.21

A Package Face Often Communicates Details of a Promotional Offer

Source: Photo by Dick Hemingway.

Packages can also be used to communicate information about promotional offers such as coupons, contests, and giveaways. Since promotions of this nature are temporary, a package "flash" is usually added to the front panel of the package to draw attention to the offer. Details of the offer would appear on the side, back, or inside of the package (see Figure 3.21).

PROVIDE CONVENIENCE

A package should be easy to carry, open, handle, and reseal (if appropriate). Liquid detergents, for example, should be easy to pour without spills (on some brands the plastic lid is the measuring device for dispensing the product). No-drip spouts on products such as mustard and ketchup also offer convenience. If a product is heavy or bulky, handles should be built into the package design (refer back to the Tide package in Figure 3.18). Other examples of convenience include resealable plastic lids on margarine containers, twist-off caps on beer and wine, and straws on fruit juice containers.

BE ENVIRONMENTALLY FRIENDLY

Packaging, or wasteful packaging, is an important issue for marketing organizations today. As many studies have shown, consumers are more willing to do business with organizations that show respect for the environment, and respect extends to marketing goods in packages that are environmentally friendly. Pepsi-Cola recently introduced a bottle made entirely of plant material. The bottle is made from switch grass, pine bark, corn husks, and other materials. The new bottle looks, feels, and protects the drink just like plastic bottles do. PepsiCo also introduced a fully compostable bag for its Sun Chips line of snacks, though the loud noise the bag makes is disturbing to some consumers. The company is investigating ways to reduce the noise factor.

Branding by Design

Not all kinds of product are sold in a package. What attributes sell an appliance, an automobile, a computer, the services offered by a bank, and so on? For durable goods like cars and computers, the key influencer in the buying decision could be the design—the look and style of the product and the image it projects about itself. For products like mutual funds, trusts, and other financial offerings—products that are truly intangible—consumers are primarily influenced by the brand image as perpetuated by effective marketing communications programs.

brand design
A concept that attempts to include an experience in the design of a product (for example, the design may trigger an emotional response).

Brand design integrates the brand experience into the product or service. It's about creatively designing innovative approaches in order to create a unique brand experience.[14] In the durable goods market, designers traditionally followed one basic premise: Form follows function. This was a good premise because consumers wanted durable goods to perform specific functions dependably and reliably. Shopping for a stove or a dishwasher involved comparing the interior and exterior features of various brands. Since all brands offered the same benefits, the decision was based largely on the brand name and the perceptions the consumer held about the brand name. But consumers now want products that fit in with their lifestyle or the decor of their home furnishings. They are more style conscious and are purchasing durable goods like automobiles, appliances, and electronics products based more on emotion and style than function. Refer to the illustration in Figure 3.22.

Advancing technology has an impact on design. In the television market, sexy-looking flat screens are in demand. The television remains the focal point of the family room, but in a very different manner. Mounted on a display stand or right on the wall, the new televisions offer a feeling of contemporary stylishness that is very attractive to consumers who now spend more money and time on home entertainment. Apple's products have always been perceived as sleek and stylish—consider the success of the iPhone and

FIGURE
3.22   **The Design of a Product Plays a Key Role in Building a Brand's Image in the Minds of Consumers**

Source: Joe Gough/Fotolia.

FIGURE
3.23

Effective Brand Design and Brand Strategy Are the Keys to Samsung Galaxy's Success in the Smartphone Market

Source: Jeon Heon-Kyun/EPA/Newscom.

iPad when they were launched. The styling of both products was an ideal fit with the lifestyle of consumers who wanted them. Have you noticed that people who hang out in coffee houses display their Apple laptops—sort of a badge of honour? Samsung also boasts sleek brand design with its Samsung Galaxy model. The slim design and larger face panel have been a hit with consumers. Refer to the image in Figure 3.23.

 SUMMARY

Developing a sound brand strategy and positioning strategy is the first step in the brand-building process. Having the right strategy is important because consumers form their impressions about a brand based on what they hear and see

about it. Therefore, marketing organizations use branding as a means of identifying products and building an image.

Over time, consumers come to trust what a brand stands for and express their satisfaction in varying degrees of brand loyalty. Loyalty is expressed in terms of brand recognition, brand preference, and brand insistence. Brand equity is the value a consumer derives from a brand beyond its physical attributes. Such equity is based on how aware consumers are of a brand, their degree of loyalty, and perceptions held about quality. Brand equity may also be described in monetary terms, as brands are a valuable asset of a company.

Branding offers several benefits for consumers. It suggests a consistent degree of quality, provides psychological rewards (for example, a better self-image) for possessing certain brands, and distinguishes competing brands from one another. Good brands are personal, and they often become integral parts of people's lives. For manufacturers, the brand name communicates a point of difference, allows for the creation of an image, and helps build brand loyalty.

The brand-building process involves four essential steps: identifying brand values and positioning strategy, planning and implementing a brand marketing program, measuring and interpreting brand performance, and growing and sustaining brand equity. Brand values are the primary attributes (descriptive features) and benefits (the values consumers attach to a brand). Positioning refers to the image a marketer wants the brand to have in the customers' minds. A positioning strategy is based on an important element of the marketing mix. Some of the common positioning strategies include product differentiation, brand leadership, head-on (comparative), innovation, price and value, and lifestyle.

When implementing a brand strategy, all elements of the marketing mix and the marketing communications mix come into play. The marketing communications mix is the voice of a brand's positioning strategy. A good strategy that is executed efficiently should instill the desired image about a brand in the customer's mind. In this regard, all elements of the communications mix work together to deliver a consistent message.

Packaging and product design play key roles in differentiating brands and help determine consumer perceptions. Therefore, it is important that a brand, in all of its different sizes, formats, and variations, have a consistent and distinctive package design. The ability of a package to stand out in a cluttered point-of-purchase environment is a key factor influencing buying decisions.

A good package design will protect the product, market the product, provide consumers convenience in handling and using the product, and be environmentally friendly. Package designs should be unique and attractive to grab the attention of consumers as they pass by. Expensive durable goods rely on the design of the product to create images in the consumer's mind. The design must be functional yet attractive to the eye. Style and appearance are important influences on buying decisions for cars, appliances, computers, and other consumer electronic goods. Goods such as these are often an expression of one's self-image.

KEY TERMS

REVIEW QUESTIONS

1. Identify and briefly explain the key components of a brand.

2. Identify two benefits of branding for consumers and two benefits of branding for organizations.

3. Identify and briefly explain the three stages of brand loyalty.

4. What is brand equity, and how does a brand build it?

5. "A brand is a set of core values." What does this statement mean?

6. Define what positioning is and state the importance of having a clearly worded positioning strategy statement.

7. What is the difference between head-on positioning and brand leadership positioning? Provide an example of each not mentioned in the chapter.
8. If a brand is using a product differentiation positioning strategy, what will the advertising message focus on? Provide an example of this strategy not mentioned in the chapter.
9. If a brand is using a lifestyle positioning strategy, what will the advertising message focus on? Provide two examples of this strategy not mentioned in the chapter.
10. What essential roles does a package perform in the marketing of a brand? Briefly explain.
11. Explain the role and influence that the design of a product can have on prospective buyers.

DISCUSSION AND APPLICATION QUESTIONS

1. "A brand is more than the physical product." Explain.
2. "Selecting the name for a new product is a critical decision." What are the essential issues in naming a brand? Conduct some online secondary research to get to the bottom of this issue.
3. Select a lifestyle advertising campaign that you think is particularly effective. Write a brief report or make a brief presentation on why you think it is effective.
4. Explain the relationship between brand positioning and the development of an effective marketing communications strategy.
5. Evaluate the marketing situation for one of the following companies or brands. What makes this company (brand) unique and what is its differential advantage(s) compared to the primary competitors? Based on what you know of this company (brand) and what you see or hear in terms of marketing communications, develop a positioning strategy statement for the company (brand).
   a) Samsung
   b) Target
   c) H&M
   d) Doritos
   e) Gatorade
6. Using a company or brand of your choosing, examine the relationship between its name, logo, and advertising slogan. Are these brand and communications elements permanently entwined or can any of them change in order to build the brand's image? What are the benefits and risks associated with any kind of change?
7. Assess the role that package design plays in building a brand's image. To justify your position, provide an example of a package design that you perceive to be good and a design that you perceive to be less than good. What is the relationship between the package design and other forms of marketing communications?

ENDNOTES

1. Definition of a Brand, About.com, marketing.about.com/od/marketingglossary/g/branddef.htm.
2. Katherine Lukovitz, "Brand Experience, Values Increasingly Drive Loyalty," *Marketing Daily*, February 6, 2012, www.mediapost.com.
3. Kristin Laird, "Hudson's Bay Gets New Logo," *Marketing Daily*, March 6, 2009, www.marketingmag.ca/news/marketer-news/hudsons-bay-gets-new-logo-7400.
4. David Dunne and Julia Moulden, "Personal Branding: Applying the Lessons of Successful Brands to Yourself," *The Globe and Mail*, October 21, 2002, p. B9.
5. "Magazine Survey Reveals Canada's 10 Most Trusted Brands," *CTV News*, August 14, 2012, www.ctvnews.ca.
6. Canadian Press, "McDonald's Canada Adds Plasma TV, Fireplaces to Revamped Stores," *Marketing*, September 8, 2011, www.marketingmag.ca/news/marketer-news/mcdonalds-canada-adds-plasma-tv-fireplaces-bmore-fire-power-to-revamped-stores-35576.
7. Dale Beckman, David Kurtz, and Louis Boone, *Foundations of Marketing* (Toronto: Holt Rinehart and Winston, 1988), pp. 316–317.
8. "Air Miles," Wikipedia, en.wikipedia.org/wiki/Air_Miles.
9. Lou Cooper, "The Top 100 Most Valuable Global Brands 2013," *Marketing Week*, May 21, 2013, www.marketingweek.com.
10. "Canada's Most Trusted Brands," *Reader's Digest*, 2011, www.readersdigest.ca/magazine/trusted-brand-2011-canadas-most-trusted-brands.
11. "Canada's 10 Most Trusted Brands," *Maclean's*, August 14, 2012, www2.macleans.ca/2012/08/14/canadas-10-most-trusted-brands.
12. Kevin Forssmann, "Is My Brand Losing Focus?" Brandchannel, July 28, 2008, www.brandchannel.com/brand_speak.asp?bs_id=198.
13. "Retail Therapy," The Australian Centre for Retail Studies, Monash University, April 2009, p. 3. "2012 Shopper Engagement Study," Point of Purchase Advertising International (POPAI), www.popai.com/engage/docs/Media-Topline-Final.pdf.
14. Larry Light, "Brand Design Takes More Than Style," *Advertising Age*, November 6, 2006, p. 74.

Planning for Integrated Media

Part 2 examines the steps, considerations, and procedures for developing message and media strategies for television, radio, newspapers, magazines, various forms of out-of-home advertising, direct response media, and interactive media.

In Chapter 4, the basic elements of the communications process are introduced along with the various stages of creative (message) planning. Because creative plans are based on clearly defined objectives, strategies, and executions, the chapter draws clear distinctions among these three planning concepts. It finishes with a discussion of various creative appeal techniques and execution techniques that advertisers employ to present compelling messages to customers.

Chapter 5 describes the media planning side of advertising. Media planning involves identifying media objectives, creating media strategies, and executing those plans. The development of a sound media strategy is crucial, so considerable time is devoted to discussing primary issues that influence the strategy. Strategic decisions are largely influenced by the budget available.

Chapter 6 examines the growing field of direct response communications. Direct response plans rely on database management techniques, and the chapter devotes considerable time to how organizations use information sources. Various direct response media options are introduced, and the strengths and weaknesses of each option are examined.

In Chapter 7, the focus is on digital communications. The various strategies for delivering effective online messages are discussed, and perspectives are offered regarding how to effectively integrate online messages with offline messages and related communications strategies. Social media and mobile communications are also examined in this chapter.

Advertising Planning: Creative

Learning Objectives

After studying this chapter, you will be able to

1. Identify the basic elements of the communications process

2. Explain the various stages of creative planning

3. Explain the role of a creative brief and describe the content of such a document

4. Distinguish between creative objectives, creative strategies, and creative execution

5. Describe the role of creative objective statements

6. Appreciate the variety of appeal techniques for developing creative strategies

7. Identify various execution techniques for best presenting creative strategies

From the previous chapter you have learned about the strategic planning process and seen how various elements of the marketing and marketing communications mix converge in a master plan of some kind. The role and nature of the individual plans—the plans for advertising, direct response, interactive, sales promotion, public relations, experiential marketing, and personal selling—are the focus of the remainder of the book. Separate external organizations may be responsible for developing these plans. Therefore, in the planning and development stages there is much communication between a company and its external suppliers.

This chapter will focus specifically on one aspect of advertising: the development and implementation of the message. The initial section discusses some fundamental communication concepts that are common to all components in the marketing communications mix. It is followed by a discussion of the creative planning process. Creative planning relies upon essential input from the marketing plan and involves the development of a separate plan that outlines the creative objectives, creative strategies, and creative execution (tactics).

Communications Essentials

The marketplace is dynamic, and consumers are exposed to hundreds of messages each day from all kinds of sources. What do consumers recognize and recall at the end of the day? Can they say with certainty they saw a television commercial for Stride gum that shows a wild chase scene in a shopping mall? Can they recall who the NHL hockey player is in a Sport Chek TV commercial? Do they recall the name of the bank that says: "You're richer than you think"? The answer is not likely. In very simple terms, there is so much commercial clutter out there that consumers remember very little. The challenge, therefore, is to develop a message that will break through the clutter and leave a lasting impression on the audience. Easier said than done!

An understanding of the communications process and how consumers receive and interpret messages is essential. In Chapter 1, various consumer behaviour concepts were introduced—concepts such as needs and motives, attitudes and perceptions, and reference groups and family influences. Knowledge and application of these concepts influence the nature and content of a commercial message and the degree to which it is accepted and retained by consumers.

100

Communication is defined as transmitting, receiving, and processing information. Communication occurs when the message that was sent reaches its destination in a form that is understood by the intended audience. Simply stated, an organization develops a message, selects the right media to deliver it, and, if all things are planned effectively, it will reach the consumers and have an impact on them. Developing the message is referred to as **encoding**; that is, the message is transformed into some attention-getting form, such as a print advertisement, a direct response mailing piece, an article about the product in a newspaper, and so on. The message is then **transmitted**, usually by the media (television, radio, newspapers, magazines, outdoor advertising, Internet, and so on). Refer to Figure 4.1 for an illustration.

In the delivery of the message, however, certain complications arise along the way. For example,

- The message was not in line with customer attitudes.

- The message did not reach the intended target with the desired frequency.

- The message delivered by the competition was more convincing.

- The competition spent more on advertising and had higher share of mind.

- New competitors entered the market and invested heavily in advertising.

Circumstances such as these are referred to as **noise** and dilute the impact of an advertiser's message. Whether or not a message breaks through the clutter is usually determined by the relationships among three separate factors: the quality of planning when developing message strategy, the execution of the plan being on target with the right timing and frequency, and the impact of competitive messages. The advertiser has control over the first two factors, but no control over the third.

Competing products are sending very similar messages to the same target market, creating noise. The objective, therefore, is to break through the noise. To do so, the message must be relevant to the consumer. For instance, the product's benefits must satisfy a need or suit the lifestyle of the target and be presented in such a manner that the brand becomes a preferred alternative.

If the message does not break through (if it is perceived as dull, uses the wrong types of appeals, or is simply confusing to the target), then no action will occur. Lack of action indicates a need to revisit the creative strategy and execution, and make changes where necessary. For example, many soap and skin care brands make similar claims and usually include good-looking females in their ads. Dove, in an effort to stand out, launched a "real beauty" campaign that encouraged women to celebrate themselves as they are. It

communication
The transmission, receipt, and processing of information between a sender and a receiver.

encoding
The transformation of a message into a meaningful format, such as an advertisement, a mailing piece, or an article in a newspaper.

transmission
The sending of a message through a medium such as television, radio, newspapers, magazines, outdoor advertising, Internet, and so on.

noise
Any potential form of disruption in the transmission of a message that could distort the impact of the message; competitive advertising or the clutter of advertising messages in a medium are forms of noise.

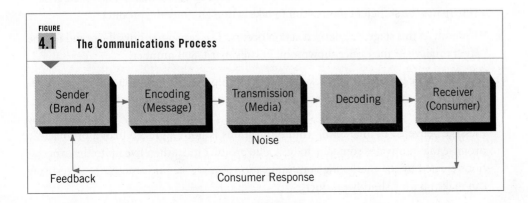

FIGURE 4.1   The Communications Process

was a bold and compelling message that regular women of all ages and sizes identified with—it broke through the clutter. The love-your-beauty attitude expressed by Dove led to the launch of several new Dove skin care products.[1]

A consumer passes through a series of stages on the way to taking action. Advertising can influence the consumer at each stage. One such model is referred to as ACCA—awareness, comprehension, conviction, and action. This model is part of a theory called DAGMAR, which stands for Defining Advertising Goals for Measured Advertising Response. An advertising goal is a specific communication task to be accomplished among a defined audience in a given period. The task should be measurable, with benchmarks in existence to assess achievements.

The effectiveness of an advertising campaign is usually linked back to this model. For example, an advertiser wants to know (in percentage terms) the level of awareness of its product among the target market, and whether or not it is perceived as being a preferred brand. Furthermore, the advertiser may want to know what percentage of the target market has tried the product (in the case of a new product campaign). Post-campaign marketing research studies measure the achievement of the objectives.

An advertisement (or campaign) that achieves good scores with respect to awareness, comprehension, and conviction is likely to succeed. The desired action in the form of someone buying the product will likely occur. To protect its investment in advertising, an organization may also conduct marketing research while the message strategy is in the development stage. The message is tested for likeability, persuasiveness, and likelihood of purchase. Research measures that exceed the norms of other products in the category would suggest the advertiser is on to something. The various marketing research techniques used to evaluate advertising effectiveness are discussed in Chapter 12. The following is a description of each behaviour stage:

- **Awareness:** In this stage, the customer learns something for the first time. In an advertising context, a message tries to plant the brand name and the primary benefit offered in the customer's mind. Awareness can be measured by aided and unaided recall tests.

- **Comprehension:** At this stage, the consumer is expressing interest. The message is perceived as relevant. The brand is evaluated on the basis of need satisfaction. It is in the consumer's cognitive realm and becomes a candidate for potential purchase. A like or dislike for a brand can be measured using attitude scales.

- **Conviction:** At this stage, the consumer expresses stronger feelings toward the brand based on the perceived benefits it offers. The brand has moved higher in the consumer's frame of reference and become a preferred brand in his or her mind. In other words, a new attitude or a change in attitude about something has occurred. There may be sufficient motivation to take action and buy the product.

- **Action:** At this stage, the desired action occurs. The consumer buys the brand for the first time, visits the dealer showroom, or calls that 1-800 number!

This is the beginning of a customer relationship. An organization will invest a considerable amount of money in advertising and other forms of marketing communications to achieve one basic goal: to get the target customers to buy the product. The message delivered by marketing communications is nothing more than a promise—a promise that motivates someone to buy. The product must then live up to the expectations created by the marketing communications. As we say, no amount of advertising can make up for a shoddy product.

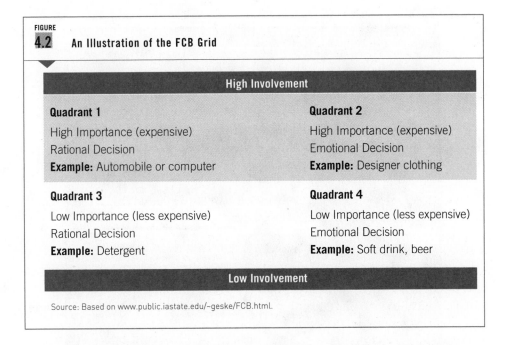

FIGURE 4.2   An Illustration of the FCB Grid

High Involvement

Quadrant 1
High Importance (expensive)
Rational Decision
Example: Automobile or computer

Quadrant 2
High Importance (expensive)
Emotional Decision
Example: Designer clothing

Quadrant 3
Low Importance (less expensive)
Rational Decision
Example: Detergent

Quadrant 4
Low Importance (less expensive)
Emotional Decision
Example: Soft drink, beer

Low Involvement

Source: Based on www.public.iastate.edu/~geske/FCB.html.

A second theory of communications revolves around the degree of involvement the consumer has with a product in the purchase decision-making process. The extent of involvement, described as either high involvement or low involvement, has implications for the development of marketing communications strategy. Referred to as the FCB Grid, the grid was developed by Richard Vaughn, a senior vice-president of Foote, Cone, and Belding Advertising (see Figure 4.2).[2]

Products that are included in Quadrant One are expensive and require a rational decision-making process during which alternatives are evaluated. Since the consumer will probably spend an extended period of time assessing alternatives, the message strategy should have an informative tone and style, and the media selected to deliver the message should be conducive to a long copy format (for example, newspapers, magazines, and websites). Products in Quadrant Two are also high involvement, but consumers evaluate alternatives more on emotion. For example, designer clothing is bought to make the consumer feel good, feel sexy, or show status. Marketing communications must generate emotional responses and create an image that people will buy. The message will appeal to higher-level needs, the looking-glass self, and the ideal self. Television ads, glossy and visual magazine ads, and special inserts are effective media for such products.

Products that are included in Quadrant Three are low-involvement products that require rational decisions. Products such as household cleaning products, paper products, and other everyday items are in this category. Marketing communications should give the consumer a compelling reason to buy (for example, it lasts longer, as in a battery; it acts quickly, as in a headache remedy; or it is convenient to use, as in a household product). The focus of the message is on the key benefit, so the message must be short. A catchy slogan might act as a reminder. The illustration in Figure 4.3 offers a good example. Here, Nestlé's Skinny Cow ice cream sandwich uses an interesting technique to deliver a simple message: great taste without the calories—a compelling message for health-conscious consumers who still want an occasional treat. Television, magazine ads with strong visuals, and point-of-purchase material are effective media choices for these kinds of products.

Products that are included in Quadrant Four are low-involvement products purchased on emotional decisions. The products are not expensive, but they make the consumer feel

good. Examples of such products include snack foods, beer and alcohol, and soft drinks. There are not many rational reasons for buying these types of products, so it is common for messages to adopt a "feel good" strategy. For example, there is an abundance of lifestyle-oriented messages among popular Canadian beer brands such as Coors Light and Bud Light. It is the image or lifestyle association that the consumer buys into. Television, outdoor advertising, interactive advertising, and point-of-purchase material play a role in delivering messages for these products.

MARKETING COMMUNICATIONS PLANNING PROCESS

The various elements of the strategic planning process were presented in Chapter 2. This chapter concentrates on the advertising planning process, but will recognize the relationships between advertising and the other forms of communication. Once the relationships are established, the chapter will then focus on creative planning. Media planning concepts for traditional media alternatives are presented in Chapter 5.

All aspects of a marketing communications plan are based on the same set of information. The current situation a brand or company faces is analyzed, a problem or opportunity is identified, and a plan of action is developed and implemented. As part of

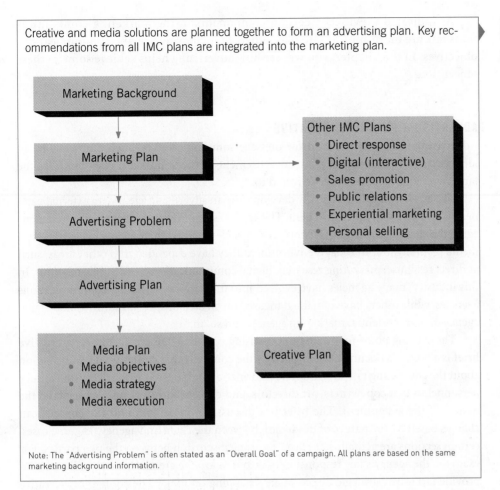

Creative and media solutions are planned together to form an advertising plan. Key recommendations from all IMC plans are integrated into the marketing plan.

FIGURE 4.4

Creative Planning

Note: The "Advertising Problem" is often stated as an "Overall Goal" of a campaign. All plans are based on the same marketing background information.

the planning process, the role and contribution of the various elements in the marketing communications mix are identified and those that are most appropriate are included in the plan. Separate plans, designed to achieve specific objectives, are developed for each element of the mix. Once completed, the key elements of these plans are integrated into the master plan—the marketing plan (see Figure 4.4).

With reference to Chapter 2 again, marketing communications plans are devised to meet a variety of challenges and are usually documented as communications objectives in the marketing communications plan. As you will see in this chapter and subsequent chapters, certain elements of the marketing communications mix are better suited to achieving certain objectives. Marketing communications objectives can be diverse and tend to involve challenges, such as

- Building awareness and interest for a product.
- Encouraging trial purchase.
- Attracting new target markets.
- Encouraging brand preference.
- Altering perceptions held by consumers.
- Creating goodwill and fostering a positive public image.
- Motivating distributors to carry a product.

As indicated previously, certain components of the marketing communications mix are more appropriate than others for achieving specific communications objectives. In this chapter, you will see how advertising helps achieve some of these objectives.

ADVERTISING PLANNING: CREATIVE

Advertising is defined as a paid-for message communicated through the media by an identified sponsor. The goal of an advertisement is it to stimulate a response from the target audience the message is delivered to.

The advertising plan is usually developed by an advertising agency, an external partner that works closely with the client. The agency is responsible for developing and managing the client's advertising. Historically, agencies focused their energy on creative and media planning, but in today's environment they have expanded into other areas, such as direct response, marketing research, digital communications, and public relations. In this industry, many agencies have evolved into full-service marketing communications agencies, while others have remained focused on an area of specialization, as in a digital agency or an experiential marketing agency, and so on.

The starting point for any new advertising project is the creative brief. A **creative brief** is a business document developed by the company that contains vital information about the advertising task at hand. The information is discussed with advertising agency personnel so that copywriters, art directors, and creative directors fully understand the nature of the assignment. The brief is a discussion document, and the content can change, based on the nature of discussion between the client and agency. In some cases, certain sections are actually left blank, awaiting discussion between the two parties. For example, the agency's key responsibility is to develop the creative strategy. Clients who provide too much strategic direction are "stepping on toes." The content of a creative brief is contained in Figure 4.5.

Information provided by the client includes essential market background information, a statement identifying the problem to be resolved or the overall goal to be achieved, and a list of communications objectives. The client also provides a positioning strategy statement to guide the development of the creative plan. The positioning strategy statement directly influences the creative objectives. For our discussions here, creative objectives deal with the content of the message to be delivered (that is, what is the primary attribute and benefit to be communicated to the target market?). The remaining elements of the creative brief—the creative strategy and creative execution—are the responsibility of the agency. That's what they get paid to do!

Once the creative brief is finalized, the spotlight shines on the copywriter and art director, a team charged with developing the **creative concept** or "big idea," as it is often referred to, that will be the cornerstone of the campaign. At this point, the agency's creative team immerses itself in details about the brand, target market, and competition so that it can fully appreciate the current situation.

Let's examine the content of the creative brief in more detail. Since the market background information is drawn from the marketing plan, that section will not be discussed in this chapter. Simply refer back to Chapter 2 if you need more details. The market background section includes information about the market, brand, key competitors, a profile of the primary target market, and budget. Knowing a brand's market position and how consumers perceive it is important to developing message strategies. Knowing how competitors advertise their products is also important. The agency wants to ensure

advertising
A paid-for media-delivered message by an identified sponsor designed to stimulate a positive response from a target audience.

creative brief
A document developed by a client organization that contains vital information about the advertising task at hand; it is a useful tool for discussions between the client and its advertising agency.

creative concept
The basic sales message (a key idea) that an advertisement communicates through verbal and visual devices.

FIGURE 4.5   **Content of a Creative Brief**

Market Information (information from marketing plan)

- Market profile
- Brand profile
- Competitor profile
- Target market profile
- Budget

Problem and Overall Objective

- Identification of the problem that advertising will resolve
- Statement of the overall goal for advertising to achieve

Advertising Objectives (based on problem or goal)

- Awareness
- Interest
- Preference
- Action
- New image
- New targets

Positioning Strategy Statement

- A statement of brand benefits, brand personality, or desired image

Creative Objectives

- Key benefit statement
- Support claims statement

Creative Strategy

- Central theme ("big idea")
- Tone and style
- Appeal techniques

Creative Execution

- Tactical considerations
- Production decisions

Note: The nature and content of a creative brief varies from company to company. A working model is presented here to show the typical content of a creative brief. Some companies include a problem statement or an overall goal, while others include both. Advertising objectives usually concentrate on one or two issues so the campaign remains focused on the problem at hand.

---

it recommends new and innovative ideas to its clients. An example of a creative brief is presented in Figure 4.6.

PROBLEM IDENTIFICATION   Advertising plans are usually designed to resolve a particular problem or pursue an opportunity. For example, an established brand will review its marketing strategy each year and make changes in strategic direction when necessary. Factors such as the stage at which a brand finds itself in the product life cycle, the intensity of competition, and changing preferences among target consumers are evaluated in the review process. Changes in these areas have an impact on marketing communications strategies.

Based on this creative brief model, the situation is encapsulated in a **problem statement**. Other models may require a statement that describes the **overall goal** of the campaign. Regardless of which option is used, advertising can only accomplish one thing at

problem statement
A brief statement that summarizes a particular problem to resolve or an opportunity to pursue and serves as the focus of a marketing strategy.

overall goal
The objective of an advertising campaign.

Harley-Davidson

Market Information
- Market volume has been affected by the economic downturn and an aging rider population; unit sales for the industry dropped 20% versus one year ago.
- Market divided into two segments: the heavyweight segment, which Harley dominates, caters to older buyers wanting style, quality, and status; the lightweight segment appeals to younger buyers seeking speed, agility, and affordability in a motorcycle.
- Harley generates 70% of its sales in the United States and 30% internationally.
- Canada accounts for 15% of Harley's international sales.

Market Shares
Harley-Davidson dominates the heavyweight segment. Current market shares are estimated to be:

Brand	Share %
Harley-Davidson	50.0
Honda	15.1
Suzuki	12.9
Yamaha	8.6
Kawasaki	6.8

Brand Profile
Harley competes on design and quality (intentionally unique-sounding engines).

Harley's past growth and continued success is closely tied to its brand loyalty (Harley owners have been known to tattoo the brand's trademark on their bodies and are members of HOG—Harley Owners Group).

Harley has distinguished itself from other brands based on its heritage, image, and reputation—a "rebellious" image the company doesn't have control over.

Harley does not promote functional benefits like power and performance; advertising messages portray the emotional connection between brand and rider.

Brand Insight from Loyal Customers
"I love everything about a Harley. From the bike and clothing to the people you meet when riding, and the instant friends everywhere you go."

"When you ride a Harley you feel a Harley. When you ride a [Honda] Gold Wing, you don't feel anything. The Harley engine has a soul. And a lot of Japanese bikes don't have soul."

Competitor Profile
Japanese competitors offer heavyweight models that appeal to price-conscious buyers more interested in the motorcycle's technology.

Features such as fuel injection and ABS brakes make Japanese bikes a sensible buy, but they lack the outlaw image of a Harley.

Target Market Profile (Current)
- Demographics: 45–59 years old; 88% male and 12% female; $75 000 plus annually; reside in urban markets
- Psychographics: adventurous; like to travel; break away from routine on weekends; enjoy the freedom of the open road
- Behaviour: current customers are extremely brand loyal and emotionally connected to brand. "Weekend Warrior" is a nickname describing the customer.

FIGURE 4.6 *(Continued)*

Problem

The current customer is aging, and younger potential customers see a Harley as a bike that looks like their father's or grandfather's bike—it is the motorcycle of choice for aging baby boomers. Future growth depends upon Harley's ability to attract new, younger customers. How does Harley-Davidson attract a younger customer?

Communications Objectives

- Attract a younger customer in the 30–45 year age range.
- Alter perceptions held by younger customers about the brand.
- Present an image more in line with the lifestyles of the younger target.

Positioning Statement

Harley-Davidson represents a sense of freedom, independence, a chance to live on your own terms for a while, even rebelliousness. For individuals wanting to be a kindred spirit with others of like mind, Harley-Davidson is the brand for you.

Creative Objectives

- To communicate an image or set of images more in line with younger lifestyles.
- To portray the feeling of freedom and independence a younger rider will enjoy when riding a Harley.
- To communicate an emotional connection between Harley-Davidson and the rider (younger rider).

Creative Strategy

Strategy is left to the discretion of the agency but it must be in line with the brand's overall positioning strategy. Emotional and lifestyle appeals that focus on freedom and independence have been successful in the past, but Harley-Davidson is open to new ideas. The recommended strategy must be suitable for print, broadcast, and digital media.

Creative Execution

- 4-colour print ads (magazine and outdoor executions).
- 30-second television spots.
- Online video ads.

All images must portray the core positioning strategy of the brand while appealing to the younger target audience.

This brief was prepared by the author for illustration purposes. Adapted from Nathan Vanderklippe and Richard Blackwell, "Passionate Riders, Few Buyers," *The Globe and Mail*, July 28, 2009, pp. B1, B4; Martin Patriquin, "Booting the Outlaw Off the Chopper," *Maclean's*, August 24, 2009, p. 53; and Joseph Tirella, "Is Harley-Davidson Over the Hill," *MSN Money*, March 30, 2009.

a time. A campaign must have a central focus. Simply stated, it's "Here's what we want to achieve!" To illustrate, consider the following examples:

- To create or increase brand awareness.
- To alter perceptions currently held by consumers about a brand.
- To present a completely new image for a brand.
- To launch a new product into the marketplace.
- To attract a new target market to a brand.
- To create awareness and trial purchase for a brand line extension.

These examples suggest focus. To demonstrate how an advertising campaign can focus on achieving an overall goal, consider the launch campaign for the all-new Honda

Accord in 2013. The look and styling of the car was completely changed with the expectations of the customer in mind. Print ads included an action-oriented beauty shot of the car. Refer to the image in Figure 4.7.

The central focus of the print campaign was to create awareness for the redesigned Honda Accord while encouraging consumers to visit Honda.ca for complete details.

FIGURE 4.7   The Central Focus of Honda's Print Campaign Is to Create Awareness for the Redesigned Honda Accord.

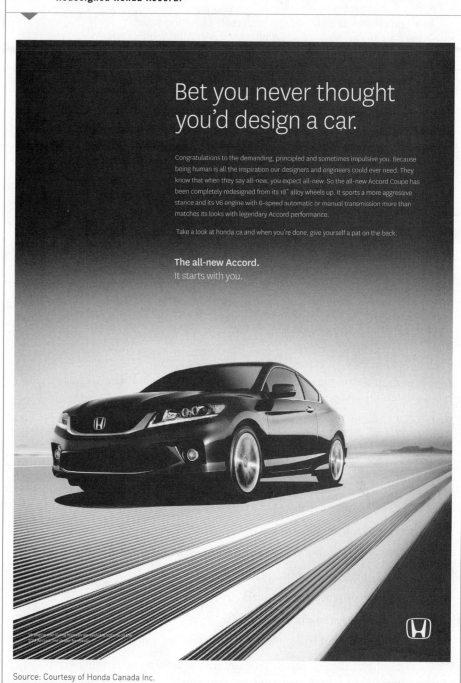

Source: Courtesy of Honda Canada Inc.

ADVERTISING OBJECTIVES   Once the overall goal is determined, specific **advertising objectives** are identified. Wherever possible, advertising objectives should be quantitative in nature so that they can be measured for success or failure at a later date. Advertising objectives may be behavioural in nature or they may focus on issues related to the overall problem. For example, an objective may focus on creating a new image or on attracting a new target market.

Advertising objectives should only deal with issues that advertising (the creative plan and media plan) can resolve. For example, a new product campaign will focus on awareness objectives. The objective is to build awareness gradually by presenting a message that informs consumers about what the product is and what it will do for them. If the market is very competitive and several brands are strong, the advertising objectives will focus on building preference. The message will focus squarely on unique attributes that show how the advertised brand performs better than other brands.

To demonstrate how advertising objectives are written, consider the following examples:

- To achieve an awareness level of 60 percent for Brand X in the defined target market within 12 months of product launch.

- To achieve a trial purchase rate of 25 percent for Brand Y in the defined target market within 12 months of product launch.

- To reposition (or re-image) Brand Z in the customer's mind by presenting images that will attract a younger target market.

The first two examples are quantitative in nature and can be easily measured for achievement at the end of the plan period. If the objectives are achieved, it indicates that current advertising strategies are working. If they are not achieved, the client and agency can re-evaluate the situation and make appropriate changes. The third example is not quantitative in nature, but it can be measured. Assuming the current image of the brand is known, a marketing research study near the end of the plan period can be conducted to determine if the brand has caught on with younger customers.

Let's examine a few of these challenges in more detail and determine how they influence the direction of creative planning and the message strategy that is ultimately employed.

CREATING OR INCREASING BRAND AWARENESS   Creating awareness is always the first challenge for advertising. The higher the level of awareness, the stronger the likelihood consumers will buy the product. Achieving high levels of awareness depends on how memorable the message is and perhaps how frequently the message is delivered. The medium used to deliver the message will also influence awareness levels. The right plan will use the right medium, but the size of the budget often dictates media selection. Nonetheless, the use of a medium such as television may create higher levels of awareness than magazines or outdoor advertising, and so on. An example of an awareness-raising ad appears in Figure 4.8.

ENCOURAGING TRIAL PURCHASE   Creating awareness and interest in a brand is one thing, but getting the wallets out is another. Sometimes incentives have to be offered to give consumers an extra nudge. If the timing of the incentive is right, positive action will be taken. Therefore, many advertisements are designed specifically to include special offers—anything from cents-off coupons to manufacturers' rebates to low-cost financing. These incentives serve a specific purpose. They help reduce the risk associated with purchasing something for the first time. For expensive goods such as cars and computers, where the risk is very high, incentives help encourage consumers to buy in a time frame that is desirable for the manufacturer.

advertising objectives
Goal statements for advertisements that include quantitative measures related to behaviour or other relevant issues.

FIGURE 4.8 **Tim Hortons Creates Awareness About a New Application for Ordering Coffee Using Digital Media**

Source: Tim Hortons and Timmy Run are trademarks of The TDL Corporation. Used with permission.

Considering how the consumer's mind works, people want to know they are making the right decision. If the product lives up to the promise presented in the advertising, subsequent purchases will be made without incentives. Consumers today are looking for better value in the products and services they buy and, as a result, incentive-oriented advertising is now more prominent than in the past.

ATTRACTING NEW TARGET MARKETS In order to attract a new target market, say a younger age group than the audience the brand currently appeals to, a new message strategy is needed. The tone and style of advertising may have to change. To illustrate, consider some recent communications from Ford automobiles in Canada. Typically, younger consumers include brands such as Toyota, Mazda, and Honda on their "to consider" list. The Ford Focus wasn't on their mind. To attract a younger (20-something) customer, Ford developed music-themed creative for television and the Internet. The new ads complemented the sportier look of the redesigned Focus model. The message promoted Ford's SYNC sound system technology as much as the car.[3]

ENCOURAGING PREFERENCE For an established brand in growth or mature markets, the objective is to stand out from competing brands. Therefore, the thrust of marketing activities is product differentiation. Advertising messages focus on the attributes the brand offers. Where continuous improvement programs are in place, it is possible for a brand to become better with age, so there may be new things to communicate. Such is the case in the potato chip market where myriad brands are available. Ruffles encourages consumers to "grip more dip" with their thicker chip. See the illustration in Figure 4.9.

The unique attributes that are important to consumers play a key role in differentiating one brand from another and in creating preference for one brand over another.

FIGURE

4.9

Messages and Images that Focus on Unique Selling Points Help Encourage Brand Preference

Source: Courtesy of PepsiCo Canada ULC.

But changes such as these must be communicated to consumers. Having advertising messages focus on something new about the brand may be just enough to position the brand in a better light with consumers.

ALTERING CONSUMERS' PERCEPTIONS   Building a brand sometimes requires consumers to adopt a different view of the brand. The quickest way to alter an image is to launch a completely new advertising campaign with an entirely different message. The style and personality of the message will be different to create a new image in the customer's mind.

Such was the case when General Electric (GE) launched a new campaign in 2012. GE wanted to broaden its image among consumers. According to Kim Warburton, vice-president of communications for GE, the campaign's objective was to tell "the bigger GE story" and to build broader awareness of the company's operations and how they contribute to economic development. Refer to the image in Figure 4.10. People overwhelmingly associated GE with appliances and lighting, but those categories only account for 10 percent of GE's business.[4] The new campaign focused on the other things the company does in business sectors such as aviation, energy, and health care.

FIGURE 4.10   GE Launched a Campaign to Broaden Consumers' Awareness of the Diverse Market Areas the Company Participates In

 Shaping Economic Growth in Canada's Remote Communities   Contribuer à l'essor économique des communautés éloignées du Canada

Source: Handout/General Electric Canada Inc./Newscom.

Positioning Strategy Statement

Positioning strategy has been discussed in the previous two chapters. Therefore, comments here will simply reinforce the necessity of having a clearly worded positioning strategy statement and discuss how to apply it in developing an ad campaign. The positioning strategy statement identifies the key benefit a brand offers, states what the brand stands for, and is a reflection of a brand's personality. These are the essential inputs assessed by the creative team when it develops the message strategy. It can be the trigger that leads to discovery of the "big idea."

To illustrate how the positioning strategy influences creative planning, consider the success a brand like Secret deodorant has experienced. You are probably very familiar with Secret's advertising tagline: "Strong enough for a man, but made for a woman." The tagline captures the positioning strategy of the brand—it is dependable, long lasting, and offers confidence to do what one must do. Secret deodorant appeals to females on an emotional level. It doesn't work any better than other brands, and it doesn't have a magical ingredient, but the slogan reaffirms femininity and a woman's ability to do anything a man can. A clever and compelling message distinguishes Secret from the other brands.

In the automotive market, Mazda's positioning statement is very clear: "The soul of a sports car is built into every car we make." Such a positioning was derived for the success of the Mazda MX-5 model—a little sports car that lots of people love to drive. Mazda wanted to transfer the MX-5 spirit to other models. For years, all Mazda automobiles (many of which have a very sporty look) used the slogan "Zoom-Zoom" to capture the

FIGURE
4.11

Mazda's Advertising Stems from a Solid Positioning Strategy: "The Spirit of a Sports Car Is Built into Every Car We Make"

Source: Handout/Mazda Canada Inc./ Newscom.

essence of the positioning strategy. Mazda vehicles appeal to people who want to have some fun when they drive.[5] Refer to Figure 4.11 for an illustration of Mazda's advertising.

CREATIVE OBJECTIVES

Creative objectives are statements that clearly indicate the information to be communicated to the target audience. What to say about a brand in general terms is usually included in the creative brief. While formats may vary, objective statements tend to involve a key benefit statement and a support claims statement, because the content of an ad or an ad campaign needs focus.

When determining what to say about a brand and how to say it, creative planners refer to the advertising objective for context. As discussed earlier in the chapter, the advertising objective may be to achieve brand awareness, encourage trial purchase, attract a new target, encourage preference, or alter a perception. Somehow, the objective and the primary reason for buying the brand must be related together so that a cohesive message is presented to the consumer.

- **Key Benefit Statement:** The key benefit statement expresses the basic selling idea, service, or benefit that the advertiser promises the consumer. This benefit should be the primary reason for buying a particular brand instead of competitive brands. The benefit can be something tangible, such as better performance, better quality, lower price, longer lasting, and so on, or it can be something intangible or psychological, such as the status and prestige that come with ownership. It is a promise to the consumer. For example, the Blue Menu Talapia entrée that appears in Figure 4.12 stresses the low levels of fat and sodium, benefits that health-conscious consumers are interested in.

creative objective
A statement that clearly indicates the information to be communicated to the target audience; usually involves a key benefit statement and a support claims statement.

key benefit statement
A statement of the basic selling idea, service, or benefit promised to the consumer by the advertiser; appears in the creative plan section of an advertising plan.

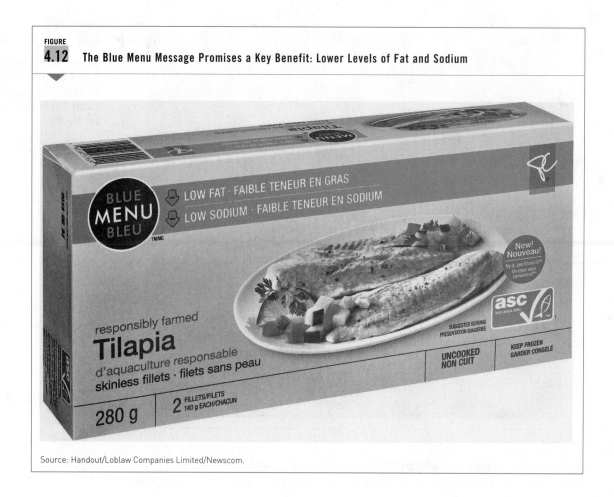

FIGURE 4.12   The Blue Menu Message Promises a Key Benefit: Lower Levels of Fat and Sodium

Source: Handout/Loblaw Companies Limited/Newscom.

support claims statement
A substantiation of the promise made in the key benefit statement; appears in the creative plan.

- **Support Claims Statement:** A support claims statement describes the characteristics that will substantiate the promise. It provides proof of the promise based on criteria such as technical performance data, comparative product testing, and any other data generated from marketing research. Good support claims give customers a real reason why they should buy the product. In the case of Blue Menu Talapia mentioned above, a strong visual illustration and supporting copy provide proof.

Support claims statements are less important for brands touting intangible benefits. Lifestyle imagery, for example, relies on the image presented and the connection between the image and the consumer who sees it to substantiate the promise. A&W has been running a series of commercials featuring a likeable manager named Allen and a young, bumbling employee named Ryan. The humorous banter between the two was building strong emotional connections with consumers, but the intended message, that A&W offered great-tasting burgers, was not getting through.

A&W and its agency created a television commercial that would create awareness (the objective) for its top-of-the-line prime rib burger. Naturally the key benefit was "great taste." But how did A&W provide proof of the great taste? The commercial introduced a new character, a fine food critic, who would pass judgement on the burger. Allen, the manager, casually leans over the critic's shoulder to peak at his notes, and learns that the critic liked the burger. The critic tells Allen (in a French accent) that it is "formidable." Yes, it is only advertising, but that's how you convince someone to try your product. It worked! Sales during the airing of the commercial increased by 4 percent, and customer counts were up 5 percent. Further, Allen's use of the word "formadoubly" to reiterate what the critic said garnered all kinds of Twitter buzz.[6]

CREATIVE STRATEGY

With the decisions about what to say in advertising determined, the creative team turns its attention to creative strategy. This is where the advertising agency starts to earn its keep. What the team searches for is the "big idea," or the central concept or theme that an entire campaign can be built around. All kinds of discussion and experimentation take place. It is an exercise in brainstorming. The guiding light is the positioning strategy. When the ad agency pitches its ideas to the client, the client evaluates the idea based on how it fits with the positioning strategy. Simply put: Is the "big idea" on strategy or off strategy?

The **creative strategy** is a statement of how the message will be communicated to the target audience. It deals with issues such as the theme, the tone and style of message that will be adopted, and the appeal techniques that will be employed. It is a statement about the personality a brand will project to consumers.

- **Central Theme:** The **central theme** is the glue that binds the various creative elements of the campaign together. As such, the theme must be transferable from one medium to another. For example, when people see an ad in print form (newspaper, magazine, or outdoor), it should conjure up images and meaning from something they have seen on television (a 30-second commercial). What the theme will be is truly the key decision the creative team makes. For the theme to see the light of day, it must be presented to the client in a very convincing manner. For a brand such as Maytag (appliances), the central theme is dependability. That is also the key benefit the brand offers. The idle Maytag repairman, a character strongly associated with the brand name, is the means by which dependability is communicated.

- **Tone and Style:** In an attempt to break through the clutter of competitive advertising, copywriters and art directors agonize over decisions about tone and style. Such fundamental decisions have a direct impact on how a campaign evolves over time and how the brand's personality gets ingrained in the customer's mind. Single words often describe the tone and style that is recommended. For example, the message will be presented in a persuasive manner, an informative manner, a conservative manner, a friendly manner, a contemporary manner, a straightforward manner, an upbeat manner, and so on. What approach will have the most impact on the target audience? Knowledge about the target audience plays a key role in this decision.

With reference to the ad that appears in Figure 4.13, the tone and style could be characterized as informative and straightforward. The combination of visual image and body copy makes the target audience think about the issue and encourages them to take action to resolve the problem.

A recent advertising campaign for Diet Pepsi aptly demonstrates how good decisions about theme, tone, and style have a positive impact on consumers. Diet Pepsi's primary target market is young adults (people in their 20s and early 30s). Marketing research revealed they didn't want to lose their spontaneity and spirit, even though they

creative strategy
A plan of action for how the message will be communicated to the target audience, covering the tone and style of message, the central theme, and the appeal techniques.

central theme
The glue that binds various creative elements of a campaign together; transferable from one medium to another.

FIGURE
4.13

A Straightforward, Informative Message Makes the Target Audience Think About the Issue and Encourages Action to Resolve It

Source: Handout/Food Banks Canada/ Newscom.

FIGURE 4.13

A Straightforward, Informative Message Makes the Target Audience Think About the Issue and Encourages Action to Resolve It

Source: Handout/Food Banks Canada/ Newscom.

were getting older. Therefore, the "big idea" had to consider the youthful feelings of a maturing audience. The creative team recommended a "Forever Young" theme. The tone and style of ads, particularly on television, were "kind of wacky." They portrayed characters on a temporary break from maturity, just longing for some crazy moments from their past. One commercial, entitled "Comb-Over," taps into the nostalgia of a balding man (see the illustration in Figure 4.14). The "Forever Young" tagline appears at the end of each commercial.

For more insight into how creative strategies are developed and evolve over time, read the IMC Highlight: **At Scotiabank, "Richer" Has New Meaning**.

FIGURE
4.14

An Illustration of Diet Pepsi's Central Theme or "Big Idea"

Source: Courtesy of PepsiCo Beverages Canada.

APPEAL TECHNIQUES

How to make an advertisement appealing to the customer is another key decision. What techniques will be employed to bring the product benefit claims and theme to life? What can we do creatively to break through the perceptual barriers in the consumer's mind? There isn't a single, definitive formula for success, but appeal techniques can be classified into different categories. For example, when you see an ad, does it make you snicker? Does it draw a tear? Does it make you think? How consumers respond to an ad is usually related to the effectiveness of the appeal. The following is a discussion of some of the more common appeal techniques.

POSITIVE APPEALS   Presenting the message in a positive manner is always a safe approach. However, it is also a very common approach. If combined effectively with the right theme, positive appeals will work. But if the creative execution lacks impact, it will wind up being just another ad. The positive appeal stresses the positive benefits of the product and how a person can gain by purchasing the product. McDonald's is one of the country's biggest advertisers and dominates its market. The company is proud of its

At Scotiabank, "Richer" Has New Meaning

You have probably seen television ads for Scotiabank telling people, "You're richer than you think." These ads have been on the air since 2006. The primary objective of the campaign was to spread a sense of optimism across the country during troubled economic times. The ads encouraged people to visit Scotiabank for a second opinion on their financial situation. When people visited the bank, they learned their situation wasn't as bad as they had thought.

The campaign was based on insights gained from consumer research that revealed people were concerned about their financial struggles—struggles that didn't necessarily depend on income level. That insight was the impetus for a marketing communications campaign to make people feel more comfortable and confident about their finances.

This campaign was successful. It raised the bank's advertising awareness level significantly and attracted new customers to the bank. So why change things? In 2012, Scotiabank recognized it was time to redefine the campaign; it was time to give new meaning to the term "richer."

Scotiabank decided it was best to let Canadians define their own wealth. Again, this strategy was based on insights from consumer research that revealed "richness" meant different things to different people. It had a lot to do with a person's stage in life, for example, having a baby, retiring, striking out on your own, or paying off a mortgage—events that involve money!

The new campaign reflects these events. One commercial, entitled "Conversation," shows young parents discussing how they want to do what's best for their baby. The copy reads, "Richness is: a 7 pound 4 ounce fresh perspective." An online digital ad showing a new mother and baby proclaims, "Richness is: The moment everything changes." The campaign includes television, print, digital, and in-bank posters.

With a sound strategy in place, the challenge for Scotiabank and its advertising agency is to bring new and fresh executions of that strategy to the consumer. The "You're richer than you think" strategy clearly demonstrates that a sound strategy considers new input (in this case new consumer insights) and evolves over time. If there's a moral to the story, it is this: If a strategy is working, resist the temptation to change it. Find new executions to keep it fresh.

Adapted from Kristin Laird, "Scotiabank Redefines 'Richer' Campaign," *Marketing*, January 23, 2012, www.marketingmag.ca.

Richness is: The moment everything changes.

Scotiabank's 5 Year Plan.
You define richness. With a 5 Year Plan that lets you adapt to anything, we can help with the money part.
scotiabank.com/5yearplan

You're richer than you think.

Scotiabank

Courtesy of Scotiabank.

accomplishments, so its ads reflect its position. The theme of McDonald's advertising does change from time to time, but the ads remain consistent in how they appeal to their target. McDonald's current campaign uses the theme and tagline "I'm lovin' it" to appeal to people in a positive manner. Typically, McDonald's ads include music and positive interactions among family members.

Kraft Canada launched a campaign for Kraft peanut butter that shows a variety of symbols drawn into the peanut butter spread on toast. A heart, happy face, and peace symbol are among 10 symbols used in the campaign. Kraft is reminding people of all the good feelings they get when eating peanut butter and telling them they should "spread the feeling." See the illustration in Figure 4.15.

FIGURE
4.15

Kraft Uses Positive Appeal to Remind People How Good They'll Feel When Eating Kraft Peanut Butter

Source: Scott P. Anderson Photography.

NEGATIVE APPEALS   Unless you are Buckley's cough mixture, you don't say bad things about your product. "Tastes awful, but it works" is now a famous slogan coined by Buckley's. Following a philosophy of "do what your momma says and you will get better," Buckley's has experienced new popularity and a positive increase in market share, based solely on its negative advertising style.

For other products, though, negative appeals usually present a situation the consumer would prefer to avoid. Nobody wants to be in a car collision. But to dramatize the safety features of the Jetta, Volkswagen created a TV spot in which two young men suddenly collide with a truck backing out of a driveway. In a split second the front of the car implodes, and the men's heads snap forward, making contact with the exploding airbags. The dramatic demonstration makes its point: In another car they would be dead.

HUMOROUS APPEALS   Taking a light-hearted approach to communicating benefits can work effectively. In fact, many critics believe that for advertising to be successful it must entertain the audience. If true, then an advertisement that causes the audience to break into a smile or giggle should break through the clutter.

A recent campaign for Boston Pizza demonstrates the effectiveness of humour. Television commercials featured a fictitious yet famous wing critic, Carl Carlson, from Flatties & Drummies. In each commercial, Carl describes the unique features of wings, using expressions such as nib, nub, meat apex, and bouchlette (as part of the wing is named after one Leroy Bouchlette). At one point in the commercial, Carl smiles and blurts out, "Nice Gil Morgan...wasn't expecting that." After diving in for a bite, he grins and says, "Knock me down and call me Susan, that's a wing!" Refer to the image in Figure 4.16. This campaign worked. By the end of the commercial run, wing sales at Boston Pizza were up 162 percent compared to the previous year.[7] Visit YouTube and enjoy a few humorous moments watching these commercials.

FIGURE
4.16

**Boston Pizza Uses a Humorous
Appeal Technique Effectively**

Source: Boston Pizza.

A major weakness of using humour is that it can wear out prematurely. After a few exposures, the audience may not find the message funny. Advertisers must also be wary of sarcastic humour that could insult cultural groups. Humour can backfire and bring on unwanted negative publicity. Since the use of humour allows for creative latitude, the creative team must ensure that the humour does not get more attention than the product. To keep the message fresh, a pool of commercials is needed so that individual spots can be rotated in and out of a media schedule.

Boston Pizza is aware of this problem. To coincide with the NHL playoffs in 2012, Boston Pizza launched a new commercial featuring a fictitious character named Terry Peters. Terry is seen on stage, lights flashing and audience screaming, praising himself for his amazing food accomplishments. "They said piggies couldn't be put in a blanket. They're in there!" he shouts. "They asked me to re-invent the chicken wing—and Terry Peters gave them All Meat Wings!" he hollers to the cheering audience. The commercial is a continuation of Boston Pizza's use of humour in advertising.

SEXUAL APPEALS   Sex in advertising! It will spark controversy, some good, some not so good. When sexual appeals are used in advertising, certain values and attitudes toward sex are being sold to consumers along with the products. To demonstrate, consider the images that Diesel shows in its jean advertisements. Diesel uses sexual imagery effectively to market jeans to 20-something males and females. Diesel's ads typically show lots of skin and couples enjoying each other's company; the ads are provocative and attention-grabbing. Refer to the image in Figure 4.17.

Sex is a strong physiological need, just behind self-preservation, so why not use it in advertising? The only real issue is the way in which it is used. Clearly, explicit sex increases the risks for the advertiser, since it may alienate consumers at large. But if core customers do not find it offensive, the advertiser may truly be on to something.

FIGURE
4.17

Diesel Effectively Uses Sexual Imagery in Print Ads to Market Its Jeans

Source: Diesel "East Meets West" FW 2005.

EMOTIONAL APPEALS   Emotional appeals presented effectively will arouse the feelings of an audience. To demonstrate, consider the style of advertising used to promote social causes: anything from drinking and driving to spousal abuse to quitting smoking. In one TV ad that encourages people to stop smoking, a mature woman talks of the perils of second-hand smoke. Her husband, a smoker, is dead, and she suffers from emphysema due to second-hand smoke. Such a message leaves the viewer with a disturbing feeling.

Tapping into people's emotions also works in a positive setting. There is no disputing the popularity and dominance of Tim Hortons in Canada. Tim Hortons uses emotion effectively to demonstrate how its outlets are part of the Canadian experience. In one commercial, called "Welcome to Canada," an apparent African immigrant waits in anticipation at an airport, laden with bags and new winter coats. From the baggage area emerge his wife and two children. After an emotional reunion he hands his wife a cup of fresh coffee. "Welcome to Canada," he says, before escorting his family into what is presumably their first snowstorm. Emotional appeals like this are an effective means for a brand to connect with consumers. Emotional messages have impact!

LIFESTYLE APPEALS   Advertisers using lifestyle appeal techniques try to associate their brand with the lifestyle or desired lifestyle of the audience they are trying to reach. Some of the appeals already discussed, such as sexual appeals and emotional appeals, are frequently included as elements of a lifestyle campaign. Other elements may include action, adventure, and excitement to stimulate desire. Lifestyle appeals are popular among advertisers owing to the greater availability of psychographic information about Canadian consumers. Many beer brands use lifestyle appeals to establish an image firmly in the minds of drinkers 19 to 29 years of age. If you are what you drink, then there is a brand of beer for you.

The automobile industry uses lifestyle messages extensively. The need to experience adventure, for example, is effectively portrayed by simply placing a vehicle in an exciting situation. As shown in Figure 4.18, the Ram truck projects an image of strength, power, and toughness. It is a truck ideally suited for a hardworking male in any kind of physical occupation or pursuit. The slogan "Guts. Glory. Ram." aptly summarizes the positioning strategy of the brand.

COMPARATIVE APPEALS In comparative advertisements, the promise and proof are shown by comparing the attributes of a given product with those of competing products—attributes that are important to the target market. The comparison should focus on the primary reason for buying the product. Comparisons can be direct, such as when the other brand is mentioned and shown, or they can be indirect, with only a reference to another leading brand or brands.

In a 2012 Super Bowl commercial, Chevy Silverado truck used a rather dramatic comparative technique to show its superiority over the Ford F-150. In the commercial, a handful of Silverado truck owners make it through a disaster (the scene looked like it was right out of the 9/11 disaster with all the dust and debris), but pause for a moment to mourn a friend who didn't make it because "he drove a Ford." Naturally, Ford didn't want the ad to air. "We don't agree with some of the claims in their ad, particularly around durability," said Mike Levine, Ford's truck communications manager.[8] For the record, Ford sold 585 000 F-150s in the United States, while General Motors only sold 415 000 Silverados. Present Ford owners may also object to the durability comparison. The entire matter is now in the hands of lawyers!

Comparative campaigns are usually undertaken by a "challenger" brand, a brand that ranks behind the category leader in terms of market share. Showing comparisons where the challenger performs better than the market leader is a convincing presentation. It will make consumers think more about the brand they currently use. This was the case in the Silverado versus Ford F-150 commercial described above. Such a strategy presents several risks. For one thing, the brand leader could fight back. If so, the brand that made the comparison may need adequate financial resources to fight an advertising war. As well, any claims must not mislead the public. If they do, the market leader could instigate legal proceedings to get the offending brand to offer proof of its claims. Critics of comparative appeals firmly believe a brand should stand on its own merits. Why cloud the issue by bringing in competing brands?

FACTUAL APPEALS   Certain product categories lend themselves to a straightforward style of advertising. The ads simply state what the product will do and back it up with information that is easy for the customer to understand. Over-the-counter pharmaceuticals use this technique frequently. Brands in this category rely on technical information or scientific data to validate claims. Advil says it's for "today's kind of pain." Advil offers fast relief for the things that slow you down. Phrases such as "safe, reliable, and doctor recommended" verify the claim. Category leader Tylenol says, "Doctors recommend Tylenol more than all other brands combined to reduce fever and temporarily relieve minor aches and pains." The third-party endorsement by doctors has a definite impact. These competitive examples aptly depict the intent of factual appeals.

For more insight into creative appeal techniques and execution decisions, read the IMC Highlight: **The Celebrity Connection**.

CREATIVE EXECUTION

In the **creative execution** stage of creative planning, specific decisions are made regarding how to best present the message. If product comparisons are used, what kind of demonstration technique will be employed? Will sexual appeals be subtle or blatant? If lifestyle appeals are used, what kind of backdrops and settings will be needed? If music is called for, what kind of music will it be? If it is a print campaign, will the ads be copy dominated or image dominated? Will artwork or photography be the key visual element? How big will the ads be? There are a host of decisions to be made.

The agency creative team evaluates specific ideas that it thinks have the potential to convert its vision of an ad into reality. In doing so, the team must answer two basic questions:

1. What is the best or most convincing way to present the brand's benefits to motivate the consumer to take action?
2. Is there a specific technique that will effectively convince consumers that this is the right brand for them?

creative execution
The stage of creative planning at which specific decisions are made regarding how to best present the message.

The Celebrity Connection

Sidney Crosby is the spokesperson for several prominent Canadian brands. Why Sidney Crosby? What did companies like PepsiCo, Tim Hortons, Sport Chek, and Adidas see in "Sid the Kid," as he is commonly known?

Gatorade was one of the first brands to jump on the Crosby bandwagon. At that time, Crosby was a newbie with great promise in the NHL. Jeff Jackett, marketing manager for Gatorade, said, "The teenagers that Gatorade targets would more easily relate to a young up-and-coming star, than a grizzled superstar." He also saw something in Crosby's character that would make him a good spokesperson for one of PepsiCo's biggest brands. Crosby would help take the brand to the next level.

Sport Chek was only known for its selection of a wide variety of sporting goods—it wasn't exactly a cool place to shop. But with Crosby on board as pitchman, the image of the retailer changed for the better. According to Mark Hindman, vice-president of marketing for Forzani Group (the parent company of Sport Chek), "Crosby's a very approachable person, and we wanted to bring that out in the television commercials he appears in."

In one commercial, Crosby is shown carrying shoe-boxes (imagine that) to presumably re-stock store shelves when he's stopped by a store clerk, who suggests names like "Sidnature" and "The Croz" for his line of clothing. Looking perplexed (he can act), Crosby responds, "How about SC87." "I like it!" the clerk responds enthusiastically. A second commercial shows a father and son rendered speechless and motionless when coming face-to-face with Crosby in a store. Crosby just smiles at both of them. Crosby is adding a human component to Sport Chek's marketing activities.

At Adidas, Crosby was a natural fit. Adidas was running a global advertising campaign using the theme "I am what I am." The campaign featured prominent athletes from various sports, but hockey was not included until Crosby got on board. In the campaign, each athlete has his or her own ad. The "I am what I am" concept celebrates authenticity and individuality, and stems from all of the blood, sweat, and tears, the dedication and determination, it took for these athletes to get to where they are today. Crosby's commercial goes right back to his childhood in Cole Harbour, Nova Scotia, and traces his climb to the NHL. Crosby has had a significant impact in developing Reebok's position in the hockey equipment market.

Is there a moral to the story? Yes. If you have the right celebrity on your side, a celebrity who fits with your product and your customer, you are on to something. But it has to be a good fit.

Adapted from Kristin Laird, "Sidney Crosby, the Approachable One for Sport Chek," *Marketing*, August 9, 2011, www.marketingmag.ca; Keith McArthur, "Crosby Follows in Gretzky's Footsteps," *The Globe and Mail*, April 17, 2006, p. B3 and "Reebok Launches Hard Hitting 'I am what I am' TV Ad Starring Sidney Crosby," *Reebok News and Media*, November 11, 2005, www.reebokhockey.com.

For example, if a decision is made to use a celebrity as a spokesperson, who will the celebrity be? Will it be a famous rock star, movie star, or sports personality? A lot of behind-the-scenes discussion goes on for decisions of this magnitude. The following are some of the more commonly used presentation tactics.

PRODUCT DEMONSTRATIONS   For products that want to make claims regarding performance (for example, dependability, reliability, speed), demonstrations work well. As mentioned above, the simplest appeal is to say or show the product and what it will do. In print advertising, "a picture says a thousand words."

On television, showing the product in use is often the simplest and most direct way to make a claim. The BMW Mini is a small automobile with a "cute" reputation, not exactly the image BMW wanted for its high-performing vehicle. A series of commercials was developed to highlight safety, speed, and spaciousness. To demonstrate how much space there is in a Mini, a commercial showed a male and female suddenly popping up in the front seat while putting their clothes back on. If that wasn't enough to make the point, a second female pops up from the back seat, also putting her clothes back on. Message delivered!

TESTIMONIALS   Advertisers that follow a traditional approach to advertising frequently use testimonials. In a **testimonial**, a typical user of the product presents the message. Real people in ads are often perceived to be more credible than models and celebrities who are paid handsomely to sell a certain brand. Walmart, for example, has developed a series of ads using people of various ethnic backgrounds to make the point that Walmart offers the value that their respective families are looking for. Such a tactic broadens the reach of Walmart in cosmopolitan markets. The Tim Hortons emotional commercials referred to earlier in the chapter effectively use testimonials to advantage. Canadians identify with the individual or family situations presented in the commercials. In each commercial, customers tell stories about why Tim Hortons plays such an important and enjoyable role in their lives.

testimonial
An ad in which a typical user of the product presents the message.

ENDORSEMENTS   Star power is the heart of an **endorsement** execution. Stars from stage, screen, music, and sports form the nucleus of celebrity endorsers.

When a celebrity is used, the advertiser capitalizes on the popularity of the star. Brands such as Gatorade, Tim Hortons, Sport Chek, and Reebok certainly see the potential of Sidney Crosby's star power. His lofty position as an NHL superstar along with his pleasant personality make him an ideal fit for these brands. For Reebok, Crosby's presence as a primary spokesperson immediately made the brand a viable competitor in the hockey equipment market. He is a significant addition to Reebok's "I Am What I Am" advertising campaign, which includes famous athletes from other sports and celebrates authenticity and individuality.[9] Refer to the Reebok image in Figure 4.19.

endorsement
A situation where a celebrity speaks highly of an advertised product.

FIGURE 4.19   Celebrities Matched with the Right Product Can Be an Effective Advertising Combination

Source: CCN Photo/Reebok/CP Images.

Do celebrities work? That's a tough question to answer, but one asked frequently by clients. There isn't a definitive answer, but let's look at a situation and try to pass judgment. Where would Nike be in the golf business without Tiger Woods? Nike has invested millions in Woods, and in return, he alone has put Nike on the golf map. To Nike's credit, it was the only company that stood by Tiger when his extramarital affairs were exposed to the public.

TAGLINES AND SLOGANS   Despite all the time, energy, and money that go into developing an ad campaign, consumers only remember bits and pieces of the message. The most important thing for them to remember is the brand name and the primary benefit. To reinforce the primary benefit and the central theme of a campaign, and to reflect the positioning strategy of the brand, the creative team develops a **tagline** for individual ads or a **slogan** that will appear in all forms of advertising. The slogan provides continuity within an advertising campaign. As described above, the slogan for Reebok's advertising campaign is "I Am What I Am." This slogan aptly summarizes the intentions of Reebok's message. Other slogans appearing in ads in this chapter include "Zoom-Zoom" for Mazda, "Good Food. Good Life." for Nestlé, and "Guts. Glory. Ram." for Ram trucks.

Of the things that consumers remember about a brand, the slogan is something they have a tendency to recall. The repetition of messages over an extended period helps ingrain the slogan in the customer's mind. From time to time the slogan will change, especially when a brand or company wants to change its image. However, it is more common for the slogan to remain in place even if the creative strategy and creative execution are completely new.

The best slogans are short, powerful summations that companies use alongside their logos to drive the brand message home to consumers. Some of the more popular and longstanding slogans appear in Figure 4.20.

tagline
A short phrase that captures the essence of an advertised message.

slogan
A short phrase that captures the essence of an entire advertising campaign; it reflects the positioning strategy of the brand and is shown in all ads in all media.

FIGURE 4.20   Some Popular Brands and Slogans

- Visa "All you need."

- MasterCard "Priceless"

- McDonald's "I'm Lovin' It"

- Nike "Just do it."

- M&Ms "Melts in your mouth, not in your hands."

- Maxwell House "Good to the last drop."

A slogan is a key element of brand identification. Many of these slogans have stood the test of time. They are strongly associated with the brand name and appear in all forms of advertising.

SUMMARY

The marketing communications process begins with a sender (the advertiser) developing a message to be sent by the media to the receiver (the consumer or business customer). The goal of marketing communications is to break through consumers' perceptual barriers while recognizing that competitors' messages are trying to do the same. When messages are developed, consideration is given to how consumers receive and interpret messages. The consumer's mind goes through a series of stages: awareness, comprehension, conviction, and action.

Creative planning is a sequential process that involves analyzing market and customer information, identifying problems and opportunities, setting goals and objectives, and developing creative strategies and tactics. The planning cycle starts with a creative brief, a document prepared by the client for discussion with the advertising agency. The brief includes relevant background information and identifies problems, goals, and advertising objectives. The document acts as a guideline for the creative team when it is brainstorming for new ideas.

Once the advertising objectives are identified, the creative team begins work on creative objectives, strategies, and execution. Advertising objectives provide focus to the creative challenge (for example, the objective is to create awareness, build preference, alter perceptions, encourage trial purchase, and so on). Creative objectives are statements that clearly identify the information to be communicated to the target market. They include a key benefit statement (a promise) and a support claims statement (proof of promise). Usually the client and agency collaborate when finalizing these statements.

Creative strategy is concerned with the theme, tone, style, and appeal techniques that are used to influence consumers to take action. Among the more commonly used strategies are positive and negative approaches using humorous, sexual, emotional, and lifestyle appeals; offering factual information; and comparisons with other products.

At the creative execution stage, specific decisions are made on how to implement the strategy. Some of the specific techniques that are commonly used include product demonstrations, testimonials from everyday users of the product, and celebrity endorsements. A good campaign will include a slogan. The slogan serves two essential roles. First, it communicates the essential idea the advertiser wants associated with the product; and second, it maintains continuity within an advertising campaign. In combination with the brand name, a good slogan helps build brand equity.

KEY TERMS

advertising   106
advertising objectives   111
central theme   117
communication   101
creative brief   106
creative concept   106
creative execution   125

creative objective   115
creative strategy   117
encoding   101
endorsement   127
key benefit statement   115
noise   101
overall goal   107

problem statement   107
slogan   128
support claims statement   116
tagline   128
testimonial   127
transmission   101

REVIEW QUESTIONS

1. Briefly explain the behavioural stages a consumer passes through prior to making the decision to buy a particular product.
2. What is a creative brief, and what role does it play in the development of an advertising campaign?
3. In the context of creative planning, what is meant by the "big idea"?
4. Ad campaigns should have focus and aim toward an overall goal. Identify and briefly explain three specific goals a campaign may try to achieve.

5. How important is a positioning strategy statement, and what role does it play in creative planning?
6. What is the difference between a key benefit statement and a support claims statement?
7. Briefly describe the various appeal techniques commonly used in advertising.
8. Briefly explain the following creative execution terms:
   a)   testimonial and endorsement
   b)   tagline and slogan

DISCUSSION AND APPLICATION QUESTIONS

1. Are humorous advertising campaigns effective? Conduct some online secondary research on humour in advertising and present a case for or against the use of humour.

2. "Lifestyle advertising strategies are ineffective because they communicate little about the product." Is this statement true or false? Conduct some online secondary research about lifestyle advertising and present a position on this issue.

3. "Good execution of a poor creative strategy will create positive results for the brand (company)." Is this statement true or false? Assemble some data that either support or refute this statement.

4. Clip an ad that catches your attention from a magazine in your household. After assessing the ad, try to determine the advertising objective, the creative objective (key benefit statement), and the creative strategy (appeal technique). Can you figure out what the advertiser intended when the ad was in the development stages?

5. Assess a series of advertisements for one brand (pick a popular brand that uses several different media). Based on everything you know about that brand and the marketing communications you are exposed to, write a positioning strategy statement that reflects the intentions of the brand. What message or image does the company want to instill in the customer's mind?

6. Select two brands that compete directly against one another. Assess the creative strategies and creative executions used by each brand. Since both brands are trying to reach and influence the same target market using advertising, which brand has more impact on consumers? Which style of advertising is more effective? Justify your position.

7. Find separate products or services that use the following creative appeal techniques:
   a) negative appeals
   b) humorous appeals
   c) comparative appeals
   d) emotional appeals
   e) lifestyle appeals

8. What is your assessment of each of the above strategies in terms of potential impact on the target market? Justify your position.

9. Assess a brand advertising campaign that features a celebrity spokesperson. Will that spokesperson have an influence on the intended target? What are the benefits and drawbacks of using a celebrity spokesperson?

ENDNOTES

1. Theresa Howard, "Ad Campaign Tells Women to Celebrate Who They Are," *USA Today*, September 7, 2005, usatoday30.usatoday.com/money/advertising/2005-07-07-dove-usat_x.htm.

2. "Ad Education," Iowa State University, www.public.iastate.edu/~geske/FCB.html.

3. Karl Greenberg, "Ford Strategy to Market Focus to Younger Set is Paying Off," *Media Post Marketing Daily*, May 12, 2008, www.mediapost.com/publications/article/82310.

4. Chris Powell, "GE Canada Launches First Branding Campaign," *Marketing*, November 17, 2011, www.marketingmag.ca/news/marketer-news/ge-canada-launches-first-branding-campaign-40382.

5. Karl Greenberg, "Mazda's Miata MX-5 Still Magnetic North for Brand," *Media Post Marketing Daily*, November 3, 2010, www.mediapost.com/publications/article/138876.

6. "A&W Goes Premium," *Strategy*, November 2011, p. 61.

7. "Boston Pizza Calls In a Critic," *Strategy*, November 2011, p. 55.

8. Stephen Williams, "Ford Versus Chevy's Super Bowl Spot: Is Any Publicity Still Good Publicity?" *Advertising Age*, February 6, 2012, adage.com/article/special-report-super-bowl/ford-chevy-proof-publicity-good-publicity/232551.

9. "Reebok Launches Hard Hitting 'I Am What I Am' TV Ad Starring Sidney Crosby," *Reebok News and Media*, November 11, 2005, www.reebokhockey.com/news-and-media/press-releases/entries/2005/Nov/11/entry/reebok-launches-hard-hitting-tv-ad.

Advertising Planning: Broadcast, Print, and Out-of-Home Media

Learning Objectives

After studying this chapter, you will be able to

1. Describe the steps involved in media planning

2. Distinguish among media objectives, media strategies, and media execution

3. Describe the various factors that influence media strategy decisions

4. Outline the characteristics, strengths, and weaknesses of various mass media advertising alternatives

As mentioned in Chapter 4, the creative plan and media plan are developed at the same time. This chapter will focus specifically on the development and implementation of the media plan. Developing a media plan is a complex process. The primary goal of the agency media planners is to reach a target market efficiently. In doing so, they consider all kinds of strategic issues, along with conditions in the marketplace and what competitors are doing.

Efficiency in media planning can be loosely defined as gaining maximum exposure at minimum cost. In following this mantra, the agency planners must develop and execute a plan that achieves the client's objectives within certain financial constraints. The media plan is part of a broader marketing communications plan and marketing plan. Therefore, the direction a media plan takes must fit in with and be coordinated (timed) with activities recommended in other marketing communications areas. Coordinating various communications activities creates synergy and maximizes the impact the plan will have on the target market.

Media planning is a complex task. With consumers' media habits changing, mainly due to technology, it is more difficult than ever to reach people with advertising messages. People are spending less time with traditional media and more time with digital media. A recent research report indicates somewhat of a divide between younger and older age groups regarding how they watch television. Young consumers, described as millennials, now consume more TV online than on regular television. The reverse is true for older age groups.[1] Since millennials are the next big group of consumers, their needs, preferences, and behaviours will have to be carefully considered by marketers and media planners. New media strategies must also consider the ever increasing mobility of consumers and their desire to stay connected. Reaching people while they are on the go is the new reality for media planners.

Media Planning

media planning
Developing a plan of action for communicating messages to the right people (the target market), at the right time, and with the right frequency.

Media planning involves developing a plan of action for communicating messages to the right people (the target market), at the right time, and with the right frequency. Both the client and the agency play a role in media planning (see Figure 5.1). The client's role focuses on providing necessary background information and then evaluating the recommendations that the agency makes. The agency assesses the information provided by the client and then prepares a strategic plan that will meet the client's objectives. Because there is a considerable amount of money involved, the client scrutinizes media plans carefully.

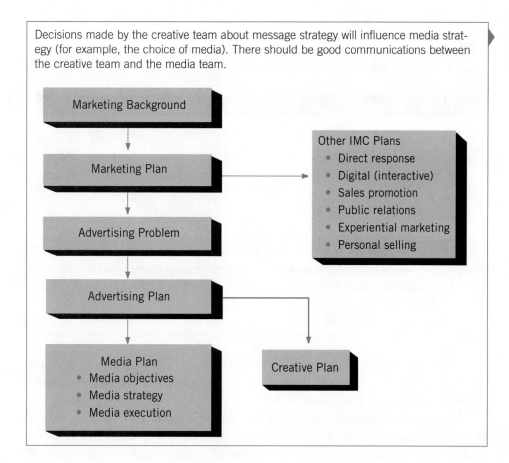

Decisions made by the creative team about message strategy will influence media strategy (for example, the choice of media). There should be good communications between the creative team and the media team.

FIGURE
5.1

Media Planning Model

Information provided by the client is contained in a **media brief** (much like the creative brief discussed in Chapter 4). The media brief is a document that contains essential information for developing the media plan and is used as a starting point in the discussion between a client and the agency. It includes some or all of the following information.

media brief
A document that contains essential information for developing a media plan; used to stimulate discussion between a client and agency.

MARKET PROFILE

Any relevant information about the current state of affairs in the market is useful to media planners. Such information includes historical sales data for leading brands, market share trends of leading brands, and rates of growth in the market. Is the market growing, flat, or declining?

COMPETITOR MEDIA STRATEGY

In general terms, what media do major competitors use, and how much money do they invest in media advertising? What the competitors are doing has some influence on the strategic directions that will be recommended. For example, if key competitors dominate a particular medium, it may be prudent to select another medium to reach the same target. Whatever competitive information is available should be in the hands of the media planners.

TARGET MARKET PROFILE

Perhaps the most important ingredient for a media plan is a thorough understanding of the target market. Targets are described on the basis of demographic, psychographic, geographic, and behaviour response variables. The target profile must be clearly defined,

FIGURE 5.2 Time Spent with Media in Canada—Selected Age Groups

Medium	18–34 Years	35–54 Years
TV	19.2	22.5
Radio	14.0	19.3
Internet	25.1	17.2
Newspaper	0.9	1.7
Magazines	0.4	0.6

All figures are hours per week spent with the medium. The Internet is the most popular medium among the 18–34 group, while TV is most popular among the 35–54 year group.

Source: BBM Analytics RTS Spring 2011.

and key variables must be expanded upon. For example, knowing the activities and interests of the target (psychographic considerations) enables a media planner to select the best times and best places to advertise.

In terms of behaviour, knowledge of how the target interacts with the media (for example, what media the target refers to most frequently) is important, as it helps the planner to allocate funds across the recommended media. As indicated above, media consumption habits are changing. A research report from TVB Canada, for example, clearly shows that people aged 18 years and older continue to spend most of their weekly media time with television, but the gap between television and the Internet is narrowing with each passing year. Among individuals aged 18 to 34, more hours per week are spent online than with television.[2] These trends have a definite impact on media planning. Refer to Figure 5.2 for details.

MEDIA OBJECTIVES

Based on marketing priorities, the client usually identifies key objectives. Objectives tend to focus on target market priorities by identifying primary targets and secondary targets, the nature of the message and its influence on media selection, the best time to advertise, and the geographic market priorities. Depending on the problem at hand or the overall goal of the campaign, the client may also identify priorities for reach, frequency, continuity, and engagement. For example, if it's a new product launch, reach and frequency over a short period may be the priority; if it's a promotional effort that invites consumer participation with a brand, engagement may be the priority.

MEDIA BUDGET

Since media advertising is but one media expenditure, the funds available come from the marketing plan budget. In most cases, the client has already identified the amount that will be allocated to media advertising. Knowing the size of the budget is essential because it provides the framework for the media planner's strategic thinking. Is there enough for television? Will this be strictly a print campaign? Is this a national campaign or will it be restricted to regional markets? The budget points the planners in a certain direction.

Once the media planners have been briefed on the assignment, they begin discussing potential alternatives. Their goal is to devise a media strategy and tactical plan (execution) that will achieve the stated objectives. Once the media plan has been presented to the client and approved, agency media buyers negotiate with the media to buy the time and space. The media buyer's task is to deliver the maximum impact (on a target audience) at a minimum cost (client's budget).

Media planning is quantitative by nature. Agency personnel are experts in media trends and have all kinds of statistical information available to figure out which media are best suited to the client's needs. Furthermore, media software enhances the ability of media planners to generate efficient media plans. Once a plan has been implemented, the agency evaluates the plan in a post-buy analysis. A **post-buy analysis** is an evaluation of actual audience deliveries calculated after a specific spot or schedule of advertising has been run. The actual audience may be different from the estimated audience that was identified in the plan. The question to be answered is whether the plan delivered the audience it was supposed to.

post-buy analysis
An evaluation of actual audience deliveries calculated after a specific spot or schedule of advertising has run.

The Media Plan

The **media plan** is a document that outlines the relevant details about how a client's budget will be spent. Objectives are clearly identified, strategies are carefully rationalized, and execution details are precisely documented. The costs associated with every recommendation are put under the microscope when the agency presents the plan to the client. Because of the money involved, media plans often go through numerous revisions before being approved by the client. The structure and content of a media plan are the focus of this section of the chapter. Figure 5.3 summarizes the content of a media plan, although the content of a media plan varies from one agency to another. This model is strictly a guideline.

media plan
A document that outlines the relevant details about how a client's budget will be spent; it involves decisions about what media to use and how much money to invest in the media chosen to reach the target audience effectively and efficiently.

MEDIA OBJECTIVES

Media objectives are clearly worded statements that outline what the plan is to accomplish. They provide guidance and direction for developing media strategies. If worded correctly, priorities will emerge. For example, there could be customer priorities, regional market priorities, and timing priorities. These priorities are based on historical information, the current situation a brand finds itself in, and the problem that the advertising plan must resolve. Such issues are part of the background information included in the media brief. For example, a plan may have a national or regional focus, or it may simply run in a few urban markets that are given priority.

media objective
A statement that outlines what a media plan is to accomplish (who, what, when, where, or how).

Media objectives typically deal with the following issues:

- **Who:** Who is the target market? The target market profile is defined in terms of demographic, psychographic, and geographic characteristics. Media planners use this profile to match the target with a compatible media profile. For example, magazines know their readership profile, radio stations know their listener profile, and television networks know who watches specific shows. If there is a means to reach the target directly (as a group with special interests or as an individual), that too is considered.

- **What:** What is the nature of the message to be communicated? Media planners must be informed about the message strategy. For example, is the message strategy information intensive (lots of copy) or image intensive (lots of visuals)? Does the budget permit television, and if so, is the creative team giving television due consideration? Issues such as these strongly suggest that basic creative and media decisions be made at the same time.

FIGURE 5.3   The Structure and Content of a Media Plan

Media Budget

- Total budget available (from client's marketing plan)

Media Objectives

- Who (is the target market)
- What (is the message)
- When (is the best time to advertise)
- Where (are the priority markets)
- How (important are reach, frequency, and continuity)

Note: Media objectives are usually clear, concise statements.

Media Strategy

- Target market matching strategy (shotgun, profile match, rifle)
- Market coverage
- Timing
- Reach considerations
- Frequency considerations
- Continuity considerations
- Engagement considerations
- Media selection rationale
- Media rejection rationale

Note: Media strategies expand upon the objectives and provide details about how the objectives will be achieved.

Media Execution

- Blocking chart (calendar showing timing, weight, and market coverage)
- Budget summary (allocations by media, time, and region)

- **Where:** Where are the market priorities geographically? The budget plays a key role in this decision. Typically, a brand has regions of strength and weakness. A media plan could be devised to correct a situation in a problem region. In such cases, a decision could be made to reduce media spending in a strong region and allocate more to a weaker region. In other situations, regions may be treated equally with media funds allocated based on population patterns, or a plan may simply consider advertising in key urban markets. The budget is a determining factor here.

- **When:** When is the best time to reach the target market? For example, is the product a seasonal product, such as suntan lotion or ski boots? If so, the media strategy will consider a heavier schedule of advertising in the pre-season, a time when consumers are starting to think about summer or winter activities. Knowledge of the target's daily schedule also plays a role in timing decisions. For instance, a busy executive who rises early and arrives home late may not have much time to spend with the media. How and when is the best time to reach this person?

- **How:** The question of how conjures up all kinds of media issues. How many people to reach, how often to reach them, and for what length of time? These are strategic issues that are best left to the media planners at the ad agency. However, some basic guidance from the client is provided. For example, if the plan is for a new product, the absolute number of people reached and how often they are reached may be given priority. If a product is firmly established and the goal of the plan is to simply remind the target, then length of time may be given priority.

MEDIA STRATEGY

Media strategy focuses on how media objectives will be achieved while outlining how to reach the target market as effectively and efficiently as possible. Given the scarcity of clients' financial resources and their demands for accountability, having the right media strategy is crucial. Clients want to see a reasonable return for their investment. A media strategy addresses how often to advertise, how long to advertise, where to advertise, and what media to use. It also rationalizes why only certain media are recommended and others rejected. Strategic decisions are linked directly to the media objectives. The various factors that influence media strategy are discussed below.

media strategy
A plan for achieving the media objectives stated in the media plan; typically justifies the use of certain media.

TARGET MARKET PROFILE   For some products and companies, the target description may be broad in scope. For example, a newspaper's primary readers include adults of all ages and income groups. In contrast, the primary buyer for a Lexus automobile may be described as a male business executive, 35 to 49 years of age, earning $75 000 annually, living in an urban market of 1 million plus. The extent of the target's description directly influences media strategy decisions.

The task of the media planner is to match the profile of the target market as closely as possible with the profile of the medium (for example, the readership profile of a magazine or the listener profile of a radio station). The more compatible the match, the more efficient the strategy will be. For example, to reach that Lexus buyer described above, executive-oriented business magazines such as *Financial Post Magazine, Canadian Business,* and *Report on Business* magazine are good matches. Figure 5.4 illustrates a readership profile. The same executive may watch television, but to place an ad in prime time hours would reach people well beyond the target description. This would not be efficient. Consideration will also be given to reaching this individual by his or her smartphone—a more efficient opportunity.

There are three basic target market matching strategies: shotgun, profile matching, and rifle.

- If a **shotgun strategy** is used, the target market's profile has a broad scope. The message is placed in media that reach a broad cross-section of the population. For example, if the target market is described as adults 18 to 49 years old with no other demographic or psychographic characteristic being important, the media selected can be more general in nature. Members of a prime time (8 pm to 11 pm) television audience watching a drama or comedy show will range in age, embrace both genders, and have a variety of incomes and varying lifestyles. Therefore, television would be a good medium for reaching the 18- to 49-year age group.

shotgun strategy
A tactic involving the use of mass media to reach a loosely defined target audience.

For advertisers with significant budgets, television can be an effective medium for reaching a broad target market. That said, the cost of reaching that audience on a national scale is expensive. A popular show such as *Grey's Anatomy* will cost an advertiser as much as $60 000 for a 30-second spot. The audience for *Grey's Anatomy*

FIGURE 5.4   Readership Profile of *Canadian Business* Magazine

Characteristic	Audience	
Circulation	90 100	
Readers per copy	9.5	
Total readership	856 000	
Male readers	558 000	
Female readers	297 000	

Demographics	Readers	Index
Household incomes $150K+	147 000	156
Managers, owners, professionals, executives	340 000	194
C-Suite (CEO, Chairman, President)	42 000	432
Business Decision Makers		
Over $100 000	45 000	316
Communications/computers	146 000	242
Services	136 000	234
Active Investors		
Securities and savings over $500K	23 000	149
Acquire mutual funds outside RRSP	54 000	218
Spend over $100 on credit cards monthly	180 000	159
Travel		
6 or more business trips	80 000	229
3 or more vacation trips outside Canada	155 000	137
Top Consumers		
Spent over $50K on most recent vehicle	58 000	195
Own vacation/retirement property	77 000	237

Notes

1. Circulation multiplied by readers per copy equals total readership.
2. The Index in the right column shows how *Canadian Business* reads compare to the Canadian average. The index is calculated by dividing the percentage of *Canadian Business* readers by the percentage of Canadian adults in various categories being measured. Canadian Business readers are well above average in all categories.

Interpretation

Based on the above readership statistics, *Canadian Business* magazine is a good profile match for advertisers wanting to reach individuals with above average incomes, including senior managers, professionals, and business owners. These individuals are decision makers in their places of employment.

Source: Adapted from Canadian Business Media Kit, 2012, Rogers Publishing.

---

averages 1.3 million people weekly (the reach factor).[3] Less popular shows would cost less, as would specialty cable channels, which reach fewer people.

For advertisers on a tighter budget but with a diverse target market, options such as daily newspapers and out-of-home advertising are attractive. They reach a diverse population in key markets and generally cost less than television.

- If a **profile-matching strategy** is used, the target market profile is carefully defined by demographic, psychographic, and geographic variables. For example, assume a target profile described as follows: female head of household, working or stay-at-home mother, college or higher education, $65 000 household income, suburban lifestyle, with interests that include home decorating, entertaining, and travel. Several magazines are good possibilities for reaching such a woman: *Chatelaine, Canadian Living, Canadian Home & Country*, and *Style at Home*. The primary reader of each magazine is reasonably close to the description of the target. In contrast, *Canadian Business* magazine appeals to upper-income males and females commonly referred to as MOPEs (managers, owners, professionals, and entrepreneurs).

  Profile matching can extend to television as well, specifically on specialty networks where content attracts a particular type of audience. Among the most-watched specialty networks are YTV (youth programs), CBC News Network (news and information programs), and TSN and Rogers Sportsnet (sports programs).[4]

- In the **rifle strategy**, a common characteristic such as an activity or interest binds a target market together. For example, golfers are golfers, whether they play at a public club, an exclusive private club, or anywhere in between. All golfers look for similar equipment. They cross both genders and most income groups. Therefore, a publication such as *Score Golf* or *Golf Canada* offers a means of reaching the target directly. Enthusiasts look to these kinds of publications for information about golf products, golf vacation destinations, and anything golf related. Most magazines also offer comprehensive websites where similar information is available. Further, about half of all magazine readers are accessing magazine content and advertising through digital channels such as tablets and cell phones—another factor that has to be considered when devising a media strategy.

profile-matching strategy
A media tactic that involves matching the demographic profile of a product's target market with a specific medium that has a similar target profile.

rifle strategy
A strategy that involves using a specific medium that effectively reaches a target market defined by a common characteristic.

NATURE OF THE MESSAGE   Creative strategy and media strategy should be developed simultaneously to ensure that the right message is delivered by the right medium. For example, if a rational appeal technique is combined with factual information in the message, then print media options take precedence. If emotional appeals are used and if action and adventure are prominent in the message, television and interactive options are good options. If engagement with the audience is a concern, then the Internet presents opportunities for delivering the message.

GEOGRAPHIC MARKET PRIORITIES   With regard to where to advertise, strategic decisions must be made on how to divide a budget among the areas where advertising will be scheduled. A company or brand rarely advertises nationally on a continuous basis. It is common for some national advertising to occur during the course of a plan, but it is supplemented by additional advertising in markets where specific problems need to be resolved. In other instances, a brand might decide just to advertise in key urban markets. The top six Canadian urban markets (Toronto, Montreal, Vancouver, Calgary, Ottawa-Gatineau, and Edmonton) reach about 45 percent of the total population—and much of the success (or failure) in Canada is governed by how successful a brand is in those six markets. Usually, the budget determines the extent of market coverage. Some of the coverage options include the following.

National Coverage   Such a strategy assumes widespread availability of the product, with all geographic areas figuring equitably in the success of the product. For example, if product sales expressed as a percentage of total sales by region are close to population splits by region, a national strategy is an option. Funds can be allocated across media that reach the national market. Network television shows in prime time, such as *Survivor, American Idol, CSI Miami,* and *Grey's Anatomy,* and national magazines, such as *Maclean's,* are good alternatives. Prime time television and general interest magazines reach a broad cross-section of the population, and the cost in absolute terms (the actual cost per ad) is high.

Regional Coverage   A regional strategy involves an evaluation of each region's contribution to a brand's (or company's) success. Funds are allocated so that no particular region has an advantage or disadvantage—at least, that's the theory. The reality is different. Some regions will over-contribute to sales, while others will under-contribute. An organization might assess the value of a region by analyzing its brand development index.

brand development index (BDI)
The percentage of a brand's sales in an area in relation to the population in that area; determines if the brand is underdeveloped or overdeveloped in each area.

A **brand development index (BDI)** is a percentage of a brand's sales in an area in relation to the population in that area. For example, if Secret deodorant has 15 percent of its Canadian sales in BC and only 12 percent of the female population lives there, the BDI for BC would be 125 (15 divided by 12). This would indicate that BC is an important area for the brand; the brand is very popular there. See Figure 5.5 for some additional calculations of the brand development index, which help explain why certain regions get disproportionate funds. There is only so much money to be allocated. For example, in a market where a brand is underdeveloped but potential for growth is present, that brand may temporarily receive additional funds that will be taken away from a region where the brand is doing well. The BDI is commonly used when determining regional media budgets.

FIGURE 5.5   Considerations for Allocating Budgets by Region

One method of determining the importance of a region for a brand (company) is to compare actual sales volume (as a percentage of total sales) to the region's population (as a percentage of Canada's population). Such an analysis is called a **brand development index (BDI)**. The BDI is determined by dividing the sales volume percentage by the regional population percentage.

Region	Sales Volume %	Population %	BDI
Atlantic Region	7.6	7.6	100.0
Quebec	21.5	23.9	89.9
Ontario	42.5	38.5	110.4
Prairie Region	13.4	16.8	79.8
British Columbia	15.0	13.2	113.6
Total	**100.0**	**100.0**	—

Example: The BDI in Ontario is 110.4. The BDI was determined by dividing 42.5 by 38.5.

Analysis: Based on the BDI in each region, Ontario and BC over-contribute to sales while Quebec and the Prairies under-contribute. The media planner can concentrate advertising dollars in areas where the brand enjoys most usage. Another option is to transfer some funds from Ontario and BC to Quebec and the Prairies to help improve sales in those regions. Other factors can influence such a decision.

In terms of media selection, a planner will focus on regional media opportunities to reach the target market. Television networks offer regional packages (for example, all stations within a region), and national magazines, such as *Chatelaine, Canadian Living,* and *Reader's Digest,* offer numerous regional editions.

Key Market Coverage   A third alternative is to give priority to those members of the target market residing in key urban markets. Usually there are predetermined criteria to establish what markets will receive media support. If population is the criterion, a planner will consider other strategic factors first and then go down the market list until the media budget is exhausted. As mentioned earlier, Canada's top six cities (Toronto, Montreal, Vancouver, Ottawa-Gatineau, Calgary, and Edmonton) account for 45 percent of the population. Given that the population is migrating steadily toward cities in Canada, a key market plan is a good option.

While this strategic approach seems equitable, smaller cities may never receive media support. Such would be the case in Atlantic Canada for the scenario described above. If the Atlantic region doesn't receive media support, expectations for the brand should be lowered appropriately. In terms of media selection, key market plans offer the most flexibility and choice. Local market television stations, daily newspapers, outdoor and transit advertising, and radio are attractive alternatives. The combination of media to recommend depends on the media preferences of the target market and the budget available in the plan.

TIMING OF ADVERTISING   Information about the target market and cyclical patterns in sales influence decisions about when to schedule advertising. The best time could refer to the time of day, day of week, or time of year. For products with a cyclical sales pattern, the media schedule may follow the ebb and flow of sales. If the media plan is for a new product, the planners may decide to hit the market heavily and frequently over a short period. Lower levels of advertising are scheduled later in the plan cycle. Typically, a media schedule is planned in flights. A **flight** is a period of time in which advertising is scheduled. There are many options available for planning the timing of a media schedule, all based on unique situations a brand (company) faces. See Figure 5.6 for an illustration of the media schedules discussed below.

flight
A period of time in which advertising is scheduled.

- A **skip schedule** calls for scheduling advertising on an alternating basis. For example, ads are scheduled one week and not the next, or one month and not the next. This cyclical pattern is maintained for the duration of the campaign. A skip schedule strategically stretches a budget over an extended period while maintaining the effect of the advertising in the marketplace.

skip schedule
The scheduling of media advertising on an alternating basis, such as every other week or every other month.

- A **pulse schedule** involves scheduling advertising in flights but with different weights (the amount invested in media) and durations (the length of time). Such a schedule looks random, but the weight and frequency of the spending patterns are carefully rationalized. To demonstrate, assume a schedule has three flights. The first is four weeks long and heavy, the second is six weeks long at a low level, and the third is four weeks long and heavy. There is a period of four weeks with no advertising between each flight. The variation in flights creates a "pulsing" effect.

pulse schedule
A scheduling of media advertising in flights of different weight and duration.

- Many products are seasonal in nature, so media advertising follows a **seasonal schedule,** with most of the advertising in the pre-season to create awareness and interest prior to the beginning of the seasonal purchase cycle. Banks and financial institutions have a heavy schedule of RRSP advertising in January and February, for example, as the tax-deduction deadline for contributions is the end of February.

seasonal schedule
Scheduling media advertising according to seasonal sales trends; usually concentrated in the pre-season or the period just prior to when the bulk of the buying occurs.

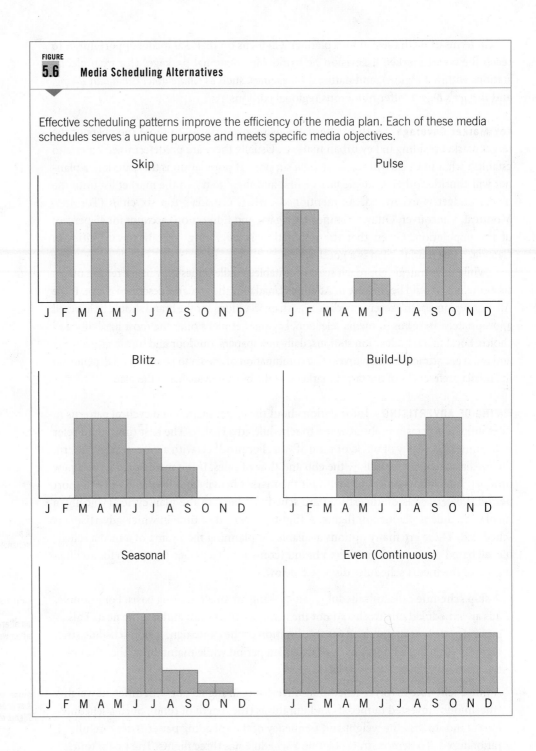

> FIGURE
> **5.6**   **Media Scheduling Alternatives**
>
> Effective scheduling patterns improve the efficiency of the media plan. Each of these media schedules serves a unique purpose and meets specific media objectives.
>
> Skip
>
> Pulse
>
> Blitz
>
> Build-Up
>
> Seasonal
>
> Even (Continuous)

blitz schedule
The scheduling of media advertising so that most spending is front-loaded in the schedule; usually involves a lot of money spent in a short period.

build-up schedule
The scheduling of media advertising so that the weight of advertising starts out light and gradually builds over a period of time; also called a teaser campaign.

- A **blitz schedule** is best suited for new products that want to hit the market with a bang—a multimedia strategy at a heavyweight level. Lots of money is spent in a very short period. Once the blitz is over, media spending tapers off considerably, and some media are dropped from the schedule.

- In a **build-up schedule**, often referred to as a teaser strategy, media advertising is scheduled at low levels initially and gradually builds (as more weight is added) over time. Often a teaser campaign is launched well before the product is available on the market (hence the name). The advertising creates a pent-up demand for the product when it becomes available. Hollywood movie releases and manufacturers of video game hardware and software frequently use this strategy.

- The **even schedule**, often referred to as a continuous schedule, involves the purchase of advertising time and space in a uniform manner over a designated period. This schedule is best suited for large advertisers that need to sustain a certain level of advertising spending due to competitive pressures. Such a spending pattern is not very common. Even in markets like the quick-serve restaurant market, where various companies seem to be advertising all the time, the level of advertising actually scheduled does vary from month to month.

even schedule
The uniform scheduling of media advertising over an extended period; also referred to as a continuous schedule.

REACH/FREQUENCY/CONTINUITY   Media planners must decide on the reach, frequency, and continuity needed to achieve advertising objectives. Much like a riddle, these three factors interact and, if planned effectively, will have a synergistic effect on the target market. It is unrealistic to have maximum reach, frequency, and continuity at the same time. Priorities are based on the situation and the budget.

- **Reach** is the total unduplicated audience (individuals or households) exposed one or more times to an advertiser's schedule of messages during a specific period (usually a week). It is expressed as a percentage of the target population in a geographically defined area. For example, a television ad on Ottawa's CJOH-TV may reach 40 percent of the households in the Ottawa region.

reach
The total unduplicated audience exposed one or more times to a commercial message during a specific period (usually a week).

- **Frequency** is the average number of times a target audience has been exposed to an advertising message over a period of time, usually a week. It is calculated by dividing the total possible audience by the audience that has been exposed at least once to the message. In newspapers, frequency would be the number of times an ad appears in a publication (for example, two ads per week in a daily newspaper); in television it is the number of times a commercial is aired in a week. The media planner must decide what combination of reach and frequency is appropriate for achieving the advertising objectives. In the case of a new product where awareness objectives prevail, the emphasis is on reach, with frequency as the budget allows. A mature product that is trying to defend its position may opt for more frequency and aim the message at a precisely defined target market where reach is lower.

frequency
The average number of times an audience has been exposed to a message over a period of time, usually a week.

- Media planners use gross rating points as a method of designing a media schedule. **Gross rating points (GRPs)** are calculated by multiplying the total reach (the unduplicated audience) of the proposed schedule by the frequency (the average amount of exposures) in the proposed schedule. It is an expression of the weight of advertising in a market. To illustrate, assume the weekly reach is 50 percent of targeted households in a particular city, and the average number of exposures is 3.5. The GRP level would be 175 (50 × 3.5). Depending on how important particular markets are, an advertiser usually varies the weight level (the GRP level) from one market to another. For more detailed illustrations of GRPs, refer to Appendix 1, "Media Buying Principles and Media Information Resources," at the end of the book.

gross rating points (GRPs)
An expression of the weight of advertising in a media schedule; calculated by multiplying reach by frequency.

- **Continuity** refers to the length of time required to ensure impact has been made on a target market through a particular medium. During that period, a consistent theme is communicated (for example, "Well Made. Well Priced. Well Dressed," the theme for Moore's, a men's clothing chain). Since advertising is scheduled in flights, continuity decisions deal with how long a flight will be. Will the schedule be four weeks, six weeks, or eight weeks?

continuity
The length of time required in an advertising medium to generate the desired impact on the target audience.

FIGURE 5.7   The Relationship Among Reach, Frequency, and Continuity

Reach is the number of people potentially exposed to a message in one week.

Frequency is the average number of times a person is exposed to a message in a week.

Continuity is the length of time required to generate impact on a target market.

The relationship among these three variables is dynamic. Since the media budget is usually a fixed amount of money, if one variable is given more priority, then another variable will be given less priority. Otherwise, you will spend beyond the budget. Examine the numbers in the chart. Each plan is different, but they all achieve the same number of gross impressions.

Gross impressions are calculated by multiplying reach × frequency × continuity.

Variable	Reach	Frequency	Continuity	Impressions
Plan 1	500 000	4	6 weeks	12 000 000
Plan 2	250 000	8	6 weeks	12 000 000
Plan 3	125 000	8	12 weeks	12 000 000

Interpretation

Each plan is different. The first plan stresses reach, the second stresses frequency, and the third stresses continuity. The costs of each plan would be about the same. It's all in the numbers!

Media planners must juggle reach, frequency, and continuity throughout a campaign. An increase in any one of these variables will increase the cost of advertising, so there would have to be a corresponding decrease in another variable to stay within budget. Very often continuity is the first of these variables to "give way" when budget becomes a factor. Figure 5.7 offers more information about the relationships between reach, frequency, and continuity.

engagement
The degree of involvement a person has with the medium when using it.

ENGAGEMENT   **Engagement** refers to the degree of involvement a person has with the medium when that person is using it. It is a response driven by emotion and whatever happens inside a person's mind. Both the message and the medium play a role in encouraging engagement.

In a fragmented media universe, planners struggle to find ways of engaging the audience. People are easily distracted, or they multi-task when using a medium. It is very common for male television watchers to avoid commercials by channel surfing during commercial breaks. In contrast, Internet users are often focused on what they are doing. They are involved and may notice advertising messages simply by glancing at them. A magazine reader may spend 30 minutes of uninterrupted time with a favourite magazine—that's engagement! Earlier in the chapter (see Figure 5.2), it was noted how much time people spend with the media. Time spent does not necessarily translate into engagement.

From a strategic point of view, creative planners and media planners have determined that online and mobile advertising messages must be entertaining if engagement is a strategic priority. As well, planners encourage engagement with the brand by using an ad in one medium (TV, radio, or print) to get consumers to go online to a website or social network page for more information. Taking the time to go online suggests engagement.

Engagement is an important strategic factor to consider. By selecting the right media, the advertiser will start to develop a relationship with the consumer, a relationship that can thrive if planned properly. For this reason media planners now recommend more use of the Internet in the media mix—a reflection of the time consumers spend with the medium and how they interact with it.

For more insight into how media objectives and various strategic media variables influence the direction of a media plan, read the IMC Highlight: **Targeted Media Work for BMW**.

IMC HIGHLIGHT

Targeted Media Work for BMW

BMWs are expensive automobiles, and the new BMW 6 series are intended for men and women who like to drive a sporty-looking luxury vehicle.

The target market is described as an "urban-dwelling middle manager or professional with relatively high income." Age is not a factor, because owning a BMW is more of an income and "mind" thing—the status of owning the car! What media strategy would BMW and its agency, The Media Company, employ to reach this target?

The key to developing the media campaign was found in new consumer insights provided by BMW. "These consumers love to drive, and because they love to drive, they are driving to work. So, we thought we could build a lot of frequency by placing messages (outdoor boards) on the routes that they take to work," says John Ware of The Media Company.

The strategy also addressed the target's emotional needs in a rational manner so that the buying decision was easy to justify. The messages suggested there was no need to settle for anything less. With reference to the image to the right, the car sells itself with a visually striking image that strongly suggests luxurious styling, sophistication, and agility—characteristics a discerning buyer is looking for.

A key market media plan was implemented in Toronto, Montreal, and Vancouver. The media mix included print ads in *The Globe and Mail*; online communications (banner ads and a brand website); and outdoor boards on busy traffic arteries to and from work and near the airports. To reach a wider audience geographically, print ads were also placed in publications such as *Report on Business* magazine, *Canadian Business*, and *Maclean's*. A profile-matching strategy was used to effectively reach the target.

This campaign offers good insight into how a media plan is strategically developed. As well it draws some relationships between message and media placement. Factors such as the target market profile, the message, reach and frequency, timing, and market coverage were all addressed when the plan was in the development stage.

Adapted from Natalie Williams, "It's All About the Insight," *Strategy*, April 2005, p. 41.

Deck Uli/DPA/ABACA/Newscom.

MEDIA EXECUTION

media execution
The translation of media strategies into specific media action plans; involves recommending specific media to be used in the plan and negotiating the media buys.

The final stage of the media planning is media execution. **Media execution** is a process of fine tuning the media strategy and translating it into specific action plans. This involves comparing various options within a class of media for cost efficiencies, finalizing a schedule in the form of a calendar or blocking chart, and allocating the budget in detail by specific activity. Then the agency buys the media time and space.

MEDIA SELECTION Selecting the right media to resolve the problem at hand is a three-step decision process: selecting the general type of media, selecting the class of media within the type, and selecting the particular medium. Of the media discussed in this chapter, the first decision involves what mix of media to use. Among television, radio, newspapers, magazines, and out-of-home, any combination is possible (direct response and interactive media are discussed in separate chapters and they too are part of the selection process). For the second decision, let's assume that magazines and television are the media chosen and that the campaign is national in scope. Will general interest magazines, men's or women's magazines, or special interest magazines be chosen? What television networks will be chosen? The characteristics of the target market will influence these decisions.

For the third decision, let's also assume the target market is men and women between 25 and 49, living in major cities across Canada. Magazines that reach both males and females would be selected: *Maclean's, Chatelaine*, and *Reader's Digest* are good candidates. Conventional television networks such as CTV, CBC, and Global are also good candidates.

cost per thousand (CPM)
The cost of delivering an advertising message to 1000 people; calculated by dividing the cost of the ad by the circulation in thousands.

When selecting specific media, the cost efficiencies of each alternative are analyzed. To demonstrate, magazines are compared on the basis of **cost per thousand (CPM)**. CPM is the cost incurred in delivering a message to 1000 readers. It is calculated by dividing the cost of the ad by the circulation of the publication in thousands. Therefore, if an ad cost $20 000 and the circulation was 500 000, the CPM would be $40 ($20 000 divided by 500). When comparing publications that reach the same target market, the ones with the lowest cost per thousand are the most efficient at reaching the target.

Media planners also assess media alternatives qualitatively. In other words, do numbers tell the complete story? Factors such as editorial content, quality of reproduction, and demographic selectivity can lead the media planner to prefer one magazine over another, even if the preferred magazine has a higher CPM. Perhaps there are more pass-along readers of one publication than another. If more people are exposed to the ad, then the real costs of reaching the target are lower than the CPM. Daily newspapers, television networks, and radio stations can be compared on a similar basis. For an illustration of a few cost comparisons within certain media, see Figure 5.8. Appendix 1, "Media Buying Principles and Media Information Resources," has additional information about media selection and how various alternatives are compared when making decisions about what media to use.

media calendar (blocking chart)
A document that shows allocation of a brand's media budget according to time of year and type of medium; shows coordination of various media recommendations.

MEDIA SCHEDULE AND BUDGET ALLOCATIONS The final stage for media planners is developing the media calendar and assigning estimated costs to all activities. A **media calendar** or **blocking chart**, as it is also referred to, summarizes in a few pages all the details of the media execution (for example, media usage, market coverage, weight levels, reach and frequency, and the timing of the campaign). Accompanying the calendar is a detailed budget. Typically, the media budget classifies spending by medium, region or key market, and time of year. Because plans change during the course of the planning

FIGURE 5.8   Comparing Media Alternatives for Efficiency

Women's Magazines	Cost (1P, 4-Colour)	Circulation	CPM
Chatelaine	$51 920	544 413	$93.37
Canadian Living	$48 890	508 480	$96.15
Canadian House & Home	$20 950	242 576	$86.35
Style at Home	$15 950	230 000	$69.35
Business Magazines			
Report on Business	$26 345	298 088	$88.38
Financial Post	$21 125	165 020	$128.03
Canadian Business	$18 915	80 064	$236.14

Observations

Among women's magazines, the lowest circulation magazine (*Style at Home*) is the most efficient at reaching women as it has the lowest CPM (the cost of reaching 1000 readers). However, advertisers with reach objectives would consider the highest circulation magazines (*Chatelaine* and *Canadian Living*), even though the CPM is higher.

Among business publications, *Report on Business* is more efficient, since its CPM is lowest. *Report on Business* is distributed for free to all *The Globe and Mail* subscribers, a significant benefit to an advertiser with reach objectives. In contrast, *Canadian Business* has a much higher CPM but its audience is paid subscribers—people who truly value the magazine's content. That too, is worth something to an advertiser.

Source: Online Media Kit for each publication, January 2012 rate cards, retrieved May 10, 2012.

cycle, clients and agencies must know how much money is committed at any point in time, in case there is a need to cancel activities. Taking the axe to the budget while the plan is in midstream is both common and frustrating for managers.

MEDIA BUYING   Once the client approves the media plan, media buyers execute the plan. Buyers work with media representatives to negotiate final prices for the various activities. If the required elements of the plan are unavailable, buyers are responsible for making replacement buys that will achieve the same objectives. The demand for key time periods in television and preferred spaces in magazines and newspapers means that good timing and effective negotiation skills on the part of the buyer are critical elements of the media buy. In the role of negotiator, the media buyer seeks favourable positions and rates to maximize efficiency and achieve the objectives set out in the plan. Appendix 2 includes an example of a media plan that shows applications of the various media strategy and execution principles discussed in this chapter.

Assessing Media Alternatives

Media planners have a variety of media alternatives to choose from: television, radio, newspapers, magazines, out-of-home advertising, and direct-response and interactive media. Typically, a planner will include several media in the plan, as people refer to more than one medium for information. In the hectic world of today's consumers, the simultaneous use of media is popular. Teens, for example, are online or texting on their cell phone while watching television. Adults frequently read the newspaper or a magazine while watching television. Knowing the right combinations for various age groups will influence media decisions.

Because consumers refer to so many different media, media planners usually recommend a **primary medium**, which will be allocated a higher percentage of the budget, and support it with **secondary media**, which complement the primary medium and receive less of the budget. As mentioned earlier, a medium such as television is ideal for creating awareness quickly, whereas print media are good for communicating detailed information over a longer period. The combination of the two media is usually effective. This section will analyze the major mass media alternatives and highlight the pros and cons of each. Chapters 6 and 7 will focus on direct response and interactive forms of communication.

primary medium
A medium that receives the largest allocation of an advertiser's budget; the dominant medium in a media plan.

secondary media
Media alternatives used to complement the primary medium in an advertising campaign; typically less money is allocated to these media.

TELEVISION

For what seems like forever, television has been the preferred medium for advertisers, assuming sufficient funds are available. To create brand awareness across a wide cross-section of the population, no medium has traditionally done it better than television. But television as a medium for advertising is in a state of transition as consumers' eyeballs move from the "big screen" to the "small screen" (laptops and mobile devices). Consequently, media planners may include an online media recommendation in combination with a television recommendation.

Many advertisers are questioning the value of television advertising. Technology such as personal video recorders (PVRs), some of which allow automatic elimination of commercials when recording shows, now threatens the very economics of the television industry. Initially, this was thought to be a threat, but only 26 percent of Canadian households have a PVR, and 95 percent of television viewing remains a real time experience.[5] For now, mainstream television remains relevant and effective, but advancing technologies will have a negative impact on the medium's effectiveness in the future.

Generally, the number of hours a person spends viewing television each week has been drifting downward. The public's preoccupation with the Internet and mobile devices is the reason for this decline. There is a correlation between these media however, as people are multi-tasking—using two or sometimes three different media devices at the same. Data compiled by BBM Nielsen Media Research show that Canadians remain avid TV watchers: Men 18 and older spend 20 hours with TV each week, while women 18 and older spend 24 hours with TV each week.[6] Figures like these suggest that television is not dead but in transition.

The biggest threat to television is audience fragmentation arising from the 300-channel universe that exists today. Television viewing of conventional English-language television networks, such as CBC, CTV, and Global, and French-language networks, such as SRC and TVA, is migrating slightly downward each year. Viewers have migrated to pay, digital, and specialty channels.[7] Among the more popular specialty channels are TSN, YTV, Discovery Channel, Showcase, Rogers Sportsnet, and many more. Channels like these are tailored to special interests and attract a particular audience, which can be a benefit to advertisers.

Budget permitting, however, advertisers are still magically drawn to television. It is a multi-sense medium that is ideal for product demonstrations and appeals to consumers on an emotional level. People perceive television to be an engaging medium, a perception not overlooked by media planners. Further, a survey conducted by BBM

Analytics (2011) reveals that consumers generally perceive television to be the most influential form of advertising.[8]

With television, media planners have four options: network advertising, selective-spot advertising, local-spot advertising, and sponsorships. Newer options such as product placement and branded content can also be added to the mix.

- **Network advertising** on networks such as CTV and Global is suitable for products and services that are widely distributed and have large media budgets. When a spot is placed on the network, the message is received in all network markets. The CTV network, for example, comprises 21 stations and reaches 99 percent of English-speaking Canadians. Popular prime time shows, such as *Big Bang Theory* (over 3 million viewers each week), *Amazing Race* (2.6 million viewers), *Survivor* (2.3 million viewers), and *The Mentalist* (2.1 million viewers), attract big-budget advertisers.[9]

network advertising
Advertising from one central source broadcast across an entire network of stations.

- At the regional or local level, stations fill the balance of their schedules with non-network programs and sell **selective spots** directly to interested advertisers. Local stations are also allocated a certain portion of a network program to sell directly to local advertisers. That's why you may see an ad for a local restaurant or retailer on *Hockey Night in Canada*.

  Strategically, selective spots benefit advertisers using a key market media strategy. For a large-budget advertiser, there is an opportunity to increase the level of advertising in local markets that are judged as priorities. Small-budget advertisers can simply choose the markets they wish to advertise in.

selective spot
Commercial time during a network show that is allocated back to regional and local stations to sell; advertisers buy spots on a station-by-station basis.

- With **local spots**, local advertisers like independent retailers and restaurants buy time from local stations. Since local market advertisers don't usually work with an advertising agency, the stations usually provide assistance in the development and production of commercials for local clients.

local spot
Advertising bought from a local station by a local advertiser.

- **Sponsorship** allows an advertiser to take "ownership" of a property that is targeted at its consumer audience. If the fit is right, the advertiser can leverage the sponsorship by extending the relationship to include consumer and trade promotions, alternate media exposure, and social media exposure.

sponsorship
The act of financially supporting an event in return for certain advertising rights and privileges.

One of the most prominent sponsorship opportunities in Canada is *Hockey Night in Canada*, a Saturday night institution on CBC television. During the broadcasts, special segments of the show are sponsored by advertisers. The preview show that precedes the game is sponsored by Scotiabank, a player biography segment is sponsored by Subway, and the dependable lines segment is sponsored by Maytag. Maytag's brand positioning is dependability! A segment featuring dependable forward lines was a natural fit for the brand.

Kraft Hockeyville has been another popular segment of *Hockey Night in Canada* for the past six years. In conjunction with the CBC, the NHL, and the NHLPA (Players' Association), Kraft pits communities across Canada against each other to be crowned Hockeyville. The winning community demonstrates how it embodies the spirit of hockey and hometown pride, and wins cash for arena upgrades and improvements. Kraft benefits from the brand mentions during the broadcast. They may also negotiate preferred positions for their commercials during the broadcast. Kraft sees the sponsorship and promotion as a way of giving back to the communities—Kraft brands have a 99 percent household penetration in Canada.[10]

Television provides advertisers a means of reaching huge numbers of people in a short space of time with a compelling message. Companies that can afford to advertise

FIGURE
5.9   Advantages and Disadvantages of Television Advertising

ADVANTAGES

- **Impact**—sight, sound, motion; demonstration; emotion
- **Reach**—high reach in short space of time
- **Some targeting**—sports and specialty cable channels reach niche targets
- **Coverage flexibility**—local, regional, and national options

DISADVANTAGES

- **High cost**—desired frequency (message repetition) increases absolute cost
- **Clutter**—too many spots in a cluster negates potential impact
- **Audience fragmentation**—abundance of channels lowers audience size (reach potential)
- **Technology**—electronic equipment records programs and edits out commercials

in prime time on shows like *Survivor, Big Bang Theory, Grey's Anatomy,* and *Hockey Night in Canada* and the *NHL Playoffs* have high reach almost instantaneously.

If reaching a well-defined target is a priority, television is not a good option. The audience in prime time, for example, spans all ages. You will reach your target, but you're also paying for everyone else who is watching. Furthermore, clutter is a problem on television. There are simply too many ads. Given that ads are scheduled in a cluster, does an advertiser want to be the third or fourth commercial in a **cluster** of six? Refer to the discussion about CPM in the "Media Execution" section for more details, and consult Figure 5.9 for a summary of the advantages and disadvantages of television advertising.

NEW STRATEGIES FOR REACHING A TELEVISION AUDIENCE   Television and television advertising is not about to disappear, but new solutions for reaching viewers must be found to retain the economics of the system. Many advertisers have already found more compelling ways of delivering advertising messages on television—product placement, branded content, and shorter commercials.

Product placement refers to the visible placement of branded merchandise in television shows, films, or video games. Hollywood has been doing product placement in movies for years, but television is now catching on to the practice fast. For example, Coca-Cola glasses or containers are prominently displayed in front of the judges on *American Idol*. Simon Cowell's newest singing show, *The X Factor,* has Pepsi-Cola as the sole sponsor. Pepsi logos and cups play a prominent role in the staging of the show. A benefit of the *X Factor* sponsorship is a cooperative marketing effort by Fox (the network) and Pepsi (the sponsor) off the air and a joint website. Pepsi also gets preferred positions for commercials during the show.[11] Refer to the image in Figure 5.10.

Branded content or **product integration** takes product placement a step further by integrating the brand into the script of the television show. The CBC offers advertisers opportunities for scripted brand content in many of its shows. Ford Canada latched on to such an opportunity on *Being Erica*. In the show, two key characters, Julianne and Erica, become co-owners of a Ford Fiesta. The ownership provided opportunities to demonstrate the key features of the vehicle over several episodes. Post-episode research

cluster
Ads grouped in a block of time during a break in a program or between programs, or in a section of a publication.

product placement
The visible placement of brand name products in television shows, movies, radio, video games, and other programming.

branded content (product integration)
The integration of brand name goods and services into the script (storyline) of a television show or movie. The brand name is clearly mentioned and sometimes discussed.

Source: PRNewsFoto/PepsiCo/AP Images.

showed consumers feeling very positive about Ford. Some 58 percent of respondents were impressed with the car's features, and 29 percent said the association with *Being Erica* changed they way they see Ford.[12] That has to be good news for Ford!

For additional insight into product placement and branded content opportunities, read the IMC Highlight: **Maytag Puts a New Spin on Things**.

Shorter commercials are another option for effectively delivering television ads. Shrinking attention spans (of multi-tasking viewers) and shrinking advertising budgets are the impetus for shorter commercials. Research is showing that shorter commercials (15 seconds long) hold onto more eyeballs than longer ones (30 seconds long), so why should an advertiser spend more on the longer format? That is an argument for a creative planner and a media planner to wrestle with!

The changes occurring in the television industry have direct implications for advertisers. Essentially, advertisers have two basic options: They can reduce investment in television advertising, making it less important in the mix than previously, or they can shift their investment entirely. While the latter option seems radical, many large advertisers are doing a lot of soul searching about their TV budgets. Other advertisers firmly

Maytag Puts a New Spin on Things

Advertisers are always looking for unique opportunities to present their brand to the public. In that regard, Maytag Canada and the CBC network devised an interesting media strategy called "Maytag Mondays."

Maytag faced a unique problem. They had been using US-produced commercials in Canada that communicated the wrong message. The US campaign focused on the fact that Maytag appliances were made in the United States. That message had little impact on Canadian buyers. The challenge for Maytag was to develop a uniquely Canadian campaign on a tight budget.

The Maytag-CBC partnership stemmed from a successful effort the previous year (2011) during the NHL playoffs. Mediacom Canada, Maytag's media agency, recommended placing ads during playoff games. Being late to the playoff party, the only inventory left was a series of 10-second gaps. The shorter spots were ideal for Maytag. They saw hockey as part of the Canadian identity, and they realized the playoffs inspire family viewing—moms would be watching! "No appliance company had ever advertised on *Hockey Night in Canada*," said Anthony Hello of Mediacom. "We knew we'd get moms' eyes."

The 10-second spots showed a hockey team coming off the ice and throwing their jerseys (branded with the *Hockey Night in Canada* logo) into a Maytag Maxima washer—the Maytag Man standing beside the machine. Sales of the Maxima model doubled while the ads were on the air.

The hockey success led to the one-night sponsorship idea. A sponsorship of this magnitude requires a significant investment. To expand the Canadian halo that CBC programming confers on the brand, the Maytag Man filmed integrated commercials, which included a 15-second spot with him watching television alongside comedian Gerry Dee of *Mr. D.*

Sponsoring an entire evening of programming is rare, but the brand integration this campaign uses is the type of extra push past the traditional 30-second spot advertisers are looking for. The CBC sees these opportunities as revenue generators at a time when advertisers are trying to find innovative ways of delivering their message on a tight budget. In this regard, both parties (the advertiser and the network) benefit.

Adapted from Susan Krashinsky, "The Maytag Man: Coming Up with a New 'Canadian Spin' Cycle," *The Globe and Mail,* March 1, 2012. P. B6.

Kevin Casey/AP Images for Boys & Girls Club of America.

believe that television will remain the dominant medium and that it's mandatory if the goal is to build brand image.

RADIO

There are just over 1200 radio stations in Canada. FM stations are much more popular than AM. FM stations reach 90 percent of persons over 12 years of age, while AM reaches 29 percent. All radio stations are self-regulating, with no restrictions on the number of commercial minutes or on the placement of those minutes.[13]

Despite the high reach figures, Canadians are listening to the radio less with each passing year. Radio's reach among younger age groups, particularly teens, continues to decline, because young people have more entertainment options available to them than before and more places to get music (for example, downloading songs to iPods and smartphones).

Where people listen to the radio is a factor a media planner must consider. Presently, about half of all radio listening hours occur in the home. A vehicle is the second most popular place to listen to radio, while work listening ranks third.

One of the major advantages of radio is its ability to reach selective target markets. In fact, radio is a one-on-one medium more in tune with the lives of its listeners than television or newspapers, which appeal to the masses. Radio's ability to personally connect with listeners helps explain why it can be effective. For advertisers, this means that messages need to speak to listeners as individuals, not as a group.[14]

The audience reached depends on the format of the station. **Format** refers to the type and nature of the programming offered by a station. Basically, the content is designed to appeal to a particular target group, usually defined by age and interests. In radio, everything is based on demographics.

format
The type and nature of the programming offered by a radio station.

The most popular radio station formats among adults are adult contemporary, golden-oldies/rock, talk, country, and contemporary. Adult contemporary (AC) stations play popular and easy-listening music, current and past, and generally appeal to an audience in the 25- to 49-year-old range.[15]

The preference for FM is largely due to the better sound quality and the transfer of many stations from the AM band to the FM band. The news/talk format has been a renaissance for AM stations that moved in that direction. The news/talk format encourages interactivity with listeners and has attracted active rather than passive listeners. This format has been extended further to all-sports stations like THE FAN 590 in Toronto and CKNW AM980 in Vancouver. These are niche stations popular with sports-minded males who like to talk about sports news and rumours.

Because of its ability to reach precisely defined demographic targets in local markets, radio can be an ideal component of a "key market" media plan. As well, it is a relatively inexpensive medium. An advertiser can achieve high frequency on a weekly basis. In fact, radio is often referred to as the "frequency medium." If frequency is the strategic priority, then radio is a good fit.

Unlike TV, which is an evening medium, radio is a morning medium. In fact, breakfast time—between 8 am and 9 am—is the highest daily period for tuning in by all demographics. There is a downward drift in listening as the day progresses, with a slight blip upward in the afternoon drive-home period (4 pm to 6 pm). Refer to Figure 5.11 for details. Listening trends such as these can influence the placement (timing) of an advertiser's message.

For additional information about the advantages and disadvantages of radio advertising, refer to Figure 5.12.

Several new technologies are having an influence on conventional radio broadcasting. Among these technologies are Internet radio, podcasting, and satellite radio. As the name suggests, **Internet radio** involves listening to audio broadcasts via the Internet. The broadcasts are streamed and played by a software media player in the computer. The broadcasts come from myriad organizations as well as traditional radio stations. Since the signal is relayed over the Internet, it is possible to access stations from anywhere in the world.

Internet radio
Listening to radio broadcasts via the Internet.

The second and already popular technology is called podcasting. **Podcasting** describes audio programming that is downloadable to iPods and other portable digital media devices. It allows listeners to tune in when it is convenient for them to do so.

podcasting
Audio programming that is downloadable to iPods and other portable digital media devices; allows listeners to tune in when it is convenient for them to do so.

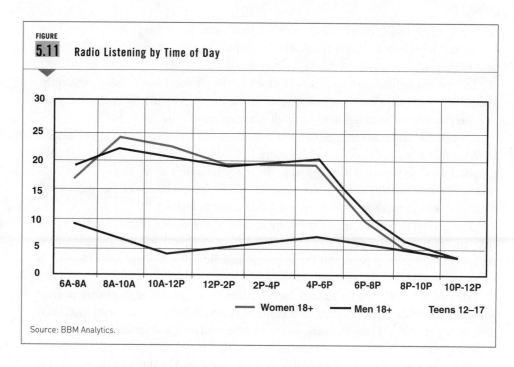

FIGURE
5.11   **Radio Listening by Time of Day**

Source: BBM Analytics.

Radio shows are recorded and posted as an MP3 file to a website where they can be downloaded to the player.

The third technology is satellite radio. **Satellite radio** offers commercial-free programming and is available through Sirius XM Canada. This service requires a special radio, and listeners must pay a monthly fee to obtain the music. Since its launch, satellite radio has had only minimal impact on conventional radio and achieved only single-digit penetration. The question remains: Are Canadians willing to pay for commercial-free radio?

satellite radio
A radio service that offers commercial-free programming for a monthly fee.

NEWSPAPERS

Canada has 122 daily newspapers, with a total average daily circulation of 5.8 million copies.[16] **Circulation** is defined as the average number of copies per issue of a publication that are sold by subscription, distributed free to predetermined recipients, carried within other publications, or made available through retail distributors.

circulation
The average number of copies per issue of a publication sold by subscription, distributed free to predetermined recipients, carried with other publications, or made available through retail distributors.

FIGURE
5.12   **Advantages and Disadvantages of Radio Advertising**

ADVANTAGES

- **Target selectivity**—station format attracts a defined audience (profile matching possible)
- **Frequency**—reach plans rotate messages through entire audience weekly
- **Cost**—very favourable compared to other media
- **Flexibility**—stations and markets selected according to priority (key market strategy)

DISADVANTAGES

- **Audience fragmentation**—multiple stations competing for the same demographic reduces station's audience potential
- **Message retention**—sound-only medium; clever creative required

Industry research indicates that 52 percent of Canada's adult population reads a daily newspaper on any given weekday. Technology is having a significant impact on the newspaper industry, as more and more reading is done online and through mobile and tablet devices. The challenge for the industry is to encourage advertisers to see the value in placing ads in digital versions of newspapers. Newspapers are a popular medium among advertisers, particularly local market advertisers. Net advertising revenue generated by newspapers on an annual basis has been declining over the past few years. Newspaper ad revenues rank third in Canada behind television and the Internet.

Newspapers are produced in two formats: broadsheets and tabloids. A **broadsheet** is a large newspaper with a fold in the middle. Most Canadian dailies are published as broadsheets, including circulation leaders such as the *Toronto Star*, *The Globe and Mail*, and the *National Post*. A **tabloid** is a smaller newspaper in terms of surface area. It is sold flat and resembles an unbound magazine. The Sun newspaper chain (*Toronto Sun*, *Ottawa Sun*, *Calgary Sun,* and others) publishes all of its newspapers in tabloid format. The country's most read newspaper is the *Toronto Star*, which attracts 1 million daily readers to its print edition. The Star.com website extends its daily reach to 1.2 million.[17]

There are 15 "free" daily newspapers, covering 11 major markets in Canada, marketed under the *Metro* banner. These newspapers have had an impact on the circulation and readership of "paid for" dailies in many urban markets. *Metro* targets YAMs—youthful, active metropolitans—through hard copy, online, and mobile formats.[18]

Community newspapers are small-circulation newspapers usually published weekly. The community paper is the voice of the community. As such, it is well read. In fact, 74 percent of adults read a community newspaper each week. The readership of community newspapers parallels the demographics of the community. For that reason, they are an excellent advertising medium for local businesses. Community newspapers are a popular medium for inserts and advertising supplements.

Newspapers generate revenues from different types of advertising:

- **National Advertising:** National ads are sold to advertisers and ad agencies by a national sales department. Advertisers in this category include products and services marketed nationally or regionally. Brand name food and beverages, automobiles, airlines, banks and financial institutions, and telecommunications products and services fall into this category.

- **Retail Advertising:** Retail advertisers include department stores, supermarkets, drug stores, restaurants, and a host of other independent retailers. These retailers usually advertise sales or re-advertise the nationally branded merchandise they sell. Retail advertising generates a majority of revenue for a newspaper.

- **Classified Advertising:** Classified ads provide an opportunity for readers and local businesses to buy, sell, lease, or rent all kinds of goods and services. Typically, the classified section is a well-read section of the newspaper.

- **Preprinted Inserts:** The preprinted **insert** (often referred to as a free-standing insert) is a dedicated piece of advertising inserted into the fold of a newspaper. Large users of inserts include department stores (Sears, Walmart, and others), drugstore chains (Shoppers Drug Mart and others), large general merchandisers (Canadian Tire and Home Depot), and electronics retailers (Best Buy and Future Shop).

For advertisers, newspapers offer geographic selectivity and high reach in local markets. Furthermore, newspapers and readers have a relationship with each other.

broadsheet
A large newspaper with a fold in its middle.

tabloid
A smaller newspaper that is sold flat (not folded).

retail advertising
Advertising by a retail store; involves advertising the store name, image, location, and the re-advertising of branded merchandise carried by the store.

classified advertising
Print advertising in which similar goods and services are grouped together in categories under appropriate headings.

insert
A preprinted, free-standing advertisement (for example, a leaflet, brochure, or flyer) specifically placed in a newspaper or magazine.

FIGURE
5.13   Advantages and Disadvantages of Newspaper Advertising

ADVANTAGES

- **Targeting capability**—reaches a diverse adult audience in key geographic markets
- **Reach**—ideal for reaching consumers in local markets frequently
- **Media environment**—readers engage with paper based on editorial content; they are receptive to messages
- **Merchandising**—national advertisers have cooperative advertising opportunities with local market retailers

DISADVANTAGES

- **Life span**—daily; exposure to message reduced if paper not read on day of publication
- **Audience diversity**—not suitable if target market profile is precisely defined (exception may be The Globe and Mail)
- **Clutter**—lots of space devoted to advertising (many ads on one page)
- **Reproduction quality**—primarily a black and white medium; adding colour does improve brand awareness and recognition scores

---

clutter
The amount of advertising in a particular medium.

Readers have a tendency to read the entire newspaper in their own unique and sequential manner—they are engaged when reading. Newspapers are an effective choice for reaching broadly defined adult target markets. Unfortunately, the papers' lifespan is very short (one day for dailies). As the old saying goes, "There's nothing as stale as yesterday's news." Newspapers also suffer from a clutter problem. **Clutter** refers to the amount of advertising in a medium. About 60 percent of newspaper space is devoted to advertising, so standing out in the crowd is a design challenge for the creative team. See Figure 5.13 for a summary of the advantages and disadvantages of newspaper advertising.

The growing popularity of tablets and mobile devices indicate that digital distribution of news, information, and advertisements will be more important to newspapers and advertisers in the future. *The Globe and Mail* and the *National Post* have discovered that mobile activity peaks when people are commuting to the office and that desktop visitors and page views increase as the day goes on. It is important for advertisers to know how and when people consume newspaper content.[19]

MAGAZINES

Magazines have managed to stay relevant with consumers in the digital media era. New titles continue to launch in Canada, readership remains stable, and magazines continue to engage large numbers of consumers from all age groups. Magazines remain relevant because they offer fresh content across all platforms and devices that matter to readers. There are magazine websites, online digital editions, social networks (Facebook pages and Twitter feeds), and a variety of mobile applications. From an advertising perspective, the combination of hard copy and digital content allows advertisers to reach and motivate readers whenever and wherever they are.

Canadian consumer magazines are distributed on the basis of paid circulation or controlled circulation. **Paid circulation** refers to subscriptions and newsstand sales. Magazines such as *Maclean's, Chatelaine*, and *Canadian Business* are paid circulation magazines and rely on subscriptions, newsstand sales, and advertising space to generate revenues. Canada's

paid circulation
The circulation of a newspaper or magazine that is generated by subscription sales and newsstand sales.

most popular consumer magazines sold by subscription or at newsstands include *Reader's Digest* (836 000 circulation), *Chatelaine* (551 000), and *Canadian Living* (511 000).

Some magazines are distributed free to a predetermined target audience based on demographic, geographic, job function, or other characteristics. These are **controlled circulation** magazines. CAA Magazine is an example of a controlled-circulation magazine. It is distributed free to all members of the CAA (Canadian Automobile Association). Entertainment magazines distributed free in movie theatres also fall into this category. *Cineplex*, for example, is distributed monthly to 700 000 Cineplex Odeon patrons.

controlled circulation
The circulation of a publication that is distributed free to individuals in a specific demographic segment or geographic area.

Business magazines are divided into various industry categories: food manufacturing and distribution, hardware trade, hotels and restaurants, engineering, and so on. These magazines are very specialized, their content appealing to people employed in a certain industry or a particular job function. Some magazine titles include *Canadian Grocer, Hotel & Restaurant, CA Magazine*, and *Marketing Magazine*.

Magazines are ideal for advertising purposes. For advertisers using a profile-matching strategy or rifle strategy, they serve a useful role. Magazines are often referred to as a "class" medium rather than a "mass" medium. In other words, readership is well defined on the basis of demographic and psychographic variables (profile matching), and there are all kinds of magazines devoted to a particular interest or activity (rifle strategy). As well, many large-circulation consumer magazines offer regional editions, so if geography is a factor influencing the media strategy, magazines can be part of the solution. Many studies have proven that readers are more engaged with magazines, and they consider advertising in magazines to be more acceptable and enjoyable than in other media. Among mass media alternatives, magazines rank first in moving readers to websites, motivating web searches, and favourably influencing attitudes toward a brand.[20]

Clutter remains a problem in most consumer magazines. The clustering of ads at the beginning of a publication, for example, may mean that a reader skips over an entire section of ads on the way to reaching editorial content. Advertisers combat the problem by requesting specific locations in a magazine. Covers, for example, are preferred positions and command a higher price. If frequency is a key objective, magazines are not a viable option. Most are published monthly or bi-monthly, so they are good for achieving reach among a defined target audience and delivering continuity of message from month to month. More information about the advantages and disadvantages of magazine advertising appears in Figure 5.14.

OUT-OF-HOME ADVERTISING

Out-of-home advertising represents a highly visible and effective alternative for advertisers. Think about it: If you drive a car, travel by transit, or stroll through shopping malls, you are constantly exposed to out-of-home advertising messages. Advertising investment in out-of-home advertising is increasing at a much greater rate than in other media. In 2010, outdoor advertising revenue in Canada totalled $482 million, a 15 percent increase over 2009.[21] Advertisers' concerns about the fragmentation of television audiences and the tuning out of broadcast messages have driven demand for out-of-home delivery.

If the goal of an advertising campaign is to reach as many people as possible, then out-of-home should be the medium of choice. Further, the emergence of digital out-of-home formats also offers advertisers creative flexibility—they can alter their message on the fly!

The major classifications of out-of-home media include outdoor advertising and transit advertising.

OUTDOOR ADVERTISING   **Posters** or **billboards**, as they are commonly referred to, are large sheets of poster paper mounted on a panel of some kind. To maximize reach

poster (billboard)
A common form of outdoor advertising; usually a picture-dominant advertisement with a minimum of copy.

> **FIGURE 5.14 Advantages and Disadvantages of Magazine Advertising**
>
> **ADVANTAGES**
>
> - **Targeting capability**—good reach based on readers' demographic (profile-matching strategy) and psychographic (rifle strategy) characteristics
> - **Coverage flexibility**—city, regional, and national magazines available
> - **Life span**—magazines tend not to be discarded right away; opportunity for multiple exposures to message
> - **Quality**—excellent colour reproduction
> - **Environment**—message benefits from the prestige of association with the magazine's quality and image
> - **Pass-along readership**—actual readership goes beyond the subscriber (added reach)
>
> **DISADVANTAGES**
>
> - **Clutter**—abundance of ads appearing in the initial section (advertising domination in some magazines)
> - **Cost**—colour is an added cost in production of ad
> - **Frequency**—distribution is usually monthly or bi-monthly

potential, they are strategically located on major travel routes leading to or within a community's business and shopping districts. To maximize the frequency of message and to extend daily viewing by consumers, posters are often illuminated. A powerful light beams upward from the bottom of the poster.

backlit (backlight) poster
A luminous outdoor sign printed on polyvinyl material.

A step up in quality is the **backlit poster**. On a backlit, the advertising message is printed on translucent polyvinyl material. When the posters are erected, lights shine through the material from behind the sign. The primary advantage is the image enhancement offered by the lighting; there is strong visual impact in the day and at night. Backlits are strategically located at major intersections and on high-volume traffic routes. For the advertiser, they cost more.

superboard (spectacular)
Outdoor advertising that is larger than a normal poster and much more expensive to produce; can include extensions beyond borders, and electronic messaging.

A **superboard** or **spectacular** is an extremely large display unit positioned at the highest-volume traffic locations. It is created to the advertiser's specifications and can include space extensions, flashing lights, rotating faces, and electronic messaging. Since superboards are one-of-a-kind structures that are illuminated and frequently include moving objects, they require a long-term commitment from the advertiser due to the high expense of designing and constructing them. Spectaculars are beyond the budgets of most advertisers, but for those inclined to use them, they offer the "wow" factor—incredibly large creative executions that create a high degree of consumer interest and media interest—and can generate buzz for a brand!

mural advertisement
A hand-painted outdoor ad seen on the side of a building.

Mural advertisements are hand-painted outdoor extravaganzas placed on the sides of buildings. They are very large—often the entire height of the building. If size really matters, these kinds of ads are real attention grabbers. See Figure 5.15 for an illustration.

Technology is providing a means for outdoor advertising to be interactive. At one time all outdoor posters were static in nature, but now they can display multiple messages at the same time. Essentially, a television advertisement could appear on a digital

FIGURE
5.15

**Mural Advertisements Are Good
Attention Grabbers**

Source: mavrixphoto.com/Keystone
Press.

board (a tactic suited for public areas where pedestrians mingle). Thus far, they are only available in major urban markets, usually in high-traffic downtown areas.

Street-level posters are rear-illuminated units consisting of two- or four-sided advertising faces. Street-level advertising includes transit shelters and blocks or columns with advertising faces. They are primarily available in urban centres. Transit shelters offer high levels of exposure to motorists, pedestrians, and transit riders. Transit shelter advertising offers the advertiser strong visual impact, as the colour reproduction is of superior quality. For an illustration see Figure 5.16.

Mall posters differ from the posters described above because they rely only on pedestrian traffic and aren't exposed to vehicle traffic. Located in shopping malls, they are directed at consumers who are actually shopping; therefore, they are a useful medium for the mall's retailers.

The various forms of outdoor advertising are ideal for advertisers using a shotgun strategy. Posters reach a large cross-section of a market's population in a short period. Frequently, outdoor boards are included in a blitz or build-up schedule because they are good for launching new products where creating awareness for the brand name, brand logo, and package are important. Outdoor posters are also ideal for advertisers who want geographic flexibility; the advertiser selects only those urban areas that are given priority.

There are a few drawbacks as well. The message must be brief, considering the circumstances in which people view outdoor boards. Since they reach a wide cross-section of the population, they are not a targeted medium. The message reaches people well beyond the target, which will increase the cost of reaching an actual target customer.

TRANSIT ADVERTISING   People who use public transit are a captive audience for advertising messages. To relieve the boredom of travelling, ads offer a form of visual

street-level poster
**A rear-illuminated unit consisting of
two- or four-sided advertising faces,
such as transit shelters and blocks or
columns with advertising faces.**

mall poster
**A form of advertising located inside
shopping malls; relies on pedestrian
traffic only.**

transit poster
A transit ad in the rack above the window or near the door of a bus or subway car.

door card
A vertically oriented poster usually found beside the doors of subway cars and light rapid transit (LRT) commuter trains.

station poster
An advertisement located on the platform or at the entrance or exit of subways and LRT systems.

station domination
One advertiser purchases all advertising inventory available in a subway station.

king poster
An oversized poster attached to the side of a bus.

seventy poster
A small poster usually affixed to the side or back of a bus.

stimulation. Passengers read the same ad over and over again while riding a subway car or bus. Transit advertising is classified as interior or exterior. Interior options include transit posters, door cards, and station posters.

Transit posters are print advertisements (horizontal format) contained in racks above the windows of transit vehicles (buses, streetcars, subway cars, and rapid transit cars). The average time spent travelling is approximately 30 minutes—ample time for brand exposure. Refer to Figure 5.17 for an illustration.

Door cards are vertically oriented posters usually located beside the doors of subway cars or light rapid transit (LRT) commuter trains. Typically the traveller sees the ad when exiting the vehicle. For both transit posters and door cards, advertisers may include take-away items such as coupons.

Station posters are advertisements located on platforms and at the entrances and exits of subway and LRT systems. They are available in a variety of sizes and are either paper posters or backlit posters. Passengers waiting on platforms are exposed to the advertising message.

Another concept called **station domination** gives a single advertiser control of all advertising space in a subway station, which includes wall murals, turnstiles, stairs, and floors. These are good options for advertisers looking for new ways of standing out amid the clutter of out-of-home advertising.

Exterior transit options include king posters, seventy posters, full wraps, bus murals, and bus backs.

Two different posters are available on the outside of buses. The **king poster** is a very large poster that stretches along the side of a bus. A **seventy poster** is smaller and located either on the side or tail end of the vehicle. The unique characteristic of bus posters is their mobility. They move through the city and are seen by lots of motorists and pedestrians.

FIGURE
5.17

Transit Posters Inside a Vehicle Have a Captive Audience

Source: *Toronto Star*/GetStock.com.

The **full wrap**, **bus mural**, and **bus back** options are vinyl coverings that take up all of the transit vehicle or parts of the vehicle. Full wraps cover both sides and the back of the vehicle; bus murals cover one side; and bus backs occupy the tail end. Due to the costs, the advertiser must commit to a long-term contract (13 or 26 weeks) with the transit company.

From an advertising perspective, transit offers continuous exposure. That 30-minute commute provides ample opportunity to deliver an advertising message while delivering both reach and frequency. Transit riders cut across all demographics, with the heaviest concentration being adults. Factors such as the increasing cost of operating a car and the increasing numbers of commuters travelling to and from a city each day have a positive effect on the reach potential of the medium. Like outdoor advertising, transit advertising is suited for media strategies designed to reach a diverse audience in key markets. Refer to Figure 5.18 for additional details about the benefits and drawbacks of the various forms of out-of-home advertising.

OTHER FORMS OF OUT-OF-HOME ADVERTISING   It's everywhere! It's everywhere! There are all kinds of unique opportunities to reach consumers when they least expect it. Among the more popular options with advertisers are washroom advertising, elevator advertising, and cinema advertising.

Washroom advertising involves the placement of mini-posters in public washrooms, usually above urinals in men's washrooms and on the backs of stall doors. They are located in colleges and universities, sporting facilities, hospitals, restaurants, and bars. Beer brands such as Budweiser and Molson Canadian have employed washroom advertising as it offers a certain degree of targeting. It is a good fit, for example, to reach college and university students on campus.

Elevator advertising is available in two forms: posters contained in display frames on the walls of elevators and slim-line televisions usually mounted in the top corner and

full wrap
An advertisement in the form of a vinyl covering that covers both sides and the back of the vehicle.

bus mural
An advertisement in the form of a vinyl covering that appears on one side of the vehicle.

bus back
A vinyl wrap advertisement that appears on the back end of a vehicle.

washroom advertising
A mini-poster ad located in a public or institutional washroom; usually placed above the urinal or on the back of the stall door.

elevator advertising
Advertising in display frames on elevator walls or on televisions mounted in the corner or above the door.

FIGURE
5.18

**Advantages and Disadvantages
of Out-of-Home Advertising**

Outdoor Posters
Advantages
Reach and frequency—reach a large general audience daily
Coverage flexibility—markets selected geographically (key market plan)
Compatibility—a good complementary medium to reinforce a message (name, logo, slogan)
Awareness—often included in teaser and blitz campaigns for new products due to reach potential
Disadvantages
Creative limitations—message must be concise; good visuals mandatory
Targeting—not suitable for reaching precisely defined targets
Cost—absolute costs high compared to other media (minimum four-week cycles)
Image—often referred to as "urban clutter"
Transit
Advantages
Reach and frequency—riders receive same message daily, weekly, and monthly
Continuous exposure—trapped riders view same ad many times
Coverage flexibility—markets selected geographically, based on priority (key market strategy)
Disadvantages
Targeting—a diverse cross-section of population, therefore some circulation wasted
Environment—cluttered and crowded environment in peak periods makes message less visible

tilted downward toward the passengers. The Captivate Network delivers up-to-date news and information along with ads on TV screens in office towers in major cities. Ads of this nature reach business decision makers in all kinds of industries.

arena and stadium advertising
Advertising within arenas and stadiums, from the door to the court, rink, or playing field.

Arena and stadium advertising opportunities extend across North America and offer targeted reach for advertisers. In arenas that are home to professional hockey teams, advertising starts right above the front door, with companies paying megabucks to have an arena adorned with their name. Rogers Arena in Vancouver, Air Canada Centre in Toronto, Scotiabank Place in Ottawa, and Bell Centre in Montreal are just some examples. See the illustration in Figure 5.19. In hockey arenas, there is also on-ice advertising and signs behind the players benches and penalty box. At ballparks, rotating signs behind home plate are popular, and there are courtside signs on basketball courts. These signs receive additional exposure when a game is broadcast on television.

cinema advertising
Print advertising inside film theatres and broadcast advertising on screens; options include television-style ads on screen, slides, posters, and ads printed on tickets.

Cinema advertising offers a variety of options, everything from 30- and 60-second full-motion commercials, digital, pre-show commercials, lobby posters, theatre promotions, ads printed on movie tickets, and more. Cineplex Odeon, Canada's largest movie distributor, reaches 8 million moviegoers monthly. There is a clear benefit to cinema advertising. Unlike most other media in which ads can be avoided, there is a captive audience in a theatre that cannot avoid the ads (unless they're on their smartphone putting in time!). A captive audience and engaging content on the big screen and in Dolby sound offer a high degree of impact.

FIGURE
5.19

Advertising Starts Right Above the Front Door

Source: Phillip MacCallum/ Getty Images.

SUMMARY

Media planning is the process of developing a plan of action for communicating messages to the right people at the right time. The end result is a media plan prepared by an advertising agency that covers all relevant media strategies and tactics. It is a document that is presented to the client for approval and, once approved, is put into action.

The key elements of the plan are media objectives, media strategies, and media execution. Media objectives deal with five key issues: who to reach, what and how to present the message creatively, where to advertise, when to advertise, and how often to advertise. Media objectives establish priorities for the plan and provide guidance for developing media strategies.

Media strategy deals with the selection of appropriate media to accomplish the objectives. Strategies are influenced by variables such as the characteristics and behaviour of the target market; the nature of the message; the degree of market coverage desired; the best time to reach the target; competitive activity; reach, frequency, and continuity; engagement; an assessment of the benefits and drawbacks of the various media options; and the available budget.

The advertising agency makes specific recommendations regarding the media a client should use. Depending on the assessment of the situation, there are numerous alternatives: television, radio, newspapers, magazines, outdoor advertising in a variety of forms, and transit advertising. Digital formats for each medium must also be considered in the media mix. Some unique and newer options are also considered: washroom advertising, elevator advertising, advertising in arenas and stadiums, and advertising in cinemas. To meet the challenge, the advertising agency usually recommends a combination of media. Typically, there is one primary medium (a medium that receives a significant portion of the budget) supplemented with secondary media.

Media execution is the section of the media plan that outlines the specific tactics for achieving the media objectives. These include the specific media usage recommendations and summaries of how media funds will be allocated. Once the plan is approved, the agency's media buyers negotiate the best possible prices with media representatives. The plan is then put into action.

KEY TERMS

REVIEW QUESTIONS

1. What are the essential differences among media objectives, media strategies, and media execution?

2. Identify and briefly describe the key issues usually covered by media objective statements.

3. What is the difference among a profile-matching strategy, a shotgun strategy, and a rifle strategy? What media are best suited for each strategy?

4. What is the difference among the following market coverage strategies: national coverage, regional coverage, and key market coverage? What media are best suited for each strategy?

5. Briefly describe how the timing and amount of spending vary in the following media schedules: pulse, skip, blitz, and build-up.

6. Briefly describe the impact of reach, frequency, continuity, and engagement on strategic media planning.

7. What role does CPM play in media selection? How is it calculated?

8. Identify two key strengths and weaknesses for each of the following media: television, radio, magazines, newspapers, outdoor boards, and transit.

9. In television advertising, what is the difference between a network spot and a selective spot?

10. What is the difference between product placement and branded content?

11. Briefly describe the following media terms:
    a) format (of a radio station)
    b) broadsheet and tabloid
    c) paid circulation and controlled circulation
    d) posters and backlit posters (outdoor)
    e) clutter and cluster

DISCUSSION AND APPLICATION QUESTIONS

1. How will technological advances affect media strategy and media execution in the future?

2. Should the budget determine the media plan or should the media plan determine the budget? Briefly explain and establish an opinion on this issue.

3. Is it possible to implement a rifle media strategy by using television advertising? Justify your position by providing branded advertising campaigns that are scheduled effectively or ineffectively on television networks and channels.

4. Assuming you can't have both high reach and high frequency, under what circumstances should reach take precedence? Under what circumstances should frequency take precedence? Be specific and provide examples.

5. Given the nature of Canada's population and where the bulk of the population is located, when is it practical to implement a national media campaign? When do regional media campaigns or key market media campaigns make economic sense?

6. Using resources that are available in your library or online, compare the CPMs for three different magazines that compete with each other. They must be magazines that reach a similar target audience and attract similar advertisers. Which magazine is the most efficient at reaching the target audience?

7. Assume you are about to devise a media plan to launch a new luxury automobile (such as a BMW, Audi, Lexus, or Infiniti). The new model is a very sleek-looking sporty car. The target market is males aged 35 to 49 living in urban markets. What media (be as specific as possible) would you use to reach this target and why would you recommend them? What target market media-matching strategy would you use? Justify your position.

ENDNOTES

1. Wayne Friedman, "Millennials Watch More TV Online," *Media Daily News*, Media Post publications, August 19, 2011, www.mediapost.com/publications/article/156252/millennials-watch-more-tv-online.html.

2. "Time Spent—Major Media 2011," TVB Canada. www.tvb.ca/pages/rts2011_htm.

3. "30 Seconds of Glory," *Report on Business* Magazine, March 2010, p. 15.

4. "Canada's Most-watched Cable Channels," *The Globe and Mail*," November 28, 2011, www.theglobeandmail.com.

5. "PVRs Will Not Eliminate TV Advertising's 30-Second Spot," TVB Canada, February 28, 2011, www.tvb.ca.

6. *TVBasics 2011-2012*, Television Bureau of Canada, p. 28, www.tvb.ca/page_files/pdf/InfoCentre/TVBasics2011-2012.pdf.

7. *Canadian Media Directors' Council Media Digest, 2011-2012, Marketing,* September 26, 2011, p. 25, bppg.rogersdigitalmedia.com/media/bppg/marketing/pdf/MediaDigest_1011.pdf.

8. *TVBasics 2011-2012*, Television Bureau of Canada, p. 12, www.tvb.ca/page_files/pdf/InfoCentre/TVBasics2011-2012.pdf.

9. "Top Programs—Total Canada (English), April 23-29, 2012," BBM Canada, www.bbm.ca/_documents/top_30_tv_programs_english/2012/nat04232012.pdf.

10. Brian Compton, "Hockeyville Growing in Popularity," NHL.com, September 19, 2008, www.nhl.com/ice/news.htm?id=382533.

11. Brian Stelter, "Pepsi to Sponsor 'American Idol' Rival," *The New York Times*, January 3, 2011, www.nytimes.com/2011/01/04/business/media/04adco.html.

12. "Ford Fiesta Gets a Lift with Erica," *Strategy*, November 2011, p. 36.

13. *Canadian Media Directors' Council Media Digest, 2011-2012, Marketing,* September 26, 2011, p. 34, bppg.rogersdigitalmedia.com/media/bppg/marketing/pdf/MediaDigest_1011.pdf.

14. Patti Summerfield, "Radio Connects with Consumers," *Strategy*, September 2, 2004, www.mediaincanada.com.

15. "Radio Listening Time by Format and Age Group," Statistics Canada, 2008, www.statcan.gc.ca/tables-tableaux/sum-som/l01/cst01/arts17-eng.htm.

16. "Daily Newspaper Circulation and Cost by Region," *Canadian Media Directors' Council Media Digest, 2011-2012, Marketing,* September 26, 2011, p. 42, bppg.rogersdigitalmedia.com/media/bppg/marketing/pdf/MediaDigest_1011.pdf.

17. Chris Powell, "Newspaper Readership (Slowly) Moving Online: NADbank," March 30, 2012, *Marketing*, www.marketingmag.ca/news/media-news/newspaper-readership-slowly-moving-online-nadbank-49686.

18. "About," metronews.ca, www.metronews.ca/about.

19. Matt Semansky, "Paper Tigers," *Marketing*, February 8, 2011, www.marketingmag.ca/uncategorized/paper-tigers-22290.

20. "Magazines Engage Across Multiple Platforms and Devices," *Canadian Media Directors' Council Media Digest, 2011-2012, Marketing,* September 26, 2011, p. 53, bppg.rogersdigitalmedia.com/media/bppg/marketing/pdf/MediaDigest_1011.pdf.

21. "Net Advertising Volume," *Canadian Media Directors' Council Media Digest, 2011-2012, Marketing,* September 26, 2011, p. 14, bppg.rogersdigitalmedia.com/media/bppg/marketing/pdf/MediaDigest_1011.pdf.

Planning for Direct Response Communications

Learning Objectives

After studying this chapter, you will be able to

1. Describe the direct response marketing communications planning process

2. Describe the various forms of direct response communications

3. Assess the role of database management techniques in the design and implementation of direct response strategies

4. Evaluate various external sources of list information and evaluate the role of lists in building an effective direct response campaign

5. Explain the role and nature, and advantages and disadvantages, of the various forms of direct response communications

Some of the discussion in previous chapters indicates that consumers' media habits are changing. There is a slow migration away from mass media such as print and broadcast media and toward direct and interactive media. As well, advancing technology has created a means for organizations to communicate with customers on an individual basis. In Chapter 1, the concepts of customer relationship management (CRM) and database marketing were introduced. Both concepts influence the development of programs that are designed to attract, cultivate, and maximize the return for each customer with whom the company does business. The end result is that companies are combining mass communications and marketing techniques with micro-marketing techniques. Database management and its influence on integrated marketing communications programs are discussed in more detail in this chapter. Information—that is, quality information—is the backbone of a direct response communications strategy.

Direct response communications involve direct mail, direct response communications in the mass media (mainly television, magazines, and newspapers), telemarketing, and catalogue marketing. Direct mail is the most common means of delivering messages directly to consumers, but advances in technology and database management techniques offer great potential for catalogues and the Internet to become more important in the mix. Internet communications are discussed in detail in Chapter 7. Using database management techniques, a company can look at a customer over an entire lifetime and plan appropriate strategies to encourage customers to buy more often or in larger quantities. Communicating directly with customers makes the entire process much more personal.

Direct Response Communications and Direct Marketing

Just how important are direct response communications and other direct marketing practices in Canada? Recent statistics suggest direct response communications and direct marketing have a significant impact on advertising expenditures and sales revenues for goods and services. Direct mail advertising alone accounts for $1.3 billion, or 9.3 percent, of net advertising revenues in Canada. As an advertising medium, it ranks fourth, behind television, the Internet, and newspapers.[1] If investments in direct response television, telemarketing, and catalogue marketing were included, the percentage of total media expenditures would be much higher.

Direct response communications are playing a more prominent role in the overall media mix of Canadian companies. Some of Canada's largest corporations have successfully integrated direct response communications with traditional forms of communications. These companies see the real value to be gained by managing customer relationships. Among these companies are Bell Canada, Rogers Communications, Shoppers Drug Mart, Mountain Equipment Co-op, and financial institutions such as RBC Financial Group and BMO Bank of Montreal.

Direct marketing and direct response communications will continue to grow for several reasons. First, companies want managers to be more accountable for the expenditures they oversee. Executives are looking for more immediate sales returns for the dollars they invest. Direct response advertising can be measured for success quickly. Second, the expanded use of customer relationship management techniques by organizations demonstrates the importance of forming good relationships with customers. Because direct response communications can be personalized, they constitute an ideal medium for nurturing relationships. Third, the availability of database management techniques provides the fuel that direct response communications run on. Specific message strategies for individual customers are now a possibility—if the organization can effectively analyze the information in its database. Advantages such as these clearly indicate why prudent marketing organizations include direct response as part of their communications mix.

It is important to remember that direct response communications is a subset of direct marketing. In other words, the communications program is a component of a much larger direct marketing program. What is the distinction between the two practices? In **direct marketing**, products are developed, messages about the products are sent directly to customers (business-to-consumer or business-to-business) through a variety of media, orders are accepted, and then products are distributed directly to customers. In true direct marketing, all wholesale and retail intermediaries are eliminated.

In contrast, **direct response advertising** is advertising placed in any medium that generates an immediate and measurable response from the intended target. A direct response advertising plan involves the design and development of appropriate messages and the placement of messages in appropriate direct response media to encourage immediate action by the intended target. Alternatively, direct response advertising may be designed to build brand image, alter a perception, or attract a new target, much like other forms of advertising. Therefore, direct response advertising can be part of a fully integrated marketing communications campaign. Figure 6.1 illustrates the direct response planning process and its relationship with other components of marketing communications.

A direct response advertisement comprises three essential components: product information, a convincing sales message, and a response mechanism. The response mechanism or call to action is the most important component. The message should include a 1-800 number, a return mail address, or a website address where more information can be obtained or an order placed. With direct response advertising, the marketer must tell the customer what to do and how they will benefit. The inclusion of time-sensitive offers is an effective means of stimulating immediate action.

Unlike other mass media, direct response advertising is capable of making a sale. Assuming adequate order taking and fulfillment strategies are in place, the entire transaction process from creating awareness to delivering the product is possible, and in a very short span of time. Further, the results of a direct response plan can be tracked and measured daily, providing a daily and weekly return on investment—significant information that is not available through other media.

direct marketing
A marketing system for developing products, sending messages directly to customers, and accepting orders through a variety of media, and then distributing the purchase directly to customers.

direct response advertising
Advertising placed in a medium that generates an immediate and measurable response from the intended target.

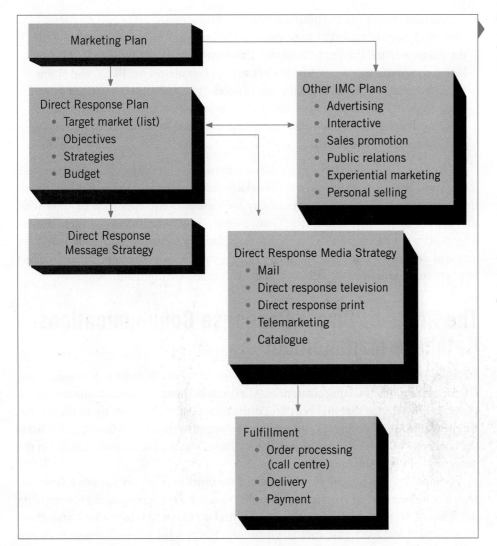

FIGURE
6.1

The Direct Response Planning Process

Direct response communications can be divided between online communications and the more traditional forms. Online communications are presented in Chapter 7. The traditional forms of direct response communications are direct mail, direct response in the mass media (TV or print), telemarketing, and catalogue marketing:

- **Direct mail** is a printed form of communications distributed to prospective consumers by Canada Post or independent delivery agents (for example, leaflets and flyers that may be dropped at a doorstep).

- **Direct response television (DRTV)** is a form of advertising communicated to prospects by television commercials that may be 30 seconds long, 60 seconds long, or more like a program that could be 30 minutes long. Call-to-action information is included in the advertisement.

- **Direct response print** refers to ads that appear in magazines or newspapers but include call-to-action information so consumers can respond immediately to the offer.

- **Telemarketing** refers to outbound sales calls (a company calls the customer) or inbound sales calls (the customer contacts the company) to secure an order. All calls are usually handled through a central call centre.

direct mail
A printed form of direct response advertising distributed by Canada Post or independent delivery agents.

direct response television (DRTV)
Advertising that appears on television and encourages viewers to respond by telephoning a toll-free number, by mail, or online; often referred to as infomercials.

Direct response print
A response-oriented ad delivered to prospects by magazines or newspaper advertisements.

telemarketing
The use of telecommunications to promote the products and services of a business; involves outbound calls (company to customer) and inbound calls (customer to company).

catalogue
A reference publication, usually annual or seasonal, distributed by large retail chains and direct marketing companies.

- **Catalogues** are important communications vehicles among retail organizations. Typically, they are mailed or hand delivered by independent agents to existing customers or they are distributed in stores. Catalogues are a key component of the marketing communications mix for retailers such as Canadian Tire, IKEA, and Home Hardware. Catalogues promote the sale of goods the retailer carries and are now designed to move customers online for more information and to encourage sales. They are also useful tools for communicating information about goods in business-to-business (B2B) situations.

There was a time when direct response communications were a last-minute strategy—a technique to be used when things weren't working well. How the times have changed! Today, marketing organizations stress accountability and measurability. They want to know what they are getting for their investment. Consequently, most large full-service agencies now offer direct response expertise or have access to it. Many traditional advertising agencies have acquired direct response agencies. Such progression reinforces the importance of direct response communications in today's competitive business environment.

The Roots of Direct Response Communications: Database Management

Whether it's mail or telephone communications, there needs to be a convenient and efficient means of contacting customers. As experts in direct response communications often state, it's the list that makes or breaks the campaign. By list, they mean the list that will be used to contact current customers or prospective customers directly. That list is the backbone of the entire campaign; the quality of the list has a direct impact on the success or failure of the campaign.

Companies recognize that it costs about six times as much to acquire a new customer as it does to keep an existing customer. Consequently, companies are compiling databases to keep track of existing customers and are forming relationships with them through mail and electronic means. Obviously, the best list is a well-maintained and well-managed internal list of customers. Such a list is referred to as a **house list**. Since the best customers are current customers, it is much easier to get them to buy more of something than it is to attract a new customer. If the goal is to generate new business from new customers, then lists can be obtained from external sources.

house list
An internal customer list.

INTERNAL DATA SOURCES

A good database management system collects and maintains relevant information about customers. The information is stored in such a manner that managers have easy access to it when developing marketing strategies. For example, managers should be able to manipulate the data so that customer profiles will emerge and future purchase patterns can be forecast from those profiles. In other words, a thorough understanding of a customer's past purchasing behaviour should provide ammunition for predicting his or her future buying patterns.

COLLECTING DATA

The names and addresses of customers are the most common forms of internal data, but simply knowing who the customers are offers little perspective when developing a strategic plan. Factor in technology, and all kinds of information about customers can be combined. Keeping track of purchasing behaviour and then linking it to a name and address is very meaningful. Therefore, the database should identify what a customer

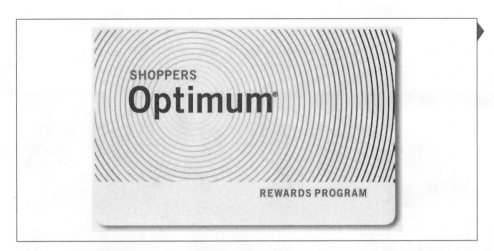

FIGURE
6.2

The Shoppers Optimum Database Provides Information that Produces Offers of Interest to Send to Shoppers Drug Mart Customers

Source: Courtesy of Shoppers Drug Mart.

purchases, how often the customer purchases, how much the customer spends on average, what brands of goods the customer prefers, and so on.

Sophisticated retail organizations update this information automatically as goods are scanned through checkouts. Shoppers Drug Mart, for example, has an exhaustive database of customer information collected via its Shoppers Optimum loyalty program. From this information, buying behaviour profiles of a customer can be developed and special offers that are unique to an individual customer can be delivered to those who have consented to receive such offers. Refer to the image in Figure 6.2.

Adding external information to the database rounds out the profile of the customer. Information about customers using credit cards for purchases is readily available. Credit card companies, such as Visa and MasterCard, are sitting on nest eggs of information that marketing organizations can purchase. Statistics Canada makes census data available, which are updated every five years. This information is available at reasonable cost to the marketing organization.

Demographic and psychographic information can also be obtained from commercial research companies like Millward Brown, or a company can hire an independent research company to conduct primary research to uncover such information. The combination of information dealing with age, gender, education, income, marital status, and household formation, along with information about attitudes, lifestyles, interests, and hobbies forms an arsenal of information ready for use in strategic planning.

ACCESSING DATA

The second step in database management is devising a storage system that allows managers to access information easily when it is needed. In the realm of marketing communications, sales representatives and sales managers need instant access to customer sales records as they prepare for sales calls. Customer service personnel need access to historical information to handle complaints or simply serve customers better. Marketing managers and marketing communications managers need to clearly identify target customers and their behaviour to communicate directly with them and design special offers. To accomplish these kinds of tasks, relevant information must be convenient and accessible to all those who work with the database. Molson Canada, for example, has more than 1 million customers in its Molson Insider database. Molson uses the database to attract insiders to Molson-sponsored events and to inform customers about new products and promotional offers.[2] Refer to the image in Figure 6.3.

The electronic era has resulted in an information explosion that allows for the storage and transfer of a large amount of business data in a short time. What has emerged is a new

FIGURE 6.3   Molson's Offers Its "Insiders" (Database Members) a Special Offer at Kelsey's Restaurants

Source: Courtesy of Molson Coors Canada.

data mining
The analysis of information to determine relationships among the data and enable more effective marketing strategies to be identified and implemented.

concept called data mining. **Data mining** is the analysis of information that establishes relationships among pieces of information so that more effective marketing strategies can be identified and implemented. Rather than looking at an entire data set, data mining techniques attempt to locate informational patterns and nuggets within the database.[3]

The goals of data mining are to produce lower marketing costs and to increase efficiency by identifying prospects most likely to buy in large volume. A firm's competitive advantage in the marketplace will increasingly depend on knowing the situation better than the competition and being able to take rapid action, based on that knowledge. Look no further than your local Walmart to see data mining at work. Walmart is the acknowledged leader in data mining, capable of tracking sales on a minute-by-minute basis. It can also quickly detect regional and local market trends. Such knowledge allows Walmart to customize each store's offerings while keeping suppliers abreast of how well their products are selling.[4]

Data mining offers an organization two essential benefits. First, it provides a means of profiling the "best" customers and the "worst" customers. Clearly, in these times, greater emphasis must be placed on customers who produce sales and high profit margins for an organization. As well, consideration can be given to dropping customers who cost more than they generate in profit. Why keep customers if they are not profitable? Second, data mining techniques give an organization a means to predict future sales. Continuous compiling and analysis of data about current customers' sales histories should result in more accurate forecasts about what the future holds. As well, when a company wants to expand its business by attracting new customers, it can use the internal customer profile information as a guideline and then rent names from lists that have similar profiles.

For some insight into how a database system is used in a marketing communications program, read the IMC Highlight: **Mountain Equipment Co-op Believes in Direct Mail Marketing**.

Mountain Equipment Co-op Believes in Direct Mail Marketing

The foundation of an effective direct marketing communications campaign is the quality of the customer list maintained by the organization. Mountain Equipment Co-op (MEC) lives and breathes by its robust member (customer) list. The list, which comprises 2.5 million members across Canada, is constantly being updated to ensure MEC can reap the most benefit from it.

MEC operates retail stores and a direct marketing division (catalogue, web, and telephone) and has annual revenues in the area of $200 million. It is a member-based national cooperative—the largest retail consumer cooperative in Canada. MEC operates with a limited advertising budget, so rather than concentrate on attracting new customers, it works diligently to get current customers to buy more. That's where database marketing plays a key role.

The focus of MEC's database marketing is on data mining—the constant refining and analyzing of data in order to effectively serve the needs of its membership. When consumers sign up for a membership, they give the retailer permission to send relevant communications to their home or email address. According to Selena McLachlan, manager of marketing and research, "When you demonstrate that you know your customer, through relevant messages that make them feel appreciated, you in turn create affection for the brand."

In terms of execution, the MEC catalogue is the key piece of communications. Members covet the catalogue, and two are distributed to members—a spring edition and a winter edition. That catalogue goes well beyond product information. It is a reflection of the socially conscious yet hip brand, with profiles of adventurers and environmental and conservation crusaders. Members retain the catalogues for 6 to 12 months, and as soon as they are mailed there is a surge in retail sales.

Being environmentally conscious, MEC doesn't mail catalogues to all members. Instead, through data mining, catalogues are only sent to members who are most engaged with the brand—those customers who buy regularly! A variety of filters are used to determine who these members are. In the database, sales data are combined with attitudinal and behavioural information collected from primary research. Collectively, the data help MEC improve the retail shopping experience and allow it to target its most profitable members with new product information and special offers.

The net result is the distribution of about 500 000 catalogues for each issue, as well as 250 000 postcards and 700 000 e-cards. MEC also produces specialty catalogues to serve members in niche sports such as canoeing and kayaking, among many others. "As much as possible, the specialty catalogues are targeted to ensure that they will land on the doorsteps of members who are engaged and active in their sport," says McLachlan.

Given the nature of the business and the niche markets that MEC serves, McLachlan knows that effective database marketing combined with catalogues will remain a key component of future success.

Adapted from "A Mountain of a Database," *Sorted*, Canada Post Publications, 2007, pp. 12–15.

Courtesy of MEC.

EXTERNAL SOURCES

People who have a history of responding to mail offers tend to be attractive prospects for new offers. Buying by mail or from offers seen on television is part of their behaviour. Therefore, the challenge is to find prospects that have a demographic profile, and perhaps a psychographic profile, that is similar to the profile of current customers. A **list broker** can

list broker
A company specializing in finding or developing lists for direct response purposes; finds prospect lists based on target market criteria established by marketing organizations.

assist in finding these prospects. The buyer provides the broker with a profile of the target customer, and the broker supplies a list of potential prospects. Generally, a high-quality list is developed through a **merge/purge** process on a computer, whereby numerous lists are purchased, combined, and stripped of duplicate names. Names are purchased (actually rented) on a cost-per-thousand basis. List brokers charge a base rate for names and charge more if additional requests are made. Additional requests, called *selects*, are usually demographic variables, interest or lifestyle variables, or geographic variables.

One of the biggest suppliers of external data about households is Canada Post. Working from postal codes that isolate a neighbourhood or a city block, prospective households are identified when census data is added. For example, relevant statistics regarding the ages and incomes of homeowners in the area and the presence of children in those households could be attractive information for marketing organizations. There are three types of lists available:

merge/purge
A process in which numerous mailing lists are combined and then stripped of duplicate names.

Response Lists   A **response list** is a list of proven direct response buyers. It's a "hot" list, so the price is high on a cost-per-thousand basis. Such lists include people who routinely place orders with cooperative direct marketing firms. Epsilon TargetSource Canada offers a list of more than 2 million Canadian adults, with a base price of $125/M (cost per thousand) and charges an additional $15/M for specific age ranges within their list.[5] Cornerstone Group of Companies is another provider of direct mail lists. For more insight into the lists and their costs, see Figure 6.4.

response list
A list of direct mail buyers who have previously made purchases based on direct response offers.

Circulation Lists   The word "circulation" indicates these lists are obtained from newspaper and magazine sources. **Circulation lists** can target consumers demographically, psychographically, and geographically. A publishing company, such as Rogers Communications, rents its list of subscribers to any other business that is interested in a similar target. A list management company is usually responsible for managing and renting all of the lists made available by the publisher.

For instance, *Chatelaine* magazine reaches women aged 25 to 49 who have children and are busy with careers and family. The *Chatelaine* list has a base cost of $125/M, which rises as certain characteristics are added. There are also additional costs for requesting specific formats for the list, such as tape, disk, email, and so on.[6]

circulation list
A publication's subscription list that targets potential customers based on specified demographic characteristics, interests, or activities.

Compiled Lists   **Compiled lists** are assembled from government, census, telephone, warranty, and other publication information. Less expensive than circulation lists and response lists, these lists are very common in B2B marketing. Names of prospects can be assembled from various print sources, such as *Fraser's Canadian Trade Index* and *Scott's Industrial Index*. Provincial and national associations like the Canadian Medical Association provide lists of their physicians, as do other associations: accountants, engineers, purchasing managers, teachers, and so on.

compiled list
A direct mail list prepared from government, census, telephone, warranty, or other publication information.

ONLINE DATABASES

Due to advancing technology, there has been a surge in developing online databases. Information from commercial sources can now be transferred to an organization almost instantly. An **online database** is an information database accessible to anyone with proper communications facilities. For example, census data from Statistics Canada are readily available online. Most of Statistics Canada data are based on census data collected every five years. The nature of the information and reporting

online database
An information database accessible online to anyone with proper communications facilities.

FIGURE
6.4   The Costs Involved in Renting a Direct Response List

CHATELAINE MAGAZINE - ENGLISH

CLASSIFICATION	MAGAZINES
TYPE	CONSUMER WOMEN
LIST SIZE	202,225
MINIMUM ORDER	5,000
BASE COST/THOUSAND	$125.00 CDN
BROKERAGE COMMISSION	20.00%
NAMES THROUGH	March 08, 2012
PROFILE UPDATED	March 12, 2012

Chatelaine - Canada's favourite women's magazine, delivers what women are looking for most - real value, real ideas, real inspiration, and real solutions.

Chatelaine subscribers index above the Canadian average for: bachelor or post grad degree (index 138); owning mutual funds (index 130); donors to Canadian charities (index 123).

Source: PMB 2010 Base: English adults 18+

Area data information has also been overlaid and a variety of averaged statistical demographic information is available. Examples include: Affluent Households over $75,000; High Contributing Donors $100-$300+. This is an ideal list for offers related to Fundraising, Entertainment, Cooking, Crafts, Education, Catalogues, Finance and a variety of additional Consumer Products and Services.

Sample Select Counts Available: Direct Mail Sold (108,529); Males (20,286); Females (154,238); Unknown Gender (17,896); Home Address (189,683; Business Address (2,737); Last 12 Month Expires (122,324). Subscription sources: direct marketing including online and agency. This list is updated bi-monthly.
Subscription Rate: $14.95/Year (12) Issues

TERMS: Duplicates between lists may not be mailed at a later date. Run charges apply to all cancelled orders. Orders cancelled after the mail date must be paid in full. Minimum quantity of 1,000 records for re-use orders. Reciprocal access to mailer's list is requested.

SELECTS	COSTS
Gender	$10.00 /M
Key Records	$5.00 /M
Nth	$0.00 /M
Province	$10.00 /M
FSA	$10.00 /M

OTHER SELECTS	COSTS
Actives (Base $125/M)	$0.00 /M
Address Type	$10.00 /M
Age	$10.00 /M
Change of Address	$10.00 /M
Donation Value	$10.00 /M
Expires (Base $95/M)	$0.00 /M
Hotline 0-3 Months	$15.00 /M
Hotline 0-6 Months	$10.00 /M
Income	$10.00 /M
New to File	$10.00 /M
Radius	$0.00 /M
Source	$10.00 /M

FORMATS	COSTS
Secure File Transfer	$60.00 /F
CD-ROM	$60.00 /F
FTP	$60.00 /F

SORTING	COSTS
Postal	$0.00 /M

SHIPPING	COSTS
Toronto Area	$50.00 /F
Other Areas	$50.00 /F
Abroad	$100.00 /F

PROVINCIAL BREAKDOWN		
ON 50.04%	QC 2.96%	BC 13.07%
AB 14.52%	MB 5.34%	NB 2.24%
NL 0.91%	NS 2.66%	PE 0.78%
SK 7.11%	NT 0.18%	YK 0.15%
NU 0.04%		

Source: Courtesy of Cornerstone Group of Companies.

of the information is very detailed, covering dozens of demographic and socio-economic topics such as family and household structures, income, occupation, education, ethnic background, and marital status. For a marketing organization, knowledge about and understanding trend data are essential skills for planning effective marketing strategies.

From commercial sources like Dun & Bradstreet (D&B), marketing organizations can access information through directory databases. A **directory database** provides a quick picture of a company and its products (for example, ownership, size in terms of sales revenue, company locations, number of employees, key management personnel, and profitability). Examples of business directories that are available electronically include the *Canadian Business Directory* and the *Canadian Trade Index*. The *Canadian Business Directory* provides some 830 000 listings of companies in Canada. These types of directories help an organization locate and qualify potential customers in Canada.

directory database
A commercial database that provides information about a company (for example, size, sales, location, number of employees).

The Tools of Direct Response Communications

Essentially, five primary media compose the direct response tool kit: direct mail, direct response television, direct response print media, telemarketing, and catalogues. Among these options, direct mail still dominates, but other options are growing in importance. Let's examine each option in more detail.

DIRECT MAIL

The use of direct mail is widespread, thanks to its ability to personalize the message by using names secured from internal databases or rented from external databases. As well, direct mail provides an opportunity to target customers demographically and geographically. For example, an organization might choose to do a mailing to a fairly general audience by distributing a magazine subscription leaflet to all households in Ontario , or it might deliver a message to very selective upper-income households in a concentrated area of a city. Moreover, direct mail provides an opportunity to "tell a story." Since the average mailing includes several pieces, an expanded story can be told about the product or service. Unlike other media, the advertiser is not restricted by time (30-second commercials on TV or radio) or space (one page or less in a newspaper or magazine). Benefits such as these make direct mail an attractive option. While direct mail is perceived by many to be "junk" mail, research clearly indicates that consumers react positively to receiving direct mail offers. Refer to Figure 6.5 for details.

A typical direct mailing has several components, each designed to serve a specific purpose:

Envelope The envelope is a critical component of the mailing. Since direct mail is usually unsolicited, the envelope has to suggest strongly why the recipient should read the contents. There should be a sense of urgency about opening the envelope.

Letter The letter introduces the prospective customer to the product or service and encourages the receiver to read more about the offer in the other pieces included in the mailing. The letter may be unaddressed (delivered to the householder) or addressed (with the person's name and address). Addressed mail offers a certain degree of personalization

---

FIGURE 6.5 Some Facts and Figures About Direct Mail in Canada

The Figures	The Facts
87	Percentage of Canadians likely to read mail that is addressed to them personally
43	Percentage of Canadians who will read most mail promotions just in case something catches their eye
24	Percentage of Canadians who pay attention to addressed direct mail
3	Time, in seconds, that a direct mail recipient takes to decide whether to keep or discard mailer.

Source: Consumer Attitudes to DM and Traditional Media, CP 09-210, March 2010; Marketing Research Fact Sheet: Canadian Attitudes towards Direct Marketing and Mail; Keith Thirgood, creative director of Capstone Communications Group, Markham, ON.

and produces a higher response. Typically, the language used in the letter is persuasive, because the goal is to generate interest and desire and, ultimately, get the receiver to respond to the offer.

Leaflets and Folders   These types of direct mailing components can vary in size and structure. By definition, a **leaflet** is one page (though it may not be a full page), printed front and back, and contains vital information about the offer: Here's what the product is and here's why you should buy it. Again the language is persuasive in nature. Visuals frequently support the copy. A **folder** can be larger in size and contain multiple pages. For example, a double page folded once results in a four-page layout. That amount of space gives the marketer ample room to sell. When an offer is put together, an **incentive** is often included to stimulate a more immediate response. An incentive might nudge a recipient interested in buying closer to taking action. The objective is to get that person to take the appropriate action, call a 1-800 number, go online, or fill in the order form. A selection of leaflets and folders is included in Figure 6.6.

Order Form   A well-designed order form is essential. It must be easy to read, and it must communicate all details regarding price, additional costs such as shipping and handling charges, and means of payment (usually credit card information). The recipient must be able to place the order effortlessly.

leaflet
A one-page flyer that offers relevant information about a direct mail offer.

folder
A direct response sales message printed on heavy stock that can be mailed with or without an envelope; may be several pages in length.

incentive
A free gift or offer included in a direct mail package.

FIGURE
6.6

A Selection of Leaflets and Folders in Various Sizes and Configurations

Source: Photo by Dick Hemingway.

Postage-Paid Return Envelope   Eliminating the need for postage is another means of encouraging the recipient to take action. The combination of a clear and concise order form with a postage-paid return envelope makes it a no-hassle process from start to finish.

statement stuffer (bounce back)
An ad or offer distributed in monthly statements or with the delivery of goods purchased by some form of direct response advertising.

Statement Stuffers   A **statement stuffer** or **bounce back** is an additional offer that rides along with the delivery of another offer or with the delivery of a monthly statement. Capitalizing on the ease of purchasing by credit or on the knowledge that the customer uses related products or services, such mailings make it convenient for the customer to take action. Bounce backs commonly arrive with Sears, The Bay, Visa, and MasterCard bills.

DIRECT MAIL STRATEGIES   There are two basic options for delivering direct mail. The first is to deliver the mailing as a standalone piece. In this option, the organization bears all of the costs associated with developing the offer and distributing it to the target market. The second option is to deliver the offer as part of a package that includes offers from other companies. In this option, the distribution costs are shared equally among all participants. That is the difference between solo direct mail and cooperative direct mail.

solo direct mail (selective direct mail)
A unique advertising offer mailed directly to a target audience by a marketing organization.

Solo Direct Mail   With **solo direct mail**, also known as **selective direct mail**, the organization prepares a unique offer and mails it directly to the target market. It is a standalone offer. As discussed earlier, today's technology makes it very convenient for organizations to assess buying information, devise unique offers for existing customers, and deliver offers directly to those customers. Such a plan of action sounds much more efficient than delivering a message blindly to all consumers on prime-time television, or through daily newspapers or national magazines. Furthermore, solo direct mail can play a key role in an organization's CRM program. It is an effective means of keeping the channel of communication open.

Personalization is an important element of solo direct mail. According to Canada Post, 84 percent of Canadians open direct mail if their name is on it, and marketers experience an increase in response and conversion rates as a result of personalization. See Figure 6.7 for details.

dimensional mail
Direct mail that can take any form other than the typical flat piece of mail.

Another type of direct mail that attracts more attention and gets higher response is dimension mail. **Dimensional mail** is a type of direct mail that can take any form other than

---

FIGURE
6.7   **Consumers Are Responsive to Personalized Direct Mail**

According to Canada Post, 84% of Canadians open direct mail if it has their name on it, and marketers experience a significant increase in response and conversion rates as a result of personalization. Canada Post also reports that:

- 89% of Canadians open direct mail if it comes from a company they know.
- 86% open it if it looks intriguing or interesting.
- 79% open it if it has their address on it.
- 66% open it if it has a postage stamp.
- 52% open it if it mentions a free draw.

Marketers should have confidence in direct mail, because consumers like receiving it.

Source: Canada Post Research as reported in "How to Get the Most Out of Your Direct Mail," *Direct Marketing Resource Guide, Marketing*, November 14, 2005, p. 4; and "Direct Mail More Likely to Be Opened than Unsolicited Mail," Center for Media Research, June 21, 2007.

A Direct Mail Piece that Combines the Elements of Solo Direct Mail and Dimensional Mail

Source: Photo by Dick Hemingway.

the typical flat piece of mail. It could be something as simple as a pen or other object in an envelope or a unique box or package that contains the mail offer. Dimensional mail is meant to stand out—it is unique and often generates buzz for the product. Figure 6.8 demonstrates elements of solo direct mail and dimensional direct mail in one mailing piece.

Cooperative Direct Mail   **Cooperative direct mail** refers to packages containing offers from non-competing products and services. Consumer goods companies commonly use this method; they are attracted to it because the costs are shared among all participants. A typical mailing might include coupons for packaged goods items, magazine subscription forms, order forms for direct mail offers, and so on. For packaged goods marketers in the food and drug industries, cooperative direct mail has proven to be an effective means of generating trial purchase. Response rates for coupon offers delivered by direct mail tend to be higher than coupon offers delivered by magazines or newspapers. The illustration in Figure 6.9 is representative of a typical cooperative direct mailing.

cooperative direct mail
A mailing containing specific offers from non-competing products.

In deciding how and when to use direct mail, a manager evaluates the benefits and drawbacks of the medium. Refer to Figure 6.10 for details.

DIRECT RESPONSE TELEVISION

Direct response television (DRTV) is gaining in popularity with advertisers. Forms of direct response television include the 30- or 60-second commercial that typically runs on cable channels and sells gadgets and music products, and the infomercial (a program-like commercial).

The nature of direct response television advertising has changed over time. Once it was regarded as the "domain of schlock"; mainstream marketing organizations would not go near it. It was perceived as a last-resort tactic when all else failed. DRTV is now looked at in a more positive light due to the acceptance of infomercials and their improved level of quality. An **infomercial** is usually a 30-minute commercial that presents, in detail, the benefits of a product or service.

infomercial
A long commercial (for example, 10 to 30 minutes) that presents in detail the benefits of a product or service; usually includes a call to action such as a 1-800 number.

FIGURE
6.10

**Direct Mail as an Advertising
Medium**

ADVANTAGES

- **Audience Selectivity**—Targets can be precisely identified and reached based on demographic, psychographic, and geographic characteristics. It is possible to secure external lists that closely match internal lists.

- **Creative Flexibility**—Unlike other media, the message can be copy oriented, visually oriented, or a combination of both. Because a mailing includes several components, there is ample time to expand on the benefits of the product.

- **Exclusivity**—Mail does not compete with other media or other ads upon receipt. In contrast, magazines and newspapers include clusters of ads and create a cluttered environment to advertise in.

- **Measurability**—Direct mail response is measured by the sales it generates. A sale can be directly linked to the mail offer (for example, receipt of a phone call or order form in the mail). The success of a campaign is determined in a relatively short period.

DISADVANTAGES

- **Image**—Direct mail is not a prestigious medium. Often perceived as junk mail, it can be easily discarded by the recipient.

- **Cost per Exposure**—When all costs are included (for example, printing, securing list, mail delivery, and fulfillment), total cost can be higher than an ad placed in another print medium, although selective targeting reduces waste circulation.

- **Lack of Editorial Support**—As a standalone medium, compared to newspapers or magazines, it can't rely on editorial content to get people to read the message.

Infomercials today are presented in a more entertaining manner. There is less "hard sell." The transfer of information is less intrusive. Consumers can simply evaluate the message and take action if they so desire. Unlike general TV advertising, direct response TV ads, including infomercials, ask the consumer to take action immediately—to make the call, grab the credit card, and make the purchase. The effectiveness of the ad can be measured for impact on the spot. Did it work or not? These ads are measured quantitatively based on response. Typical measures include cost per order, cost per lead, cost per call, or some other criteria.

Well-produced and highly informative infomercials are now being run by serious mainstream marketing organizations. By industry, pharmaceutical marketers, automotive marketers, packaged goods marketers, and financial institution marketers are all on board. Companies within these industries that are using DRTV include Pfizer and GlaxoSmithKline, General Motors and Ford, Procter & Gamble and Unilever, and RBC Financial and TD Canada Trust.

These organizations evaluated the returns from their respective investments in mainstream advertising and decided that direct response communications would play a more vital role. For some companies, the message could not be adequately conveyed in the usual 30-second television spot. Manulife Financial recently produced three 120-second commercials. According to Ian French, president and executive creative director at Northern Lights Direct Response, "We wanted to more clearly articulate the types of life circumstances that people would be in that lend themselves to insurance." For example, one commercial depicts a family facing child health care costs that are not covered by government insurance.[7]

Direct response commercials do not always have to sell something. In fact, a good infomercial can serve many different marketing communications objectives: It can establish leads, drive retail traffic, launch new products, create awareness, and protect and enhance brand image. Procter & Gamble, for example, is not selling direct to consumers, but uses infomercials to promote products sold by retailers. Essentially, advertisers are pursuing a dual benefit—they are combining a brand message with a DRTV technique of encouraging action, either immediately or when the viewer visits a store.

Getting into direct response television, however, is not cheap. Experts say it costs at least $150 000 to produce a 30-minute infomercial, and if celebrities are included, the costs can go much higher. To keep media placement costs reasonable, shorter commercials (up to 60 seconds long) usually employ a station's run-of-schedule option where the ad is placed at the discretion of the station. Advertisers also use **remnant time**, which is unsold television inventory available on short notice at a lower cost.

remnant time
Unsold television inventory available at lower cost to an advertiser.

For more insight into the effectiveness of direct response television, read the IMC Highlight: **Infomercials Move the Merchandise**.

DIRECT RESPONSE PRINT MEDIA

The print media—mainly newspapers and magazines—are good choices for communicating direct response offers or for fielding leads for future marketing programs. Given the local nature of daily newspapers, an organization can target prospects geographically. If the size of the budget restricts activity, then markets can be assigned priorities until the budget is exhausted. Local market retailers that want to take advantage of direct response techniques have a good option in newspapers.

A majority of magazines are targeted at specific audiences based on demographic and psychographic characteristics, so the direct response message can be sent to specific

Infomercials Move the Merchandise

There are those who believe television is dead. They claim it's an old medium—it's out of touch with on-demand consumers who want to watch programs when they want to watch, not when the station wants them to watch. Not so fast, says Amir Tukulj, chairman and CEO of Thane Direct Inc., a Toronto-based direct marketing company.

Stop and think about those infomercials that have grabbed your attention late at night or on weekend mornings: the FlavorWave Oven or the Ab Doer Twist exercise machine. Ads like those carry the classic boast: "As seen on TV."

Tukulj agrees that the television universe is becoming fragmented with so many stations available, but he prefers to turn that negative into a positive. "For us it will mean the ability to target consumers in a more accurate manner and at lower cost," he says. With traditional forms of advertising such as a 30-second TV spot, a radio commercial, or a print ad, it is difficult to directly link the ad to sales since too many other variables come into play. With an infomercial, the phones start to ring right away, so the impact of the ad and the resulting sales are known almost immediately. For clients concerned about financial accountability, direct response television is an ideal fit.

So what makes a consumer pick up the phone to place an order? According to Tukulj, "The message has to be clear and concise; it has to resolve a specific problem which the consumer is experiencing. It has to provide the consumer instant gratification, it has to be a good price point, it has to provide value, and it has to be demonstrable."

The success of a direct response campaign also considers consumer behaviour. With direct response television, it's an impulse buy. "When they're passive, watching TV, that's when we get their attention, strike a chord, and cause them to purchase," says Tukulj.

Seasonality is also a factor in planning a direct response campaign. In the first quarter of the year (January to March), many national advertisers pull back their advertising. This allows direct response advertisers to buy better time at lower cost. If people are staying inside, they will be watching television. "People make New Year's resolutions," says Tukulj, "And one of those is to lose some weight and get fit." You can have the Total Flex fitness system on a 30-day trial for a down payment of $14.95. And it's yours to keep for only five more payments of $49.95 each. Are there any takers?

Adapted from Simon Houpt, "Call Now to Take Advantage of This Special TV Advertising Offer," *The Globe and Mail*, December 16, 2011, p. B5.

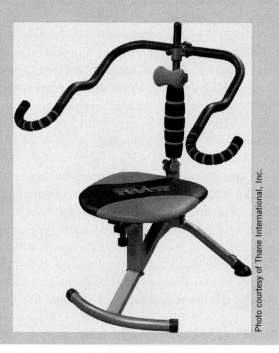

Photo courtesy of Thane International, Inc.

audiences based on criteria established by the advertiser. For example, a company marketing floating docks or cottage designs might want to reach cottage owners. A direct response ad placed in *Cottage Life* magazine will reach that target market. The basic point is that it is possible to identify magazines that closely match the profile of a company's best customers. Resort destinations such as Whistler Blackcomb and Mont Tremblant adopt similar strategies, as do provincial governments wanting to promote

FIGURE
6.11

**An Illustration of Direct
Response Print Advertising**

Source: Courtesy of NWT Tourism.

tourism. The print media are ideal for showing colourful pictures of local tourist attractions. See the ad in Figure 6.11 for an illustration.

Another option to consider is the insert, which was briefly discussed in Chapter 5 in the discussion of newspapers. An **insert** can be a single-page or multiple-page document that is inserted into the publication (see Figure 6.12). In some cases, the insert is actually glued onto a page (rubber-like glue that is easily removed when the insert is removed from the page). This type of insert is referred to as a **tip-in**.

Advertisers pay the publication insertion fees on a cost-per-thousand basis. A single-page insert in the *Toronto Star*, for example, costs $44.50/M, and a 16-page insert costs $60.50/M. Costs increase with the page count.[8] Preprinted inserts can be used for other communications purposes—they are good handouts at trade shows and other promotional events, and can be used to draw attention to products at the point of purchase. They can also be mailed directly to customers in the company's database.

insert
A preprinted, free-standing advertisement (for example, a leaflet, brochure, or flyer) specifically placed in a newspaper or magazine.

tip-in
An insert that is glued to a page in the publication using a removable adhesive.

FIGURE
6.12   Inserts Are Flexible and Can Be Used in Print Media, Direct Mail, and at Point of Purchase

Source: Jesse Johnston/CP Images.

TELEMARKETING

Telemarketers seem to call at the worst times, like suppertime, or just as you are sitting down to watch a favourite program. Can't telemarketers call at a more suitable time? Doesn't that sound like a common complaint? To a telemarketer, it's simply a fact of life. The best time to call is when the prospect is at home, and that's suppertime or shortly thereafter. Despite the negative feelings consumers have about telemarketing's practices, it is growing in popularity with marketers as a means of communicating with customers. Telemarketing communications are often directly linked to direct response television and direct mail campaigns. Working together, they are a potent combination for achieving all kinds of marketing objectives.

Most telemarketing activities are conducted by call centres. A **call centre** is a central operation from which a company conducts its inbound and outbound telemarketing programs. In Canada, the revenues generated by call centres climbed rapidly from just over $424 million in 1998 to $2.76 billion in 2006.[9] Such growth suggests telemarketing practices are having a positive impact on Canadian marketing strategies.

There are two forms of telemarketing: inbound and outbound. **Inbound telemarketing** refers to the calls received by an order desk, customer inquiries, and calls generated from toll-free telephone numbers promoted on direct response television commercials. **Outbound telemarketing** refers to calls made by a company to customers to develop new accounts, generate sales leads, and even close a sale.

call centre
A central operation from which a company conducts its inbound and outbound telemarketing programs.

inbound telemarketing
The calls received by a company from consumers, whether to place an order, inquire about products or services, or in response to a toll-free telephone number promoted on a direct response television commercial.

outbound telemarketing
Calls made by a company to customers to develop new accounts, generate sales leads, and even close a sale.

The call centre is a vital link in the database management system because the telephone is a quick and convenient tool for capturing information about customers. Any information that is obtained can be added instantly to the database. Cost-effective software is available to manage this task.

In direct response communications, much emphasis is placed on message and media decisions. For example, how will the offer be communicated to entice the target market, and what media will it be placed in? Managing the inbound sales calls generated by commercials has traditionally been a weak link. Therefore, an organization must effectively plan its activities to meet call volume, capture data, present selling opportunities, and handle closing calls. The better a company can do these things, the better the economics of the direct response campaign. To illustrate, consider that a national TV spot on a cable network for a direct response lead generation campaign can easily generate 500 or more inbound inquiries, 85 percent of which will occur within the first three minutes of airing.[10] The call centre has to be ready! If it has to drop the call, or if the consumer hears a busy signal and hangs up, the marketer's return on investment is undermined. The ability to manage an inbound call requires precision planning to maximize returns.

The primary advantage of telemarketing is cost. Compared to traditional forms of mass advertising and the cost of having a salesperson make a business call, telemarketing offers considerable savings. In comparison to direct mail, the response rate for telemarketing is about 100 times higher. Even though direct mail may appear to be cheaper than telephone solicitation, it is actually more costly in the long run. To be effective, however, the telemarketing call must be carefully planned. There must be proper training and preparation for telemarketing representatives, just as there is for field sales representatives. Figure 6.13 summarizes the activities that can involve telemarketing.

FIGURE 6.13   Telemarketing Performs Many Marketing Roles

Fundraising

- Inbound (donations)
- Outbound (solicitations)

Sales Support

- Generating leads
- Qualifying prospects
- Securing appointments
- Marketing research

Personal Selling

- Opening new accounts
- Selling existing accounts
- Selling marginal accounts

Fulfillment

- Accepting orders
- Maintaining customer records
- Invoicing and payment processing

Customer Service

- Handling inquiries and complaints
- Help lines

Earlier in this section, the negative image of telemarketing was mentioned. Image is perhaps telemarketing's biggest drawback. People who react negatively to the calls simply hang up. In Canada, a National Do Not Call List (DNCL) was established in 2008 to protect consumers from unwanted telephone calls. By calling the registry number or by registering online, consumers can have their telephone number included on the DNCL. The registry requires that telemarketers check the registry at regular intervals. The Canadian Marketing Association (CMA) supports the registry, stating that "without reasonable laws regulating organizations that use the telephone to market goods and services, the industry risks losing this valuable marketing channel."[11] Telemarketers who call individuals or households on the list are subject to fines of "up to $15 000 per call"—ouch![12]

CATALOGUES

Catalogues are reference publications, often annual, distributed by large retail chains and other direct marketing organizations. Catalogue marketing involves the merchandising of products through catalogue sales. When someone thinks of catalogues, the Sears catalogue comes to mind immediately, and for good reason. The Sears catalogue is the largest in Canada and is distributed to more than 3 million households. Sears publishes two semi-annual catalogues (Fall & Winter and Spring & Summer) as well as numerous seasonal catalogues, such as the *Christmas Wish Book,* and sale catalogues. To facilitate catalogue buying, Sears has two 24-hour call centres (Belleville and Montreal) that process customer orders.[13]

Sears is now a fully integrated marketing communications organization that generates $5 billion in revenues annually. Much of its business is generated from catalogue sales. Sears also operates one of the busiest commercial websites in Canada. The company accepts orders by fax, email, and online. Its 1-800 number is the most frequently called toll-free number in Canada. Refer to Figure 6.14 for an illustration.

FIGURE
6.14   **Sears Effectively Integrates Retail, Catalogue Marketing, and Web Marketing**

Source: Used with permission of Sears Canada Inc. Steve White/CP Images.

Other prominent catalogue retailers in Canada include Mountain Equipment Co-op and IKEA. Both retailers are merging their retail operations with online buying. The catalogues they distribute drive traffic to their respective websites or to their retail stores.

These and other catalogue retailers see the value in catalogue and online marketing activities. Refer back to the IMC Highlight: **Mountain Equipment Co-op Believes in Direct Mail** for more information. Sales through catalogues definitely take away from store sales, but companies are responding to their customers' demand for convenience. Customers today are into multi-channel shopping. These companies effectively combine media advertising (television, print, and flyers), which creates awareness, with direct response and digital communications, which are designed to stimulate immediate action.

Rather than distribute catalogues, some companies have taken the concept a step further and are publishing their own magazines for distribution to current customers. The purpose is to stay in touch with customers after the sale. Harry Rosen, a prominent, upscale menswear store, distributes *Harry* magazine in hard copy and online to customers and prospective customers. The magazine keeps customers informed about fashion, health and lifestyle trends, and stories of interest to them. The magazine provides a means of building a sound relationship with customers and is part of Harry Rosen's customer relationship management program. Refer to the image in Figure 6.15.

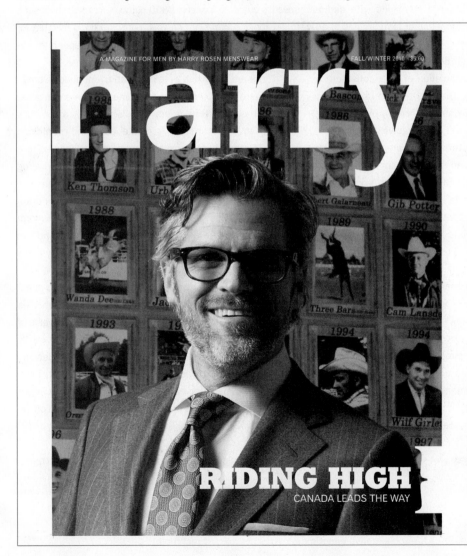

FIGURE
6.15

Harry Rosen Builds a Relationship with Customers Through *Harry* Magazine

Source: Courtesy of Harry Rosen, Inc.

SUMMARY

Direct response advertising is the fourth-largest advertising medium in Canada and growing at a pace faster than other mass media. Several factors are contributing to this growth: Companies are looking for tangible returns for the money they invest in communications; direct response communications are a natural extension of database management programs; and direct response is a personalized medium that is ideal for enhancing customer relationships. The key components of direct response communications are direct mail, direct response television (DRTV), telemarketing, and catalogue marketing.

The foundation of direct response communications is the organization's database. An organization collects and analyzes data from internal and external sources. Customer or house lists record data about purchase transactions made by customers. This information is combined with demographic and psychographic information to form profiles of an organization's best customers. These customers are then targeted and reached through direct response communications. The analysis and manipulation of data constitute a process called data mining. The goal of data mining is to lower marketing costs and increase efficiency by identifying those customers most likely to buy in large volume.

The success of a direct response campaign depends on the quality of the list used by the advertiser. Lists are available from list brokers and other secondary sources such as directories and trade indexes. Lists provided by brokers are rented on a cost-per-thousand basis. Advertisers can choose between response lists (the most expensive), circulation lists, and compiled lists.

Direct mail is the most common form of direct response advertising. A direct mailing usually includes an envelope, letter, leaflet or folder, order form, and postage-paid return envelope. Each component performs a specific role in trying to get the recipient to take action. Advertisers choose between solo direct mail and cooperative direct mail. Solo distribution is more expensive but produces a higher response rate than cooperative distribution. An organization also has the option to use dimensional mail, which is mail of a different size and shape than traditional flat pieces. Dimensional mail draws attention to something inside the mailing piece and tends to break through the clutter of other mailings.

In recent years, direct response television has captured the attention of blue-chip marketing organizations. An advertiser can choose between 30- and 60-second direct response commercials and infomercials, which are much longer and are more like a program than a commercial. Direct response commercials are effective if an organization wants to establish leads, build image, and launch new products. Infomercials are effective in situations where there are lots of details to communicate or for explaining complex products. By definition, direct response ads are capable of completing a transaction with the recipient.

Direct response ads in the print media are another option. Advertisers frequently use the print media to encourage prospective customers to call 1-800 numbers or to visit websites to get more information. As well, print is a good medium for distributing inserts. By selecting the right newspaper or magazine, the advertiser can target its primary customer.

There are two types of telemarketing. Inbound telemarketing refers to calls made by customers to an order desk. Outbound telemarketing refers to calls made by a company to prospective customers to generate leads and even close a sale. Telemarketing programs are usually outsourced to a call centre. Companies are attracted to telemarketing because of its low costs. It is much less expensive than face-to-face personal selling and mass advertising. Its major drawback is the negative perception people hold about this form of communication. Recent government legislation and the establishment of a National Do Not Call List now play a key role in determining whom a direct marketer may call.

Catalogues are an underdeveloped alternative in direct response communications in Canada. However, companies such as Sears and Mountain Equipment Co-op see the value of producing catalogues. As well, there are all kinds of specialty companies that produce catalogues, which include descriptions, pictures, and prices of the products they market. Time-pressed consumers appreciate the convenience of catalogue shopping, and catalogues help direct consumers toward offline purchases (at retail) and online purchases (at a website).

KEY TERMS

bounce back 178	circulation list 174	data mining 172
call centre 184	compiled list 174	dimensional mail 178
catalogue 170	cooperative direct mail 179	direct mail 169

REVIEW QUESTIONS

1. What is the difference between direct marketing and direct response advertising?
2. What are the major forms of direct response advertising?
3. Explain the concept of data mining. What impact does data mining have on marketing and marketing communications?
4. What is the role of the list broker in direct response advertising?
5. In the context of mailing lists, what does merge/purge refer to?
6. What are the differences among a response list, a circulation list, and a compiled list?
7. Briefly explain two advantages and two disadvantages of direct mail advertising.
8. Identify and briefly explain the components of a typical direct mail piece.
9. What is a statement stuffer?
10. What is the difference between a solo direct response campaign and a cooperative direct response campaign?
11. Identify and briefly explain how dimensional mail is different from other forms of direct mail.
12. Identify and briefly explain the various direct response television alternatives.
13. What is the difference between an insert and a tip-in?
14. What is the difference between inbound telemarketing and outbound telemarketing?

DISCUSSION AND APPLICATION QUESTIONS

1. Will direct response communications play a more significant role in the marketing communications mix in the future? Through secondary research, identify those factors that will encourage or discourage the use of direct response communications and formulate your position on the issue.
2. Direct mail advertising remains a popular medium for many profit-based and not-for-profit organizations. Why? What are the benefits and drawbacks of using direct mail? Identify some organizations that successfully use direct mail advertising to help achieve their marketing goals.
3. Collect two or three direct mail pieces that have been delivered to your household address. Did the mailing reach the appropriate target market? What components did the mailing include, and how effective were they in communicating the message? Is the message convincing enough to act upon?
4. Assume you are about to develop a direct response advertising campaign that will encourage a select target audience to visit an Audi dealer to test drive a new Audi TT. The target is defined as male and female managers and executives who earn $100 000 or more and live in large metropolitan markets. The priority markets are Toronto, Montreal, and Vancouver. What direct response media would you use in the campaign? Assuming direct mail will be a component of the campaign, how would you find names for the mailing?
5. Conduct some research to find a company that has successfully used direct response advertising as part of an integrated marketing communications campaign (such as a major bank, financial services company, or not-for-profit fundraising campaign). What role did direct response communications play? Describe the successes that resulted from the direct response effort.

ENDNOTES

1. *Canadian Media Directors' Council Media Digest, 2011-2012, Marketing*, September 26, 2011, p. 14, bppg.rogersdigitalmedia.com/media/bppg/marketing/pdf/MediaDigest_1011.pdf.

2. Mary Dickie, "Change Is Brewing," *Strategy*, July1, 2007, strategyonline.ca/2007/07/01/biz-20070701/.

3. Ross Waring, "The Promise and Reality of Data Mining," *Strategy*, June 7, 1999, strategyonline.ca/1999/06/07/25818-19990607.

4. Susan Pigg, "Diapers, Drinking, and Data," *Toronto Star*, August 16, 2002, pp. E1, E10.

5. Epsilon TargetSource Canada, Demographics: Adult Ages, November 16, 2012, lists.epsilon.com/market?page=research/datacard&id=363761.

6. Costs obtained from Cornerstone Group of Companies, 2012.

7. Matt Semansky, "Manulife Financial Flexes DRTV Muscle," *Marketing*, January 9, 2008, www.marketingmag.ca/news/marketer-news/manulife-financial-flexes-drtv-muscle-12715.

8. *Toronto Star*, Media Kit, 2012, http://mediakit.thestar.ca.

9. Richard Vincent and Larry McKeown, "Study: Trends in the Telephone Call Centre Industry," Statistics Canada, www.statcan.gc.ca/pub/63f0002x/63f0002x2008053-eng.pdf.

10. Maria Eden, "One Call, Multiple Sales Opportunities," *Direct Marketing News*, August 30, 2002, www.dmnews.com/one-call-multiple-sales-opportunities/article/78517.

11. "Do Not Call Has Strong Support," *Marketing Daily*, November 1, 2007, www.marketingmag.ca/daily.

12. "FAQ: Canada's Do-Not-Call List," *CBC News*, December 20, 2010, www.cbc.ca/news/canada/story/2010/12/20/f-do-not-call-list.html.

13. Sears Canada, "About Sears," www.sears.ca/content/corporate-info/about.

Planning for Online and Interactive Communications

Learning Objectives

After studying this chapter, you will be able to

1. Assess strategies for delivering effective messages using online advertising

2. Describe the various roles played by online communications in a marketing and marketing communications environment

3. Evaluate the various advertising alternatives that are available online

4. Assess the potential of the Internet as an advertising medium

5. Assess the role of mobile media, video games, and social media networks as alternatives in integrated marketing communications campaigns

Online communications offer a high degree of personalization. Since personalization is one of the cornerstones of customer relationship management (CRM) programs, the Internet is becoming an attractive communications alternative for marketers. The medium is unique, as it allows an organization to listen to customers, learn from them, and then deliver content and services tailored to their responses and actions. These benefits must be considered when devising an integrated marketing communications plan.

In the digital universe, control has shifted from the advertiser to the customer, a situation that marketing organizations must adapt to. It's no longer about delivering a message, but rather about allowing customers to participate in developing messages and interacting with brands—a concept referred to as engagement. As well, viewers now have unprecedented choice. They can access the Internet by computer, tablet, or mobile phone.

A recent study prepared for the Interactive Advertising Bureau in Canada found that the Internet provides marketers with a "mirror image" of the age profile for users of other major media, particularly when comparing the Internet and television.[1] Thinking strategically, therefore, media planners see Internet communications as complementary to traditional media and expect that, when used together, they will more effectively and efficiently achieve desired communications objectives.

This chapter examines in detail a host of new interactive marketing communications opportunities that should be considered when planning an integrated marketing communications campaign.

Internet Penetration

When compared to most other countries, Canada has one of the highest levels of Internet penetration and broadband access. The latest survey conducted by Statistics Canada reveals that 79% of Canadian households have access to the Internet, and over one-half of connected households use more than one type of device to go online (a combination of computer and wireless device).[2] Such high Internet penetration is having an impact on time spent with other media, but it seems that Canadians have seamlessly adopted digital media technologies while maintaining a strong appetite for traditional media.

Canadians spend more time online than any other country, including highly wired societies such as China, South Korea, and the United States. The average Canadian spends about 45 hours a month browsing the Internet, with a majority of that time spent on social network sites such as Facebook.[3] The Internet now ranks a strong second to television in terms of time spent with media on a weekly basis. Time spent with the media is an important factor that media planners consider when making recommendations

Medium	Adults 18+	Adults 18–34	Adults 35–49	Adults 50+
Television	23.7	19.2	21.6	28.0
Radio	18.3	14.0	19.0	20.8
Internet	17.2	25.1	17.8	11.6
Newspapers	2.5	0.9	1.5	4.2
Magazines	0.8	0.4	0.5	1.1

FIGURE
7.1

Time Spent with the Media by Canadians

Source: BBM Analytics Spring 2011.

to their clients about what media to use. By age category, younger people spend much more time online than older people. In fact, the 18- to 34-year-old group now spends more time online than they do with television. For more insight into who's spending time with what media, refer to Figure 7.1.

The trend data presented in this section strongly suggest the inclusion of online media in a marketing communications plan. The Internet is an ideal medium for reaching younger Canadians as well as middle- to upper-income households. Just around the corner is the emerging wireless communications market. Mobile media, such as smartphones and tablets, represent additional screens consumers use to access information and watch video content. Soon, wireless communications will be the preferred method of connecting to the Internet, which will enable consumers to be exposed to advertising messages anywhere at any time.

Online and Interactive Marketing Communications

Based on the data presented in the previous section, it is clear that the Internet is a mass reach medium, much like television, radio, and print. Data from Canada's Internet Use Survey show that 80 percent of Canadians or 27.2 million people use the Internet for personal reasons. To further demonstrate the reach of the Internet, consider that about 50 percent of the Canadian population are on Facebook, some 17 million people.[4] In comparison, Canada's most watched television shows, such as *Big Bang Theory* and *Grey's Anatomy*, average 2.5 million viewers per episode.

In terms of targeting, the Internet is absolutely essential for reaching an audience under the age of 35 years. The Internet is now the number one medium for this age group in terms of time spent with media each week. For more insight into the reach capabilities of the Internet, refer to Figure 7.2.

Factors such as time spent and reach are forcing advertisers to invest more dollars in online advertising; they are shifting funds from conventional media to online, mobile, and social media campaigns. By industry, the largest investors in online advertising include automotive companies, packaged goods companies, financial institutions, and retailers. It is now readily apparent that some combination of traditional media with digital media produces a more effective and efficient media strategy. Some organizations are going a step further. PepsiCo, for example, is transferring a full third of its advertising budget online and is even using the Internet as a primary medium for launching new products. From Pepsi's perspective, the Internet and social media, such as Facebook and Twitter, are now essential components of its marketing communications mix.

In Canada, net revenues for online advertising total $2.6 billion (2011). The Internet has surpassed daily newspapers and is now second only to television in terms of share of total Canadian media advertising revenue.[5] Advertisers such as Unilever, Molson,

FIGURE
7.2

Daily Reach of Various Media in Canada

Source: BBM Analytics RTS Spring 2011.

Medium	Adults 18+	Adults 18–34	Adults 35–49	Adults 50+
Television	84.4	78.0	83.3	89.6
Radio	80.5	75.7	84.2	81.3
Internet	72.5	86.6	79.7	58.4
Newspapers	48.3	31.4	43.7	62.8
Magazines	30.0	22.7	27.1	36.8

Figures represent the percentage of adults reached by each medium.

PepsiCo, RBC Financial, Canadian Tire, Procter & Gamble, and McDonald's have participated in cross-media research programs that have convinced them online advertising deserves an important place in the marketing communications mix.[6] Simply stated, if your target market is online, you had better be there with your advertising message.

The challenge facing marketers is two-fold. First, they must devise a plan that effectively integrates online advertising into the marketing communications mix. In doing so, they must understand certain differences in consumer behaviour that people exhibit when using digital media. Second, they must determine how much to invest (share of budget) in online advertising. For details on how Canadian companies spend their Internet advertising dollars, refer to Figure 7.3.

Unlike any of the traditional mass media, online advertising provides immediate feedback to advertisers regarding how effectively their message reached the target; it automatically gears ads to viewers' personal tastes, and it generally reaches receptive consumers—at least those consumers who click on the ads. Target marketing capabilities are discussed in more detail in the next section. Beyond targeting, the Internet delivers on the corporate mandate for marketers to be more accountable; since online advertising is measurable, it is attractive to marketing organizations. Finally, the expansion of broadband capabilities and the growing penetration of smartphones and tablets will make video downloading a very attractive option for advertisers who have relied on television advertising in the past.[7]

FIGURE 7.3   Online Advertising Revenues by Types of Advertising

Type of Advertising	$M 2009	$M 2010	% Change
Search	741	907	+22
Display	578	688	+19
Classifieds/Directories	467	587	+26
Video	20	37	+85
Email	13	11	−15
Video Games	3	2	−33
Total	1822	2232	+23

Source: IAB Canada, Canadian Online Advertising Revenue Survey, detailed report.

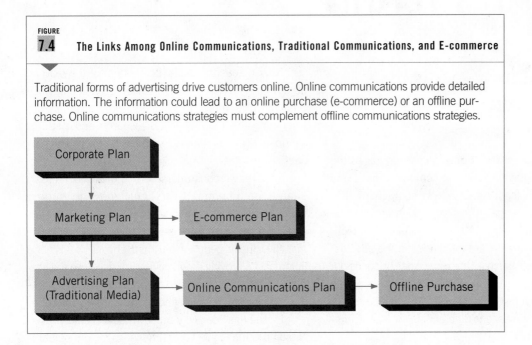

FIGURE 7.4   The Links Among Online Communications, Traditional Communications, and E-commerce

Traditional forms of advertising drive customers online. Online communications provide detailed information. The information could lead to an online purchase (e-commerce) or an offline purchase. Online communications strategies must complement offline communications strategies.

As consumers continue to embrace the Internet and other interactive media as an integral part of their everyday lives, marketers have little choice but to acknowledge that anything interactive is a critical medium to engage consumers and create deeper brand experiences. At the same time, online communications can go further than many other media because they can secure a purchase and make arrangements to have goods delivered. They are capable of closing the loop, from initial awareness to a buying decision, in a very short period, assuming a website has e-commerce capabilities. Figure 7.4 illustrates how Internet communications link with traditional advertising and e-commerce.

For more insight into the benefits of adding online advertising to the marketing communications mix, see the IMC Highlight: **Nissan Altima Goes with Digital Media**.

THE INTERNET AND TARGETING

The reality of the Internet is that consumers voluntarily visit specific websites. To get what they want, they also divulge valuable information about themselves. Smart companies use the Internet as a means of obtaining information for their databases. Once the information is analyzed, it can be translated into specific messages, and marketing offers can be tailored to specific customer needs.

The Internet is much like any other medium. Audiences can be targeted based on demographic and geographic variables, by time of day, day of week, and by behaviour. All websites accumulate data on who visits and how long they visit. Such information aids media planners when they are devising target audience reach and frequency scenarios. In terms of **demographics**, a popular website like TSN.ca attracts a male audience and is over-indexed for males in the 18- to 24-year age category. On a daily basis, it attracts about a half a million visitors.[8] It's no wonder that Molson Canadian is a heavy advertiser on this website—it reaches the company's primary demographic! A website like HGTV.ca has a strong female reach, particularly in the 35- to 49-year age category—an attractive target for any marketing organization in the home furnishing and decorating business.

demographics
The characteristics of a population that include gender, age, education, income, occupation, and culture.

Nissan Altima Goes with Digital Media

The 2013 launch of the Nissan Altima embraced the concept of integrated marketing communications and included a significant digital media component. The creative for the campaign revolved around the tagline "Innovation that Excites." Naturally, the latest in technological developments are mentioned in the advertising; improvements such as the redesigned suspension; a category-unique, tire-fill alert system; zero-gravity seats; and a 3D driver display. Nissan decided to use "innovation" as a means to differentiate the Altima from competitor brands.

The campaign was launched with a 60-second spot shown on cinema screens and 3D cinema screens. Computer graphics show how the car has evolved from its predecessor. On the digital front, animated banners say things like "Wouldn't it be cool if your car was as smart as your smartphone?" and "Wouldn't it be cool if your car was as fast as it looked?" Print ads use phrases like "Go further. Go faster. Go lighter." Out-of-home ads use short messages like "38 miles per gallon" and "Vroomier," and include a beauty shot of the vehicle.

Source: Mark Lennihan/AP Photo/CP Images.

Nissan sees the digital component of the plan as absolutely vital. According to director of marketing Vinay Shahani, "We know the majority of our customers are leveraging the Internet to do research and perform shopping tasks, so it makes sense to be there. The percentage of digital is much higher than in the past."

To engage consumers with the brand, Nissan offered an opportunity for customers to submit personal essays on why they should be chosen to participate in an Altima driving experience. In a contest format, five lucky people were then chosen to visit the automaker's proving grounds in Arizona to drive the new Altima. Videos of their driving experiences were produced and placed on Facebook, Twitter, and YouTube.

Nissan has been very active in social media; in fact, Nissan has the highest consumer engagement percentage on its Facebook brand page of any automaker. If "likes" are an important measure of success in social media, then Altima is a clear winner, with more than one million of them. According to Nissan's director of interactive and social media marketing Erich Marx, "Everybody at Nissan understands that social space is different and quirky, and we are trying to take advantage of that with what we do there."

Vinay Shahani acknowledges that the Honda Accord and Toyota Camry are key competitors and that the objective of the campaign is to gain market share at their expense. He says the Altima buyer is typically younger and more interested in the performance and uniqueness of a vehicle. The all-new Altima meets these buying criteria, and the new marketing communications campaign was designed to connect with the target audience on an emotional level. "We'll have to wait and see how the market responds," says Shahani.

Adapted from Karl Greenberg, "Nissan Rolls Out Biggest Campaign for Altima," *Marketing Daily*, June 18, 2012, www.mediapost.com; and Rich Thomaselli, "Nissan Looks to Facebook to Help Launch Five New Models," *Advertising Age*, June 25, 2012, www.adage.com.

Once targets are identified demographically, they can be qualified further by geography. Advertisers can zero in on users in specific regions, cities, or postal codes. For example, the Ontario Lottery Corporation (www.olg.ca) reaches Ontario. Toronto.com (www.toronto.com), a site that offers information about restaurants, entertainment, hotels, and shopping, reaches a Toronto audience.

Targeting by daypart is another planning decision. Unlike television, where prime time is night time, prime time online is during the day—when people are at work. Not only is the at-work online audience vast, it is comprises a demographically attractive group of individuals who have higher-than-average incomes, education, and tendencies to shop and buy online. To demonstrate the impact of daypart targeting, Best Buy ran a three-week campaign on Yahoo! Its ads ran Monday to Friday between 5 am and 11 am in Ontario and Quebec. The campaign generated a 200 percent conversion lift (consumers who took action based on the advertising) over previous campaigns.[9]

Unlike other media, the Internet is a medium that allows marketers to target customers on the basis of their behaviour. In its simplest form, **behavioural targeting** means delivering ads based on a consumer's previous surfing patterns. An individual's surfing behaviour is tracked by placing a **cookie**, which is a small text file uploaded to a consumer's web browser and sometimes stored on that person's hard drive. The cookie can be used to remember a user's preferences. By tracking preferences, an organization can directly tailor messages to reach specific consumers.

behavioural targeting
A means of delivering online ads based on a consumer's previous surfing patterns.

cookie
An electronic identification tag sent from a web server to a user's browser to track the user's browsing patterns.

When targeting based on behaviour, the reach component of an advertising campaign is less important. In mass media campaigns, advertisers typically want to reach as many people as possible at a frequency that will motivate some kind of action. Behavioural targeting online allows an advertiser to reach fewer people, and the actual results can be measured and evaluated immediately.

To demonstrate the impact of behavioural targeting, an automotive insurance advertiser targeted consumers who recently visited automotive sites in order to generate leads. Two different plans were used: demographic targeting and behavioural targeting. The demographic targeting option resulted in 183 million impressions and generated 47 leads per 1 million impressions. An **impression** or **ad view** is defined as a measurement of responses from a web server to a page request from a user's browser. When behavioural targeting was employed, only 6 million impressions were made (at much lower cost), but those impressions generated 116 leads per 1 million impressions. Behavioural targeting produced three times the number of leads that demographic targeting did.

impression (ad view)
An ad request that was successfully sent to a visitor. This is the standard way of determining exposure for an ad on the web.

Behavioural targeting is ideal for reaching consumers when they are researching a purchase. The sheer amount of research done online by consumers is reason enough for a company to be actively engaged with consumers through online communications. A user who sees something of interest (that is, an advertising message that creates awareness) can obtain information immediately by clicking the ad. Therefore, well-designed, well-placed, and well-targeted messages are useful tools for consumers who engage in online product research. The potential of the Internet is huge—it is becoming the medium of choice for companies wanting to reach their target audience in a cost-efficient manner.

Beyond reaching people efficiently, an organization can complete a sale online. In terms of securing action, the Internet is very similar to direct response advertising (discussed in Chapter 6). Online storefronts such as those for Sears and Chapters/Indigo fall into this category. Finally, the Internet deals with the concept of mass customization. **Mass customization** refers to the capability of personalizing messages and, ultimately, products to a target audience of one—the ultimate form of targeting! The marketer has the potential to deal with each customer individually. For example, Dell Computer does not produce a computer until it hears directly from a customer. Once the exact specifications are determined through a process of interaction at the Dell website, a unique computer is produced and shipped directly to the consumer.

mass customization
The development, manufacture, and marketing of unique products to unique customers.

Online and Interactive Communications Planning

interactive communications
The placement of an advertising message on a website, or an ad delivered by email or through mobile communications devices.

Interactive communications refers to the placement of an advertising message on a website, usually in the form of a banner, rich media ad, video ad, sponsorship at a website, or an ad delivered by email. Advertising messages may also be communicated through other electronic devices such as cell phones, tablets, and video games.

When devising an interactive communications plan, decisions about which medium to use are largely based on the communications objectives and the budget available. Refer to Figure 7.5 for a visual review of the interactive planning process. The first step in the process is to establish the objectives. The second step is to evaluate the various media options strategically. Will it be an online campaign, a mobile media campaign, a video game campaign, a social media campaign, or any combination of alternatives? Once the strategy is determined, the next step is execution. Here, decisions are made on specific media, how much to spend, and how to schedule media activities during the year.

Online and Interactive Communications Objectives

Online advertising performs the same or similar roles as traditional media advertising. It can help create brand awareness, build or enhance brand image, generate sales leads, provide a means to make a purchase, improve customer service and communications between customers and the company, and acquire meaningful data about potential customers (as in database management).

CREATING BRAND AWARENESS

portal
A website that serves as a gateway to a variety of services such as searching, news, directories, email, online shopping, and links to other sites.

Given the amount of time and the frequency with which consumers go online, there is ample opportunity for a company or brand to develop advertising that will generate brand awareness. The most obvious way to achieve awareness is to advertise on a web portal where the reach is extremely high. A **portal** is a website featuring several commonly used services, such as news or searching, and serves as a starting point or gateway to other services, such as shopping, discussion groups, and links to other sites. These sites are among the most visited sites on the web and include Facebook.com (880 million unique visitors monthly); Youtube.com (800 million), and Yahoo.com (590 million).[10] These are sites that people are automatically routed to when they launch their browser.

To create brand awareness and awareness of a brand's promise, a variety of advertising alternatives are available. Among the options are banner ads, rich media, and sponsorships (all options are discussed later in the chapter). Recent research indicates that Internet advertising works best when utilized as part of a media mix. To illustrate, when Dove launched a new line of skin care products, a media mix of magazine, outdoor, television, and online advertising was employed. Key findings of the Dove study provided insight into how various media can work together in a synergistic manner. The key findings were:

- The addition of online and/or outdoor advertising to a combination of television and magazines improved awareness scores by 33 percent.

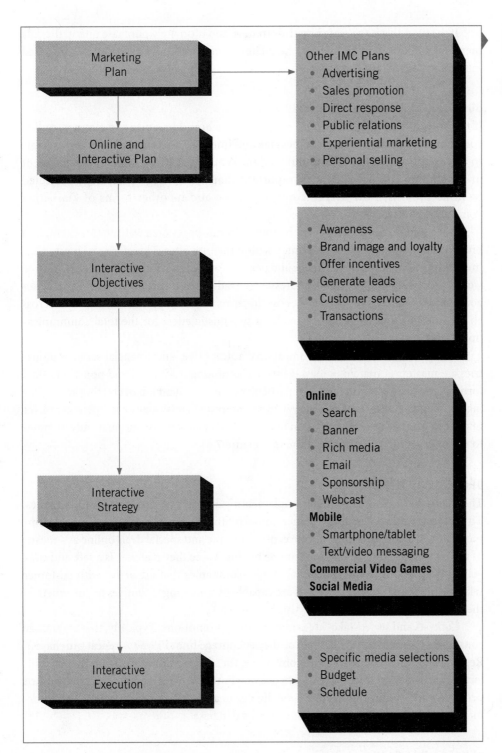

FIGURE
7.5

The Online and Interactive Communications Planning Process

- The combination of television, print, and online was especially effective in increasing brand attribute scores among a very specific female target group versus television alone.

- Online advertising outperformed television in terms of raising purchase intent; however, the combination of television, magazine, and online maximized purchase intent an astounding 47 percent higher than what was achieved by using television alone.

If the objective is to create brand awareness, and ultimately purchase intent, the data mentioned above strongly suggest the inclusion of online advertising in an integrated marketing communications plan.

BUILDING AND ENHANCING BRAND IMAGE

If the objective is to have the public perceive the brand in a positive manner, online communications must present a message and image consistent with and comparable to any traditional form of communication. Whether it be an online advertisement or brand/company website, it is important that the message and image projected be in keeping with the overall company image and its other forms of marketing communications.

It is common for consumers to be routed to sub-pages on a website (for example, a brand page) as they search for the information they are after. Therefore, the brand page must comply with the brand's image and persona. Since it is common practice to include website addresses and Facebook addresses on traditional forms of advertising, it makes good sense to have an integrated message in terms of look, appearance, and style across all media. Such a practice helps produce a synergistic effect for the total communications effort.

Companies in the telecommunications, automotive, and financial services industries are masters at matching message strategies among traditional and non-traditional forms of media. Automotive sites in particular do an excellent job of creating and building an image for a new car model. When an interested consumer or tempted car buyer first sees a new car in a print ad or on television, he or she almost automatically migrates to the Internet for more information. (see Figure 7.6).

OFFERING INCENTIVES

The Internet is a good medium for implementing a variety of sales promotion activities. To encourage consumers to make their initial online purchase, price discounts are commonplace. Canadian Tire, for instance, offers unique and special deals online as a means of getting people comfortable with online buying. Once they realize it is a safe and convenient way to buy, they go back for more. Companies that are active with customer relationship management programs are capable of delivering incentives to customers in their database by using email advertising.

Contests and sweepstakes are popular online promotions. Typically, they encourage consumers to buy for the first time, or they encourage brand loyalty (repeat purchases). Regardless, the true benefit to the company is the names and information that are collected through entry forms. For the chance of winning a prize, it is surprising how much personal information an individual will divulge to a marketing organization. This information can be used either to start or expand a database.

GENERATING LEADS

In a business-to-consumer or business-to-business marketing situation, the Internet is a useful medium for generating leads. As already indicated, consumers willingly disclose information when entering contests. Consumers and business people will also leave the same vital information when they are searching for information online. The stumbling block in retrieving the information they want is the transfer of personal or business information. However, online visitors are known to give out more details about themselves, or the business they are part of, so that they may retrieve

FIGURE

7.6   An Integrated Approach to Message Strategy Across All Media Has Greater Impact

Source: Courtesy of Mercedes-Benz Canada Inc.

the information they are searching for. Business sites often request information such as company size, number of employees, type of business, location, postal code, email address, and so on. It's a fact of life in doing business online. This type of information, once analyzed and mined (data mining), can be used to identify potential targets (one-to-one marketing) and to customize messages and products that are suited to that target. It's the start of CRM.

PROVIDING CUSTOMER SERVICE

In any form of marketing, offering good customer service is crucial. Satisfied customers hold positive attitudes about a company and are likely to return to buy more goods. Again, the Internet plays a pivotal role. It can be an efficient and cost-effective way of providing service, assuming a company's website is well organized. Service demands by customers tend to be high. Therefore, any frustration a customer experiences when searching for service on a website will only compound the problem. Speed of service is a primary benefit offered by the Internet. It goes without saying that customers should have quick and open access to service information. Carefully indexed FAQs (frequently asked questions) or key word searches are common ways to access online information quickly.

For specific questions and concerns, email is another good option. Of course, response time for handling email has unfortunately become a real issue. Making customers wait a few days for a response is not the type of service they expect. Successful online businesses don't forget that online activities must be backed up by a human component. They must pay close attention to inbound sales, order tracking, out-of-stock issues, deliveries and returns, and all the service issues associated with these tasks. All of these activities are part of a good CRM program.

CONDUCTING TRANSACTIONS

In Canada, the business-to-business market is booming with online transactions, but the business-to-consumer market lags behind the United States, even though Canada is one of the most connected countries in the world. As of 2010, Canadian consumers purchased $15.3 billion worth of goods and services online, a figure that is double that of 2005. Some 13.2 million Canadians used the Internet to make an online purchase in 2010.[11] The busiest group of online shoppers are the 25- to 34-year-old age category—people with money, good credit ratings, and a high degree of comfort with online buying.

Having a website with e-business capabilities is important today. While shoppers remain concerned about security aspects of the Internet, they are using their credit cards online. Companies such as Canadian Tire, Sears, and Chapters/Indigo use the Internet to communicate effectively with shoppers, and they have combined e-marketing and e-business with their traditional methods of conducting business. Canadian Tire recently launched a new online tire store that allows customers to quickly compare tires for their vehicle on the basis of brand, price, type, size, load range, mileage rating, and speed rating. If the tires are purchased online, they are shipped to the store nearest the customer at no additional charge, where they can be picked up or installed. Some businesses remain skeptical about the Internet and are not making the necessary investment to tap into the Internet's potential. Businesses that do not make the investment risk losing business to those businesses that do.

Online and Interactive Communications Strategies

As indicated by the increase in advertising revenues from year to year and the amount of time consumers spend online each week, advertisers must embrace online communications from a strategic perspective. Today's media planners are technologically savvy; they recognize the value of online communications and other forms of interactive communications, and make appropriate recommendations when devising an integrated marketing communications strategy.

From a media strategy perspective, the Internet and other forms of interactive communications offer high reach and frequency, though advertisers have to be careful about budgets when the various cost models are evaluated (see later section of the chapter for cost models). At portal sites such as Google and Yahoo, the number of unique visitors on a daily basis is incredibly high. In contrast, niche sites that focus on a particular interest, hobby, or activity reach smaller numbers of people, but they are more targeted. Both scenarios may be considered when devising an online media plan.

There are a variety of creative opportunities available to online advertisers. In terms of advertising, the options include search advertising, banner advertising, rich media ads, video ads, sponsorships, and email advertising. Beyond the Internet, an advertiser may consider mobile communications opportunities, advertising in video games, and social media networks. As with other media, the planner must evaluate the alternatives and devise a media selection and rejection rationale for the online and interactive components of a media plan.

Prior to examining the various online advertising alternatives, some basic terminology should be understood. All terms relate to how Internet ads are measured for strategic variables such as reach, frequency, and engagement:

- **Impression (Ad Views):** An ad request that was successfully sent to a visitor. This is the standard way of determining exposure for an ad on the web.

- **Frequency (Online):** The number of times an ad is delivered to the same browser in a single session or time period. A site can use cookies to manage frequency.

- **Clicks (Clickthroughs):** This refers to the number of times that users click on a banner ad. Such a measurement allows an advertiser to judge the response to an ad. When viewers click the ad, they are transferred to the advertiser's website or to a special page where they are encouraged to respond in some way to the ad.

- **Click (Clickthrough) Rate:** The ratio of clicks to impressions. It is calculated by dividing the total number of clicks by the total number of impressions. For example, if during 1 million impressions, there are 20 000 clicks on the banner, the clickthrough rate is 2 percent. A high click rate indicates the banner ad was effective in its purpose.

- **Unique Visitor:** The number of unduplicated (counted only once) visitors to a website over a course of a specified time period. Visitors are determined by cookies, a small text file stored in a user's browser.

- **Visit:** A sequence of page requests made by one user at one website. A visit is also referred to as a session or browsing period.

A site's activity is described in terms of the number of unique visitors, the time they spend visiting, and how often they return to the site. A site that can report, for example, that it had 8 million page views, 100 000 visitors, and 800 000 visits last month would be

impression (ad view)
An ad request that was successfully sent to a visitor. This is the standard way of determining exposure for an ad on the web.

frequency (online)
The number of times an ad is delivered to the same browser in a single session or time period.

clicks (clickthroughs)
The number of times users click on a banner (clicking transfers the user to another website).

click (clickthrough) rate
The percentage of impressions (ad views) that resulted in a click; determines the success of an ad in attracting visitors to click on it.

unique visitor
The number of unduplicated visitors to a website during a specified period.

visit
A sequence of page requests made by a visitor to a website; also called a session or a browsing period.

doing very well. It means that the average visitor returns to the site 8 times each month and views 10 pages on each visit. That's incredible "stickiness" (most sites don't do that well)! **Stickiness** (or sticky content) refers to the notion that the website has a compelling reason for users to stay for a longer visit or to come back frequently for more information. Offering relevant and interesting content is a key factor in getting visitors to return to a website.

Among social networks, Facebook dominates in term of visitors (reach), time spent, and stickiness. In Canada, for example, 60 percent of the population (20.4 million people) have a social networking profile, and 85 percent of those people (17.3 million) have a profile on Facebook.[12] Visitors to Facebook spend an average of 6.5 hours on the site each month. Keeping users coming back is a constant challenge for Facebook, and to do so they constantly introduce new features such as the timeline interface rolled out in 2012.[13]

stickiness
A website's ability to keep people at the site for an extended period or to have them return to the site frequently.

SEARCH ADVERTISING

With **search advertising**, the advertiser's listing is placed within or alongside search results in exchange for paying a fee each time someone clicks on the listing. This is also known as **pay-per-click advertising**. Google, for example, offers a service called AdWords, which allows companies, for a small fee, to have a link to their website when a user searches for a word that company has specified. For example, if a user types in outboard motors and Yamaha has bought that term, an ad for Yamaha would appear on the screen. Google sets advertisers against one another in auction-style bidding for the highest positions on the search page. If Yamaha bid the most for the word, it would appear first on the listing of ads. Other manufacturers such as Johnson, Mercury, and Suzuki may also appear lower on the list if they paid for the word. When a consumer clicks on the sponsored link, that consumer is immediately directed to the advertiser's webpage where detailed information is provided. Presently, search advertising ranks first in terms of revenue among the various online advertising options.

search advertising (pay-per-click advertising)
An advertiser's listing is placed within or alongside search results in exchange for paying a fee each time someone clicks on the listing.

BANNER ADVERTISING (DISPLAY ADVERTISING)

A **banner** refers to advertising on a website, usually placed by a third party. A standard banner ad resembles an ad on an outdoor board or an ad that stretches across the bottom of a newspaper—it stretches across a webpage. Not much copy can be included in a banner. The combination of brand name, short message, and visual must convince the user to click on the ad, which links to another website.

The industry, through the Interactive Advertising Bureau (IAB), has established standard ad sizes to reduce costs and inefficiencies associated with planning, buying, and creating online media. The size of an ad is based on Internet Measurement Units (IMU), an expression of the width and depth of an ad. Refer to Figure 7.7 for a visual illustration of the four ad sizes established in the initial standardization phase.

banner
Online, a graphic advertising image (usually horizontal or vertical in shape) that appears on a webpage.

- **Rectangle Ad:** A larger, box-style ad (180 × 150 IMU) that offers more depth than a standard-sized banner.

- **Big box:** A large rectangle (300 × 250 IMU) that offers greater width and depth to an ad.

- **Leaderboard (Super Banner):** An ad that stretches across the entire top of a webpage (728 × 90 IMU).

- **Skyscraper:** A tall, slim, oblong-shaped ad that appears at the side of a webpage (160 × 600 IMU).

rectangle ad
A large ad, slightly wider than it is tall, on a webpage.

big box
An online ad shaped like a large rectangle that offers greater width and depth to an ad.

leaderboard (super banner)
An ad that stretches across the entire top of a webpage.

skyscraper
A vertical, box-shaped ad that appears on a webpage.

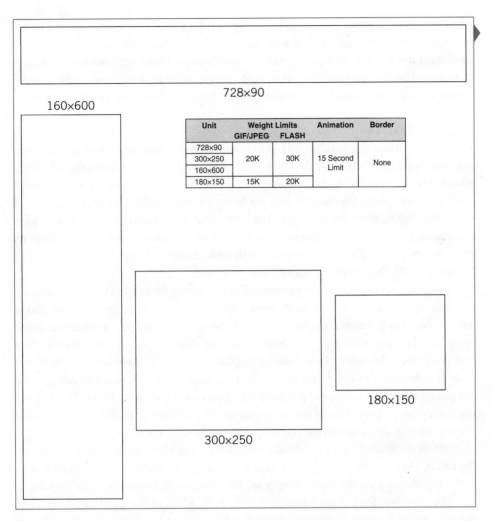

728×90

160×600

Unit	Weight Limits		Animation	Border
	GIF/JPEG	FLASH		
728×90				
300×250	20K	30K	15 Second Limit	None
160×600				
180×150	15K	20K		

180×150

300×250

FIGURE
7.7

Universal Ad Package Sizes for Internet Advertising

Source: IAB Canada – Ad Standards & Creative Specs – Universal Ad Package + Rich Media Ad Units, January 2012.

Advertising research conducted by the IAB has concluded that larger formats, which are naturally more visible and provide more creative freedom, are more effective than smaller, standard-sized banners across all campaigns. Because of their size and better performance, they command a higher price. Cost must be factored into the equation when an advertiser decides to use online advertising.

Given the interactive nature of the medium and the behaviour of Internet users who like to avoid ads if possible, the results achieved from banner ads have fallen short of expectations. The average click rate for a banner ad is now 0.09 percent, meaning only one person in a thousand actually clicks on an ad, even though the ad, by its presence on the page, made an impression on the person. Consequently, advertisers are migrating toward video advertising (a TV style of advertising online) and sponsorships as a means of reaching their target market more effectively.

RICH MEDIA

Rich media are banner ads that include animation, sound, video, and interactivity. There are several inside-the-banner rich media options. An *expandable banner* employs multiple panels that are launched when the banner is clicked on. A *video strip* shows a strip of video in the banner space but, when clicked on, expands to reveal the video and audio in a full-sized panel. A *push down banner* slides advertising out of the way to reveal additional content rather than covering it up.

rich media
A form of online communication that includes animation, sound, video, and interactivity.

There are also some outside-the-banner options. A *floating ad* moves within a transparent layer over the page and plays within a specific area of the page. A *window ad* downloads itself immediately and plays instantly when a page is loading. A *wallpaper ad* is a large image that replaces the web background. Such a variety of styles can grab the viewer's attention in different ways. They can also irritate the viewer if they are too intrusive.

VIDEO ADVERTISING

Video advertising is a smaller but fast-growing component of online advertising. Advertisers are comfortable with online video ads because they are similar to television advertising—they offer the opportunity to connect with consumers on an emotional level. Now that more television shows are being streamed online, as well as news and sports highlights, there are some good opportunities for advertisers—streamed video content includes commercial breaks! The CTV Network offers popular shows from its main network on CTV.ca as well as many of its cable channels that include TSN, Comedy Network, MTV, Discovery, and Bravo, among others.

streaming
Audio or video delivered online in small, compressed packets of data that are interpreted by a software player as they are received.

Video ads are delivered by a process called streaming. **Streaming** involves continuous delivery of small packets of compressed data that are interpreted by a software player and displayed as full-motion video. Having shows available online is a reflection of the on-demand nature of the present television market. People want to watch shows when and where they like rather than abide by preplanned network schedules. Online shows include video ads. **Pre-roll ads** refer to ads at the start of a video, **mid-roll ads** refer to ads placed during the video, and **post-roll ads** appear after the video. When TV-style ads are embedded in programs or on news and sports highlight clips, it ensures an ad is viewed. To view the desired video content, viewers have no choice.

pre-roll ad
An ad placed at the start of a video.

mid-roll ad
An ad placed during a video.

post-roll ad
An ad that appears after the video.

For an illustration of how various online advertising alternatives work together, see Figure 7.8. The figure includes a banner ad and video ad for the Suzuki Vitara. When the banner ad is clicked, it links the viewer directly to a full-motion video commercial for the vehicle.

The challenge for the advertiser is to effectively adapt offline creative strategies to the online environment. Shorter messages that are of less-than-perfect visual quality can be effective. Simply duplicating the quality of television commercials is not the answer, though many advertisers do this to save money. In terms of objectives, many advertisers are shifting video ads away from brand awareness and toward brand engagement, as evidenced by a 2011 survey conducted by eMarketer. In this way, marketers can use video ads with social sharing and other calls to action as a springboard to additional engagement on social networks, their website, or mobile apps.[14]

SPONSORSHIPS

online sponsorship
A commitment to advertise on a third-party website for an extended period.

An **online sponsorship** is a commitment to advertise on a third-party website for an extended period. Advertisers are attracted to sponsorships on the basis of web content. If the content of a site is particularly interesting to an advertiser's target market, visitors are apt to visit the site frequently. For example, investors in the stock market frequently visit BNN.ca, which broadcasts business news online, and sports junkies frequently visit TSN.ca. Brands that are closely linked to the content of these networks pursue sponsorships. TSN, for example, runs various sports contests during the year. Kraft Canada sponsors the annual Kraft Celebration Tour on TSN and TSN.ca. Each year, Kraft and TSN go on the road to visit 10 towns in 10 days. A TSN live sportscast and numerous community events occur in each town. The winning communities, as voted by the public, each receive $25 000 to upgrade local sports facilities. Refer to the image in Figure 7.9.

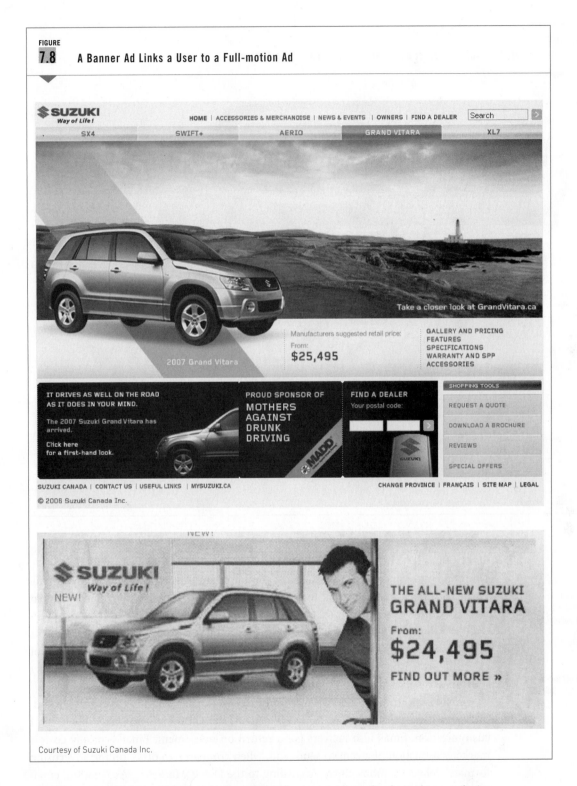

Courtesy of Suzuki Canada Inc.

In sponsorship arrangements such as these, the sponsor benefits from the popularity of the website and the traffic it draws (high reach and frequency). TSN is one of the busiest websites in Canada and is a key site for reaching a young male audience that visits regularly. Consumers trust the sites they visit frequently on the web, so a brand associated with the site through a sponsorship could be perceived more positively. The Kraft sponsorship on TSN.ca. described in the previous paragraph demonstrates this principle.

FIGURE 7.9 Kraft Sponsors the Kraft Celebration Tour on TSN and TSN.ca

Source: Handout/Kraft Celebration Tour/Newscom.

EMAIL ADVERTISING

One of the most promising applications in online advertising is permission-based email. **Permission-based email** is sent to recipients who agree to receive information in that form. In other words, people actively subscribe to the email service. This form of advertising is relatively inexpensive, response rates are high and easy to measure, and it is targeted at people who want information about certain goods and services. An offshoot of email advertising is sponsored email. With **sponsored email**, the email includes a short message from a sponsor along with a link to the sponsor's website.

Email is an attractive opportunity for businesses of all sizes. It is less expensive than direct mail, and allows for greater frequency of distribution and an incredible level of customization. Email also delivers good return on investment. Email typically costs a marketer a fraction of a cent to send, and, when compared to other online advertising formats, delivers a good return. According to the Direct Marketing Association, email produces $40.56 for every dollar spent on it; mobile $10.51; social media $12.71; and display ads $19.72.[15] Email is an efficient method of delivering new product information and information about promotional offers.

Email advertising is similar to direct mail advertising, but at the same time it is very different. Email advertising programs operate from a list contained in a database and target customers specifically interested in something. This type of advertising generates

permission-based email
Email sent to recipients who have agreed to accept email advertising messages.

sponsored email
Email that includes a short message from a sponsor along with a link to the sponsor's website.

higher responses—and that is attracting advertisers' attention. Unlike other forms of online advertising, sending messages by email seems quite acceptable to Internet users. Users can subscribe and unsubscribe to email lists as they wish. How often a marketer communicates with customers by email is an issue. "Many experts say there is a fine line between sending emails to customers on a consistent basis and crossing into annoyance marketing territory."[16]

Similar to direct mail, the success of an email campaign depends on the quality of the list. The lists are called **opt-in lists**, an appropriate name because consumers agree to have their names included. There are two kinds of opt-in lists. A *first-party list* comprises people who have specifically agreed to receive email from an organization. A *third-party list* is composed of names and addresses compiled by one company and sold to another.

In the age of database marketing, the compilation of an in-house list is essential. Sending email to customers and prospects who specifically request it will almost always work better than using a rented list. Online promotions and contests sponsored by companies are another way of securing names and addresses. However, organizations should be careful how they distribute names to other organizations. There's a saying these days: "Permission rented is permission lost."

Although email advertising is attractive, that third-party list is what promotes spam. **Spam** is unsolicited email, even from reputable sources, and third-party lists can result in people receiving mail they do not expect. The use of the Internet to send large volumes of email has infuriated many consumers, forced employees in organizations to waste precious time deleting junk email, and hurt the business of legitimate Internet marketers.

Email also opens up opportunities for viral marketing. **Viral marketing** is a situation where the receiver of an online message is encouraged to pass it on to friends. A research study in the United States reports that 89 percent of adult Internet users share content with others via email.[17] Should an organization pursue a viral campaign, the goal is to create content that people feel compelled to pass around. Advertisers also have to be wary of the degree to which bad news about a company or brand can spread virally. As is often said, "Bad news travels fast, even faster online."

One of the key objectives of email advertising is to establish and maintain a relationship with customers, and ultimately generate sales. As shown in Figure 7.10, Staples sends email offers to customers in its database. Typically, these mailings include financial incentives to encourage customers to take action within a certain period.

WEBCASTING (WEBISODES)

Webcasting or **webisodes** involve the production of an extended commercial that includes entertainment value in the communications. While consumers are using digital video recorders to skip television ads they don't like, they are using the Internet to tune in to commercials they want to see—an interesting phenomenon!

Mercedes-Benz Canada devised an integrated campaign to reach a younger audience, which included online webcasting and mobile applications. A spy-themed movie, entitled *Drive & Seek,* features a James Bond–like character and his female accomplice eluding police—by employing fancy driving maneuvers in a C-Class coupe—to deliver a mysterious suitcase. Viewers participate in the movie by using keyboard sequences to drive the action.[18] The mobile application included a contest that used GPS technology to guide users to one of 10 virtual briefcases in their vicinity. When they approach the briefcase, the driver will see a 3D rendering of the car espousing the latest technological advancements. The grand prize for one of the top 125 game players was a new C-Class coupe. Refer to the image in Figure 7.11.

opt-in list
A list of people who have agreed to receive messages via email.

spam
Unsolicited email.

viral marketing
Online marketing that encourages the receiver of a message to pass it along to others to generate additional exposure.

webcasting (webisodes)
The production of an extended commercial presented on the web that includes entertainment value in the communications.

Source: Courtesy of Staples, Inc.

Webisodes are a form of online entertainment; used effectively, they present a great opportunity to develop a better relationship with consumers. Under the guise of entertainment, people will watch as long as the content is enjoyable and engaging. It isn't necessary to camouflage the brand—people expect the brand to play a key role. The Mercedes webisode demonstrates how consumers will engage with a brand, either online or through a mobile device.

COMPANY AND BRAND WEBSITES

Traditional media communications and online communications encourage users to visit a company or brand website. Clicking on an ad automatically takes you to the website. The purpose of the ad is to attract attention; once the person is at the website, the purpose is to deliver more meaningful and detailed information in an entertaining manner. The website provides an opportunity to tell a story. A company cannot tell or show as much through traditional media as inexpensively as it can on the website. Advertising in the traditional media should provide a website address or Facebook page address and encourage potential customers to contact those sites for additional information.

FIGURE 7.11 A Spy-themed Web Movie Attracts a Younger, Tech-savvy Consumer to Mercedes-Benz C-Class Coupe

Source: Courtesy of Mercedes-Benz Canada Inc.

Information on a website must be presented in such a manner that effectively combines imagery with information. For example, Toyota Canada overhauled its website to tap into the consumer's online information-gathering process. According to David Brimson, national manager for public relations and marketing, "Consumers are increasingly turning up at retail with an almost predestined vision of what they want. We have

> **FIGURE 7.12   Advantages and Disadvantages of Online Marketing Communications**
>
> **ADVANTAGES**
>
> - **Targeting Capability**—Advertiser reaches individuals based on browsing behaviour and preferences.
> - **Broad and Flexible Reach**—The online audience is growing rapidly; since ads can be bought by the impression, you can buy as much or as little of the audience as you desire.
> - **Timing**—Messages can be delivered 24 hours a day, 7 days a week.
> - **Interactivity**—Messages encourage consumers to interact with brands while online (performing a task, playing a game, and so on).
> - **Tracking and Measurement**—Detailed information on who saw an ad, in what context, and how many times, is available immediately.
> - **Transaction**—Assuming e-business capability at a website, an online purchase can occur.
>
> **DISADVANTAGES**
>
> - **Low Click Rates**—Average click rates of only 1 percent are common, which significantly reduces the number of visitors to a website (the intended action).
> - **Advertising Overload**—Too much advertising clutter on a webpage reduces the potential impact of any ad appearing on the page.
> - **Consumer Frustration**—The barrage of unexpected banner ads and unsolicited emails frustrates, even harasses, consumers; advertisers must deal with their wrath.
> - **Too Measurable**—A marketer can be overburdened with the amount of data available from an online advertising campaign.

to ensure that we provide the best knowledge and information to help them make decisions." Toyota's website was redesigned from a consumer's perspective. Consumers move from the welcome page, to different car models, to information areas such as safety and colour choice, to a car configuration page, and finally to a price quote.[19]

microsite
An individual page or series of pages that is a supplement to a primary website.

Organizations also establish microsites that serve unique purposes. A **microsite** is an individual webpage or series of pages that functions as a supplement to a primary website. For example, Unilever has a corporate website in which all brands may have a page. However, for new product launches or high-profile brands, the company will create a microsite with its own address. For example, Axe, a very popular grooming product line, has its own microsite that encourages males to "Get Clean. Get Styled. Get Noticed. Get Close." All it takes is a visit to the AXE.ca website. Similar content is also available by following Axe on Facebook, Twitter, or its YouTube channel. Axe is a leading brand, and web communications have contributed to the brand's success.

For a summary of the advantages and disadvantages of the various forms of online communications, refer to Figure 7.12.

Mobile Media

The screen is small, the audience's attention span is short, and the environment—a park bench or a busy subway station—is variable. Yet the possibilities of mobile marketing are capturing the attention of advertisers. In 2010, there were 25.9 million mobile subscribers in Canada, and 45 percent of them (approximately 11.6 million people) had a smartphone. By 2011, mobile advertising had reached $82 million, almost four times what it was just two years earlier. According to former IAB Canada president Paula Gignac, mobile ad growth is driven by several factors: the penetration of smartphones; Canadians' willingness to complete online transactions; and the ability to deliver location-specific messages; not to mention it's a 24/7 medium.[20] Thus far, the consumer packaged goods industry, retailers, telecommunications companies, and automotive companies are leading the charge to mobile advertising.

Earlier in the chapter, the issue of time spent with the media was discussed. People spend most of their time with television (40 percent of the average adult's media time); the Internet ranks second (23 percent of time). Mobile only represents 7.5 percent of the average adult's time, but it is growing at a much faster rate than all other media.[21] Time spent with a medium is an important consideration when devising a media plan.

Smartphones such as the iPhone, BlackBerry, or Google's Android typically offer many features: send email messages and access the web; take photographs and videos; download applications; and play music and video games. Therefore, marketers can reach consumers through text messaging, video messaging, downloaded applications, and online video games—and they can do so in a highly targeted manner.

Through mobile media, an advertiser can reach targets where they are located at any point in time—a concept referred to as **location-based targeting**. Essentially, a person's location information (available through GPS chips in smartphones) is factored into a marketing communications effort. Let's assume that a fast-food restaurant such as Dairy Queen or A&W knows where you are; they can instantly send you an incentive (coupon) to encourage you to visit a nearby location.

location-based targeting
An effort to integrate consumers' location information into a marketing communications strategy.

Let's examine the primary means of communicating with consumers through mobile media.

TEXT MESSAGING

Text messaging refers to the transmission of text-only messages. The popularity of electronic devices such as the iPhone and BlackBerry has allowed text messaging to emerge as a popular communications tool. Believe it or not, Canadians send 186 million text messages a day.[22] Texting is popular because of its speed, portability, and low cost.

text messaging
The transmission of short text-only messages via cell phone.

Marketers interested in reaching younger targets are experimenting with text messaging, running promotions that include "call to action" short codes. Codes are usually mentioned in other media used to create awareness for the promotion. Cell phone users can punch in their codes to participate in contests, download free music, and get ring tones and prizes.

Marketers must consider some potential drawbacks of a text message strategy. Too much commercial contact via text messaging could ultimately backfire on the advertiser. If the messages are too intrusive, they could be perceived much like a telemarketing call and have a negative impact on brand image. Further, wireless companies must be careful about renting their databases to commercial interests without having an *opt-in* from their customers. Opt-in means customers agree to allow calls or messages to be sent to them.

Scotiabank entered the cell phone arena successfully. Its initial effort was a contest in support of the bank's sponsorship of the Canadian Football League. Contest entrants earned the chance to win a VIP Grey Cup Experience and a selection of secondary prizes. Objectives of the promotion were to encourage participation, broaden reach beyond that of traditional media channels, and drive the brand's association with the sponsorship among consumers. The campaign was a multimedia effort with web, email, online media, TV, stadium advertising, and mobile components. A full 20 percent of all entries were through the text short code "Scotia" (726842). The mobile component helped make the contest a success.[23]

VIDEO MESSAGING

video messaging
The transfer of video messages and other content (for example, television shows) via cell phones and other personal electronic devices.

Video messaging is the next generation of cell phone communications. Surprisingly, or not surprisingly, people are watching long-form video content on their mobile phones—in fact, some 40 percent of all video viewing occurs on a smartphone. Such a high figure runs counter to conventional wisdom that mobile viewers want "bite-size content." Apparently, mobile users will watch television shows, sports events, and YouTube videos on their phones. About half of all video viewed on mobile phones are watched in the home.[24] These same consumers want the largest flat screen television in their living room!

The sweet spot for mobile users is the 15- to 29-year-old age category, but the industry is growing across all demographics. Teens and young adults have grown up with technology. Mobile phones are ubiquitous among teens and are becoming popular with younger kids. These consumers will carry their mobile behaviour forward, and it will have a dramatic impact on how they learn about and buy products. Already, smartphones are performing like "butlers" for Canadian shoppers, assisting them with everything from finding a retailer's nearest store to checking product availability and price. A recent study conducted by Solutions Research Group revealed that 8 million Canadians used a smartphone to help them shop in the last month. Further, 39 percent of smartphone users took a picture or video of a product while shopping and sent it to someone for an opinion.[25] The influence of the smartphone seems to be everywhere already!

Are mobile ads effective? Recent research indicates that mobile ads are outperforming standard banners on the Internet. MediaMind, an organization that tracks the performance of online and mobile campaigns, reports that the clickthrough rate for mobile banners is 0.61 percent, almost eight times as high as the clickthrough for standard online banners in campaigns that had at least one mobile ad.[26] For additional insight see Figure 7.13.

FIGURE 7.13   Mobile Ads Have an Impact on Canadian Consumers

A survey commissioned by Bell Media Digital among 1064 Canadians revealed the following about mobile communications:

- 82% of mobile media users said mobile media is a good way to learn about products and brands
- 80% said mobile media could persuade them to investigate products and brands
- 71% said mobile media could change their perceptions of a product or service
- 53% of mobile media users said they could not leave home without their mobile devices

The results of the survey suggested that smartphone penetration in Canada is accelerating and that marketers would be well advised to ensure their brands deliver a high quality mobile media experience to consumers.

Source: Matt Semansky, "Topline: Bell finds mobile drives brand awareness," *Marketing*, August 18, 2011, www.marketingmag.ca.

MOBILE APPLICATIONS

All smartphone suppliers, such as Apple and Google, offer applications that encourage in-application advertising. Apple's system is called iAd, and it allows for full-screen video and interactive advertising content to be served within an application. The advertisements are wirelessly delivered to the phone. In other systems, it is common for users to be bounced to a company website for the video message. Apple created a new advertising category called Apple Apps. With some 500 000 and counting applications (2012 data), Apple has the means to deliver advertising messages.

There's a common complaint about applications among consumers, however. They say, "There's so much choice, but nothing I really want." Well here's one that Canadians will love—from Tim Hortons, it's the Timmy Run application. Timmy Run was initially launched as a web-based application, but there are plans for a mobile extension. The application allows users to take orders for up to 20 people. It makes the run easier and more convenient for those who volunteer on behalf of friends and colleagues. Logistically, when a member of a group initiates a run, everyone in the group is notified by email and given a specified period of time to opt-in. When the time's up, the runner is notified of the order, which is compiled on one list.[27]

Among media companies, Rogers-owned City (formerly Citytv) launched a video application that allows iPhone, iPad tablet, and iPod, touch users to view live and on-demand content on their mobile devices. Regular, scheduled programs are available to mobile users. The application gives advertisers the ability to reach consumers on a greater variety of platforms—online, tablet, and mobile. Pre-roll and mid-roll video ads are sold to advertisers.[28]

QR CODES

A **quick response (QR) code** is a two-dimensional barcode that can be scanned and read by smartphones. Made up of small squares with black and white patterns, the code allows for sharing of text and data. To read the code, a person needs to download a QR code reader, available at various app stores (for example, Tag Reader for an iPhone).

To secure information, a user takes a picture of a code and is then linked to a website, a phone number, or perhaps a YouTube video that offers more information about a product or service. Thus far, Canadian advertisers have enjoyed mixed results when using the codes; their effectiveness in stimulating interest and ultimately a desired action is yet to be determined.

QR codes offer an advertiser several benefits: Additional information is communicated to the customer in a cost-efficient manner; when customers snap the picture, they are instantly engaged with the brand; and the codes are environmentally friendly, since they save on printed materials and potential waste. Refer to the illustration in Figure 7.14.

quick response (QR) code
A two-dimensional barcode that can be scanned and read by smartphones to allow sharing of text and data.

VIDEO GAME ADVERTISING (ADVERGAMING)

Advertising in video games, or **advergaming**, refers to the placement of ads in commercially sold games or in games played online or on mobile devices. The notion that video games are a male (young male)-dominated activity has somewhat restricted the level of interest in the medium by marketing organizations. However, new data suggest that video games are growing in popularity across both genders and all age categories. Games are becoming an accepted form of family and adult entertainment.[29] That could be an important targeting consideration for a media planner.

advergaming
The integration of brands into video games, which are either played online or on mobile devices, or purchased directly by consumers.

From a planning perspective, integrating a brand into games helps achieve several objectives: It can generate positive brand awareness and higher brand preference ratings, as well as help stimulate purchases. The tactic is seen as being more effective than product placements in TV shows, mainly due to the intensity of the behaviour while gamers are playing—they see and recall the brand messages!

Gamers do not seem to mind the presence of ads. In fact, they expect to see ads, and they are receptive to their presence. A study conducted by IGA Worldwide (a game vendor) discovered 70 percent of respondents felt that the ads made them feel better about the brands. Further, brands running ads in games experienced an average 44 percent increase in brand recall among consumers, when compared to awareness prior to seeing the brand in the game.[30]

With video games, an organization can go in two directions: create its own branded game or place ads in commercially produced games. Many brands have developed their own games for visitors to play at their website. Such games promote interactivity and offer good entertainment value—things people are looking for when they visit a website. In commercially sold games, there is a diverse range of possibilities, including fully integrated opportunities (having a game designed around a brand or brands), interactive product placements, outdoor-style billboards, and 30-second video spots.

Social Media Networks

A **social media network** connects people with different kinds of interests at a website. Social networking is a bit of a phenomenon—in a very short period it has become a fundamental aspect of the online experience. Social network sites, such as Facebook, Twitter, and YouTube, are among the most visited sites in the online world.

While it is difficult to stay abreast of social media statistics, the latest count for Facebook users is about 900 million worldwide, 158 million in the United States, and 17 million in Canada. Figures like these suggest significant potential for advertisers to reach a large audience. To illustrate how fast things are happening online, consider that social networks are actually reaching maturity—at least the most popular networks mentioned above are Facebook's user growth rate in the United States is slowing dramatically, and the amount of time people spend on the network is decelerating.[31] Like any product, Facebook has to find ways of remaining relevant—it must continuously offer new things to keep people coming back.

With businesses operating in an era of social media marketing, you would think that all companies and brands would be actively devising strategies to engage consumers on social networks. Many have jumped in and enjoyed success, while others have struggled. A study by The Creative Group among marketing and advertising executives found that 71 percent of executives feel it is "somewhat challenging" to stay abreast of social media trends. These executives seem unprepared for the changes that are happening.[32]

Social media is extremely important today and can't be viewed as an add-on in a marketing communications strategy. Executives need to understand the medium, even though it is difficult for them to view things through the lens of social media. Another obstacle to moving forward with social media strategies is the uncertainty surrounding return on investment. What is the value of a "like"? Do people actively engage with brands on social networks? What is the impact on sales? Executives need answers to these questions before they commit to the medium.

Social networks fall into two categories. Broad-based sites, such as Facebook, Twitter, and YouTube, offer an interactive, user-created network of friends, personal profiles, blogs, music, and videos. A lot of content sharing occurs on these sites. Niche sites also exist. LinkedIn is a site where business professionals can network. Pinterest lets people post pictures (on a pinboard) of things they love. Users can also browse pinboards created by other people—a fun way to discover new things and share interests.

social media network
A social website (for example, Facebook and Twitter) that connects people with different interests together.

ADAPTING TO THE SOCIAL MEDIA ENVIRONMENT

Organizations are operating in an era where consumers have more control over marketing communications. In previous eras, marketers would push their communications on to consumers. In the social media era, the communications process is more participative—the goal is to get consumers talking about brands and promoting brands on behalf of the organization. This shift in control is often referred to as **brand democratization**.

Once the marketer adapts to this change and sees the benefit of allowing consumers to participate in the creation of brand content, the easier it will be to integrate social media into a marketing communications strategy. For example, if a marketer puts out a call for input based on some broad-stroke direction (for example, request that consumers submit a video and enter a contest), the public may submit some very worthy content that the marketer could use. It is often surprising what a brand enthusiast can do for a brand!

Much of the content on social media networks is created by amateurs. **Consumer-generated content** is content created by consumers for consumers. It is done without provocation and, in many cases, presents the brand effectively. People who do this are often called "brand evangelists" and will do anything to promote their favourite brand—visit YouTube for video examples! For many people, this type of content carries more weight than marketer-generated content.

When a company invites the public to participate in the marketing of its brands, it is employing a technique referred to as crowdsourcing. **Crowdsourcing** uses the "collective intelligence of the public at large to complete business-related tasks that a company would normally perform itself or outsource to a third-party provider (for example, an ad agency or production company)."[33] Crowdsourcing capitalizes on the vision, creativity, and enthusiasm people have for the brand.

Harley-Davidson, a famous brand with a unique image, adapted and is using the techniques described above. A recent Twitter campaign was sourced from a member of the brand's Facebook-based Fan Machine. The fan suggested that having actual Harley riders show off their own chrome would provide instant credibility with new customers. Dino Bernacchi, Harley's director of marketing, says, "Our fans know how to express our brand. They live it everyday." Harley riders were encouraged to tweet about who they are and why they ride. The objective of the campaign was to challenge assumptions about Harley riders and showcase the Harley community's surprising diversity. Bernacchi says, "Many of Harley's 3.3 million Facebook fans don't yet own bikes. All it takes is a little push to awaken the hog within."[34] Since entering the social media arena, Harley's unit sales have been much higher than the industry average.

Marketers must take advantage of this shift in power. There's an expression, "Any publicity is good publicity," that applies here. If consumers can create and upload content that is viewed by millions of people, there must be some benefit for the brand. Moving forward, marketers must find ways to tap into this phenomenon and to strategically add social media to their marketing communications arsenal. It sounds almost frightening to let consumers take charge, but consumer control is the ultimate form of engagement that consumers are searching for.

For insight into what Durex is doing with social media, read the IMC Highlight: **Durex Gets Couples In Sync via Facebook App.**

OPTIONS FOR SOCIAL NETWORK ADVERTISING AND MARKETING COMMUNICATIONS

Several advertising and marketing communications opportunities exist on social networks. Many of the online advertising options discussed earlier are available, along with

brand democratization
A concept that states consumers are now in charge of brand marketing (because of the amount of consumer-generated content produced and distributed online) rather than brand marketers being in control.

consumer-generated content
Online content, often brand oriented, that is created by consumers for consumers.

crowdsourcing
A technique that uses the collective intelligence of the public at large to complete business-related tasks a company would normally perform itself or outsource to a third-party provider.

Durex Gets Couples In Sync via Facebook App

No laughing now, for this is a serious matter! Durex hopes to get loving couples in sync with one another by offering an application that helps them find the perfect love song for their style of lovemaking. The Facebook application is part of the marketing strategy for the new Durex Performax range of products that are designed to "speed her up and slow him down." Developing the marketing strategy for a line of condoms sounds interesting, doesn't it?

The application called "The Durex In-Sync Song Generator" asks a series of questions about preferences for time of day in lovemaking as well as how varied, energetic, and loud one's routine is. Then, the user sends a request to his or her partner on Facebook to complete the survey, or has the partner fill in the questions at the same time if they are together.

Source: Alanah M. Torralba/EPA/Newscom.

Here's an example of how it works. If a couple is identified as "Romantic & Racy" (one partner is eager in the evening and the other likes to get naughty at night), the generator selects a song with a titillating tempo and a sensuous sound. Peter Gabriel's "In Your Eyes" might be the song recommended.

This innovative social media effort is part of a bigger campaign to reposition Durex in the condom market. According to Kevin Harshaw, personal care marketing director for Reckitt Benckiser, "Lovers are a neglected group in this market. Going forward, we want to be the brand of choice for lovers age 25 to 39."

To achieve that goal, Durex is offering a suite of products to get lovers in sync. The "speed her up" condom has extra ribs and dots for added sensation. The "slow him down" condom has a climax-delay lubricant on the inside. Another condom is touted as the "ring of bliss," a feather-like design to hit the spot for her. A lot of serious thinking goes into this kind of product development!

The marketing objective for Reckitt Benckiser is to improve market share. Durex (15% market share) is a distant second to Trojan (69% share) in a North American market worth about $430 million. Harshaw hopes for the best when he says, "We're filling a true need in the market, and we're coming with true innovation for that target group."

Other components of the $15 million marketing communications campaign include digital and social media, radio, public relations, and product placement.

Adapted from Jack Neff, "Durex Offers Facebook App to Find Just the Right Song to Go with Condom," *Advertising Age*, June 28, 2012, www.adage.com.

some interesting brand-sponsored opportunities, such as blogs, which allow an organization to publish ongoing information about its brands.

DISPLAY ADVERTISING

Display advertising in the form of banner ads is available on social networks. Consumers are adapting to the notion that advertising is necessary to sustain their social practices and ultimately for the financial survival of a network like Facebook. Given the abundance of information that social networks collect about users, there is a significant targeting advantage available to advertisers. Facebook offers a sophisticated demographic filtering process. For example, if an advertiser wants to reach females 35 to 49 years old who are interested in home decorating and renovations, that target request could be entered into the Facebook database. The advertiser would know the approximate number of women fitting the profile and plan a campaign to reach them.

Click rates on Facebook are relatively low—about half that of standard banners on other websites. Presently, about one click is generated for every 2000 impressions (the number of times the banner appears on a browser page). Low click rates are causing advertisers to look at other marketing communications options on social networks.

BRAND PAGE (FAN PAGE)

Marketers can create their own page on Facebook that users choose to join. Users who click on a brand's like button become members of the brand's fan page. Contests or other forms of incentives motivate fans to visit the page, resulting in an expanded base that can be used for future marketing programs.

The value of a "like" is often questioned by advertisers. Presently, many marketers equate social media success to the number of likes they have, and they implement programs to build their number of likes. But the value of a like remains elusive. Apparently, only 5 percent of people who "like" a brand go back to that brand page.[35] The limited consumer engagement with brands on Facebook suggests there may be a disconnection between the reasons why consumers "like" a brand and the reasons brands think consumers are "liking" their page.[36] A prudent marketer must shift his or her way of thinking and devise strategies that give "engagement" a priority over "likes."

In 2012, Facebook announced a new format for business pages. No longer will a brand page have a static tab as a default landing page; instead, a timeline design will be in effect. The timeline design forces marketers to frequently post fresh and engaging content. Specific posts will appear at the top of the page, but they will be removed after seven days. Marketers will also have to be more engaged since they must post, monitor, and respond more often on their brand page.[37]

REFERRALS FROM A FRIEND NETWORK

Referrals from friends have proven to be an important influencer in social media; they play a role in creating interest in a brand. A news feed about someone buying something new, for example, could be received by countless numbers of friends. Word of mouth is often cited as more influential than company-sponsored communication. Too much word of mouth may not be good, as users become skeptical of the source or see it as exploitation of personal relationships with friends.

sponsored post
A sponsored ad circulated by friends in a social network.

Facebook launched **sponsored posts** (sponsored stories) that are served to friends of users who have engaged with a brand. The new format requires marketers to pay for exposure for their posts—something they might once have gotten for free. Initial reaction has been positive among many Facebook advertisers, as click rates have been about four times higher than those of traditional Facebook ads.[38]

COMPANY BLOGS

blog
A frequent, chronological publication of personal thoughts at a website.

A **blog** is a website where journal entries are posted on a regular basis and displayed in reverse chronological order. Blogs provide commentary on news or particular subject areas of interest—politics, food, fashion, even marketing-related material! A blog can include text, images, video, and links to other blogs.

A company blog is proving to be an effective means of presenting relevant information in a positive manner. It gives an organization an opportunity to be part of the discussion on matters that are important to customers. People access blogs because they want the content. With a blog, an organization can communicate with customers in a more relaxed way. With a blog, a brand has an opportunity to develop an online personality that goes beyond what can be accomplished in traditional media communications.

YOUTUBE CHANNELS

Everyone views video content on YouTube, don't they? With that in mind, doesn't it make sense for an organization to have its own YouTube channel, where it can show some dazzling videos about its brands. On YouTube, a channel is the word used for a user's profile. Other users can access a channel/profile to find out what videos have been uploaded. You can also subscribe to a user's profile and be notified when that user uploads new videos to the site.[39]

The principle just described can certainly apply to a company and its brands. Axe, a very popular brand of male grooming products, is all over social media and recently launched a dedicated channel on YouTube: www.youtube.com/AXECanada. Similar to Axe communications in other media, the YouTube channel offers a highly sexualized perspective on topics of male interest. According to Shelley Brown, president and CEO of CP+B (Axe's ad agency), "Axe is a brand that, as it moves through social space, needs to stay very relevant, very fresh. It needs to be in a state of continual renewal."[40]

KEY BENEFITS OF SOCIAL MEDIA MARKETING COMMUNICATIONS

There are several key benefits available for a marketing organization that engages in social media communications. From a targeting perspective, all age groups are engaged with social networks. Therefore, it is a complementary medium in the marketing communications mix. More specifically, millennials are on social networks in droves: 91 percent are on the Internet, and 86 percent of those participate on a social network.[41] Now and in the future, social media communications that reach this group are absolutely essential in the mix.

One of the most potent forms of influence on brand decisions is word-of-mouth, a situation that marketers have no control over. As demonstrated earlier in the chapter, a significant amount of word-of-mouth happens among friends on social networks. Perhaps the primary benefit is an intangible one—the fact that consumers willingly engage with brands. While such engagement may not produce an immediate sale, it is part of the relationship-building process that could produce a sale later on.

Despite these benefits, many companies are reluctant to invest in social media communications. The absence of sound metrics (beyond click rates) to determine return on investment is a stumbling block. Erich Marx, director of interactive and social media at Nissan, effectively puts social media communications into perspective for modern-day advertisers. He says, "From an ROI standpoint, are we selling hundreds of cars through social? No. But, you have to be there. It's not about ROI, it's about COI—cost of ignoring. It's too big to ignore."[42]

SUMMARY

A stronger understanding of the role and importance of the Internet and other forms of interactive media in the daily lives of consumers has resulted in more integration of digital media in marketing communications plans. With the younger generation of consumers being avid users of technology, there is little doubt that digital media will play a more dominant role in the future.

As Internet penetration continues to rise, Canada tops the world in Internet usage. Canadians are spending more time online than any other country; the Internet ranks second only to television in terms of time spent with the media. The interactive nature of the medium allows a brand to engage consumers and create deeper brand experiences. The challenge for advertisers is to create useful and entertaining messages that will capture the imagination of Internet users who want to be entertained. Advertisers must also understand that control of the message is in the hands of consumers in social media. The differences in consumer behaviour when using social media must be considered when planning communications strategies.

The Internet is a medium that allows marketers to target customers on the basis of demographics, geographics, and behaviour. Of particular interest to advertisers is the concept of behaviour targeting. By tracking preferences, unique messages are delivered to consumers on an individual basis. As well, there is the capability to design unique products for customers, a concept referred to as mass customization.

Interactive marketing communications refers to the placement of an advertising message on a website in a variety of different formats. The messages are communicated by computer, cell phones, tablets, MP3 players, and video games. Advertising online plays a key role in achieving specific marketing objectives. It will help create brand awareness for the launch of new products and is an excellent medium for building and enhancing brand image. Companies also find the Internet ideal for distributing buying incentives and for promoting contests. In both cases, information about consumers is collected and added to a database for use at a later date. In a business-to-business context, online advertising is a means of generating leads and completing transactions.

There are a variety of advertising alternatives to choose from. Among the options are search advertising, banner ads in static and rich media formats, video ads, sponsorships at other websites, email ads, and webcasting. Video ads are growing in popularity mainly due to their similarity to television ads. Permission-based email is also growing in popularity. Using lists generated from in-house databases or from other sources (rented lists), email advertising represents a cost-efficient way to reach prospects and current customers. Beyond these advertising options, companies also use company and brand websites to communicate detailed information.

As an advertising medium, the Internet provides targeting capability at a very reasonable cost and also offers tracking capabilities that measure effectiveness in a variety of ways (for example, impressions, clicks, clickthrough rates, leads, and purchases). It is also a 24/7 medium, offering ample opportunity for brand and company exposure and engagement with consumers. Some drawbacks of the Internet include low click rates for ads and advertising overload (the sheer number of ads that may appear on a webpage).

Mobile media represent new opportunities to deliver advertising messages. With smartphone penetration growing rapidly in Canada, the potential to deliver messages to consumers while they are on the go, a concept referred to as location-based targeting, represents significant opportunity for advertisers. Marketers are attracted to mobile media based on the immediacy and intimacy they offer. Mobile media advertisers must be careful regarding the frequency of communications with consumers. If the advertiser is too intrusive, there could be a negative impact on brand image. Other mobile opportunities include advertising on applications or using QR codes in other forms of communication.

Video games are proving to be an effective means of reaching all age groups. People are spending more time playing games (often in prime time) than they are watching television. Gamers don't mind the presence of ads. In fact, they say ads make the game more real. Recall scores for brands that appear in games are quite high.

Finally, social media networks are increasing in popularity due to their social nature and intimate environment. Many advertisers have jumped in and enjoyed much success, while others have struggled to find the right formula. Marketing executives say that it is challenging just to stay abreast of the changes that are occurring in the social media environment, and claim that their lack of knowledge is what's holding them back. Nonetheless, people are spending considerable time with social media, so advertisers must be there. In the social media era, the communications process is more participative, a situation that advertisers must adapt to. The goal is to get consumers talking about the brands and promoting the brands on behalf of the organization.

Advertising options in social media include display advertising, brand pages, referrals from a friend network, blogs, and YouTube channels. Social media reach all age groups, a key benefit to advertisers. As well, social media encourage word-of-mouth about brands, among friends. The ability to measure return on investment is a common concern that advertisers raise about social media.

KEY TERMS

REVIEW QUESTIONS

1. What is behavioural targeting, and how is it applied in online marketing communications programs?

2. What is mass customization, and how do online communications facilitate its practice?

3. What are the primary marketing and marketing communications roles that the Internet can provide marketing organizations? Identify and explain each role briefly.

4. In the context of online marketing communications, briefly explain what viral marketing is. Is it a worthwhile pursuit for marketing organizations?

5. Explain the following terms as they relate to online advertising:
   a) impressions
   b) clicks
   c) click rate
   d) visits

6. What is banner advertising, and how does it work?

7. Identify and briefly describe the various types of banner ads.

8. What does rich media refer to, and how does it work? What does streaming media refer to?

9. Briefly explain how an online advertising sponsorship works. What benefits does it provide? Illustrate the benefits with some examples.

10. Briefly explain the following email advertising terms:
    a) permission-based email
    b) sponsored email
    c) opt-in list
    d) spam

11. What is a cookie, and what role does it perform in online communications and marketing?

DISCUSSION AND APPLICATION QUESTIONS

1. Identify and briefly explain two advantages and two disadvantages of Internet-based advertising.

2. What future lies ahead for email advertising? Will it continue to grow, or will consumers and businesses turn away from it? Conduct some online research on the issue and present a brief report on your findings.

3. "Persistent invasions of consumer privacy will be the undoing of online advertising." Is this statement true or false? Conduct some online secondary research on this issue. Report on your findings.

4. Visit some commercial websites of your choosing. Evaluate these websites in terms of their ability to

achieve certain marketing and marketing communications objectives such as building brand image, offering incentives, generating leads, and providing customer service. Are communications on the websites coordinated with any other form of marketing communications?

5. Assess how consumer goods marketing organizations are using social media communications to their advantage. Can it be an effective medium for building relationships with customers?

6. Will consumers accept or reject the notion of delivering advertising messages via cell phones and other portable devices? Examine the issues surrounding this emerging practice and formulate a position on the matter.

7. Is it possible to launch a new product using online communications as the primary medium for creating awareness and interest? What strategies would be necessary to make such a plan work?

ENDNOTES

1. Gariné Tcholakian, "Internet Top Media Time Grabber Among Canadian Youth, Says New IAB study," Media in Canada, February 2, 2009, www.mediaincanada.com.

2. "Canadian Internet Use Survey," 2010, Statistics Canada, www.statcan.gc.ca/daily-quotidien/110525/dq110525b-eng.htm.

3. Steve Ladurantaye, "Canada Tops Globe in Internet Usage," The Globe and Mail, March 1, 2012, www.theglobeandmail.com/technology/tech-news/canada-tops-globe-in-internet-usage/article551593.

4. Michael Oliveira, "Fewer Canadians Using Facebook," Toronto Star, June 13, 2011, www.thestar.com/business/2011/06/13/fewer_canadians_using_facebook.html.

5. "2010 Canadian Online Advertising Revenue Grows to $2.23 Billion, Surpassing Daily Newspaper," IAB Canada, press release, August 2, 2011, www.iabcanada.com.

6. "Interactive Marketing + Online Advertising," IAB Canada Conference, May 20, 2009, p. 50.

7. "What's Driving Growth?" Interactive Advertising Bureau, www.iab.com.

8. Website Looker, www.websitelooker.com/www/tsn.ca.

9. "Interactive Marketing + Online Advertising," IAB Canada Conference, May 20, 2009, p. 145.

10. "Doubleclick Ad Planner," Google, www.google.com/adplanner/static/top1000.

11. "Individual Internet Use and E-Commerce, 2010" Statistics Canada, www.statcan.gc.ca/daily-quotidien/111012/dq111012a-eng.htm.

12. "Social Networking Usage Patterns: Canada," New Media Trend Watch, www.newmediatrendwatch.com.

13. Justin Lafferty, "Facebook Unique Visitors Dropped in May," AllFacebook, June 20, 2012, allfacebook.com/facebook-unique-visitor-dropped-in-may_b92492.

14. "Marketers Use Online Video to Complement, Not Cannibalize, TV Ads," eMarketer, December 28, 2011, www.emarketer.com/Article/Marketers-Use-Online-Video-Complement-Not-Cannibalize-TV-Ads/1008755.

15. Maureen Morrison, "Consumers Balance on Verge of Offer Anarchy," Advertising Age, February 13, 2012, p. 24.

16. Ibid., p. 24.

17. Kris Orser, "Study Finds Consumers Fans of Emails," Advertising Age, February 13, 2006, p. 35.

18. Chris Powell, "Mercedes Take an 'Appy' Path to Younger Consumers," Marketing, October 14, 2011, www.marketingmag.ca/news/marketer-news/mercedes-take-an-'appy'-path-to-younger-consumers-37945.

19. Samson Okalow, "Marketers Retool Sites to Exploit Web Research Boom," Strategy, May 3, 2004, p. 11.

20. Chris Powell, "Mobile Ad Spend to Reach $82 Million in 2011: IAB," Marketing, September 20, 2011, www.marketingmag.ca/news/media-news/mobile-ad-spend-to-reach-82-million-in-2010-iab-36379.

21. Lisa Phillips, "Trends in Consumers' Time Spent with the Media," eMarketer, December 28, 2010, www.emarketer.com/Article/Trends-Consumers-Time-Spent-with-Media/1008138.

22. Ian Hardy, "Canadians Sent 56.4 Billion Text Messages in 2010," Mobilesyrup, May 16, 2011, www.mobilesyrup.com.

23. "Take Possession," Mobile Marketing Supplement to Strategy, August 2008, p.S32.

24. Daisy Whitney, "Prime Time is Mobile Time; Study Shows Mobile Online Video Use Skyrocketing," VidBlog, May 31, 2012, www.mediapost.com/publications/article/175889/prime-time-is-mobile-time-studies-show-mobile-onl.html.

25. Chris Powell, "Mobile Devices Becoming a Bigger Part of Retail: Study," Marketing, May 31, 2012, www.marketingmag.ca/news/media-news/mobile-devices-becoming-a-bigger-part-of-retail-study-53799.

26. "Mobile Ads Outperform Standard Banners," eMarketer, July 13, 2011, www.emarketer.com/Article/Mobile-Ads-Outperform-Standard-Banners/1008494.

27. Kristin Laird, "Updated: Tim Hortons Makes Group Buying a Little Easier," Marketing, April 17, 2012, www.marketingmag.ca/news/marketer-news/tim-hortons-makes-group-buying-a-little-easier-50546.

28. Matt Semansky, "Citytv Goes Mobile with Video App," Marketing, December 8, 2011, www.marketingmag.ca/news/media-news/citytv-goes-mobile-with-video-app-41991.

29. Aaron Barr, "Video Games Becoming a Mainstream Choice," MediaPost, January 19, 2009, www.mediapost.com/publications/article/98599.

30. Mike Shields, "IGA: Most Gamers Cool with In-game Ads," AdWeek, June 17, 2008, www.adweek.com.

31. Shayndi Rice, "Days of Wild User Growth Appear Over at Facebook," The Wall Street Journal, June 11, 2012, online.wsj.com.

32. Chris Powell, "Marketers Struggling with Speed of Social Media: Study," Marketing, August 26, 2010, www.marketingmag.ca/news/marketer-news/marketers-struggling-with-speed-of-social-media-study-4590.

33. Jennifer Alsever, "What Is Crowdsourcing?" MoneyWatch, CBSNews, March 7, 2007, www.cbsnews.com/8301-505125_162-51052961/what-is-crowdsourcing.

34. Robert Klara, "Tweeters of the Pack: Harley-Davidson Turns to Its Riders and Twitter in New Social Effort," Adweek, March 6, 2012, www.adweek.com/news/harley-davidson/tweeters-pack-138690.

35. Mark Walsh, "Engagement: Brands Should Drive Traffic to Facebook Page," *Online Media Daily*, June 14, 2012, www.mediapost.com/publications/article/176841/engagement-brands-should-drive-traffic-to-faceboo.html.

36. "Does 'Liking' a Brand Drive User Loyalty?" *eMarketer*, February 8, 2012, www.emarketer.com/Article/Liking-Brand-Drive-User-Loyalty/1008822.

37. Clara Shih, "Facebook's New Business Pages Means Marketers Must Evolve," *Advertising Age*, March 19, 2012, adage.com/article/digitalnext/facebook-s-business-pages-means-marketers-evolve/233387.

38. Cotton Delo for *Advertising Age*, "Apps Move Facebook Beyond the 'Like,'" *Marketing*, January 19, 2012, www.marketingmag.ca/news/media-news/apps-move-facebook-beyond-the-like-44660.

39. Michael Miller, "Joining the YouTube Community—And Creating Your Own Channel," May 4, 2007, www.quepublishing.com.

40. Chris Powell, "Axe Launches Its Own Web Channel," *Marketing*, August 25, 2011, www.marketingmag.ca/news/marketer-news/axe-launches-its-own-web-channel-34902.

41. "Social Networking Doubles Among Boomers and Seniors," *eMarketer*, September 3, 2010, www.emarketer.com/Article/Social-Networking-Doubles-Among-Boomers-Seniors/1007908.

42. Rich Thomaselli, "Nissan Looks to Facebook to Help Launch Five New Models," *Advertising Age*, June 25, 2012, adage.com/article/digital/nissan-facebook-launch-models/235616/.

Planning for Integrated Marketing

Part 3 looks at marketing communications choices beyond the media that enhance the communications plan.

Chapter 8 introduces various sales promotion alternatives that are frequently used in integrated marketing communications plans. Discussion is divided between consumer promotions and trade promotions, with each area examined for its ability to achieve marketing and marketing communications objectives.

Chapter 9 describes the role of public relations communications in the marketing communications mix. Various public relations techniques are introduced. The process of planning public relations activities is examined in detail, along with various measurement techniques used to determine the effectiveness of public relations messages.

Chapter 10 discusses the role of experiential marketing techniques that embrace street marketing strategies along with event marketing and sponsorships. The criteria for participating in event marketing, and the steps and procedures for planning an event are introduced, along with evaluation techniques for this activity.

In Chapter 11, the role of personal selling in a variety of business settings is examined. Personal selling adds a human component to the integrated marketing communications mix and, for this reason, plays a very important role in an era where customer relationship management practices dominate.

Sales Promotion

Learning Objectives

After studying this chapter, you will be able to

1. Distinguish between consumer promotions and trade promotions

2. Describe the steps in the sales promotion planning process

3. Assess the role of consumer promotions in achieving specific marketing communications and marketing objectives

4. Assess the role of trade promotions in achieving specific marketing communications and marketing objectives

5. Outline the nature of various consumer promotion and trade promotion activities

6. Assess various criteria for integrating sales promotion strategies with other integrated marketing communications strategies

This chapter examines the role of sales promotions in the marketing communications mix. Promotions are activities that focus on making a sale, usually in a short period of time. When planning and implementing promotions, the marketing organization provides an offer to customers in return for something they must do. Because the offer is valid only for a certain period, the impact of the offer—and its success or failure—can be measured quickly.

A wide variety of promotion offers are presented here, all of which are suited to achieving specific marketing and marketing communications objectives. The right promotion must be offered at the right time if the offer is to bring true benefit to the brand or company. In order to create awareness and interest in the promotion, there must also be media advertising to support it, and possibly some publicity generated by public relations and social media campaigns. A coordinated effort is usually required to make a sales promotion a success. This chapter focuses on two distinct yet related areas of sales promotion: consumer promotion and trade promotion. An organization must consider strategies for both if it is to grow and prosper.

Sales Promotion

Sales promotion is defined as an activity that provides special incentives to bring about immediate response from customers, distributors, and an organization's sales force. It is a strategy that encourages action by the recipient. According to the definition, three distinct groups are considered when planning sales promotion strategies. First, the consumer or final user must be motivated to take advantage of the offer. Second, the distributor (reseller of goods) must be motivated to support the offer by providing merchandising support. Third, the company's sales force must be motivated to sell the promotion to its trade customers. Because the intent of a promotion is to provide some added excitement to the product, an organization's sales representatives must present it enthusiastically to the trade distributors.

Consumer promotions are designed to stimulate purchases or to encourage loyalty. Among the options readily available are coupons, free samples, contests, rebates, price incentives, and rewards programs. These types of promotions are planned to help **pull** the product through the channel of distribution. An organization creates demand for the product by directing its promotional efforts directly at the consumer. The combination of advertising and promotions, for example, creates demand and causes consumers to look for the product in stores or request a service; by asking for it specifically, they put

sales promotion
An activity that provides incentives to bring about immediate response from customers, distributors, and an organization's sales force.

consumer promotion
An incentive offered to consumers to stimulate purchases or encourage loyalty.

pull
Demand created by directing promotional activities at consumers or final users, who in turn pressure retailers to supply the product or service.

FIGURE
8.1

Pull and Push Promotion Strategies

Pull—The promotion strategy is directed at consumers, who in turn request the product or service from distributors and pull it through the channel.

| Marketing Organization | Wholesaler | Retailer | Consumer |

Push—The promotion strategy is directed at distributors, who resell the product. Incentives help push the product from one distributor to another.

pressure on the retailer to provide it. Many companies now include experiential marketing activities in their promotion strategies. Experiential marketing is presented in detail in Chapter 9.

Consumers express a favourable opinion about the effectiveness of various consumer promotions, so they should play a key role in an integrated marketing communications plan. A poll conducted by Delvinia Data Collection asked a sampling of Canadian consumers, "What would best convince you to try a new brand of beer?" Product sampling and tasting events garnered a 42.6 percent response; giveaways (clothing and hats) 20.6 percent; and contests 14.3 percent. In comparison, television advertising only garnered a 7.8 percent response.[1]

Trade promotions are less visible activities, given that they are offered to members of the channel of distribution. These promotions include options such as discounts and allowances, cooperative advertising funds, dealer premiums and incentives, and point-of-purchase materials. Offering financial incentives to distributors encourages them to support a manufacturer's promotion plans. Such promotions **push** the product through the channel of distribution. Refer to Figure 8.1 for a visual image of pull and push promotion strategies.

To be successful, an organization must determine what type of promotion will contribute the most to achieving its objectives. In most cases, it is a combination of both consumer and trade promotions. The real decision is to determine the extent to which each type of promotion is offered. Such a decision is based on the market analysis that precedes the development of any sales promotion plan. Sales promotion planning is discussed in the following section.

trade promotion
An incentive offered to channel members to encourage them to provide marketing and merchandising support for a particular product.

push
Demand created by directing promotional activities at intermediaries, who in turn promote the product or service among consumers.

Sales Promotion Planning

Like any other component of the marketing communications mix, a sales promotion plan is but one component of a much larger plan. It must directly fit into the marketing communications plan and play a role in achieving the specific objectives that are identified in that plan. Whereas advertising plans have a long-term perspective and longer-term objectives, the sales promotion plan adopts a short-term view and achieves objectives of a more immediate nature. While advertising is building a brand's image, sales promotions are implemented to encourage a spike in sales.

To demonstrate the difference between the roles of advertising and sales promotions, consider a recent campaign by Deeley Harley-Davidson in Canada. Harley's "Live the Dream" campaign combined the renowned Harley mystique with a more friendly tone to attract newcomers to the brand. The theme of the television advertising captured a young boy's love of his bicycle and drew parallels to the feelings of riding a Harley motorcycle. Harley also used advertising to connect with the individuality and rebel in everyone. The promotion side of the campaign included a dedicated website that offered a chance to win a made-to-measure Harley. The contest encouraged consumer engagement with the brand, as sharing information with friends via Facebook, Twitter, or email increased a person's chances of winning the motorcycle.[2]

Sales promotions are activities that complement advertising. When you consider the primary goals of advertising—awareness, comprehension, conviction, and action—the primary goal of sales promotion is to focus on one specific area—action. A well-timed promotional offer that coincides with an image-building advertising campaign, as described in the Harley-Davidson example above, could be just the incentive needed to get the customer's money out of that wallet or purse. Such a relationship suggests that integration of advertising strategies and promotional strategies is essential and, on a larger scale, that their integration with online communications, events and sponsorships, and public relations is what promotes a brand or company with a sense of continuity.

Sales promotion planning involves developing a plan of action for communicating incentives to the appropriate target markets (consumers and trade customers) at the right time. Very often, an external company that specializes in sales promotion will assume responsibility for developing and implementing the consumer promotion plan. As with developing an advertising plan, the specialist must be briefed. The client's role is to provide the necessary background information and then evaluate the promotion concepts put forth by the agency. The promotion agency must assess the information provided by the client and then prepare a strategic plan that will meet the client's objectives. Figure 8.2 outlines the promotion planning process. A sales promotion brief typically includes some or all of the following information.

MARKET PROFILE

An overview of sales and market share trends provides market perspective to the promotion planners. Knowing if the brand is a leader, challenger, or follower has an impact on the nature of the promotion they will ultimately recommend. It is important to know if the market is growing and what brands are growing in the market.

COMPETITOR ACTIVITY PROFILE

In general terms, what marketing communications strategies do key competitors rely upon? The role of the various elements of the mix will vary from one brand to another. What brands dominate the market, and what are their mixes? An evaluation of this kind of information may suggest that various combinations of activities have more or less impact on customers. A review of competitors' recent sales promotion activities is essential.

TARGET MARKET PROFILE

Perhaps the most important aspect of planning a promotion is a good understanding of the target customer. As discussed earlier in the text, customers are described according to demographic, psychographic, geographic, and behavioural characteristics. Additional information about shopping behaviour usually plays a role in developing a sales promotion plan. For example, many of today's consumers are time challenged and value conscious, and are looking for good deals they can take advantage of quickly. When planning the promotion, the value must be immediately evident to the consumer.

FIGURE
8.2

**The Sales Promotion Planning
Process**

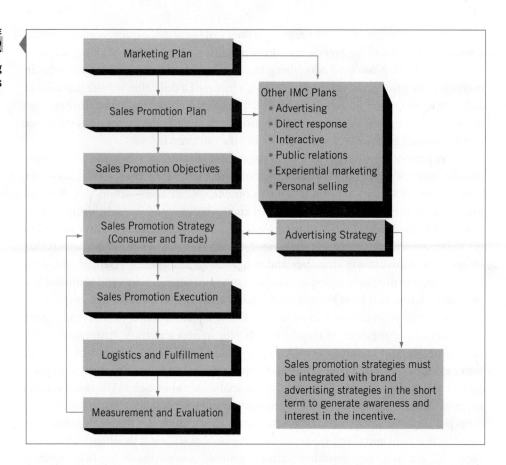

SALES PROMOTION OBJECTIVES

A variety of background factors will determine the objectives of the promotion campaign. Essentially, sales promotion plans focus on three distinct objectives: generating trial purchases, encouraging repeat or multiple purchases, and building long-term brand loyalty. Objectives for trade promotion plans concentrate on building sales and achieving merchandising support. These objectives are discussed in more detail in the "Consumer Promotion Execution" and "Trade Promotion Execution" sections of this chapter.

BUDGET

Funds for the sales promotion plan come from the overall marketing budget. In most cases, the client has already determined how much money is available for promotions. Knowing the size of the budget is crucial when the promotion agency is thinking about potential concepts. Will this be a large-scale national promotion, or will it be restricted to specific regions? Will it involve an expensive grand prize, or will there be a series of smaller prizes? How much media advertising support will be needed to create awareness for the promotion?

The Sales Promotion Plan

sales promotion plan
An action plan for communicating incentives to appropriate target markets at the right time.

The **sales promotion plan** is a document that outlines the relevant details about how the client's budget will be spent. Objectives are clearly defined, strategies are justified, and tactical details are precisely documented. Similar to direct response communications plans, back-end considerations are very important. For example, if a fulfillment program is part of the package, details about how the offer will be handled from the

FIGURE 8.3 The Content of a Sales Promotion Plan

Situation Analysis
- Market profile
- Competitor activity profile
- Target market profile

Budget
- Funds available

Sales Promotion Objectives

A. Consumer Promotion
- Trial purchase
- Repeat purchases
- Multiple purchases
- Brand loyalty

B. Trade Promotion
- New listings
- Sales volume
- Merchandising support

Sales Promotion Strategy
- Incentive or offer (save, win, or reward)
- Merchandise, cash, or combination
- Balance between consumer and trade

Advertising Strategy
- Broadcast
- Print
- In-store
- Digital and interactive

Sales Promotion Execution
- Details of consumer offer (coupon, sample, contest, premium, rebate, loyalty promotion)
- Details of trade offer (trade allowance, performance allowance, cooperative advertising funds, dealer premiums, collateral materials, display materials, trade shows)

Logistics and Fulfillment
- Back-end plan to administer and implement the promotion

Budget and Timing
- Activity costs
- Calendar of events

time the consumer responds to the time the goods are delivered must be precisely planned. Promotions that include coupons, free samples, contests, rebates, and premiums might involve other companies that handle various aspects of the promotion. The structure and content of a sales promotion plan are the focus of this section. Figure 8.3 summarizes the content of a sales promotion plan, but because the content of a plan varies from one company to another, it is only a guideline.

SALES PROMOTION OBJECTIVES

Sales promotion objectives are statements that clearly indicate what the promotion plan is to accomplish. Similar to other communications plans, objective statements should be realistically achievable, quantitative in nature to facilitate measurement, and directed at a carefully defined target market.

The nature of the promotion plan (that is, consumer promotion versus trade promotion) determines the objectives. Although objectives for both are quite different, they complement each other when implemented. Let's start with consumer promotion objectives.

The most common objective of consumer promotion is to encourage consumers to make a *trial purchase*. When a product is new, for example, an organization wants to establish acceptance as quickly as possible. Therefore, trial-oriented promotions are common (see Figure 8.4). Even when a product is in the growth stage of development, there is a need to distinguish one brand from another. At that stage, incentives that

encourage purchase of a specific brand remain essential. Media-delivered coupons are an excellent promotion tool for encouraging trial purchase, as are product samples.

The second objective is to stimulate **repeat purchases** by existing customers. An extension of this objective is to encourage consumers to make multiple purchases at one time. To illustrate, a well-conceived contest will encourage **multiple entries** by consumers. Persistent purchases of the brand in the contest tie the consumer to the brand for a period of time. Those consumers won't be buying a competitor's brand! To demonstrate, the Tim Hortons "Roll Up the Rim" promotion encourages consumers to visit Tim's more often—more visits mean more sales! Refer to the image in Figure 8.5.

The third objective deals with customer relationship management (CRM). Here, the objective is to encourage **brand loyalty** for an extended period. Traditionally, promotions encourage instant activity, but there are promotion alternatives that can meet both short-term and long-term brand objectives. Something as simple as the loyalty card offered by a local coffee shop helps keep a customer. Rewards bring customers back.

The overall goal of trade promotions is to give sales a jolt in the short run. But such an accomplishment is usually the result of promotion strategies combined with other marketing strategies to influence trade customers and consumers. Therefore, trade promotion objectives must be confined to what they can realistically achieve. Generally speaking, trade promotion plans are designed to encourage distributors to carry a product and then sell it to retailers, and to increase the volume sold for products they already carry.

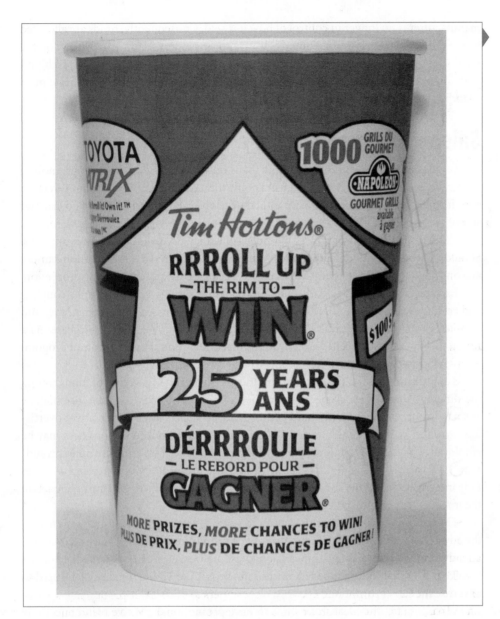

FIGURE
8.5

**A Consumer Promotion
Designed to Encourage Repeat
Purchases**

Source: Handout/Tim Hortons Inc./
Newscom.

In the case of a new product, the first objective is to *secure a listing* with distributors. A listing is an agreement made by a wholesaler to distribute a manufacturer's product to the retailer it supplies. For example, when the head office of Canada Safeway or Sobeys agrees to list a product, it is then available to all of their retail outlets. Typically, trade promotions in the form of financial incentives are used to secure listings.

A second objective is to *build sales volume* on either a seasonal basis or a predetermined cyclical basis throughout the year. For example, baking products are promoted in the pre-Christmas season, and there are usually displays of such products in retail stores. In other cases, it is common for a company to offer temporary discounts for its key brands on a quarterly basis because it recognizes that consistent activity keeps a popular brand in a preferred position with the trade and consumers. The nature of competition often dictates such a strategy.

A third trade objective is to *secure merchandising support* from distributors. Their support is crucial, because once the product leaves the manufacturer's warehouse, the manufacturer is no longer in control of how it is sold. Consequently, funds are allocated to activities that get the product out of a distributor's warehouse and into displays on the retail sales floor. As well, the manufacturer will look for a sale price and perhaps a brand mention of the sale price in a retailer's advertising flyer. These activities constitute merchandising support.

Sales Promotion Strategy

Decisions about sales promotion strategy focus on the selection of the best promotion activity to meet the objectives. Decisions point the organization in a certain direction and, if agreed to, the tactical details are then developed. For example, on the consumer side of things, an organization can choose among coupons, free samples, contests, rebates, premiums, and loyalty programs. Other decisions may involve the selection of prizes. Should they be cash, merchandise, or a combination of both? The organization can use any one of these options or combine several to maximize the potential of the promotion.

Each of these options provides a different kind of incentive. For example, coupons and rebates save people money; contests give people a chance to win something; and samples, premiums, and loyalty programs offer something free with a purchase. As a result, the first decision relates directly to the incentive. Should the promotion program offer savings, a chance to win something, or a reward?

Key decisions about trade promotion strategy involve the allocation of funds among the different alternatives. Depending on the promotion objectives, preference may be given to listing allowances, trade and performance allowances, and cooperative advertising allowances. Alternatively, some combination of several of these allowances may be employed. The manager must also decide about the balance between consumer promotions (pull) and trade promotions (push). Successful promotions use both and are carefully integrated with other forms of marketing communications to maximize impact on the intended target audience.

The second component of the sales promotion strategy involves integration with the advertising strategy. You need to promote a promotion! In many cases, a brand will already be planning a brand-image campaign, and several different media may be involved. Is special creative needed for the sales promotion? What media will be used to advertise the sales promotion?

With creative, the ideal situation is to have promotional creative blend effectively with existing brand creative. For example, in March each year, Tim Hortons implements its "Roll Up the Rim to Win" promotion. Separate creative and a variety of media (television, outdoor boards, online communications, and in-store signage) are employed to announce details of the promotion. A promotion is an added incentive, so it temporarily becomes the brand's unique selling point. The combination of a strong ongoing sales message with the added bonus of a special offer will help achieve short-term and long-term objectives. Refer back to Figure 8.5.

Marketing research by Resolve Corporation observes that consumers should be able to immediately see that a promotion offer provides significant real value. This means that the savings have to be meaningful in relation to the purchase price of the product and must also make sense in relation to the market strength and purchase frequency of the brand.[3] For a promotion to be successful, it must be a good fit for the product and the target market.

A sales promotion will only work if it receives the necessary media support, so another decision must be made about allocating funds specifically for promotion-related programs. Once that decision is made, the media strategy will focus on two objectives:

creating awareness for the promotion and providing details about how the consumer can take advantage of the promotion (for example, how to send in order forms for premium offers or entry forms for contests).

Typically, a variety of broadcast, print, and online media are selected. Television is an ideal medium for creating instant awareness of the promotion. High-impact television advertising in a short period (a blitz strategy) is common. In the case of a contest or sweepstakes promotion, television is ideal for creating excitement and for conveying a sense of urgency to consumers. It encourages them to take advantage of the offer right away. Social media can also play a role in generating buzz for the promotion.

In-store advertising can also assist in achieving awareness objectives while playing a key role in communicating details of the offer. Consumers are conditioned to look for details at point of purchase. In conjunction with trade promotion strategies, the ideal situation is to have brand displays in stores supported by posters and shelf cards at the product's regular shelf location to draw attention to the promotion. See the illustration in Figure 8.6.

FIGURE
8.6

In-store Displays and Signage Draw Attention to an Old Dutch/ Humpty Dumpty Products Promotion

Source: Jesse Johnston/CP Images.

Obviously, the nature and size of the promotion will dictate the degree of media support. It is common for brands such as Pepsi-Cola, Gillette, and Kellogg's cereals to invest in media advertising to promote contests that offer huge grand prizes. In contrast, a premium offer may simply be announced to the target market on the package itself and by shelf cards at point of purchase. The investment in media advertising in this case would be low. Refer to the illustration in Figure 8.7. In this illustration, it is the package that advertises the premium offer.

Trade customers must be made aware of consumer promotion offers, a task that falls on the shoulders of the manufacturer's sales representatives. The manufacturer commonly prepares specific sales literature such as brochures, pamphlets, and display material for representatives to use to introduce the promotion. The sales representatives will integrate the consumer promotion offer with their trade promotion plans (a combination of pull and push) to maximize the impact of the dollars being invested in the promotion. The sales representatives must sell the promotion to the distributors and show how it will affect their business positively. Their objective may be to secure a listing for a new product or to ensure the distributor orders sufficient inventory of an existing product to cover the anticipated demand and to encourage adequate merchandising support in its stores. If the trade customers are on board, the promotion will be successful. Their support is crucial.

LOGISTICS AND FULFILLMENT

The final phase of planning a promotion campaign involves working out all of the details of the offer. Depending on the nature of the promotion, there will be a variety of dates and deadlines, there will be other companies involved in planning and implementing the offer, and there will need to be a system in place to deliver the goods to consumers, if the promotion so dictates. These are only a sampling of the potential decisions that are made.

To demonstrate the fulfillment process, let's assume that a major contest is the sales promotion offer. The grand prize is a trip to Disneyland with a series of smaller prizes to be awarded to runners-up. Answers to the following questions start to create a plan of action for implementing the awareness and fulfillment sides of the promotion:

- When will the promotion be announced to the trade and to consumers?
- Who are the contest prize suppliers, and what are the costs?
- How will consumers enter the contest? Who will design the entry form? Will it be an online entry form?
- What is the deadline for receiving entries?
- Who will draw the prizes?
- How will the prizes be delivered to the winners?
- What costs are associated with contest administration by a third-party organization?
- Who will the third-party organization be?
- Who will prepare in-store promotional materials?
- Who will print the promotional literature, and what will it cost?
- How will media advertising be coordinated with the sales promotion offer?

Such a list of questions reveals the logistical implications for running a sales promotion offer. Needless to say, the entire promotion must operate seamlessly from the front end (announcing the promotion) to the back end (delivering prizes to winners). Smart marketing organizations outsource the administration of the promotion to a specialist in this industry.

MEASUREMENT AND EVALUATION

Similar to any other marketing communications program, sales promotion activities must be evaluated for success or failure. As indicated earlier, a boost in sales is the immediate goal of most forms of promotion, but other factors beyond promotion also influence sales. Therefore, a promotion must be evaluated based on the objectives that were established for it. If the objective was to generate trial purchases, how many new users were attracted to the product? If the objective was loyalty, are current customers buying the product more frequently? To answer these questions, some pre- and post-promotion marketing research is necessary.

Specific promotions are also measured by response rates of consumers. For example, a coupon promotion could be assessed by the number of coupons returned. If the average return rate for coupons distributed by magazines is 1 percent and an offer draws a 2 percent response, the promotion could be judged a success. A contest is evaluated on the basis of the number of entries received. If the objective was 10 000 entries and only 7500 were received, the promotion could be judged a failure.

If there is a method of projecting revenues generated by a promotion, then it is possible to estimate some kind of financial payout from the promotion. The difference between revenues and costs would be the return on investment, because the costs of the promotion are known. Figure 8.8 illustrates how to evaluate the financial payout of a coupon offer.

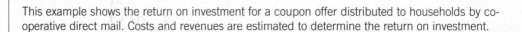

FIGURE 8.8   Evaluating the Financial Impact of a Sales Promotion Offer

This example shows the return on investment for a coupon offer distributed to households by co-operative direct mail. Costs and revenues are estimated to determine the return on investment.

Coupon Plan	
Face value of coupon	$1.00
Handling charge for retailer	$0.15
Handling charge for clearing house	$0.05
Distribution cost	$18.00/M
Distribution	2 million households
Printing cost (digest-sized ad with perforated coupon at bottom)	$12.00/M
Redemption rate (estimated)	5.0%
Retail price of product	$3.89
(Manufacturer receives about 65% of retail price when distributors' mark-ups are deducted.)	

Costs	Cost Calculation	Total	Grand Total
Distribution	2 000 000 x $18/M	$36 000	
Printing	2 000 000 x $12/M	$24 000	
Coupon redemption	2 000 000 x 0.05 x $1.20	$120 000	
Total cost		**$180 000**	**$180 000**
Cost per coupon redeemed	180 000/100 000	$1.80	

Revenues			
Per unit of revenue	$3.89 x.065	$2.53	
Total revenue*	**2 000 000 x 0.05 x 0.80 x $2.53**	**202 400**	**$202 400**
Return on investment			**$22 400**

*With any coupon offer, there is a risk of coupons being returned without a purchase being made. This is referred to as *misredemption*. In this example, the misredemption rate is 20%, hence the 0.80 factor in the revenue calculation equation.

A side benefit of consumer promotions is the collection of names. The names on entry forms from contests and order forms for premium offers and rebate offers can be added to the organization's database. Smart marketers seek additional information about consumers on promotion entry forms to develop more thorough customer profiles and determine who their primary target market is. Having more and better information about customers will assist in the development of customer relationship management programs.

For more insight into the role sales promotion strategies play in building market share, read the IMC Highlight: **Quick Serves Battle with Promotions**.

Quick Serves Battle with Promotions

There's a breakfast war going on between several big names in the quick-serve restaurant market. Breakfasts are the fastest growing segment of the industry, so the battle for market share means lots of trial incentives for consumers!

Burger King, a late entrant to the breakfast market, offered free breakfasts to get things rolling, but has retreated to something less expensive recently—free coffee every Friday. The free coffee makes sense, since the customer is bound to buy a food item at the same time.

McDonald's has been very active in the past two years, with periodic free coffee offers lasting at least a week or two. McDonald's coffee is good, and they want people to know about it. The target is a customer of Tim Hortons.

These types of promotions were originally cast as traffic builders during the recession, but the restaurants have continued with them because they have an impact on market share. In other words, satisfied customers return to the restaurant and buy meals at regular prices. Mission accomplished!

McDonald's is very pleased with the results of its free coffee offers. "Aggressive trial tactics have brought people in at record numbers and dramatically changed the way people look at our brand," says Louis Payette,

spokesperson for McDonald's. McDonald's objective is to change one's breakfast routine, that is, to get people to stop at McDonald's instead of Tim Hortons. Tasting McDonald's coffee for free helps make that happen.

Tim Hortons controls about 60 percent of the breakfast market, but it can't be complacent about its lofty position. McDonald's has very deep pockets and can keep the battle for market share alive!

At Tim Hortons, sales and profits declined marginally in the final quarter of 2010. Ironically, the company blamed the profit slide on the increased costs associated with its extremely popular "Roll Up the Rim" contest. Apparently, a beefed-up prize structure in which one in six people won a prize instead of the usual one in nine people was the culprit. There were a lot more happy customers, however!

Adapted from Jason Kirby, "Free Food Fight," *Maclean's*, June 13, 2011, p. 42.

Source: Mario Beauregard/CP Images.

CONSUMER PROMOTION EXECUTION

As indicated earlier, an organization will combine various consumer promotion activities with trade promotion activities so that there is balance between the pull and push strategies. It is that combination of pull and push that creates a synergistic effect in the marketplace. This section will discuss the various forms of consumer promotions that are often included in sales promotion plans.

The major types of consumer promotions include coupons, free samples, contests, cash rebates and related incentives, premiums, and loyalty programs. The popularity of the various alternatives varies from one industry to another. In the packaged goods industry, all alternatives are used, but coupons and free samples tend to be very popular. In the appliance and automobile industries, rebates are the preferred tactic. Automobile manufacturers frequently offer cash-back rebates and extremely low financing terms. Does anyone actually buy a car that doesn't have some kind of incentive offer attached to it? Let's analyze the various consumer promotions and determine the conditions for which each type of promotion is best suited.

COUPONS   **Coupons** are price-saving incentives offered to consumers to stimulate quick purchase of a designated product. The motivation for distributing the coupons is the same across all industries, although the value of the coupons varies considerably. Grocery coupons, for example, may only be valued at $0.75 or $1.00, while a trial coupon for a restaurant may be valued at 50 percent of the cost of the meal. See Figure 8.9 for an illustration.

coupon
A price-saving incentive offered to consumers to stimulate quick purchase of a specified product.

FIGURE
8.9

Coupons Are Commonly Used by Packaged Goods Brands to Stimulate Trial Purchases

Source: Karen Bleier/AFP/Getty Images.

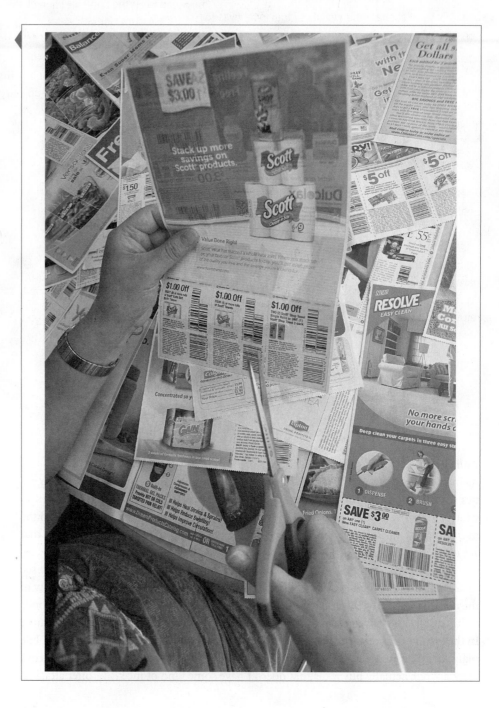

In packaged goods markets, coupons are the dominant form of sales promotion activity. According to a 2012 coupon report published in the United States, 80 percent of adult consumers said they used coupons regularly the year before. That figure was a significant increase from a year earlier. Apparently, coupon usage was positively influenced by the recession in 2008 and the weak recovery that followed. Consumers are looking for ways to save money on household expenditures.[4]

Data available from the Canadian Deals Association, which keeps records on coupon distribution and redemption rates in Canada, reveal that more than 6.8 billion coupons are distributed annually. A total of 86 million are returned, for an average redemption rate of 1.26 percent. The most popular categories for distributing coupons are food, personal care, and household products.[5]

Coupons are an excellent medium for achieving several marketing objectives at various stages of the product life cycle. First, coupons can encourage *trial purchase* among new users (and encourage competitive brand users to switch brands), and they can encourage *repeat purchases* by current users. In the latter situation, the coupon is a means of building brand loyalty.

The method by which the coupons are distributed to consumers is based on the objectives of the coupon offer. When a product is new or relatively new, trial purchase is the marketer's primary objective, so **media-delivered coupons** are popular. Options for delivery include **free-standing inserts (FSI)** in newspapers, magazines, direct mail, and in-store distribution. Websites such as Save.ca distribute coupons on behalf of manufacturers. Many companies distribute coupons to consumers who request them while visiting their website. Procter & Gamble firmly believes in the power of coupons and distributes them online at www.pgbrandsaver.com and www.pgeveryday.com.

The distribution of digital coupons online or by mobile devices is becoming very popular. For example, location-based check-in services such as Groupon and Foursquare bring special deals to consumers in real time on their mobile devices. Groupon uses the power of scale to negotiate sizeable discounts for shoppers and takes a cut of the revenues from retailers that participate. Groupon broadcasts the offer to its subscribers. Restaurants, spas, automotive repair shops, and other retailers have participated with Groupon and offered savings as high as 50 percent to attract new customers. On average, the retailer makes only about 25 percent of what it would normally make.[6] While this may not be financially attractive, the real objective is to get satisfied customers to return and pay regular prices.

Once a product moves into the late growth and early mature stages of its life cycle, a marketer's attention shifts from trial purchase to *repeat purchase*. By now there are many competing brands, all of which have a certain degree of consumer loyalty. As a defensive measure, it is important to reward current customers in one form or another. The package itself becomes an important medium for distributing coupons. The insertion of a coupon in or on a package, for example, is an incentive for a customer to keep buying the product.

Coupons contained inside a package are called **in-pack self-coupons**, because they are redeemable on the next purchase. Usually the face panel of the package makes mention of the coupon contained inside. A coupon that appears on the side panel or back panel is called an **on-pack self-coupon**. Another option is the **instantly redeemable coupon**, which is attached to the package in some fashion and can be removed immediately and used on the purchase of the product. Sometimes two different products collaborate on a coupon offer. To illustrate, Tetley includes an in-pack coupon for Christie cookies, and Christie places a Tetley tea coupon in its package. The relationship between the two brands is obvious. Each brand capitalizes on the other's consumer franchise in its effort to attract new users. This type of coupon is called a **cross-ruff** or **cross-coupon**.

media-delivered coupon
Coupon packaged with another medium, such as newspapers, magazines, direct mail, in-store distribution, and the Internet.

free-standing insert (FSI)
A booklet featuring coupons, refunds, contests, or other promotional advertising distributed by direct mail or with newspapers, magazines, or other delivery vehicles.

in-pack self-coupon
A coupon for the next purchase of a product that is packed inside the package or under a label.

on-pack self-coupon
A coupon that is printed on the outside of a package redeemable on the next purchase of the product.

instantly redeemable coupon
A removable coupon often located on the package or a store shelf that is redeemable on the current purchase of the product.

cross-ruff (cross-coupon)
A coupon packed in or with one product that is redeemable for another product. The product the coupon is packed with is the means of distributing the coupon.

redemption rate
The number of coupons returned expressed as a percentage of the number of coupons that were distributed.

The success or failure of a coupon offer is often determined by the redemption rate that is achieved. The **redemption rate** refers to the number of coupons returned to the manufacturer expressed as a percentage of the total coupons in distribution. If, for example, 1 million coupons were distributed and 45 000 were returned, the redemption rate would be 4.5 percent (45 000 divided by 1 000 000).

For budgeting purposes, it is important to know the average redemption rates for the various methods of delivering coupons. For example, Resolve Corporation research shows the average redemption rate for addressed direct mail coupons to be 6.5 percent, while the range can be anywhere from 1.9 percent to 22.6 percent. Magazine coupons have a range of 0.1 percent to 7.0 percent, with an average of only 0.8 percent. A key factor that influences the redemption rate and causes such variations in the rate is the perceived value of the offer in relation to the regular price of the product. If it is not a worthwhile incentive, it will not be acted upon.

PRODUCT SAMPLES

Product sampling is a powerful, yet expensive, way to promote a product. It is an effective strategy for encouraging trial purchase, but due to the costs involved, many manufacturers do not select this option. Traditionally, **free sample** programs involved the distribution of trial-size packages (small replicas of the real package) or actual-size packages. The latter option is obviously an expensive proposition.

free sample
Free distribution of a product to potential users.

In order to implement a sampling program, the marketer must appreciate the true benefit of such an offer. In a nutshell, it is unlike any other form of promotion in that it is the only alternative that will convert a trial user to a regular user solely on the basis of product satisfaction. Essentially, the marketing organization has eliminated any perceived risk the consumer may have about buying the product. That's a compelling reason for using samples. There are less expensive ways to implement sample programs, but they lack the impact of household distribution of free goods. A tried and true approach, particularly for food products, is in-store sampling. Costco uses this approach extensively by setting up sample stations at the ends of food aisles. A smart shopper can practically have a free lunch while shopping at Costco on a Saturday! When packaged goods grocery manufacturers do sample tasting in local supermarkets, they usually outsource the promotion to an independent company that specializes in this activity. Booths are strategically set up in stores to intercept customers as they shop. Refer to the image in Figure 8.10.

Larry Burns, co-chair of U.S.-based Promotion Marketing Association (PMA), says, "Targeted, well-thought-out sampling programs are the way to go in today's market." He cites research findings to back up his claim. From a survey conducted by the PMA, 94 percent of respondents view sampling as a way of increasing their comfort level when buying a product. A further 68 percent said they were "excited" about receiving the sample.[7]

When deciding whether to use a free sample program, a review of the benefits and drawbacks is essential. Samples are an expensive proposition due to product, package, and handling costs. In spite of these costs, samples rank second to coupons among marketers, so clearly the long-term benefit outweighs the short-term costs. The fact that samples eliminate the risk usually associated with new product purchases is a key benefit. On the downside, a sample is the fastest and surest way to kill an inferior product. In terms of timing, sample programs are best suited to the early stage of the product life cycle, when the primary objective is to achieve trial purchase. For certain, the delivery of samples adds excitement to any new product launch.

contest
A promotion that involves awarding cash or merchandise prizes to consumers when they purchase a specified product.

CONTESTS **Contests** are designed and implemented to create temporary excitement about a brand. For example, offering a grand prize such as an automobile, vacation, or

FIGURE
8.10

In-store Sampling Motivates Consumers to Purchase a Product

Source: Casey Rodgers/AP Images for Kellogg Company.

dream home can capture the consumer's imagination, even though the odds of winning are very low. Contests can be classified into two categories: sweepstakes and games. A **sweepstakes** is a chance promotion involving the giveaway of products and services such as cars, vacations, and sometimes cash. It's like a lottery—winners are randomly selected from the entries received. Typically, consumers enter a contest by filling in an entry form that is available at point of purchase, through print advertising, or at a website.

When companies are searching for the right sweepstakes idea, their objective is clear: It must light a fire under sales. In the world of promotional contests, experts generally agree that offering cash, cars, and travel are effective. PepsiCo broke away from this principle with a more community-minded contest called "Bring the Stanley Cup Home." What could be more Canadian than that? Three finalists in the contest had to create an online video that explained why they deserved votes to bring home a Stanley Cup Champion and the Stanley Cup. Canadians viewed the videos and voted online for their favourite finalist. "Spending the day with the Stanley Cup is something most people only dream about, and few actually get the experience," according to Kyle McMann, vice-president of Partnership Marketing, NHL. Julie Raheja-Perara, senior director of marketing, PepsiCo Beverages Canada, adds, "The participation of Canadians in this year's program (2011) has been overwhelming."[8] Among the Stanley Cup champions who visit the community with the cup are Mark Messier, Doug Gilmour, and Guy Carbonneau. Refer to the image in Figure 8.11.

Games are also based on chance, but can be more involving because they often require repeat visits for game pieces. This makes them a good device for encouraging continuity of purchase by consumers. McDonald's is somewhat of an expert in this area. Its "Monopoly" game is a regular feature in annual marketing plans. As the saying goes, "You have to play to win," and the only way to play is to go to a McDonald's restaurant.

An offshoot of the game contest is the **instant-win promotion**, which involves pre-determined, pre-seeded winning tickets in the overall fixed universe of tickets.

Tim Hortons' annual "Roll Up the Rim to Win" is an example of an instant-win promotion. While most of the prizes involve food products, it is the roster of bigger prizes that draws the consumer in. "Roll Up the Rim to Win" is an example of a longstanding successful promotion. It delivers a consistent theme and has a catchy and memorable

sweepstakes
A chance promotion involving the giveaway of products or services of value to randomly selected participants.

game (instant-win promotion)
A promotional contest that includes a number of pre-seeded winning tickets; instant-win tickets can be redeemed immediately.

FIGURE
8.11

PepsiCo's Contest Involving the Stanley Cup Was a Hit with Consumers

Source: Handout/PepsiCo Canada/ Newscom.

slogan. According to Tim Hortons, the promotion is now less of a promotion and more like a brand unto itself: "Roll Up the Rim to Win" is recognized as an entity, much like a product is. The promotion is an integral part of Tim Hortons' annual marketing plan. It increases sales by 10 to 15 percent during the promotion period.

Planning any kind of contest is a challenge. Most manufacturers rely on external suppliers to develop and implement a contest. In this regard, there is much upfront discussion with suppliers to ensure proper briefing on objectives and expectations. The success of a contest depends on the consumer's perception of the value and number of prizes being awarded and on the odds of winning. As well, the prizes must match the image of the product and the lifestyle of the target market. Contests that are combined with other purchase incentives provide added stimulus for consumers to take action. Refer to the illustration in Figure 8.12.

A cost–benefit analysis should be done prior to getting involved with a contest. In terms of benefit, a contest is a good device for achieving repeat purchase objectives. A well-designed contest encourages customers to come back or buy more frequently. By returning or buying more goods, consumers exhibit a certain degree of loyalty. As such, contests are ideal promotions for products in the mature stage of the product life cycle. They can boost brand sales in a time of need.

On the cost side of things, a contest requires a significant investment in media advertising to create awareness and interest. Contests such as "Roll Up the Rim to Win" are

FIGURE
8.12

An Example of a Promotion that Combines a Coupon and Contest Communicated by In-Store Shelf Pads

Source: Photo by Keith J. Tuckwell.

supported by multimedia advertising campaigns. A combination of media advertising and in-store promotional materials tends to be effective. When the cost of prizes and the cost of having an external organization implement the contest are factored in, the amount required for a contest promotion can be a sizeable portion of a marketing budget.

Legal issues are another concern for marketers when they get involved in contests. The manager must be familiar with some of the basic laws that govern contests in Canada. Section 189 of the *Criminal Code* and sections 52 and 59 of the *Competition Act* regulate most contests in Canada, and there are certain fairly standardized rules and regulations for what information must be communicated to participants. The following information must be clearly conveyed:

- The number of prizes and the value of each.
- The odds of winning, if known.
- Whether a skill-testing question will be administered.
- Whether facsimiles are acceptable in the case of a sweepstakes.
- How to enter, and what proof of purchase is required.
- The contest's closing date.

For some tips on planning an effective contest, see Figure 8.13.

REBATES   A **rebate** is a predetermined amount of money returned directly to the customer by the manufacturer after the purchase has been made. It is an incentive to get consumers to buy in greater volume during the promotion period. Initially, rebates were the promotion of choice among packaged goods marketers, but they are now an integral

rebate
A predetermined amount of money returned directly to customers by the manufacturer after the purchase has been made.

Tips for Planning an Effective Contest

> Effective contests do not happen by chance. They are carefully planned to spark interest and action, and to achieve specific marketing objectives. Here are some pointers from those in the business:
>
> - Choose prizes that spark wish-fulfillment fantasies.
> - Give consumers a decent chance of winning (low odds of winning create ill will).
> - Plan an engaging media component to drive consumer awareness and generate publicity.
> - Keep the company name in the contest moniker (again for positive press).
> - Use strategic partnerships; co-brand the contest to leverage each other's equity.
> - Make sure contest rules are clear and unambiguous.
> - Ensure that fulfillment (awarding of prizes) occurs quickly.
> - If it ain't broke, don't fix it! Stay with a successful contest if it's producing desired results.
>
> Source: Adapted from "Tips for Creating Killer Contests," Special Report on Premiums and Incentives, *Strategy*, August 26, 2002, p. 24.

element of marketing programs for durable goods such as automobiles, major appliances, and consumer electronics.

The most common type of rebate is the ***single-purchase refund***, in which consumers receive a portion of their money back for the purchase of a specified product. Such an offer is one method of achieving trial purchases. Other variations of rebates include making an offer according to an escalating schedule. For example, an offer could be structured as follows: Buy one and get $1.00 back, buy two and get $2.00 back, and buy three and get $5.00 back. The nature of the offer encourages consumers to buy three items at one time, thus helping achieve multiple purchase objectives.

Though many people buy a product because of the possibility of a rebate, many rebates go uncollected due to the hassle of filling out the form and mailing it in with the proof of purchase documentation a manufacturer requires. This phenomenon is referred to as **slippage**, when the consumer collects labels but fails to follow through and request the refund, even for a refund with a $100 value. Time-pressed consumers often forget about the rebate offer. Technology at point of purchase is now eliminating problems associated with slippage. Once a transaction is complete in a retail store, for example, it can transfer appropriate information about the customer to the source of the rebate offer.

In recent years, incentives and rebates have become commonplace among automobile manufacturers. Automobile companies trying to recover from the recent recession offered "cash back" rebates as high as $5000 on cars and $8000 on trucks. The rebates move the cars but place a financial strain on the company. Consumers are adapting to rebates so well, it seems they won't buy a new car without some kind of financial incentive. In the long term, this promotion tactic is not in the best interests of the industry.

Rebate offers are best suited to products in the mature stage of the product life cycle. As indicated above, they are a good incentive for encouraging multiple purchases of inexpensive packaged goods products. Encouraging multiple purchases or building frequency of purchases is a common objective for mature products. At this stage in the life cycle, maintaining customer loyalty is critical. Apart from the rebates offered by automobile companies, which tend to be very high, a rebate promotion is not that expensive to implement. Since it is current users who tend to take advantage of rebate offers, advertising support can be confined to the package and various in-store opportunities, such as shelf cards and product displays.

PREMIUM OFFERS   A **premium** is an additional item given free, or greatly discounted, to induce purchase of the primary brand. The goal of a premium is to provide added value to tempt consumers to buy.

slippage
A situation in which a consumer collects labels in a promotion offer but fails to follow through and request the refund.

premium
An additional item given free, or greatly discounted, to induce purchase of the primary brand.

FIGURE
8.14

On-pack Premiums Encourage Impulse Purchases at Point of Purchase

Source: Photo by Keith J. Tuckwell.

Premiums are offered to consumers several ways: as a mail-in, by sending in proofs of purchase so the item can be delivered by mail; as an in-pack or on-pack promotion, where the item is placed inside or attached to a package; by an order form that is usually available at point of purchase; or by electronic registration at a website. Packaged goods companies frequently use their packages to distribute free premiums. Refer to the illustration in Figure 8.14. In this figure, Listerine offers an on-pack premium, a bonus item attached to the bottle of Listerine.

Many marketers firmly believe that there is something to be said for offering a tangible, quality gift, which can surprise the consumer and build long-term equity through association. Others see the benefits of premiums as largely misleading, citing large increases in sales followed by an equally large tumble once the giveaway ends. Both Molson and Labatt experienced this feast-or-famine phenomenon when they packed everything from golf balls, to T-shirts, to ball caps in their beer cases. Both companies found the promotions expensive, and rather than create loyalty, they simply encouraged drinkers to switch brands constantly.[9]

An offshoot of a premium offer is the **bonus pack**. The traditional bonus pack offers the consumer more for less. For example, a brand offers a package size that gives the consumer 20 percent more product for the regular price. Another option is to bundle a product in pairs and offer a deal like "Buy One, Get One Free." Offers like these, if implemented properly, will attract new users and reward current users. If done wrong, they can cheapen the image or value perception of the brand.

Marketing managers tend to rank premiums lower in terms of popularity, but they do offer some tangible benefits. They achieve several marketing objectives: They can increase the quantity of brand purchases made by consumers during the promotion period; they help to retain current customers, therefore building brand loyalty; and they provide a merchandising tool to encourage display activity in stores. A good premium offer will help differentiate one brand from another at a crucial point in time, the time when consumers decide which brand to buy.

bonus pack
The temporary offering of a larger package size (for example, 20 percent more) for the same price as the regular size.

LOYALTY PROGRAMS

loyalty program (frequent buyer program)
A program that offers consumers a small bonus, such as points or play money, each time they make a purchase; the bonus accumulates and can be redeemed for merchandise or some other benefit.

Loyalty programs take the short-term premium offer a step further—they encourage long-term brand loyalty. How many loyalty cards do you have in your wallet? It seems that consumers are collecting points to obtain something for free years from now. In the meantime, we keep going back to the loyalty sponsor to earn more points. By definition, a **loyalty program** (**frequent buyer program**) offers consumers a small bonus, such as points or play money, each time they make a purchase. The bonus accumulates and can be redeemed for merchandise or some other benefit at a later date.

Shoppers Drug Mart has a frequent buyer program that is updated electronically. Member customers swipe their Shoppers Optimum card each time they make a purchase. Shoppers can cross-reference transaction data electronically, and tailor offers and services to specific customers. One such offer included free samples of a variety of brand-name grooming and personal care products. These samples were distributed by mail to a select group of Shoppers Drug Mart customers. As discussed elsewhere in this book, the true benefit of a loyalty program is the information it collects for database marketing. See the illustration in Figure 8.15.

The Intercontinental Group of Hotels, which operates in all price and quality segments of the lodging industry, has a program called "Priority Club Rewards." In this program the customer can redeem accumulated points on merchandise such as coffee makers, food processors, and small consumer electronic items, or the points can be used for hotel rooms and special travel packages sponsored by the hotel chain and its airline partners.

Perhaps the longest-running and most successful loyalty program in Canada is Canadian Tire money. Canadian Tire rewards regular shoppers who pay by cash or Canadian Tire credit card with Canadian Tire money, worth up to 4 percent of the value of the purchase. Now at an advanced stage, the program allows customers to collect virtual money at Canadian Tire's website. Canadian Tire money represents the true essence of a loyalty program: Customers can actually receive something for free. In contrast, a program like AIR MILES takes considerable time before the consumer can get even the smallest of rewards. For insight into its program, read the IMC Highlight: **Canadian Tire Money Keeps Customers Happy.**

FIGURE
8.15

An Illustration of a Rewards Loyalty Program at Shoppers Drug Mart/Pharmaprix

Source: Courtesy of Shoppers Drug Mart.

Canadian Tire Money Keeps Customers Happy

Canadian Tire money . . . a simple concept. Yet it is the cornerstone of Canadian Tire's marketing mix. Canadian Tire money is a most successful and popular customer reward program, with a 90 percent redemption and participation level. It is the very heart of what Canadian Tire stands for in today's competitive marketplace.

The program has evolved since it was introduced in 1958, but stays true to its original premise: reward good customers for their loyalty! To keep customers truly happy, the program lets customers determine what their reward will be. Unlike many other loyalty programs that are much more complex and only allow customers to select rewards from predetermined merchandise, Canadian Tire's program allows customers to claim their reward anytime and on anything the store sells. That formula still works today. Collecting Canadian Tire money represents a successful promotion that people have come to know, expect, and love. It encourages people to come back to the store.

Canadian Tire retains a focus on its loyalty program because the money is an important element of the customers' shopping experience. From a marketing perspective, it allows the company to differentiate itself and provides immense competitive advantage. For the record, Canadian Tire is the most-shopped store in Canada: 90 percent of Canadians shop there. And the Canadian Tire brand is one of the top five most recognized brands in Canada.

Canadian Tire money actually feels like money, and it should because it is printed on paper with the same rag content as real money. The "money" is extremely popular among older customers, who feel deep connections to the currency. Moving forward, Canadian Tire wants to bring its rewards program into the digital era so that it can do what loyalty programs are designed to do: Track customer purchase patterns to help customize marketing and select products for shelves.

Canadian Tire is presently testing an electronic loyalty card, "The Canadian Tire Money Advantage" card, in Nova Scotia. To encourage Nova Scotia consumers to switch to the electronic card, the discount incentives are much higher. Nova Scotia customers will get 1 percent back on their purchases with the Advantage card (instead of 4 percent with paper money) and 3 percent back if they use Canadian Tire's Options MasterCard (instead of the present 2 percent). If the test is successful, the long-term plan would be to phase out paper money gradually.

As a loyalty program, and regardless of whether it's paper money or electronic money, the Canadian Tire rewards program is successful because of its simplicity. It offers instant rewards to its customers, and it keeps them coming back!

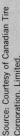

Source: Courtesy of Canadian Tire Corporation, Limited.

Adapted from Marina Strauss, "Canadian Tire's 'Funny Money' Dilemma," *The Globe and Mail*, February 16, 2012, p. B3; and Sharon Adams, "Canadian Tire Got the Ball Rolling," *Loyalty & Its Rewards*, supplement in the *National Post*, April 26, 2007, p. IS6.

Given that our wallets are bulging with loyalty cards, it is safe to say that loyalty programs are popular with consumers. In fact, a recent study revealed that 86 percent of Canadians participate in at least one loyalty program, while the average Canadian household is active in more than nine programs. Small wonder that Canadian companies have jumped on the rewards bandwagon as they seek to shape customers' spending habits.[10] Offering a rewards program does add to the costs of doing business, but, as it turns out, the cost of points and rewards are small compared to the potential profit of getting customers to buy more often or buy more expensive goods, where margins are higher.

A plastic card can function as both a loyalty card and a gift card. Gift cards are a booming market. Presently, the gift card market is estimated to be worth $6 billion. Card buyers benefit from having a convenient option for gift giving. Retailers benefit through what is known as float and slippage. **Float** refers to the fact that the issuer of the card receives the money without offering goods or services right away. **Slippage** (often called **breakage** as well) refers to those cards that go unredeemed; it is estimated that 10 to 15 percent of cards are not redeemed—easy money in the pocket of the card seller![11] Retailers like gift cards because they could be in the hands of a brand-new customer, a starting point of a long-term relationship.

The true benefit of a loyalty card program for the organization is the information it is collecting about customers. Members of loyalty programs voluntarily submit profiles with their age, gender, address, and consumer preferences. This information can be combined with transaction data. When the data is mined at a later date, it can be extremely useful as organizations move toward individualized marketing programs. Once an organization starts a loyalty program, it is an ongoing program.

TRADE PROMOTION EXECUTION

Trade customers are the link between manufacturers and consumers, and in Canada they have incredible control in many markets. In the grocery industry, for example, the combination of two large wholesale/retail operations, Loblaw and Sobeys, controls more than half of all food store sales. In the hardware market, the combination of Canadian Tire and Home Hardware controls a significant portion of volume. Distributors make money by selling your products, but they are also in business to sell anyone's products. Consequently, their loyalty to any supplier can waver if they do not receive trade promotion offers they feel they deserve.

Simply stated, the trade looks for the best offers from suppliers and makes buying decisions accordingly. As with consumer promotions, trade promotions must be designed to deliver the highest possible value to the trade while costing as little as possible for the manufacturer. Manufacturers have a variety of trade promotion offers to choose from when developing a promotion plan. Typically, the offers work together to generate a high degree of impact during the promotion period. This section explores the various trade promotion options.

TRADE ALLOWANCES   A **trade allowance** is a temporary price reduction that encourages larger purchases by distributors. It can be offered several ways: a percentage reduction from the list price, a predetermined dollar amount off the list price, or free goods. A free goods offer may be something like "Buy 10 cases and get 1 free."

In addition to encouraging larger volume purchases, the manufacturer would like to see a portion of the allowance devoted to lowering the price of the product at retail for a short period. In the grocery industry, products are commonly offered on sale for one week. The manufacturer absorbs the discount offered to consumers. Trade allowances can be deducted from the invoice immediately, and in such cases are called *off-invoice allowances*. Or they can be offered on the basis of a *bill-back*, in which case the manufacturer keeps a record of all purchases shipped to the distributor and, when the deal period expires, reimburses the distributor for the allowances it earned.

PERFORMANCE ALLOWANCES   A **performance allowance** is a discount that encourages the distributor to perform a merchandising function on behalf of the manufacturer. As indicated above, a trade allowance helps lower prices, but additional incentives are

---

float
Money received by the issuer of a gift card without yet having offered any goods or services.

slippage (breakage)
Gift cards that go unredeemed.

trade allowance
A temporary price reduction that encourages larger purchases by distributors.

performance allowance
A discount offered by a manufacturer that encourages a distributor to perform a merchandising function on behalf of the manufacturer.

required to make the promotion a real success. It is common for the manufacturer to request automatic distribution of goods to retail stores, displays in stores, and a mention of the sale price in the retailer's weekly advertising flyer. The additional funds provided in the performance allowance help cover the distributor's costs of implementing these activities. The distributor may or may not comply with all of the manufacturer's requests, but some kind of deal is negotiated and agreed to. Before paying the allowance, the manufacturer requires proof of performance by the distributor.

Given this information, you can now appreciate that many of the advertising flyers and in-store promotional activities that are undertaken by large retail chain stores are actually subsidized by the manufacturers' brands involved in the promotions. The costs of trade promotions are significant and take a considerable portion of a brand's marketing budget each year.

COOPERATIVE ADVERTISING ALLOWANCES   A **cooperative advertising allowance**, or **co-op allowance** as it is commonly referred to, is a fund allocated to pay for a portion of a distributor's advertising. Marketing organizations often pay a percentage (often 50 percent or more) of the distributor's ad cost, provided the marketer's brand is featured prominently.

> **cooperative advertising allowance (co-op allowance)**
> The sharing of advertising costs by suppliers and retailers or by several retailers.

To maximize the effectiveness of allowances offered to the trade, the above allowances are frequently combined to develop an integrated promotion plan. If a bigger plan is in place, the trade promotion plan will be integrated with consumer promotions and brand advertising. Combining the allowances is attractive to the retailers. The financial rewards will be much greater, and the funds available are sufficient to support their own advertising and merchandising activities. Financial incentives are a great motivator among distributors.

DEALER PREMIUMS   A **dealer premium** is an incentive offered to a distributor by a manufacturer to encourage the special purchase of a product or to secure additional merchandising support from a retailer. Premiums are usually offered in the form of merchandise and distributed by sales representatives of the company offering the premium. Some common premiums include golfing equipment, cameras, audio equipment, and leisure clothing. The offering of premiums is a controversial issue. Some distributors absolutely forbid their buyers to accept them. They argue that the buyer is the only beneficiary and that the buying organization might be purchasing more goods than it really needs. Many believe the practice of offering premiums, often referred to as "payola," to buyers is unethical. However, dealings between sellers and buyers sometimes occur under the table.

> **dealer premium**
> An incentive offered to a distributor to encourage the special purchase of a product or to secure additional merchandising support from the distributor.

An offshoot of a premium offer is a **spiff**. Next time you're in a sporting goods store, ask yourself why that retail sales representative recommended an expensive pair of Reebok (or any other popular brand) running shoes over the others. It could be that the manufacturer encouraged the sales representative to promote its brand by providing some kind of incentive. The retail sales representative stands to gain if more Reebok products are sold. Such a practice is common in product categories where consumers have a tendency to ask for recommendations. Since there are so many good running shoe brands to choose from, you value the salesperson's advice, but you may also play right into their hand by doing so!

> **spiff**
> An incentive offered to retail salespeople to encourage them to promote a specified brand of goods to customers.

Clearly, the use of premiums and spiffs achieves certain marketing objectives. Many companies employ them when they are facing unusual circumstances, such as when trying to meet year-end sales objectives and it's a touch-and-go situation. Compared to other forms of sales promotion, though, they are not the kinds of activities that will be used regularly.

COLLATERAL MATERIAL   The role of the sales representative cannot be underestimated, particularly in business-to-business selling situations. Companies invest significant sums in programs that tell consumers about their goods and services but, as indicated above, it is also important to invest in programs that help push the product through the channel. Sales representatives need selling resources, and that's where collateral material comes into play. **Collateral materials** are visual aids that are specific to special promotions or simply ongoing aids for the variety of products being sold. Collateral materials include price lists, catalogues, sales brochures, pamphlets, specification sheets, and digital sales aids.

collateral materials
Visual aids used by sales representatives in sales presentations, such as price lists, sales brochures, and digital materials.

DEALER DISPLAY MATERIAL   As indicated earlier, one of the objectives of trade promotion is to encourage merchandising support from retail distributors. The manufacturer can assist in this area by providing **dealer display material** or **point-of-purchase material** as it is often called. Dealer display material includes posters, shelf talkers (mini-posters that hang or dangle from store shelves), channel strips (narrow bands that fit into the side of a store shelf), and advertising pads (tear-off sheets that hang from pads attached to shelves).

dealer display (point-of-purchase) material
Temporary display material placed in retail stores that advertises a product and encourages impulse purchasing.

Material of a more permanent nature includes display shippers (shipping cases that convert to display stands when opened and erected properly) and permanent display racks. One of the problems with display material is that it frequently goes to waste. In many retail outlets, permission to erect displays must be granted by the store manager and sometimes by the head office of the retailer. Some retailers do not allow manufacturer-supplied display material at all. To be effective, displays must be erected in a visible location. The retailer makes the location decision, and it may not be to the liking of the manufacturer. A poor location will diminish the intended impact of the display. Refer to Figure 8.16 for an illustration of a display shipper.

trade show
An event that allows a company to showcase its products to a captive audience and generate leads.

TRADE SHOWS   **Trade shows** are an effective way for a company to introduce new products to the marketplace. There is no better opportunity to showcase something special than at a trade show. Where else will a manufacturer find as many customers, all in one place, actively and willingly seeking product information? All industries seem to have trade shows, and in many cases they move around the country to make it more convenient for prospective customers to visit. Depending on the nature of the show, it may attract consumers, trade distributors, or both.

The automobile industry and the recreation and leisure products industry are among the largest users of trade shows. Here, all manufacturers gather to show their latest models (see Figure 8.17). Auto shows are magnets for the media, so they generate all kinds of positive press for the participating companies. From a manufacturer's perspective, a trade show provides an opportunity to develop a prospect list that the sales force can follow up on. When visiting a trade show, customers leave a trail of valuable information about themselves, which can be quickly added to a database for analysis and use later. The very nature of a trade show, however, requires considerable planning by participants, along with a considerable financial investment. There is a simple rule of thumb about participating in trade shows: "If you are going to do it, do it right." It's a great opportunity to outshine the competition.

Additional Considerations for Sales Promotion Planning

Sales promotions are not usually the focal point of a brand's marketing communications strategies but, as mentioned above, play a complementary role in achieving certain objectives. Therefore, sales promotions must be carefully planned so they effectively integrate with advertising, public relations, and any other marketing communications

FIGURE
8.16

Temporary In-store Displays Draw Attention to a Product and Encourage Impulse Purchases

Source: Steve White/CP Images.

plans. Decisions must be made regarding how frequently promotions are offered, what types of promotions will have a positive effect on brand image, and how they will build brand value in the long term. Let's look at each situation briefly.

FREQUENCY OF PROMOTIONS

How frequently should a brand offer sales promotions? All kinds of factors influence this decision: the type of product, the activities of the competition, the stage of the product life cycle the brand is in, and the receptiveness of customers toward promotions. A theme running throughout this chapter is that promotions are complementary in nature, so they should never disrupt the flow of regular and more dominant communications

FIGURE 8.17 Trade Shows Bring the Customer to the Marketer

Source: Courtesy of Toronto Sportsmen's Show.

activities. There is a risk that too many promotions could cheapen the image of a brand—short-term gain for long-term pain! In general, coupon activity can be implemented more frequently than cash refunds, premium offers, and contests. It is less disruptive to the regular message expressed through media advertising.

BRAND IMAGE AND PROMOTIONS

Much of the discussion about promotion strategies in this chapter mentioned lowering prices so that consumers get a better deal. In the short run, such a strategy brings positive results. However, if this practice becomes frequent, consumers will perceive the sale price to be more of a regular price. In the long term, such a practice will hurt the brand's image and lower profit margins. Domestic automobile manufacturers are facing this dilemma right now. Advertising is so focused on rebates and low financing packages that much less time is devoted to building an image, the former priority of these companies. That said, these manufacturers have to deal with the economic realities that exist today.

BUILDING BRAND EQUITY

The cumulative force of all marketing communications is a key factor in building brand equity. Marketers must be aware that sales promotions are a rather chaotic sequence of deals and events that create noise in the marketplace. They are not a sustaining message. It is preferable to adopt a view about promotions that will pay attention to long-term brand values and a consistent approach that will build good relationships with the trade and consumers. A few of the promotions mentioned in this chapter do just that. Among them are Tim Hortons' "Roll Up the Rim to Win", Shoppers Drug Mart's Optimum Card loyalty program, and Canadian Tire's reward money. Promotions like these become a positive part of the brand's heritage and reinforce relationships with customers.

SUMMARY

Sales promotions are incentives offered to consumers and the trade to encourage more immediate and larger purchases. Strategically, consumer promotions are designed to help pull a product through the channel of distribution, while trade promotions help push a product through the channel of distribution. A good sales promotion plan usually balances between pull and push.

Sales promotion planning involves a series of steps or decisions. After an assessment of the situation is made, specific objectives and strategies are established and the appropriate offers or incentives are determined. The plan must also consider fulfillment obligations at the back end, and a means of assessing the effectiveness of the plan must be in place.

A key to a successful sales promotion plan lies in how it is integrated with other marketing communications strategies. For certain, sales promotion strategies must be integrated with advertising strategies. Because sales promotions are short term in nature, they often become the focus of the advertising message while the promotion is in place. When the overall plan is implemented, advertising creates awareness for the promotion, while in-store displays and websites provide additional details.

Some specific objectives of consumer promotions are to achieve trial purchase by new users and repeat and multiple purchases by current users. The types of activities commonly used to achieve these objectives include coupons, free samples, contests, rebates, premium offers, and loyalty programs.

Specific marketing objectives of trade promotions are to secure new listings and distribution, build volume on a preplanned cyclical basis, and encourage merchandising support at point of purchase. Trade promotion activities that help achieve these objectives include trade allowances, performance allowances, cooperative advertising funds, dealer premiums, point-of-purchase display materials, collateral materials, and trade shows.

The impact of sales promotions is short term in nature, and therefore promotions complement other integrated marketing communications strategies. As such, sales promotions should not disrupt regular brand advertising. They must be integrated into advertising strategies to enhance the overall impact on consumers and trade customers. When planning promotions, a manager should guard against running them too frequently so as to not harm the image of the brand. A good sales promotion concept will fit with the brand's image and help build brand equity.

KEY TERMS

REVIEW QUESTIONS

1. What is the difference between a pull strategy and a push strategy, and how do sales promotions complement both strategies?

2. What are the primary objectives of a consumer promotion plan?

3. What are the primary objectives of a trade promotion plan?

4. Briefly explain how sales promotion strategies are integrated with advertising strategies. Why is such integration essential?

5. In sales promotion planning, what is meant by logistics and fulfillment?

6. Briefly describe the following consumer promotion terms:
   a) redemption rate
   b) in-pack self-coupon
   c) cross-ruff
   d) instant-win promotions
   e) slippage
   f) bonus pack

7. What types of coupon distribution are appropriate for the early stages of the product life cycle? What distribution is appropriate for the later stages? Why?

8. What are the benefits and drawbacks of a free sample offer?

9. What elements contribute to the success of a contest offer?

10. What is the objective of a consumer premium offer, and when is the best time to implement such an offer?

11. What are the benefits and drawbacks of loyalty promotions?

12. How do trade allowances, performance allowances, and cooperative advertising funds complement each other when implementing a trade promotion plan?

13. Briefly describe the following trade promotion terms:
    a) spiff
    b) dealer premium
    c) collateral materials
    d) point-of-purchase material

DISCUSSION AND APPLICATION QUESTIONS

1. Assume you are a brand manager launching a new snack food or confectionary product. What balance would you recommend among consumer promotion, trade promotion, and media advertising? What specific sales promotion activities would you recommend? Justify your choices.

2. Conduct some secondary research on consumer and trade promotion budgets and spending patterns in various industries. Is there undue pressure placed on marketing organizations to spend more on trade promotions and less on other activities? Does the situation vary from one industry to another?

3. A common criticism of consumer premium offers is that they only encourage temporary brand switching.

Once the offer is over, consumers switch back to their regular brand. Therefore, in the long run, the promotion will not contribute to sales objectives. Conduct some secondary research on this issue and determine if such a criticism is valid.

4. Consumers could be suffering from "loyalty promotion fatigue." Conduct some secondary research on loyalty promotions to find out how organizations view loyalty promotions. Do loyalty promotions provide real benefits to consumers and the sponsor? What are the elements that make a loyalty promotion a success?

5. What forms of sales promotion are best suited for the following brands? (Hint: you may want to consider

the life cycle stage the brand is in). Justify your position.

   a) Secret deodorant
   b) Quaker Chewy Granola Bars
   c) Blue Mountain Resort (or any similar ski or golf resort)
   d) Valvoline motor oil
   e) Gatorade
   f) New Balance running shoes

6. Evaluate the sales promotion strategies employed by Canadian Tire. What marketing and marketing communications objectives do they meet? How effective are the programs? How does Canadian Tire integrate sales promotions with other components of its marketing communications plan?

7. Evaluate the sales promotion strategies used by Tim Hortons. What marketing and marketing communications objectives do they meet? How does Tim Hortons integrate sales promotions with other components of the marketing communications mix?

8. Automobile manufacturers have used rebate programs for years to provide consumers with an incentive to buy (and buy now!). Is this an effective sales promotion strategy? Conduct some secondary research on rebate incentives and develop some kind of cost–benefit analysis for using this form of promotion.

ENDNOTES

1. "Asking Canadians," *Strategy*, March 2008, p. 12.

2. Evra Taylor, "Harley-Davidson Rides Out with 'Live the Dream' Promotion," *Marketing*, April 13, 2012, www.marketingmag.ca/uncategorized/harley-davidson-says-let's-rumble-with'live-the-dream'-promotion-50296.

3. Wayne Mouland, "Coupon Convenience," *Marketing*, May 9, 2005, p. 16.

4. Jack Neff, "Coupons Are Hot, But Are They a Bargain for Brands?" *Advertising Age*, July 11, 2011, p. 10.

5. "Coupon Redemption Canada: Some Interesting Data," Canadian Deals Association, www.canadiandealsassociation.com/coupon-redemption-in-canada-some-interesting-data.

6. Daniel Lyons, "Click and Save," *Newsweek*, November 29, 2010, p. 25.

7. Geoff Dennis, "Sampling Growth Spurs Creativity," *Strategy*, May 20, 2002, pp. 1, 10.

8. "Which Lucky Canadian Hockey Fan will Bring Home a Stanley Cup Champion and the Stanley Cup?" press release, PepsiCo Canada., www.pepsico.ca.

9. John Heinzl, "Beer Firms Rethink Giveaways," *The Globe and Mail*, March 3, 2003, p. B5.

10. Chris Atchison, "What Small Businesses Can Learn from Shoppers' Optimum Program," *The Globe and Mail*, August 24, 2011, m.theglobeandmail.com/report-on-business/small-business/sb-marketing/what-small-businesses-can-learn-from-shoppers-optimum-program/article4258806.

11. Rob Carrick, "Not All Gift Cards Are Created Equal," *The Globe and Mail*, December 1, 2009, m.theglobeandmail.com/globe-investor/personal-finance/not-all-gift-cards-are-created-equal/article-4310949.

Public Relations

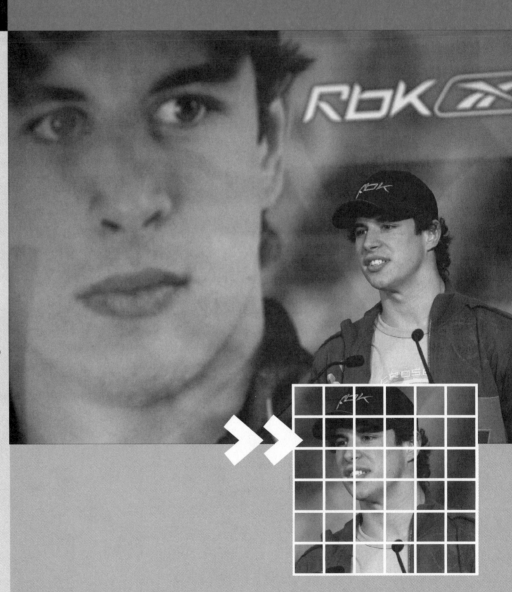

Nathan Denette/CP Images

Learning Objectives

After studying this chapter, you will be able to

1. Identify and assess the various roles of public relations communications in achieving marketing and business objectives

2. Describe the various steps in public relations planning

3. Identify and evaluate various public relations execution techniques for potential application in public relations plans

4. Identify and assess the various techniques that evaluate and measure the impact of public relations strategies

Public relations (PR) are an often misunderstood form of marketing communications. The term often conjures up negative images of a company trying to cover something up or trying to put its own spin on a situation. Certainly, with all the news coverage that companies receive when they are in trouble, there is some truth to such perceptions. But public relations can have a very positive impact on a brand or company's performance, and are responsible for communicating all kinds of positive information.

The theme of this book deals with how messages from various disciplines in communications are integrated and how, whatever the discipline, all must work together to give the consumer a unified message. In fact, with the media landscape and technology transforming the way in which consumers receive information, many PR experts believe public relations should be at the forefront of the communications mix. With social media, public relations communications can move from earned media (the traditional press coverage they still desire) to shared media (where consumers interact and exchange information they find interesting with others).

Technology and social media are changing the nature of public relations practice. It is taking off as a profession! Organizations are now using new job titles such as "strategists" and "connectors" to reflect how things are changing. Public relations now play a key role in building brand image and brand equity.

In the age of heightened competition and advancing electronic technology, marketers are looking for multiple solutions to brand building. This position further suggests the need for the integration of various forms of marketing communications. To rely on any one medium or channel of marketing communications could be harmful, since consumers' media habits are constantly changing. An organization must embrace all communications channels in order to build better relationships with consumers and to achieve its business objectives.

Defining Public Relations

Public relations are a form of communication that is primarily directed toward gaining public understanding and acceptance. Unlike advertising, which is a form of communication paid for by the company, public relations use publicity that does not necessarily involve payment. Public relations communications appear in the news media and, as such, offer a legitimacy that advertising does not have. Recently, companies have been using public relations to extol the merits of a product by assisting in new product launches or reporting eventful occurrences of the product. This form of communications is often referred to as marketing public relations or marketing PR.

public relations
A form of communication designed to gain public understanding and acceptance.

The practice of public relations is used to build rapport with the various publics a company, individual, or organization may have. These publics are either internal or external. **Internal publics** involve those with whom the organization communicates regularly and include employers, distributors, suppliers, shareholders, and customers. **External publics** are more distant and are communicated with less frequently. They include the media, governments, prospective shareholders, the financial community, and community organizations.

The goal of public relations is to conduct communications in such a way that an organization builds an open, honest, and constructive relationship with its various publics. In comparison to advertising, public relations communications are not controlled by the organization. Instead, the media determine what is said about the company, regardless of what information the company provides. In other words, the media act as a "filter" for the information an organization releases.

In the age of social media, an organization can actually bypass the traditional media channel and post information directly online through Facebook, YouTube, and Twitter. That said, it takes a significant investment in time, people, and money for an organization to keep information fresh in the social media. As well, organizations must adapt to the reality that consumers will comment on brand communications. A shift in who controls the message is taking place.

The Role of Public Relations

One of the largest automobile companies in the world saw the value in good public relations in 2010. That year, Toyota had to recall 4 million vehicles in North America because of sticky gas pedals. The recall would certainly damage Toyota's reputation as the leader in automotive quality, and, needless to say, Toyota experienced much negative publicity in the media initially. After carefully analyzing the situation, Toyota implemented a well-thought-out public relations plan over a long period. The plan helped re-establish its quality position in the minds of consumers. Toyota's case demonstrates how public relations communications fit into an organization's overall marketing communications plans.

As a management function, public relations will help an organization anticipate and interpret public opinion that will have an impact on its actions. PR will also provide the means to plan and implement communications strategies that are in the best interest of the organization—for example, to devise communications intended to change public attitudes if necessary. Good PR will help launch new products, and create awareness and excitement for them, just like advertising can, and at a much lower cost. In an era where marketing budgets are being squeezed, that's music to an executive's ears!

The role of public relations is varied, but generally falls into six key categories: corporate communications; reputation management; product publicity; product placement, branded content, and product seeding; community relations; and fundraising. The diversity of this list indicates how public relations can be company oriented or product oriented. Let's examine each category in more detail.

CORPORATE COMMUNICATIONS

A good public relations plan strives to maximize communications in an unpaid manner, but there are times when paid communications are necessary. Such communications may be in the form of **corporate advertising**, a paid form of advertising designed to convey a favourable image of a company to its various publics.

---

internal publics
The publics with which an organization communicates regularly; can include employees, distributors, suppliers, shareholders, and customers.

external publics
Those publics that are distant from an organization and are communicated with less frequently.

corporate advertising
Advertising (paid for) designed to convey a favourable image of a company among its various publics.

Corporate advertising shows how the resources of the organization resolve customers' problems by promoting goodwill or by demonstrating a sense of social responsibility. The Good Purpose survey conducted by global PR firm Edelman shows that Canadians support brands that have a societal purpose associated with them. Some 70 percent of Canadians are more likely to recommend a brand that supports a good cause than one that doesn't.[1] Domtar Canada shows how it integrates economic progress with environmental issues, often a delicate challenge for a company in the pulp and paper business (see Figure 9.1). This advertisement is an example of social responsibility marketing and reflects an attitude of corporate conscience that anticipates and responds to social problems.

A company can also be active in the area of issue management. In such cases, the company delivers messages to the public to show where it stands on a particular issue, usually an issue that is important to its various publics. The Domtar example in Figure 9.1

FIGURE
9.1

An Illustration of Corporate Advertising with a Social Responsibility Message

Source: Handout/Domtar Corporation/Newscom.

shows a proactive stance on protecting the environment. Companies also engage in corporate advertising to generate goodwill in the communities they serve.

REPUTATION MANAGEMENT

Chances are that a company in the headlines is there for all the wrong reasons. Something went wrong and key executives are being called upon to defend the company's position. Public relations play a vital role when a company finds itself in a crisis situation, because the final outcome often depends on how effectively an organization manages its communications during the crisis.

A crisis Toyota faced was mentioned earlier. Here are a few details about the crisis and what Toyota did to resolve it. Toyota had a sticky gas pedal problem and was accused of not acting quickly enough in announcing their recall. Key executives of the company and the global CEO were on the hot seat. Toyota eventually put a plan into action and recalled more than 4 million vehicles in North America.

In terms of public relations communications, Toyota placed full-page ads in daily newspapers advising the public of the action the company was taking to correct the mechanical problem. The ad stated that direct contact would be made with all current customers to offer reassurance. Other communications included a four-minute video outlining the action plan, a television commercial, and print ads in major daily papers nationwide.

Part of the action plan called for a halt in sales of all vehicles for a two-week period. By year's end, Toyota sales dropped 15 percent. According to Larry Smith from the Institute of Crisis Management, the key issue in this situation was "how Toyota expresses its plan and executes the repairs. They are a good company with a great reputation, so there is no reason they shouldn't bounce back."[2] By 2012, sales of Toyota vehicles returned to normal levels, a sure sign they were on the road to recovery.

When facing a crisis situation, acting quickly and decisively is the approach recommended by experts. The objective is to reassure the public that everything possible is being done to correct the situation. Maple Leaf Foods faced a serious crisis a few years ago, a crisis that put considerable strain on the company's resources. But Maple Leaf responded in a quick and professional manner. For details, read the IMC Highlight: **Maple Leaf Effectively Manages Crisis**.

Situations like these clearly show how important it is for organizations to be prepared. Having a plan in place to meet disaster head on makes more sense than simply reacting to an unforeseen circumstance. Senior executives must be ready to act instantly and demonstrate they are in control of the situation. Company executives must be ready to meet the demand of a more sophisticated and more demanding consumer audience, or suffer the consequences of its wrath. Some tips for handling a crisis situation appear in Figure 9.2.

PRODUCT PUBLICITY

publicity
News about an organization, product, service, or person that appears in the media.

Publicity is news about an organization, product, service, or person that appears in the media. There is a tendency for people to confuse publicity and public relations, thinking they are one and the same. Publicity is but one aspect of many public relations activities. Essentially, publicity is something that a company and the media deem to be newsworthy. Newsworthy information may include things like a discovery, securing a significant contract that will generate new jobs, and celebrating product or company success.

Maple Leaf Effectively Manages Crisis

When it comes to handling a crisis situation, the best strategy for an organization is to be open, honest, and forthcoming. That philosophy was adopted by Johnson & Johnson back in 1982, when some Tylenol capsules had been intentionally tainted with cyanide. The company recalled 30 million bottles, halted sales of the product, and reached out to hospital and medical practitioners to tell people not to use the product. Through effective public relations, Tylenol rebuilt its reputation and leadership position in the market.

Clearly, Maple Leaf Foods adopted the right strategy in dealing with a listeriosis outbreak in 2008. Tainted meat from a Toronto processing plant was responsible for the deaths of 20 people. Michael McCain, CEO of Maple Leaf, took quick and decisive action, and did so in a manner much like Johnson & Johnson did for Tylenol.

McCain's first step was to apologize publicly. At a press conference, McCain stated, "Tragically our products have been linked to illnesses and loss of life. To Canadians who are ill and who have lost loved ones, I offer my deepest sympathies. Words cannot begin to express our sadness for your pain. We have an unwavering commitment to keeping your food safe with standards well beyond regulatory requirements, but this week our best efforts failed and we are deeply sorry." His apology was heartfelt.

McCain went on to explain the actions the company would be taking to ensure the safety of the public. His plan included an immediate recall of all meat products produced at the plant. The announcement received national coverage and helped position the company positively in the eyes of the public. To reassure the public and to inform the public of the actions the company was taking, Maple Leaf ran full-page newspaper ads in all major daily newspapers in Canada.

Much is at stake if a company is less than forthcoming. Michael Dunne, a marketing professor at the University of Toronto, commends Maple Leaf for its proactive approach. He says, "They were very proactive about it, unusually so, because most companies that go through crises of this nature tend to hide. Maple Leaf is protecting the brand, and it's the brand that matters in the long term for Maple Leaf. Without the brand they don't have anything."

Maple Leaf suffered a serious blow in this situation. Sales of Maple Leaf products declined by 35 percent following the recall, and the profits of the meat division were wiped out. The recall alone cost the company about $30 million. The company's stock price dropped to $6.15 from a high of $15.00. McCain also decided to quickly settle the class-action lawsuits by agreeing to pay $27 million. McCain said settling the lawsuit was part of understanding that "you can't accept accountability without accepting a consequence."

To summarize, hiding from the public doesn't work. The best approach for handling a crisis is to clearly and quickly communicate to the public an action plan that will reassure them that all that can be done is being done. Having the CEO, who is the face of the organization, deliver the message is an effective strategy to employ.

Adapted from Kristine Owram, "A Real Example of How to Do It Right," *The Kingston Whig-Standard*, January 3, 2009, p. 24; Hollie Shaw, "On Road to Recovery," *National Post*, September 5, 2008, p. FP15; and "Maple Leaf Brand Should Rebound in Months: Experts," *Marketing Daily*, August 27, 2008, www.marketingmag.ca.

To demonstrate how publicity works: Kraft wanted to celebrate the hundredth anniversary of its popular Oreo cookie. Everybody loves Oreos, don't they? An anniversary itself isn't that special to the media, but the events that surround it are. Once there's consumer involvement with the anniversary, the press takes note. Celebrating the anniversary on a global scale is not easy, but, to the credit of Kraft, it kept things fairly simple. There was a special website with lots of interactivity, tons of social media tie-ins on Facebook and Twitter, special events and music concerts featuring popular country

FIGURE
9.2

Tips for Handling a Crisis Situation

Adapted from David Menzies, "Silence Ain't Golden: Media Crisis Dos and Don'ts," *Marketing*, August 1/8, 2005, p. 18.

An organization never knows when it will be caught off guard. Circumstances can arise quickly and get out of control if an organization is not prepared. Here are some tips for handling a crisis situation properly.

1. Take responsibility. If your name is on the problem, you have to take responsibility for it. This is different from accepting blame. The public respects an organization that accepts responsibility.

2. Respond quickly and communicate directly and sincerely. Show the public you are going to resolve the problem.

3. Embrace the three fundamentals of good crisis communication:
   - Communicate very clearly what has gone wrong.
   - Communicate what you are doing about it.
   - Describe the steps you are taking to ensure it doesn't happen again.

4. Have access to a former journalist who knows how to deal with the media (knowing what to expect when the media calls is essential).

5. Offer an apology if an apology is warranted. If the public is satisfied with your efforts in rectifying the problem, they will forgive and move on.

music bands, live special events that included flash mobs, and an oversized Oreo birthday cake.[3] Refer to the image in Figure 9.3.

The Oreo celebration is indicative of two trends reshaping marketing. First, there's a growing interest in authenticity and consumers are searching for brands that have stood the test of time. Second, heritage brands are changing their marketing strategies to demonstrate how they have stayed in touch with change. Kraft set out to do something authentic yet fresh for today.[4] The Oreo campaign used the theme "Celebrate the kid inside," which appeared in video and print ads, online at oreo.com/birthday, and in social media such as Facebook, where the brand has more than 25 million "likes" on its fan page. The Oreo celebration campaign included television advertising, online video ads, experiential marketing, and sales promotions—a truly integrated marketing communications campaign!

PRODUCT PLACEMENT, BRANDED CONTENT, AND PRODUCT SEEDING

product placement
The visible placement of brand-name products in television shows, movies, radio, video games, and other programming.

Product placement refers to the visible placement of branded merchandise in television shows, video games, films, or other programming. Product placement was discussed in Chapter 5 as it is also part of a well-planned media strategy—a strategy that stems from public relations roots. It seems that no brand does product placement better than Apple. It's no accident, for example, that *Gossip Girl*'s characters went from carrying Verizon phones to the Apple iPhone. Unlike many other companies, Apple does not pay for its products to appear in television shows or movies. Apple products appeared 891 times on television shows in 2011, twice the number of times of Chevy and Ford, who were next in line.[5] In Apple's case, the show is actually capitalizing on the aura of Apple.

Product placement is a growing form of marketing communications. In the United States alone, spending on product placement in television, movies, and video games reached $7.6 billion in 2010. Product placement offers an organization two key benefits. First, the product is present at a time when the audience is paying attention—they can't avoid the brand impression. Second, there may be an opportunity to associate the brand with the show's character beyond the television show. It presents an opportunity to

FIGURE
9.3

Oreo's 100th Anniversary Is Celebrated by Legions of Fans Across the Country

Source: JJ Thompson/Kraft Canada Inc./Newscom.

extend the brand/actor relationship and build buzz for the brand elsewhere, not to mention the brand chatter that could follow on Facebook.

Branded content, or **product integration**, takes product placement a step further by weaving the name of the brand right into the storyline of a show, movie, or video game. In Canada, the CBC presents marketers with opportunities to integrate their brands into Canadian-produced shows. TD Canada Trust signed on early. The bank was carefully written into the script for three shows: *Being Erica, Heartland,* and *Little Mosque on the Prairie*. TD briefed the CBC on the brand and suggested some integration ideas,

branded content (product integration)
The integration of brand-name goods and services into the script (storyline) of a television show or movie. The brand name is clearly mentioned and sometimes discussed.

because it wanted the bank to be presented accurately. In the end, however, it was the CBC writers who controlled the message and presentation of the bank.[6]

How much TD Canada Trust paid for the integration hasn't been divulged, but the CBC looks at the show and the audience it draws and quotes a price based on the cost of a typical 30-second spot for the show. In the age of tight budgets everywhere, the public can expect more brand integration in the future. Showing cast members doing real things with real products doesn't seem objectionable; if anything, it makes the show more real.

Product seeding is an activity that involves giving a product free to a group of trendsetters who, in turn, influence others to become aware of the product and, one hopes, purchase the product. The trendsetters or influencers are people who marketers use to pass on product information. These people use technology and their own social networks to spread their opinions about products. Marketers, therefore, can take advantage of their knowledge and their access to consumers—a concept referred to as **word-of-mouth marketing**.

Putting a product in the hands of trendsetters helps create buzz for the brand. Their role is to chat about the brand whenever the opportunity arises. BMW experimented with product seeding when it partnered with Fairmont Hotels & Resorts. Members of Fairmont's loyalty program were granted complimentary access to a BMW X5 during their stay with the hotel. They didn't drive the vehicle, but were chauffeured around town in an X5. "The most powerful marketing tool we can do is have prospects experience the vehicle," says Kevin Marcotte, director of marketing at BMW Canada.[7]

Product seeding offers several advantages. First, it is a low-cost strategy that is nowhere near the cost of an advertising campaign. Second, it can reach a narrowly defined target. There is a potential disadvantage as well. If the product does not meet expectations, influencers could tell others about that experience—word of mouth can backfire!

COMMUNITY RELATIONS

Companies today are operating in an environment where social responsibility is very important. Consequently, they place much higher value on programs that foster a good public image in the communities where they operate. Sponsoring community events, local groups, and sports teams is part of being a good corporate citizen. The effect of such an investment on sales is indirect and long term in nature. Very often, being part of the fabric of a community takes precedence over sales. Leaders of companies that place a high value on public relations will tell you that the public has to "like you before they will buy you." Tim Hortons is a good example of a community-minded company. It supplies sports jerseys to local hockey and soccer teams through its Timbits Sports program, offers free ice skating in local communities during the Christmas break, and sends thousands of needy children to camps each summer through the Tim Horton Children's Foundation.

FUNDRAISING

In the not-for-profit sector, public relations play a key role in fundraising. National organizations such as the Canadian Cancer Society, the Canadian Heart and Stroke Foundation, and the United Way face huge financial challenges each year. For these and similar organizations, public relations help educate the public about how funds are used. The message is designed to predispose people to give, to solicit commitment, and to make people feel good about giving. The overall goal of such campaigns is to create a positive image and secure support by sending a message that clearly states what the organization is all about. Such campaigns require an integrated communications plan and employ a variety of techniques to deliver the message. In addition to public relations

FIGURE
9.4   A Public Relations Advertisement Encouraging the Public to Support an Important Social Cause

I believe
in possibility.

Please give to United Way's Community Fund

www.unitedwayhalifax.ca

United Way

Source: United Way Halifax.

FIGURE 9.4   A Public Relations Advertisement Encouraging the Public to Support an Important Social Cause

communications, media strategies include direct mail, telemarketing, print advertising (outdoor, newspapers, and magazines), and websites (see Figure 9.4).

Public Relations Planning

As a component of the integrated marketing communications mix, public relations plans are designed to fit directly with the needs of the organization's marketing objectives. They can be active (help support a brand or company positively) or reactive (help out in a crisis situation). Regardless of the situation, as already stated, a plan must be in place.

A good public relations plan can help build an image and assist in developing relationships with customers. Furthermore, a well-timed public relations plan can play a key role in the launch of a new product, especially in times when budget resources are scarce. Advertising is a very expensive endeavour; public relations are much more economical. To companies searching for greater effectiveness at lower cost, public relations look like a better option than advertising, or, at the very least, the two disciplines must work effectively together to achieve objectives efficiently.

To demonstrate how public relations and advertising should work together, Richard Edelman, president and CEO of Edelman Public Relations Worldwide, says it often makes sense for public relations to take the lead in marketing communications campaigns. "We are going first more often than not," he says. Edelman's firm was engaging bloggers and fans with the Microsoft Xbox gaming system 10 months before the advertising campaign was launched. He says his job "is no longer doing a press conference to break the ads, it's to engage with enthusiasts to create a runway of credibility for a new brand or campaign."[8]

The planning of public relations communications is best left to specialists. It is not an area of expertise in most organizations, though many have a senior-ranking officer assigned the responsibility. Typically, the in-house public relations specialist is a liaison with outside agencies that prepare and implement public relations plans. For the preparation and implementation of corporate and product public relations plans, there is a tendency to hire an organization that specializes in these areas. Hill and Knowlton, Edelman Canada, and NATIONAL Public Relations are examples of leading public relations agencies in Canada. The specialist is briefed by the organization on its needs and expectations. Then, the specialist assesses the information and prepares a strategic plan that will meet the client's objectives. Such a plan must consider the timing of other components of the marketing communications mix—all plans must fit together. Figure 9.5 illustrates the public relations planning process. Let's discuss each stage of the planning process in more detail.

PUBLIC RELATIONS OBJECTIVES

Public relations objectives typically involve creating awareness, shaping attitudes, and altering behaviour. As marketing campaigns become more integrated and seamless, the ability both to quantify and to measure objectives becomes more difficult. On the surface, public relations objectives are very similar to advertising objectives. Therefore, to try to distinguish between the two is difficult. Increased awareness and predisposition to buy are influenced by numerous factors well beyond the scope of public relations, so trying to evaluate public relations in terms of sales and increased market share is next to impossible.

What can be measured is the level of publicity generated (or earned media) by a public relations plan. Typically, the goal of public relations is to achieve media exposure, so quantifiable objectives can be established in this area. Publicity objectives should consider the media through which the message will be communicated and the target audience reached by the media. Surprisingly, even very targeted public relations plans can catch the attention of the national media, because good stories, no matter where they come from, are good stories on national news broadcasts, in national newspapers, and in general interest magazines.

Media exposure can be measured in terms of **gross impressions**, the number of times an item was potentially seen. If a news story appears in a large-circulation newspaper, what is the circulation or readership (circulation multiplied by the readers per copy) of that newspaper? An objective can be stated in terms of impressions. For example, the objective may be to achieve 10 million gross impressions nationally in Canadian daily newspapers.

Alternatively, publicity can be measured for its **equivalent advertising value**. For example, when a horse named Big Brown won the Kentucky Derby, UPS, the

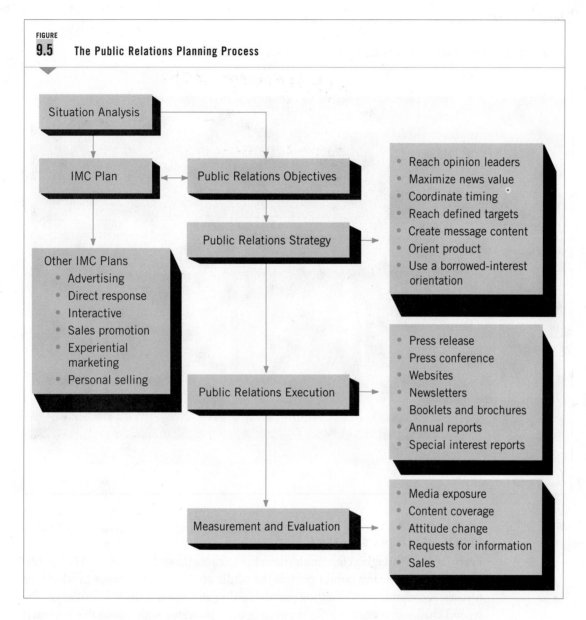

FIGURE 9.5   The Public Relations Planning Process

Situation Analysis

IMC Plan ↔ Public Relations Objectives

Other IMC Plans
- Advertising
- Direct response
- Interactive
- Sales promotion
- Experiential marketing
- Personal selling

Public Relations Strategy
- Reach opinion leaders
- Maximize news value
- Coordinate timing
- Reach defined targets
- Create message content
- Orient product
- Use a borrowed-interest orientation

Public Relations Execution
- Press release
- Press conference
- Websites
- Newsletters
- Booklets and brochures
- Annual reports
- Special interest reports

Measurement and Evaluation
- Media exposure
- Content coverage
- Attitude change
- Requests for information
- Sales

horse's sponsor, reaped an estimated $4 million in advertising value. Fortuitously for UPS, Big Brown was named after the shipping company by its original owner, a New York trucking agent. The sponsorship arrangement was struck just weeks before the Derby.[9]

Another objective could focus on *engaging consumers* with a brand. Degree deodorant did just that when it devised a campaign centred on content that "guys" were interested in. Unilever decided to split its Degree brand of deodorant into specific men's and women's lines. The PR challenge was to engage the male target—men in their twenties—in a manner relevant to them. Unilever's PR agency Weber Shandwick recommended a dedicated website called "The Adrenalist." The site featured news, videos, and information on gear and gadgets for the target audience. Degree enticed males to the website by reaching them where they hang out. The plan included links to the company's Facebook pages, earned media (publicity), and paid ads online. The word "Adrenaline" was also added to the package. Refer to the illustration in Figure 9.6. Within four months of the launch, The Adrenalist tallied more than 750 000 unique visitors, representing nearly 18 500 hours of engagement.[10]

FIGURE
9.6 **Degree Adrenaline Appeals to Males in Their Twenties in a Manner Relevant to That Target**

Source: Jesse Johnston/CP Images.

PUBLIC RELATIONS STRATEGY

Every form of marketing communications has its strengths and weaknesses. With public relations, the company cannot control the media or dictate the manner in which the message is communicated. Getting past the media gatekeepers is the first challenge. The second challenge is ensuring the message is communicated with reasonable accuracy. On the positive side, public relations messages provide enhanced credibility. When the consumer reads a story in a newspaper, hears and sees something positive on a news broadcast about a product or company, or receives branded information from friends in their social network, it is much more authentic than an advertisement.

The role of public relations is determined in advance and is outlined in the marketing communications plan. Typically, that role is to reach influential individuals such as industry analysts, key media representatives, and early adopters of products (refer back to the discussion about product seeding).

The strategic role of public relations should be examined based on how best to

- Reach the opinion leaders, including professionals, industry analysts, trade audiences, and media, well in advance of the public.

- Maximize the news value of new product introductions, new advertising campaigns, and event sponsorships. Messages must be written creatively and visuals must grab attention.

- Time public relations events to reinforce advertising and promotion campaigns, and to maintain visibility between campaigns.

- Reach markets that are defined by demographics, psychographics, or geographic locations that might not be targeted by advertising.[11]

A public relations strategy allows an organization to tell a longer story about itself and its products. Strategy deals more with informing and educating rather than motivating someone to buy something. Therefore, when claims are made about a product, proper substantiation should be provided. Unlike advertising, where time and space are often restricted, public relations communications can spend additional time expanding on something of importance. Granted, a news editor may shorten the story.

A company may employ a **borrowed-interest strategy** to generate publicity. A borrowed-interest strategy will typically promote a newsworthy marketing activity that is related to the product. For example, participation in and sponsorship of a community event or national event is news, as is the launch of a national sales promotion offer designed to stimulate sales. Old Dutch, for example, generates interest in its brands by advertising a contest that would be of interest to many Canadians—the chance to win $1 000 000 for shooting pucks into an empty net within a certain time frame. In this situation, marketing communications shift away from image advertising to focus on the promotion, the goal of which is to stimulate immediate purchases. Refer to the image in Figure 9.7.

borrowed-interest strategy
A plan to promote a marketing activity that is related to a product.

PUBLIC RELATIONS EXECUTION

The tools available to execute public relations programs are diverse. Some are used routinely to communicate newsworthy information, and some are brought out periodically or only on special occasions. This section examines some of the more routinely used media tools.

FIGURE 9.7 Old Dutch Uses a Borrowed-interest Strategy (a Contest) to Stimulate Brand Purchases

Source: Handout/Old Dutch Foods Ltd./Newscom.

press release
A document prepared by an organization containing public relations information that is sent to the media for publication or broadcast.

PRESS RELEASE   A **press release** is a document containing all the essential elements of the story (who, what, when, where, and why). Editors make very quick decisions on what to use and what to discard, so the release must grab their attention quickly. Copies of the release are delivered to a list of preferred editors, for example those with whom an organization has a good relationship. Alternatively, the release could be distributed to a national wire service as well as posted on the company's website. A press release is a quick way to spread the news about a company and its products.

A good press release should be clearly written with key details carefully explained in the opening few paragraphs (editors receive all kinds of releases). The goal is to grab attention early. Many practitioners follow a very simple formula: Focus on who, what, when, and where, and then end the release with whom to contact should more information be needed. Refer to the illustration in Figure 9.8.

press conference
A meeting called by an organization to present information to representatives of the media.

PRESS CONFERENCE   A **press conference** is a meeting of news reporters invited to witness the release of important information about a company or product. Because a conference is time consuming for the media representatives, it is usually reserved for only the most important announcements. A crisis, for example, is usually handled by an initial press conference (see the IMC Highlight about Maple Leaf Foods that appeared earlier in the chapter). When a professional sports team is about to announce a new star player entering the fold, a press conference is very common. A conference allows the media to interact by asking questions, which results in the transfer of additional and perhaps more meaningful information for the story they will publish or broadcast.

media kit
A package of relevant information associated with a product or organization that is distributed at a press conference.

A media kit is usually distributed at a press conference. A **media kit** can include a schedule of conference events, a list of company participants including biographical information, a press release, a backgrounder that tells something about the character of the organization and the nature of what it does, a page of stand-alone facts about the company, sample products, photographs, digital material, contact information, and any other relevant information. The key to developing a good media kit is to evaluate who will use it and what that person is likely to need. For example, a media kit for a special event or new sales promotion activity would be very different in tone, style, and content from one needed for a crisis situation.

WEBSITES   Since the primary purpose of a website is to communicate information about a company or brand, it can be a very useful public relations tool. Visitors to a website quickly form an impression about the company based on the experience they have at the site. Therefore, the site must download quickly and be easy to navigate. Providing some kind of entertainment or interactive activity also enhances the visit. Unlike other media, the website can be updated easily and quickly, so the very latest news about a company and its products can be made available for public consumption. In large companies, it is now common to have dedicated pages for specific brands. All press releases about the company and its brands are also posted at the company website, usually in chronological order starting with the newest releases.

newsletter
A document sent to a predetermined audience that contains news about an organization (for example, a newsletter sent to alumni of a school or to all employees of an organization).

NEWSLETTERS   The **newsletter** is a very common public relations tool. By nature, it is a concise reporting of the news related to the organization and is very clear and to the point. A successful newsletter conveys information in a unique way so that the people who receive it pay attention to it. Newsletters are distributed regularly to their intended audience, so they are an efficient method of conveying information.

There are various types of newsletters, but most are published by companies that want to communicate regularly with employees and customers, by recreation and sports

FIGURE
9.8

The Essential Elements of a Good Press Release: Who, What, When, and Where

Source: Nova Scotia Community College.

clubs that wish to keep in touch with their members, and by professional associations that regularly convey information to members who are geographically dispersed. Typically, a newsletter is distributed by internal or external mail or email, and relies on an accurate database of names and addresses. Many organizations now distribute their newsletters in a digital format instead of hard copy. The frequency of publication is based on budget, timelines, and serialization. Small budgets may dictate quarterly distribution as opposed to monthly; if timeliness is an issue, then more frequent distribution is required. *Special interest newsletters* are distributed by a wide variety of lifestyle clubs and organizations, and by professional associations. Investors in the stock market, for instance, often receive newsletters from a bank or other financial institution.

booklet (brochure)
A multiple-page document distributed to consumers and other interested stakeholders.

BOOKLETS AND BROCHURES   A **booklet** or **brochure** is a brand-sponsored, multiple-page document that is distributed to consumers and other interested stakeholders. The information in a booklet is usually related to a product or service. For example, it may promote usage of a product in a variety of ways, or it may appeal to the lifestyle of the target audience it is intended for. Campbell's Soup is well known for distributing recipe booklets in food stores, through direct mail, and through its website. These booklets encourage consumers to use Campbell's products more frequently in cooking recipes as well as in other non-traditional ways. Greater usage equals greater sales.

In the automobile market, Mazda Canada publishes a semi-annual magazine that is distributed in a digital format to all car owners in its database. The magazine can also be read by visitors to the Mazda Canada website. The publication, appropriately titled *Zoom Zoom*, has a lifestyle orientation and includes general interest articles along with articles and advertisements about the company's newest models. See the illustration in Figure 9.9.

annual report
A document published annually by an organization primarily to provide current and prospective investors and stakeholders with financial data and a description of the company's operations.

ANNUAL REPORTS AND SPECIAL INTEREST REPORTS   The primary purpose of an **annual report** is to provide current and prospective investors and stakeholders with financial data and a description of an organization's operations. But it can do much more to promote the company. In terms of public relations, it is a good opportunity for the organization to tell the public where it stands on social and environmental issues, for example. In fact, the annual report is often seen by audiences beyond the primary target, such as the media, community leaders, and employees. Word can spread fast about what a company stands for.

Special interest reports can be integrated into an annual report or can be stand-alone documents. For companies that want to portray to the public that there is more to business than a healthy bottom line, a special interest report is an ideal vehicle to get a different message out. To illustrate, RBC Financial Group issues a Corporate Responsibility Report each year. The report focuses on issues such as integrity in business; commitment to clients, employees, and the community; commitment to diversity; and commitment to the environment. The information is also published online at the RBC Financial website. Refer to the illustration in Figures 9.10 and 9.11 for illustrations of RBC Financial's public relations initiatives.

social media
Online tools that people use to share content, insights, experiences, and various media, thus facilitating conversations and interaction online between groups of people.

SOCIAL MEDIA   If you have read a blog, joined an online discussion group, sent a tweet via Twitter, or uploaded a photo to Flickr, you have participated in social media. **Social media** are the online tools that people use to share content, profiles, opinions, insights, experiences, perspectives, and media itself, thus facilitating conversations and interaction online between groups of people.[12] The emergence of social media has shifted control of the message from the organization to the consumer—the consumer can read the message, formulate an opinion on it, and communicate that opinion to others. Social media have changed communication from monologue (one to many) to dialogue (many to many).

**FIGURE
9.9   Mazda Distributes a Magazine to Current Customers to Keep Them Informed About New Car Models**

Source: Used with the permission of Mazda Canada Inc.

FIGURE
9.10

RBC Financial Group Publishes Information About How It Contributes to Community and Sustainability Issues

Source: Reproduced with permission of Royal Bank of Canada.

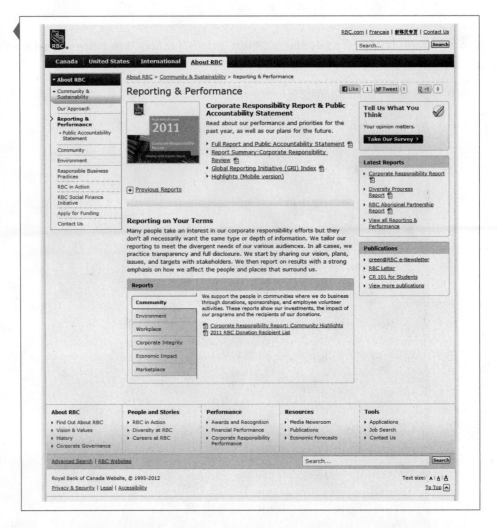

Social media have had a significant impact on public relations practice. Furthering the evolution is a shift in the way people relate to news. They don't just read it. They want to interact with it and influence opinions. That explains why many of the top websites are social media sites, such as YouTube, Facebook, and Twitter. Organizations that understand this concept now use these popular social media sites to their advantage.

Public relations have long been associated with the word "spin." Spin implies that marketers can deliver the message in a tone and manner to their liking. In a social media environment, that approach has to change. Many experts recommend "less spin and more humility in their PR communications."[13] Their rationale for this change is based on the fact that millions of Internet users simultaneously scrutinize a brand in the public domain. Therefore, being as transparent as possible while engaging consumers in the conversation is an important consideration when using social media communications.

Many organizations now use blogs to communicate with their publics. A **blog** is a frequent, chronological publication of personal thoughts on a website. They can be the property of everyday people who like to rant and challenge the integrity of an organization. Blogs of this nature can harm an organization's reputation—one of the perils of social media. An organization must learn to deal with the idea that negative things will be said about it.

Viewed more positively and in a public relations context, a corporate blog can be an effective way to deliver the company's message. Today, corporate blogs that include video

blog
A frequent, chronological publication of personal thoughts at a website.

FIGURE 9.11

RBC Financial Employs Advertising to Inform the Public About One of Its Sustainability Programs

Source: Reproduced with permission of Royal Bank of Canada.

FIGURE
9.12 **Companies Are Now Employing Corporate Blogs to Communicate Current and Relevant Information**

Source: General Motors LLC. Used by permission of GM Media Archives.

content and blogs from everyday people (people who are intensely engaged with specific subjects) and that include consumer-generated content can be an effective combination in delivering a brand's message. A corporate blog is also a means for an organization to regain some message control in the social media arena. See Figure 9.12 for an illustration.

With social media, an organization must adapt to the shift in control and recognize the power that the public has regarding message. "Consumers are in control, and consumers are the media. It's a paradigm shift that's going to change PR forever," says Steve Rubel, vice-president of client services at PR firm CooperKatz."[14] Organizations that disregard this principle face the wrath of the public. To demonstrate the power of social media, consider the dilemma Carnival Cruise Corp. faced when one of its ships was grounded and ultimately tipped over off the Italian coast. Instead of using the social media to its advantage, the company retreated from its own social media (Facebook, Twitter, YouTube, LinkedIn, and Google+). Without communications, the public response became hostile, and conversations across social media platforms were extremely negative about Carnival. Conversation grew rapidly, and public sentiment about the company dropped from 91 percent positive/neutral to 66 percent positive/neutral.[15] This incident clearly demonstrates the immediacy and influence of social media communications!

Richard Edelman, president and CEO of Edelman Public Relations Worldwide, has much to say about how public relations will change in the social media era. He believes, "PR practitioners must become more like journalists and rely less on the media to get the message out. If we are putting information online and people are reading it and accepting it as truth, then we should have a journalist-level quality as our objective."[16] Instead of persuading the media to report a story, practitioners must speak directly to the public, or try to influence bloggers to post messages on their behalf.

Online video sharing sites are one of the fastest-growing media sectors, with sites such as YouTube attracting millions of visitors daily. Therefore, an organization must evaluate the benefits of including web-style videos in the communications mix. Many companies now have their own YouTube channel, where they can deliver video content non-stop. A web video is an enticing proposition, since production and distribution costs are much lower than the costs of creating traditional broadcast material. Unfortunately, a majority of web video content is simply an edited version of conventional broadcast material, an organizational cost-savings strategy that many online communications experts question. For smaller businesses that compete with larger businesses, online video helps level the playing field.

Press releases for traditional media were discussed earlier. Social media provide an opportunity to communicate more detailed information. A social media news release can include a variety of social media elements such as photos and video, links to blogs, digital tags, and RSS feeds. These opportunities were discussed in Chapter 7.

In summary, social media offer new and innovative ways to help a business achieve its marketing communications objectives. The techniques described in this section are much less expensive than traditional advertising. When using social media, an organization must consider that some control of the message may be lost. That loss can be weighed against additional exposure and engagement opportunities with potential customers.

TIMELINE AND BUDGET

A timeline is essential so that all activities can be carefully coordinated with other marketing communications activities. In the case of a new product launch, for example, public relations programs can be put in place well before the product is actually available. One strategy is to start the public relations communications in a small way, slowly building credibility, and proceed with a slow rollout. This strategy creates demand in such a manner that the public is eager to buy the product once it is launched. Apple uses this approach all the time!

Public relations programs cost much less than advertising programs, but, nonetheless, there are costs that must be accounted for. If a company employs corporate advertising, the costs are similar to brand advertising programs. There are costs associated with producing print and broadcast materials, and with buying time in the broadcast media, space in the print media, and in developing and maintaining websites and blogs.

MEASUREMENT AND EVALUATION

To justify a financial investment in any form of marketing communications, certain expectations and results must be delivered. There must be some kind of financial return, increase in awareness, or change in behaviour. Walter K. Lindenmann, senior vice-president and director of research at Ketchum Public Relations, has identified levels for measuring public relations effectiveness: outputs, outgrowths, and outcomes.[17]

- **Outputs** measure the transmission, that is, the amount of exposure in the media, the number of placements and audience impressions, and the likelihood of reaching the target audience.

- **Outgrowths** measure message reception by the target audience. Did the target pay attention to, understand, and retain the message?

- **Outcomes** measure attitude and behavioural change. Was there a change in attitude and did the recipient do something as a result of the message?

Output measures are the most common means of evaluating public relations effectiveness. There are companies that specialize in tracking everything that is written and broadcast about a company and its brands. For example, if an article appears in the front section of the *Toronto Star*, a newspaper with a weekday circulation of more than 400 000, how many impressions will be made? If there are 2.5 readers for every newspaper, the potential number of impressions is 1 million (400 000 × 2.5). If a similar story appears in other newspapers, the total impressions accumulate.

It is also possible to attach an *equivalent advertising value* to such an article. The tracking firm examines the size of the article, the location in the publication, the number of brand mentions, and so on, and through the magic of mathematical calculations, determines the value in terms of advertising. While this may not be exact science, it does appease senior executives who are looking for some kind of return on their investment. Many public relations experts believe that a good article about a product is worth anywhere from three times to ten times as much as an equivalent-sized ad in the same publication.

Measuring for outgrowths involves determining if the target audience received and understood the message. Collecting this information involves a combination of qualitative and quantitative research methodologies, so it is much more costly. As with research conducted for any other marketing activity, this form of evaluation involves pre-campaign and post-campaign research. The initial research firmly establishes a benchmark, and the post-research measures any change. Since creating awareness is the primary objective of most public relations campaigns, many firms do not proceed with research in this area.

More detailed information about specific procedures for measuring and evaluating public relations activities is included in Chapter 12.

Public Relations as a Communications Medium

Senior executives today have a much better understanding of the role played by public relations in achieving their organization's marketing objectives. As a communications discipline, the status of public relations has been considerably elevated. The examples in this chapter show how public relations can play a key role in specific situations. That role will certainly continue to grow in terms of its contribution to marketing communications strategies and the achievement of an organization's objectives. Those responsible for corporate and brand communications should be aware of the basic benefits and drawbacks of public relations communications.

For insight into some successful PR campaigns using some of the newer PR techniques, see the IMC Highlight: **Special Events and Social Media Create Buzz for Brands**.

ADVANTAGES OF PUBLIC RELATIONS

If public relations are done properly, they can be a *credible source* of information. Unlike advertising, public relations messages are delivered by third parties who have no particular interest in the company or product. They are communicating information that they deem useful to their readers, listeners, viewers, and so on. Consumers reading or viewing such messages perceive those messages to be more objective than advertisements.

Third-party endorsements by trusted media personalities can have a *positive impact on sales*. To illustrate, consider what happened when Oprah spoke positively about Sears on her popular daytime television show. The Sears placement on the show involved providing Christmas gifts to foster children in a small Texas community. On the show, Oprah proclaimed "We love Sears." Through pre- and post-show surveys, Sears found

Special Events and Social Media Create Buzz for Brands

Senior marketing executives want results. They look for tangible benefits gained from their investment in any form of marketing communications. Public relations are no different. In planning a PR program, specific objectives are established; the campaign is implemented and then evaluated. Here are a few campaigns that really clicked using some of the newer PR techniques.

Reebok set out to change how people think of fitness. The objective of their communications campaign was to change the way people define, view, and experience fitness. Reebok wanted to show people that fitness can be a sport itself. To launch "The Sport of Fitness" campaign in Toronto, an elaborate stunt was employed in Dundas Square, a very busy downtown public park. Using a crane, Reebok hoisted a 15 000-pound shipping container above the square to raise public curiosity. A week later, it was lowered to reveal a mobile CrossFit-branded gym and equipment, which the public was encouraged to try. CrossFit is Reebok's strength and conditioning program.

Rich Froning Jr. and Graham Holmberg, both recent winners of the "Fittest Men on Earth" competition, were there to promote the CrossFit program and encourage consumer participation. Uli Becker, president of Reebok, says "Fitness is tedious and uninspiring to many people, but it doesn't have to be. Our event in Toronto shows people that CrossFit has all the elements that fuel people's love of sport—community, competition, and challenge." Television commercials showing young people working out strenuously together were another key element of the integrated campaign.

A&W jumped into social media with a campaign for its new sirloin Uncle Burger. The restaurant's "Ultimate Uncle Contest" invited customers to tell A&W why they have the best uncle at UncleBurger.ca. The site included a number of coupons for free Uncle Burgers, and visitors could send their uncle an electronic "Uncle's Day" greeting card and print a coupon for a free Uncle Burger.

The objective of the promotion was to get people talking about the Uncle Burger, drive people to the website, and generate some excitement for the product. Soon after the launch, details and discussion of the offer were all over Twitter, Facebook, and other message boards. The site attracted 10 000 visitors in 48 hours, and 2000 free burgers were claimed. By the end of the contest, there were 41 000 entries.

A&W targets baby boomers and saw social media as a new way to connect with them. According to David Waterfall, director of marketing, "Research shows increasing numbers of baby boomers are involved with social media. It's not just teens who are texting and using Twitter." Tom Shepansky, the creator of the promotion, said, "You want to be where people young or old will be going, either to get a deal or join a discussion. Put the deal out there, and people will talk. Is it a good deal or not? Is it something worth eating? People will talk about the strangest things."

Adapted from Alicia Androich, "Reebok to Put Focus on Fitness in Toronto," *Marketing*, February 13, 2012, www.marketingmag.ca and Eve Lazarus, "A&W Puts Social Media on Marketing Menu," *Marketing Daily*, April 13, 2009, www.marketingmag.ca.

Souce: Ryan Emberley/Reebok Canada Inc./Newscom.

the show provided incentive to move viewers from neutral to positive intent to shop at Sears during the holidays.

Indirectly, public relations also play a role in developing sound ***customer relationships***. Public relations campaigns offer a means to build rapport through ongoing dialogue with consumers and other stakeholders. Such a benefit is important, considering the rising costs of media advertising, the fragmentation of the media, and the clutter of commercial messages.

DISADVANTAGES OF PUBLIC RELATIONS

One of the biggest drawbacks of public relations is the ***absence of control*** experienced by the sponsoring organization. Through press releases and press conferences, the company does its best to ensure that factual information is available and presented accurately to the public. In the process of communicating the information, however, the media might add their own opinions, which detract from the intent of the original message. Companies facing crisis situations often see stories in the media that misrepresent the company or mislead the public. In the case of blogs and other social media options, consumers act as publishers and control what is said about the product or company, be it good, bad, or indifferent.

A second disadvantage deals with the sheer ***waste*** of time, energy, and materials that go into a public relations campaign. This is not to say that the effort isn't worthwhile, but the challenge of catching the attention of editors (the media gatekeepers) is an onerous one. Enormous amounts of material flow into media newsrooms daily, so standing out in the crowd is part of the public relations challenge. The same can be said about the clutter of information that is present in the diverse social media universe. Senior management must recognize the waste factor and be prepared to absorb the costs that go along with it. Finally, what is important to management may not be perceived as important by the media. End of story!

>> SUMMARY

Public relations are a form of communications directed at gaining public understanding and acceptance. They are used by organizations to change or influence attitudes and behaviour. Unlike advertising, which is very costly, public relations go largely unpaid for. The organization presents information to the media in the hopes they will publish or broadcast it in a news story.

The primary roles of public relations are diverse. They constitute a useful channel for communicating corporate-oriented messages designed to build or repair an organization's image. At the product level, public relations help generate positive publicity by distributing news releases and holding press conferences when there is newsworthy information to announce. As well, relatively new communications alternatives, such as product placement, branded content, product seeding, and social media opportunities, fall under the umbrella of public relations. Social media tools provide an opportunity for the public to engage and interact with an organization's message.

Public relations planning begins with a situation analysis. Usually, the client organization provides a brief containing all relevant background information to a public relations agency. The public relations firm establishes the goals and objectives, develops the communications strategy, selects the best execution techniques, and, after receiving the client's approval, implements the plan.

The primary objectives of public relations programs tend to dwell on creating awareness, altering attitudes, and motivating a change in behaviour. The public relations strategy focuses on reaching opinion leaders, maximizing the news value of the story, and reinforcing other communications campaigns such as advertising, sales promotions, and experiential marketing activities. There are several techniques for getting a story into distribution. The most commonly used options include the press release, press conferences, websites, newsletters, booklets and brochures, and social media. Social media options include the use of blogs, postings on Facebook and Twitter, and video sharing websites such as YouTube.

The impact of public relations is measured several ways. Output measurements are the most common technique.

They measure message transmission—that is, the amount of exposure in the media, the number of placements and audience impressions, and the likelihood of the message reaching the intended target audience. If pre-campaign and post-campaign research is conducted (budget permitting), an organization can measure the impact of public relations messages in terms of influencing attitudes and altering behaviour.

Public relations communications offer several benefits: They help build credibility for a product or company with its various publics; they help build brand awareness and interest; and they have an indirect impact on brand sales. There are some drawbacks as well. The organization has little control over the message that is delivered by the media, and there is often a lot of waste in the preparation of materials that are not distributed by the media.

KEY TERMS

annual report   276

blog   278

booklet   276

borrowed-interest strategy   273

branded content   267

brochure   276

corporate advertising   262

external publics   262

internal publics   262

media kit   274

newsletter   274

press conference   274

press release   274

product integration   267

product placement   266

product seeding   268

public relations   261

publicity   264

social media   276

word-of-mouth marketing   268

REVIEW QUESTIONS

1. What are the essential differences between media advertising and public relations communications?
2. Identify and briefly explain the role of public relations in the following areas:
   a) corporate communications
   b) reputation management
   c) product publicity
   d) product seeding
   e) community relations
3. What is the difference between product placement, branded content, and product seeding?
4. What are the key elements of a public relations strategy?

5. What is a borrowed-interest public relations strategy? Provide an example of this strategy that isn't in the text.
6. What is a media kit, and what role does it serve?
7. What are the roles of special interest newsletters and special interest reports that are distributed by companies, organizations, and associations?
8. Public relations effectiveness is measured based on outputs, outgrowths, and outcomes. Briefly explain each form of measurement.
9. What are the advantages and disadvantages of using public relations as a marketing communications medium? Briefly explain.

DISCUSSION AND APPLICATION QUESTIONS

1. Considering the nature of the business environment today, do you think that public relations will play a more significant role or less significant role in future marketing communications strategies? State your position and justify it, based on your vision of the future business environment.
2. What is your opinion of the newer PR techniques such as product placement, product seeding, and social media communications? Will these techniques continue to grow in importance as PR tools? Review the

IMC Highlight: **Special Events and Social Media Create Buzz for Brands** for essential insights into a few of these techniques.

3. What role will social media play in future public relations practice? Will it change the very nature of the way an organization communicates with its publics? Conduct some secondary research on this issue and formulate an opinion on it.
4. Conduct some secondary research that involves an organization using public relations strategies to

launch a new product. How important was public relations in the marketing communications mix? What were the objectives of the public relations effort? Was the plan effective in achieving its goals?

5. Identify two different companies that compete with each other (Coca-Cola and Pepsi-Cola, Nike and Adidas, and so on) in the same industry or markets. Analyze the information they provide on their Facebook pages in terms of public relations value. Are these companies maximizing the potential of Facebook in communicating vital information to customers?

6. Visit a company website of your choosing. Usually, there is a link to the press release section of the site. Review that company's five latest press releases. What subject matter did they deal with? Try to determine how the company uses public relations to its advantage.

ENDNOTES

1. Rebecca Harris, "Canadians Support Brands that Do Good," *Marketing*, May 16, 2012, www.marketingmag.ca/news/marketer-news/canadians-support-companies-that-do-good-survey-52792.

2. "Toyota Launches Ad Blitz to Reassure Customers," *Marketing*, February 1, 2010, www.marketingmag.ca/news/marketer-news/toyota-launches-ad-blitz-to-reassure-customers-987.

3. Tim O'Brien, "Oreo's 100th: An Anniversary Campaign with Taste," April 2, 2012, simplifyingpr.blogspot.ca/2012/04/oreos-100th-anniversary-campaign-with.html.

4. Stuart Elliott, "The Oreo Turns 100, with a Nod to the Past," *The New York Times*, February 27, 2012, www.nytimes.com/2012/02/28/business/media/the-oreo-turns-100-with-a-nod-to-the-past-advertising.html.

5. Peter Burrows and Andy Fixmer, "How Apple Became a Cult in Hollywood," *San Francisco Chronicle*, May 14, 2012, www.sfgate.com/business/article/How-Apple-became-a-cult-in-Hollywood-3555741.php.

6. Matt Semansky, "Mosque and State," *Marketing*, September 29, 2009, p. 27.

7. Kristin Laird, "Fairmont Puts Guests Behind the Wheel with BMW," *Marketing*, November 3, 2009, www.marketingmag.ca/news/marketer-news/fairmont-puts-guests-behind-the-wheel-with-bmw-11784.

8. Julie Liesse, "The Big Idea," Special advertising section of *Advertising Age*, November 28, 2011, p. C4.

9. Michael Bush, "Win or Lose, UPS Sees Big Payoff in Belmont," *Advertising Age*, May 26, 2008, p. 8.

10. Julie Liesse, "The Big Idea: Unilever/Degree," Special Advertising Section of *Advertising Age*, November 28, 2011, p. 25.

11. Thomas L. Harris, "Value-Added Public Relations" (Chicago: NTP Publications, 1998), p. 243.

12. Brian Solis, "The Definition of Social Media," *WebProNews*, June 29, 2007, www.webpronews.com/the-definition-of-social-media-2007-06.

13. Kenneth Evans, "Stop the Spin," *Marketing*, Public Relations Report, June 1, 2009, p. 11.

14. Kenneth Newcomb, "MWW Debuts Blog Marketing Practice," ClikZ, January 4, 2005, www.clickz.com/clickz/news/1695856/mww-debuts-blog-marketing-practice.

15. Glenn Engler, "Carnival Retreats from Social Media Following Disaster," *Marketing*, February 14, 2012, www.marketingmag.ca/news/media-news/carnival-retreats-from-social-media-following-disaster-46326.

16. Keith McArthur, "Online Era Leaves Media Out of the Loop: PR Expert," *The Globe and Mail*, March 21, 2005, p. B5.

17. Walter K. Lindenmann, Ketchum Public Relations, "It's the Hottest Thing These Days in PR," presentation at PRSA Counselors Academy, Key West, Florida, April 25, 1995.

Experiential Marketing, Events, and Sponsorships

Learning Objectives

After studying this chapter, you will be able to

1. Explain the role of experiential marketing as a vehicle for building relationships with customers

2. Explain the importance of event marketing and sponsorships in contemporary marketing

3. Differentiate among the various forms of event sponsorships

4. Evaluate the role of event marketing and sponsorships in the marketing communications mix

5. Assess the criteria that a marketing executive considers before participating in event marketing and sponsorships

6. Identify and assess the various evaluation techniques that determine the effectiveness of event marketing and sponsorship activities

7. Describe the steps in event marketing planning

8. Evaluate various marketing strategies for making an event successful

9. Identify and explain the key elements of event marketing execution

Traditional forms of marketing communications tend to bombard consumers with messages. They emphasize reach and frequency, and the brand that barks the loudest gets the consumer's attention. In that scenario, there isn't a true connection between the brand and the consumer. In contrast, experiential marketing focuses on giving a target audience a brand-relevant customer experience that adds value to their lives. It involves effective two-way communications between the brand and consumer. Consequently, marketers are rethinking how marketing budgets are allocated, and there is a shift in the direction of engagement-oriented activities.

Experiential marketing embraces several tried and true concepts such as event marketing, sponsorships, and product sampling, but it is the event itself rather than the product that becomes the key component of an integrated marketing campaign. The ultimate goal of experiential marketing is to get consumers to actively engage with the brand and, based on the experience, talk about the brand to others. A well-planned and implemented experiential marketing campaign can be the fuel for effective word-of-mouth marketing. This chapter explores the emerging world of experiential marketing, events, and sponsorships, and shows how a variety of companies reap the benefits of these forms of marketing communications.

An Introduction to Experiential Marketing

experiential marketing
A form of marketing that creates an emotional connection with the consumer in personally relevant and memorable ways.

Experiential marketing is a form of marketing that creates an emotional connection with the consumer in personally relevant and memorable ways. Using one or more senses such as touch, taste, smell, sight, and hearing, it establishes a touch-point or connection with consumers in the form of experiences that are personal, memorable, and interactive.[1] The experience could be something as simple as a free sample distributed at an event or something as complex as a planned event where the brand is the centrepiece of the event.

The term *experiential marketing* is relatively new, but the fundamental concepts behind it are not. Brands have always employed product sampling, special product promotions, public relations stunts, product seeding, and special events in their marketing arsenal, but it is just recently that the concept of consumer engagement with a brand has taken hold. To engage consumers requires a carefully designed and emotive experience that often integrates various forms of marketing communications.

FIGURE
10.1   **To Encourage People to Visit the Yukon, Can-Can Girls Brought the Yukon Experience to Urban Canada**

Source: © Gunter Marx Stock Photos.

The event itself may be the centrepiece of an experiential marketing campaign. To encourage travellers to visit the Yukon, Tourism Yukon brought the Yukon "feeling" to urban centres. If you visited the Yukon, what would you experience? The campaign employed street teams of can-can girls dressed in historical garb. Refer to the image in Figure 10.1. The girls greeted passersby next to images of the aurora borealis and the gold rush. To further engage people, there was a contest incentive to win a free road and air trip to the land of the midnight sun. The experiential component was part of a fully integrated communications campaign that included cinema ads, outdoor posters, transit shelters, print, social media, and digital advertising.[2]

In an effort to show young males the "manly art of grooming," Philips (a marketer of electric grooming products) developed an experiential program involving a cross-Canada campus tour to engage a younger male target. A squad of Philips Groom U cheerleaders led the charge. Refer to the image in Figure 10.2. A two-day crash course in the art of grooming took place on 11 university campuses across the country. At each campus, the Groom U cheerleaders looked for students who embodied a unique element of self-expression. They awarded products from the Groom U tool box to 10 standout students from each campus. A $10 000 cash scholarship offer encouraged students to visit the Groom U website at PhilipsGroomU.ca for more information about grooming. Social media also played a role in the campaign. Coach Niki posted grooming updates on the brand's YouTube page and by tweets on #PhilipsGroomU. The campaign

shopper marketing
Understanding how consumers behave as shoppers in all channels (retail, catalogue, and web) and then targeting these channels with appropriate marketing communications to enhance the sales of a brand.

also included ads in *The Hockey News* and various *Score* properties. Both of these media attract the male target Philips was pursuing.

Another component of experiential marketing is shopper marketing. **Shopper marketing** involves understanding how consumers behave as shoppers in all channels (retail, catalogue, and web) and then targeting these channels with appropriate marketing communications to enhance the sales of a brand. Shopper marketing is essential since three out of four purchase decisions are made in-store. These purchase decisions are broken down into categories: 55 percent of the decisions are unplanned; 15 percent are generally or specifically planned; and 6 percent are substitutes.[3] This data, when combined with other known information about shopping behaviour (that is, shoppers feel time stressed and in a hurry to make purchase decisions), reinforces the importance of an effective shopper marketing communication strategy. The goal is to make the purchase decision easier.

Samsung Canada has benefited from shopper marketing in a number of ways. According to marketing director Robert Gumiela, "The consumer is of critical importance and needs a positive buying experience. Essentially, customer experience is a new medium. We do more training in-store and spend more money with retailers than all of our competitors, and our sales results have made this investment worthwhile."[4] To illustrate, Samsung televisions are displayed on Samsung walls in all Future Shop and Best Buy stores. How Samsung televisions perform can be seen in an environment similar to the home environment.

A successful shopper marketing campaign calls for collaboration between a supplier and a retailer. To demonstrate, Procter & Gamble and Walmart collaborated on a program of "preparedness" to maximize sales of the Vicks family of products. Well in advance of the cold season, shoppers were encouraged to stock up on Vicks when they were in Walmart. Product displays that utilized point-of-purchase materials created by

One of the greatest challenges facing a company is where to invest its marketing dollars at a time when there are more choices than ever.

Experiential marketing is growing in popularity, and companies are investing in it because consumers respond to it. Nine out of ten consumers say they would purchase a good or service if they experienced it and were satisfied.

Here are a few unique examples of experiential marketing:

Tylenol PM

The over-the-counter drug product that makes a person sleep better reached 1 million target consumers by having packaged samples of the product placed on beds in resorts throughout the United States. A note with the sample said, "We know how long you've waited for this vacation, and we know how much you want to catch up on your sleep. Enjoy."

Lipton Brisk Green Tea with Apple

The Lipton tea beverage got some street marketing exposure by serving samples of "forbidden fruits" to "Adams and Eves" in the streets of key Canadian markets. Street teams, adorned in fig-leaf uniforms and accompanied by apple carts and trees, invited passersby to pick fruit and win prizes.

Stride Gum

Stride is a "ridiculously long-lasting" gum. To engage consumers, two "Stride Guys" visited 28 cities in a Volkswagen van, enticing people to play ping-pong with them wherever they stopped. Free gum was distributed at all stops to those who watched, and participants were given headbands and wristbands. The fun series of events engaged Canadians, according to Cadbury Adams, the maker of the gum.

FIGURE 10.3

Some Unique Experiential Marketing Campaigns

Source: Based on Brian F. Martin, "Give It a Try: Put Brands in Consumers' Hands (Literally)," *Advertising Age*, October 22, 2007, www.adage.com; Jonathan Paul, "Stride Gum: Ping Pong Anyone?" *Media in Canada*, May 1, 2008, www.mediaincanada.com; and Jesse Kohl, "Forbidden Fruit Campaign Drives Online with Street Media," *Media in Canada*, August 13, 2007, www.mediaincanada.

Procter & Gamble brought attention to the program, and coupons encouraged consumers to buy right away. The campaign ran for several years, and Walmart reported sales increases for Vicks products in the +30 percent range.[5]

Organizations are investing more money in experiential marketing, and that investment is justified based on changing market conditions. In the past, an organization was concerned about making impressions on people (a staple means for measuring the effectiveness of advertising and public relations communications). Presently, emphasis has shifted so that the objective is to make quality impressions (fewer but better impressions) while engaging the consumer with the brand. When consumers interact with the brand, it creates a stronger reason to buy the product and to build a relationship over an extended period. For some additional examples of experiential marketing refer to Figure 10.3.

For more insight into the nature of experiential marketing campaigns, read the IMC Highlight: **Experiential Marketing Pays Off**.

Event Marketing and Sponsorships

Event marketing and sponsorships are important components of many experiential marketing programs. Over the past five years, investment in these areas has continued to grow—a sure sign that marketers see the value in such activity. In 2010, total investment in event marketing and sponsorships in Canada amounted to $1.55 billion, up from $1.1 billion in 2006. Over a five-year period, the average annual increase for spending in events and sponsorships is about 8 percent a year.[6]

IMC HIGHLIGHT

Experiential Marketing Pays Off

According to Aidan Tracy, president of Mosaic Experiential Marketing, the key to experiential marketing is engaging with your consumers in a manner that leaves them with an impression that changes their perception of the brand. "It's about immersing the consumer in an experience circle—where the consumer learns about the product and tries the product."

Procter & Gamble provides a good example of how an experiential marketing program works. P&G uses the term "shopper marketing" to describe how it engages consumers with its brands. Shopper marketing is based on two key concepts. First, a distinction needs to be made between consumers who receive brand messages from various media while not shopping and shoppers who are consumers in action. Since three out of four purchasing decisions are made in-store, the second concept of shopper marketing becomes clear: Retail space must be viewed as a media platform and used to advantage to get customers interested in the brand. The marketing challenge is to devise the content needed to change consumers' behaviour while they are on the retail floor. How can stores serve as an effective communications channel?

Procter & Gamble worked with Walmart on a shopper marketing program to boost the profile of its Olay brand of beauty products. The program was based on the insight that the typical Walmart shopper buys for the family and neglects herself in the shopping process—not a good situation for a brand like Olay. That knowledge spawned a program theme: "Everything for the family,

something for you." A series of health and wellness fairs were held in selected Walmart locations across Canada. Women entering the store were issued a passport-style card and were encouraged to visit the health and beauty aisles during their trip. Shoppers who picked up Olay items earned passport stamps, and those reaching the checkout with a fully stamped passport were entered in a grand prize draw. The passports forced the women to think about themselves for a moment.

Walmart was very satisfied with the sales the program generated and decided to bring it back for a second spin. This program demonstrates how marketers must think beyond traditional channels of communications and find new ways of motivating consumers to buy their brands. The sales floor as a communications channel opens up a new realm of possibilities at a critical time in the buying decision process. There is little doubt that experiential marketing, or shopper marketing, as P&G calls it, will play a more dominant role in its marketing communications mix.

Adapted from Matt Semansky, "All Hail the Shopper," *Marketing*, May 12, 2008, p. 31, and Matt Semansky, "First-Hand Experience," *Marketing*, May 12, 2008, p. 34.

Source: Rebecca Sapp/WireImage/Getty Images

---

event marketing
The process, planned by a sponsoring organization, of integrating a variety of communications elements with a single event theme.

Event marketing is the design and development of a "live" themed activity, occasion, display, or exhibit (such as a sporting event, music festival, fair, or concert) to promote a product, cause, or organization.[7] Both of Canada's leading breweries, Molson Coors and Labatt, include events as a key component of their marketing mix. Both companies see events as a means of creating excitement for their brands. For example, when Bud Light Lime was launched in Canada, a flash mob event was organized in downtown Montreal. Some 100 people encouraged passersby to participate in the action. In conjunction with Kawartha Fest, a Peterborough, Ontario, summer festival, Molson Coors plans and implements an annual wakeboard event. The event is billed as "Coors Light presents Wolfstock at the Molson Canadian Wakeboard Festival" (that's quite a handle)! The event includes music by popular Canadian bands, sports tournaments, and kids' activities. An event of this nature is an ideal fit for a brand that relies heavily on the summer selling season.

Event sponsorship is the financial support of an event, say a sports event, theatre production, or cause marketing effort, in return for advertising privileges associated with the event. On the grandest scale, the Olympics is the most expensive sponsorship investment a company can make. Referred to as partners, these organizations commit to Olympic sponsorship investment continuously (summer and winter games). Companies in this group include Coca-Cola, Omega, Procter & Gamble, Visa, and Samsung. As global marketing organizations, these companies see true value in being involved with a global event.

> **event sponsorship**
> The financial support of an event in exchange for advertising privileges associated with that event.

Usually, an event marketer offers sponsorships on a tiered basis. For instance, a lead or title sponsor or sponsors would pay a maximum amount and receive maximum privileges. When Vancouver hosted the 2010 Winter Olympic Games, the lead Canadian sponsors included Bell, Hudson's Bay Company, RBC Financial, GM Canada, Petro-Canada, and Rona. Other sponsors, classified as official supporters, paid less and received fewer privileges. Some companies in this group included Air Canada, Canadian Pacific, and British Columbia Lottery Corporation.

Event marketing is big business! According to IEG, LLC, a Chicago-based sponsorship measurement firm, the North American sponsorship market is estimated to be valued at $18.1 billion (2011).[8] As mentioned earlier, the Canadian sponsorship market is estimated to be worth $1.55 billion. Growth in event marketing is being fuelled by deals with traditional broadcast properties that include a sponsorship element. As well, marketers today are reluctant to rely on traditional forms of marketing communications. With television viewership waning and newspaper and magazine readership declining each year, marketers are shifting their dollars to other alternatives.

A recent survey among North American marketing executives indicates that events deliver the greatest return on investment over other customary tools, including advertising. There are a few other reasons why sponsorships offer value to an organization. First, the company or brand can form an emotional connection with the fans simply by being there and participating (fans expect sponsors to be at events). Second, an event can reach or target a certain demographic more effectively than advertising. Maybelline cosmetics derives these benefits from its role as a lead sponsor of World MasterCard Fashion Week, an annual event in New York City. The connection between the brand, the event, and the target market is quite clear. Refer to the image in Figure 10.4.

Investment in event marketing and sponsorships is mainly divided among five areas: sports, entertainment, festivals and fairs, culture and the arts, and causes. Ongoing sponsorships on television shows can also be included in the sponsorship mix. A list of the leading event marketing and sponsorship companies in North America appears in Figure 10.5. In Canada, RBC Financial is a leading sponsor of sports and community events. Each year RBC invests some $100 million in a variety of national and local programs. RBC's sponsorships include the Olympics and Paralympics, the RBC Play Hockey program, RBC Canadian Open (golf), the Canadian Freestyle Ski Association, and the Canada Snowboard Federation. RBC has a philanthropic side, making annual contributions to educational, civic, social, and environmental causes.

SPORTS MARKETING SPONSORSHIP

Sports sponsorship occurs at amateur and professional levels, and can be subdivided into classifications from local events to global events (see Figure 10.6). Among the various

FIGURE
10.4

Maybelline Sees Great Value in Sponsoring an Annual Fashion Event, Ideal for Reaching Its Primary Target Market

Source: Handout/Maybelline New York/Newscom.

FIGURE
10.5

Leading Sponsorship Investors in North America

Source: Based on *IEG Sponsorship Report*, Chicago, 2010.

Rank	Company	Amount ($ million)
1	PepsiCo.	$340M–$345M
2	The Coca-Cola Co.	$265M–$270M
3	Anheuser-Busch Cos.	$255M–$260M
4	Nike, Inc.	$215M–$220M
5	AT&T Inc.	$175M–$180M
6	General Motors Co.	$17M–$175M
7	Toyota Motor Sales	$150M–$155M
8	Miller Coors LLC.	$135M–$1405M
9	Ford Motor Co.	$ 125M–$130M
10	Adidas North America Inc.	$ 120M–$125M

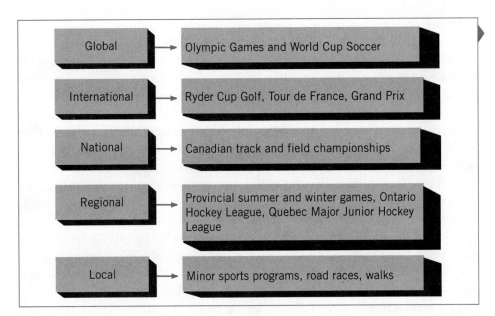

FIGURE
10.6

The Various Levels of Sports Event Marketing

categories of sponsorships, sports sponsorship is by far the largest in terms of dollars invested by marketing organizations. In Canada, sports presently accounts for about 46 percent of all sponsorship investments; festivals and fairs accounts for 24 percent; the arts 13 percent; cause marketing 7 percent; and entertainment 6 percent.[9]

Sports sponsorships tend to be dominated by certain industries and manufacturers. In Canada, for example, the automobile industry is well represented by General Motors and Ford, the brewing industry by Molson and Labatt, and the financial industry by RBC Financial Group, BMO Financial Group, Scotiabank, Visa, and MasterCard.

Sponsorships are a key component of BMO's marketing mix. BMO partners with organizations that help create brand exposure nationally and regionally. BMO is actively involved in soccer sponsorships across Canada at the grassroots level—over 15 000 jerseys carrying the "BMO" logo are provided to youth house leagues. BMO is a partner of the Canadian Soccer Association, a premier partner and jersey sponsor of both Toronto FC and Montreal Impact (professional teams), and a founding partner of Vancouver Whitecaps FC.[10] Soccer is a growing sport that appeals to diverse target markets that BMO is interested in.

The investment in sports sponsorship increases at each level moving upward on the chart. Organizations choose between spending locally to support community events at relatively low cost to investing in national and international sponsorships at significantly higher cost. Such decisions are based on how sponsorships fit with other marketing communications strategies and the overall marketing strategy of the organization.

An organization's involvement in sports sponsorship does not have to be extravagant; involvement and commitment depend upon the organization's marketing objectives and its overall strategy. To illustrate, Visa associates with national and international events, a reflection of the card's status around the world, while Tim Hortons prefers to sponsor local sports programs all across Canada. The company's Timbits Minor Sports Program provides team jerseys for community-based youth soccer and hockey leagues. The local sponsorship program fits nicely with the target audience the company is trying to reach.

A recent phenomenon associated with event sponsorship is the practice of ambush marketing. **Ambush marketing** is a strategy used by non-sponsors to capitalize on the prestige

ambush marketing
A strategy used by non-sponsors of an event to capitalize on the prestige and popularity of the event by giving the false impression they are sponsors.

and popularity of an event by giving the false impression they are sponsors. The ambush of all ambushes was a Nike effort at the 1996 Atlanta Olympics. Saving the US$50 million that an official sponsorship would have cost, Nike plastered the city with billboards, handed out Swoosh banners to wave at the competitions, and erected an enormous Nike Centre overlooking the stadium. The tactics devastated the International Olympic Committee's credibility.

Such tactics have led to more assertive anti-ambushing strategies by subsequent Olympic organizing committees and by organizers of other world events such as the FIFA World Cup of Soccer. In the 2010 Winter Olympics, US goaltender Ryan Miller was ordered to remove the phrase "Miller Time" from his mask under IOC ambush marketing rules. "Miller Time" is the slogan of Miller Lite beer, which was not a sponsor of the games.

venue marketing (venue sponsorship)
Linking a brand name or company name to a physical site, such as a stadium, arena, or theatre.

Venue marketing or **venue sponsorship** is another form of event sponsorship. Here, a company or brand is linked to a physical site such as a stadium, arena, or theatre. See the illustration in Figure 10.7. In Canada, there is the Air Canada Centre (home of the Toronto Maple Leafs and Raptors), Rogers Arena (home of the Vancouver Canucks), and Rexall Place (home of the Edmonton Oilers). Pre-eminent title positions like these break through the clutter of other forms of advertising, but they do come at a cost. Air Canada spent $20 million for a 20-year agreement for the naming rights to the Leafs' home rink. Sony, the Japanese electronics giant, paid $10 million to have its name on a performing arts centre in downtown Toronto (formerly the O'Keefe Centre, then Hummingbird Centre). As part of the deal, the centre will be fitted with the most technically advanced audio and video equipment made by Sony.[11]

FIGURE 10.7   The Branding of Sports Venues Helps Improve Brand Awareness

Source: Tom Szczerbowski/Zuffa LLC/Zuffa LLC via Getty Images.

FIGURE
10.8

Venue Marketing Is Popular Among Canadian Corporations

AIR CANADA CENTRE ($20 MILLION, 20-YEAR DEAL)

Sponsor: Air Canada
Toronto Maple Leafs (hockey), Toronto Raptors (basketball), Toronto Rock (lacrosse)

BELL CENTRE ($60 MILLION, 20-YEAR DEAL)

Sponsor: Bell Canada
Montreal Canadiens (hockey)

JOHN LABATT CENTRE ($2.9 MILLION, 10-YEAR DEAL)

Sponsor: Labatt Breweries of Canada
London Knights (Ontario Hockey League)

TD GARDEN ($80 MILLION, 20-YEAR DEAL)

Sponsor: TD Bank
Boston Bruins (hockey) and Boston Celtics (basketball)

Source: Data from Revenues From Sports Venues, 2009.

There are also sponsorship opportunities within an arena or stadium. PepsiCo recently signed a multiyear partnership with the Vancouver Canucks and Rogers Arena (where the Canucks play). PepsiCo secured exclusive beverage and snack rights (through its Lay's brand) for a five-year period. The partnership gives Pepsi branding and advertising placements at all concessions, restaurants, bars, and other outlets in the arena; branded cups; LED rink board signage; and spectator stairwell branding. "The partnership is a major win because of the sheer volume of visitors to Rogers Arena," says Robb Hadley, director of marketing for PepsiCo Beverages Canada.[12]

Many prominent Canadian companies have invested in venue sponsorships in Canada and the United States. For a list of some of these companies and the costs involved, see Figure 10.8.

What's thriving in sports marketing is the concept of *value-added sponsorships*, where hefty doses of public relations and media exposure accompany a marketer's sponsorship agreement. The key in this strategy is a lucrative player endorsement. Reebok International was quick to strike an endorsement deal with young hockey sensation Sidney Crosby—a five-year deal worth $2.5 million, more money than any hockey company has ever paid established stars. Crosby is part of Reebok's global advertising campaign that uses the slogan, "I am what I am." Reebok invested heavily in Crosby's ability to help build its hockey business, and for marketing purposes Reebok sees him as "the total package." When interviewed by the media, Crosby is always seen wearing a Reebok hat. Crosby also participates in a variety of company business-building functions.[13] Crosby is also a spokesperson for Sport Chek, a leading sporting goods retailer in Canada. Crosby appears in commercials (quite humorous ones) promoting his SC87 line of equipment. Refer to the image in Figure 10.9.

How effective is an organization's investment in sports marketing? The true benefits of event marketing are discussed later in the chapter. For now, simply consider that key indicators of success are brand awareness and brand association with the event or, in some cases, celebrity. For example, which quick-serve restaurant sponsors the Olympics? Which company sponsors the men's national curling championships each year, an event called the Brier? If you can or can't answer these questions, it helps a company justify the benefits and drawbacks of investing in sports sponsorships.

FIGURE 10.9   Celebrities Matched with the Right Product Can Be an Effective Motivator in Brand Purchase Decisions

Source: CCN Photo/Reebok/CP Images.

ENTERTAINMENT SPONSORSHIPS

Canadian corporations invest huge amounts of money to sponsor concerts and secure endorsements from high-profile entertainment personalities in the hopes that the celebrity–company relationship will pay off in the long run. Companies like Molson and PepsiCo, which are interested in targeting youth and young adult segments, use entertainment sponsorship as a vehicle for developing pop-music and youth-lifestyle marketing strategies.

Pepsi-Cola recently decided to end its sponsorship of the *Academy Awards* because it is not a distinct enough platform for reaching younger people. Typically, shows such as the *Academy Awards* present opportunities to launch a big-event commercial or a new campaign. Coca-Cola replaced Pepsi on the broadcast, citing the "continuing marketing power" of the show and the "diverse audience" it reaches as reasons to get involved.[14] Other key sponsors of the Academy Awards are General Motors and JC Penny (a department store). The median age of an *Academy Awards* viewer is 50.5 years. While that age may be old for some advertisers, others see it as an age when consumers have discretionary income to spend. Since viewers are primarily female as well, the show is an ideal fit for both GM and JC Penny. Advertising insiders refer to the show as the "Super Bowl for women."

FESTIVAL AND FAIR SPONSORSHIPS

Festivals that embrace film, theatre, and comedy are enticing because they reach a cross-section of adult target audiences. At a top film festival, a corporate sponsor hitches a ride on the most glamorous coattails of all—movie stars! For two prominent film festivals, the Toronto International Film Festival and the Festival des Films du Monde in Montreal, there are waiting lists for platinum sponsorships. These events showcase branded products not only to filmgoers, but also to the thousands of deep-pocketed domestic and international wheeler-dealers who do business at festivals. Key clients get to hobnob with the movie stars.

Sponsorship revenue for the Toronto International Film Festival (TIFF) averages $4 million annually, with the top sponsor spot occupied by Bell Canada. The theatre in which many of the films are shown is called the Bell Lightbox. Refer to the image in Figure 10.10. Other major sponsors of TIFF include RBC Royal Bank, L'Oréal Paris, and Visa. Visa provides its cardholders with exclusive benefits. Visa cardholders can purchase tickets and special ticket packages in advance of the general public, get access to exclusive ticket passes, and enjoy priority access to the Visa Screening Room—Visa-branded theatres during the film festivals. Visa Premium cardholders (Visa Gold, Visa Platinum, and Visa Infinite cardholders) also have exclusive access to the Visa Premier Lounge in Toronto, where they can enjoy refreshments and complimentary snacks one hour before evening screenings at the Visa Screening Room.

Film and other types of theatre festivals are now popular with marketing decision makers, as organizers are offering customized packages better suited to a sponsor's unique needs. From a marketing strategy perspective, a festival like the Toronto

FIGURE
10.10 Bell Capitalizes on Entertainment Sponsorships to Reach a More Exclusive Audience

Source: Christopher Drost/ZUMAPRESS.com/Keystone Press.

International Film Festival reaches a "class" audience rather than a "mass" audience. The TIFF audience is described as young, urban, and affluent: 47 percent are 18 to 34 years old; 92 percent have a university education; 73 percent have a household income of $50 000+, 33 percent in excess of $100 000; and all are culture and experience seekers who spend money on entertainment.[15]

CULTURE AND THE ARTS SPONSORSHIPS

Arts and cultural event opportunities embrace such areas as dance, film, literature, music, painting, sculpture, and theatre. What separates cultural events from sports and entertainment events is the audience size. Depending on the sponsor, this is an advantage or a disadvantage. A company such as Molson might prefer the mass audience reach of a sports event, whereas Mercedes-Benz and BMW might prefer to reach a more selective and upscale audience through an arts event. Perhaps only 2500 people attend the arts event, but those people can be powerful. Typically, their education level would be above average, as would their income. Such an audience profile would be a good match for promoting a new luxury car. A financial services company such as RBC Financial Group or MasterCard may sponsor both large-audience and small-audience events given the diversity of age and income of its customers.

The primary benefit these companies gain by sponsoring the arts is goodwill from the public. Most firms view this type of investment as part of their corporate citizenship objectives; that is, they are perceived as good, contributing members of society. The Shaw Festival, a live theatre event in Niagara-on-the-Lake, relies on the corporate citizenship of sponsors. At Shaw, various productions are sponsored by prominent corporations. For example, in 2012 *Ragtime* was sponsored by TD Financial; *Present Laughter* by CIBC; and *Trouble in Tahiti* by Vintage Hotels. Financial institutions and upscale hotels are attracted by the type of audience attending Shaw productions.

CAUSE MARKETING SPONSORSHIPS

Cause-related marketing is relevant in the minds of consumers, corporations, and not-for-profit organizations that mean something to consumers. This feeling, when associated with a brand or company, can have a positive effect on the consumer's perception of the brand. Such is the benefit that the CIBC derives from its ongoing title sponsorship of the Canadian Breast Cancer Foundation CIBC "Run for the Cure," where the overall goal is to raise funds to help find a cure for breast cancer. Refer to the image in Figure 10.11. Other sponsors of this cause include New Balance, East Side Mario's, Running Room, Egg Farmers of Canada, and Revlon.

In today's competitive business world, brands drive marketing. But as brand loyalty diminishes, marketing executives are searching for new ways to connect with consumers emotionally. By associating with causes that have a high degree of interest among the public, even the biggest of corporations can connect with consumers on an emotional level. As indicated above, CIBC has been doing it for years.

TELEVISION SPONSORSHIPS

Due to the waning impact of the 30-second TV commercial, the television industry and programs are offering branded sponsorship opportunities. One of the hottest sponsorship properties in Canada is on CBC and TSN hockey broadcasts. Hockey is a natural fit for companies such as Molson, General Motors, Canadian Tire, and Tim Hortons. These brands have been associated with hockey and hockey broadcasts for years.

FIGURE

10.11 CIBC Is the Ongoing Title Sponsor of the Canadian Breast Cancer Foundation's Run for the Cure

Source: Canadian Breast Cancer Foundation.

Within the *Hockey Night in Canada* broadcast, there is an opportunity to sponsor special segments as well. During the 2011–2012 broadcasts, Maytag sponsored the "Dependable Lines" contest segment—Maytag's brand positioning is dependability. The segment was a bracket-style tournament, where lines faced off against each other to win votes from viewers. Video clips of each line in action were shown during the segment. Each week, the line with the most votes moved on to the next bracket until a winner was decided. The grand prize was an entire line of Maytag appliances valued at $8500.

Perhaps the biggest event on *Hockey Night in Canada* is the annual "Hockey Day in Canada" sponsored by Scotiabank. That broadcast, which involves three games broadcast in one day, culminates a week of community activities and events celebrating the grassroots of the game—what could be more Canadian than that! Refer to the image in Figure 10.12.

Considerations for Participating in Event Marketing

When companies enter into events and sponsorships, there are typically two key objectives they are trying to achieve. First, they are trying to create a favourable impression (build awareness and/or enhance their image) with their target audience. Second, they

are trying to engage the target audience directly with the brand. Unlike other forms of communication, an event provides an environment where people are more receptive to the message—they expect to hear from the sponsors when they attend. To achieve these objectives, the fit between the event and the sponsor must be a good one. The most effective sponsors generally adhere to the following principles when considering participation in event marketing:

- **Select Events Offering Exclusivity:** If a company needs to be differentiated from its competition within the events it sponsors, it calls for exclusivity so direct competitors are blocked from sponsorship. For example, McDonald's ongoing sponsorship of the Olympic Games shuts out all other quick-serve restaurants from the event. Also, sponsors are often concerned about the clutter of lower-level sponsors in non-competing categories that reduce the overall impact of the primary sponsor. There is a lot of clutter, for example, in sports events such as NASCAR (brand logos seem to be everywhere, as can be seen in Figure 10.13).

- **Use Sponsorships to Complement Other Promotional Activities:** The roles that advertising and promotion will play in the sponsorship must be determined first. Sponsoring the appropriate event will complement the company's other promotional activities. For example, Pepsi-Cola and Frito Lay (both PepsiCo brands) sponsor the Super Bowl and place several ads during the broadcast. To leverage the association with the Super Bowl, both brands combine to advertise a Super Bowl contest (game tickets and other major prizes) in the months preceding the game. Huge in-store displays often accompanied by coupon or cash refund offers promote the Super Bowl connection, and encourage consumers to buy product. Pepsi's integrated strategy embraces advertising, sales promotion (consumer and trade promotion), and event marketing and sponsorships across key company brands.

- **Choose the Target Carefully:** Events reach specific targets. For example, while rock concerts attract youth, symphonies tend to reach audiences that are older, urban,

10.13

Brand Logos Seem to Be Everywhere at NASCAR Races

Source: Christa L. Thomas/ZUMApress.com/Keystone Press.

and upscale. As suggested earlier, it is the fit—or matching—of targets that is crucial, not the size of the audience.

- **Select an Event with an Image That Sells:** The sponsor must capitalize on the image of the event and perhaps the prestige or status associated with it. For example, several brands of automobiles place a high value on associating with professional golf and sponsor various tour events: BMW Championship Tournament, Buick Open, and Honda Classic are examples. The prestigious image and status of such events have an impact on the sale of products that project a comparable image: the image and status that come with ownership of a BMW automobile, for example.

- **Formalize Selection Criteria:** In addition to using the criteria cited here, companies should make sure they formalize the decision process. For example, the short-term costs must be evaluated against the long-term return on investment that sponsorship offers. Before committing financial resources to an event, a company should also consider whether it is likely to receive communications exposure through unpaid media sources and whether the event organizers will be able to administer the event

---

FIGURE

10.14 Companies Have Different Reasons for Participating in Event Marketing and Sponsorships

General Motors Canada

Sponsorship

Chevrolet Canada is sponsoring the Toronto 2015 Pan/Parapan American Games. The company will provide 1000 vehicles for event organizers and volunteers leading up to and during the event. The vehicles will feature various green technologies.

Rationale

"This partnership allows Chevrolet to be part of an event that will inspire and engage a generation of Canadians," said Kevin Williams, president of GM Canada. "This major commitment is an extension of Chevrolet's long history of supporting Canadian athletes, from novice players to elite players at an international level."

Molson Coors Brewing Company

Sponsorship

Molson Coors is now the beer sponsor of the National Hockey League. Cost of the sponsorship deal over a five-year period is $375M.

Rationale

"Hockey is something that is very central to Canadian culture and really helps us with Molson Canadian and the Coors Light brand," said David Perkins, president of Molson Coors Canada. "It's a very reasonable deal for us. It's one that we feel will be an important part of building the health of our portfolio."

Pizza Pizza

Sponsorship

Pizza Pizza formed a partnership with True North Sports and Entertainment to sponsor the Winnipeg Jets. Pizza Pizza will have onsite concessions at the MTS Centre, home of the Jets.

Rationale

"It's about doing good work together to benefit the fans, and to have fun as a team. It will have a positive impact on our business in the region," said Pat Finelli, chief marketing officer of Pizza Pizza. The company is trying to grow its presence in the region and has plans to expand from five restaurants to ten by the end of 2012.

Source: Adapted from Evra Taylor, "Pizza Pizza Sponsors Jets to Build Western Footprint," *Marketing*, December 5, 2011, www.marketingmag.ca; Evra Taylor, "Chevrolet Teams Up with Pan/Parapan American Games," *Marketing*, November 11, 2011, www.marketingmag.ca; and Canadian Press, "Molson Coors Optimistic that NHL Sponsorship Will Drive Sales of Key Brands," *Marketing*, November 2, 2011, www.marketingmag.ca.

---

efficiently. The company must establish objectives in terms of awareness and association scores, image improvement, sales, and return on investment, so it can properly evaluate its participation in the activity.

For insight into how various organizations make sponsorship decisions, refer to Figure 10.14. For additional insight into the role and impact of sponsorships, read the IMC Highlight: **Hockey Sponsorships Recession-Proof**.

Measuring the Benefits of Event Marketing and Sponsorship

One reason many companies are reluctant to enter into sponsorship programs is that results are difficult to measure. Large sums of money are spent at one time for a benefit that may be short-lived. Will the investment produce a reasonable return on investment (ROI)? The basic appeal of event marketing is that it provides an opportunity to communicate with consumers in an environment in which they are already emotionally involved. Beyond this, companies conduct marketing research to determine the impact

Hockey Sponsorships Recession-Proof

Scotiabank is very active in the sports sponsorship arena in Canada, but one might question the bank's strategy when it agreed to be the official bank of the Toronto Maple Leafs. Does the association risk alienating customers who don't like the team? It may, but there are other factors to consider beyond what teams Canadian fans cheer for.

From Scotiabank's perspective, all that matters is a good return on their sponsorship investment, and right now hockey is the best bet in sports, particularly in Canada. "Hockey is highly relevant to Canadians, and our love of hockey aligns with that of our customers and prospective customers," says Duncan Hannay, marketing executive at Scotiabank.

Hockey is the biggest sponsorship investment at Scotiabank; the bank is involved right up the ladder from youth hockey programs to sponsorship deals with the seven Canadian National Hockey League (NHL) teams. Sellout crowds in all Canadian cities make the relationship financially attractive for Scotiabank. Sponsorship revenue is very important to the teams as well. Ticket sales only account for about half of the revenue that Canadian NHL teams generate each year, and the costs of operating a team are very high.

There is something about hockey that attracts corporate sponsors. If it were just patriotism, then sports like football and baseball would be doing better on the sponsorship front. According to Alan Middleton, professor at York University, "When money gets tight, we focus on the big stuff. Hockey is protected, and it gives the sponsor coverage right across the country." It seems that a tried and true sport like hockey offers stronger appeal than a merely popular sport like UFC (Ultimate Fighting Championship).

BMO recently extended its relationship with junior hockey in Canada. As part of the deal, BMO will have on-ice advertising at each of the Canadian Hockey League's 46 arenas and a presence in CHL telecasts, the CHL website, and each of the team's websites. According to Sandy Bourne, vice-president of sponsorships, advertising, and corporate events, "It's really important for us to be localized and show that we are part of the community, because that's important to our customers and our employees." He sees the CHL as a great fit, suggesting they will reach young families seeking a mortgage or older couples in the market for RRSPs or loans for home renovations. He says "the CHL relationship shows our commitment to a good many communities across Canada."

Part of the sponsorship deal includes a contest called "Score a Trip to the Memorial Cup," the annual Canadian junior championship tournament.

Adapted from Morgan Campbell, "Why the Maple Leafs Remain a Safe Bet for Corporate Sponsors," *Toronto Star*, October 21, 2011, pp. Si, S4; and Chris Powell, "BMO Expands Partnership with CHL," *Marketing*, October 17, 2011, www.marketingmag.ca.

Source: Francis Vachon/CP Images.

of the sponsorship association. The following indicators, many of which are obtained from research, are used to measure the benefits of sponsorship.

- **Awareness:** How much awareness of the event is there within each target group? How well do people recall the brand or product name that sponsored the event?

- **Image:** What change in image and what increase in consumer perception of leadership or credibility result from the sponsorship?

- **New Clients:** How many new clients were generated as a result of the company's sponsoring an event? Entertaining prospective clients in a luxury box at an event goes a considerable way in building a relationship.

- **Sales:** Do increases in sales or market share occur in the period following the event? Be aware that the real sales benefit may take years. It takes time for a sponsor to become closely associated with an event.

- **Specific Target Reach:** Do the events deliver constituency? Carefully selected events reach specific targets that are difficult to reach by conventional communications. For example, pre-teens and teens are difficult to reach through conventional media but can be reached effectively through sponsorship of concerts and music tours. As discussed earlier, events need not be big in terms of attendance to attract constituency.

- **Media Coverage:** What value was derived from editorial coverage? Did the sponsorship result in free publicity for the sponsor? The industry benchmark for sports sponsorship is currently four to one, meaning $4 in exposure (for example, free air time) for every $1 spent on sponsorship and its marketing support.

For sponsorships to be successful, they must be seamlessly integrated into corporate marketing and marketing communications plans. All forms of communications must be complementary. The organization must leverage the use of its website, Facebook page, and Twitter feed; incorporate the sponsorship into public relations campaigns; and run thematic promotions to get all customer groups (trade and consumers) involved. Above all, it has to make a financial commitment above and beyond the rights fees. A general ratio for spending should be three to one: $3 should be spent to promote the relationship to the event for every dollar spent on securing the rights.[16]

For smaller events, success or failure is determined by the financial outcome of the event. Key indicators of success would be the profit the event generated. The event planner and perhaps a financial executive would scrutinize all the revenues and costs associated with planning and operating the event to determine if a profit or loss was ultimately generated.

An organization must choose between event marketing (planning and implementing its own event) and event sponsorships (providing financial support in return for advertising privileges). Either option presents challenges and opportunities.

Planning the Event

Should an organization decide to develop its own event, it must be comfortable with an exhaustive planning process. Putting the plan into place is one thing—executing it is quite another! As in the case of many other forms of marketing communications, a more prudent approach may be to outsource the activity, allowing experts in this field to do the job.

An organization's marketing team carefully considers the role of an event or sponsorship to ensure it is an appropriate opportunity for achieving the company's business objectives. The organization's primary role is to identify the overall goal and marketing objectives, identify the target audience and timing, consider the financial implications (revenues, costs, and profit), and evaluate the results. Working with the client organization, the event planner develops the event theme, identifies the best venue, and establishes the marketing strategy and implementation plan. The event planner's role is tactical in nature at the implementation stage, as all kinds of concerns need to be addressed. Among these are staging the event, having adequate and trained staff, operations and

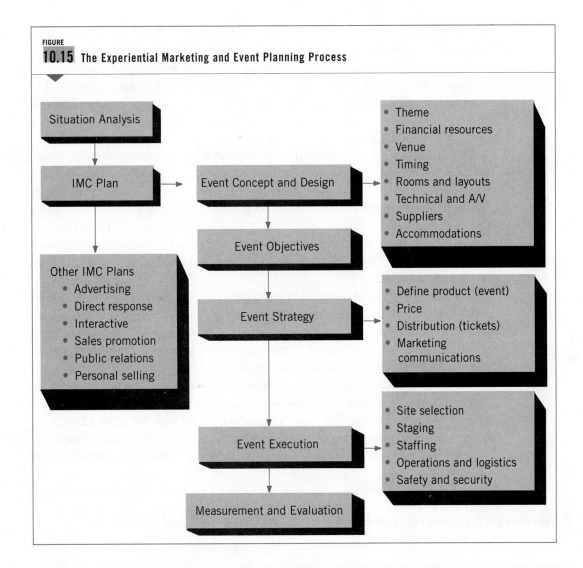

FIGURE 10.15 The Experiential Marketing and Event Planning Process

logistics planning, and safety and security. Successful events run smoothly, moving like clockwork from one activity to another. A successful event requires careful planning down to the minutest of details (see Figure 10.15).

EVENT CONCEPT DEVELOPMENT

The initial stage of planning is developing the concept. In determining the nature of the event, the planner considers the event's purpose, the audience it will reach, available resources, potential venues, and timing. In terms of ***purpose***, an event that is designed to transfer information to prospective clients would be much different from one intended to entertain an audience. The former might have a business tone and style, while the latter would be much more upbeat and participative. To illustrate, an event with a trade show orientation (for example, some kind of business fair where new products are introduced to the market) is much different from the annual Calgary Stampede. The Calgary Stampede is a community event that is presented with all the enthusiasm and passion that the people of Calgary and all of Alberta can muster. The Stampede represents the historical and cultural fabric of the West.

The ***theme*** of the event should be linked to the purpose and consider the needs of the audience. Events tend to adopt a colour scheme and a tagline that tie various components of the event together. For example, tickets, programs, promotional literature, and signs are usually designed to look like they are all part of a package. Key influences on theme development are one's imagination and money. The latter always brings a sense of reality to one's imagination! Potential themes could involve history (the organization's history), geography and culture (the location of the organization or the event), sports (being part of a sports event that fits with the product), music and entertainment (offers significant appeal for younger audiences), and so on.

Once the theme is determined, the next decision is *venue*. Will the venue be a traditional setting such as a hotel, convention centre, arena, or stadium (see Figure 10.16)? Or will it be something unusual, such as a parking lot or a site at a company facility? Or will it move from location to location, as in the case of branded product promotional tours? Regardless of the venue, the planner must carefully consider factors such as sound, lighting, other technical issues, and availability of parking and public transportation. And of course, there's always the unpredictability of the weather. Should the event be inside or outside?

The *financial resources* must be considered immediately. The event's budget quickly determines the degree of extravagance. What an event planner would like to do and what the planner can actually do are usually quite different—a good idea is only a good idea if it is financially viable. Therefore, the event planner must carefully balance creative instincts with the financial resources of the organization.

The *timing* of an event is often linked to the season or weather. For example, the National Home Show, an annual show held at the Direct Energy Centre in Toronto, is held mid-March each year. The show is timed to coincide with the public's interest in home improvements and renovations, which tends to peak in the early spring. Essentially, there are four time-related factors to consider: season, day of the week, time of day, and

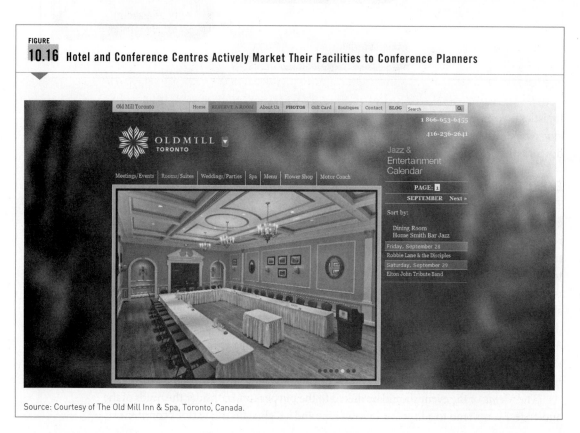

FIGURE 10.16   Hotel and Conference Centres Actively Market Their Facilities to Conference Planners

Source: Courtesy of The Old Mill Inn & Spa, Toronto, Canada.

duration of the event. Business trade shows, for example, are usually scheduled on weekdays. In contrast, home and leisure shows cover weekends as well as weekdays, with traffic at the show peaking on the weekends.

DESIGNING THE EVENT

Once the concept decisions have been made, the next stage is design. For the purpose of illustration, let's assume we are planning a two-day business conference at which several prominent business speakers will make presentations about various aspects of marketing communications. Attendees will include advertising agency personnel, marketing executives, as well as managers employed in digital communications, sales promotion, and public relations. The theme of the conference is "How to Communicate Effectively with Youth," a hot topic among marketing communications practitioners.

In designing this conference, key decision areas include venue, room layout, technical requirements, food and beverage requirements, material suppliers, and hotel room availability. Regarding *venue*, a downtown hotel location in a major city would likely be a logical choice because the target audience works in that environment. The hotel's banquet room facilities will be considered, because a room for 250 to 300 attendees is required, and an additional banquet room will be needed for some of the meals. For example, it is common for keynote speakers to make their presentations after a meal in the main banquet room. Meals without keynote speakers are often in an adjacent room where the atmosphere is less formal.

The *layout* of the banquet room has a bearing on how well the audience and speakers interact with each other. A common layout at this type of conference includes carefully spaced round tables with eight people seated at each. Attendees usually like this arrangement because a table can be reserved for a large group from one company. Such an arrangement encourages collegiality at the table, even if the people did not know each other initially. The speakers usually address the audience from an elevated podium at the front of the room.

In today's technologically driven world, the use of proper and effective *technology* is crucial. Most speakers today use slides or video presentations as their primary visual aid to illustrate their key points. Therefore, an event planner must consider all possible audiovisual needs in advance. Typically, the audiovisual aspect of the conference is outsourced to an expert company in this field. This company brings in the equipment (sets it up and tears it down) and is responsible for coordinating the visual aspect of the presentation with the speaker. For extremely large conferences where attendees are distant from the speaker, it is common to have additional screens that display the speaker making the presentation.

Food and beverage requirements are another decision area. Since attendees are investing their time and money in the conference, they expect good-quality food and efficient service by hotel staff. A poor experience in this area can negate any other positive experiences the attendee has at the conference. Buffet-style meals, for example, seem efficient, but only if there are enough serving stations so the lineups aren't too long. If the meal is served directly to tables, adequate staff must be on duty so that the meal is served within the time allocated. Conferences must stick to their schedule. Light snacks and beverages must be readily available in convenient locations during the break periods.

Dealing with *suppliers* behind the scenes is another key decision area. With our example of the marketing communications conference, print materials are prepared and copied by a printing company to be distributed at registration. It is quite common to have a booklet containing an event schedule, profiles of the various speakers, information about the host sponsor, and copies of the various presentations. As indicated earlier, audiovisual supply requirements must also be confirmed in advance. Food and beverage supplies are the responsibility of the hotel, but all meal requirements must be confirmed ahead of time between the event planner and catering manager.

The final decision area involves having adequate **hotel rooms** available for the anticipated number of attendees. Hotels usually block off rooms until a specified date before the conference. If there aren't enough rooms at the host hotel, additional rooms should be reserved nearby. All promotional materials should include hotel information and indicate the key dates and reservation procedures.

SETTING OBJECTIVES

As indicated earlier in the chapter, an organization must establish concrete objectives to justify any financial investment in event marketing. Therefore, quantitative objectives are identified—objectives that are realistic, achievable, and measurable. They must be within the realm of what event marketing is capable of achieving. A direct link to sales is not possible, but it may be possible to measure changes in awareness or intentions to purchase a company's product as a result of event participation.

Other objectives might relate to the size of audience reached, the ability to reach a specific target audience (for example, the quality of reach), sponsor recognition levels, sales of sponsor products, the economic impact of the event, and profit. In the example of the marketing communications conference, the event's objective may have been to attract 300 participants (perhaps any number above 200 participants would produce a profit for the event). Since the event will attract a quality target audience of marketing communications practitioners, it could attract additional sponsors who will help defray the costs of planning and executing the conference.

PLANNING TOOLS

The initial stage of planning is the preparation of an event proposal. The **proposal** should include the objectives of the event as well as details about organization, layout, venue, technical requirements, and any other key considerations (see Figure 10.17). Certain planning tools are essential in the planning stages. Most important is a **timeline chart** that indicates when various planning activities start and finish. As well, a schedule of daily events, often called a **run sheet**, is essential to list the various dates, times, and locations of activities (see Figure 10.18). The importance of the timeline chart will become clear in the discussion of execution issues later in this chapter. With so many logistical things to consider, it is important to identify a critical path for those elements of the plan that are essential for a successful outcome.

timeline chart
A chart indicating when various planning activities start and finish.

run sheet
A schedule of daily events that shows the various dates, times, and locations of activities at an event.

Marketing the Event

Marketing an event is no different from marketing a product; an integrated plan is needed. The key decisions involve carefully defining the product (event) and then positioning it in the minds of the target audience in a favourable way. Motivating people to attend the event depends on the quality and quantity of marketing communications activities. This section examines some of the essential strategic planning elements.

PRODUCT STRATEGY: DEFINING THE EVENT

In defining the event, the planner must identify the essential features and benefits of the event that can ultimately be used in messages directed at the target audience. For example,

An event proposal is drafted in the preliminary stages of planning to highlight key elements. As planning progresses, the proposal becomes more detailed and execution oriented.

FIGURE

10.17

Key Elements of an Event Proposal

EVENT DESCRIPTION

- Type of event and event name
- Location
- Timing
- Event concept (including goals and objectives)

EVENT MANAGEMENT

- Management responsibilities
- External supplier requirements
- Facility requirements (venue, rooms, layout)
- Identification of target audience

MARKETING

- Assessment of audience needs
- Competitor analysis (similar events, timing)
- Product (event definition)
- Price strategy (price ranges, ticket availability)
- Marketing communications strategy (media advertising, web, public relations)
- Distribution strategy (registration procedures, methods)

FINANCIAL

- Budget (consideration of all associated costs)
- Profit-and-loss statement

STAGING

- Theme
- Decor
- Layout

- Sound and lighting
- Catering
- Services (parking, transportation, vehicle requirements, electricity)

STAFFING

- Recruitment of staff
- Staff training (roles and responsibilities)
- Recruitment of volunteers
- Volunteer training

SAFETY AND SECURITY

- Risk identification and management
- Safety strategy (audience, presenters, entertainers)
- Security strategy (premises, equipment, cash)
- Reporting procedures and communications
- First aid

OPERATIONS AND LOGISTICS

- Bump-in (setup)
- Room layout
- Technical execution (sound, lighting, computers, projectors)
- Attendee traffic flow (venue layout, room locations, meeting rooms)
- Contingencies (weather, technology failure, accidents)
- Bump-out (teardown)

EVALUATION

- Actual versus plan (based on objectives)
- Profitability

is the purpose to entertain, to provide a learning experience, or to simply have fun with friends? The marketing communications conference cited earlier offers a learning experience for participants, who gain from the success and expertise of others. In contrast, attending the Rogers Cup Tennis Championships brings tennis enthusiasts together to cheer and celebrate tennis at the highest level of performance. Clearly, the nature of communications to motivate attendance for these two events would be very different. Promotional information for the Rogers Cup stresses words such as intense competition, excitement, and emotion.

In defining the product (event) and understanding the motivation of the target audience, the event planner discovers what buttons to press to motivate participation.

PRICING STRATEGY

Price also plays a role in motivating attendance. Literature promoting professional seminars and conferences is easily discarded if the price–value relationship is incongruent. Charge too much for a conference, and the value is questioned. Charge too little, and

FIGURE

10.18

A Sample Run Sheet

A run sheet is an indispensable planning tool that is updated as needed during planning. It is particularly useful for hotels and conference centres at the execution stage of an event. The schedule below was used at the Ambassador Resort Hotel and Conference Centre, Kingston, Ontario, when it hosted the Ontario Colleges' Marketing Competition.

THURSDAY, NOVEMBER 14, 2002	
2:00–4:00 pm	Registration and Team Photographs (Atrium)
5:30–7:00 pm	Complimentary Buffet Dinner (Ballroom)
7:00–7:15 pm	Opening Ceremonies (Ballroom)
7:15–9:30 pm	Marketing Quiz Bowl (Ballroom)
10:00–11:30 pm	Faculty Social (Prime Minister's Suite)

FRIDAY, NOVEMBER 15	
7:00–8:00 am	Judges' Breakfast (East Ballroom)
7:00–8:00 am	Continental Breakfast, Students and Faculty (West Central Ballroom)
8:00 am	First Participants Enter Prep Rooms (refer to event schedules)
8:00 am–12:00 pm	Judging Begins for Cases, Job Interview, and Sales Presentation
12:00–1:00 pm	Judges' Lunch and Faculty Lunch (East Ballroom)
1:00–4:00 pm	Competition Continues
6:30–7:30 pm	Reception (Ballroom)
7:30–10:00 pm	Awards Banquet (Ballroom)

All activities take place at the Ambassador Resort Hotel and Conference Centre.

people may think they won't learn anything important by attending. All things considered, the pricing decision is a delicate one. To put things in perspective, the registration fee for our example of the one-day marketing communications conference could be in the range of $500 to $600. Such an event might attract 200 people and could prove to be profitable for the sponsoring organization. However, if the price were lowered to less than $500 (say $495), would it attract a larger audience? Pricing an event is much like pricing a product—a lot of psychology is involved.

In contrast, the RBC Canadian Open (a Professional Golf Association tour event) offers tickets in a range of prices starting as low as $80 for a single day grounds pass at the low end, but provides upgraded packages for those wanting a better experience. A Golf Canada House Single package is priced at $300; a 2-Some package at $550 and 4-Some package at $1000. Package prices include upgraded food and beverage choices, indoor seating with big-screen TVs, and reserved washrooms.[17] Pricing for an event sometimes has to be flexible and meet a variety of customer needs.

A second pricing consideration involves a plan for purchasing tickets. The sale and distribution of tickets for an event or the registration process for a business conference must be convenient for the participant. As well, the planning organization must decide if it will sell the tickets directly or outsource this task to a specialist, such as Ticketmaster. Consumers find online ticket buying and event registration very convenient. Therefore, registration could be handled by an organization's website or by the website of a ticket intermediary. All details about pricing and how to buy tickets should be clearly stated on the organization's website (see the tickets page at www.rbccanadianopen.com).

MARKETING COMMUNICATIONS STRATEGY

The success of any event is often dictated by the effectiveness of the marketing communications strategy. What message will be delivered to the target audience to motivate participation, and what media will be used to efficiently reach that audience? A separate budget must be drawn up for marketing communications, because it may take a considerable portion of the event's overall budget.

The initial marketing communications decisions are basically ***branding*** decisions. Typically, an event will adopt a distinctive name, logo, colour scheme, and image. Several examples appear in various figure images in this chapter. Every component of the communications mix, including tickets, will bear the same logo and colour scheme. Such consistency of presentation gives the event a branded look. For the CN Canadian Women's Open (a national golf championship conducted by Golf Canada and sponsored by CN), all forms of marketing communications have a common look. The CN logo appears in all communications materials related to the Open, and the website for the event includes links to other golf partnerships that CN is involved with, including its relationship with Golf Canada and the LPGA Tour. CN is a strong supporter of Golf Canada's development programs. Refer to the illustration in Figure 10.19.

Among the various elements of the marketing communications mix, advertising, public relations, and Internet communications frequently play key roles in promoting an event. The ***advertising strategies*** for the event are based on the target market profile and how best to reach the target given the financial resources available. The content of the message and the style of delivery must combine effectively to meet the motivational needs of the audience. Media alternatives include television and radio advertising, magazine and newspaper advertising, direct mail (letters, brochures, and pamphlets), and the Internet.

FIGURE
10.19 **An Event Is a Brand with a Branded Look**

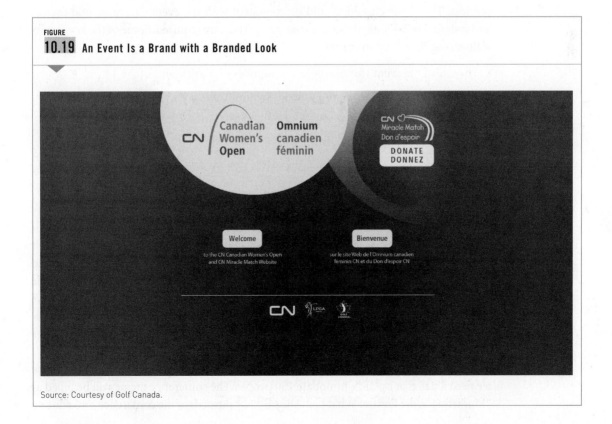

Source: Courtesy of Golf Canada.

The size of the media budget obviously dictates media decisions. An event like the Rogers Cup Tennis Championships for both men and women, which attracts a broad cross-section of ages, will adopt a multimedia strategy to create awareness and will rely heavily on the Internet to communicate specific information and sell tickets.

Public relations are also essential in generating positive publicity for an event. Organizers of large events frequently hold press conferences, timed appropriately, to build some pre-event publicity. Organizers may also issue press releases, as in the case of the Tim Hortons Brier, held in Edmonton in 2013, to stimulate interest in the community where the event is taking place and among people who may wish to attend the event. Refer to Figure 10.20 for an illustration. Smaller and more local events send a press release to all local media and then hope for the best—and take care to invite the press to the actual event.

Event Marketing Execution

Execution involves dealing with specific details about an event. A planner usually works from a checklist to ensure that all details are taken care of in the planning stage and the execution stage of an event. For the purpose of illustrating event execution, this section assumes that a planner is planning a marketing conference. Discussion will focus on several key areas, including site selection and staging, staffing, operations and logistics, and safety and security. Event execution is complex, and a full discussion of such a topic is beyond the scope of this textbook.

SITE SELECTION AND STAGING

In the theatre, the *stage* is the scene of action. The same is essentially true in event marketing. The scene of action for an event involves a site selected according to considerations such as theme development, sound and lighting, and availability of essential services. The venue chosen should be consistent with the event's purpose and theme, and it should provide all of the essential services that are required. Some of the key factors influencing site selection include

- The size of the event (for example, the number of participants).
- The suitability of the site for planned activities (for example, formal and informal activities).
- The primary field of play (for example, the theatre or conference room where the main event will be held).
- The availability of or proximity to accommodation, food, and attractions.
- The availability of on-site technical support and venue management experience.

Theme development was discussed earlier. At the event, the theme should be supported in every aspect, including sound and lighting, decor, and special effects. For example, the theme at a marketing conference could be very subtle and communicated only by signage and colour schemes. At much larger events of a longer duration, music and entertainment (for example, specific acts revolving around the theme) could be included, along with special props appropriately placed around the venue. If the latter is the choice, an event planner is wise to seek advice from staging and rental companies that offer specialized services in this area.

For the purpose of illustration, let's assume for our one-day marketing conference we need a hall that can accommodate 150 people. The conference theme will be billed as "Marketing in the Future: What Lies Ahead?" The purpose of the conference is to educate

FIGURE

10.20 **A Press Release Announcing Details of the Tim Hortons Brier (*continued*)**

 Edmonton to stage 2013 Tim Hortons Brier

Edmonton to stage 2013 Tim Hortons Brier

Wednesday, 23 November 2011 - Posted by **Jeff Timson**

Tweet ⟨3⟩   **Like** ⟨4⟩   **Print this Article**

The City of Edmonton will stage the 2013 Tim Hortons Brier, it was announced today by the Canadian Curling Association (CCA).

The Tim Hortons Brier, presented by Monsanto, will be played March 2-10 at Rexall Place. It will mark the sixth time that Edmonton has hosted the Canadian Men's Curling Championship, the last in 2005, and the 13th time it has been staged in Alberta, since the event began in 1927 in Toronto.

Edmonton joins Calgary, Halifax, Saskatoon and Toronto as the only cities to host the Brier on at least six occasions. It also will be the fourth major curling event held in the city in the last eight years, following the inaugural Tim Hortons Brier in 2005, the Ford World Men's in 2007 and the Tim Hortons Roar of the Rings (Canadian Curling Trials) in 2009. In fact, event attendance records were established at all three.

Rexall Place in Edmonton will host the 2013 Tim Hortons Brier

"The City of Edmonton has proven to be one of the most successful hosts for the Season of Champions properties over the past decade," stated Greg Stremlaw, Chief Executive Officer of the Canadian Curling Association. "The success of the 2005 Brier still resonates with curling fans across Canada as the largest attended curling event in history. As the most recent major curling event hosted in Edmonton, the 2009 Tim Hortons Roar of the Rings was yet another stellar event that served as the springboard for the selection of our Olympic curling teams in 2010.

"Building on these results, the CCA is expecting the 2013 Tim Hortons Brier to be a massive event and we look forward to putting on a show for all spectators to remember."

In 2005, a record 281,985 fans attended the Brier. In 2007, the World Men's attracted 184,970 fans, the best-ever for a men's only world event, while the 2009 Trials drew a record 175,852.

"In 1973, I was throwing rocks at the old Edmonton Hillcrest Country Club when Danny Fink and his team from Manitoba stepped out onto the ice next to me to practice for the Edmonton Brier," said Mark Johnson, host committee chair for the 2013 Tim Hortons Brier and also the 2010 Canadian Seniors and 2011 World Seniors champion.

"I was in awe watching them throw and then when I attended my first Brier game only days later, I was hooked on the Brier dream. It took me 33 years before I was able to fulfill that dream and represent Alberta in the 2006 Regina Brier. Believe me, I soaked up every minute of that amazing experience.

"I can't tell you how much of an honour it is to now have the opportunity to be the Chairman of the 2013 Tim Hortons Brier. Edmonton and the surrounding communities have an excellent reputation for supporting and hosting major events. I fully expect the calibre of play at the Brier to be the best. The Brier offers players the unique experience of representing their province or territory in a national championship and with the 2014 Sochi Winter Olympic Games taking place not long after, get ready, curling fans, because it's going to be a great show!"

Tim Hortons began its title sponsorship of the Brier in 2005 and earlier this year extended its agreement through 2014.

"The 2013 season marks Tim Hortons' ninth year as title sponsor of the Brier – a title that we are very proud of," said Bill Moir, Chief Brand and Marketing Officer, Tim Hortons. "The Brier is a true Canadian tradition and it's our pleasure to cheer them on through another championship."

Tickets for the 2013 Tim Hortons Brier, the 84th edition of the championship, are expected to go on sale in February of 2012. The winning team will represent Canada at the Ford World Men's Curling Championship, March 30-April 7 in Victoria, British Columbia. Edmonton also hosted the Brier in 1954, 1973, 1987 and 1999.

"Monsanto Canada remains a committed sponsor of Canadian Curling Association events because curling is a sport that is embraced by our farm customers and rural communities across the country," said Trish Jordan, Public and Industry Affairs Director with Monsanto Canada, based in Winnipeg.

FIGURE
10.20 *(continued)*

"We remember the excitement of the Roar of the Rings in 2009, which was also hosted by the City of Edmonton, and we look forward to returning to Edmonton for the 2013 Tim Hortons Brier."

The Brier will be televised exclusively and extensively in Canada by TSN, from the round robin, through the Page Playoffs, semi-final, bronze medal and gold medal games.

The Brier has been played in 31 cities across Canada, from Victoria to St. John's. Manitoba has won a leading 27 Briers, after last season's win by Winnipeg's Jeff Stoughton in London. Alberta is next with 25 victories, the latest by Edmonton's Kevin Koe in 2010 in Halifax. New Brunswick, Prince Edward Island and Yukon/Northwest Territories have yet to win.

Meanwhile, the 2012 Tim Hortons Brier, presented by Monsanto, will be held March 3-11 at Credit Union Centre in Saskatoon.

For further information:

Greg Stremlaw
Chief Executive Officer
Canadian Curling Association
Office: 613.834.2076 x 117
Cell: 613.799.9993
gstremlaw@curling.ca
www.curling.ca

Warren Hansen
Director, Event Operations and Media
Canadian Curling Association
Cell: 604.329.9850
whansen@curling.ca

TAGS: 2013, EDMONTON, NEWS FROM THE TIM HORTONS BRIER, TIM HORTONS

Source: Courtesy of Canadian Curling Association.

and inform concerned marketing managers about what trends and external environments will influence marketing strategies over the next decade. Influential guest speakers from the ranks of industry, government, and the services sectors will present their views on what the future holds and provide insights into how they are already responding.

At this type of conference, most of the speakers' presentations involve computer-generated shows, so a planner must be concerned about room layout—the stage where the speakers are positioned, sound, lighting, and vision. Let's start with **room layout**. Since a standard, rectangular-shaped banquet room is the theatre, the speakers will be placed at one long side of the room, reducing the distance between the front and back of the room. The seating will be laid out in a way conducive to taking notes. For this type of a presentation, there are four basic seating layouts: cabaret, banquet, classroom, and theatre (see Figure 10.21). Of the options available, the cabaret layout seems most appropriate because it allows for good eye contact for all participants and encourages communication among participants at each table.

The guest speakers will be on an elevated platform at one side of the room. The height of the platform considers the sight lines of the audience. The audience must be able to see the speaker and the screen clearly. Appropriate backdrops should be on stage to isolate the presentation area and create a more intimate feeling. At such a conference, the speaker rarely controls the slide presentation—technical coordination is usually the responsibility of an audiovisual expert who is located at the side of the room.

Proper **sound** and **lighting** are essential to create mood and ambience. Professional advice from a sound and lighting expert is recommended. Such advice is usually readily available at conference centres. If audience communication is going to be important, microphones should be strategically situated throughout the conference room.

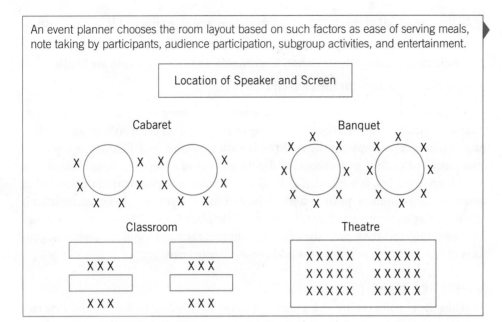

FIGURE
10.21

An Event Planner Can Choose from a Variety of Room Layouts

An event planner chooses the room layout based on such factors as ease of serving meals, note taking by participants, audience participation, subgroup activities, and entertainment.

With all details addressed, the final aspect of staging is *rehearsal*. The rehearsal is an opportunity for everyone to integrate their efforts and to ensure that all technical glitches are remedied. Contingency plans should be established in case the unexpected occurs, which it often does! For example, there should be a plan in place in case a speaker falls ill at the last minute or the projector breaks down.

Additional staging considerations include making arrangements for catering and *accommodations*. Since the marketing conference is being held at a conference centre, food and beverages are readily available. Decisions involve the style of service (for example, buffet or set menu with table service), the timing and availability of snacks and beverages (for example, during planned breaks), and choosing the menu for each meal. Hotels and conference centres usually offer food and beverage packages that are available in a range of prices. Of course, the planner must negotiate room rates with the host hotel or conference centre. Typically a group rate is negotiated based on number of rooms that will be booked.

STAFFING

Planning and executing an event are complex undertakings and, depending on the size and scope of the event, the human resources required can vary considerably. Can you imagine the number of people who are required (paid and volunteers) when a city hosts the Olympic Games or a national sports championship? For large-scale events, the roles and responsibilities of all individuals must be spelled out in detail. Therefore, organization charts are needed for various stages of event planning: pre-event, event, and post-event. In the pre-event stage, the focus is on planning, so anyone connected with marketing, financial, and human resources planning is involved. During the event itself, human resources capacity expands to its fullest, so it is essential that reporting relationships for all operations be delineated. After the event, only those people involved with evaluation and financial planning play a key role.

OPERATIONS AND LOGISTICS

To illustrate the importance of operations and logistics, consider the planning required to get a major golf championship, such as the RBC Canadian Open, up and running. For the participants alone, a plan is needed to ensure that

• All golfers, their entourage, and their equipment arrive on time.

- Golfers are settled in the correct accommodation, and all equipment is safe and secure.

- The golf course is in immaculate condition (a process that starts months before the competition), and spectator stands, scoreboards, and crowd barriers are in place.

- Golfers arrive in time for their tee-off each day.

bump-in (setup)
The setting up of structures and other equipment at an event.

This set-up process is referred to as the bump-in. **Bump-in**, or **setup**, involves setting up structures and facilities required for an event. For an event such as our marketing conference example, tasks such as installing sound and lighting equipment, computers, projectors, and screens involve the services of a specialist. Regardless of how the bump-in occurs, it is essential that all facilities and equipment are in place and in good working condition prior to the official start of the event. Simply stated, logistics is about getting equipment and people into the right place at the right time so that things run smoothly, and then, once the event is complete, taking everything down. The process of dismantling is referred to as **bump-out**, or **teardown**.

bump-out (teardown)
The process of dismantling everything after an event.

SAFETY AND SECURITY

Imagine the potential safety and security concerns there would be for a Grand Prix racing car event where the race is conducted on city streets. For that matter, any sports event where large numbers of fans congregate requires a detailed plan outlining safety and security measures. The plan must consider potential crowd behaviour and methods for controlling crowds, should the need arise.

At an event, everyone must feel safe, including the audience, the staff, and the subcontractors (for example, technical crews). At large events, accidents can occur, people might fall ill, or something completely unexpected may happen. Potential risks include fires, bomb threats, gas leaks, overzealous fans (even riots), and so on. A few years back, some NBA basketball players and fans were involved in an ugly brawl, a situation that threatened the safety of both fans and players. Crowd management—the orderly flow of spectators in and out of the venue—is very important. Signage indicating direction and staff barking out commands where necessary play a key role in moving audience pedestrian traffic smoothly.

Proper security measures for property, equipment, and cash must also be planned for. As well, the planner must ensure that only certain people have access to specific areas and must act responsibly in case of emergency. Typically, people in positions of authority or special responsibility wear badges identifying their role at the event. Vehicles may be necessary to transport security personnel to areas where emergencies occur. Event planners have a choice of hiring private security firms or members of the local police force. Since safety and security is such a critical issue, it is recommended that organizers of large events employ external organizations that are experts in this field to take care of all of the planning and implementation.

SUMMARY

Experiential marketing is a growing component of marketing communications campaigns. Organizations see greater value in activities that actively engage a target audience with a brand, and that is what experiential marketing does. Activities such as free product samples, product promotional tours, shopper marketing programs, and event marketing and sponsorships are potential components of an experiential marketing campaign. Typically, experiential marketing strategies reach fewer consumers than traditional advertising strategies, but the quality of the association a brand develops with consumers is stronger.

Event marketing and sponsorships are now an important element of a firm's marketing communications mix. Sponsorships tend to be concentrated in five areas: sports, entertainment, festivals and fairs, culture and the arts, and causes. Ongoing sponsorships on television shows can also be included in the sponsorship mix. Events and sponsorships can be local in nature, or they can be expanded to become regional, national, or international in scope. Sports sponsorships and events draw the majority of the sponsorship pie, but interest is now growing faster in the other areas.

Prior to getting involved with sponsorships, an organization should establish specific criteria for participation. Factors to consider include product category exclusivity, relationships with other marketing communications programs, the event's ability to reach the desired target market effectively, and the image-building potential offered by the event.

Once the event is over, attention turns to evaluation. In relation to objectives that were established for the event, measures are determined for criteria such as awareness, image enhancement, new business clients, product sales, target market reach, and media coverage. There will be an assessment of all revenues and costs to determine profitability and to make recommendations for improvements should the event be planned for another occasion.

Should an organization decide to plan its own event, it must be comfortable with a rather exhaustive planning process. The first decision is to evaluate the role of the event or sponsorship to ensure it offers a good opportunity for achieving business objectives. The organization is responsible for establishing goals and objectives, identifying the target audience, determining the best time for the event, providing adequate financial resources, and evaluating the event for effectiveness. The event planner develops strategies for staging the event, making available properly trained staff to execute the event, planning operations and logistics to make sure everything runs smoothly, and preparing for safety and security issues that could arise during an event.

The first stage in developing an event is to determine the event's concept and design. This involves decisions about the type of event, the name, and the theme of the event. Once these decisions are made, attention focuses on issues such as venue alternatives, financial resources required, timing, room layouts, and technical requirements. Technical support is commonly outsourced.

As with other forms of marketing communications planning, objectives are established. Typically, event marketing objectives focus on target audience reach, potential new business and product sales, the economic impact of the event, and profit. Event marketing strategies involve carefully defining the product (the event) and then positioning it in the minds of the target audience. A good event title and theme become the foundation for building an effective communications strategy for motivating attendance at the event. An effective price strategy is also crucial because prospective participants evaluate the potential benefits against the cost of attending. To promote the event, a combination of media advertising and public relations is an effective mix. All communications must have a branded look and present a similar message to the target audience.

At the execution stage, concerns focus on specific details in the following areas: site selection and staging, staffing, operations and logistics, and safety and security. All details must be checked and rechecked to ensure a smooth flow of activities and people.

KEY TERMS

ambush marketing 295	experiential marketing 288	timeline chart 310
bump-in 318	run sheet 310	venue marketing 296
bump-out 318	setup 317	venue sponsorship 296
event marketing 292	shopper marketing 290	
event sponsorship 293	teardown 317	

REVIEW QUESTIONS

1. Briefly explain how experiential marketing is different from other forms of marketing communications activities. What benefits does it offer?
2. What is shopper marketing? Briefly explain and offer a new example of this concept.
3. What is the difference between event marketing and event sponsorship?
4. What is ambush marketing, and what benefits does it offer?
5. Identify and briefly explain the main classifications of event marketing.
6. Briefly explain the criteria an executive considers before pursuing an event marketing opportunity.

7. What are the measures commonly used to evaluate the effectiveness of event marketing participation?
8. Identify the basic steps in the event marketing planning process.
9. Developing the event concept is the initial stage of planning an event. What are the key decision areas in this stage? Briefly explain each.
10. Designing the event is the second stage of event planning. What are some of the key decision areas in this stage? Briefly explain each.
11. Briefly explain the purpose of the following planning tools:

a) timeline chart
b) run sheet

12. A key element of event marketing strategy is defining the event. What decisions are associated with defining the event?
13. Briefly explain the following stages of event marketing execution:

a) site selection and staging
b) staffing
c) operations and logistics
d) safety and security

DISCUSSION AND APPLICATION QUESTIONS

1. Why are companies becoming more actively involved in cause-related event sponsorships? Conduct some secondary research on this issue and formulate a position on the matter.
2. Do value-added sponsorships, such as the one between Reebok and Sidney Crosby, offer significant benefits to the sponsoring organization? If so, what are the benefits? Discuss.
3. What classification of event sponsorship is appropriate for the following companies or brands? (More than one can apply.) Justify your decision.

a) Becel margarine
b) Michelin tires
c) BMW automobiles
d) McDonald's

4. Assume you are responsible for planning an event such as a marathon/half-marathon race to raise funds for the Alzheimer's Association of Canada or some similar not-for-profit organization. What are your objectives? Consider both qualitative and quantitative objectives. Provide examples of a few objective statements. What marketing strategies will you employ to create awareness and interest in the event? Provide details of the activities you recommend.
5. Provide some examples of companies and brands that are involved with "experiential marketing." Based on your observations of their activities, identify the strengths and weaknesses of this form of marketing communications.

ENDNOTES

1. Adapted from Levon Guiragossian, "The Definition of Experiential Marketing," *Web 2.0 Marketing*, March 31, 2008, web2pointzero-marketing.blogspot.ca/2008/03/definition-of-experiential-marketing.html.
2. "Yukon Tourism Calls City Folk Northward," *Marketing*, April 25, 2012, www.marketingmag.ca/uncategorized/yukon-tourism-calls-city-folk-northward-51094.
3. "2012 Shopper Engagement Study," Point of Purchase Advertising International (POPAI), www.popai.com/engage/docs/Media-Topline-Final.pdf.
4. Robert Gumiela, comments from a presentation at the Experiential Marketing Conference, Toronto, 2009.
5. "What Is Shopper Marketing? Examples of It in Action." *Visualise News*, January 20, 2012, www.visualise.ie/what-is-shopper-marketing-examples-of-it-in-action.
6. Norm O'Reilly and Benoit Seguin, *Canadian Sponsorship Landscape Study*, University of Ottawa, 2011, www.sponsorshipmarketing.ca/CSLS_5thannual_2011.pdf.
7. "Event Marketing," Business Dictionary, www.businessdictionary.com/definition/event-marketing.html.
8. Simon Ward, "North American Sponsorship Growth to Slow in a Year Full of Contradictions," IEG, January 11, 2011, www.sponsorship.com/About-IEG/IEG-In-The-News/North-American-Sponsorship-Growth--To-Slow-In-Year.aspx.
9. "Lesson 4: Where the Money Goes; Lessons Learned in 2011: *Canadian Sponsorship Landscape Study*," Canadian Sponsorship Forum, www.canadiansponsorshipforum.com/lesson-4-where-the-money-goes.
10. "Corporate Responsibility: Community Sponsorship," BMO Financial Group, www.bmo.com/home/about/banking/corporate-responsibility/community/sponsorships.
11. "Sony Takes Over from Hummingbird," *Marketing Daily*, September 10, 2007, www.marketingmag.ca.
12. "Pepsi Ousts Coke in Rogers Arena Deal," *Marketing*, October 5, 2011, www.marketingmag.ca/uncategorized/pepsi-ousts-coke-in-rogers-arena-deal-37322.
13. Paul-Mark Rendon, "Hot Properties," *Marketing*, June 27, 2005, p. 11.
14. Kate Macarthur, "Pepsi is Out, Coke is In as 2006 Oscars Sponsor," *Advertising Age*, June 2, 2005, adage.com/article/news/pepsi-coke-2006-oscars-sponsor/45952.
15. Toronto International Film Festival, "Lights, Camera, Festival!" cdn.media.tiff.net/contents/pdfs/SponsorshipFestival2013.pdf.
16. Wendy Cuthbert, "Sponsors Pump ROI with Experiential Approach," *Strategy*, March 12, 2001, p. B7.
17. RBC Canadian Open, www.rbccanadianopen.com.

Personal Selling

1. Understand the role of personal selling in retail, business-to-business, and direct selling environments, and its relationship to integrated marketing communications

2. Describe the evolution of personal selling strategies and evaluate the role that relationship selling plays in integrated marketing communications programs

3. Identify the human variables that contribute to the successful application of personal selling strategies

4. Learn how to apply this knowledge to a variety of personal selling situations

5. Identify the fundamental roles and responsibilities of a sales representative

6. Identify the essential steps in the selling process and the key elements required for preparing a successful sales presentation

7. Assess how selling strategies need to adapt to a changing business environment

Among the various components of the integrated marketing communications mix, personal selling differentiates itself due to its personal nature. Other forms of marketing communication are non-personal. Advertising and promotions rely on the media to deliver a message; public relations use various tools to seek the media's support in spreading the word; and direct response communications rely on the mail, the Internet, and mobile communications. In spite of all of the changes that have occurred in the marketplace and in spite of the fact that industry has come to rely on technology as a means of communication, personal selling still remains a vital component. Organizations continue to sell—they just sell differently than they used to.

To demonstrate, customer relationship management (CRM) practices affect all forms of communication, but none more than personal selling. The human contact and the ability to negotiate form the foundation of CRM practices. Furthermore, all the technical wizardry in the world can only go so far. Once the show is over, someone has to ask for the order. And that's the responsibility of the sales representative. This chapter examines the role of personal selling in the context of integrated marketing communications.

Personal Selling and Integrated Marketing Communications

personal selling
Face-to-face communication involving the presentation of features and benefits of a product or service to a buyer; the objective is to make a sale.

Personal selling is a personalized form of communications that involves sellers presenting the features and benefits of a product or service to a buyer for the purpose of making a sale. It is an integral component of marketing communications because it is the activity that in many cases clinches the deal. Advertising and promotions create awareness and interest for a product; personal selling creates desire and action. In creating desire and action, the interaction between the seller and buyer is crucial.

Personal selling can be divided into three main areas: retail selling, business-to-business (B2B) selling, and direct selling, either to consumers or other businesses (see Figure 11.1). In all these areas, personal selling is connected to other aspects of integrated marketing communications planning. For example, a sales representative for Kraft Foods who calls on the head office of a grocery chain such as Safeway or Sobeys does more than just communicate the benefits of various product lines. If the salesperson's

FIGURE
11.1

Classifications of Personal Selling

Retail Selling	Involves single or repeat transactions at point-of-purchase. Key ingredients are knowledgeable staff and efficient, courteous service.
Business-to-Business	Involves highly trained salespeople calling on manufacturers, wholesalers, and institutions. It is important to establish and build relationships with customers.
Direct Selling	Involves contacting customers directly by telephone or other electronic means. Effective database management systems encourage direct selling.

presentation involves a new product launch, the objective is to get the product listed by the chain's head office so that retail stores in the chain can order it. Buyers want to know what kind of marketing support will be provided by Kraft. In the sales presentation, the salesperson will include information about advertising plans and sales promotion plans (both consumer and trade promotions) that will help create demand for the new product. Details about when advertising is scheduled, what markets it will run in, and what incentives will be offered to the consumer and the trade are all critical factors that influence the buying decision.

RETAIL SELLING

Transactions occur on the sales floor of a department store, at the teller's wicket in a bank, at an insurance agent's office, and at the service desk of an automobile maintenance shop, to name just a few examples of retail selling. In these situations, the nature of the sale is defined as a single transaction or a repeat transaction. The quality of service offered at the point of purchase and the degree of satisfaction the customer receives usually influence repeat transactions. In fact, the retail salesperson is the face of the organization. How that person deals with customers affects the buyer's experience.

Successful retailers continuously stress the importance of customer contact at point of purchase. How a retail salesperson interacts with the customer has a significant impact on how the customer perceives the retailer and helps determine if that individual will make a purchase. It is the seller's responsibility to clarify what the customer actually needs, usually by politely asking a few questions. The seller must then offer some product suggestions and demonstrate knowledge by presenting the essential benefits of the products to the customer.

The nature of information offered and the level of service provided will also influence whether or not a person will return to the retail store. People like to feel comfortable when making important buying decisions. For example, customers will return to the same automobile repair shop after getting to know the people who are working on their cars. The customer wants to avoid the potential risk in dealing with different repair shops. The relationship between the buyer and seller is usually based on factors such as trust, respect, and satisfaction with the goods or services provided.

When the purchase decision is made, the seller should look for opportunities for add-on sales or suggest service warranties to protect the customer's long-term interests.

In doing so, the seller should not be too aggressive, as that may lead to customer frustration. Generally speaking, a low-key approach involving positive customer contact in a pleasant and courteous manner is the main ingredient for retail selling success. In retail, the salespeople are the most essential point of contact in the purchasing process—integral to a well-planned integrated marketing communications program.

BUSINESS-TO-BUSINESS SELLING

Business-to-business salespeople either sell products for use in the production and sale of other products, or sell finished products to channel members who in turn resell them. For example, a Xerox sales representative sells photocopiers to another business for use in its daily operations; a representative from Sun Life sells a health insurance plan to another company that will benefit all the buying company's employees.

Thoroughly trained and adequately prepared sales representatives are crucial in these examples. Investment in other forms of marketing communications could be all for naught if the personal selling execution is weak. B2B organizations usually have different types of sales personnel. A **field sales force** is composed of sales representatives who call on customers regularly. They make presentations to existing and new customers, and provide ongoing customer contact to establish a good business relationship. A company may also operate with an **inside sales force**, often referred to as order takers, who seek out new customers and provide useful information to them. Working from the organization's premises, an order taker handles orders that are received by telephone, fax, or online.

DIRECT SELLING

Direct selling to customers either by telephone or the Internet can be accommodated in the retail selling and B2B selling situations described above. **Telemarketing** involves using the telephone as an interactive medium for a marketing response. It uses highly trained people and database marketing techniques to seek and serve new customers. Figure 11.2 summarizes the role that telemarketing can play in the selling process. Telemarketing improves productivity by reducing direct-selling costs, specifically the costs associated with keeping sales representatives on the road (automobiles, accommodations, and related travel expenses). It is also useful in screening and **qualifying** incoming leads, generating leads from various database directories and mailing lists, calling on current customers to secure additional orders, and determining the level of customer satisfaction.

Online selling refers to the use of websites to conduct sales transactions. Consumers who are looking for convenience now include the web as part of their shopping experience. E-commerce in Canada in the business-to-consumer sector is growing gradually each year. In 2010, 51 percent of Internet users ordered goods or services for personal or

field sales force
An organization's external sales representatives who regularly call on customers to pursue orders.

inside sales force
An internal group of sellers, often referred to as order takers, who accept orders from customers by telephone or other means.

telemarketing
The use of telecommunications to promote the products and services of a business; involves outbound calls (company to customer) and inbound calls (customer to company).

qualifying (a customer)
Assessing if a prospect needs a product, has the authority to buy it, and has the ability to pay for it.

online selling
Using the Internet to conduct sales transactions.

FIGURE 11.2

Some of the Roles Played by Telemarketing in Personal Selling

Sales Support	Selling	Customer Service
• Generate leads	• Open new accounts	• Operate customer help lines
• Qualify leads	• Call marginal accounts	• Handle inquiries and complaints
• Schedule appointments	• Sell to existing customers	• Offer after-sales service
• Collect market intelligence		• Conduct satisfaction surveys

FIGURE

11.3

Online Selling Offers Convenience to Consumers

Source: Courtesy of Grocery Gateway.

household use—orders valued at $15.3 billion.[1] Consumers now use their mobile devices to purchase goods. As the penetration of smartphones increases in Canada, more people will be purchasing their goods and services directly. To stay relevant, marketing organizations must adapt their selling strategies accordingly.

Figure 11.3 shows how Grocery Gateway, an online supermarket, provides its consumers convenience. Websites like Grocery Gateway's are capable of accepting and processing orders, receiving payment, and arranging for the delivery of goods and services directly to consumers and businesses. Indigo Books & Music, operator of Chapters and Indigo stores, sells goods in a similar fashion. Since all transactions are electronically recorded, companies accumulate huge databases of information that can be used for marketing purposes in the longer term.

The Evolution of Selling

Over the years, the nature of selling has changed dramatically. Since the 1970s, personal selling has passed through four distinct stages: consultative selling, strategic selling, relationship selling, and partnership selling.[2] Organizations now operate in an era where buyers have already done their homework on potential suppliers and their products and services before a sales representative even gets in the door. Furthermore, transactions between buyers and sellers are so automated today salespeople are struggling to make themselves relevant in the transaction process.[3]

Changes in the marketplace have dictated changes in selling strategies. Products are now more sophisticated and complex, competition is more intense and occurs on a broader (global) scale, and customer expectations of quality, price, service, and individualized solutions have increased considerably. Similar to other components of the marketing

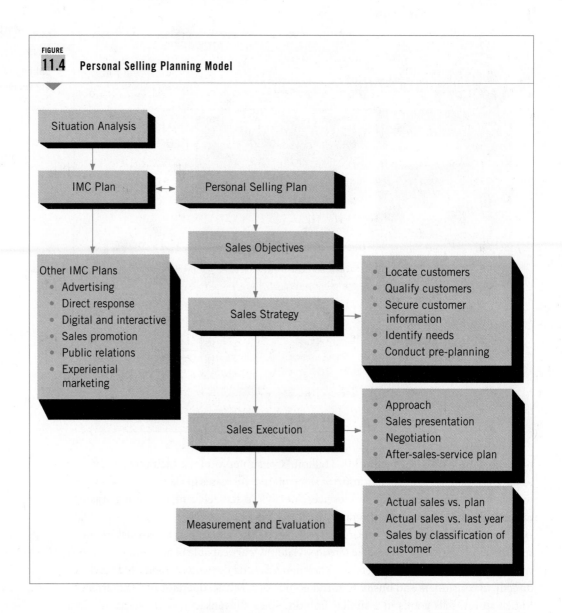

FIGURE 11.4   Personal Selling Planning Model

Situation Analysis

IMC Plan ↔ Personal Selling Plan

Sales Objectives

Other IMC Plans
- Advertising
- Direct response
- Digital and interactive
- Sales promotion
- Public relations
- Experiential marketing

Sales Strategy
- Locate customers
- Qualify customers
- Secure customer information
- Identify needs
- Conduct pre-planning

Sales Execution
- Approach
- Sales presentation
- Negotiation
- After-sales-service plan

Measurement and Evaluation
- Actual sales vs. plan
- Actual sales vs. last year
- Sales by classification of customer

communications mix, strategic selling strategies are influenced by an organization's strategic marketing plan. The marketing plan acts as a guide for the strategic selling plan. Refer to Figure 11.4 for an illustration of the planning model.

Consultative selling stresses open, two-way communication between sellers and buyers. The initial task of the seller is to discover a need or set of needs by asking questions and listening carefully. The seller then uses that information to formulate appropriate product recommendations—acting as a consultant. Once the sale is complete, the seller gets involved with after-sales service and customer care programs. A satisfied customer remains a customer!

Strategic selling takes consultative selling to the next level. It considers the most recent yet continuously changing conditions in the marketplace, adds technology to enhance the methods of presenting products to buyers, and focuses on serving customers one customer at a time. The goal is to remain flexible while providing solutions that are unique to each customer. There are three key factors to be considered when formulating a strategic sales strategy. First, the seller must do what is necessary to form a good relationship with the customer. Second, the seller must effectively match products and position them so that they

consultative selling
A form of selling that stresses open, two-way communication between a buyer and seller.

strategic selling
A form of consultative selling that involves dealing with each customer as an individual, stressing that in the transfer of product information.

meet customer needs. Third, the seller must develop a compelling presentation that will clearly portray the usefulness of a product in resolving a customer's problem.

In **relationship selling**, the goal is to develop a plan of action to establish, build, and maintain customers. In involves taking a long-term perspective on selling and considers the fact that good relationships don't necessarily form very quickly. Instead, a seller must take the necessary steps to form a relationship, such as establishing rapport and building trust and respect, over a long period of time. Having a positive attitude, projecting a good image, and being able to get along with all kinds of different people and personalities are key factors that contribute to a sales representative's ability to build a solid relationship with customers.

relationship selling
A form of selling with the goal of developing a plan of action that establishes, builds, and maintains a long-term relationship with customers.

Establishing a good relationship depends on how well the seller positions products in the minds of customers, how effectively (persuasively) the product's benefits are presented, and how well the seller guards the relationship in the long run. The latter requires ongoing customer contact and the implementation of customer care programs. Figure 11.5 reviews the key aspects of relationship selling.

With relationship selling, it is the seller's responsibility to match the right product to the customer and then develop the communications strategy that will position it appropriately in the customer's mind. A sales representative for Apple, for example, will capitalize on the user-friendly positioning strategy that Apple uses in other forms of marketing communications to sell computers. The representative differentiates Apple from other brands based on benefits such as uniqueness, degree of innovation, performance capabilities (speed of performing functions), and reliability. A wise representative will also build in the lifestyle imagery associated with the brand—for example, it is perceived as a sleek and sexy brand, a lifestyle brand compared to PCs.

The formation of the right positioning strategy depends largely on the seller's knowledge of the customer. The more knowledge the seller has going into the presentation, the easier it is to structure the presentation. A good salesperson continuously updates customer files with new information. In the age of technology, such a practice is easy to do and vital to success. People in organizations move around, so it is very important to be constantly on top of who is responsible for what.

A good salesperson formulates a **presentation strategy** that focuses on what to say to customers when presenting the product. A good plan is based on the seller's knowledge

presentation strategy
A plan of what to say to a customer in a sales presentation to identify customer needs, summarize benefits, and prepare for potential objections.

FIGURE
11.5

The Key Elements of Relationship Selling

Overall Goal	To establish, build, and maintain customers.
Personal Strategy	The seller must initiate steps that will build rapport with customers. The seller must earn the trust and respect of the customer. The salesperson must have a strong and positive self-image and be flexible when dealing with many different people and personalities.
Selling Strategy	The salesperson must effectively position the product (a solution) in the customer's mind by relating the right benefits to a unique problem or situation that the customer presents. The benefits should be related to the rational needs of the buying organization and the emotional needs of the buyer. A salesperson must make a convincing presentation and be flexible enough to adapt to the unexpected while the presentation is in progress. A persuasive presentation should lead the buyer to the right decision.
Building Relationships	Customers not only want good products, but also want good relationships. Selling today is not about selling products—it's about selling solutions!

of the customer and the customer's immediate needs; it summarizes potential benefits that will be stressed (often prioritized from most important to least important) and considers potential objections that the buyer might raise. As with most marketing communications strategies, a sales strategy must remain flexible. The seller, for example, must be able to adapt the presentation based on new information that surfaces during a presentation, or to rephrase relevant benefits if the buyer introduces the benefits of a competitor's product. The importance of knowledge in a variety of areas and the key elements of a presentation are discussed in more detail later in this chapter.

PARTNERSHIP SELLING

partnership selling
A strategically developed long-term relationship that involves selling products and providing comprehensive after-sales service and effective two-way communications to ensure complete customer satisfaction.

Partnership selling is an extension of relationship selling. It involves a strategically developed, long-term relationship to sell products, provides comprehensive after-sales service, and encourages effective two-way communications to ensure complete customer satisfaction. The goal is to form partnerships with customers in a manner that fosters prosperity among partners.

Changing conditions in the marketplace have fostered the concept of partnership selling. There was a time when companies could rely on the strength of their company, product, and service components to secure stability and growth. Now, however, the intensity of competition, the availability of copycat products, the need to constantly reduce costs, and the speed with which innovative products are introduced necessitates strong buyer–seller partnerships. As well, buyers are simply more informed today. With so much information available online, they can access information about competing brands and formulate opinions prior to even meeting with a sales representative.

In today's business environment, sellers are transforming their selling procedures and methods to build formal relationships with other organizations in the channel of distribution.[4] These procedures and methods are part of the CRM philosophy discussed earlier in this book.

Selling organizations today must be willing to invest time and money into finding good solutions. It's not about selling products any more—it's about selling solutions! To operate successfully in this environment, a salesperson must show a deep understanding of a prospect's business needs. According to Mark Stuyt, a successful sales force trainer, "A sales representative needs to understand how the business operates. Industry content is absolutely critical. Sales people know their product but not much about the industry they are selling into. Today, business acumen trumps traditional sales tactics."[5]

To illustrate, consider separate cases of two competing courier companies. Purolator changed its selling practices by moving away from a transactional approach to a value-based selling strategy. In the courier market, price is an important element of the decision process, but the VP of sales at Purolator said, "If you win customers on price, you'll typically lose them on price."[6] So, instead of focusing on price when selling its services, Purolator began offering customers customized large-freight shipping services that required a much more intensive style of selling. Since 2005, Purolator has grown its large-freight business from nothing to $70 million annually. (see Figure 11.6).

UPS has moved from being a courier service to become a supply chain management company with the goal of assisting customers with their long-range growth needs. The company has evolved with changes in the marketplace and with the changing needs of its customers. Shipping goods is a complex business that many organizations prefer to outsource. UPS is equipped to serve those organizations.

In a marketing communications context, smart managers know that customers rely on different pieces of information as they proceed through the buying process. Various components of the mix may take priority. For example, an event may be more important than advertising, depending on the target audience. An event combined with effective personal selling strategies may be just the right mix to motivate a potential buyer. For more insight into how various components of the communications mix may be combined, read the IMC Highlight: **Personal Connections Work for Jaguar and Jeep**.

Personal Connections Work for Jaguar and Jeep

With the help of some good database marketing, Jaguar Canada was able to identify prospective customers it would invite to an invitation-only test-drive event. Imagine driving a 400-horsepower Jaguar around a track, sampling gourmet pasta, and relaxing over drinks. Jaguar's mission: get owners of competitors' vehicles inside a Jaguar—kind of a "try it and you will like it" marketing strategy.

Jaguar is a small brand that doesn't advertise all that much. Given the upscale nature of the vehicle and the selective audience that has the means to buy the car, Jaguar prefers relationship marketing events. Jaguar president Gary Moyer says, "Someone buying a $100 000 car doesn't watch TV ads or read magazine ads. But this kind of thing makes their hair stand up on the back of their neck."

Test-drive events are growing in importance, and for some companies they now take centre stage in the overall marketing strategy. These events are costly to plan and implement, but there is a payoff. People who test drive a vehicle are more likely to consider that brand when they buy. In fact, some research indicates they are three times more likely to buy the test-drive vehicle.

At Chrysler, the Jeep brand runs a three-day event called Camp Jeep and invites brand loyalists and prospective customers to it. Lou Bitonti, a marketing executive at Chrysler, says, "You have to keep that human connection and passion point. We show them the Jeep in real conditions and have specialists there to answer all their questions." He adds that events help dispel false impressions about Jeep while creating positive new ones.

To promote the Toyota Tundra truck, Toyota participates in farm, fishing, and outdoor shows. At these events, Toyota shows how the truck complements the lifestyle of the target audience by showing a Toyota Tundra packed and ready to go on a fishing trip. That gets the prospect excited!

From a strategic perspective, auto marketers like these kinds of events for three reasons: First, there is a personal connection with the customer; second, they can convey the vehicle's character; and third, events break through the cluttered media landscape and can target hard-to-reach targets, such as young trendsetters. More to the point, the automaker has the complete attention of the buyer, who can actually touch and feel the car, interact with the brand at a relaxed pace, and test the vehicle to discover in a very personal way what it has to offer. Marketing today is about reaching people wherever they are. Test-drive events do just that, but in a very personal and creative manner.

Adapted from Jeremy Cato, "Automakers Finding New Ways to Move Metal," *The Globe and Mail*, August 16, 2007, www.globeauto.com.

Personal Selling: The Human Communications Element

If establishing and building effective relationships are the keys to modern-day success, what strategies must the salesperson use to form a good working relationship with customers? To be successful, a salesperson must focus on three primary areas: personal characteristics, verbal communications, and non-verbal communications. A well-prepared and energetic salesperson knows how to communicate effectively both verbally and non-verbally, and, as a result, will be successful. Let's examine each area briefly.

PERSONAL CHARACTERISTICS

To survive in selling, certain personal characteristics are required. Typically, successful salespeople are self-confident, motivated, flexible, optimistic, and project a good image when confronted with social and business situations. These characteristics can be learned and practised. Given time and proper training, poorly performing salespeople can be transformed into prosperous salespeople. All that is required are dedication and a desire to confront the challenges of selling.

Self-image is a psychological term referring to one's attitude and feelings about oneself and one's roles in relation to others. It certainly plays a key role in selling. Perhaps the most important aspect of self-image is confidence. For example, an individual who approaches a challenge with enthusiasm, or possesses that "I'm going to win" attitude, is likely to succeed. In contrast, an individual who tends to forecast failure, or has a "doom and gloom" attitude, will almost certainly get disappointing results. To succeed, therefore, you have to think you can succeed.

self-image
One's own idea about oneself and one's relationship with others.

Among all the theories about building self-confidence that exist, three essential strategies stand out. First, a positive self-image will exist if a person does not dwell on past mistakes. Instead, people must learn from their mistakes and move forward. Second, a salesperson should develop some expertise in a certain area, because there is special status in being an expert. Others will call upon you for advice. Third, a salesperson should develop a positive outlook. For example, taking courses that reinforce the principles of success and simply associating with other positive and successful people are both good practices to follow.

VERBAL AND NON-VERBAL COMMUNICATIONS

Typically, good salespeople have good **verbal skills**. They are generally comfortable when addressing a buyer, buying committee, or even a larger audience. When one thinks of a salesperson, the stereotype of the fast talker often comes to mind, but the reality is that listening skills are just as important. A salesperson who listens carefully to what the buyer says can respond better. Communications in a selling situation is a two-way street.

verbal skills
Comfort and ability with speaking and listening.

Non-verbal communication or **body language** is another essential aspect of self-confidence. Non-verbal communication refers to the imparting of thoughts, opinions, or information without using spoken words. An observer (in this case the buyer) will notice non-verbal cues such as body movement, facial expressions, and eye contact.[7] A buyer's perceptions of a salesperson are often determined by body language. For example, does the seller squirm in the chair while conversing, or does the seller fidget with a small object while speaking? Such body language could be perceived as a lack of confidence. Alternatively, does the seller make direct eye contact? Was that handshake firm and friendly? Such body language suggests positive self-confidence. For a summary of some essential characteristics and traits for successful selling, refer to Figure 11.7.

non-verbal communication (body language)
The expression of thoughts, opinions, or information using non-verbal cues such as body movement, facial expressions, and eye contact.

Other non-verbal characteristics that influence buyers' perceptions include facial expressions, personal appearance, and manners. The old expression that "the lips say one thing, but the eyes say another" applies to selling situations. Facial gestures can communicate confidence, as does a smile; boredom, as does a grin; or evaluation or judgment, as in a frown or perplexed expression. Given that the goal in selling is to express confidence, successful salespeople always wear a sincere and winning smile when they approach customers and when they present information to them.

Dress codes have changed drastically in recent years. The business world moved away from formal attire (business suits) and toward informal attire (business casual) for a period of time. The "Casual Friday" concept spread to the entire week. Recently,

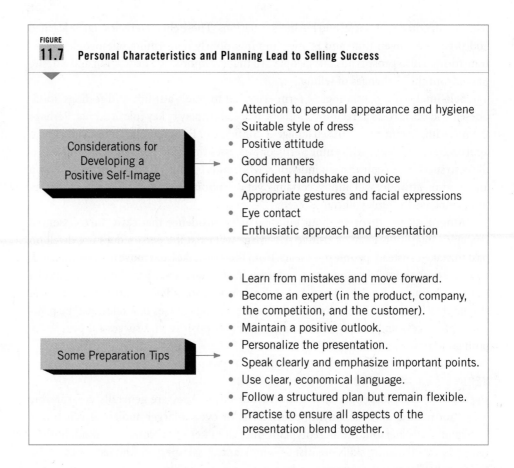

FIGURE 11.7   Personal Characteristics and Planning Lead to Selling Success

Considerations for Developing a Positive Self-Image

- Attention to personal appearance and hygiene
- Suitable style of dress
- Positive attitude
- Good manners
- Confident handshake and voice
- Appropriate gestures and facial expressions
- Eye contact
- Enthusiatic approach and presentation

Some Preparation Tips

- Learn from mistakes and move forward.
- Become an expert (in the product, company, the competition, and the customer).
- Maintain a positive outlook.
- Personalize the presentation.
- Speak clearly and emphasize important points.
- Use clear, economical language.
- Follow a structured plan but remain flexible.
- Practise to ensure all aspects of the presentation blend together.

however, there has been a return to more formal dress. Wardrobe experts believe clothing makes a significant difference in building one's credibility and likeability with customers. Experts offer different opinions on how to dress, but generally there is one common theme: The situation (or appropriateness) dictates the style of dress. For example, if you are meeting your customer in a business office or boardroom setting, formal dress is appropriate. If the meeting is in a factory or at a construction site, less formal attire is suitable. Other traditional guidelines for wardrobe focus on simplicity, quality, and the selective use of accessories. Accessories such as earrings, necklaces, and facial jewellery could be a distraction for the buyer, and anything causing a distraction should be avoided.

There is a relationship between verbal communication and non-verbal communication in a selling situation. Successful salespeople effectively blend together verbal and non-verbal communications. They communicate the message in a positive and enthusiastic manner, and reinforce it with body language that is consistent with what they say. Such a combination builds confidence in the buyer and gives the buyer the impression the salesperson can be trusted. Such perceptions certainly go a long way in building and maintaining a business relationship.

Beyond these personal characteristics, good salespeople possess other intangible characteristics that have an impact on their performance. For some insight into these characteristics, see the IMC Highlight: **What Separates Successful Salespeople from Everyone Else?**

What Separates Successful Salespeople from Everyone Else?

Successful salespeople possess intangible skills that go beyond product, company, and competitor knowledge. These salespeople know it is the "little things" that separate successful salespeople from the rest of the pack. So, what are some of these intangibles? Here are a few of them.

They Are Persistent

Successful salespeople don't let obstacles stand in their way. They are tenacious and are constantly looking for new solutions.

They Set Goals

Successful salespeople establish specific goals, then visualize their target, determine how they will achieve their goals, and take action daily.

They Listen

Effective salespeople know the customer will tell them what they need to know; therefore, they listen and learn.

They Are Passionate

When you love what you do, you put more passion into it. Effective salespeople are passionate about their company and products.

They Are Enthusiastic

Effective salespeople remain positive, even in tough times. When faced with negative and challenging situations, they always focus on the positives.

They Keep in Touch

Effective salespeople go well beyond routine follow-up. They keep track of key dates, such as birthdays and anniversaries, and deliver communications on a more personal level in order to enhance the relationship.

They Work Hard

Successful salespeople start early, make more calls, and stay late when necessary. They know that making more presentations will produce more sales.

Adapted from Kelley Robertson, "Characteristics of Successful Salespeople," *SOHO*, Summer 2006, pp. 14, 15.

PREPARATION AND THE IMPORTANCE OF KNOWLEDGE

In a nutshell, the primary task of a salesperson is to provide a customer with a solution to a problem by matching the right product or service at a price that is agreeable to the customer. It sounds so simple! But it requires much advance preparation. That preparation is divided into three primary areas: product knowledge, company knowledge, and competitor knowledge. With regard to product knowledge, the salesperson must become an expert and know exactly what benefits to stress with any particular customer. For example, two different customers might require the same product, but one customer is motivated by quality, the other by service. The salesperson would have to adapt the presentation to offer different perspectives based on each buyer's unique needs and priorities. In complex situations, such as when various products must be combined to form a solution, the salesperson must be capable of bringing the right products and services together. This process is called **product configuration**.

product configuration
The bringing together of various products and services to form a solution for the customer.

PRODUCT KNOWLEDGE

Essentially, product knowledge can be classified into four key areas: product development and quality improvement processes, performance data and specifications, maintenance and service, and price and delivery. The various combinations of this information make up the essential elements of a planned sales presentation. To grow, companies develop new products to solve new needs. It is important for a salesperson to know how a product was developed, how much it cost to develop, and why it was developed. This sort of information strongly suggests to a customer that the company takes research and development seriously and strives to build better products for its customers. In terms of performance and quality, a salesperson should be familiar with quality control standards so that information regarding product claims can be substantiated and compared with claims made by competitors. Knowing that a product meets or exceeds certain standards often provides a competitive advantage in a sales presentation.

A buyer usually poses questions or raises objections about performance data and specifications in the middle of a sales presentation. To illustrate, assume you are planning a business conference and considering various conference centres. What kinds of questions would you ask the sales manager of a potential conference centre? Here are a few examples:

- Does the conference centre offer technical support if we need it?
- Is there an Internet connection available to delegates and at what cost?
- Is there sufficient accommodation available for 200 delegates?
- How efficient is the catering department in serving a buffet dinner to 200 people?

Certainly the list could be longer and much more diverse. And that is the key point. A good salesperson must be ready to respond to the expected and the unexpected.

If the competing products are similar, it could be that information about maintenance and service provide product differentiation. If service is provided as part of a package deal, all specifications regarding additional services must be part of the sales presentation. Specifications must be agreed upon about who is responsible for what service, when it will happen, how often it will happen, and so on. It is very common for selling companies to draw up official service contracts based on specific requirements provided by the buying organization. Such contracts play a vital role in the relationship-building process.

Other knowledge that helps differentiate one product from another is knowledge about price and delivery. The easiest and most common objection that buyers raise is price: "Your price is too high!" Knowing how to respond appropriately is crucial to closing the sale. If your price is higher than the competition, that fact must be acknowledged, and additional and tangible product benefits must be presented to justify the higher price. In such situations, the buyer simply wants more information; the salesperson must show good product knowledge.

COMPANY KNOWLEDGE

Since the salesperson is the customer's primary source of contact, the salesperson is the company. The perceptions formed by a customer or prospective customer about a company depend largely on the attitude, style, behaviour, and communications ability of the salesperson. If perceptions are positive, there is a stronger likelihood of making the sale and developing a long-term business relationship. A salesperson, therefore, should integrate essential information about the company into a sales presentation.

Business organizations exist to serve their customers, and all employees must recognize that they contribute to this effort. This attitude, often referred to as **corporate culture**, is defined as the values, norms, and practices shared by all employees of an organization. A good corporate culture always puts the customer first. A successful and diversified organization such as 3M thinks "customer" all the time. All employees are part of a

corporate culture
The values, beliefs, norms, and practices shared by all employees of an organization.

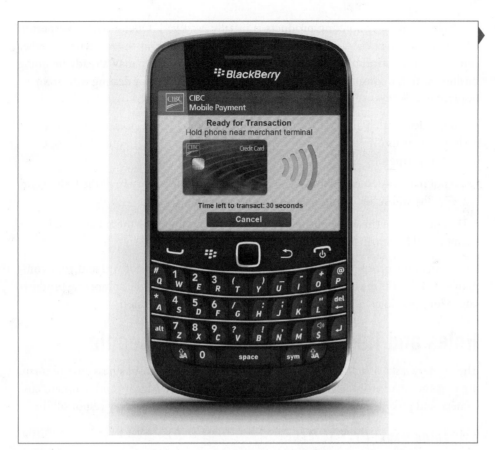

FIGURE
11.8

CIBC Responds to the Challenge of Developing New and Innovative Products for a Changing Marketplace

Source: Handout/Giesecke & Devrient/Newscom.

marketing team and consider themselves to be in the customer care business. In fact, 3M uses phrases such as "Commitment to Innovation" and "3M Innovation" in its marketing communications to suggest its leadership role in the markets it operates in.

CIBC identifies customer needs and develops innovative products to satisfy those needs. Such information should be passed on to prospective customers by sales representatives because it sends out a clear signal about the type of company CIBC is: a company willing to develop new products and to respond to new challenges in an ever-changing marketplace. Introducing mobile payments for retail purchase transactions is but one example of how CIBC responds to a changing marketplace. Refer to the image in Figure 11.8.

What services a company provides after the sale is also crucial information to provide to customers. As many experts say, "The relationship begins once the sale is made." Therefore, after-sales service, which is a function that is usually implemented by other departments of a company, must be integrated into a sales presentation. It is important for a company to track the level of satisfaction that customers are experiencing, so it is quite common for organizations to contact customers directly by telephone or mail. The results of surveys, for example, can be passed on to sales representatives for follow-up.

COMPETITOR KNOWLEDGE

Good salespeople know the competitor's products almost as well as their own. In a sales presentation, comparisons inevitably crop up, making it essential to know the benefits and weaknesses of competing products and adapt the selling strategy accordingly. If a seller cannot respond to the challenges posed by a buyer, the chances of making a sale are lost.

Talking about competing products is usually awkward. Obviously, a salesperson does not want to acknowledge a competitor's strengths, but at the same time a seller cannot be too critical of competitors' products. The customer may already be doing business with the competition. Here are a few basic guidelines for dealing with competing products:[8]

- Do not deliberately include reference to competitors in your presentation as it shifts the focus off your own product. Do, however, respond to questions about the competition.
- Do not make statements about the competitor if you are uncertain of the facts. Your credibility will suffer if you make inaccurate statements.
- Do not criticize the competition. State the facts as you know them and avoid emotional comments if you have to make a comparison.

Remember, prospective customers are forming perceptions of you and your company when you are making the sales presentation. How you handle competing products goes a long way in creating a favourable or unfavourable impression.

Roles and Responsibilities of Salespeople

The primary tasks of a salesperson, particularly in a business-to-business environment, are to gather market intelligence, solve customers' problems, locate and maintain customers, and provide follow-up service. This section examines each key responsibility.

GATHERING MARKET INTELLIGENCE

In a competitive marketplace, salespeople must be attuned to the trends in their industry. They must be alert to what the competitor is doing, to its new product projects, and to its advertising and promotion plans, and they must listen to feedback from customers regarding their own products' performance. As indicated earlier, competitive knowledge is important when the salesperson faces questions involving product comparisons. Data collected by a salesperson can be reported electronically to the company's head office. Managers can retrieve the information and use it appropriately at a later date.

PROBLEM SOLVING

The only way a salesperson can make a sale is to listen to what a customer wants and ask questions to determine the customer's real needs. Asking, listening, and providing information and advice that is in the best interests of the customer are what relationship selling is all about. The seller must demonstrate a sincere concern for the customer's needs.

LOCATING AND MAINTAINING CUSTOMERS

Salespeople who locate new customers play a key role in a company's growth. A company cannot be satisfied with its current list of customers, because aggressive competitors are always attempting to lure them away. To prevent shrinkage and to increase sales, salespeople actively pursue new accounts. Their time is divided between finding new accounts and selling and servicing current accounts.

FOLLOW-UP SERVICE

The salesperson is the first point of contact should anything go wrong or should more information be required. Maintenance of customers is crucial and, very often, it is the quality of the follow-up service that determines if a customer will remain a customer.

Since the salespeople are the company's direct link to the customer, it cannot be stressed enough how important it is that they handle customer service well. The sale is never over! Once the deal has closed, numerous tasks arise: arranging for delivery, providing technical assistance, offering customer training, and being readily available to handle any problems that might emerge during and after delivery. The personalized role of the sales representative is instrumental in building relationships.

Personal Selling Strategies

Before discussing the various steps involved in successful personal selling, let's first explore the difference between features and benefits. A product **feature** is anything that can be felt, seen, or measured. Features include such things as durability, design, and economy of operation. They provide a customer with information, but do not motivate a customer to buy. A **benefit** provides the customer with advantage or gain, and shows how a product will help resolve a specific problem. Benefits provide motivation! To demonstrate, consider all the technical features usually associated with a laptop or desktop computer. The list seems endless and includes much technical jargon. Assuming the customer wants quick access to information when using the computer (information the seller would seek out by asking a few questions), the seller can quickly zoom in on the appropriate features and translate them into benefits that are appropriate for and meaningful to the customer.

Regardless of the sales situation—whether retail selling, business-to-business selling, or direct selling—the steps in the selling process are similar. They are simply adapted to each situation. This section covers the seven essential steps in the selling process (see Figure 11.9).

PROSPECTING

The first step is **prospecting**, which is a procedure for systematically developing sales leads. If salespeople do not allocate enough time to finding new customers, they risk causing a decline in sales for their company. If their income is geared to the value of the business they produce, they risk the loss of personal compensation as well. Prospecting is also important because of attrition. Attrition refers to the loss of customers over a period of time. Even with extensive CRM programs in place as a means of retaining customers, buyers switch suppliers when better products and services become available.

Potential customers, or prospects, are identified by means of published lists and directories, such as Scott's Industrial Directories, the *Frasers Trade Index*, and the *Canadian Key Business Directory*. Another strategy for seeking new customers is the referral. A **referral** is a prospect who is recommended by a current customer. The salesperson also seeks new customers by **cold canvass**, the process of calling on people or organizations without appointments or advance knowledge of them. Other sources of leads include names obtained from trade shows, advertising, direct response communications, telemarketing and online communications, sales promotion entry forms, and channel members.

PRE-APPROACH

The **pre-approach** involves gathering information about potential customers before actually making sales contact. During the pre-approach stage, customers are qualified, which is the procedure for determining if a prospect needs the product, has the authority to buy it, and has the ability to pay for it. There is little sense in pursuing customers

feature
Tangible aspect of a product, such as durability, design, and economy of operation.

benefit
The value a customer attaches to a brand attribute.

prospecting
A procedure for systematically developing sales leads.

referral
A recommendation by a current customer of a potential new customer to a sales representative.

cold canvass
The process of calling on people or organizations without appointments or advance knowledge of them.

pre-approach
The gathering of information about customers before actually making sales contact.

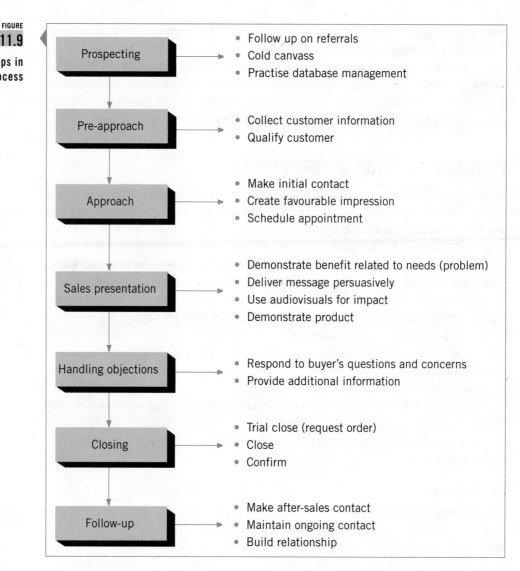

FIGURE
11.9

The Seven Essential Steps in
the Personal Selling Process

Prospecting
- Follow up on referrals
- Cold canvass
- Practise database management

Pre-approach
- Collect customer information
- Qualify customer

Approach
- Make initial contact
- Create favourable impression
- Schedule appointment

Sales presentation
- Demonstrate benefit related to needs (problem)
- Deliver message persuasively
- Use audiovisuals for impact
- Demonstrate product

Handling objections
- Respond to buyer's questions and concerns
- Provide additional information

Closing
- Trial close (request order)
- Close
- Confirm

Follow-up
- Make after-sales contact
- Maintain ongoing contact
- Build relationship

who lack the financial resources or have no need to make the business relationship successful. In the process of qualifying customers, the seller also gains insights that can be used in the sales presentation: information such as the buyer's likes and dislikes, personal interests and hobbies, buying procedures, and special needs and problems.

APPROACH

approach
The initial contact with a customer.

The **approach** is the initial contact with the prospect, often in a face-to-face selling situation. Since buyers are usually busy, little time should be wasted in the approach. In the first few minutes of a sales interview, the salesperson must capture the attention and interest of the buyer and create a favourable first impression so that there is an effective environment for the presentation of the product's benefits.

SALES PRESENTATION

It is common for a salesperson to make presentations to individuals (one-on-one selling) or to buying teams (one-on-group selling). Buying teams are classified as buying centres (an informal grouping of people in the buying group) or buying committees (a formal group with a structured buying procedure in place). In dealing with buying committees, the salesperson must listen attentively and observe body language to determine which members of the group are the real influencers and decision makers.

The actual **sales presentation** consists of a persuasive delivery and demonstration of a product's benefits. An effective sales presentation shows the buyer how the benefits of the product satisfy specific needs or help resolve a particular problem. In doing so, the seller focuses on the benefits that are most important to the buyer. Critical elements usually focus on lower price, the durability of the product, the dependability of supply, the performance of the product, and the availability of follow-up service.

At this stage, asking proper questions and listening attentively are particularly important to uncover real needs. A salesperson listens to and analyzes what buyers are saying, then uses what has been discovered when presenting the appropriate benefits. Being flexible and adapting a presentation in mid-stream could be the difference between making a sale and not making a sale.

Demonstrations play a key role in a sales presentation. A **demonstration** is an opportunity to show the product in action and substantiate the claims being made about the product. A good demonstration (something the buyer can see) adds to the convincing nature of the presentation. It helps hold the buyer's attention and creates interest and desire. It is wise to rehearse the demonstration so that what the salesperson says and what the salesperson demonstrates are in harmony with each other. Laptop computers and changing technology now allow for multimedia presentations and very effective demonstrations.

A useful tactic in the presentation is to let the prospect handle the product and the materials relevant to it. This action results in a feeling of ownership and helps in the decision-making process. In situations where technology is part of the presentation, the salesperson must be certain all equipment is in good working condition. A failure with the technology is embarrassing for the salesperson and costly in terms of potential time lost for the presentation. Figure 11.10 lists useful reminders for planning a sales presentation.

HANDLING OBJECTIONS

An **objection** is an obstacle that the salesperson must confront during a presentation and resolve if the sales transaction is to be completed. An objection is a cue for more information. The buyer is suggesting that the presentation of a product has not revealed how the product will satisfy a particular need. The objection, therefore, is feedback to be analyzed and used. It may enable the salesperson to discover another benefit in the product, a benefit that can then be presented to the buyer.

Typical objections involve issues related to the following: product quality and the level of service and technical assistance; the price or the level of discounts suggested, for

---

sales presentation
A persuasive delivery and demonstration of a product's benefits; shows buyers how the product's benefits will satisfy their needs.

demonstration
A sales technique that involves showing the product in action to portray its benefits to a buyer.

objection
An obstacle that a salesperson must confront during a sales presentation.

- Ask the buyer questions and listen attentively to the responses.
- Include useful information about the company.
- Watch for cues by observing body language.
- Include a product demonstration (rehearse to make sure it works).
- Involve the buyer in the presentation.
- Remain flexible throughout the presentation and adapt it based on feedback.
- Add technology where appropriate to enhance the presentation.
- Respond to objections pleasantly (be prepared for the expected and unexpected).
- Ask for the order (always be closing).

FIGURE 11.10

Useful Reminders for Planning a Sales Presentation

example, the price may be too high, discount too low, or credit terms unacceptable; and sourcing issues such as how the buyer feels about the company in comparison to other potential suppliers. Objections are a normal response from buyers, so salespeople should not take them personally. Instead, the salesperson should ask questions to confirm the buyer's understanding of the situation, answer the objection, and then move on to the next benefit or attempt to close the sale.

A good salesperson develops effective strategies for handling objections; being prepared for the expected and unexpected is essential. When responding to objections, the salesperson can call upon the product itself, testimonials and case histories of success, test results shown in a variety of formats (for example, graphs and charts), and other forms of audiovisual support.

CLOSING

closing
Asking for the order at the appropriate time in a sales presentation.

Does the buyer voluntarily say, "Yes, I'll buy it"? The answer is "rarely"! Getting the buyer to say "yes" is the entire purpose of the sales interview, but this task is only accomplished if the salesperson asks for the order. **Closing** consists of asking for the order; it is the most difficult step in the process of selling. Salespeople are reluctant to ask the big question, even though it is the logical sequel to a good presentation and demonstration. In fact, a good salesperson attempts a close whenever a point of agreement is made with the buyer. If the buyer says "no," the close is referred to as a **trial close**, or an attempt to close that failed. The salesperson simply moves on to the next point in the presentation.

trial close
A failed attempt at closing a sale; the buyer said "no."

The close can occur at any point in a sales presentation. Knowing when to close is essential. Therefore, as the sales presentation progresses, the salesperson must be alert to closing cues. A **closing cue** is an indication that the buyer is ready to buy. The cue may be verbal or non-verbal. If a cue is detected, a close should be attempted. Verbal cues include statements such as "What type of warranty do you provide?" Such a statement shows that the buyer is thinking ahead. Another cue is "The delivery and installation schedule fits well with our factory conversion schedule." Such a statement suggests confirmation of a key benefit. Or another could be "We need the product in one week." In other words, if you can supply it, we'll buy it! Statements such as these are closing cues that must be acted upon.

closing cue
An indication that the buyer is ready to buy; can be expressed verbally or non-verbally.

Positive non-verbal communications include changing facial expressions, a change in the buyer's mood (for example, the buyer becomes more jovial), or the buyer nods in agreement or reads the sales information intently. Good salespeople do not miss such opportunities, even if they have not finished their presentation. The buyer is telling you it is time to close—do it!

Timing a close is a matter of judgment. Good salespeople know when to close—it is often referred to as the "sixth sense" of selling. The salesperson assesses the buyer's verbal and non-verbal responses in an effort to judge when that person has become receptive, and at the right moment, asks the big question with a high degree of self-confidence. A list of commonly used closing techniques appears in Figure 11.11.

Once the sale has been closed, it is time to reassure the customer that a good decision has been taken and to confirm that you will provide all the essential services that were promised in the presentation. Parting on a positive note is crucial, because buyers very often experience cognitive dissonance. **Cognitive dissonance** refers to a feeling of doubt or regret once the buying decision has been made. The buyer wants to be reassured that the best choice has been made. This is the start of the relationship-building process.

cognitive dissonance
A feeling of doubt or regret in a consumer's mind once a buying decision has been made.

FIGURE
11.11

Successful Closing Techniques

The objective of the sales presentation is to get the order. To do so, the seller must close the sale by asking for the order. Asking for the order can be accomplished in a variety of ways.

Assumptive Close

The seller assumes the buyer has already decided to buy. The seller says, "I'll have it delivered by Friday," or "What is the best day for delivery?" An agreement or answer confirms the seller's assumption.

Alternative-Choice Close

The seller assumes the sale is made but asks for clarification on another point. For example, the seller may say, "Would you prefer metallic blue or cherry red?"

Summary-of-Benefits Close

At the end of the presentation, the seller calmly reviews the key points the buyer has already agreed to (price, service, quality, reliability, and so on). Once the summary is complete, the seller says, "When would you like it delivered?"

Direct Close

No beating around the bush here. The seller confidently says, "Can I deliver it on Friday?" Then the seller stops talking and awaits the response.

Take-Away Close

It is human nature to want what one can't have. The seller says, "This product isn't for everyone. It's a certain kind of person who can appreciate the finer qualities of this product."

FOLLOW-UP

There is an old saying: "The sale never ends." There is truth to this statement, because a new sale is nothing more than the start of a new relationship. Keeping current customers satisfied is the key to success. Effective salespeople make a point of providing **follow-up**; that is, they keep in touch with customers to ensure that the delivery and installation of the goods were satisfactory, that promises were kept, and that the expectations of the buyer were met. When problems do occur, the salesperson is ready to take action to resolve the situation.

In the current competitive business environment, good follow-up strategies help reduce customer attrition. Companies realize that a satisfied customer is a long-term customer. As discussed elsewhere in this textbook, customer relationship management programs now act as a foundation for long-term business success. Keeping track of customer transactions and customer preferences provides an opportunity for incremental sales. Larry Rosen, president of upscale clothier Harry Rosen, firmly understands this concept. Harry Rosen has implemented programs that ensure the utmost in customer service and care. "We don't look at a person in terms of an immediate sale. We look at him in terms of potential lifetime value."[9]

Success in selling requires dedication, determination, and discipline. What separates the successful salesperson from the unsuccessful one usually boils down to how well an individual follows an established set of principles. While the wording of these principles might vary from one source to another, the intent behind them is consistent. See Figure 11.12 for some pointers on what separates the professionals from the average salespeople.

follow-up
Maintaining contact with customers to ensure that service has been satisfactory.

FIGURE
11.12

Tips for Successful Selling

1. Selling skills are learned skills

Successful salespeople take the time to develop their skills. They ask meaningful questions, listen attentively, and observe buyer behaviour. Through learning, they can relate appropriate product benefits to the customer's needs. Knowledge of the product, company, customer and their industry, and competition is essential.

2. The salesperson is the most important product

Successful salespeople sell themselves. They project a positive image about themselves and their company. A customer who isn't sold on you won't buy your product.

3. Emotions, feelings, and relationships are important

Successful salespeople present more than just facts. They create positive emotions about themselves, their products and services, and their company. Through effective communications, they bring the buyers into the relationship, showing how their problems will be resolved.

4. Preparation is crucial

Be prepared! A sales presentation is like a stage performance. You may not get a second chance. Command the buyer's attention immediately and encourage participation throughout the presentation. Through participation, the buyer will discover the product's benefits. Ensure that all components of the presentation are coordinated and all electronic aids are in working condition.

5. Negotiation skills are important

A successful salesperson can deal with any and all concerns raised by the buyer. Be prepared to meet challenges by offering additional information, and package together all points of agreement in order to close the sale.

6. Always be closing

Closing begins at the start of a presentation. The challenge is to build agreement and help the prospect decide how to buy, not whether to buy. When the prospect agrees, ask for the order. If the buyer refuses, continue with the presentation and ask for the order again when the prospect agrees. Persistence pays off!

Selling in a Changing Business Environment

The nature of selling is changing rapidly. To be successful in the future, the salesperson and the company must consider the importance of teamwork in communicating with customers (another aspect of integration), the importance of building long-term relationships, and the importance of adapting to technologies that directly influence the selling process.

SELLING IS A TEAM EFFORT

Traditionally, selling has been thought of as an individual effort (for example, the salesperson calling on the customer and presenting a product to an individual or to a committee of buyers). Today, selling is often a team effort involving people from different departments of an organization. To sell sophisticated technical equipment in a B2B environment requires a team of experts, including research and design specialists, engineers, and other marketing personnel in addition to the salesperson. They all bring different expertise to the presentation and make the customer feel more at ease with the decision-making process.

Buyers also form teams, referred to as a buying committee composed of members from across an organization who share responsibility for making a decision. A committee can better evaluate the product offerings of sellers, as the product can be evaluated from different perspectives. The use of a committee also reduces the risks that are associated with large and complex buying decisions.

COMPANIES SELL RELATIONSHIPS, NOT PRODUCTS

Organizations abiding by contemporary corporate culture—that is, those that believe in relationship marketing—actively pursue relationships in the selling process. Making a sale or getting the order is simply one step in the sales continuum. It symbolizes the start of a new relationship or the solidification of an existing one.

The key for the seller is to determine how the company's resources can give the customer an edge. It is a consultative process in which the seller proves to the buyer that there is an advantage in doing business together. The search for a good fit between sellers (suppliers) and buyers stems from customers' relentless search for value in everything they purchase.

TECHNOLOGY IS CHANGING SELLING

The nature of selling is changing in many industries due to the advances in communications technology. Members of a channel of distribution that includes raw material suppliers, manufacturers, wholesalers, retailers, and end users are working cooperatively on supply chain management programs. By electronically transferring information among the participants in the supply chain—a cornerstone of true CRM programs—basic buying decisions are automated. Therefore, the challenge facing creative sellers is how to get their products into such a system.

Technology-based CRM programs and a company's ability to sell goods online also have consequences for salespeople and the way they communicate with customers. Technology makes it possible to use fewer people in personal selling, and these sellers find themselves spending less time in personal contact with customers and more time in electronic contact with them. Companies using technology to help market goods and services are finding that geographical boundaries are being eliminated as buyers search for the best value in what they require. Because customers contact companies in a variety of ways (such as by telephone, in person, by email, or through websites), it is important to send out a consistent and integrated marketing communications message.

In summary, even though business operates in an era of automated purchasing, downsized sales teams, and state-of-the art customer relationship management technology, many experts still insist the human element remains important. People like to buy from people they like.

SUMMARY

Personal selling refers to personal communications between sellers and buyers. Typically, personal selling is divided into three main areas: retail selling, business-to-business selling, and direct selling. In all forms, the immediate goal is to complete a sales transaction and then adopt appropriate strategies to encourage repeat transactions, thus building a relationship with the customer that will last for an extended period.

The nature of selling has evolved with the changing marketplace. Selling has moved from consultative selling to strategic selling to relationship selling. Relationship selling involves strategies to establish, build, and maintain customers. It approaches selling from the perspective of the lifetime value of a customer and the concept that retaining satisfied customers is much more profitable than constantly finding new ones. Relationship selling has extended into partnerships between sellers and buyers. Partnership selling is but one aspect of customer relationship management programs and is strategically developed to encourage a profitable long-term relationship.

There are several essential attributes for successful selling today. A good salesperson possesses the right combination of personal characteristics (characteristics that can be learned and practised) and communication skills (both speaking and listening). A good self-image and positive approach to selling are essential—a successful outlook breeds success! The ability to read a customer is also necessary. Observing and interpreting verbal and non-verbal cues from the customer allow the salesperson to adapt a presentation while in progress and to close the sale at the appropriate time.

Adequate advance preparation is another key to successful selling. A good salesperson possesses sound knowledge of the product and company they represent, the customer and the industry they operate in, and the competition. The task of the salesperson is to match the right product or combination of products and services with the customer's needs. In doing so, the salesperson plans a presentation strategy that shows how the products meet customer needs better than the competition's products. Other essential roles of the salesperson include gathering market intelligence, solving problems, locating and maintaining customers, and providing follow-up service.

The selling process involves seven distinct steps: prospecting, pre-approach, approach, sales presentation, handling objections, closing, and follow-up. Contemporary selling strategies involve the presentation of appropriate product benefits to meet customer needs. A benefit provides the customer with a gain or advantage and shows how the product will resolve a specific problem. Product benefits that are identified as important for a particular buyer are built into a pre-planned presentation designed to resolve a unique problem. During the presentation, a seller's negotiation skills are called upon to respond to the buyer's objections and concerns. Once those are answered, the seller closes the sale by asking for the order. Assuming a satisfactory response, the sale is confirmed and follow-up strategies are implemented. This is the start of the CRM process that, if nurtured carefully, will be profitable for both parties.

Advances in technology are changing the nature of personal selling. Less time is now spent in personal contact while more time is devoted to electronic contact and activities designed to service and retain customers. As in other forms of marketing communications, the challenge is to develop effective strategies to solidify relationships.

KEY TERMS

approach   338
benefit   337
body language   331
closing   340
closing cue   340
cognitive dissonance   340
cold canvass   337
consultative selling   326
corporate culture   334
demonstration   339
feature   337

field sales force   324
follow-up   341
inside sales force   324
non-verbal communication   331
objection   339
online selling   324
partnership selling   328
personal selling   322
pre-approach   337
presentation strategy   327
product configuration   333

prospecting   337
qualifying (a customer)   324
referral   337
relationship selling   327
sales presentation   339
self-image   331
strategic selling   326
telemarketing   324
trial close   340
verbal skills   331

REVIEW QUESTIONS

1. What are the fundamental differences among consultative selling, strategic selling, and relationship selling?
2. In relationship selling, what is meant by the phrase "positioning the product in the customer's mind"?
3. Briefly define partnership selling and explain its importance.
4. What personal and non-personal characteristics are essential for successful selling?

5. Advance preparation is crucial to successful selling. Briefly describe the importance of knowledge in the following areas: product, company, and competition.
6. Briefly explain the roles and responsibilities of a salesperson.
7. List and briefly describe the seven steps in the selling strategy process.

DISCUSSION AND APPLICATION QUESTIONS

1. "Advances in communications technology will dramatically change the role and nature of selling in the future." Discuss this statement and provide examples of changes that are already influencing selling strategies or will have an influence on them in the future.

2. Conduct some secondary research on the concept of partnership selling. How prevalent is partnership selling in business today? Provide some examples of organizations that have adopted this strategy.

3. Assess the role of follow-up in the context of customer relationship management practices. How important is it, and how much emphasis do sales representatives place on this aspect of selling?

4. Evaluate the personal selling strategies of the following retail businesses: Future Shop, Best Buy, and Canadian Tire. Do the style and nature of personal selling vary from one business to the other? Which approach is more effective at selling goods at retail? Justify your opinion.

5. Conduct a brief interview with a business-to-business sales representative for a company in your area. Inquire about the representative's role in the context of integrated marketing communications. Are there links to other aspects of marketing communications that offer assistance in selling goods and services? Explain the various links as best you can.

6. Pre-planning is an essential step in making a sales presentation. Assume you are working for Apple (or any other marketer of desktop and laptop computers) and plan to make a sales presentation to your school. The school is going to purchase or lease desktop computers for a new 50-station lab and is in the process of securing information from various computer suppliers. What questions would you ask to determine your prospect's specific needs? What benefits would you stress when planning the sales presentation and why? What objections do you foresee being raised by the buyer? You may wish to discuss this question with the individual responsible for information technology at your school.

ENDNOTES

1. "Individual Internet Use and E-Commerce," Statistics Canada, October 12, 2011, www.statcan.gc.ca/daily-quotidien/111012/dq111012a-eng.htm.

2. Gerald Manning, Barry Reece, and H.F. MacKenzie, *Selling Today*, 3rd Edition (Toronto: Prentice Hall, 2004), pp. 7–14.

3. John Lorinc, "Death of the Salesman," *Canadian Business*, November 2, 2011, pp. 49–50.

4. Terrance Belford, "Re-arm Your Sales Force," *National Post*, May 5, 2003, p. BE1.

5. John Lorinc, "Death of the Salesman," *Canadian Business*, November 21, 2011, pp. 50, 51.

6. John Lorinc, "Death of the Salesman," *Canadian Business*, November 2, 2011, p. 50.

7. *Dictionary of Marketing Terms* (Barron's Educational Series Inc., 1994), p. 367.

8. Gerald Manning, Barry Reece, and H.F. Mackenzie, *Selling Today*, 3rd Edition (Toronto: Prentice Hall, 2004), p. 137.

9. "Relationship Marketing," *Venture* (Canadian Broadcasting Corporation), broadcast on April 7, 1998.

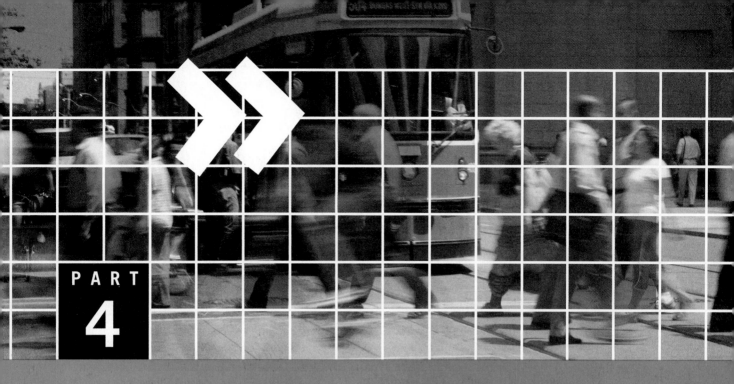

Measuring Performance

Part 4 takes a look at the role of marketing research in evaluating the effectiveness of marketing communications programs. Because so much of the evaluation process relies on the collection of qualitative and quantitative data, it is essential to develop an appreciation of the various research techniques and procedures available.

Chapter 12 introduces some fundamental methodologies for collecting primary research data and distinguishes between qualitative and quantitative data. It discusses the relationship between data analysis and interpretation, and their impact on the development and evaluation of marketing communications strategies and executions.

Learning Objectives

After studying this chapter, you will be able to

1. Define the role and scope of marketing research in contemporary marketing organizations

2. Describe the methodologies for collecting primary research data

3. Distinguish between qualitative data and quantitative data

4. Determine the influence of primary data and information on the development of marketing communications plans

5. Assess a variety of marketing research procedures and methodologies that measure and evaluate behavioural responses to communications messages

6. Identify the unique methods that measure the effectiveness of individual components of marketing communications

Because a considerable amount of money is invested in marketing communications activities, a marketing organization is very concerned about protecting its investment. In addition, its desire to remain competitive and be knowledgeable about consumers' changing needs makes it necessary to collect appropriate information before and after critical decisions are made. Certainly, a firm understanding of relevant and contemporary consumer behaviour will play a major role in the development of a marketing communications campaign (refer to Chapter 1 for details). Carefully planned and well-timed marketing research is the tool that provides organizations with the insight necessary to take advantage of new opportunities. This chapter will discuss some fundamental concepts about the marketing research process and present various specific research techniques that are used to measure and evaluate the effectiveness of marketing communications programs.

The Role and Scope of Marketing Research

Research provides an organization with data. The data do not guarantee that proper decisions and actions by the firm will be taken, because data are always open to interpretation. The old saying that "some information is better than no information" puts the role of marketing research into perspective. A vital marketing tool, market research is used to help reduce or eliminate the uncertainty and risk associated with making business decisions. Of course, this principle applies to marketing communications decisions as well.

In many ways, marketing research is a form of insurance. It ensures that the action a company might take is the right action. For a multi-million-dollar advertising decision, a manager would want to have good information (a foundation, so to speak) available to make sure the right decision is made. To demonstrate, consider a problem and decision made by Procter & Gamble. When the company launched Febreze, it quickly became a leader in a market for products that eliminated pesky odours. When demand in the market dropped, sales of Febreze were adversely affected. Marketing managers talked with consumers and discovered many of them did not believe odours lived in fabric, and, therefore, didn't see a need for the product. To learn more, marketers conducted shop-alongs (following and observing people as they shopped) and focus groups. From the research, the managers concluded that a greater emphasis on the brand's functionality was needed. A new marketing communications campaign was created around the idea that Febreze "eliminates odours and freshens."[1]

marketing research
A marketing function that links the consumer/customer/public to the marketer through information; the information is used to define marketing opportunities and problems, generate marketing strategies, evaluate marketing actions, and monitor performance.

Marketing research links the consumer/customer/public to the marketer through information—information used to define marketing opportunities and problems; to generate, refine, and evaluate marketing actions; to monitor marketing performance; and to improve the understanding of marketing as a process. It designs the method for collecting information, manages and implements the information collection process, analyzes the results, and communicates the findings and their implications.[2]

The scope of marketing research seems endless. In a marketing communications setting, research is useful for identifying consumer insights that can be considered when developing message strategies, for measuring the impact and effectiveness of message and media strategies, for tracking brand awareness during the life of a campaign, for pre-testing and post-testing advertising strategies, and for measuring changes in behaviour based on the effects of all forms of marketing communications. Any information obtained will assist managers in their decision making.

The very nature of marketing research, however, requires a significant investment by a marketing organization. Due to the diversity of marketing communications and the complementary ways in which the various components blend together, it is difficult to isolate one communications component and state definitively that it determined success or failure.

reliability (of data)
Degree of similarity of results achieved if another research study were undertaken under similar circumstances.

validity (of data)
A research procedure's ability to measure what it is intended to measure.

How do managers go about collecting information? Prudent marketing decision makers combine their intuition and judgment with all other information sources available. They use the scientific method, which implies that the data generated are reliable and valid. **Reliability** refers to the degree of similar results being achieved if another study were undertaken under similar conditions. **Validity** refers to the research procedure's ability to measure what it was intended to measure.

Research Techniques for Marketing Communications

When an organization attempts to measure the potential impact of its advertising messages on consumers, it implements a variety of primary research techniques. Students should be aware of the basic steps involved in planning various research procedures to appreciate the value of the data. Essentially, the evaluation of advertising messages or any other form of marketing communications involves the collection of primary data.

PRIMARY RESEARCH

primary research
The collection and recording of primary data.

primary data
Data collected to resolve a problem and recorded for the first time.

Once the organization decides it requires input from customers and potential customers before making a decision, the research process moves to the stage of collecting primary data. **Primary research** refers to the process of collecting and recording new data, called **primary data**, to resolve a specific problem, usually at a high cost to the sponsoring organization. Primary research is custom designed and focuses on resolving a particular question or obtaining specified information. A procedure is developed and a research instrument designed to perform the specific task. Figure 12.1 summarizes the steps involved in collecting primary data.

research objective
A statement that outlines what the marketing research is to accomplish.

hypothesis
A statement of outcomes predicted in a marketing research investigation.

In directing the primary research, the marketing organization identifies the precise nature of the problem, the objectives of the study, and the hypotheses associated with it. **Research objectives** are statements that outline what the research is to accomplish, while **hypotheses**, which are statements of predicted outcomes, are confirmed or refuted by the data collected. The outcome of the research often leads to certain actions being taken by the marketing organization. Refer to Figure 12.2 for an illustration of research objectives, hypotheses, and action standards.

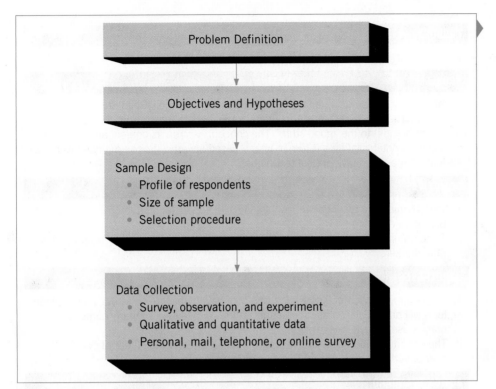

FIGURE
12.1

The Steps Involved in Primary Research

SAMPLE DESIGN

Prior to implementing a research study, the researchers identify the characteristics of the people they would like to participate in the study. This process is referred to as sample design. A **sample** is defined as a portion of an entire population used to obtain information about that population. The sample must form an accurate representation of the population if the information gathered is to be considered reliable. Some basic steps must be taken to develop a representative sample:

- **Define the Population (Universe):** A **population (universe)** is a group of people with specific age, gender, or other demographic characteristics. It is usually the description of the target market or audience under study. For the purposes of primary research, a description of a population might be "single or married females between the ages of 21 and 34 years living in cities with more than 500 000 residents."

- **Identify the Sampling Frame:** The **sampling frame** refers to a list that can be used for reaching a population. If Canadian Tire wanted to conduct research among its current customers about the style of advertising it uses, it could use its credit card account holder list as a means of access. Canadian Tire could also survey visitors to its website. Online feedback is quick, convenient, and less costly than traditional forms of research.

- **Determine the Type of Sample:** The researcher has the option of using a probability sample or a non-probability sample. If a **probability sample** is used, the respondents have a known or equal chance of selection and are randomly selected from across the population. For example, the researcher may use a predetermined, systematic procedure for picking respondents through a telephone directory. The known chance of selection enables statistical procedures to be used in the results to estimate sampling errors.

sample
A representative portion of an entire population that is used to obtain information about that population.

population (universe)
In marketing research, a group of people with certain age, gender, or other demographic characteristics.

sampling frame
A list used to access a representative sample of a population; it is a means of accessing people for a research study.

probability sample
A sample of respondents who are known to have an equal chance of selection and are randomly selected from the sampling frame.

FIGURE
12.2

A Sample of Research
Objectives, Hypotheses, and
Sample Design for a Marketing
Communications Study

PRODUCT

Labatt Blue

PROBLEM

Labatt Blue has been using a tactical style of advertising—its "Good Stuff" advertising campaign. The attack style ads encourage consumers to switch from the "okay stuff" (discount brands) to the "good stuff." The concept has run its course, and the brand manager is contemplating a return to image-based advertising. The manager wants to evaluate some alternative appeal techniques.

OBJECTIVES

1. To determine the potential impact of a lifestyle appeal technique on current Labatt Blue drinkers.
2. To determine the potential impact of a sexual appeal technique on current Labatt Blue drinkers.

HYPOTHESES

1. The communication of lifestyle appeals may have impact initially, but over the long term will not be viewed as unique and distinctive because so many competing brands use lifestyle imagery.
2. The communication of sexual appeal will break through the clutter of competitive beer advertising and separate Blue from other leading brands.

ACTION STANDARD

Given the assumption that research results indicate a preference for either the lifestyle appeal technique or the sexual appeal technique, and preference can be sustained for an extended period, then a new creative campaign will be devised for Labatt Blue. The implementation date for a new campaign will be May 2014.

SAMPLE DESIGN

Population

Input will be sought from Blue's primary target market, described as males, 19 to 29 years old, living in urban markets.

Sampling Frame

Current Blue drinkers will be recruited by telephone and by using telephone directories in three cities: Toronto, Edmonton, and Vancouver. A series of qualifying questions will be asked of potential respondents to determine their degree of brand loyalty.

Type of Sample

A probability sample is essential to ensure accurate and reliable data. A systematic procedure will be devised to recruit respondents in each city.

Sample Size

It is anticipated that a mixture of qualitative research and quantitative research will be employed. A focus group will be conducted in each city to derive qualitative information. Survey research will require a minimum of 200 respondents in each city to secure accurate quantitative data.

The above is a hypothetical example and is intended for illustration purposes only.

non-probability sample
A sample of respondents who have an unknown chance of selection and are chosen because of factors such as convenience or the judgment of the researcher.

In a **non-probability sample**, the respondents have an unknown chance of selection, and their selection is based on factors such as convenience for the researcher or the researcher's judgment. The researcher relies on experience to determine who would be most appropriate. For example, Canadian Tire could randomly stop shoppers inside its stores to seek their input on a variety of marketing concerns. Factors such as cost and timing are other reasons for using non-probability samples.

- **Determine the Sample Size:** Generally, the larger the sample, the greater the accuracy of the data collected and the higher the cost. The nature of the research study is a determining factor in the number of participants required. Some researchers use a 1 percent rule (1 percent of the defined population or universe), while others state absolute minimums of 200 respondents. The accuracy of the sample is usually calculated statistically and stated in the research report. Therefore, a researcher considers the margin of error that is acceptable and the degree of certainty required.

Figure 12.2 contains a sample design. It should be noted that errors in the design and implementation of a research sample could distort the validity and reliability of the data collected.

DATA COLLECTION METHODS

There are three primary methods a researcher can use to collect data: surveys, observation, and experiments (see Figure 12.3). The data collected can be qualitative or quantitative in nature.

For **survey research**, data are collected systematically through some form of communication with a representative sample by means of a questionnaire that records responses. Most surveys include predetermined questions and a selection of responses that are easily filled in by the respondent or the interviewer. This technique is referred to as **fixed-response (closed-ended) questioning**. Surveys may also include space at the end of a question where verbatim comments by the respondent are recorded, referred to as **open-response (open-ended) questioning**. Survey research can be conducted by personal interview, telephone, mail, or online. Computer software is now available that allows researchers to conduct surveys on electronic devices. The use of electronic devices ensures error-free transfer of data.

In **observation research**, the behaviour of the respondent is observed and recorded. In this form of research, participants do not have to be recruited; they can participate in a study without knowing it. In other situations, respondents are usually aware of being observed, perhaps through a two-way mirror, by a hidden camera while being interviewed, or by electronic measurement of impulses. All of these techniques can be used when consumers are asked to evaluate advertising messages.

survey research
The systematic collection of data by communicating with a representative sample by means of a questionnaire.

fixed-response (closed-ended) questioning
Predetermined questions with set answers for the respondents to choose from.

open-response (open-ended) questioning
Space available at the end of a question where the respondents can add their comments.

observation research
A form of research in which the behaviour of the respondent is observed and recorded; may be by personal or electronic means.

FIGURE 12.3

Data Collection Methods

SURVEYS
- Data are collected systematically by communicating with a representative sample, usually using a questionnaire.
- Questionnaires can be disguised (purpose hidden) or undisguised (purpose known), and structured (fixed responses provided) or unstructured (open-ended question format).

OBSERVATION
- The behaviour of the respondent is observed by personal, mechanical, or electronic means.

EXPERIMENTS
- Variables are manipulated under controlled conditions to observe respondents' reactions.
- Experiments are used to test marketing influences such as product changes, package changes, and advertising copy tests.

The Ford Motor Company found that observing online chatter provided insights for developing better marketing communications strategies. From its observations, Ford learned that information presented on blogs (information that is either positive or negative) quickly becomes the subject of much online discussion. Ford was so impressed with the discussion about the Ford Edge (a crossover vehicle) it decided to add consumer-generated content to its professionally produced creative executions.[3]

In **experimental research**, one or more factors are manipulated under controlled conditions, while other elements remain constant so that respondents' reactions can be evaluated. Test marketing is a form of experimental research. In a marketing communications context, **test marketing** involves placing a commercial or set of commercials in a campaign (could include print ads as well) in one or more limited markets, representative of the whole, to observe the potential impact of the ads on consumers. Do the ads generate the desired level of awareness and preference? Do they provide sufficient motivation so that consumers take the desired action? Good test marketing provides valuable experience prior to an expensive regional or national launch of the campaign.

QUALITATIVE DATA VERSUS QUANTITATIVE DATA

According to the nature of the information sought, research data are classified as either qualitative or quantitative. There are significant differences between these two classifications.

Qualitative data are usually collected from small samples in a controlled environment. They result from questions concerned with "why" and from in-depth probing of the participants. Typically, such data are gathered from focus group interviews. A **focus group** is a small group of people (usually eight to ten) with common characteristics (for example, a target market profile), brought together to discuss issues related to the marketing of a product or service.

The word "focus" implies that the discussion concentrates on one topic or concept. A trained moderator usually conducts the interview over a period of a few hours. The role of the moderator is to get the participants to interact fairly freely to uncover the reasons and motivations underlying their remarks. Probing uncovers the hidden interplay of psychological factors that drive a consumer to buy one brand rather than another. With regard to advertising evaluations, it provides views on how effective a message might be. Consumers' reactions to the message, the characters that present the message, and the campaign theme and slogan can be discussed at length.

The major drawback of using focus groups concerns the reliability of the data. The sample size is too small to be representative of the entire population, and most people in a focus group do not like to show disagreement with a prevailing opinion. For that reason, interviews are usually held in several locations.

Marketing decisions involving considerable sums of money are very risky if based on such limited research. One of the most spectacular focus group failures, the launch of new Coke in the 1980s, came about because the soft-drink maker was not asking the right questions. Worried that archrival PepsiCo had a better-tasting product, Coca-Cola asked consumers if they liked its new formulation without ever asking if they wanted its tried-and-true beverage changed.[4] The new version of Coca-Cola failed miserably when it was launched, and the public backlash was so significant that Coca-Cola had to reintroduce the original Coke as Coca-Cola Classic.

Quantitative data provide answers to questions concerned with "what," "when," "who," "how many," and "how often." This research attempts to put feelings, attitudes, and opinions into numbers and percentages. The data are gathered from structured questionnaires and a large sample to ensure accuracy and reliability. The interpretation

---

experimental research
Research in which one or more factors are manipulated under controlled conditions while other elements remain constant so that the respondent's actions can be evaluated.

test marketing
Placing a commercial, set of commercials, or print ad campaign in one or more limited markets that are representative of the whole to observe the impact of the ads on consumers.

qualitative data
Data collected from small samples in a controlled environment; the data describe feelings and opinions on issues.

focus group
A small group of people with common characteristics brought together to discuss issues related to the marketing of a product or service.

quantitative data
Measurable data collected from large samples using a structured research procedure.

FIGURE
12.4

A Comparison of Qualitative and Quantitative Data

QUALITATIVE DATA
• Collected from a small sample, usually in a focus-group environment.
• Unstructured questions.
• Questions seek attitudes, feelings, and opinions.
• Data not always reliable because of small sample.

QUANTITATIVE DATA
• Collected from a large, representative sample of target market.
• Structured questions with predetermined responses.
• Deals with who, what, when, how many, and how often.
• Statistically reliable, with calculated degree of error.

of the results is based on the numbers compiled, not on the judgment of the researcher. Quantitative research will statistically confirm the attitudes and feelings that arose in qualitative research. Therefore, a manager will have more confidence in research-based decisions. Figure 12.4 briefly compares qualitative and quantitative research.

The wise organization should use both forms of data collection. Molson Coors, for example, does focus groups and qualitative research, but it also does quantitative research on all television ads before production of the ad takes place. Each ad must hit a specific persuasion level or it will not be used in a campaign.[5]

SURVEY METHODOLOGY

There are four primary means of contacting consumers when conducting surveys to collect quantitative data: telephone, personal interview, mail, and the Internet. **Personal interviews** involve face-to-face communication with groups (for example, focus groups) or individuals and are usually done through quantitative questionnaires. Popular locations for interviews are shopping malls and the homes of respondents.

personal interview
The collection of information in a face-to-face interview.

Telephone interviews involve communication with individuals over the phone. Usually, the interviews are conducted from central locations (that is, one location that can reach all Canadian markets), and, consequently, there is supervised control over the interview process. Telephone technology is now so advanced that research data can be transferred from the telephone directly to a computer. There is a very high refusal rate for telephone surveys. A recent study by the Professional Marketing Research Society observed that 78 percent of people contacted refuse to participate.[6]

telephone interview
In marketing research, the collection of information from a respondent by telephone.

Mail interviews are a silent process of collecting information. Using the mail to distribute a survey means that a highly dispersed sample is reached in a cost-efficient manner. The main drawbacks are the lack of control and the amount of time required to implement and retrieve the surveys.

mail interview
In marketing research, the collection of information from a respondent by mail.

Online surveys allow an organization to be much less invasive in collecting information. Some companies have found that consumers seem more willing to divulge information over the Internet compared with the more traditional means of surveying.

online survey
In marketing research, using an online questionnaire to collect data from people.

Online research is proving effective in terms of testing new product concepts and getting feedback on new advertising ideas. Online research now accounts for about 20 percent of all research spending. For marketers, if time is an imperative and money is in short supply, online research answers the bell—you can quickly access and analyze information. On the downside, recruiting respondents can be a lot like fishing—participation is left to the fish. Consequently, the validity of information collected is questionable.

Figure 12.5 summarizes the advantages and disadvantages of each survey method.

FIGURE
12.5

The Advantages and
Disadvantages of Various
Survey Methods

ADVANTAGES	DISADVANTAGES
Personal Interview	
• High rate of participation • Visual observations possible • Flexible (can include visuals)	• Higher cost due to time needed • Respondents reluctant to respond to certain questions • Interviewer bias possible
Telephone Interview	
• Convenient and allows control • Costs less • Timely responses	• Observation not possible • Short questions and questionnaires • Privacy concerns (bad time of day)
Mail Surveys	
• Cost efficient • Large sample obtainable • Relaxed environment • Impersonal nature produces accurate responses	• Lack of control • Potential for misinterpretation by respondent • Time lag between distribution and return • Low response rates
Online Surveys	
• Efficient and inexpensive • Less intrusive (respondent driven) • Convenient for respondent • Fast response time (days)	• Respondent voluntarily participates, so respondent authenticity is questioned • Limited sample frame (Internet users only) • Research by bulk email associated with spam • Reliability of information suspect

For insight into how primary research can influence brand strategy and marketing communications strategy, see the IMC Highlight: **Mark's New Shopping Experience**.

DATA TRANSFER AND PROCESSING

editing stage
In marketing research, the review of questionnaires for consistency and completeness.

data transfer
In marketing research, the transfer of answers from the questionnaire to the computer.

tabulation
The process of counting various responses for each question in a survey.

frequency distribution
The number of times each answer in a survey was chosen for a question.

cross-tabulation
The comparison of answers to questions by various subgroups with the total number of responses.

data analysis
The evaluation of responses question by question; gives meaning to the data.

Once the data have been collected, then editing, data transfer, and tabulation take place. In the **editing stage**, completed questionnaires are reviewed for consistency and completeness. In the **data transfer** stage, answers from questions are transferred to a computer. Answers are pre-coded to facilitate the transfer.

Once the survey results have been entered into a computer, the results are tabulated. **Tabulation** is the process of counting the various responses for each question and arriving at a frequency distribution. A **frequency distribution** shows the number of times each answer was chosen for a question. Numerous cross-tabulations are also made. **Cross-tabulation** is the comparison and contrast of the answers from various subgroups or from particular subgroups with the total response group. For example, a question dealing with brand awareness could be analyzed by the age, gender, or income of respondents.

DATA ANALYSIS AND INTERPRETATION

Data analysis refers to the evaluation of responses question by question, a process that gives meaning to the data. At this point, the statistical data for each question are reviewed,

Mark's New Shopping Experience

Successful retailers today have added online communications and web-based transaction capabilities to their marketing mix strategy. And what they have learned in the online environment is having an impact on their traditional bricks and mortar business.

Some online research conducted by Mark's (formerly Mark's Work Wearhouse), a division of Canadian Tire, unveiled some important insights that led to an overhaul of their website. Customers want easy navigation, readily available information, and entertaining interactivity. If they don't enjoy the experience, they won't buy.

The research also revealed branding issues that needed to be addressed. For example, the name Mark's Work Wearhouse conjured up the image of a men's clothing and shoe store. Since Mark's had been selling women's clothing for some time, they realized a more effective communications campaign was needed to alter perceptions of the brand.

The first change was the name. Simply calling the store Mark's presents new opportunities. As you have learned earlier in the textbook, all communications start with the brand, so Mark's now had a clean slate to work with. The second change was the website, which was redesigned to meet the consumer expectations described above.

What Mark's learned from the research was also applied to the in-store experience. Their goal was to make the shopping experience more pleasant. Mark's developed a prototype store in Edmonton that was easier to navigate and included some unique interactive elements. In terms of communications, there were overhead banners to direct customers to specific product families. As well, there were overhead towers housing interactive LED video screens with additional information about specific products. Finally, the most unique recommendation involved a walk-in freezer that customers could use to test cold-weather clothing. Now that's innovative thinking!

Mark's won't disclose the impact the changes had on sales, but sales in the prototype store did increase thanks to the buzz generated by the interactive features. Mark's has embarked on a store remodelling plan based on the success of the prototype store.

Adapted from Bill Mah, "Mark's Gets a Fashion Makeover," *Edmonton Journal*, September 16, 2010, www.edmontonjournal.com; Chris Atchison, "Retail Stores Download Lessons from the Net," *The Globe and Mail*, February 15, 2011, p. B11.

Courtesy of Canadian Tire Corporation, Limited.

and the researcher makes observations. Typically, a researcher makes comparisons between responses of subgroups on a percentage basis.

Data interpretation, on the other hand, involves relating the accumulated data to the problem under review and to the objectives and hypotheses of the research study. The process of interpretation uncovers solutions to the problem. The researcher draws conclusions that state the implications of the data for managers.

data interpretation
The relating of accumulated data to the problem under review and to the objectives and hypotheses of the research study.

RECOMMENDATIONS AND IMPLEMENTATION

The recommendations outline suggested courses of action that the sponsoring organization should take in view of the data collected. Once a research project is complete, the research company will present its findings in a written report and highlight the key findings in a visual presentation.

Measuring and Evaluating Advertising Messages

One of the first steps in measuring advertising messages is an evaluation of agency creative ideas by the client. It seems that a creative idea is just that—an idea—until it is sold to the client for approval. Very often, these kinds of evaluations are subjective in nature because they rely on opinions put forth by brand managers, marketing directors, and presidents of companies. The chain of command for approving advertising creative and media expenditures can go very high in an organization.

CLIENT EVALUATION

Creative can be tested at several stages of the development process. The first step is usually a qualitative assessment by the client to determine if the message conforms to the strategic direction that was provided to the agency. This evaluation is conducted by means of a *managerial approach* whereby certain criteria are established and the advertising ideas are measured against them. Typically, a client reserves the right to conduct research prior to making a decision to proceed.

Clients using the managerial approach for evaluating creative may apply some or all of the criteria listed below:

1. **In terms of content, does the advertisement communicate the creative objectives and reflect the positioning strategy of the brand (company)?** The client reviews the creative for its ability to communicate the key benefit and support claims that substantiate the benefit. The client would determine if the message strategy and execution conform to the overall positioning strategy of the brand. If it is off strategy, the ad will be rejected.

2. **In terms of how the ad is presented (strategy and execution), does it mislead or misrepresent the intent of the message? Is it presented in good taste?** The client must be concerned about the actual message and any implied message since it is responsible for the truthfulness of the message. Legal counsel often has the final say regarding message content.

    Taste is always in the eyes of the beholder, and very often consumers complain if an ad is too offensive. Advertisers must be conscious of potential negative feedback and avoid it if they can.

3. **Is the ad memorable?** Breaking through the clutter of competitive advertising is always a challenge, and a lot of advertising that is approved doesn't quite cut it. Is there something that stands out that people will remember? For instance, characters in ads often build momentum for a brand and become strongly associated with the brand itself. For example, think of the "most interesting man in the world" who performs many impressive stunts in the Dos Equis beer commercials. Always surrounded by beautiful women he says, "I don't often drink beer, but when I do, I prefer Dos Equis."

4. **Is the brand recognition effective?** There must be sufficient brand registration in the ad. Some companies go as far as to stipulate how many times the package should be shown in a television commercial or how many times the brand name should be

mentioned. The creativity of the commercial or print ad should not outweigh the product—it should complement the product. For example, people often recall funny ads, but when asked what brand was in the ad they can't remember. So much for the laughs!

5. **Should the advertisement be researched?** When it comes to assessing the impact and effectiveness of the advertisement, subjective judgments by the client have the disadvantage of not being quantifiable. Prior to spending money on production, the client may decide to conduct consumer research to seek quantifiable data that will help the decision-making process. Better safe than sorry!

The evaluation process can occur at any stage of the creative development process. A television commercial, for example, could be evaluated by consumers at the storyboard, rough-cut, or finished commercial stage. Although it is not practical to test commercials at all stages, if the quality or effectiveness of the commercial is ever in question, the client should conduct research to avoid costly and embarrassing errors in judgment.

EXTERNAL RESEARCH TECHNIQUES AND PROCEDURES

Creative evaluation involves a variety of research techniques. The objective of most creative research is to measure the impact of a message on a target audience. Creative research is conducted based on the stage of creative development. It is either a pre-test or a post-test situation. **Pre-testing** is the evaluation of an advertisement, commercial, or campaign before it goes into final production or media placement to determine the strengths and weaknesses of a strategy and execution. **Post-testing** is the process of evaluating and measuring the effectiveness of an advertisement, commercial, or campaign during its run or after it has run. Post-testing provides information that can be used in future advertising planning.

Common techniques used to measure the effectiveness of creative are recognition and recall testing, opinion-measure testing, and physiological-response testing.

pre-testing
The evaluation of commercial messages prior to final production to determine the strengths and weaknesses of the communications.

post-testing
The evaluation and measurement of a message's effectiveness during its run or after the message has run.

RECOGNITION AND RECALL TESTING

In **recognition tests**, respondents are tested for awareness. They are asked if they can recall an advertisement for a specific brand or any of the points made in the advertisement. For example, consumers who have read a publication in which an ad has appeared are asked if they remember what brand was advertised and what the basic message being communicated was.

Several factors affect the level of recognition of an ad. For example, a large print ad occupying a full page usually has a higher level of recognition than an ad occupying only a portion of a page. The inclusion of a celebrity might draw more attention to an ad simply because consumers like the celebrity.

In **recall tests**, respondents are tested for comprehension to measure the impact of advertising. The test can be an *aided* situation (some information is provided to the respondent to stimulate thinking) or an *unaided* situation (no information is provided). In either situation, respondents are asked to name or recall ads and asked to recall specific elements of an advertisement or commercial, such as its primary selling points, the characters in it as presenters, and its slogan. Test scores are usually higher when some form of aid is provided.

Recognition and recall both help develop a brand's image with consumers over a period of time. Therefore, once an advertiser finds an ad or advertising campaign that is performing well, it must resist the temptation to make changes. In the long run, effective advertising plays a role in building sales and market share.

recognition test
A test that measures a target audience's awareness of a brand, copy, or the advertisement itself after the audience has been exposed to the message.

recall test
A test that measures an ad's impact by asking respondents to recall specific elements (for example, the selling message) of the advertisement; can be aided (some information provided) or unaided.

Starch readership test
A post-test recognition procedure that measures readers' recall of an advertisement (noted), their ability to identify the sponsor (associated), and whether they read more than half of the written material (read most).

Two of the most common methods for collecting recognition and recall information are Starch readership tests and day-after recall tests. A **Starch readership test** is a post-test recognition procedure applied to both newspaper and magazine advertisements. The objectives of the test are to measure how many readers saw an ad and how many actually read the ad.

In a Starch readership test, a consumer is given a magazine to read, after which an interviewer goes through it ad by ad with the respondent. For each advertisement in the magazine (the entire magazine is "starched"), responses are divided into three categories:

- **Noted:** the percentage of readers who remembered seeing the ad in this issue.

- **Associated:** the percentage of readers who saw any part of the ad that clearly indicated the brand or advertiser.

- **Read Most:** the percentage of readers who read half or more of the written material.

The Starch readership test offers several benefits. The client can measure the extent to which an ad is seen and read; by reviewing the results of other ads that were tested, the extent of clutter breakthrough can be determined; and by reviewing scores obtained by other products in previous tests, various layouts and design options can be evaluated for effectiveness.

day-after recall (DAR) test
Research conducted the day following the respondent's exposure to a message to determine the degree of recognition and recall of the advertisement, the brand, and the selling message.

In the broadcast media, particularly television, the use of **day-after recall (DAR) testing** is common. As the name implies, research is conducted the day after an audience has been exposed to a commercial message for the first time. By means of a telephone survey technique, a sampling of the client's target market is recruited and asked a series of questions to determine exposure to and recall of particular commercials. Respondents who saw the commercial are asked what the ad actually communicated.

For additional details about the research methodologies described above, visit the websites for Gallup and Robinson (www.gallup-robinson.com) and Starch Research (www.starchresearch.com).

OPINION-MEASURE TESTING

Measuring attitudinal components is another means of evaluating advertising effectiveness. Attitudes and opinions can be gathered from surveys or focus groups. The intent of attitude surveys is to delve a bit deeper with consumers to determine their true feelings about an ad and the product.

opinion-measure testing
A form of research yielding information about the effect of a commercial message on respondents' brand name recall, interest in the brand, and purchase intentions.

With television commercials, **opinion-measure testing** exposes an audience to test-commercial messages in the context of special television programs. In a research setting, respondents view commercials on a large screen (theatre) or on television monitors. Once all of the ads are viewed, participants respond to a series of questions.

The test commercial is usually presented twice during the program, in cluster situations. Also included in the cluster is a set of control commercials against which the test commercial or commercials (sometimes more than one commercial is being tested) can be compared. The position of the test commercial is different in each cluster. The test measures three key attributes: the audience's awareness of the commercial based on brand name recall, the extent to which the main idea of the ad is communicated, and the effect the commercial could have on purchase motivation—that is, the likelihood of the respondent buying the brand. This final measure is based on a comparison of pre-exposure brand purchase information and post-exposure brand preference data. Millward Brown, a marketing research company, uses a procedure it calls TVLink™ to predict how well an ad will perform. Visit its website (www.millwardbrown.com) for additional details.

PHYSIOLOGICAL-RESPONSE TESTING

Advertisers also have access to a variety of physiological testing methods that measure involuntary responses to a specific element of an advertisement. In an **eye movement–camera test**, consumers read an advertisement while a hidden camera tracks their eye movements. Such a test gauges the point of immediate contact, how a reader scans the various components of an ad, and the amount of time spent reading it. The **pupilometer test** measures the dilation of a person's pupil to see how it changes based on emotional arousal. For example, a person's pupils widen when frightened or excited and are smaller when the response is negative.

These types of tests are popular with researchers because emotions trigger physiological responses that can be measured. Physiological responses to something a person sees or hears are difficult to mask. In the two tests mentioned above, reactions are monitored with no words being spoken. Sometimes respondents try to hide their true feelings by saying something that contradicts their physiological reaction. For example, a person might respond in the desired way physiologically to a print ad with sexual imagery, but might state that the ad should not be shown in a magazine. In such a case, physiological reactions speak louder than words.

Testing procedures and the need for them are controversial issues in the industry. Many creative directors argue that too much testing defeats the creative process (because it stifles creativity) and that what people say in research and do in the real world can be completely different. These same creative directors also realize it is the client's money at stake, so if the client is inclined toward research, the ad agency must deal with the situation as best it can.

Measuring and Evaluating Sales Promotions

The overall goal of sales promotions is to produce an increase in sales in the short term and to build brand loyalty in the long term. As discussed in Chapter 8, promotions are classified as consumer promotions and trade promotions. Consumer promotions (for example, coupons, contests, free samples, cash rebates, premium offers, and loyalty card programs) are designed to encourage trial purchase by new customers, repeat purchases by existing customers, and, generally, brand loyalty. Therefore, consumer promotions are measured against these objectives.

Trade promotions include activities such as trade allowances, performance allowances, cooperative advertising allowances, dealer premiums, and dealer display materials. These activities are designed to secure listings of new products with distributors, build sales volume in the promotion period, and secure merchandising support from distributors. Trade promotions are measured against these objectives.

Specific sales promotion measures include response rates to coupon offers, the number of entries received for a contest, and the number of cash rebate forms returned to the company. A marketing manager typically compares response rates for current promotions to response rates received for past and similar promotions. For example, some brands may run a major contest each year in the peak season. Brands like Pepsi-Cola and Coca-Cola, and Coors Light and Bud Light usually run a summer contest. If a particular contest generates significantly more entries than usual, the manager will attempt to isolate the elements of the promotion that led to the higher degree of interest.

Coupon offers are usually evaluated based on the **redemption rate**, which is defined as the number of coupons returned, expressed as a percentage of the number of coupons

eye movement–camera test
A test that uses a hidden camera to track eye movement to gauge the point of immediate contact in an advertisement, how the reader scans the ad, and the amount of time spent reading.

pupilometer test
A device that measures pupil dilation (enlargement) of a person's eye when reading; it measures emotional responses to an advertisement.

redemption rate
The number of coupons returned expressed as a percentage of the number of coupons that were distributed.

distributed. The higher the redemption rate, the more successful the coupon promotion was. For example, if a magazine coupon draws a 2 percent return rate and the norm for magazine coupons is only 1 percent, the offer is an overwhelming success. Historical redemption rates for coupon offers are used to develop budgets for new coupon offers. For an illustration of such a calculation, refer to Figure 12.6.

The absolute number of entry forms received from a contest or rebate offer is a means of measuring the effectiveness of these types of offers. Post Cereal recently offered consumers a high value premium on their packages—a free Reebok PlayDry T-shirt for just two proofs of purchase. Managers estimated that 60 000 T-shirts would be given away over the duration of the promotion. All of the shirts were gone in a matter of weeks! This case demonstrates that the perceived value of an offer has a significant impact on a promotion's success.

The names collected from a contest, premium, or rebate offer provide an additional marketing benefit, as they can be added to the company's database and used for marketing purposes at a later time.

The use of dealer display materials affects the success of sales promotions. Point-of-purchase advertising helps create awareness of promotion offers and reminds

FIGURE 12.6

Measuring the Effectiveness of a Coupon Promotion

ASSUMPTION

A manufacturer offers a $1.00 coupon on a branded box of cereal that has a regular retail price of $4.59. The coupon is distributed through a cooperative direct mail package. For the purposes of budgeting, an average coupon redemption rate for cooperative direct mail will be used. A misredemption rate of 20% is considered, because on average only 80% of coupons redeemed are on valid purchases. The manufacturer receives about 65% of the retail price when wholesale and retail profit margins are considered.

COUPON INFORMATION

Face value	$1.00
Handling charge (retailer)	$0.10
Handling charge (clearing house)	$0.03
Distribution cost	$15.00/M
Printing cost	$10.00/M
Total coupons in distribution	2.5 million
Redemption rate	5.0%

COSTS

Distribution	2 500 000 × $15.00/M	$37 500
Printing	2 500 000 × $10.00/M	$25 000
Redemption	2 500 000 × 0.05 × $1.13	$141 250
Total cost		**$203 750**

REVENUES

Revenue from each purchase	$4.59 × 0.65	$2.98
Total revenue	2 500 000 × 0.05 × 0.80 × $2.66	**$266 000**

PAYOUT

Total revenue minus total cost	$266 000 − $203 750	**$62 250**

From the total revenue line, it can be determined that the coupon offer generated 100 000 purchases (2 500 000 × 0.05 × 0.80).

FORM OF COMMUNICATION	INCREMENTAL RESPONSE RATE
Brand signage	+2%
Sign plus base wrap	+12%
Display stand and sign	+27%
Display stand, sign, and mobile	+40%
Display stand plus sign about sports tie-in	+65%

On average, point-of-purchase communication generates incremental sales ranging from +2% to +65%, independent of any price reductions. The above figures were based on research in 250 stores in 22 cities, and 94 brands in eight different product categories (beer, salty snacks, cold and allergy products, dog food, soft drinks, laundry detergent, shampoo, and conditioner).

FIGURE 12.7

Measuring the Effectiveness of Point-of-purchase Communications

Adapted from "Initial Results from Supermarket Phase of POPAI/ARF Study Reveal Insights into POP Advertising," *Point-of-Purchase Advertising International*, March 27, 2000.

consumers about a product at precisely the right time—the purchase decision time. Figure 12.7 shows that a significantly higher purchase response is achieved if various combinations of in-store merchandising activities are implemented. The importance of these activities is highlighted by the fact that 70 percent of brand purchase decisions are made in-store.[7]

Measuring and Evaluating Direct Response and Internet Communications

One method of measuring direct mail and direct response television messages is to include a toll-free telephone number or website address. The number of inquiries received or the actual sales that result from a particular offer can be compared to those of offers in the past. From this, an observation can be made about the effectiveness of a new offer. As well, a great deal of information can be collected about consumers responding to phone calls. Sales data can be recorded and demographic information gathered. Sales data can be tied to demographic information to determine who is actually buying the product. Knowing who is responding to each offer helps a firm better understand its customers and provides insight into how to develop better marketing communications strategies to reach particular targets.

Response cards are another means of assessing impact and collecting information about customers. Typically, these cards are filled in at the time of purchase. Any information that is collected can be added to the organization's database and be combined with other information that may be available on a particular customer.

In an online environment, a **cookie** (an electronic identification tag sent from a web server to a user's browser to track the user's browsing patterns) enables an organization to track online responses. The Internet is a unique communications medium that has built-in technology, unlike any other medium. That technology allows for all communications to be measured for effectiveness. In fact, Internet communications are much easier to measure in terms of hard numbers than any other form of media advertising.

Currently, online advertising campaigns are measured based on impressions, clicks (or clickthroughs), and click rates. An **impression** (also called an **ad view**) refers to the number of times a banner ad image is downloaded onto a user's computer.

response card
A card filled in, usually at the time of purchase, that collects information about customers that can be added to the organization's database.

cookie
An electronic identification tag sent from a web server to a user's browser to track the user's browsing patterns.

impression (ad view)
The number of times a banner ad image is downloaded onto a user's computer.

clicks (clickthroughs)
The number of times users click on a banner (clicking transfers the user to another website).

Impressions are the standard way of determining exposure of an Internet ad. **Clicks** or **clickthroughs** refer to the number of times that users click on a banner ad. Such a measurement allows an advertiser to judge the response to an ad. When viewers click the ad, they are transferred to the advertiser's website or a special page where more information is available.

click (clickthrough) rate
The percentage of impressions (ad views) that resulted in a click; determines the success of an ad in attracting visitors to click on it.

The **click (clickthrough) rate** is the percentage of impressions that result in a click (or clickthrough). It indicates the success of an advertiser in attracting visitors to click on an ad. The click rate is calculated by dividing the number of clicks by the number of impressions. For example, if during 1 million impressions there are 10 000 clicks on the banner, the click rate is 1 percent (10 000/1 000 000). Google reports that click rates for banners are not that high. In 2010, the click rate for a standard banner ad was 0.09 percent, down from 0.1 percent a year earlier. That means about one person in 1000 actually clicks on a banner ad.[8] Such a low click rate leaves many advertisers pondering the value of online advertising.

Measuring the effectiveness of search ads is relatively easy since advertisers only pay for the ads' placement when people click on them, and they can also track when clicks translate into purchases. The impact of video and display ads on the web is as difficult to measure as the impact of television spots. Various research studies have determined that placing an advertising message mid-roll is better than pre-roll or post-roll. A person watching video content of their choosing stays near the screen during commercial breaks.[9]

Measuring and Evaluating Public Relations Communications

There are several ways to evaluate public relations communications: counting clippings, calculating the number of impressions based on the numbers of clippings, and employing a mathematical model that equates public relations to an advertising value. The latter is referred to as an advertising equivalency.

clipping service
An organization that scans the print and broadcast media in search of a company's or brand's name.

Many organizations that are active in public relations subscribe to a **clipping service**, which scans the print and broadcast media in search of a company's name. Each time the name is found, it is recorded and compared to the number of press releases that were issued. For example, if 500 press releases were issued and there were 50 clippings, the return rate would be 10 percent. The success of the campaign would be based on historical comparisons of return rates.

The number of impressions generated is based on the circulation of the medium in which the organization's name is mentioned. For example, if an article appears in the *Toronto Star* on a Tuesday and the circulation that day is 450 000, the total number of impressions is 450 000. A company may also "gross up" the number of impressions by considering the actual readership of the paper. If the average number of readers is 2.5 per copy, the gross impressions would be 1 125 000 (450 000 × 2.5).

Counting clippings and impressions is a form of measurement, but the procedure ignores the nature of the article written or broadcast about the organization. Was it positive or negative? There is a presumption that an article critical of a company is of equal value to one that praises a company. It could be argued that positive articles and negative articles should be separated. For certain, companies receive a lot of negative publicity when they face a crisis situation, and such publicity negates much of the positive publicity that is generated by planned public relations

Good Turns to Bad for Jaguar

Since you are taking a marketing communications course, perhaps your interest has been piqued by the television show called *Mad Men*. The popular series portrays what advertising was like in the 1960s. Well, at least a TV version of it: Desire, power, and sexuality are key themes throughout. The show features a team of executives lead by creative director Don Draper. To add a sense of reality, the show features real products in the storyline—a branded content strategy many brands could only wish for.

During the 2012 season, one of the main storylines had the agency pitching for the Jaguar account, so there were ongoing references to the car and the company. "It's a car," says Don Draper. "And every agency on Madison Avenue is defined by the moment they get their car." The car is presented as an object of desire, a creative strategy that remains quite common for luxury cars today.

In one episode, Joan Holloway (an agency character) and Don Draper posed as man and wife, and took a Jaguar for a test drive. Suddenly Jaguar was seen as a hot property—lots of social media buzz was happening! The real-world Jaguar got involved and issued *Mad Men*-themed tweets that promoted its new slogan, "Feel Alive." There were links to galleries of *Mad Men*'s Jaguars and explanations about how Jaguars make Don Draper and Joan Holloway "feel alive." Jaguar couldn't be happier.

The next episode caught real-world Jaguar off guard. A new character playing the role of the Jaguar dealer association president had the power to make or break the account for the agency. His price for giving the agency the account: a one-night stand with Joan. Draper pitches the account using the line, "Jaguar: At last, something beautiful you can own." Joan takes the offer while extracting a partnership in the agency. Is this really the way advertising operated in the sixties?

Jaguar suffered some fallout. They had hitched a ride on the positive a week earlier, but were now in the middle of a sexually themed advertising pitch on the show. In trying to explain things away, Jaguar tweeted, "We loved the pitch but didn't like the process." Comments abounded on Twitter, and bloggers had a field day with Jaguar's reaction. The company found itself in a situation it had no control over—it was being associated with a tawdry prostitution racket. Perhaps that's an exaggeration, but in social media, comments can get out of control quickly.

The issue here deals with the impact of social media on a brand and how to measure it. You be the judge. Will this situation have a positive or negative impact on Jaguar's business?

Adapted from Ivor Tossell, "How following Mad Men backfired on the real Jaguar," *The Globe and Mail*, June 15, 2012, p. L4.

---

communications. On the other hand, there are also those who believe that any publicity is good publicity.

Trying to equate public relations to a corresponding advertising value is an attempt to eliminate the problems associated with clippings and impressions. A technique called **advertising equivalency** involves an evaluation of the space occupied by a public relations message and relating it to a similar amount of advertising space. To demonstrate, assume that a one-page article about a company appeared in *Canadian Business* magazine. If a one-page ad costs $25 000, then that is the value of the public relations to the organization. Similar calculations can be made for the broadcast media. Based on this type of calculation, the sum total of a public relations campaign can be considerable. Specialist companies exist to provide this service.

For more insight into public relations and its positive and negative impact on a company, read the IMC Highlight: **Good Turns to Bad for Jaguar**.

advertising equivalency
A mathematical model that equates public relations to an advertising value by evaluating the space occupied by a public relations message in relation to advertising space.

Measuring Experiential Marketing, Events, and Sponsorships

Among all of the integrated marketing communications components, event marketing and sponsorships are the most difficult to evaluate, particularly on a quantitative basis. At their best, sponsorships are a high-profile way to increase sales and improve brand recognition. At their worst, they're a haphazard form of promotion.[10]

Event marketing is attracting a bigger piece of the marketing communications pie each year, but it doesn't get the respect it deserves because there aren't any widely accepted, standardized methods of measuring its results. Despite the lack of measurement, event marketing and sponsorship programs continue to be a valued element in many marketing plans.

The most common measures of an event's success are **how well the event reaches the target audience** and **how well the brand or company is associated with the event**. If some form of return on investment can be added to the evaluation mix, so much the better. But, unless you are establishing leads or selling something at the event, the true impact of the sponsorship won't be felt immediately. Nowhere are sponsorships more visible than in the world of sports. In professional football, basketball, and hockey leagues, there is no shortage of sponsors willing to jump in. The Olympics are also a hot ticket, resulting in a sponsorship battle among bidding advertisers. McDonald's was very pleased with the results of its sponsorship of the Beijing Olympics (2008). McDonald's garnered the highest unaided recall among Olympic sponsors in a post-Olympics survey. In a survey of 1000 Canadians 12 years and older, 33 percent recalled McDonald's as a major Olympic advertiser (ahead of Coca-Cola, Visa, Bell, and RBC).[11]

Most managers rely on less concrete evidence to justify investing in event marketing and sponsorships. Having Tiger Woods walking around a golf course wearing a Nike hat, for example, has a positive impact for all kinds of Nike products that extends well beyond golf products. Seeing Sidney Crosby wearing Reebok attire and equipment when he's being interviewed enhances the credibility of Reebok as a manufacturer of hockey equipment.

How beneficial are naming rights on a building? Scotiabank has the name rights to the building where the Ottawa Senators play, which is called Scotiabank Place. Will it enhance Scotiabank's brand image? Industry experts believe Scotiabank will get lots of media exposure for its $20 million investment at Ottawa's Scotiabank Place. Media exposure is a true benefit of event marketing, since hockey games are broadcast and covered by newspapers, radio, and TV stations.

As discussed in Chapter 10, certain indicators are commonly used to measure the benefits of sponsorship. As described above in the McDonald's example, an organization might look at *awareness* and *association* measures as well as changes in *image perceptions* among its customers. To do so, a company will have to conduct some of the pre- and post-test research described earlier in the chapter.

Another common measure is the impact on *brand sales*. Is it immediate, during the event period, or will it happen after the event? When Roots was an Olympic sponsor, clothing sales rose considerably during the Olympic period and the few months that followed the Olympics, a clear indication that the association with Canada's Olympic team paid dividends. For a variety of reasons, however, Roots is no longer associated with the Olympics. Perhaps the costs started to outweigh the benefits.

Measuring the Impact of Social Media Advertising

With social media, advertisers have to look at a softer set of measurement tools to judge whether or not a communications effort was successful. For example, the amount of time a person spends at a social media site and the extent of involvement they might have with a brand while at a site become meaningful ways of measuring the effectiveness of a social media campaign. The Interactive Advertising Bureau (IAB) is actively promoting a new set of terms to measure social media efforts.[12] The terms are:

- **Interaction Rate:** The proportion of users who interact with an ad or application.

- **Time Spent:** The time spent during a specific visit or session.

- **Conversation Reach:** The number of unique visitors per month in all sites related to the conversation in which the client (brand advertiser) is participating.

- **Conversation-Relevant Links:** The number of links to and from content that contains phrases from all sites identified as part of the client's campaign.

Facebook, the largest social media network by far, recommends that companies measure five key areas: volume, reach, engagement, influence, and share of voice.[13] *Volume* refers to the number of messages there are about a brand and the number of people talking about a brand. Facebook offers a tool called "people talking about this," so tracking volume is an easy task. *Reach* measures the extent of social media conversation about a brand and is a measure of potential audience size. *Engagement* assesses how people are participating with a brand and what they are doing to spread the content to others. Facebook shares and posts help determine who is spreading brand content, while comments and likes determine who is replying to your content. *Influence* refers to the degree of impact a person may have when discussing a brand. For example, many bloggers may converse about the automobile industry, but certain bloggers will have more influence and a larger following.

Finally, *share of voice*, or how well a brand is doing in terms of conversation compared to competitors, can be an important measure. Dividing a brand conversation by industry conversation will give a brand its share of voice. If a competitor has a much higher share of voice, it would be wise to analyze the social media practices of that competitor.

Marketers who realize the difference between offline communities and online communities will reap the benefits of online communications. Generally speaking, content that is innovative tends to grab the attention of people in the social media universe. The communications objective is to grab attention and point the conversation in the right direction.

Measuring the Integrated Marketing Communications Effort

Because integrated marketing communications is a coordinated and collaborative effort among many different individuals and organizations and many different communications disciplines, perhaps the best form of measurement and evaluation is to look at the big picture. In other words, how healthy is a particular brand or the company as a whole, based on all the marketing and marketing communications strategies that have been implemented over the past year (a typical planning cycle)?

Some typical indicators of success or failure include market share, productivity, sales and profitability, customer satisfaction levels, and social responsibility. As in most evaluation systems already discussed in this chapter, the organization should look back at the corporate objectives it established in these areas to see how well it performed.

An increase in **market share** would indicate greater acceptance by more customers, a higher degree of brand loyalty among current customers, and a strong competitive position. A well-planned integrated marketing communications program would have contributed to such an outcome. *Productivity* measures are more difficult to come by, but where tangible results can be attributed to a specific communications activity, it should be noted. Did the integrated marketing communications program generate new customers? Was brand awareness higher than it was previously? Was the company's or brand's image altered in a positive way? These kinds of measures indicate whether or not a plan is working.

Marketing managers are responsible for producing sales while keeping marketing and marketing communications investments at reasonable levels. Sales must generate an adequate level of *profit* for the company to thrive and survive in the long term. Most brands in an organization have their own profit and loss statement, which is reviewed continually to ensure that sales, costs, and profit targets are always within sight. Alterations and adjustments to a marketing plan or marketing communications plan will occur during the year when necessary.

As discussed elsewhere in the text, every employee of an organization plays a role in providing *customer satisfaction*; all employees must adopt a marketing attitude. Therefore, it is very important for all employees to be aware of the marketing and marketing communications strategies. Informed employees play a key role in implementing the strategies; they thus directly influence how customers perceive the organization.

With regard to *social responsibility* objectives, planned public relations programs play a key role. An organization must promote its positive contributions while eliminating, as best it can, the negative outcomes. Brand equity and company image are directly influenced by the quality of social programs and ethical behaviour that a company and its employees demonstrate to the public.

market share
The sales volume of one product or company expressed as a percentage of total sales volume in the market the company or brand is competing in.

▶▶ SUMMARY

Marketing research must be viewed as a tool that assists the manager in the decision-making process. It is a systematic procedure that, if used properly, will produce reliable and valid data.

The research process begins with a firm becoming aware of a problem situation. Problems associated with evaluating marketing communications typically involve primary research. Primary research is the gathering of new data from a representative sample. Primary data are collected from surveys, observation, and experiments. Survey data are either qualitative or quantitative in nature. Qualitative data are collected by focus group or one-on-one interviews and answer the question "why." Quantitative data are obtained by questionnaires through personal interview, telephone, mail, or online surveys and involve translating thoughts and feelings into measurable numbers. Once the data are secured, they are processed for analysis and interpreted by the researcher.

Experimental research involves testing a marketing mix activity within a controlled situation to measure the effectiveness of the activity. Test marketing is an example of experimental research. In a test market involving marketing communications, an advertisement, commercial, or set of ads in a campaign is placed in designated geographic markets to evaluate the potential impact on consumers. Knowledge gained from such tests allows an organization to make changes to a campaign before it is launched in additional markets.

In order to measure the effectiveness of marketing communications programs, various research procedures are implemented. In advertising, several pre-test and post-test techniques are available. If recognition and recall are a concern, a Starch readership test, a day-after recall test, and opinion-measure tests can be applied. These tests generate data on brand identification and message comprehension.

Sales promotion measures include response rates to coupon offers and the number of entries received for contest, premium, and cash rebate offers. Response rates for current promotions are compared to response rates for previous promotions. The manager will evaluate the various elements of the promotion to determine what elements contributed to success or failure.

Direct response communications can be measured quantitatively since they include a toll-free telephone number, a website address, or response cards. Inquiries can be tracked, and any sales that occur can be attributed to specific customers. With Internet communications, the use of cookies allows an organization to track responses. Other forms of Internet measures include impressions, clicks, and the actual click rate an ad generates.

The most common ways of measuring public relations communications include counting actual clippings that appear in the print and broadcast media, calculating the number of impressions that the press clippings generate, and converting the press coverage (the size of space or amount of time it occupies) to some kind of advertising equivalency. The latter places a monetary value on public relations and is a popular means of justifying investment in public relations.

Event marketing and sponsorships remain difficult to measure, but they are perceived as a high-profile way to increase sales and improve brand recognition. The most common measure of an event's success is determined by how well the event reaches the target audience. Other commonly used measures include changes in brand awareness levels and image, both of which are based on how well a brand associates with an event.

Social media measures include interaction rates, time spent (with a brand), and conversation reach. On Facebook, the largest social media network, five key measures are recommended: volume, reach, engagement, influence, and share of voice. Generally speaking, social media measures are softer than those in traditional media. An organization must adjust to the differences between social media and mainstream media.

When measuring the success of an integrated marketing communications campaign, an organization looks at the bigger picture. Typical indicators of success or failure include shifts in market share, productivity, sales and profitability, employee performance and attitude, and the public's perceptions of an organization's social responsibility. A carefully planned marketing communications program contributes to achieving objectives in all of these areas.

KEY TERMS

REVIEW QUESTIONS

1. In the context of marketing research, what is the relationship between each of the following sets of terms?
   a) research objectives and hypotheses
   b) observation and experimental research
   c) population and sampling frame
   d) qualitative data and quantitative data
   e) probability sample and non-probability sample
   f) frequency distribution and cross-tabulation
   g) tabulation and cross-tabulation
   h) data analysis and data interpretation
2. What is the problem-awareness stage of the marketing research process?
3. Briefly explain the four steps in the sample design process.
4. What is a focus group? What are the benefits of focus group research?
5. Under what circumstances would you use the telephone for collecting survey data? When would you use the personal interview?
6. In terms of measuring the effectiveness of advertising, what is the difference between pre-testing and post-testing? What benefits does each form of research provide?
7. What is the difference between a recognition test and a recall test?
8. What are the three categories of measurement in a Starch readership test? Briefly explain each category.
9. What does opinion-measure testing refer to?
10. What are the three primary ways of measuring the effectiveness of public relations campaigns? Briefly discuss each form of measurement.
11. What are the primary ways of measuring the effectiveness of event marketing and sponsorship participation? Briefly discuss each form of measurement.

DISCUSSION AND APPLICATION QUESTIONS

1. Compare and contrast the nature of qualitative data and quantitative data. Is it essential to have both types of information prior to investing in a new advertising campaign? Prepare a position and provide appropriate justification for it.
2. You are about to devise a new advertising strategy (a message strategy) for the Porsche 911 Carrera. You do not know how to present the automobile to potential customers and would like to find out more about them. What information would you like to obtain, and what procedure would you recommend to obtain it?
3. "Too much information obtained from marketing research ultimately stifles creative thinking and the production of innovative creative." Many creative directors have expressed this opinion. Conduct some secondary research and present an opinion on the issue. Justify your position with appropriate examples.
4. Companies are now using online surveys to learn more about their customers and how they feel about the company's products. What are the benefits and drawbacks of using online research? Is it as useful and effective as traditional survey methodologies? Briefly discuss the key issues.
5. If event marketing and sponsorships are so difficult to measure for tangible business results, why do so many large and prosperous companies pursue such associations? What are the advantages and disadvantages of being involved in this form of marketing communications? Is it a worthwhile investment? Present an opinion supported with appropriate justification.

ENDNOTES

1. Mary Maddever, "P&G's Trevor Thun: Selling Fresh Air," *Strategy*, November 1, 2008, p. 10.
2. American Marketing Association, *Dictionary of Marketing Terms*, www.marketingpower.com.
3. Jean Halliday, "Car Talk: Ford Listens to Consumer Chatter," *Advertising Age*, February 5, 2007, p. 3.
4. "Managers Should Rethink the Power and Limitations of Focus Groups," *Financial Post*, December 14, 1999, p. C4.
5. Wendy Cuthbert, "Hold the Numbers," *Strategy*, June 4, 2001, pp. B6, B7.
6. Colin Flint, "Market Researchers Facing a Lot of Hang-ups," *Financial Post*, March 26, 2004, p. FP4.

7. Sarah Mahoney, "Companies Shifting More Funds, Brain Cells to Shopper Marketing," *Marketing Daily*, October 16, 2007, www.mediapost.com/publications/article/69231.

8. "Google: Click-through Rates Fell in 2010," *Mashable.com*, August 19, 2011, mashable.com/2011/08/19/google-click-through-rates-fell-in-2010-study.

9. Gavin O'Malley, "Web Watchers Ditch Video Ads," *Online Media Daily*, May 17, 2012, www.mediapost.com/publications/article/174988.

10. Patrick Maloney, "Do Sponsorships Measure Up?" *Marketing*, July 8, 2002, p. 13.

11. Chris Powell, "McDonald's Wins Canadian Olympic Recall," *Marketing*, September 10, 2008, www.marketingmag.ca/news/marketer-news/mcdonalds-wins-canadian-olympic-recall-17575.

12. "The Social Media Metrics Glossary," *Marketing*, June 15, 2009, p. 27.

13. "5 Most Essential Facebook Marketing Metrics, *AllFacebook*, April 17, 2012, www.allfacebook.com/facebook-metrics-essentials_b86156.

Media Buying Principles and Media Information Resources

This appendix presents the essential aspects of media buying and acquaints the student with a variety of media rate cards and how to read them. The rate cards used in this section have been gathered from online sources and *Canadian Advertising Rates and Data (CARD)*. Rate cards are usually posted on a media company's website under a title like "Advertise with Us" or "Media Kit." Students can refer to *CARD*, a publication usually available in the reference section of college and university libraries, or by visiting cardonline.ca. *CARD* contains summary rate cards for all print and selected out-of-home media in Canada.

In addition, this section exposes the student to a variety of media information sources often referred to by marketing organizations and communications agencies. In most cases, specialized software available by subscription is required to access specific data. However, students are encouraged to visit the various websites listed under "Media Information Resources" to gain exposure to basic information that is available for free.

A set of review questions dealing with various media calculations is included at the end of the appendix.

Media Buying Principles

NEWSPAPER ADVERTISING

agate line
A non-standardized unit of space measurement, equal to one column wide and 1/14″ deep, used in newspaper advertising.

broadsheet
A large newspaper with a fold in its middle.

tabloid
A smaller newspaper that is sold flat (not folded).

modular advertising
Selling advertisements based on standardized sizes.

Newspaper space is sold on the basis of agate lines or modular agate lines. An **agate line** is a non-standardized unit of space measurement, equal to one column wide and 1/14″ deep. For **broadsheets**, a standard page ranges from 10″ to 11″ wide by 20″ to 22″ deep. A page may have anywhere from 6 to 10 columns, with the norm being 10 columns.

In **tabloids**, the page is generally 10″ wide and ranges from 11″ to 14″ in depth. The number of columns range from 6 to 10. Most broadsheets and tabloids use agate lines to determine the size of an advertisement.

An alternative to the agate line format is modular advertising. **Modular advertising** involves selling ads by standardized sizes. To illustrate, an advertisement could be described as a 1/2 page vertical or 1/3 page horizontal.

Note that in this context "lines" and "columns" are not physical lines and columns. They are invisible lines and columns that the newspaper industry uses to measure the size of an ad.

The basic procedure for buying newspaper space is to determine the size of the ad, either in agate lines or by buying a standardized size offered by the newspaper.

In the agate line situation, the cost is calculated by multiplying the width of the ad (number of columns) by the depth of the ad (inches of depth). One column inch of depth equals 14 agate lines. Other factors that influence costs include the number of insertions, creative considerations such as the use of colour, and position charges, if applicable.

Some newspapers offer standard-size ads that are easier to understand in terms of size. With reference to *The Globe and Mail* (see Figure A1.1), some of the standard-size options include full page (2800 agate lines), 1/2 page horizontal (1400 agate lines), 1/3 page (930 agate lines), and 1/4 page horizontal (700 agate lines).

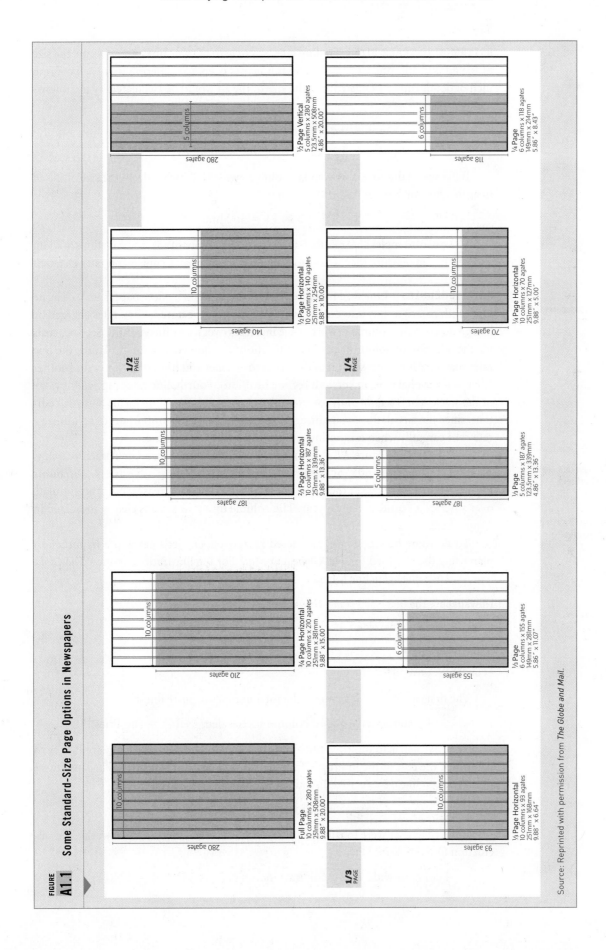

FIGURE A1.1   Some Standard-Size Page Options in Newspapers

Source: Reprinted with permission from *The Globe and Mail*.

DETERMINING SPACE SIZE To illustrate the concept of agate lines, let's assume the size of the ad is 4 columns wide by 10 column inches deep. Considering that each column inch of depth equals 14 agate lines, the size of the ad would be calculated by the following formula:

$$\text{Number of columns wide} \times \text{Inches of depth} \times 14$$
$$4 \times 10 \times 14 = 560 \text{ agate lines}$$

If the size of the advertisement is 5 columns wide by 8 inches deep, the size of the ad in agate lines will be:

$$5 \times 8 \times 14 = 560 \text{ lines}$$

These two examples illustrate that different configurations of ads (combinations of width and depth) can produce the same size of ad in terms of space occupied and rates charged.

line rate
The rate charged by newspapers for one agate line.

RATE SCHEDULES **Line rate** is defined as the rate charged by newspapers for one agate line. With regard to rate schedules, several factors must be noted. First, rates charged by line go down as the volume of the lineage increases over a specified period. Second, costs for the addition of colour or preferred positions are quoted separately. Third, the line rates may vary from one section of the paper to another and from one edition to another (that is, a national edition versus a regional edition). Fourth, line rates may vary by day of the week. The *Toronto Star*, for example, charges more per line for its Saturday edition, since the circulation is significantly higher that day. It is important to scrutinize a rate card carefully when estimating costs of newspaper advertising.

transient rate
A one-time rate, or base rate, that applies to casual advertisers.

In the chart in Figure A1.2, the rates quoted start with a **transient rate**, which is defined as a one-time rate, or base rate, that applies to casual advertisers. *Discounts* are offered to advertisers as the number of lines purchased increases. Lines accumulate over a period of time, usually a year. The volume discount scale is clearly indicated in Figure A1.2.

To illustrate how costs are calculated in newspapers, let's develop a hypothetical plan using the rate card for *The Globe and Mail*. For the illustration, assume *The Globe and Mail* uses the agate line format.

Newspaper: *The Globe and Mail*—News Section, National Edition

Size of ad: 4 columns wide x 10 column inches deep

Rate: Transient rate

Frequency: Once

The first calculation determines the total number of agate lines:

$$4 \text{ columns wide} \times (10 \text{ column inches deep} \times 14) = 560 \text{ lines}$$

The next step is to multiply the number of lines by the line rate by the frequency to determine the cost of the insertion. In this case, the transient rate applies because there is not enough lineage to earn a discount.

$$560 \times \$31.25 \times 1 = \$17\,500$$

If the advertiser were to run the ad four times over a period of a few weeks, the calculation for costs would be

$$4 \text{ columns wide} \times (10 \text{ columns inches deep} \times 14) \times 4 = 2240 \text{ lines}$$
$$2240 \times \$31.25 = \$70\,000$$

FIGURE A1.2 *The Globe and Mail* **Rate Card**

NATIONAL RATES 2013

National Advertising Rates

ADVERTISING RATES EFFECTIVE JANUARY 1, 2013. ALL RATES ARE GROSS $ CANADIAN PER LINE (UNLESS OTHERWISE NOTED), BASED ON ANNUAL DOLLAR VOLUME CONTRACT COMMITMENT
BEFORE BOOKING YOUR AD, PLEASE BE SURE TO REFER TO THE GLOBE ADVERTISING INFORMATION ON PAGE 12 AND THE TERMS AND CONDITIONS ON PAGE 16

FULL PAGE SIZE
10 COLUMNS X 280 AGATE LINES

- **NEWS** appears daily, in all editions
- **REPORT ON BUSINESS** appears daily in the National Edition
- **GLOBE T.O.** appears Saturday in the Metro edition

	MONDAY TO FRIDAY			SATURDAY		
	NATIONAL	CENTRAL (ON/QC)	METRO	NATIONAL	CENTRAL (ON/QC)	METRO
Transient	$31.88	$27.42	25.18	$35.06	$30.16	$27.71
$15,000	27.91	24.00	22.04	30.69	26.38	24.24
$25,000	27.09	23.32	21.40	29.81	25.63	23.54
$50,000	26.30	22.62	20.78	28.94	24.88	22.85
$100,000	25.51	21.93	20.16	28.06	24.13	22.15
$150,000	24.70	21.26	19.52	27.18	23.38	21.48
$250,000	23.91	20.56	18.89	26.30	22.62	20.78
$350,000	22.96	19.75	18.14	25.26	21.72	19.94
$500,000	21.99	18.92	17.37	24.18	20.81	19.13
$750,000	21.03	18.09	16.61	23.14	19.91	18.29
$1,000,000	20.08	17.27	15.87	22.09	19.00	17.45
$1,500,000	19.14	16.46	15.12	21.03	18.09	16.61
$2,000,000	18.17	15.63	14.37	19.97	17.19	15.80
$2,500,000	17.22	14.80	13.61	18.94	16.29	14.95

COLOUR	HALF PAGE PLUS			LESS THAN HALF PAGE		
MON – SAT	NATIONAL	CENTRAL (ON/QC)	METRO	NATIONAL	CENTRAL (ON/QC)	METRO
	$10,697	$9,727	$8,950	$8,557	$7,782	$6,846

- **GLOBE BOOKS** appears Saturday in the National edition within Globe Arts
- **GLOBE FOCUS** appears Saturday in the National edition
- **GLOBE FILM** appears Friday in the Metro edition
- **GLOBE LIFE & ARTS** appears Monday through Friday in the Metro and National editions
- **GLOBE ARTS** appears Saturday in the Metro and National editions
- **GLOBE SPORTS** appears daily in the Metro and National editions

	MONDAY TO FRIDAY		SATURDAY	
	NATIONAL	METRO	NATIONAL	METRO
Transient	$14.99	$11.84	$16.48	13.03
$15,000	13.10	10.37	14.42	11.40
$25,000	12.73	10.06	14.03	11.07
$50,000	12.36	9.76	13.61	10.74
$100,000	11.99	9.47	13.19	10.42
$150,000	11.61	9.17	12.76	10.09
$250,000	11.24	8.87	12.36	9.76
$350,000	10.79	8.52	11.86	9.36
$500,000	10.32	8.17	11.37	8.99
$750,000	9.88	7.81	10.87	8.59
$1,000,000	9.45	7.47	10.39	8.20
$1,500,000	9.00	7.10	9.88	7.81
$2,000,000	8.54	6.75	9.40	7.43
$2,500,000	8.09	6.40	8.90	7.12

COLOUR	HALF PAGE PLUS		LESS THAN HALF PAGE	
MON – SAT	NATIONAL	METRO	NATIONAL	METRO
	$8,557	$7,782	$6,846	$5,477

- **GLOBE STYLE** appears Saturday in the National edition

	SATURDAY		SATURDAY	
	NATIONAL			NATIONAL
Transient	$20.56		Transient	$20.56
$15,000	20.56		$500,000	15.45
$25,000	18.00		$750,000	14.95
$50,000	17.69		$1,000,000	14.47
$100,000	17.27		$1,500,000	13.96
$150,000	16.84		$2,000,000	13.48
$250,000	16.44		$2,500,000	12.98
$350,000	15.94			

- **GLOBE REAL ESTATE** appears Friday in the Metro edition
- **GLOBE TRAVEL** appears Tuesday within Life section in Metro and National editions and Saturday in the Metro, Central and National editions
- **GLOBE DRIVE** appears Thursday in the Metro edition

	MONDAY TO FRIDAY			SATURDAY		
	NATIONAL	CENTRAL (ON/QC)	METRO	NATIONAL	CENTRAL (ON/QC)	METRO
Transient	$19..77	$17.00	$15.62	$21.73	$18.70	$17.18
$15,000	17.29	14.86	13.75	19.02	16.36	15.03
$25,000	16.80	14.44	13.27	18.48	15.89	14.60
$50,000	16.31	14.04	12.88	17.94	15.42	14.17
$100,000	15.81	13.61	12.50	17.39	14.95	13.74
$150,000	15.32	13.18	12.11	16.85	14.48	13.31
$250,000	14.82	12.74	11.70	16.31	14.04	12.88
$350,000	14.23	12.24	11.24	15.65	13.45	12.36
$500,000	13.64	11.74	10.78	15.00	12.90	11.85
$750,000	13.05	11.22	10.30	14.36	12.34	11.33
$1,000,000	12.46	10.71	9.83	13.69	11.79	10.82
$1,500,000	11.86	10.20	9.36	13.05	11.22	10.30
$2,000,000	11.26	9.69	8.90	12.38	10.66	9.80
$2,500,000	10.69	9.17	8.44	11.75	10.10	9.27

COLOUR	HALF PAGE PLUS			LESS THAN HALF PAGE		
MON – SAT	NATIONAL	CENTRAL (ON/QC)	METRO	NATIONAL	CENTRAL (ON/QC)	METRO
	$8,557	$7,782	$6,846	$6,846	$6,225	$5,477

FIGURE
A1.2 (*Continued*)

NATIONAL RATES 2013

Globe Advertising Information

COLOUR MANDATORY POSITIONS

Certain positions are colour mandatory. Please contact your Globe and Mail representative for more details.

PREMIUM STOCK SURCHARGE

$5,000.00 net per page except for Globe Style.

- The Front News section is wrapped in semi-gloss premium stock Monday through Saturday. These pages feature our front banner, page 2, inside back cover (IBC) and outside back cover (OBC) advertising positions.
- The Globe Style (Saturday) section is printed on our semi-gloss premium stock.
- The Globe Life & Arts section is wrapped in semi-gloss premium stock Monday through Friday. These pages feature our front page banner, page 2 and facts and arguments advertising positions.

ADDITIONAL INFORMATION

- Double Trucks: Gutter is charged as full column.
- Regional material changes: $579 per split. Not available in Report on Business, Style, Books or Careers.
- Position charge: +25 per cent.
- Front News Banner: +50 per cent.
- Page 3, News: +40 per cent.
- Front Report on Business banner: +25 per cent.
- Pages 2 & 3, Report on Business: +40 per cent.
- Floating Banners: +50 per cent.
- Charge for Globe and Mail box number: $100.
- Charge for affidavits: $100.
- Cancellation charge: 50 per cent for ads cancelled after deadline. No cancellations accepted the day prior to publication.
- The Publisher shall not be liable for errors in advertisements beyond the actual space paid. No liability for non-insertions of any advertisement.
- There is a $100 production charge for ads under 50 MAL that are not camera-ready.

ADVERTISING SPECIFICATIONS

Page dimensions: 9.88˝ wide x 20˝ deep
Number of columns: 10
Column depth: 280 modular agate lines for full page ads (2,800 lines per 10 column page)

For complete layout, mechanical and digital specifications, please visit

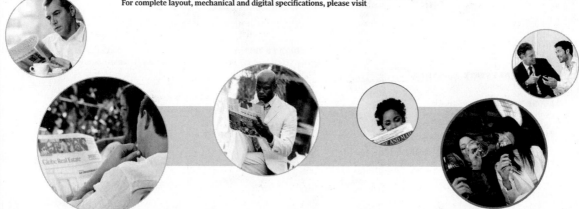

In this situation, the advertiser remains in the transient rate range even though the total number of lines purchased increased.

Advertisers earn discounted line rates based on annual dollar volume line commitment. To demonstrate, assume an advertiser commits to $100 000. At that level, the line rate drops to $25.01 if the ads are placed in the News section or Report on Business section. Therefore, if the dollar commitment is divided by the line rate ($100 000/$25.01), the advertiser can place ads in various sizes totalling approximately 4000 lines. From the previous example, the total line space was 560 lines for one ad, which means that this ad could run seven times (560 lines × 7) for a total of 3920 lines. When an advertiser commits (typically by a contract) to a certain dollar volume, a greater number of ads can be placed with the newspaper.

POSITION CHARGES   Since one disadvantage of newspaper advertising is clutter, advertisers and agencies can request positions in the newspaper that are deemed to be favourable. The request may be for a particular type of ad that commands a higher rate, or it could be for the first few pages of the newspaper. With reference to Figure A1.2, *The Globe and Mail* charges more for preferred locations. A general request for a specific section will increase rates by 25 percent, while a request for an ad to appear on page 3 (news section) will increase the rates by 40 percent. A banner on the front page of the news section will increase by 50 percent.

The privilege of having a preferred position in a newspaper at a higher cost incurs a **position charge**. An advertiser usually justifies the additional expense of a position request by referring to the improved recognition and recall that will result from the better position.

position charge
The cost of requesting a preferred position in a newspaper.

COLOUR CHARGES   Although newspapers are often referred to as the black-and-white medium, colour is available to advertisers willing to pay for it. With reference to *The Globe and Mail*'s rate schedule in Figure A1.2, a separate cost of $8557 is added if the ad runs in colour. The colour charge applies each time the ad is run. Other newspapers quote cost increases for each additional colour that is added. The addition of a particular colour is often referred to as **spot colour**. A newspaper will also indicate if there is a minimum size requirement for ads running in colour. Make sure you read the fine print on the rate cards!

spot colour
The addition of one colour to an otherwise black-and-white newspaper or magazine ad.

Generally speaking, there is higher recognition and recall of ads that appear in colour, but given the constraints of most budgets, the use of colour in newspaper advertising is reserved for very large advertisers.

PREPRINTED INSERTS   Preprinted inserts, such as advertising supplements for supermarkets, drug stores, and mass merchandisers, are inserted into most newspapers and distributed by them. Rates are usually quoted on cost per thousand (CPM). As the size of an insert increases (number of pages) or the delivery circulation increases, the rates on a cost-per-thousand basis also increase. For example, a 24-page catalogue insert would cost more than a 4-page folded insert. Insert rates are quoted separately on newspaper rate cards. In many cases, there is only a reference to the rates on the rate card. Advertisers must contact the newspaper for details.

COMPARING NEWSPAPERS FOR EFFICIENCY   In large metropolitan markets where several newspapers compete for advertising revenue, advertisers must decide which papers to place advertising with. For instance, the *Toronto Star* and *Toronto Sun* compete for ad dollars in Toronto as do the *Calgary Herald* and *Calgary Sun* in Calgary. If using a shotgun strategy, the advertiser may use all newspapers. Conversely, if the budget is limited and the target market is more precisely defined, the advertiser might be more selective.

Since the circulation and the cost of advertising (line rates) vary among newspapers, the advertiser must have a way of comparing the alternatives. To make this comparison, the advertiser may use a standard figure called the **cost per thousand** (**CPM**). CPM is the actual cost of reaching 1000 readers in a market. The formula for calculating CPM is as follows:

$$\frac{\text{Cost}}{\text{Circulation (in thousands)}} = \text{CPM}$$

cost per thousand (CPM)
The cost of delivering an advertising message to 1000 people; calculated by dividing the cost of the ad by the circulation in thousands.

To illustrate the concept of CPM, assume an advertiser wants to reach adults in the Calgary market and is considering both the *Calgary Herald* and the *Calgary Sun*. Refer to Figure A1.3 for specific details on how the newspapers are compared.

As shown by Figure A1.3, the newspaper CPM is strictly a quantitative figure and the results vary considerably. If the advertiser bases the decision of which newspaper to use solely on this principle, the decision is an easy one—the *Calgary Herald* has a much lower CPM than the *Calgary Sun*. However, to reach the adult population of Calgary effectively, the advertiser will realize that the circulation of both newspapers will be needed. Even though the *Calgary Sun* costs more, it will help an advertiser expand its reach in that market.

MAGAZINE ADVERTISING

The procedure for buying magazine space begins with deciding on the size of the ad, which involves choosing from among the variety of page options sold by the magazines under consideration. The rates quoted are based on the size of page requested. Other factors that influence the cost of advertising in magazines include the frequency of insertions and appropriate discounts, the use of colour, guaranteed-position charges, and the use of regional editions.

SIZE OF AN ADVERTISEMENT AND RATE SCHEDULES   Magazines offer a variety of page options or page combinations. For example, *Canadian Geographic* sells space in the following

**FIGURE
A1.3**

Comparing Newspapers for Efficiency

The CPM, or cost per thousand, is used to compare newspaper alternatives. It is calculated by dividing the cost of the advertisement by the circulation (in thousands) of the newspaper.

Specifications	Calgary Herald	Calgary Sun
Ad size	1000 lines	1000 lines
Cost per line	$6.68	$4.11
Ad cost (rate × lines)	$6680	$4110
Circulation	129 043	57 207
CPM	$51.78	$71.85

Interpretation: Both newspapers reach adult males and females in Calgary, but the *Calgary Herald* reaches the audience in a more cost-efficient manner. An advertiser would have to place ads in both newspapers to effectively reach an adult target in Calgary.

Source: Adapted from rate card information published in *CARD*, Winter 2009, pp. 7–8.

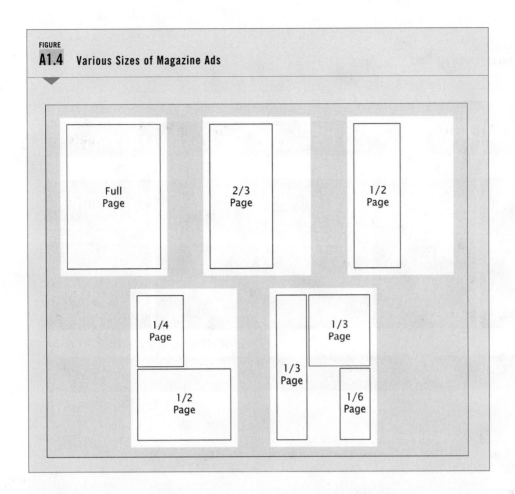

A1.4   Various Sizes of Magazine Ads

formats: full page, double-page spread, 2/3 page, 1/2 page, and 1/3 page. See Figure A1.4 for illustrations of various magazine ad sizes. The size selected for the advertisement determines the rate to be charged. Magazine rates are typically quoted for all page combinations.

To illustrate how costs are calculated, let's consider a simple example. Assume an advertiser would like to purchase a one-page, four-colour ad in *Canadian Geographic* for January/February and July/August editions (see Figure A1.5 for rate card details). *Canadian Geographic* is issued six times a year. The column headings on the rate card (1X, 3X, 6X, and so on) refer to frequency (one time, three times, six times). In this example, the frequency is only two. Therefore, the rates in the 1X column are used to calculate the campaign. A discount does not apply until the advertiser commits to three advertisements. The cost calculation would be as follows:

$$\text{One-page rate} \times \text{Number of insertions} = \text{Total cost}$$
$$\$17\,290 \times 2 = \$34\,580$$

DISCOUNTS Advertisers purchasing space in specific magazines with greater frequency will qualify for a variety of discounts. The nature of these discounts varies from one publication to another. Some of the more common discounts include frequency, continuity, and corporate discounts. In magazines, a **frequency discount (print)** refers to a discounted page rate, with the discount based on the number of times an advertisement is run. The more often the ad is run, the lower the unit cost for each ad. In the *Canadian Geographic* rate card, the unit rate is reduced when the ad is run three times, six times, nine times, and twelve times.

A **continuity discount (print)** is an additional discount offered to advertisers that agree to purchase space in consecutive issues of a magazine (such as buying space in 12

frequency discount (print)
A discounted page rate based on the number of times an advertisement runs.

continuity discount (print)
A discount offered to advertisers purchasing space in consecutive issues of a publication.

FIGURE
A1.5 *Canadian Geographic* Rate Card

2013 NATIONAL RATES AND DATA

www.canadiangeographic.ca

    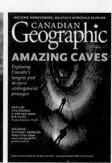

PUBLISHING SCHEDULE 2013-2014

6 ISSUES ANNUALLY	CANADIAN GEOGRAPHIC EDITORIAL FEATURES	CLOSING DATES (insertion orders & material)	IN MARKET
January/February 2013	Arctic Expedition	December 5, 2012	December 26, 2012
April 2013	Rouge River National Park	February 26, 2013	March 19, 2013
June 2013	Annual Environment Issue: Hydro Power	April 24, 2013	May 15, 2013
July/August 2013	TBD	June 5, 2013	June 26, 2013
October 2013	TBD	August 21, 2013	September 11, 2013
December 2013	Annual Wildlife Issue	October 30, 2013	November 20, 2013
January/February 2014	TBD	December 4, 2013	December 26, 2013

NATIONAL ADVERTISING RATES 2013

NATIONAL	1X	3X	6X	9X	12X
Full Page	$17,290	$16,770	$16,250	$15,730	$15,210
Double-Page Spread	$32,845	$31,855	$30,875	$29,885	$28,910
2/3 Page	$13,830	$13,415	$12,995	$12,585	$12,170
1/2 Page	$12,965	$12,575	$12,190	$11,790	$11,405
1/3 Page	$8,640	$8,385	$8,120	$7,865	$7,595
IFC Spread	$38,035	$36,895	$35,750	$34,610	$33,465
OBC	$22,470	$21,795	$21,125	$20,450	$19,780
IBC	$20,745	$20,015	$19,415	$18,840	$18,265

EAST/WEST SPLIT RUNS	1X	3X	6X	9X	12X
Double-Page Spread	$24,685	$23,950	$23,215	$22,530	$21,880
Full Page	$12,995	$12,610	$12,220	$11,865	$11,515

*GROSS CANADIAN DOLLARS

Source: Courtesy of Canadian Geographic Enterprises.

issues of a monthly magazine). When continuity discounts are combined with frequency discounts, lower unit costs per page of advertising result.

Large advertisers using the same magazine to advertise a variety of products (note that such an advertiser would likely be a multi-product firm with products that share similar target markets) may qualify for corporate discounts. A **corporate discount** involves consideration of the total number of pages purchased by the company (all product lines combined), and gives a lower page rate for each product. Companies such as Procter & Gamble or Unilever that advertise extensively in women's magazines such as *Chatelaine* and *Canadian Living* would earn preferred rates for the advertising pages they buy in those magazines.

corporate discount
A discount based on the total number of pages purchased by a single company (all product lines combined).

COLOUR AND POSITION CHARGES Most magazines publish in colour. Therefore, rates for black and white ads or ads that only include spot colour are usually quoted separately. Additional costs for requesting a guaranteed position are also quoted separately on the rate card. For a guaranteed position, such as the outside back cover (OBC) or the inside front cover (IFC) and inside back cover (IBC), the additional costs are usually in the +20 percent range. With reference to the *Canadian Geographic* rate card, the rate for the inside back cover is $20 745, compared to a full-page ad inside the magazine at $17 290. The outside back cover costs even more.

To illustrate the cost calculations of buying magazine space, let's develop a couple of examples based on the *Canadian Geographic* rate card (see Figure A1.5) and the following information:

Example 1:

Magazine:	*Canadian Geographic*
Size of ad:	full-page, 4-colour ad
Number of insertions:	full-page ad to run in 6 consecutive issues

The calculation for this buying plan will be as follows:

Costs for full page, four colour:

Base rate	6X rate applies
$16 250 × 6	= $97 500

Example 2:

Magazine:	*Canadian Geographic*
Size of ad:	double-page spread, 4-colour ad
Number of insertions:	6 issues

The calculation for this buying plan will be as follows:

Costs for double-page spread (DPS), four colour:

Base rate	6X rate applies
$30 875 × 6	= $185 250

COMPARING MAGAZINES FOR EFFICIENCY Let's assume the advertiser has decided to use magazines because they usually have a well-defined target audience based on demographic variables. The advertiser still must choose particular magazines in which to advertise. Because costs and circulation figures vary, the advertiser needs a way to compare alternatives. As with newspapers, CPM is an effective quantitative means of comparing competing magazines.

Similar to newspapers, CPM (cost per thousand) comparisons are made between magazines that reach similar target markets. In this case, *Chatelaine* and *Canadian Living* compete head-to-head for advertisers.

Specifications	Chatelaine	Canadian Living
1 time, 4-colour rate	$51 920	$48 890
Circulation	551 000	511 000
CPM	$94.22	$95.67

Both magazines charge different rates and have different circulations. In this comparison, it appears that *Chatelaine* is marginally more efficient at reaching female adults. If the objective were to maximize reach, an advertiser would have to include both magazines in the media mix. Similar CPM comparisons can be made on the basis of total readership for each magazine (circulation × the number of readers per copy = total readership).

Source: Calculation based on data published in *CARD* Winter 2009, Rogers Publishing Limited.

In most magazine classifications, there is usually a group of publications competing for the same market. For example, *Chatelaine* and *Canadian Living*, among others, compete against each other in the women's classification. Although the editorial content varies from one magazine to another, each reaches a similar target, so advertisers must look at the efficiencies of each.

Figure A1.6 contains the comparative calculations for two of the magazines in the women's classification. In terms of a purely quantitative measure, both magazines are almost equal, which is why they attract the same types of advertisers. Advertisers wanting to reach the demographic profile of readers of these magazines have little choice but to allocate dollars to both. They reach different readers, but readers with the same profile. Therefore, to advertise in both increases the reach of the magazine campaign.

TELEVISION ADVERTISING

As indicated earlier, stations and networks tend not to publish a rate card. Therefore, it is difficult to demonstrate media buying procedures in this textbook. Simply stated, television rates are negotiated between buyers (advertising agencies) and sellers (television networks and local market stations). A variety of factors that influence the costs of television advertising: the supply of advertising time available and the demand for that time, the type of program, the time of day the ad will appear, and the length of the commercial.

SUPPLY AND DEMAND For major networks such as CTV, CBC, and Global, fundamental economic principles rule the cost of advertising. The network's objective is to maximize revenue from top-rated shows. Top-rated shows like *Big Bang Theory* (CTV), *American Idol* (CTV), *Grey's Anatomy* (CTV), *Glee* (Global), *NCIS* (Global), and *Hockey Night in Canada* (CBC) attract advertisers willing to pay a premium price for being on a popular (highly watched) show. The low supply and high demand for the space drives the rates upward. Canada's top-rated shows are determined weekly by research organizations such as the BBM and Nielsen Media Research. A sample of their research appears in Figure A1.7.

The rates ultimately paid for popular shows depend largely on the advertising agency's ability to negotiate with the networks. To illustrate, the quoted 30-second spot on a popular show like *Big Bang* might be $60 000 or more, an indication of the show's popularity.

FIGURE
A1.7   Canada's Top TV Shows

Measuring Audiences. Delivering Intelligence.

Auditoires mesurés. Décisions éclairées.

Top Programs – Total Canada (English)
February 11, 2013 - February 17, 2013
Based on confirmed program schedules and overnight audience data, Demographic: All Persons 2+

Rank	Program	Broadcast Outlet	Weekday	Start	End	Total 2+ AMA(000)
1	BIG BANG THEORY	CTV Total	...T...	20:00	20:31	3877
2	TWO AND A HALF MEN	CTV Total	...T...	20:31	21:00	2391
3	AMAZING RACE 22	CTV Total	......S	20:00	21:00	2283
4	HNIC PRIME EAST	CBC Total	.....S.	19:03	22:01	2248
5	SURVIVOR: CARAMOAN	Global Total	..W....	20:00	21:30	2116
6	C.S.I.	CTV Total	..W....	22:00	23:00	1873
7	BONES	Global Total	M......	20:00	21:00	1792
8	CTV EVENING NEWS	CTV Total	MTWTF..	18:00	19:00	1719
9	GREY'S ANATOMY	CTV Total	...T...	21:00	22:01	1713
10	HAWAII FIVE-O	Global Total	M......	22:00	23:00	1704
11	C.S.I. NEW YORK	CTV Total	....F..	20:00	21:00	1587
12	BLUE BLOODS	CTV Total	....F..	22:00	23:00	1572
13	CASTLE	CTV Total	M......	22:00	23:00	1542
14	AMERICAN IDOL 12 AP	CTV Total	..W....	20:00	22:00	1512
15	THE MENTALIST	CTV Total	......S	22:00	23:00	1457
16	ARROW	CTV Total	..W....	19:00	20:00	1423
17	BIG BANG THEORY	CTV Total	M..TF..	19:30	20:00	1386
18	ELEMENTARY	Global Total	...T...	22:01	23:00	1368
19	CTV EVENING NEWS WKD	CTV Total	.....SS	18:00	19:00	1350
20	THE FOLLOWING	CTV Total	M......	21:00	22:00	1328
21	ONCE UPON A TIME	CTV Total	......S	19:00	20:00	1289
22	MURDOCH MYSTERIES	CBC Total	M......	21:00	22:00	1168
23	CTV NATIONAL NEWS	CTV Total	MTWTFSS	23:00	23:30	1159
24	AMERICAN IDOL 12 AR	CTV Two Total	...T...	20:00	21:00	1132
25	PERSON OF INTEREST	City Total	...T...	21:01	22:02	1114
26	HOT IN CLEVELAND	CTV Total	.T.....	21:30	22:00	1013
27	MOTIVE	CTV Total	......S	21:00	22:00	1012
28	SHARK TANK	CTV Total	....F..	21:00	22:00	991
29	BIG BANG THEORY	CTV Total	M......	20:30	21:00	990
30	W5	CTV Total	.....S.	19:00	20:00	987

Understanding this report ...
This chart shows the Top 30 TV programs for all national networks and Canadian English specialty networks for the week indicated. Programs are ranked based on their AMA(000). AMA(000) is the average minute audience in thousands. The chart also indicates the broadcast outlet on which the program aired and the program's start and end time (shown in Eastern Time).

Source: BBM Canada, Top Programs—Total Canada (English), February 27–March 4, 2012.

negotiated rate
The rate ultimately paid by an advertiser as a result of negotiations between an ad agency and a particular medium.

But big budget advertisers often get lower rates. The **negotiated rate**, typically given to larger year-round advertisers after negotiations, packaging strategies, and agency agreements, will be much lower, possibly in the $35 000 to $40 000 range. Again, negotiation skills play a key role in the rates an advertiser actually pays.

TYPES OF PROGRAMS   Special programs such as drama specials, sports events, and miniseries are usually distinguished from regular programming. They are designated as special buys and are sold separately from regular programs. In the case of sports programs, for example, hockey and baseball broadcasts tend to appeal to a particular demographic: males between 18 and 49. They are attractive shows for certain types of advertisers. For these shows, networks need sponsors that are willing to make a long-term commitment, and there are separate rates and discount schedules for those that make such a commitment. For instance, Scotiabank, Canadian Tire, Tim Hortons, and Kraft are regular sponsors of *Hockey Night in Canada*.

Rates for one-time annual sports programming are usually separate from rates for regular programming because these special events attract a particular audience. For example, advertising rates for a special event like the Super Bowl command extremely high prices. In the United States, networks such as CBS and NBC charge between $3.5 million and $4 million for a 30-second spot. Advertisers are attracted to the large audience—usually around 115 million people.[1] In comparison, the cost of a Super Bowl spot broadcast in Canada on the CTV network is around $130 000. That's still expensive for a Canadian advertiser.

TIME OF DAY   Television is divided into three time categories: *prime time*, *fringe time*, and *day time*. Prime time is usually between 7 pm and 11 pm, fringe time between 4 pm and 7 pm, and day time from sign-on to 4 pm. Because television viewing is highest in prime time, the advertising rates are higher for that time period. Rates vary from show to show and are based solely on the size of viewing audience each show reaches. As indicated above, shows like *NCIS*, *Grey's Anatomy*, and *American Idol* reach a very large audience, so their rates are among the highest. Less popular shows (based on the audience size) command lower advertising rates.

Television viewing in fringe time and day time is much lower, so the advertising rates are adjusted downward. Program content is of a different nature: talk shows, children's shows, reruns of popular programs, and so on.

LENGTH OF COMMERCIAL   Most advertisers run 30-second commercials, so rates are normally quoted based on that length. Due to the rising costs of television advertising, however, advertisers are starting to use 15-second commercials more frequently. There is a slight premium for using 15-second commercials; rates are normally about 65 percent of the cost of a 30-second commercial on the same network or station. If an advertiser can accomplish creatively what is desired by using 15-second commercials, the cost to advertise will be less in absolute dollars. This is an important budget consideration.

gross rating points (GRPs)
An expression of the weight of advertising in a media schedule, calculated by multiplying reach by frequency.

GROSS RATING POINTS   The weight of advertising in a market is determined by a rating system referred to as gross rating points. **Gross rating points (GRPs)** are an aggregate of total ratings in a schedule, usually in a weekly period, against a predetermined target audience. GRPs are based on the following formula:

$$GRPs = Reach \times Frequency$$

FIGURE

A1.8

Calculating GRPs for Television

The weight of advertising in a market or on a particular show is determined by a rating system. Media weight is expressed in terms of gross rating points (GRPs). GRPs consider two key variables: the size of the audience reached and frequency with which the ad is run against that audience. The chart shows some sample calculations to arrive at total GRPs.

Audience Demographic	Rating	Number of Spots	GRPs
18–49	15	2	30
18–49	20	2	40
18–49	10	2	20
18–49	18	2	36
Total		**8**	**116**

If the eight spots were scheduled in a one-week period, the weight level for the advertising would be expressed as 116 GRPs for the week.

To illustrate how GRPs work, assume a message reaches 40 percent of target households three times in one week. The GRP level would be 120 (40×3). If the message reaches 30 percent of households with an average frequency of 3.5 per week, the GRP level would be 105 (30×3.5). The reach of a television show is referred to as a rating. For example, if *Big Bang Theory* reaches 15 percent of households during its weekly time slot, the show has a 15 rating. Therefore, another way to calculate GRPs is to multiply a show's rating by the frequency of messages on that show. See Figure A1.8 for an illustration of this calculation.

To demonstrate a television media buy at a local market CBC station, refer to the information in Figure A1.9. This is a fictitious plan that was created to reach an adult target 25 to 54 years old in Nova Scotia. Thirty-second spots were placed on a variety of prime time shows all with different ratings. The media buy was scheduled over a three-week period. The unit price per spot shown in the schedule is the price for a local market spot (in this case on the Halifax station) during a network broadcast. Depending on the show, the number of spots purchased vary from week to week, as do the ratings for each show.

A variety of discounts are usually available to television advertisers. A **frequency discount (television/radio)** is usually earned by purchasing a minimum number of spots over a specified period. A **volume discount** is linked to the dollar volume purchased over an extended period. The greater the volume purchased, the greater the discount. A **continuity discount (television/radio)** is earned when advertisers purchase a minimum number of spots over an extended period. With reference to the CBC discount schedule that appears in Figure A1.10, dollar volume discounts and continuity discounts are calculated based on 13-, 26-, and 52-week intervals.

RADIO ADVERTISING

The rates paid by radio advertisers are affected by several factors: the season or time of year in which commercials are placed, the time of day at which the commercials are scheduled, the use of reach plans, and the availability of discounts offered by individual stations.

SEASONAL RATE STRUCTURES Radio stations use grid-rate schedules that reflect seasonal listening patterns and reach potential. Refer to Figure A1.11 for

frequency discount (television/radio)
A discount earned by purchasing a minimum number of spots over a specified period.

volume discount
A discount linked to the dollar volume purchased over an extended period; the greater the volume purchased, the higher the discount.

continuity discount (television/radio)
A discount earned when purchasing a minimum number of spots over an extended period.

CBC

Purchaser: Time and Space Media
Attn: ANGIE REID

CHANNEL: CBHT - Halifax

Plan ID:	9568472
From:	Mar-18-2013 To: Apr-07-2013
Rev #:	0
	Apr-07-2013
Target Grp:	A 25-54 / Primary demo
Source:	BBM
Advertiser:	Quest Vitamins
Phone:	
Fax:	
PO/Product:	

Submitted on:
Booked on:
Revised on:

GENERAL AVAILS CHART

Line #	Selling Component	Commercial Type	F/M	Unit	MTWTFSS	Time	Brk*	Pos	# Week	Unit Price	By spot GRPs	By spot AUD	CPP $	CPM $	Mar 18	Mar 25	Apr 01
4	Ron James Series	Regular	L	30	.W....	20:30-21:00		N	3	49.33	1.1	14.0	46.98	3.52	X	X	X
5	Cracked	Regular	L	30	.T....	21:00-22:00		N	2	78.33	1.6	12.0	50.21	6.53	X	X	X
6	Murdoch Mysteries	Regular	L	30	M.....	21:00-22:00		N	3	103.33	1.8	13.6	58.38	7.60	X	X	
8	Coronation St - Prime	Regular	L	30	MTWTF..	19:30-20:00		N	1	223.67	3.2	25.0	71.01	8.95	X	X	X
9	Dragons' Den	Regular	L	30	......S	20:00-21:00		N	2	168.00	2.7	31.3	61.31	5.36		X	X
11	HNIC Prime West	Regular	L	30	......S	23:00-26:00		N	3	80.67	1.2	10.5	67.23	7.68	X	X	X
12	CBC News: @ Six	Regular	L	30	MTWTF..	18:00-18:30		N	1	240.00	3.8	16.5	63.16	14.55	X	X	X
14	Disney	Regular	L	30	......S	17:00-19:00		N	1	28.33	0.8	8.5	37.77	3.33	X		
15	Republic Of Doyle	Regular	L	30	......S	21:00-22:00		N	1	120.67	1.5	18.0	80.45	6.70			X
16	CBC Evening News	Regular	L	30	MTWTF..	17:00-18:00		N	3	79.67	2.4	14.5	33.90	5.49	X	X	X
17	Cdn Reflections - Sun	Regular	L	30	......S	24:00-24:30		N	3	1.00	0.1	1.0	10.00	1.00	X	X	X
18	Fifth Estate - Sun	Regular	L	30	......S	23:30-24:30		N	3	1.00	0.1	1.5	10.00	0.67	X	X	X
19	Dragons' Den Rotation	Regular	L	30	MTWTF..	16:00-17:00		N	2	8.00	0.2	1.5	40.00	5.33	X	X	X
23	HNIC Afternoon	Regular	L	30	.....SS	15:00-19:00		N	1	44.33	1.4	9.8	31.22	4.54			X

Sales Rep.:	Wilson, Alexandra	(902) 420-4315 /	GST/HST:	10076 0909 RT0001
Sales Admin.:	Veysey, Catherine	(506) 451-4132 /	QST:	1006030706 TQ0005

Email:
Email: VEYSEYC@fredericton.cbc.ca

Accepted on behalf of Purchaser

Date:

X -

Rates protected for 5 working days from the date submitted

FIGURE A1.9 (Continued)

CBC

PROPOSAL

CHANNEL: CBHT - Halifax

Purchaser: Time and Space Media
Attn: ANGIE REID

Plan ID:	9568472
From:	Mar-18-2013
Target Grp:	A 25-54 / Primary demo
Source:	BBM
Advertiser:	Quest Vitamins
Phone:	
Fax:	
PO/Product:	

Rev. #:   0
To: Apr-07-2013

Submitted on: February 14, 2013
Booked on: -
Revised on: February 14, 2013

RATING SUMMARY

Line#	Selling Component	By spot AUD
ProRata		%
Total Cost (000's)		$
Avg Weekly Cost (000's) $		$
Total AUD/GRP		
CPM/CPR		$
Avg Weekly AUD/GRP		

WEEKLY MARKET RATINGS

	Week Of	Occasions	By Week AUD
		Total Delivery	

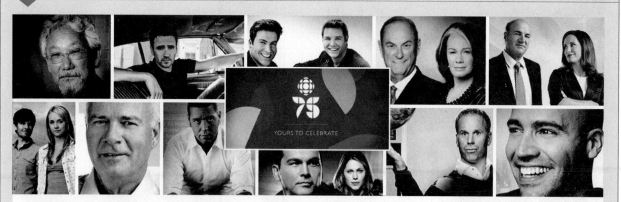

DVD Rate Card

DVD THRESHOLDS ARE BASED ON INDIVIDUAL MARKET

Effective May 10, 2012

CBC CLIENT DEAL FLEXIBILITY 2012-13 BROADCAST YEAR	13 Week	26 Week Entire Regular Season	Full Season = Regular Season + Entire Playoffs
Continuity – HNIC only	5%	10%	15%
	13 Week	26 Week	52 Week
Continuity	5%	10%	15%
DVD	5%	10%	15%
Market/Tier Spend Thresholds	Gross $'s	Gross $'s	Gross $'s
National Tiers			
Network (incl. Mainchannel, Specialty & Digital*)	$750,000	$1,500,000	$2,500,000
CBC News Net	$75,000	$150,000	$300,000
Selective Markets (Mainchannel & Regional Digital)			
Pacific Region	$75,000	$125,000	$250,000
CBRT Calgary	$50,000	$100,000	$200,000
CBXT Edmonton	$40,000	$75,000	$175,000
CBKT Regina/Saskatoon	$10,000	$30,000	$80,000
CBWT Winnipeg	$15,000	$25,000	$50,000
Ontario Region	$80,000	$200,000	$600,000
CBLT Toronto	$75,000	$150,000	$400,000
CBET Windsor	$5,000	$15,000	$40,000
CBOT Ottawa	$20,000	$50,000	$100,000
CBMT Montreal	$20,000	$50,000	$100,000
Maritime Region	$10,000	$25,000	$50,000
CBHT Halifax	$10,000	$25,000	$50,000
CBCT Charlottetown	$7,500	$20,000	$40,000
CBAT Saint John/Moncton	$5,000	$12,500	$25,000
CBNT St John's/Cornerbrook	$15,000	$25,000	$50,000

*Digital Investment can count to overall Volume of spend on either your National buy or your Regional buy. However DVD is NOT applied to the Digital elements, ONLY the broadcast schedule. First calculate DVD discount and then apply Continuity discount on the new total.

Contact your account manager today

cbcrevenuegroup.ca

CBC

an illustration of specific grid-level rates. Generally, radio rates fluctuate with the seasons as follows:

Time Period	Rate
May–August (summer) and December	Higher
September–October	Mid-range
March–April	Mid-range
January–February	Lower

DAYPARTS Since the size and nature of the audience vary according to the **daypart** (a broadcast time period or segment), different rates are charged for each. Generally, the dayparts are classified as follows:

Classification	Time
Breakfast	6 to 10 am
Midday	10 am to 4 pm
Drive	4 to 7 pm
Evening	7 pm to midnight
Nighttime	Midnight to 6 am

Dayparts vary from one station to another, with some stations having more or fewer classifications than those listed above. In addition, weekend classifications are often different from weekday ones, as the listening patterns of the audience change on weekends.

REACH PLANS Radio advertisers can purchase specific time slots and schedule a particular rotation plan during the length of the media buy, or they can purchase a reach plan. For the first option, a **rotation plan**, the advertiser specifies the time slots and pays the rate associated with them. Two types of rotation plans are available:

- **Vertical Rotation:** the placement of commercials based on the time of day (within various dayparts).

- **Horizontal Rotation:** the placement of commercials based on the day of the week (same daypart on different days).

Radio stations sell reach plans so that advertisers can maximize reach. In a **reach plan**, commercials are rotated through the various dayparts according to a predetermined frequency to reach different people with the same message. As shown in Figure A1.11, the reach plan divides spots equally between breakfast, daytime, drive time, and evening/Sunday dayparts. For the advertiser, the benefit of the reach plan is twofold. First, the reach potential is extended; and second, the rates charged for the reach plan collectively are lower (because of the discounts) than those that would result from the individual purchase of similar time slots. Reach plans do require a minimum spot purchase on a weekly basis (16 spots per week is common).

DISCOUNTS OFFERED BY RADIO Advertisers that purchase frequently from specific stations qualify for a variety of discounts.

A **frequency discount** is a discounted rate earned through the purchase of a minimum number of spots over a specified period of time, usually a week. Having earned such a discount, advertisers are referred to a lower-rate grid schedule, or could be quoted a percentage discount, such as 5 percent for 15 to 20 spots per week, 8 percent for 21 to 30 spots per week, 10 percent for over 31 spots, and so forth. With a **volume discount**, the advertiser is charged a lower rate for buying a large number of spots; the discount

daypart
A broadcast time period or segment on radio or television.

rotation plan
The placement of commercials in time slots purchased on radio; can be vertical according to the time of day or horizontal according to the day of the week.

vertical rotation
The placement of radio commercials based on the time of day (within various dayparts).

horizontal rotation
The placement of radio commercials based on the day of the week (same daypart on different days).

reach plan
Rotation of commercials in various dayparts on radio according to a predetermined frequency.

CJAZ-FM RADIO
101.7 JAZ-FM

Jazz that Rocks!

30-sec spot rates

Daypart/Grid	1	2	3	4	5
Breakfast 6:00 to 10:00 am	300	275	250	225	200
Daytime 10:00 am to 3:00 pm	245	225	205	185	165
Drive 3:00 to 7:00 pm	250	230	210	190	170
Evening and Sunday	220	200	180	160	140

Reach Plan - 30 sec spots

	1	2	3	4	5
Breakfast 25% Daytime 25% Drive 25% Evening and Sunday 25%	250	225	200	175	150

Discount Schedule

Contract Buy (Continuity)		*Volume (Spots)*	
14 to 26 weeks	Grid 3	250	Grid 3
27 to 39 weeks	Grid 4	450	Grid 4
40 to 52 weeks	Grid 5	700	Grid 5

might be 5 percent for 260 spots, for example, or 10 percent for 520 spots. A **continuity discount** applies when an advertiser agrees to place ads over an extended period such as intervals of 26, 39, and 52 weeks.

Advertisers can increase reach by buying a reach plan. The **reach plan** offers a minimum number of weekly spots across all dayparts in return for a packaged discount rate. Refer to Figure A1.11 for examples of discounts.

BUYING RADIO TIME   A strategic plan guides the purchase of radio commercial time. To get the best possible rate from a station or network of stations, all details of the plan must be known by the radio station. Factors such as volume and frequency (the total number of spots in the buy), the timing of the schedule (in terms of time of day or season in which the plan is scheduled), and continuity (the length of the plan) collectively affect the spot rate that is charged the advertiser. It places an advertiser on a particular grid with the station. Refer to Figure A1.11 for a listing of grid rates and how an advertiser arrives at a certain grid. For advertisers that purchase large amounts of time, the discounts described above usually apply.

To illustrate some basic cost calculations used in buying radio time, let's develop some examples based on the CJAZ-FM rate card in Figure A1.11.

Example 1:

30-second spots

10 breakfast spots per week

15 drive spots per week

12-week schedule

Cost Calculations:

The advertiser does not qualify for a continuity discount. Therefore, the first calculation is to determine the total number of spots in the buy to see if a volume discount applies.

Total number of spots	= Spots per week × Number of weeks
Breakfast	= 10 per week × 12 weeks = 120
Drive	= 15 per week × 12 weeks = 180
Total spots	= 300

Based on the total number of spots (300), the rate charged will be from Grid 3. In this case, the 30-second rate is $250 for breakfast and $210 for drive time. The cost calculations are as follows:

Total cost	= Number of spots × Earned rate
Breakfast	= 120 spots × $250 = $30 000
Drive	= 180 spots × $210 = $37 800
Total cost	= $67 800

Example 2:

The advertiser would like to evaluate a reach plan (involving 16 commercials per week) against a specific buying plan. Details of each plan are as follows:

Plan A: Reach Plan (30-second spots)

16 spots per week (reach plan)

Rotated between breakfast, drive, day, and evening/Sunday

Schedule over 16 weeks, June through September

Plan B: Specific Plan (30-second spots)

8 breakfast spots per week

8 drive spots per week

16-week schedule

Cost Calculations for Plan A:

The advertiser qualifies for a continuity discount because of the 16-week schedule. The rate would be in Grid 3 in the reach plan. The earned rate is $200 per spot.

Total Cost	= Total number of spots × Earned rate
	= (16 spots per week × 16 weeks) × $200
	= $51 200

Cost Calculations for Plan B:

The total number of spots is as follows:

Breakfast	= 8 spots per week × 16 weeks = 128 spots
Drive	= 8 spots per week × 16 weeks = 128 spots
Total spots	= 256

Based on this calculation, the advertiser qualifies for either a volume or a continuity discount. The advertiser is charged the rate from Grid 3.

Breakfast	= 128 spots × $250 = $32 000
Drive	= 128 spots × 210 = $26 880
Total cost	= $58 880

In conducting a comparative evaluation of Plan A and Plan B, the advertiser must weigh the more selective reach potential of Plan B against the savings of Plan A. Perhaps the advertiser wants to reach business commuters in drive time to and from work. With Plan A, the advertiser can reach a somewhat different audience by means of a daypart rotation of spots. The net result is a cost difference of $7680 in favour of Plan A. Should the advertiser decide to go with the cost savings of Plan A, or with the more selective reach of Plan B at greater cost?

OUT-OF-HOME ADVERTISING

Out-of-home advertising offers a variety of outdoor poster options, street-level advertising, wall murals, transit shelters, vehicles, and station advertising. Regardless of the alternative, the media buying procedure is similar. Out-of-home rates can be based on GRPs or on a per-panel basis.

Referring to Figure A1.12, a rate card for CBS Outdoor transit shelters, let's assume an advertiser wants to buy 50 GRPs in Toronto. That means the advertiser will reach the equivalent of 50 percent of Toronto's population. The word "equivalent" is important because vehicle and pedestrian traffic in a city is partly habitual; that is, people tend to travel the same routes each day. Therefore, in the Toronto example, the advertiser might reach 25 percent of the population twice a day for a total of 50 daily GRPs.

All out-of-home advertising rates are quoted on a four-week basis and are sold on a market-by-market basis. Posters and transit shelters are typically sold on the basis of a four-week minimum purchase. More elaborate outdoor executions such as a superboard will have an extended minimum time requirement. To illustrate outdoor cost calculations, let's consider a couple of media buying examples. Rates and data from Figure A1.12 (transit shelter rates) and Figure A1.13 (outdoor poster rates) are used to calculate costs.

Example 1: Outdoor Buying Plan

Medium:	Transit shelters (CBS)
Markets:	Toronto (CMA), Vancouver (CMA), Calgary (CMA), and Edmonton (CMA)
Weight:	25 GRPs weekly in Toronto and Vancouver; 50 GRPs weekly in Calgary and Edmonton
Contract length:	16 weeks in all markets

Cost Calculations:

The costs for a four-week period for each market would be as follows:

Toronto	$71 431
Vancouver	$36 997
Calgary	$56 430
Edmonton	$29 440
Total	$194 298

FIGURE A1.12 Outdoor Rate Card for Transit Shelters

2013 CBS Outdoor RATEBOOK: Street Furniture - Transit Shelters, APTs, Mapstands, Kiosks, Mediacolumns (68 1/4" x 47 1/4")

Province	Code	Market	Operator	2013 Est. Population	Avg. Daily Circ. In-Market Oct '12 CDR	Single Panel Rate $ Net	25	50	75	100	25 GRPs (+5%) @25	50 GRPs flat @50	75 GRPs (-5%) @75	100 GRPs (-10%) @100
							Average # of Panels to deliver GRPs				4 week net rate			
Newfoundland	005	St. John's CMA (Nfld.)	St. John's Trans.Co	190,500		$ 530	6	11	17	23	$ 3,180	$ 5,214	$ 8,058	$ 10,534
Nova Scotia	019	Halifax CMA	CBS	393,600	9,451	$ 750	11	21	32	42	$ 4,686	$ 8,925	$ 12,718	$ 16,065
Nova Scotia	025	Cape Breton CA (Sydney)	CBS	95,600	12,274	$ 709	2	4	6	8	$ 851	$ 1,620	$ 2,309	$ 2,916
Nova Scotia	23	Annapolis Valley & Region	Atcom	61,900	8,200	$ 613								
New Brunswick	48	Saint John CMA (NB)	CBS	125,300	9,047	$ 667	4	8	11	15	$ 1,600	$ 3,048	$ 4,343	$ 5,486
Quebec	065	Saguenay (Chicoutimi-Jonquiere) CMA	CBS	153,700	10,247	$ 613	4	8	12	16	$ 1,470	$ 2,800	$ 3,990	$ 5,040
Quebec	77	Trois-Rivieres CMA	CBS	150,000	7,386	$ 548	6	11	16	21	$ 1,808	$ 3,443	$ 4,906	$ 6,197
Quebec	088	Sherbrooke CMA	CBS	198,500	14,869	$ 740	4	7	10	14	$ 1,555	$ 2,961	$ 4,219	$ 5,330
Quebec	057	Blainville (Montreal CMA)	Imagi	53,510		$ 510								
Quebec	123	Boucherville (Montreal CMA)	Imagi	40,753		$ 510								
Quebec	118	Brossard (Montreal CMA)	Imagi	79,273		$ 510								
Quebec	141	Chambly/Richelieu/Carignan (Montreal CMA)	Imagi	39,004		$ 365								
Quebec	130	Chateauguay (Montreal CMA)	Imagi	45,904		$ 365	non standard format size 55 1/4" H x 48"W							
Quebec	070	La Prairie (Montreal CMA)	Imagi	23,357		$ 365								
Quebec	119	Longueuil (Montreal CMA)	Imagi	231,409		$ 450								
Quebec	135	Repentigny (Montreal CMA)	Imagi	82,000		$ 450								
Quebec	081	St. Constant/Ste.Catherine/Delson (Montreal CMA)	Imagi	49,204		$ 365	non standard format size 55 1/4" H x 48"W							
Quebec	085	St-Jérôme (Montreal CMA)	Imagi	68,456		$ 365	non standard format size 55 1/4" H x 48"W							
Quebec	136	Saint-Philippe (Montreal CMA)	Imagi	5,495		$ 365								
Quebec	111	Terrebonne & Mascouche (Montreal CMA)	Imagi	148,813		$ 510								
Quebec	105	Varennes (Montreal CMA)	Imagi	20,994		$ 365	non standard format size 55 1/4" H x 48"W							
Quebec	144	Ottawa-Gatineau CMA-Quebec (incl. Gatineau, Hull & Aylmer)	Imagi	265,349			9-11	19-21	27-31	37-41	$ 4,477	$ 8,550	$ 12,000	$ 15,765
Quebec	108	Drummondville CA	Imagi	71,852		$ 450								
Quebec	098	Joliette CA	Imagi	19,621		$ 365	non standard format size 55 1/4" H x 48"W							
Quebec	137	Mercier/Ste-Martine/Ormstown	Imagi	20,145		$ 365	non standard format size 55 1/4" H x 48"W							
Quebec	143	St-Hyacinthe CA/Ste-Madeleine	Imagi	58,777		$ 365								
Quebec	139	Saint-Jean-Sur-Richelieu Terminal	Imagi	92,394		$ 510								
Quebec	100	Shawinigan CA	Imagi	50,060		$ 365	3	5	7	9	$ 1,535	$ 2,500	$ 3,405	$ 4,235
Quebec	140	Sorel (Sorel-Tracey CA)	Imagi	34,600		$ 365								
Ontario	182	Toronto CMA	CBS	5,572,700	20,962	$ 1,790	67	133	199	265	$ 71,431	$ 136,059	$ 193,884	$ 244,906
Ontario	199	Hamilton CMA (+ 10% discount with Toronto)	CBS	705,700	9,320	$ 912	19	37	56	74	$ 10,120	$ 19,277	$ 27,470	$ 34,699
Ontario	224	London CMA	CBS	462,800	12,538	$ 781	10	19	28	38	$ 4,449	$ 8,474	$ 12,075	$ 15,253
Ontario	243	Windsor CMA	CBS	304,100	10,617	$ 901	8	15	22	29	$ 4,056	$ 7,725	$ 11,008	$ 13,905
Ontario	284	Sault Ste. Marie CA	Superior 7	77,100	7,300	$ 503								
Ontario	309	Timmins CA	BK Corp. Mktg.	41,500		$ 700	2	4	6	8	$ 1,300	$ 2,500	$ 3,600	$ 4,600
Ontario	311	Greater Sudbury CMA	BK Corp. Mktg.	155,900	13,700	$ 850	3	6	9	12	$ 2,250	$ 4,350	$ 6,300	$ 8,100
Manitoba	318	Winnipeg CMA	CBS	722,800	18,829	$ 726	10	20	29	39	$ 4,358	$ 8,300	$ 11,828	$ 14,940
Alberta	362	Calgary CMA	CBS	1,218,200	9,199	$ 1,500	33	66	99	131	$ 29,626	$ 56,430	$ 80,413	$ 101,574
Alberta	387	Red Deer CA	Reid Signs	96,600		$ 400								
Alberta	395	Edmonton CMA (Mediacolumns/kiosks)	CBS	1,165,500	13,462	$ 1,120	23	46	69	92	$ 15,456	$ 29,440	$ 41,952	$ 52,992
British Columbia	430	Vancouver CMA	CBS	2,338,000	20,084	$ 2,126	29	58	87	116	$ 36,997	$ 70,470	$ 100,420	$ 126,846
British Columbia	431	Vancouver Core	CBS	600,000		$ 2,755								

Source: Courtesy of CBS Outdoor Canada.

FIGURE A1.13 Rate Card for Outdoor Horizontal Posters

2013 CBS Outdoor RATEBOOK: Horizontal Posters (10' X 20')

Province	Code	Market	Operator	2013 Est. Population	Avg. Daily Circ. In-Market Oct '12 CDR / Circ In-Market	Single Panel Rate $ Net / $ Rate	Avg # Panels 25	50	75	100	4 week net rate (+5%) @25	flat @50	(-5%) @75	(-10%) @100
Newfoundland	004	St. John's CMA	E.C. Boone	190,500	13,800	$ 1,325	3-4	7	9-11	100				
Nova Scotia	019	Halifax CMA	CBS	393,600	14,377	$ 1,400	7	14	21	28	$ 8,232	$ 15,680	$ 22,344	$ 28,224
Nova Scotia	020	Acadian Peninsula	Media 2000	15,700	4,100	$ 850								
Nova Scotia	023	Bridgewater/Lunenburg County	Atcom	47,300		$ 700								
Nova Scotia	025	Cape Breton CA (Sydney)	CBS	95,600	9,807	$ 1,456	3	5	8		$ 3,058	$ 5,825	$ 8,301	
New Brunswick	024	Bathurst CA	Media 2000	32,800	5,400	$ 950								
New Brunswick	026	Miramichi CA	Media 2000	27,300	10,200	$ 950								
New Brunswick	039	Fredericton CA	CBS	93,400	7,348	$ 1,350								
New Brunswick	043	Moncton CMA	CBS	137,600	9,738	$ 900	4	7	11	14	$ 2,646	$ 5,040	$ 7,182	$ 9,072
New Brunswick	048	Saint John CMA	CBS	125,300	11,060	$ 900	3	6	9	12	$ 2,268	$ 4,320	$ 6,156	$ 7,776
New Brunswick	049	St. Lawrence Basin/Matapedia (see below)	CBS	60,000		$ 700								
Quebec	051	Rimouski CA	CBS	50,100	6,118	$ 1,000								
Quebec	063	Riviere du Loup CA	CBS	27,300	7,603	$ 1,500								
Quebec	050	Matane CA	CBS	17,800	2,280	$ 1,000								
Quebec	074	Charlevoix	CBS	26,000		$ 1,000								
Quebec	056	Baie-Comeau CA	CBS	27,800	6,536	$ 1,000								
Quebec	059	Sept Iles CA	CBS	27,500	1,996	$ 1,000								
Quebec	054	Beauce District (see below)	CBS	28,400	3,480	$ 700								
Quebec	073	Saint-Georges CA	CBS	33,900	4,826	$ 1,500								
Quebec	071	Thetford Mines CA	CBS	27,300		$ 1,000								
Quebec	072	Victoriaville CA	CBS	45,900	4,974	$ 1,500								
Quebec	113	Plessisville	CBS	6,500		$ 930								
Quebec	114	Princeville	CBS	5,300		$ 930								
Quebec	117	Saint-Eulalie	CBS	900		$ 950								
Quebec	060	Quebec City CMA	CBS	756,200	21,165	$ 3,150	9	18	27	35	$ 19,845	$ 37,800	$ 53,865	$ 68,040
Quebec	065	Saguenay CMA (Chicoutimi-Jonquiere)	CBS	153,700	9,330	$ 1,403	5	9	13	17	$ 5,301	$ 10,098	$ 14,390	$ 18,176
Quebec	069	Alma CA	CBS	32,400	5,104	$ 1,000								
Quebec	082	Saint Bruno	CBS	2,400		$ 720								
Quebec	077	Trois-Rivieres CMA	CBS	150,000	12,105	$ 2,265	4	7	10	13	$ 6,659	$ 12,684	$ 18,075	$ 22,831
Quebec	078	Shawinigan CA	CBS	53,400	7,589	$ 1,545								
Quebec	084	Drummondville CA	CBS	87,200	7,000	$ 1,590								
Quebec	089	Granby CA	CBS	76,700	9,949	$ 1,590								
Quebec	088	Sherbrooke CMA	CBS	198,500	15,001	$ 2,265	4	7	11	14	$ 6,659	$ 12,684	$ 18,075	$ 22,831
Quebec	090	Montreal CMA	CBS	3,744,300	36,635	$ 4,418	26	52	78	103	$ 80,399	$ 153,140	$ 218,225	$ 275,652
Quebec	094	Joliette CA	CBS	46,900	13,538	$ 1,390								
Quebec	106	Saint-Hyacinthe CA	CBS	55,800	13,746	$ 1,390								
Quebec	109	Sorel-Tracy CA	CBS	47,200	8,960	$ 1,340								
Quebec	110	Salaberry de Valleyfield CA	CBS	39,200	7,994	$ 1,390								
Quebec	080	Cadillac/Malartic	CBS	3,500		$ 950								
Quebec	096	Rouyn-Noranda CA	CBS	40,700	3,463	$ 1,270								
Quebec	097	Val d'Or CA	CBS	32,200	4,397	$ 1,030								
Quebec	146	Ottawa-Gatineau CMA (Quebec)Hull	CBS	311,300	15,800	$ 1,794	6	11			$ 8,287	$ 15,785		
Ontario	125	Kingston CMA	CBS	157,000	14,362	$ 1,500	3	6	9	11	$ 3,780	$ 7,200	$ 10,260	$ 12,960

Source: Courtesy of CBS Outdoor Canada.

FIGURE A1.13 (Continued)

2013 CBS Outdoor RATEBOOK: Horizontal Posters (10' X 20')

Province	Code	Market	Operator	2013 Est. Population	Avg. Daily Circ. In-Market Oct '12 CDR Circ In-Market	Single Panel Rate $ Net $ Rate	Average # of Panels to deliver GRPs 25	50	75	100	4 week net rate (+5%) @25	flat @50	(-5%) @75	(-10%) @100
Ontario	124	Belleville CA/Trenton	CBS	89,300	10,786	$ 1,000								
Ontario	126	Brockville CA	CBS	37,600	5,248	$ 1,000								
Ontario	150	Picton/Prince Edward County	CBS	26,700		$ 950								
Ontario	149	Napanee	CBS	16,040		$ 950								
Ontario	148	Gananoque	CBS	5,600		$ 950								
Ontario	147	Ottawa-Gatineau CMA (Ontario)	CBS	919,600	14,000	$ 3,680	17	33	49	65	$ 42,498	$ 80,949	$ 115,352	$ 145,708
Ontario	134	Smith Falls	CBS	8,500		$ 1,000								
Ontario	132	Beckwith /Carleton Place	CBS	6,900		$ 1,000								
Ontario	131	Arnprior	CBS	7,200		$ 1,000								
Ontario	133	Perth	CBS	6,000		$ 1,000								
Ontario	165	Kawartha Lakes CA/Lindsay & Emily	CBS	70,400	6,474	$ 1,100								
Ontario	166	Peterborough CMA	CBS	115,900	5,904	$ 1,386	5	10			$ 5,822	$ 11,090		
Ontario	280	Beaverton/Brock	CBS	12,000		$ 650								
Ontario	182	Toronto CMA	CBS	5,572,700	24,964	$ 4,191	56	111	166	222	$ 139,569	$ 265,845	$ 378,829	$ 478,521
Ontario	195	Oshawa CMA	CBS	353,200	11,150	$ 1,769	8	16	24	31	$ 8,492	$ 16,176	$ 23,051	$ 29,117
Ontario	199	Hamilton CMA (additional 10% if sold with Toronto)	CBS	705,700	11,897	$ 1,871	15	29	43	57	$ 16,276	$ 31,001	$ 44,176	$ 55,802
Ontario	203	Kitchener CMA/Cambridge -distribution issues - check with charti	CBS	467,700	12,403	$ 1,695	10				$ 11,865			
Ontario	219	Brantford CMA	CBS	131,900	4,852	$ 1,255								
Ontario	211	St. Catharines/Niagara CMA	CBS	379,600	9,582	$ 1,511	10	20	30	40	$ 10,574	$ 20,140	$ 28,700	$ 36,252
Ontario	224	London CMA	CBS	462,800	16,398	$ 1,641	8	15	22	29	$ 8,615	$ 16,410	$ 23,384	$ 29,538
Ontario	243	Windsor CMA	CBS	304,100	12,900	$ 1,416	6	12	18	24	$ 7,138	$ 13,596	$ 19,374	$ 24,473
Ontario	242	Chatham-Kent CA	CBS	97,900	3,719	$ 850								
Ontario	252	Leamington CA/Kingsville	CBS	47,600	3,900	$ 850								
Ontario	258	Essex	CBS	20,400		$ 850								
Ontario	250	Sarnia CA	CBS	86,600	7,844	$ 700								
Ontario	265	Collingwood CA	CBS	19,500	2,016	$ 1,400								
Ontario	264	Owen Sound CA	CBS	31,000	4,699	$ 1,400								
Ontario	266	Blue Mountain District (see below)	CBS	133,500		$ 1,000								
Ontario	278	Barrie CMA	CBS	183,800	9,236	$ 1,500	6	11	16	21	$ 6,930	$ 13,200	$ 18,810	$ 23,760
Ontario	281	Orillia CA	CBS	39,400	11,236	$ 1,400								
Ontario	277	Midland CA	CBS	34,400	5,374	$ 1,400								
Ontario	274	Muskoka District (see below)	CBS	62,000		$ 1,000								
Ontario	284	Sault Ste. Marie CA	Superior 7	77,100	10,200	$ 1,326	2	4	6	8	$ 2,652	$ 5,304	$ 7,956	$ 10,608
Ontario	295	Greater Sudbury CMA/North Bay CA/North Shore & Dist.	Outdoor Exposure	238,100	7,700	$ 1,100	8	16	23	31	$ 8,200	$ 17,600	$ 22,885	$ 29,400
Ontario	303	Thunder Bay CMA	CBS	116,800	9,687	$ 1,000								
Ontario	305	Timmins CA & District	Woodgreen	80,800	5,400	$ 1,005	4	8	11	15	$ 5,027	$ 8,684	$ 11,946	$ 16,830
Ontario	308	Timmins CA	Woodgreen	41,500	6,500	$ 1,100	2	3	5-8	8-10	$ 2,200	$ 4,200	$ 7,630	$ 8,864
Manitoba	318	Winnipeg CMA	CBS	722,800	21,614	$ 1,733	9	17	26	34	$ 8,836	$ 16,830	$ 23,983	$ 30,294

FIGURE A1.13 *(Continued)*

2013 CBS Outdoor RATEBOOK: Horizontal Posters (10' X 20')

Province	Code	Market	Operator	2013 Est. Population	Avg. Daily Circ. In-Market Oct '12 CDR / Circ In-Market	Single Panel Rate $ Net / $ Rate	Average # of Panels to deliver GRPs				4 week net rate			
							25	50	75	100	(+5%) @25	flat @50	(-5%) @75	(-10%) @100
Saskatchewan	346	Prince Albert CA	20-twenty.ca	39,600		$ 950								
Saskatchewan	347	Yorkton CA	CBS	17,900	3,548	$ 715								
Saskatchewan	349	Regina CMA	CBS	207,000	15,156	$ 1,400	4	7	11	14	$ 4,116	$ 7,840	$ 11,172	$ 14,112
Saskatchewan	350	North Battleford CA	CBS	18,800	3,448	$ 715								
Saskatchewan	351	Rural Saskatchewan (Minimum 8 week buy)	CBS	437,000		$ 870								
Ontario	355	Moose Jaw CA	CBS	33,700	7,321	$ 1,060								
Saskatchewan	358	Saskatoon CMA	CBS	257,300	18,039	$ 1,400	4	8	11	15	$ 4,704	$ 8,960	$ 12,768	$ 16,128
Alberta	362	Calgary CMA	CBS	1,218,200	17,829	$ 1,938	18	35	52	69	$ 28,481	$ 54,250	$ 77,306	$ 97,650
Alberta	395	Edmonton CMA	CBS	1,165,500	16,923	$ 1,938	18	35	52	69	$ 28,481	$ 54,250	$ 77,306	$ 97,650
British Columbia	425	Vancouver CMA	CBS	2,338,000	30,720	$ 3,000	19	37	55		$ 46,601	$ 88,763	$ 126,487	

St. Lawrence Basin (049) includes: Cacouna, Grand Metis, Ile-Verte, Mont-Joli, Montmagny, Notre-Dame-Des-Neiges, Sayabec, St-Fabien, St-Simon, Ste-Luce, Trois-Pistoles, Val-Brillant

Beauce District (054) includes: Beauceville, Notre-Dame-Des-Prins, St-Come-Liniere, St. Joseph De Beauce, Ste-Marie Beauce, Vallee Jonction

Blue Mountain District (266) includes: Durham, Hanover, Hepworth, Kincardine, Markdale, Meaford, Nottawa, Port Elgin, Singhampton, Southampton, Stayner, Sunnidale Corners, Thornbury, Walkerton

Muskoka District (274) includes: Oro Township, Parry Sound, Ramara Township, Tiny Township, Wasaga

Because the contract is for 16 weeks, the costs are multiplied by four (16 weeks divided by four-week rates). The gross cost would be as follows:

$$\$194\ 298 \times 4 = \$777\ 192$$

Although not shown in this particular illustration and rate card, outdoor media usually offer advertisers volume discounts (for example, a reduced rate based on dollar volume purchased) and continuity discounts (for example, a reduced rate for extended buys such as 12 weeks, 16 weeks, and so forth).

Example 2: Outdoor Buying Plan

Medium:	Horizontal posters (CBS)
Markets:	Toronto (CMA), Montreal (CMA), and Winnipeg (CMA)
Weight:	Toronto, Montreal, and Winnipeg 50 GRPs
Contract length:	12 weeks in Toronto; 8 weeks in Montreal and Winnipeg

Cost Calculations:

Using the data from Figure A1.13, the appropriate costs for each market over a four-week period would be as follows:

Toronto	$\$265\ 845 \times 3 = \$797\ 535$
Montreal	$\$153\ 140 \times 2 = \$306\ 280$
Winnipeg	$\$16\ 830 \times 2\ = \$33\ 660$
Gross costs	$= \$1\ 137\ 475$

Because the length of the contract in Toronto is 12 weeks, the costs are multiplied by three (12 weeks divided by the four-week rate). In Montreal and Winnipeg, the contract is 8 weeks. Therefore, the costs are multiplied by a factor of two (8 weeks divided by the four-week rate).

DIRECT MAIL ADVERTISING

Three basic steps are involved in buying direct mail: obtaining a proper prospect list, conceiving and producing the mailing piece, and distributing the final version.

OBTAINING DIRECT MAIL LISTS   The direct mail list is the backbone of the entire campaign. Both the accuracy and definition of the list can have a significant bearing on the success or failure of a campaign. Since it is much less expensive to keep a current customer than to find a new one, companies should compile accurate lists of customers in their database and form relationships with customers through mail and electronic means. Internal lists compiled from a database management system are referred to as **house lists**.

Prospective names are also gathered from external sources. People with a history of responding to mail offers tend to be attractive prospects for new offers. Buying by mail is part of their behaviour. Therefore, the challenge is to find prospects that have a demographic profile and, perhaps, a psychographic profile that mirror the profile of current customers. A **list broker** can assist in finding these prospects. The buyer provides the broker with the profile of the target customer, and the broker supplies a list of possible prospects on a cost-per-name basis. Generally, a high-quality list is developed through a **merge/purge** process on a computer, whereby numerous lists are purchased, combined, and stripped of duplicate names.

Cornerstone Group of Companies, a database management company, compiles lists for various consumer, business, and professional targets. A consumer list can be

house list
An internal customer list.

list broker
A company specializing in finding or developing lists for direct response purposes; finds prospect lists based on target market criteria established by marketing organizations.

merge/purge
A process in which numerous mailing lists are combined and then stripped of duplicate names.

compiled based on predetermined criteria such as income, home ownership, marital status, and type of dwelling. Business lists can be developed based on the type or size of business (for example, small, home-based businesses). Professional lists are available for medical, legal, and engineering practitioners, among many others.

Canada Post also supplies information vital to the accurate targeting of messages. For example, a postal code can isolate a small geographic area—say, a city block—and can then be combined with census data to provide relevant statistics regarding the ages and incomes of homeowners in the area and whether children are present in the households.

A few types of lists are available: response lists, circulation lists, and compiled lists. A **response list** is a list of proven mail-order buyers. Such lists include book-of-the-month-club buyers, CD music buyers, or people who order from cooperative direct mailing firms. Because these lists include proven mail-order buyers, they tend to cost more. A minimum rental of 5000 names is required in most cases.

Circulation lists are magazine subscription lists that target potential customers according to an interest or activity. A publishing company, for example, might sell its list of subscribers to another business interested in a similar target. Rogers Media offers a consumer database composed of unduplicated active subscribers to a host of its publications, including *Maclean's*, *Chatelaine*, and *Flare*.

Compiled lists are prepared from government, census, telephone, warranty, and other publication information. These are the least expensive of the lists and are not always personalized. Provincial and national associations, such as the Canadian Medical Association, commonly provide mailing lists of their members. A list broker, for example, could compile a list of a cross-section of professionals from various occupations, if required by a client.

PRODUCTION Direct mail packages are usually designed by a specialist agency. Once the mailing package is designed, it is ready for printing. Various factors that influence cost include size, shape, number of pieces, use of colour, and so on. Costs are usually quoted CPM or on a cost-per-unit basis, with larger runs incurring lower unit costs. Once printed, the mailing pieces are turned over to a letter shop that specializes in stuffing and sealing envelopes, affixing labels, sorting, binding, and stacking the mailers. Once this task is complete, the mailing units are sent to the post office for distribution.

DISTRIBUTION Distribution costs of direct mail replace placement costs in traditional forms of media advertising. The most common means of delivery is Canada Post. Several options are available through the postal system: first-class mail, third-class mail, and business-reply mail. Obviously, the quicker the means of delivery, the higher the costs will be. Most direct mail pieces—whether single pieces, bulk items, catalogues, or cooperative mailings—are delivered third class. The advantage over first class is the cost savings.

DIRECT MAIL BUYING ILLUSTRATION The procedures for estimating the cost of solo direct mail and cooperative direct mail are similar. However, with a solo direct mail campaign, the advertiser absorbs all the costs rather than sharing them with other advertisers. Taken into consideration are factors such as costs of renting a mailing list, distribution costs, printing costs, mailing costs, and costs associated with fulfillment. For this example, we will assume a cooperative direct mail program will be undertaken in the Valassis Canada cooperative mailing package (see Figure A1.14). The Valassis Canada mailer is distributed to a predetermined list of households across Canada and contains offers from non-competing brands in various product categories.

response list
A list of direct mail buyers who have previously made purchases based on direct response offers.

circulation list
A publication's subscription list that targets potential customers based on specified demographic characteristics, interests, or activities.

compiled list
A direct mail list prepared from government, census, telephone, warranty, or other publication information.

Buying Information:

Valassis Canada Cooperative Mailings

The offer:	One-page premium size (5.5 × 8.25) that includes a $1.50 coupon
Redemption rate:	2.5 percent
Distribution:	2 000 000 households
Frequency:	Once
CPM:	$8.00 (from rate card)

Cost Calculations:

Distribution costs

2 000 000 units to be delivered, therefore,

2 000 × $8.00 = $16 000

Printing costs (estimated at $7.50/M)

2 000 × $7.50 = $15 000

Redemption costs (based on a 2.5 percent redemption rate)

2 000 000 × 0.025 × $1.50 = $75 000

Total cost   = $106 000

Depending on how the coupon offer is returned, there could be additional costs for the advertiser. For example, there is a handling fee provided to the retailer for conducting the coupon transaction. As well, coupons are usually sent from the retailer to a clearing

Direct Responsel Rate Card—Valassis Canada Inc.

Valassis is a full range media and marketing services company. We deliver value to consumers how, when, and where they want, achieved through exceptional targeting insights, results analysis and our diverse media portfolio.

Advertising Rates are effective **January 1, 2013**.

Rates are based on 1 side of page and exclusivity for one product category only. Additional categories extra. Multiple page, volume or frequency discounts available on request. Regional buys subject to a 10% surcharge with a minimum of $500 in each market purchased. Our Red Plum free standing insert delivers advertising messages and coupons through home delivered newspapers.

Rate Card

Size	Rate Per M
1P	$8.00
1/2P	$5.20
Front Cover	$12.50
Back Cover	$11.50
Front Tab	$9.50
Back Tab	$9.00

Note: Per M = $ cost per thousand

Source: CARDonline, www.cardonline.com.

house for processing. The clearing house pays the retailer and provides periodic reports to the advertiser about how many coupons are being redeemed. The advertiser pays a fee for this service.

INTERNET ADVERTISING

The most common model for quoting advertising rates on the Internet is CPM. An advertiser may pay each time an ad is downloaded to a browser, creating an impression or ad view. Or the advertiser may only pay when an ad is clicked on, a pay for performance model.

CPM (online)
The price charged for displaying an ad 1000 times. The calculation for CPM is cost divided by impressions (number of impressions divided by 1000).

CPM MODEL **CPM** is the price charged for displaying an ad 1000 times. The calculation for CPM is cost divided by impressions (number of impressions divided by 1000). For online advertising, an organization pays a rate for every 1000 impressions made. Therefore, if the total number of impressions desired is 500 000 and the CPM is $30, the total cost of the advertising campaign will be $15 000 (500 000 impressions/1000) × $30. In this pricing model the ad appears on a user's screen, so it makes an impression. The person may or may not click on the ad.

CPM rates vary according to the level of targeting desired by the advertiser. Typical options include *run of site*, *run of category*, *geographic targeting*, and *keyword targeting*. With reference to the rate card for globeandmail.com shown in Figure A1.15, if run of site is selected, the rates charged are those quoted for the various sizes and creative formats that appear anywhere on the site (see the column titled "Net CPM rate" on the rate card). For example, a big box ad is $37/M, a skyscraper is $35/M, and so on. The difference in rates is indicative of the effectiveness of the different sizes of ads—bigger ads are more effective.

targeting request
An ad placed to reach a specific target audience of a website, for which a premium is usually paid.

If **targeting requests** are applied, a 15 percent premium is charged for each targeted request (see the "Geo-targeting" column on the rate card). Also note that there is an additional 15 percent charge for rich media ads. Volume discounts might be offered based on the total dollar value of the advertising space that is purchased (see the volume discount scale at the bottom of the rate card).

CPM rate cards vary from one site to another, but the high-traffic sites of course charge a higher CPM. Popular portal sites, like Google and MSN, and various sports and media sites, such as TSN and Rogers Sportsnet, attract significant traffic and price their CPMs accordingly.

Here are a few illustrations to show how online advertising costs are calculated. Rate information is obtained from Figure A1.15.

Example 1:

Type of ad:	Leaderboard
Impressions desired:	3 000 000
CPM:	$37

Cost Calculation:

(3 000 000/1000) × $37 = $111 000

Since a volume discount of 20 percent applies in this situation (see volume discount section of the rate card), there is an additional calculation:

Volume discount:	$111 000 × 0.20 = 22 200

Therefore, the net cost is $88 800 ($111 000 − $22 200).

Once the ad achieves the desired number of impressions, it will be removed from the website.

Example 2:

Type of ad:	Half-page skyscraper
Impressions desired:	3 000 000
CPM:	$50
One geographic target request	+15%

Cost Calculation:

(3 000 000 / 1000) $\times$ $50 $\times$ 1.15 = $172 500

In this example, a volume discount of 25 percent applies (see the dollar volume discount scale in the rate card). Therefore, the additional calculation would be:

Volume discount: $172 500 $\times$ 0.25 = $43 125

Therefore, the net cost would be $129 375 ($172 500 − $43 125).

Although these are the quoted rates, the reality of the situation is similar to offline advertising. CPM rates are negotiable and depend on factors such as length of the campaign, season, and relationship between client and vendor. Effective negotiation skills in the media buying process could result in lower CPM rates.

PAY FOR PERFORMANCE MODEL   Advertisers must remember that the purpose of the banner is to create interest so that the viewer clicks the ad for more information. Once clicked, the viewer sees the ad in its entirety or is linked to the advertiser's website. Since clicking is the desired action, many pricing models are based on a **cost-per-click (CPC)** basis instead of CPM. The benefit of such a system is clear: The degree of clicking achieved by an ad indicates the effectiveness of the ad.

> cost-per-click (CPC)
> An Internet advertising pricing strategy where advertisers pay based on the number of ad clicks received.

The question is often asked: What is a good click rate? The answer depends on a host of factors such as the size of the banner, whether or not animation or video content was included, and where the ad was located on a page. A recent report by MediaMind observes that standard banner click rates have stabilized at 0.09 percent, meaning there is just one click for every 1000 impressions made.[2] The same study showed click rates for mobile banner ads to average 0.64 percent. While the click rates may seem low, an advertiser has to assess the targeting capabilities of online and mobile ads. The ability to target individuals based on location and behaviour is a positive factor to consider when deciding to use mobile advertising.

FLAT-FEE MODEL   Some websites charge a flat fee for advertising—typically, it is a set amount for the length of time the ad appears on the site. Sponsorships, for example, are usually sold on a flat-rate basis rather than on the number of impressions. For example, a site such as TSN.ca may offer a flat-fee sponsorship opportunity to an advertiser in combination with a CPM or CPC (cost-per-click) advertising package. The TSN Playoff Hockey Challenge was recently presented by KIA Canada, and the TSN Stock Car Challenge was presented by VTech. Fee structures for sponsorships vary from one site to another and are open to price negotiations between the advertiser and the site.

SOCIAL MEDIA NETWORK ADVERTISING

Since Facebook is by far the largest social media network, it will be used as the base for discussing some media buying options. There are two basic options on Facebook: banner ads and promoted posts for brand pages. The banner option is similar to the online banners discussed in the previous section. In terms of budget, the advertiser chooses

FIGURE
A1.15 The Globe and Mail Online Advertising Rate Card

Online Rates and Deadlines

ADVERTISING RATES EFFECTIVE JANUARY 1, 2012

GENERAL ADVERTISING RATES

CREATIVE FORMAT	PIXEL SIZE	MAX FILE SIZE ANIMATIONS	NET CPM RATE**	EXPANDING CREATIVE +15%	GEO-TARGETING +15%	FREQUENCY CAPPING +15%
Big Box†	300 x 250	40k – 5 rotations	$37	600 x 250*	yes	yes
Leaderboard†	728 x 90	40k – 5 rotations	$37	728 x 360*	yes	yes
Superbanner	960 x 90	40k – 5 rotations	$43	960 x 360*	yes	yes
Skyscraper	160 x 600	40k – 5 rotations	$35	—	yes	yes
Half Page Skyscraper †	300 x 600	40k – 5 rotations	$50	—	yes	yes
Tile	120 x 240	15k – 3 rotations	$13	—	yes	yes
Pre-Roll Video***	576 x 324	2 Mbps (minimum)	$52	—	yes	yes
Top Layer (Voken)	500 x 500 max	40k – no rotations	$40	—	yes	included
Pop Up	250 x 250 max	40k – no rotations	$37	—	yes	included
Full Screen Transition	640 x 480	40k – no rotations	$70	—	yes	included
Text Link	95 characters	—	$2	—	yes	—
Smartphone banners	300 x 50	7k – 3 rotations	$20	300 x 150*	no	no

*For complete expanded ad specs go to: www.globelink.ca/onlinespecs **Rich media +15% ***With companion Big Box (300 x 250) †Tablet rate same as display

NEWSLETTERS

E-MAIL NAME	SITE	SUBSCRIBERS	FREQUENCY
News Update	GAM	64,000	Daily
Business Ticker	GAM	50,000	Daily
Personal Finance Reader	GI	130,000	Friday
Advisor Focus	GA	12,000	2nd Friday
Berman's Market Update	GI	3,500 x 3	3 x daily
Wine & Spirits	LIFE	99,800	Friday
Globe Life Newsletter	LIFE	104,100	Daily
Drive Newsletter	GD	21,700	Sunday
Weekly Tech Alert	GT	29,000	Thursday
Small Business	ROB	570	Friday
Politics	GAM	3,120	Daily
Jets Games Report	GS	304	After game day

ADVERTISER EXCLUSIVE E-MAILS

E-MAIL CATEGORY	SUBSCRIBERS
Arts & Entertainment	26,900
Auto	18,000
Consumer Electronics	17,200
Computer Hardware/Software	21,200
Fashion & Style	16,900
Food & Groceries	19,100
Health & Well-Being	28,400
Personal Finance & Investing	35,900
Sporting Goods & Events	16,900
Travel & Accommodations	29,700
Wine & Spirits	24,400
Real Estate	21,700
Rates	$250 per 1000 subscribers

*targeting +15%

VOLUME DISCOUNT

VOLUME DISCOUNT BY	DISCOUNT
$0 – $4,999	0%
$5,000 – $9,999	5%
$10,000 – $49,999	10%
$50,000 – $99,999	15%
$100,000 – $149,999	20%
$150,000 – $199,999	25%
$200,000 – $249,999	30%
$250,000 – $349,999	35%
$350,000 – $499,999	40%
$500,000 – $749,999	45%
$750,000 – $999,999	50%

CONTRACT AND MATERIAL DEADLINES

DUE 2 DAYS PRIOR TO LAUNCH	DUE 5 DAYS PRIOR TO LAUNCH
Standard Ad: *impression-based material* Creative Updates	Sponsorship Ad: *time-based ownership* Rich Media Ad Exclusive

SIGNED CONTRACT DEADLINE

Signed online contracts must arrive a minimum of 1 business day prior to the above material deadlines

between a CPM (cost per thousand) model and the CPC model (cost per click). If the CPC model is chosen, an advertiser establishes a daily budget (the maximum the advertiser is willing to spend) and a bid price within or above the selected range. The **bid (bid price)** is a predetermined maximum amount an advertiser is willing to pay for each click. On Facebook, advertisers can target their ads based on criteria such as location, age, gender, education, likes, and interests (for example, hiking, camping, skiing, and so on). Click rates on Facebook are lower than traditional banner ads. A recent study by Webtrends observed an average click rate of only 0.051 percent on Facebook.[3]

The promoted posts for brand pages option allows advertisers to pay for posts to be more prominently displayed on news feeds. Facebook determined that the average brand page is only seen by 16 percent of fans. Promoted posts will help businesses reach and engage more of their fan base. A brand can now pay $5, $10, $15, or $20 to get more people who like a brand's page to see a promoted post.[4]

Bid (bid price)
A predetermined maximum amount an advertiser is willing to pay for a click.

Media Information Resources

Media planners rely on secondary research data provided by specialist media organizations. **Secondary research** refers to data compiled and published by others for purposes other than resolving a specific problem. In advertising, secondary sources are frequently used to gain access to media information that benefits media analysis and planning. This information is available through various media associations, specialized media research companies, and individual media outlets (for example, a daily newspaper, national magazine, or a local television station).

Most organizations that provide media data also provide appropriate software that can be used to sift through the data (for example, data can be cross-tabulated with product and service consumption data to determine the best way of reaching a specific target audience). Much of the information is made available through the media research companies and organizations mentioned below, or through specialist companies that develop software for use with database information provided by these organizations. Agencies pay for the data provided by the various media research organizations.

secondary research
Data compiled and published by others for purposes other than resolving a specific problem. In advertising, secondary sources are frequently used to gain access to media information that benefits media analysis and planning.

TELEVISION RESOURCES
The organizations that compile television media data on a continuous (year-to-year) basis include BBM Canada, Nielsen Media Research, and the Television Bureau of Canada.

BBM CANADA BBM Canada is the leading supplier of television and radio audience ratings services to the Canadian broadcast advertising industry. The service is divided into two divisions for recording and analyzing data: BBM TV and BBM Radio. BBM TV collects audience data through a combination of electronic observation (portable people meter or PPM) and diaries that are returned by mail.

When the **diary system** is used, participants complete a seven-day log by recording the television viewing for all television sets in the household for each quarter hour of the day from 6 am to 2 am. Information from returned diaries is keyed into computers for processing and verification.

In the case of the **portable people meter (PPM)**, a form of electronic observation is employed. BBM Canada and Nielsen Media Research launched a joint venture that measures television network viewing nationally as well as viewing in five major markets: Toronto, Vancouver, Montreal (French), Edmonton, and Calgary. The meter registers

diary system
A system to collect audience data where participants complete a seven-day log by recording the television viewing for all television sets in the household for each quarter hour of the day from 6 am to 2 am.

portable people meter (PPM)
A form of electronic observation where electronic metering devices are carried by household members that register what is being watched on television every minute of every day.

what is being watched (programs and advertisements) every minute of every day in every metered household. Because the households are a representative sample, extrapolations are made about how people view programs on local, regional, and national bases.

BBM data focus on national and local markets. BBM conducts its surveys three times a year—fall, winter, and spring—in 40 television markets. Its reports contain current audience ratings and share data, as well as full coverage data for local market stations. The data are presented in four sections: time block, program, time period, and trend.

BBM also conducts a "sweep" survey in the fall and spring that covers the national market (television viewers two years of age and older). The data collected during the ratings period are used to estimate the audiences of programs on individual stations and networks. **Ratings** are audience estimates expressed as a percentage of a population in a defined geographic area. For example, if a show has a rating of 20, it reaches 20 percent of that market's population. Each year BBM publishes *The TV Data Book*, which provides an overview in graphic and table form of national and regional television viewing habits in Canada. The data provide valuable trend information to advertisers and agencies. For some examples of basic trend data available from BBM, visit www.bbm.ca.

rating
Television and radio audience estimates expressed as a percentage of a population in a defined geographic area.

NIELSEN MEDIA RESEARCH Nielsen Media Research provides advertising information services including advertising expenditures, GRP analysis, and creative monitoring services for advertising messages. Its advertising expenditure estimates are available for television (network and spot), radio, magazines, daily newspapers, and out-of-home media. These data allow an advertiser to compare its expenditures against those of its competitors.

Nielsen Media Research also offers a variety of competitive tracking services that provide the quantitative information necessary for strategic determination and tactical execution of communications plans. Advertisers and agencies use Nielsen Media's audience analyses and applications to estimate the future performance of television shows, to execute television buys, and to measure the performance of campaigns. Nielsen's software can be used to perform reach/frequency, duplication, and quintile delivery analyses.[5] For additional information about Nielsen Media Research, visit www.nielsenmedia.com/ca.

TELEVISION BUREAU OF CANADA The Television Bureau of Canada (TVB) is a sales and marketing resource centre for the commercial television industry. Its mandate is to promote television as an effective advertising medium. Each year, this organization publishes a booklet, *TV Basics*, that contains the latest data on television trends. It covers viewing trends by demographic and geographic variables, programming preferences by demographic variables, and television-station circulation by gender and age for all station markets. The TVB provides such data as viewing by time of day, day of week, and time of year. For additional information about the data provided by the TVB, visit www.tvb.ca.

RADIO RESOURCES

BBM CANADA BBM Canada compiles consumption data for radio on a continuous basis. The radio division of BBM Canada measures radio audiences in 115 Canadian markets up to four times a year, in eight-week periods, using seven-day personal diaries. In addition to collecting tuning data, the diary contains questions collecting product usage and lifestyle data.

Twice yearly, BBM Radio produces a *Reach Report*. The report contains reach, hours, and share data for each member station in each measured market for five standard demographics. This allows advertisers to plan their buys better, since they will know the exact profile of each station's audience. Audience data are available based on hours tuned per week, listening by daypart, and listening by location (for example, home, automobile, and other locations). For some samples of basic trend data published by the BBM, visit www.bbm.ca.

The BBM also publishes a *Radio Data Book*, which provides an overview of national, provincial, and local radio tuning based on the latest fall radio survey and the previous fall survey. The book offers a picture of tuning habits over the past five years and is useful for people planning radio campaigns.

MAGAZINE RESOURCES   The companies and organizations involved in magazine research and data collection include the Audit Bureau of Circulations, BPA Worldwide, and the Print Measurement Bureau.

ALLIANCE FOR AUDITED MEDIA   The Alliance for Audited Media (AAM) issues standardized statements verifying circulation statistics for paid-circulation magazines (consumer and business publications) and most daily newspapers in Canada. All publications that are members of the AAM receive an audited **publisher's statement**. This statement is the authority on which advertising rates are based (verified circulation is used to establish the advertising rate base as shown in the publication's rate card). The statement is issued twice each year. A publisher's statement includes the following information: average paid circulation for the past six months, paid circulation for each issue in the last six months, an analysis of new and renewal subscriptions, paid circulation by county size, and geographic analysis of total paid circulation. For a selection of sample data published by the AAM, refer to www.auditedmedia.com.

The AAM publishes five-year circulation data for newspapers and annual circulation data for magazines.

publisher's statement
A statement published by the Alliance for Audited Media (AAM) twice a year that is the authority on which advertising rates are based.

CANADIAN CIRCULATIONS AUDIT BOARD (CCAB)   The CCAB, the Canadian division of BPA Worldwide, audits all paid, controlled, or any combination of paid and controlled circulation for over 450 business and farm publications, consumer magazines, and community and daily newspapers throughout Canada.

Statements include type of circulation (for example, paid or controlled circulation), recipient qualification (for example, distribution to a predetermined target based on demographic data), circulation for the past six months, average paid circulation per issue, and a geographical breakdown of the circulation. Additional information about the CCAB is available at www.bpaww.com.

The CCAB also audits web traffic for 12 daily newspapers. The metrics available include page impressions, user sessions, unique browsers and their frequency, page duration, and user session duration. The availability of web traffic data lets media buyers and advertisers evaluate greater brand reach instead of just circulation.

PRINT MEASUREMENT BUREAU   The Print Measurement Bureau (PMB) provides standardized readership information for members, a group that includes advertisers, agencies, publishers, and other related companies in the Canadian media industry. The PMB publishes Canada's leading single-source multimedia study.

The major data component of the annual PMB study is the detailed readership data for more than 125 magazines and newspapers, and the linking of those data with information on readers' product usage patterns, their usage of brands, their retail shopping habits, extensive demographic data, and their lifestyles.

The study also provides general usage data on other media such as television, daily newspapers, outdoor, transit, and the Internet. Data provided by the PMB study benefit advertisers and agencies in the media planning process. Based on cross-tabulations of data concerning media, product, brand, and lifestyle, the information can be used to identify target markets more precisely, to assist in budget allocation, and to make better decisions regarding media selection and placement. PMB information is available to clients electronically and requires special software to access it.

The PMB's full two-year database is fused with comScore website visitor data to provide combination reach data for PMB-measured titles and their websites. Such data allow a media planner to assess options for both print and web advertising for magazines of interest. For additional information about the PMB, visit www.pmb.ca.

NEWSPAPERS

As stated in the magazine section, newspaper circulation and readership data are available from the Audit Bureau of Circulations and the Canadian Circulations Audit Board (a division of BPA Worldwide). Readership information is also compiled by an industry-sponsored measurement organization known as NADbank.

NADBANK—NEWSPAPER AUDIENCE DATABANK
NADbank provides advertisers, advertising agencies, and daily newspapers with accurate and credible information on newspaper readership, retail data, and consumer behaviour. NADbank is an annual survey among Canadian adults 18 years and older. It compiles relevant data about newspaper circulation and readership. In conjunction with Nielsen IMS, it also compiles online readership data, which, when combined with hard copy readership data, give a media planner useful reach information for individual newspapers. NADbank members have access to readership data for 84 daily newspapers in 53 markets and 59 community newspapers in 34 markets.

The nature of information produced by NADbank includes weekday and weekend readership, demographic profiles of readers, product ownership and purchase intentions, media habits (for example, other media referred to), and shopping habits (for example, malls visited and frequency of visits). Additional information and some sample data published by NADbank are available at www.nadbank.com.

OUT-OF-HOME MEDIA

CANADIAN OUT-OF-HOME MEASUREMENT BUREAU
The Canadian Out-of-Home Measurement Bureau (COMB) audits the circulations of outdoor posters and backlight posters, outdoor digital, mural advertising, furniture advertising, and superboards. COMB also audits indoor media that include backlight boards, mini-boards, digital screens, and mall posters.

Audience data are location specific, full coverage, and in-market in nature. Circulation data concerning all outdoor media are based on municipal and provincial traffic counts and converted to circulations according to an established traffic-variation factor. A 2009 survey sets the average occupation factor for light vehicles in Canada at 1.62, which represents the average number of people in an automobile.[6] Mall counts are based on observation (head counts) in each location by an independent research firm.

COMB publishes the *COMB Data Report* on a semi-annual basis. The report contains daily and weekly audience averages for each product in each market. Verification reports are also provided. These reports verify that suppliers are delivering what they are contracted to deliver and compare the percentage of audience delivered to what was contracted. Media planners can access COMB Navigator, a planning and reach-frequency analysis tool that adds insight to the outdoor advertising planning process. For more information about COMB, visit www.comb.org.

DIGITAL DATA SOURCES (INTERNET, SOCIAL, AND MOBILE)

Both the Interactive Marketing Bureau (IAB) and comScore Media provide useful information about online media and advertising consumption.

INTERACTIVE ADVERTISING BUREAU

The Interactive Advertising Bureau (IAB) is a national organization of Internet publishers, advertisers, and agencies acting as the collective voice to represent companies engaged in selling advertising on Internet-based media. IAB promotes the value of Internet advertising to advertisers and agencies, and serves as an educational resource through which advertisers can increase their knowledge and gain a competitive edge in the marketplace.

The IAB actively promotes advertising standards and guidelines that make it easier to plan, buy, execute, track, and evaluate online advertising plans. As well, it provides cross-media usage data via an annual research study and other interactive research.[7] The IAB reports that the Internet is the second-most popular medium in terms of time spent with the media by Canadians.

Research studies conducted by independent organizations for IAB show the effectiveness of online advertising. When online is added to the media mix, scores for various brand measurements increase. Tests among many leading brands in various product categories are the foundation of the research findings. Details of these studies are available at the IAB website. For more information about the IAB, visit www.iabcanada.com.

COMSCORE CANADA

comScore Canada is an Internet audience measurement service that reports details of website usage, visitor demographics, and detailed information for online search behaviour.

A variety of quantitative data is available to advertisers, including measures for a website's unique visitors; reach; average usage days per user; average unique pages per user per month; average minutes spent per person per page per month; and age, gender, and other demographic characteristics of visitors.

Other services offered by comScore include online buying power metrics based on actual consumer purchases made online, local audience measurement for major Canadian markets, and detailed measurements of online search behaviour. With the Internet growing in importance as a medium, the research that supports it is becoming more sophisticated.

comScore also provides an array of media insights aimed at understanding and leveraging social media conversations and provides a full suite of media measurement metrics that can be directly compared to other types of media. comScore data include demographic and behavioural composition of a brand's social media audience, the reach and frequency of social media brand impressions, and the ability to tie social media exposure to desired consumer behaviours, including brand engagement and spending propensity. Similar information is available for mobile web audiences.[8] For more information, go to www.comscore.com.

Research Data by Individual Media

The specific media vehicles often conduct their own marketing research or use research data provided by independent sources such as those just described. These data provide advertisers and agencies with objective, reliable information showing the relative strengths of the given medium as an advertising vehicle. In local market situations, a daily newspaper or a local radio station provides advertisers and agencies with data to assist them in the decision-making process. Here, local media compete with each other for advertising revenue, so comparisons on criteria such as reach, readership, number of people listening and watching, and so on are inevitable. When assessing this type of data, the advertiser should ensure that it is audited data and that it has been verified by an independent organization. Much of this data is available at the website of the particular magazine, newspaper, radio station, and so on.

The same situation exists for magazines and newspapers. All magazines and newspapers have their circulation and readership data readily available for review by advertisers and agencies. The viewer of such information should ensure it is audited data, possibly audited by the various research organizations cited in this appendix.

KEY TERMS

agate line 374	diary system 405	position charge 379
bid (bid price) 405	frequency discount (print) 381	publisher's statement 407
broadsheet 374	frequency discount	rating 406
circulation list 400	(television/radio) 387	reach plan 391
compiled list 400	gross rating points (GRPs) 386	response list 400
continuity discount (print) 381	horizontal rotation 391	rotation plan 391
continuity discount	house list 399	secondary research 405
(television/radio) 387	line rate 376	spot colour 379
corporate discount 383	list broker 399	tabloid 374
cost-per-click (CPC) 403	merge/purge 399	targeting request 402
cost per thousand (CPM) 380	modular advertising 374	transient rate 376
CPM (online) 402	negotiated rate 386	vertical rotation 391
daypart 391	portable people meter (PPM) 405	volume discount 387

REVIEW QUESTIONS

1. Calculate the cost of the following newspaper campaign. Refer to Figure A1.2 for rate card information.

   Newspaper: *The Globe and Mail*,
   National Edition,
   Sports Section
   Ad Size: 4 columns wide by 6 column inches deep
   Colour: All ads are black and white
   Frequency: 2 ads per week (Wed. and Fri.)
   Continuity: 8 weeks
   Rate: Transient

2. Calculate the total cost of the following magazine campaign. Refer to Figure A1.5 for rate card information.

   Magazine: *Canadian Geographic*
   Ad Size: Double-page spread
   Frequency: 4 insertions

3. Calculate the total cost of the following magazine campaign. Refer to Figure A1.5 for rate card information.

   Magazine: *Canadian Geographic*
   Ad Size: 1/2 page
   Frequency: 8 insertions

4. Calculate the total cost of the following radio campaign. Refer to Figure A1.11 for rate card information.

   Station: CJAZ-FM
   Nature of Plan: Specific times requested during breakfast and drive periods
   Breakfast: 8 spots per week
   Drive: 8 spots per week
   Continuity: 6 weeks

5. Calculate the total cost of a 16-spot weekly reach plan for the same period of time as in Question 5 on CJAZ-FM radio. Refer to Figure A1.11 for rate card information. When the total costs of the reach plan are compared to the total costs of the specific request plan in Question 5, how much does the advertiser save by using the reach plan?

6. Calculate the total cost of the following outdoor campaign. Refer to Figure A1.12 for rate card information.

   Medium: CBS Outdoor Transit Shelters
   Markets and GRPs:
   Toronto (CMA), 25 GRP
   Calgary (CMA), 50 GRP
   Halifax (CMA), 50 GRP

   Vancouver (CMA), 25 GRP
   Continuity: 20 weeks in all markets

7. Calculate the total cost of the following outdoor campaign. Refer to Figure A1.13 for rate card information.

   Medium: CBS Outdoor Posters
   Markets and GRPs:
   St. John's, 50 GRP
   Quebec City, 50 GRP
   Hamilton, 75 GRP
   Winnipeg, 50 GRP
   Continuity: Quebec City and Hamilton, 16 weeks; Edmonton, St. John's, and Winnipeg, 12 weeks.

8. Calculate the total cost of delivering a $2.00 coupon to 4 million Canadian households using Valassis Canada cooperative mailings. The estimated redemption rate for the offer is 2.5 percent. Refer to Figure A1.14 for rate card information.

9. Calculate the total cost of the following online banner campaign. Refer to Figure A1.15 for rate card information.

   Medium: globeandmail.com
   Ad Type: Big box
   Impressions: 10 million

ENDNOTES

1. Rob Neill, "Despite $4 Million Price Tag, Marketers Clamor for Super Bowl Ads," NBC News, January 6, 2012, www.nbcnews.com/business/despite-4-million-price-tag-marketers-clamor-super-bowl-ads-1C7100946.

2. Esther Shein, "Banner Ads: Past, Present, and...Future?" CMO.COM, April 24, 2012, www.cmo.com/articles/2012/4/24/banner-ads-past-present-and-future.html.

3. Todd Wasserman, "Facebook Ads Perform Half as Well as Regular Banner Ads [STATS]," Mashable.com, January 31, 2011, mashable.com/2011/01/31/facebook-half-click-throughs.

4. Lauren Drell, "Facebook Promoted Posts: A Step-by-Step Guide," Mashable.com, May 31, 2012, mashable.com/2012/05/31/facebook-promoted-posts-tips.

5. "Television Data Sources," Canadian Media Directors' Council Media Digest, 2011-2012, Marketing, September 26, 2011, p. 32,

6. "2009 Canadian Vehicle Survey," Natural Resources Canada, Cat. No. M141-18/2009E-PDF, p. 16, oee.rncan.gc.ca/publications/statistics/cvs09/pdf/cvs09.pdf.

7. www.iabcanada.com.

8. www.comscore.com.

Integrated Marketing Communications Plan: Mr. Sub

Market Background

MARKET ANALYSIS

The quick-serve restaurant (QSR) market is a mature market. The degree of competition among the various banners is intensive and extensive.

- The restaurant industry is growing only marginally (+3.0 percent a year).
- Quick-serve segment sales totalled $22.0 billion in Canada (2011).
- The quick-serve segment is saturated and offers limited growth potential over the next five years.
- The casual dining segment, composed of mid-range establishments like Montana's and Kelsey's, is experiencing higher growth (+6 percent a year).
- The sandwich segment of the market is presently worth $2.1 billion and accounts for about 10 percent of the quick-serve restaurant market.
- The sandwich segment is growing at the rate of +4.0 percent a year.

EXTERNAL INFLUENCES ON THE MARKET

ECONOMIC TRENDS The cyclical nature of the economy influences the volume of business in the QSR market segment. Generally, the Canadian economy is growing at a moderate rate, as is the restaurant industry. There is a variation in trends within the various segments of the restaurant industry.

DEMOGRAPHIC TRENDS

- With the population aging, restaurants must reposition themselves to maintain customers.
- Youthful generations who are influenced less by traditional marketing methods are the next generation of customers.
- Ethnic Canadians are creating a demand for ethnic dishes in QSR establishments.

SOCIAL TRENDS

- The health boom associated with the late 1990s appears to be over, but in general terms, a healthier lifestyle is an ambition for many people.
- People are maintaining an active lifestyle, but are subject to indulgences.
- Youthful generations favour non-traditional methods for learning about products; peer influences are very important.
- Time-pressed consumers are constantly searching for products and services offering convenience.

TECHNOLOGY

- Non-traditional methods of communication are popular with younger generations of consumers.

- Multi-tasking consumers refer to several media at the same time, so reaching consumers is now more challenging for marketing organizations.

CONSUMER DATA   Consumers indicate that the following criteria are important when selecting a quick-serve restaurant:

- Value (in terms of food quality at competitive prices).
- Reduced wait times.
- Convenience (location in time of need is important).
- Food served "their" way.

COMPETITIVE ANALYSIS

Mr. Sub competes directly with Subway and Quizno's in the fresh sandwich segment. Quizno's is somewhat different, as it specializes in hot-served or toasted sandwiches.

Subway dominates the sandwich segment. Much of its strength can be attributed to the number of restaurant locations it operates across Canada.

McDonald's and Tim Hortons compete in the sandwich segment, but sandwiches account for only a portion of their business. Both restaurants offer only a limited selection of fresh and toasted sandwiches, but are very popular destinations for quick meals.

Market shares for the national chains (in the sandwich segment only) are as follows:

Chain	Share	Locations
Subway	25.0	2800
Tim Hortons	10.0	3000
Mr. Sub	6.5	375
McDonald's	3.5	1400
Quizno's	3.0	325

SUBWAY   As the commercials say, "Subway...Eat Fresh." Subway is positioned as the premier destination for fresh sandwiches. Subway's success in the QSR market is due to the following factors:

- The brand name is synonymous with fresh food.
- High-quality and healthy food products are available.
- It has an association with social responsibility causes such as childhood obesity.
- It has an ability to react quickly to consumer preferences (for example, introducing healthier breads).
- Financial resources are available for marketing and marketing communications.
- The "Jared" ad campaign (weight-loss message) was a success.
- It has extensive distribution with 2800 restaurants coast to coast.
- Its successful rewards program encourages loyalty.

QUIZNO'S   The market share for Quizno's has tripled in the past two years. The company's success is based on the following factors:

- It claims to own the "toasted" and "grilled" segment (even though other brands offer similar items).
- An advertising campaign that included celebrities such as Don Cherry and Tie Domi helped establish the brand.

- A focus on quality justifies higher prices; consumers seem willing to pay more for a sandwich.

BRAND ANALYSIS (MR. SUB)

Mr. Sub was the original submarine sandwich retailer in Canada, but over the years it has not maintained marketing and marketing communications support at a sufficient level to build the brand. Mr. Sub has lost considerable market share to Subway.

Mr. Sub's present position in the marketplace is a result of the following factors:

- It is a popular destination for former generations of young people.
- Quality products are offered at competitive prices.
- Its product range includes popular items such as sandwiches, wraps, salads, and hot and cold beverages.
- Its present positioning fits with customer expectations and is based on "quality, freshness, and quantity."
- It has a loyal following among older age groups (40+ years).
- The brand is not well known among younger age groups.
- Only 375 locations (1:7.5 ratio of stores compared to Subway) exist coast to coast, with more than 60 percent of locations in Southern Ontario.
- Investment in advertising and marketing communications is much lower than that of its competitors.

SWOT ANALYSIS

BRAND STRENGTHS

- Products offered are as good as the leading brand.
- The brand is well known with older consumers (a sense of loyalty exists).
- Its good reputation will enhance new marketing initiatives.

BRAND WEAKNESSES

- Young consumers are unfamiliar with the brand and its offerings.
- It has low visibility among primary targets due to lack of marketing communications activity.
- Lack of availability (convenience); its key competitor has a significant distribution advantage.

MARKETING OPPORTUNITIES

- Fit the brand into healthier and contemporary lifestyles.
- Take a fresh marketing approach to attract a younger target audience.
- Appeal to consumer demand for value (a combination of convenience and quality).

THREATS

- The marketing and financial resources of direct competitors are extensive.
- Taste preferences among consumers (less demand for fresh) shift.
- Further encroachment from other fast-food restaurants and casual dining establishments is possible.

Marketing Communications Plan

TARGET MARKET

To rebuild/rejuvenate Mr. Sub requires that greater attention be given to younger generations of consumers, for they are the primary consumers of QSR establishments.

PRIMARY TARGET

Demographic

- Males and females 15 to 29 years old.
- Secondary and post-secondary education level.
- Students and newly employed graduates.
- Income not important.

Psychographic

- Time-pressed and fast-paced daily routines.
- Socially active (peer groups are influencers).
- Technologically savvy (online and mobile communications generation).
- Active with a healthy outlook.

Geographic

- All across Canada, with emphasis on major urban markets.

SECONDARY TARGET

- Males and females 35+ years old.
- Young families.
- Active lifestyles.
- Located in major urban markets.
- More inclined to refer to traditional media for information.

MARKETING OBJECTIVES

1. To increase market share from 6.5 percent to 7.5 percent.
2. To position Mr. Sub as a restaurant offering healthy and hearty sandwiches at reasonable prices.

MARKETING COMMUNICATIONS GOAL (CHALLENGE)

- To create more top-of-mind awareness for Mr. Sub among younger generations of consumers and secure a place on their "consideration list."
- To associate Mr. Sub with a contemporary urban lifestyle that will appeal to the primary and secondary targets.

MARKETING COMMUNICATIONS OBJECTIVES

1. To achieve a 70 percent brand awareness level among the primary target market.
2. To achieve a trial purchase rate of 20 percent among the primary target market.

3. To communicate the quality, variety, and freshness of the various menu items offered by Mr. Sub.
4. To create an image for Mr. Sub that is in keeping with contemporary lifestyles.
5. To build buzz for Mr. Sub among a new generation of consumers currently unfamiliar with the brand.

MARKETING COMMUNICATIONS STRATEGY

BUDGET For the first year of the campaign, a budget of $3.0 million is available to cover all marketing communications expenditures. The budget will cover a multimedia campaign and will include various integrated marketing communications activities.

POSITIONING STRATEGY STATEMENT The current positioning strategy will be retained and is described as follows:

> "Mr. Sub is a restaurant that offers the best in terms of fresh, healthy food served quickly. Mr. Sub prides itself on giving the customer a little bit more for their money."

MARKETING COMMUNICATIONS MIX A mix of marketing communications elements will combine to create a synergistic impact on the primary and secondary target markets. The various elements of the mix will each contribute to achieving the marketing communications objectives. The marketing communications mix will include traditional media advertising, sales promotions, event marketing, and online and interactive communications. The rationale for this combination of media is as follows:

- **Advertising:** Traditional forms of media advertising are needed to make a "visual impression" in key urban markets and to achieve the awareness objective.

- **Sales Promotion:** A variety of "incentives" are needed to achieve the trial purchase objectives. Some street-level activities will help achieve the "brand buzz" objective.

- **Event Marketing:** A significant event will be staged in Toronto that will start an association between Mr. Sub and basketball (a popular and growing sport). Basketball appeals directly to the primary male target, and the street-level marketing event will create buzz for Mr. Sub.

- **Online Communications:** The primary target audience is the biggest user of online and mobile technologies; therefore, these media are both effective and efficient for delivering Mr. Sub's message.

ADVERTISING PLAN: CREATIVE

CREATIVE OBJECTIVES

1. To communicate that Mr. Sub offers quality sandwiches, wraps, and salads.
2. To portray Mr. Sub as an appealing restaurant destination suited to a contemporary urban lifestyle.

CREATIVE STRATEGY Mr. Sub does not have the physical presence of its primary competitor; therefore, the message will focus on the quality of the food (scrumptious shots of sandwiches and wraps) and people (teens and 20-somethings) enjoying the food. It's worth searching a little harder for!

Selected messages in various media will also include members of the secondary target enjoying the Mr. Sub experience.

Central Theme   All messages, regardless of media, will show the sandwich being created or the finished product; a mouth-watering selection of sandwiches that will satisfy any type of hunger will be visually presented in advertisements.

Appeal Technique   The message will combine a positive appeal (with an emphasis on the product and what it looks like) with a lifestyle appeal (the target will be shown enjoying the food).

Tone and Style   A straightforward approach will be used. All messages will be clear, product focused, and easy to understand. Print media will stress visual imagery by showing the "scrumptious" aspect of the sandwiches.

Tagline   Some options to summarize the message strategy include:

"Mr. Sub. More than enough."

"Mr. Sub. Enough and then some."

"Mr. Sub. It's all about the sandwich."

CREATIVE EXECUTION   The campaign will include 30-second television spots, 4-colour print advertising, 4-colour newspaper inserts, outdoor posters, online banner ads, and an interactive component. Selected messages will encourage consumers to visit the Mr. Sub website to participate in a selection of new video games.

Print and outdoor media will be product focused, while broadcast media will feature consumer enjoyment and the fun associated with the Mr. Sub experience.

Integrated aspects of the campaign will include trial incentives delivered by newspaper inserts, a contest, a street-level marketing program in Toronto, and a television and online sponsorship element. Creating awareness for the brand and tagline will be a priority throughout the campaign.

ADVERTISING PLAN: MEDIA

BUDGET   A budget of approximately $2.0 million has been allocated for media advertising to cover a one-year period from January 2014 to December 2014.

MEDIA OBJECTIVES

Who   As described earlier, the primary target is teens and 20-somethings residing in urban locations. The secondary target is adults 35+ years residing in urban markets.

What   The message to be communicated will focus on the scrumptious quality of the food and people enjoying the Mr. Sub experience.

When   The launch phase of the plan will be given heavier support to set the new campaign in motion. Spending will be slightly higher than normal in the summer when promotions are in progress. A steady spending pattern will be implemented at other times of the year.

Where   The campaign will be national in scope with additional emphasis placed on key urban markets.

How   Creating awareness and developing a new image for a brand takes time; therefore, reach and frequency will be a priority in the initial phase of the campaign (the first three months). Continuity will be more important as the campaign progresses.

MEDIA STRATEGY

Target Market Strategy   In the initial phase of the campaign, a shotgun strategy is recommended to reach the primary and secondary target markets. A multimedia approach will be employed to achieve reach objectives. As the campaign progresses, there will be a shift to a profile-matching strategy to effectively reach the primary target.

Market Coverage   Since this is a national campaign, media that reach the national market will be used. Supplementary media will be added in urban markets to increase reach and frequency against the primary and secondary targets. The budget available will determine the extent of key market coverage.

Timing   Spending will be heavier in the initial phase (first three months), reflecting a blitz strategy. Spending will then taper off for a few months but rebound upward during the summer months when various integrated marketing activities are scheduled. For the remaining months of the campaign, spending will follow a moderate but steady pattern.

Reach/Frequency/Continuity   The initial phase of the campaign is devoted to attracting a new target market to Mr. Sub. Therefore, reach and frequency are the priorities. Various media will be employed to reach the target market in different ways. As the campaign progresses, continuity of message will be more of a priority. Media advertising will be scheduled in flights to ensure maximum impact, regardless of the media employed.

MEDIA SELECTION RATIONALE   A multimedia campaign that embraces network television, specialty television stations, national (targeted) magazines, key market daily newspapers (for inserts), out-of-home advertising, and online media is recommended.

Television   Television reaches the national target audience with a strong visual message (the message emphasis on food and friends is best delivered by television). Prime-time ad placements will ensure a high level of brand recognition. A television sponsorship opportunity will associate Mr. Sub with basketball, a popular and growing sport in Canada.

Print   A combination of targeted lifestyle magazines, newspapers, and inserts in selected daily newspapers will assist in creating brand awareness and distributing trial incentives. Inserts will be used exclusively to announce discounted meal combinations and special coupon offers to encourage trial visits.

Out-of-Home   In major markets, outdoor posters will deliver the message while people are "on the move." The decision about where to dine is often made when people are in transit, presenting an ideal opportunity to remind them about Mr. Sub.

Online   Since the primary target market spends a lot of time online, there is an opportunity for consumers to interact directly with the brand. In conjunction with messages delivered by other media, the target will be encouraged to visit a new Mr. Sub website to play a selection of new sports games. Banner ads will also appear on two third-party sites that will move viewers to the Mr. Sub website.

MEDIA EXECUTION   The CTV Network and TVA Quebec are recommended to reach a broad cross-section of the population. TSN and The Score are recommended to reach the primary target market.

Network	# of Spots	Cost/Spot	Total Cost
CTV	40	$16 500	$660 000
TVA	30	$3 000	$90 000
TSN	50	$3 500	$175 000
The Score	65	$300	$19 500
Total	**185**		**$944 500**
The Score TV Sponsorship			$25 000
Total TV Costs			**$969 500**

Note: All ads are 30-second spots.

FIGURE A2.1

Television Advertising

Outdoor posters will complement television ads and reach a broad cross-section of the population in 12 major markets across Canada.

Both *Tribute* and *Inside Entertainment* magazines are recommended, as they effectively reach males and females in the primary target. *Maclean's* is also recommended, since it effectively reaches a cross-section of the adult population regardless of age.

For a summary of all media activity (timing and expenditures), refer to Figures A2.1 to A2.3.

Market	GRPs	Weeks	Total Cost
Toronto/Hamilton	25	12	$295 800
Vancouver	25	12	$223 500
Ottawa	25	12	$108 600
Calgary	25	12	$64 800
Edmonton	25	12	$57 600
Quebec City	25	8	$40 800
Winnipeg	25	8	$20 800
London	25	8	$19 600
Kitchener	25	8	$22 200
Halifax	25	8	$13 400
Regina	25	8	$7 200
St. John's	25	8	$8 600
Total Cost			**$882 900**

Note: All ads are horizontal outdoor posters.

FIGURE A2.2

Outdoor Advertising

Magazine	# Inserts	Cost/Insert	Total Cost
Maclean's	4	$25 400	$101 600
Tribute	4	$18 900	$75 600
Inside Entertainment	4	$15 000	$60 000
Total	**12**		**$237 200**

Note: All ads are 1-page, 4-colour

SALES PROMOTION PLAN

PROMOTION OBJECTIVES

1. To encourage trial purchase among primary and secondary targets.
2. To secure interactivity between the consumer and the brand by encouraging consumers to visit the Mr. Sub website.

PROMOTION STRATEGY Trial coupons offering a discounted price for any sandwich or wrap will be distributed by daily newspapers in major urban markets. In many cases, the daily newspapers offer reach well beyond their designated market area.

Consumers visiting a Mr. Sub restaurant during the first two months of the campaign will receive a coded entry form for a contest. Consumers must visit the Mr. Sub website to enter their contest code.

SALES PROMOTION EXECUTION

Trial Coupon A $1.50 coupon for the purchase of any sandwich or wrap (with a two-month expiry date) will be circulated. The initial coupon drop is timed for February/March.

Contest A grand prize and two secondary prizes will be awarded:

• Grand Prize: $25 000 cash.

• Second Prize: One of three all-expenses-paid ski trips for two to Whistler/Blackcomb (value: $5000 each).

• Third Prize: One of five Sony HDTV flat-screen televisions (value: $2000 each).

The contest is open to all residents of Canada, with winners randomly drawn from all entries received. Winners will be announced at the Mr. Sub website the day following the closing date of the contest. Complete contest details are available at the Mr. Sub website and all restaurant locations.

Trial Coupon A second wave of $1.50 coupons (with a two-month expiry date) will be distributed by national daily newspapers in the August/September period.

The coupon inserts will be distributed via daily newspapers in the following markets: Toronto, Hamilton, Vancouver, Ottawa, Calgary, Edmonton, Quebec City, Winnipeg, London, Kitchener, Halifax, Regina, Saskatoon, St. John's, and Windsor.

Coupon inserts will be distributed by community newspapers in the following markets: Oshawa/Whitby/Clarington, St. Catharines, Niagara Falls, Cambridge, Barrie, Kingston, Peterborough, and Sudbury.

For cost details on these sales promotion activities, see Figures A2.4 and A2.5.

Component	Circulation	Cost/M	Frequency	Total Cost
Distribution	2 785 000	$40	2	$222 800
Printing	2 785 000	$10	2	$55 700
Coupon Redemption*				$83 500
Total Cost				**$362 000**

* Circulation × Redemption Rate × Value of Coupon × Frequency = Coupon Cost
2 785 000 × .01 × $1.50 × 2 = $83 500

FIGURE
A2.4

Sales Promotion Costs for Coupon Inserts

Prize	# Winners	Prize Cost	Total Cost
Cash Grand Prize	1	$25 000	$25 000
Ski Trip	3	$5 000	$15 000
Sony HDTV Flat Screens	5	$2 000	$10 000
Total Cost			**$50 000**

FIGURE
A2.5

Sales Promotion Costs

ONLINE AND INTERACTIVE PLAN

OBJECTIVES

1. To increase brand awareness among teens and 20-something males.
2. To associate the Mr. Sub brand with a sporting activity popular with young urban males.

STRATEGY   A combination that involves online banner advertising, a combination television and online sponsorship, and a brand new website will help build awareness among the primary target and help associate the brand with an urban lifestyle.

EXECUTION

Banner Ads   Banners will be scheduled on the TSN and The Score sports websites, which are popular with a younger male audience.

Sponsorship   In conjunction with The Score television channel, Mr. Sub will sponsor a highlight segment shown once a week. Each Wednesday night during the last four months of the basketball season, The Score broadcasts a show called *NBA Court Surfing*. During the show, Mr. Sub will sponsor a segment called "Dunks of the Week" that features all the exciting dunks from the previous week's NBA action. The same video clip sponsored by Mr. Sub will be available on The Score's website, www.thescore.com.

Mr. Sub Website   An entirely new and exciting website will be constructed. The new site will offer essential product information and provide opportunities for consumers to engage in some entertaining activities. A selection of sports and action video games will be available for play at the site.

Refer to Figure A2.6 for online and interactive cost details.

EVENT MARKETING PLAN

To further develop the association between Mr. Sub and basketball, a street-level marketing event is planned in conjunction with the Toronto Raptors basketball team. This

Site	Impressions/Month	CPM	# Months	Total Cost
TSN.ca	500 000	$40	6	$120 000
thescore.com	125 000	$20	6	$15 000
Mr. Sub website				$200 000
Total Cost				**$335 000**

Note: Mr. Sub website costs include development and maintenance costs of the site.

event fits with the Raptors objective of being "more visible in the community" and provides an opportunity to generate positive publicity for the Raptors in the off-season.

OBJECTIVES

1. To encourage members of the primary target market to participate in a "3-on-3" basketball tournament.
2. To create buzz for Mr. Sub in a key urban market.

STRATEGY To associate Mr. Sub with the growing sport of basketball (playground, high school, college, and university level) in a key urban market.

To associate Mr. Sub with the Toronto Raptors (an exciting team that is creating its own "buzz" in Toronto, based on recent player acquisitions and performance).

EXECUTION

- The Mr. Sub Toronto Raptors 3-on-3 Tournament (straight elimination) will be held on half-size courts at Exhibition Place, Toronto, over one weekend in July.

- A predetermined number of teams (128 teams) will compete against each other in four age categories: 8 to 12 years; 13 to 16 years; 17 to 21 years; and 21 to 30 years. The youngest age category will attract the children of Mr. Sub's secondary target, while the older categories will attract the primary target. A total of 32 teams will be entered in each age category.

- Toronto Raptors players will participate in a skills competition to determine "the most skilled Raptor."

- Prizes will be awarded to each member of the winning team (five members on each team) in each category.

- Mr. Sub kiosks will be set up at the event to serve meals.

- The general public will be invited to the event, though all viewing of the games and Raptor skills competition will be on a "stand and watch" basis.

- A one-month outdoor ad campaign just prior to the event will create awareness and recruit teams for the event. A press release will also be issued to the media outlining all event-related details.

Cost details for this event marketing activity are included in Figure A2.7.

For summary details of all marketing communications expenditures and the timing of all activities, refer to Figures A2.8 through A2.11.

The marketing communications budget will be reviewed quarterly. Adjustments to the budget will be made when necessary.

Item or Activity	Estimated Cost
Equipment Rental	$50 000
Site Rental	$25 000
Bump-in (Setup)	$10 000
Staffing	$10 000
Security	$8 000
Bump-out (Teardown)	$10 000
Administration Costs	$15 000
Prizes	$40 000
Miscellaneous Costs	$10 000
Total Cost	**$178 000**

FIGURE A2.7

Event Marketing Costs

Activity	Expenditure	% of Total
Television	$969 500	32.2
Outdoor	$882 900	29.3
Magazine	$237 200	7.8
Sales Promotions (Coupons and Contest)	$412 050	13.7
Online and Interactive	$335 000	11.1
Event Marketing	$178 000	5.9
Total	**$3 014 650**	**100.0**

FIGURE A2.8

Marketing Communications Expenditures by Activity

Month	Expenditure	% of Total
January	$211 300	7.0
February	$708 900	23.5
March	$426 850	14.2
April	$169 150	5.6
May	$117 000	3.9
June	$398 700	13.2
July	$264 000	8.8
August	$261 050	8.7
September	$100 500	3.3
October	$144 300	4.8
November	$118 500	3.9
December	$94 400	3.1
Total	**$3 014 650**	**100.0**

FIGURE A2.9

Marketing Communications Expenditures by Month

FIGURE
A2.10

Marketing Communications Budget (Actual versus Plan)

Estimated Budget (Based on Activities)	$3 014 650
Plan Budget	$3 000 000
Expenditure Over Budget	$(14 650)

FIGURE
A2.11 **Marketing Communications Calendar**

Activity	Jan.	Feb.	Mar.	Apr.	May	June	July	Aug.	Sept.	Oct.	Nov.	Dec.
Television												
CTV	8	8	8	4	4				4	4		
TVA	5	5	5							5	5	
TSN	10	10					10				10	10
The Score	15	15	10	10					5	10		
The Score Sponsorship	←			→								
Outdoor												
Top 5 Markets		←→				←→						
Remaining Markets		←→				←→						
Magazines												
Maclean's				1		1	1		1			
Tribute						1		1		1		1
Inside Entertainment					1		1		1		1	
Sales Promotions												
Coupon Insert		←→						←→				
Contest		←→										
Online												
TSN.ca						←→					←→	
thescore.com		←→									←→	
Mr. Sub Website	←											→
Event Marketing												
3-on-3 Basketball							←→					

Notes:

Television: Figures represent the number of spots on each network each month. All spots are 30-seconds long and run in prime time.

Outdoor: Top five markets include Toronto/Hamilton, Vancouver, Ottawa, Calgary, and Edmonton. Remaining markets include Quebec City, Winnipeg, London, Kitchener, Halifax, Regina, and St. John's. All ads are outdoor posters.

Magazines: Figures indicate one insertion in each month scheduled (*Maclean's* is a weekly magazine; others are monthly). All ads are 1P, 4-colour.

Online: 500 000 impressions monthly on TSN.ca and 125 000 impressions monthly on the thescore.com.

Coupon Insert: Coupons will be distributed in key market daily newspapers or community newspapers. Dailies include: *Toronto Star, Toronto Sun, Vancouver Sun, Vancouver Province, Ottawa Citizen, Ottawa Sun, Calgary Herald, Calgary Sun, Edmonton Journal, Edmonton Sun, Regina Leader Post, Saskatoon Star Phoenix, Winnipeg Free Press, Hamilton Spectator, Kitchener Record, London Free Press, Windsor Star, Halifax Chronicle Herald,* and *St. John's Telegram.* Community newspapers include: *Oshawa/Whitby/Clarington This Week, St. Catharines News, Niagara This Week, Cambridge Times, Barrie Examiner Complimentary, Kingston This Week, Peterborough This Week,* and *Sudbury Northern Life.*

Glossary

Acquisition strategy – A plan of action for acquiring companies that represent attractive financial opportunities.

Ad view – See Impression.

Advergaming – The integration of brands into video games, which are either played online or on mobile devices, or purchased directly by consumers.

Advertising – A paid-for media-delivered message by an identified sponsor designed to stimulate a positive response from a target audience.

Advertising equivalency – A mathematical model that equates public relations to an advertising value by evaluating the space occupied by a public relations message in relation to advertising space.

Advertising objectives – Goal statements for advertisements that include quantitative measures related to behaviour or other relevant issues.

Advertising plan – A plan that includes creative and media components.

Agate line – A non-standardized unit of space measurement, equal to one column wide and 1/14" deep, used in newspaper advertising.

Ambush marketing – A strategy used by non-sponsors of an event to capitalize on the prestige and popularity of the event by giving the false impression they are sponsors.

Annual report – A document published annually by an organization primarily to provide current and prospective investors and stakeholders with financial data and a description of the company's operations.

Approach – The initial contact with a customer.

Arena and stadium advertising – Advertising within arenas and stadiums, from the door to the court, rink, or playing field.

Attitude – An individual's feelings, favourable or unfavourable, toward an idea or object.

Attribute – A descriptive feature of a product.

Backlit (backlight) poster – A luminous outdoor sign printed on polyvinyl material.

Banner – Online, a graphic advertising image (usually horizontal or vertical in shape) that appears on a webpage.

Behavioural targeting – A means of delivering online ads based on a consumer's previous surfing patterns.

Benefit – The value a customer attaches to a brand attribute.

Bid (bid price) – A predetermined maximum amount an advertiser is willing to pay for a click.

Big box – An online ad shaped like a large rectangle that offers greater width and depth to an ad.

Billboard – see Poster.

Blitz schedule – The scheduling of media advertising so that most spending is front-loaded in the schedule; usually involves a lot of money spent in a short period.

Blocking chart – See Media calendar.

Blog – A frequent, chronological publication of personal thoughts at a website.

Body language – See Non-verbal communication.

Bonus pack – The temporary offering of a larger package size (for example, 20 percent more) for the same price as the regular size.

Booklet (brochure) – A multiple-page document distributed to consumers and other interested stakeholders.

Borrowed-interest strategy – A plan to promote a marketing activity that is related to a product.

Bounce back – See Statement stuffer.

Brand – An identifying mark, symbol, word or words, or combination of mark and words that separates one product from another product; can also be defined as the sum of all tangible and intangible characteristics that make a unique offer to customers.

Brand democratization – A concept that states that consumers are now in charge of brand marketing (because of the amount of consumer-generated content produced and distributed online) instead of brand marketers being in control.

Brand design – A concept that attempts to include an experience in the design of a product (for example, the design may trigger an emotional response).

Brand development index (BDI) – The percentage of a brand's sales in an area in relation to the population in that area; determines if the brand is underdeveloped or overdeveloped in each area.

Brand equity – The value (monetary or otherwise) of a brand to its owners; influenced by brand name awareness, degree of customer loyalty, perceived quality, and the brand's association with a certain attribute.

Brand insistence – A situation where the consumer searches the market for the specific brand.

Brand logo – A symbol that plays a key role in branding and creating an image.

Brand loyalty – The degree of attachment to a particular brand expressed by a consumer. There are three stages of brand loyalty: brand recognition, brand preference, and brand insistence.

Brand manager – An individual assigned responsibility for the development and implementation of marketing programs for a specific product or group of products.

Brand name – That part of a brand that can be spoken.

Brand preference – The situation where a brand is perceived as an acceptable alternative by a customer and will be purchased if it is available.

Brand recognition – Customer awareness of the brand name and package.

Branded content (product integration) – The integration of brand name goods and services into the script (storyline) of a television show or movie. The brand name is clearly mentioned and sometimes discussed.

Breakage – See Slippage (breakage).

Broadsheet – A large newspaper with a fold in its middle.

Brochure – See Booklet.

Build-up schedule – The scheduling of media advertising so that the weight of advertising starts out light and gradually builds over a period of time; also called a teaser campaign.

Bump-in (setup) – The setting up of structures and other equipment at an event.

Bump-out (teardown) – The process of dismantling everything after an event.

Bus back – A vinyl wrap advertisement that appears on the back end of a vehicle.

Bus mural – An advertisement in the form of a vinyl covering that appears on one side of the vehicle.

Business-to-business (B2B) market – A market of goods and services needed to produce a product or service, promote an idea, or operate a business.

Buying centre – An informal purchasing process in which individuals in an organization perform particular roles but may not have direct responsibility for the actual decision.

Buying committee – A formal buying structure in an organization that brings together expertise from the various functional areas to share in the buying decision process.

Call centre – A central operation from which a company conducts its inbound and outbound telemarketing programs.

Catalogue – A reference publication, usually annual or seasonal, distributed by large retail chains and direct marketing companies.

Central theme – The glue that binds various creative elements of a campaign together; transferable from one medium to another.

Cinema advertising – Print advertising inside film theatres and broadcast advertising on screens; options include television-style ads on screen, slides, posters, and ads printed on tickets.

Circulation – The average number of copies per issue of a publication sold by subscription, distributed free to predetermined recipients, carried with other publications, or made available through retail distributors.

Circulation list – A publication's subscription list that targets potential customers based on specified demographic characteristics, interests, or activities.

Classified advertising – Print advertising in which similar goods and services are grouped together in categories under appropriate headings.

Click (clickthrough) rate – The percentage of impressions (ad views) that resulted in a click; determines the success of an ad in attracting visitors to click on it.

Clicks (clickthroughs) – The number of times users click on a banner (clicking transfers the user to another website).

Clickthroughs – See Clicks.

Clipping service – An organization that scans the print and broadcast media in search of a company's or brand's name.

Closed-ended questioning – See Fixed-response questioning.

Closing – Asking for the order at the appropriate time in a sales presentation.

Closing cue – An indication that the buyer is ready to buy; can be expressed verbally or nonverbally.

Cluster – Ads grouped in a block of time during a break in a program or between programs, or in a section of a publication.

Clutter – The amount of advertising in a particular medium.

Cognitive dissonance – A feeling of doubt or regret in a consumer's mind once a buying decision has been made.

Cold canvass – The process of calling on people or organizations without appointments or advance knowledge of them.

Collateral materials – Visual aids used by sales representatives in sales presentations, such as price lists, sales brochures, and digital materials.

Communication – The transmission, receipt, and processing of information between a sender and a receiver.

Compiled list – A direct mail list prepared from government, census, telephone, warranty, or other publication information.

Consultative selling – A form of selling that stresses open, two-way communication between a buyer and seller.

Consumer behaviour – The combined acts carried out by individuals choosing and using goods and services, including the decision-making processes that determine these acts.

Consumer promotion – An incentive offered to consumers to stimulate purchases or encourage loyalty.

Consumer-generated content – Online content, often brand oriented, that is created by consumers for consumers.

Contest – A promotion that involves awarding cash or merchandise prizes to consumers when they purchase a specified product.

Contingency plan – The identification of alternative courses of action that can be used to modify an original plan if and when new circumstances arise.

Continuity – The length of time required in an advertising medium to generate the desired impact on the target audience.

Continuity discount (print) – A discount offered to advertisers that purchase space in consecutive issues of a publication.

Continuity discount (television/radio) – A discount earned when purchasing a minimum number of spots over an extended period.

Controlled circulation – The circulation of a publication that is distributed free to individuals in a specific demographic segment or geographic area.

Cookie – An electronic identification tag sent from a web server to a user's browser to track the user's browsing patterns.

Co-op allowance – See Cooperative advertising allowance.

Cooperative advertising allowance (co-op allowance) – The sharing of advertising costs by suppliers and retailers or by several retailers.

Cooperative direct mail – A mailing containing specific offers from non-competing products.

Core values – The primary attributes and benefits a brand delivers to the customer.

Corporate advertising – Advertising (paid for) designed to convey a favourable image of a company among its various publics.

Corporate culture – The values, beliefs, norms, and practices shared by all employees of an organization.

Corporate discount – A discount based on the total number of pages purchased by a single company (all product lines combined).

Corporate objective – A statement of a company's overall goal; used to evaluate the effectiveness or ineffectiveness of a company's strategic plan.

Corporate plan – A strategic plan formulated at the executive level of an organization to guide the development of functional plans in the organization.

Corporate strategy – see Strategic planning.

Cost-per-click – An Internet advertising pricing strategy where advertisers pay based on the number of ad clicks received.

Cost per thousand (CPM) – The cost of delivering an advertising message to 1000 people; calculated by dividing the cost of the ad by the circulation in thousands.

Coupon – A price-saving incentive offered to consumers to stimulate quick purchase of a specified product.

CPM (online) – The price charged for displaying an ad 1000 times. The calculation for CPM is cost divided by impressions (number of impressions divided by 1000).

Creative brief – A document developed by a client organization that contains vital information about the advertising task at hand; it is a useful tool for discussions between the client and its advertising agency.

Creative concept – The basic sales message (a key idea) that an advertisement communicates through verbal and visual devices.

Creative execution – The stage of creative planning at which specific decisions are made regarding how to best present the message.

Creative objective – A statement that clearly indicates the information to be communicated to the target audience; usually involves a key benefit statement and a support claims statement.

Creative plan – A plan that outlines the nature of the message to be communicated to the target audience; involves the development of creative objectives, creative strategies, and creative execution.

Creative strategy – A plan of action for how the message will be communicated to the target audience, covering the tone and style of message, the central theme, and the appeal techniques.

Cross-coupon – See Cross-ruff.

Cross-ruff (cross-coupon) – A coupon packed in or with one product that is redeemable for another product. The product the coupon is packed with is the means of distributing the coupon.

Cross-tabulation – The comparison of answers to questions by various subgroups with the total number of responses.

Crowdsourcing – A technique that uses the collective intelligence of the public at large to complete business-related tasks a company would normally perform itself or outsource to a third-party provider.

Customer relationship management (CRM) – A process that enables an organization to develop an ongoing relationship with valued customers; the organization captures and uses information about its customers to its advantage in developing the relationship.

Data analysis – The evaluation of responses question by question; gives meaning to the data.

Data interpretation – The relating of accumulated data to the problem under review and to the objectives and hypotheses of the research study.

Data mining – The analysis of information to determine relationships among the data and enable more effective marketing strategies to be identified and implemented.

Data transfer – In marketing research, the transfer of answers from the questionnaire to the computer.

Database management system – A system that collects information about customers for analysis by managers to facilitate sound business decisions.

Day-after recall (DAR) test – Research conducted the day following the respondent's exposure to a message to determine the degree of recognition and recall of the advertisement, the brand, and the selling message.

Daypart – A broadcast time period or segment on radio or television.

Dealer display (point-of-purchase) material – Temporary display material placed in retail stores that advertises a product and encourages impulse purchasing.

Dealer premium – An incentive offered to a distributor to encourage the special purchase of a product or to secure additional merchandising support from the distributor.

Demographics – The characteristics of a population that include gender, age, education, income, occupation, and culture.

Demonstration – A sales technique that involves showing the product in action to portray its benefits to a buyer.

Diary system – A system to collect audience data where participants complete a seven-day log by recording the television viewing for all television sets in the household for each quarter hour of the day from 6 am to 2 am.

Digital (interactive) communications – The placement of an advertising message on a website, or an ad delivered by email or through mobile communications devices.

Dimensional mail – Direct mail that can take any form other than the typical flat piece of mail.

Direct competition – Competition from alternative products and services that satisfy the needs of a target market.

Direct mail – A printed form of direct response advertising distributed by Canada Post or independent delivery agents.

Direct marketing – A marketing system for developing products, sending messages directly to customers, and accepting orders through a variety of media, and then distributing the purchase directly to customers.

Direct response advertising – Advertising placed in a medium that generates an immediate and measurable response from the intended target.

Direct response communications – The delivery of a message to a target audience of one; the message can be distributed by direct mail, direct response television, or telemarketing.

Direct response print – A response-oriented ad delivered to prospects by magazines or newspaper advertisements.

Direct response television (DRTV) – Advertising that appears on television and encourages viewers to respond by telephoning a toll-free number, by mail, or online; often referred to as infomercials.

Directory database – A commercial database that provides information about a company (for example, size, sales, location, number of employees).

Divestment strategy – Selling off divisions or product lines that no longer fit the strategic direction an organization is taking.

Door card – A vertically oriented poster usually found beside the doors of subway cars and light rapid transit (LRT) commuter trains.

Double targeting – Market strategies that reach both genders effectively.

Editing stage – In marketing research, the review of questionnaires for consistency and completeness.

Elevator advertising – Advertising in display frames on elevator walls or on televisions mounted in the corner or above the door.

Encoding – The transformation of a message into a meaningful format, such as an advertisement, a mailing piece, or an article in a newspaper.

Endorsement – A situation where a celebrity speaks highly of an advertised product.

Engagement – The degree of involvement a person has with the media when using it.

Even schedule – The uniform schedule of media advertising over an extended period; also referred to as a continuous schedule.

Event marketing – The process, planned by a sponsoring organization, of integrating a variety of communications elements with a single event theme.

Event sponsorship – The financial support of an event in exchange for advertising privileges associated with that event.

Execution – See Tactics.

Expandable banner – A rich-media banner ad employing multiple panels that are launched when the banner is clicked on.

Experiential marketing – A form of marketing that creates an emotional connection with the consumer in personally relevant and memorable ways.

Experimental research – Research in which one or more factors are manipulated under controlled conditions while other elements remain constant so that the respondent's actions can be evaluated.

External publics – Those publics that are distant from an organization and are communicated with less frequently.

Eye movement–camera test – A test that uses a hidden camera to track eye movement to gauge the point of immediate contact in an advertisement, how the reader scans the ad, and the amount of time spent reading.

Feature – Tangible aspects of a product, such as durability, design, and economy of operation.

Field sales force – An organization's external sales representatives who regularly call on customers to pursue orders.

Fixed-response (closed-ended) questioning – Predetermined questions with set answers for the respondents to choose from.

Flight – A period of time in which advertising is scheduled.

Float – Money received by the issuer of a gift card without yet having offered any goods or services.

Floating ad – A rich-media ad that moves within a transparent layer over the page and plays with a specific area of the page.

Focus group – A small group of people with common characteristics brought together to discuss issues related to the marketing of a product or service.

Folder – A direct response sales message printed on heavy stock that can be mailed with or without an envelope; may be several pages in length.

Follow-up – Maintaining contact with customers to ensure that service has been satisfactory.

Format – The type and nature of the programming offered by a radio station.

Free sample – Free distribution of a product to potential users.

Free-standing insert (FSI) – A booklet featuring coupons, refunds, contests, or other promotional advertising distributed by direct mail or with newspapers, magazines, or other delivery vehicles.

Frequency – The average number of times an audience has been exposed to a message over a period of time, usually a week.

Frequency (online) – The number of times an ad is delivered to the same browser in a single session or time period. A site can use cookies to manage frequency.

Frequency discount (print) – A discounted page rate based on the number of times an advertisement runs.

Frequency discount (television/radio) – A discount earned by purchasing a minimum number of spots over a specified period.

Frequency distribution – The number of times each answer in a survey was chosen for a question.

Frequent buyer program – See Loyalty program.

Full wrap – An advertisement in the form of a vinyl covering that covers both sides and the back of the vehicle.

Game (instant-win promotion) – A promotional contest that includes a number of pre-seeded winning tickets; instant-win tickets can be redeemed immediately.

Gross rating points (GRPs) – An expression of the weight of advertising in a media schedule; calculated by multiplying reach by frequency.

Head-on positioning – A marketing strategy in which one product is presented as an equal or better alternative than a competing product.

Horizontal rotation – The placement of radio commercials based on the day of the week (same daypart on different days).

House list – An internal customer list.

Hypothesis – A statement of outcomes predicted in a marketing research investigation.

Image positioning – See Lifestyle positioning.

Impression (ad view) – An ad request that was successfully sent to a visitor. This is the standard way of determining exposure for an ad on the web.

Inbound telemarketing – The calls received by a company from consumers, whether to place an order, inquire about products or services, or in response to a toll-free telephone number promoted on a direct response television commercial.

Incentive – A free gift or offer included in a direct mail package.

Indirect competition – Competition from substitute products that offer the same benefit as another type of product.

Infomercial – A long commercial (for example, 10 to 30 minutes) that presents in detail the benefits of a product or service; usually includes a call to action such as a 1-800 number. See also direct response television.

Innovation positioning – A marketing strategy that stresses newness (based on a commitment to research and development) as a means of differentiating a company or a brand from competing companies and brands.

In-pack self-coupon – A coupon for the next purchase of a product that is packed inside the package or under a label.

Insert – A preprinted, free-standing advertisement (for example, a leaflet, brochure, or flyer) specifically placed in a newspaper or magazine.

Inside sales force – An internal group of sellers, often referred to as order takers, who accept orders from customers by telephone or other means.

Instantly redeemable coupon – A removable coupon often located on the package or a store shelf that is redeemable on the current purchase of the product.

Instant-win promotion – See Game.

Integrated marketing communications – The coordination of all marketing communications in a unified program that maximizes the impact on the intended target audience.

Interactive communications – The placement of an advertising message on a website, or an ad delivered by email or through mobile communications devices.

Internal publics – The publics with which an organization communicates regularly; can include employees, distributors, suppliers, shareholders, and customers.

Internet radio – Listening to radio broadcasts via the Internet.

Key benefit statement – A statement of the basic selling idea, service, or benefit promised the consumer by the advertiser; appears in the creative plan section of an advertising plan.

King poster – An oversized poster attached to the side of a bus.

Leaderboard (Super banner) – An ad that stretches across the entire top of a webpage.

Leadership positioning – A marketing strategy in which a product presents itself as a preferred choice among customers.

Leaflet – A one-page flyer that offers relevant information about a direct mail offer.

Lifestyle (image) positioning – A marketing strategy based on intangible characteristics associated with a lifestyle instead of tangible characteristics.

Line rate – The rate charged by newspapers for one agate.

List broker – A company specializing in finding or developing lists for direct response purposes; finds prospect lists based on target market criteria established by marketing organizations.

Local spot – Advertising bought from a local station by a local advertiser.

Location-based targeting – An effort to integrate consumers' location information into a marketing communications strategy.

Loyalty program (frequent buyer program) – A program that offers consumers a small bonus, such as points or play money, each time they make a purchase; the bonus accumulates and can be redeemed for merchandise or some other benefit.

Mail interview – In marketing research, the collection of information from a respondent by mail.

Mall poster – A form of advertising located inside shopping malls; relies on pedestrian traffic only.

Market share – The sales volume of one product or company expressed as a percentage of total sales volume in the market the company or brand is competing in.

Marketing communications plan – A plan that identifies how the various elements of marketing communications will be integrated into a cohesive and coordinated plan.

Marketing control – The process of measuring and evaluating the results of marketing strategies and plans, and of taking corrective action to ensure marketing objectives are achieved.

Marketing objective – A statement that identifies what a product will accomplish in a one-year period, usually expressed in terms of sales, market share, and profit.

Marketing plan – A short-term, specific plan of action that combines strategy and tactics.

Marketing planning – The analysis, planning, implementing, and controlling of marketing initiatives to satisfy target market needs and achieve organizational objectives.

Marketing research – A marketing function that links the consumer/customer/public to the marketer through information; the information is used to define marketing opportunities and problems, generate marketing strategies, evaluate marketing actions, and monitor performance.

Marketing strategy – A plan of action that shows how the various elements of the marketing mix will be used to satisfy a target market's needs.

Mass customization – The development, manufacture, and marketing of unique products to unique customers.

Media brief – A document that contains essential information for developing a media plan; used to stimulate discussion between a client and agency.

Media calendar (blocking chart) – A document that shows allocation of a brand's media budget according to time of year and type of medium; shows coordination of various media recommendations.

Media execution – The translation of media strategies into specific media action plans; involves recommending specific media to be used in the plan and negotiating the media buys.

Media kit – A package of relevant information associated with a product or organization that is distributed at a press conference.

Media objective – A statement that outlines what a media plan is to accomplish (who, what, when, where, or how).

Media plan – A document that outlines the relevant details about how a client's budget will be spent; it involves decisions about what media to use and how much money to invest in the media chosen to reach the target audience effectively and efficiently.

Media planning – Developing a plan of action for communicating messages to the right people (the target market), at the right time, and with the right frequency.

Media strategy – A plan for achieving the media objectives stated in the media plan; typically justifies the use of certain media.

Media-delivered coupon – Coupon packaged with another medium, such as newspapers, magazines, direct mail, in-store distribution, and the Internet.

Merge/purge – A process in which numerous mailing lists are combined and then stripped of duplicate names.

Microsite – An individual page or series of pages that is a supplement to a primary website.

Mid-roll ad – An ad placed during a video.

Mission statement – A statement of an organization's purpose and operating philosophy; provides guidance and direction for the operations of the company.

Modular advertising – Selling advertisements based on standardized sizes.

Monopolistic competition – A market in which there are many competitors, each offering a unique marketing mix; consumers can assess these choices prior to making a buying decision.

Motive – A condition that prompts an individual to take action to satisfy a need.

Mural advertisement – A hand-painted outdoor ad seen on the side of a building.

Need – The perception of the absence of something useful.

Negotiated rate – The rate ultimately paid by an advertiser as a result of negotiations between an ad agency and a particular medium.

Network advertising – Advertising from one central source broadcast across an entire network of stations.

New product development strategy – A marketing strategy that calls for significant investment in research and development to develop innovative products.

Newsletter – A document sent to a predetermined audience that contains news about an organization (for example, a newsletter sent to alumni of a school or to all employees of an organization).

Noise – Any potential form of disruption in the transmission of a message that could distort the impact of the message; competitive advertising or the clutter of advertising messages in a medium are forms of noise.

Non-probability sample – A sample of respondents who have an unknown chance of selection and are chosen because of factors such as convenience or the judgment of the researcher.

Non-verbal communication (body language) – The expression of thoughts, opinions, or information using non-verbal cues such as body movement, facial expressions, and eye contact.

Objection – An obstacle that a salesperson must confront during a sales presentation.

Objectives – Statements of what is to be accomplished in terms of sales, profit, market share, or other measures.

Observation research – A form of research in which the behaviour of the respondent is observed and recorded; may be by personal or electronic means.

Oligopoly – A market situation in which only a few brands control the market.

Online database – An information database accessible online to anyone with proper communications facilities.

Online selling – Using the Internet to conduct sales transactions.

Online sponsorship – A commitment to advertise on a third-party website for an extended period.

Online survey – In marketing research, using an online questionnaire to collect data from people.

On-pack self-coupon – A coupon that is printed on the outside of a package redeemable on the next purchase of the product.

Open-ended questioning – See Open-response questioning.

Open-response (open-ended) questioning – Space available at the end of a question where the respondents can add their comments.

Opinion-measure testing – A form of research yielding information about the effect of a commercial message on respondents' brand name recall, interest in the brand, and purchase intentions.

Opt-in list – A list of people who have agreed to receive messages via email.

Outbound telemarketing – Calls made by a company to customers to develop new accounts, generate sales leads, and even close a sale.

Overall goal – The objective of an advertising campaign.

Paid circulation – The circulation of a newspaper or magazine that is generated by subscription sales and newsstand sales.

Partnership selling – A strategically developed long-term relationship that involves selling products and providing comprehensive after-sales service and effective two-way communications to ensure complete customer satisfaction.

Pay-per-click advertising – See Search advertising.

Peer group – see Reference group.

Penetration strategy – A plan of action for aggressive marketing of a company's existing products.

Perception – The manner in which individuals receive and interpret messages.

Performance allowance – A discount offered by a manufacturer that encourages a distributor to perform a merchandising function on behalf of the manufacturer.

Permission-based email – Email sent to recipients who have agreed to accept email advertising messages.

Personal interview – The collection of information in a face-to-face interview.

Personal selling – Face-to-face communication involving the presentation of features and benefits of a product or service to a buyer; the objective is to make a sale.

Personality – A person's distinguishing psychological characteristics that lead to relatively consistent and enduring responses to the environment in which that person lives.

Podcasting – Audio programming that is downloadable to iPods and other portable digital media devices; allows the listener to tune in when it is convenient for them to do so.

Point-of-purchase material – See Dealer display material.

Population (universe) – In marketing research, a group of people with certain age, gender, or other demographic characteristics.

Portable people meter (PPM) – A form of electronic observation where electronic metering devices are carried by household members that register what is being watched on television every minute of every day.

Portal – A website that serves as a gateway to a variety of services such as searching, news, directories, email, online shopping, and links to other sites.

Position charge – The cost of requesting a preferred position in a newspaper.

Positioning – The selling concept that motivates purchase or the image that marketers desire a brand to have in the minds of consumers.

Positioning strategy statement – A summary of the character and personality of a brand and the benefits it offers customers.

Post-buy analysis – An evaluation of actual audience deliveries calculated after a specific spot or schedule of advertising has run.

Poster (billboard) – A common form of outdoor advertising; usually a picture-dominant advertisement with a minimum of copy.

Post-roll ad – An ad that appears after the video.

Post-testing – The evaluation and measurement of a message's effectiveness during or after the message has run.

Pre-approach – The gathering of information about customers before actually making sales contact.

Premium – An additional item given free, or greatly discounted, to induce purchase of the primary brand.

Pre-roll ad – An ad placed at the start of a video.

Presentation strategy – A plan of what to say to a customer in a sales presentation to identify customer needs, summarize benefits, and prepare for potential objections.

Press conference – A meeting called by an organization to present information to representatives of the media.

Press release – A document prepared by an organization containing public relations information that is sent to the media for publication or broadcast.

Pre-testing – The evaluation of commercial messages prior to final production to determine the strengths and weaknesses of the communications.

Price positioning – A marketing strategy based on the premise that consumers search for the best possible value given their economic circumstances.

Primary data – Data collected to resolve a problem and recorded for the first time.

Primary medium – A medium that receives the largest allocation of an advertiser's budget; the dominant medium in a media plan.

Primary research – The collection and recording of primary data.

Probability sample – A sample of respondents who are known to have an equal chance of selection and are randomly selected from the sampling frame.

Problem statement – A brief statement that summarizes a particular problem to resolve or an opportunity to pursue and serves as the focus of a marketing strategy.

Product advertising – Advertising that provides information about a branded product to help build its image in the minds of customers.

Product configuration – The bringing together of various products and services to form a solution for the customer.

Product differentiation strategy – A plan of action for communicating meaningful attributes and benefits of a product to a target market.

Product integration – See Branded content.

Product placement – The visible placement of brand name products in television shows, movies, radio, video games, and other programming.

Product seeding – Giving a product free to a group of trendsetters who promote the product to others by word of mouth.

Profile-matching strategy – A media tactic that involves matching the demographic profile of a product's target market with a specific medium that has a similar target profile.

Promotional advertising – Advertising that communicates a specific offer to encourage an immediate response from the target audience.

Prospecting – A procedure for systematically developing sales leads.

Public relations – A form of communications designed to gain public understanding and acceptance.

Publicity – News about an organization, product, service, or person that appears in the media.

Publisher's statement – A statement published by the Alliance for Audited Media (AAM) twice a year that is the authority on which advertising rates are based.

Pull – Demand created by directing promotional activities at consumers or final users, who in turn pressure retailers to supply the product or service.

Pulse schedule – A scheduling of media advertising in flights of different weight and duration.

Pupilometer test – A device that measures pupil dilation (enlargement) of a person's eye when reading; it measures emotional responses to an advertisement.

Push – Demand created by directing promotional activities at intermediaries, who in turn promote the product or service among consumers.

Push down banner – A rich-media banner ad that slides advertising out of the way to reveal additional content rather than covering it up.

Qualifying (a customer) – Assessing if a prospect needs a product, has the authority to buy it, and has the ability to pay for it.

Qualitative data – Data collected from small samples in a controlled environment; the data describe feelings and opinions on issues.

Quantitative data – Measurable data collected from large samples using a structured research procedure.

Quick response (QR) code – A two-dimensional barcode that can be scanned and read by smartphones to allow sharing of text and data.

Rating – Television and radio audience estimates expressed as a percentage of a population in a defined geographic area.

Reach – The total unduplicated audience exposed one or more times to a commercial message during a specific period (usually a week).

Reach plan – Rotation of commercials in various dayparts on radio according to a predetermined frequency.

Rebate – A predetermined amount of money returned directly to customers by the manufacturer after the purchase has been made.

Recall test – A test that measures an ad's impact by asking respondents to recall specific elements (for example, the selling message) of the advertisement; can be aided (some information provided) or unaided.

Recognition test – A test that measures a target audience's awareness of a brand, copy, or the advertisement itself after the audience has been exposed to the message.

Rectangle ad – A large ad, slightly wider than it is tall, on a webpage.

Redemption rate – The number of coupons returned expressed as a percentage of the number of coupons that were distributed.

Reference group (peer group) – A group of people who share common interests that influence the attitudes and behaviour of its members.

Referral – A recommendation by a current customer of a potential new customer to a sales representative.

Relationship selling – A form of selling with the goal of developing a plan of action that establishes, builds, and maintains a long-term relationship with customers.

Reliability (of data) – Degree of similarity of results achieved if another research study were undertaken under similar circumstances.

Remnant time – Unsold television inventory available at lower cost to an advertiser.

Repositioning – Changing the place a product occupies in the customer's mind, relative to competing products.

Research objective – A statement that outlines what the marketing research is to accomplish.

Response card – A card filled in, usually at the time of purchase, that collects information about customers that can be added to the organization's database.

Response list – A list of direct mail buyers who have previously made purchases based on direct response offers.

Retail advertising – Advertising by a retail store; involves advertising the store name, image, location, and the re-advertising of branded merchandise carried by the store.

Rich media – A form of online communication that includes animation, sound, video, and interactivity.

Rifle strategy – A strategy that involves using a specific medium that effectively reaches a target market defined by a common characteristic.

Rotation plan – The placement of commercials in time slots purchased on radio; can be vertical according to the time of day or horizontal according to the day of the week.

Run sheet – A schedule of daily events that shows the various dates, times, and locations of activities at an event.

Sales presentation – A persuasive delivery and demonstration of a product's benefits; shows buyers how the product's benefits will satisfy their needs.

Sales promotion – An activity that provides incentives to bring about immediate response from customers, distributors, and an organization's sales force.

Sales promotion plan – An action plan for communicating incentives to appropriate target markets at the right time.

Sample – A representative portion of an entire population that is used to obtain information about that population.

Sampling frame – A list used to access a representative sample of a population; it is a means of accessing people for a research study.

Satellite radio – A radio service that offers commercial-free programming for a monthly fee.

Search advertising (pay-per-click advertising) – An advertiser's listing is placed within or alongside search results in exchange for paying a fee each time someone clicks on the listing.

Seasonal schedule – Scheduling media advertising according to seasonal sales trends; usually concentrated in the pre-season or the period just prior to when the bulk of the buying occurs.

Secondary media – Media alternatives used to complement the primary medium in an advertising campaign; typically less money is allocated to these media.

Secondary research – Data compiled and published by others for purposes other than resolving a specific problem. In advertising, secondary sources are frequently used to gain access to media information that benefits media analysis and planning.

Selective direct mail – See Solo direct mail.

Selective spot – Commercial time during a network show that is allocated back to regional and local stations to sell; advertisers buy spots on a station-by-station basis.

Self-image – One's own idea about oneself and one's relationship with others.

Setup – See Bump-in.

Seventy poster – A small poster usually affixed to the back of a bus.

Shopper marketing – Understanding how consumers behave as shoppers in all channels (retail, catalogue, and web) and then targeting these channels with appropriate marketing communications to enhance the sales of a brand.

Shotgun strategy – A tactic involving the use of mass media to reach a loosely defined target audience.

Skip schedule – The scheduling of media advertising on an alternating basis, such as every other week or every other month.

Skyscraper – A vertical box-shaped ad that appears on a webpage.

Slippage – A situation in which a consumer collects labels in a promotion offer but fails to follow through and request the refund.

Slippage (breakage) – Gift cards that go unredeemed.

Slogan – A short phrase that captures the essence of an entire advertising campaign; it reflects the positioning strategy of the brand and is shown in all ads in all media.

Social media – Online tools that people use to share content, insights, experiences, and various media, thus facilitating conversations and interaction online between groups of people.

Social media network – A social website for example, Facebook and Twitter that connects people with different interests together.

Solo direct mail (selective direct mail) – A unique advertising offer mailed directly to a target audience by a marketing organization.

Spam – Unsolicited email.

Spectacular – See Superboard.

Spiff – An incentive offered to retail salespeople to encourage them to promote a specified brand of goods to customers.

Sponsored email – Email that includes a short message from a sponsor along with a link to the sponsor's website.

Sponsored post – A sponsored ad circulated by friends in a social network.

Sponsorship – The act of financially supporting an event in return for certain advertising rights and privileges.

Spot colour – The addition of one colour to an otherwise black-and-white newspaper or magazine ad.

Starch readership test – A post-test recognition procedure that measures readers' recall of an advertisement (noted), their ability to identify the sponsor (associated), and whether they read more than half of the written material (read most).

Statement stuffer (bounce back) – An ad or offer distributed in monthly statements or with the delivery of goods purchased by some form of direct response advertising.

Station domination – One advertiser purchases all advertising inventory available in a subway station.

Station poster – An advertisement located on the platform or at the entrance or exit of subways and light rail transit (LRT) systems.

Stickiness – A website's ability to keep people at the site for an extended period or to have them return to the site frequently.

Strategic alliance – A relationship between two companies where the resources of those companies are combined in a marketing venture for the purpose of satisfying the customers they share.

Strategic planning (corporate strategy) – The process of determining objectives (setting goals) and identifying strategies (ways to achieve the goals) and tactics (specific action plans) to help achieve objectives.

Strategic selling – A form of consultative selling that involves dealing with each customer as an individual, stressing that in the transfer of product information.

Strategies – Statements that outline how objectives will be achieved, such as the direction to be taken and the allocation of resources needed to proceed.

Streaming – Audio or video delivered online in small, compressed packets of data that are interpreted by a software player as they are received.

Street-level poster – A rear-illuminated unit consisting of two- or four-sided advertising faces, such as transit shelters and blocks or columns with advertising faces.

Subcultures – Subgroups within the larger cultural context that have distinctive lifestyles based on religious, racial, and geographical differences.

Super banner – See Leaderboard.

Superboard (spectacular) – Outdoor advertising that is larger than a normal poster and much more expensive to produce; can include extensions beyond borders and electronic messaging.

Support claims statement – A substantiation of the promise made in the key benefit statement; appears in the creative plan.

Survey research – The systematic collection of data by communicating with a representative sample by means of a questionnaire.

Sweepstakes – A chance promotion involving the giveaway of products or services of value to randomly selected participants.

SWOT analysis – An analysis procedure that involves an assessment of an organization's strengths, weaknesses, opportunities, and threats; strengths and weaknesses are internal variables, whereas opportunities and threats are external variables.

Tabloid – A smaller newspaper that is sold flat (not folded).

Tabulation – The process of counting various responses for each question in a survey.

Tactics (execution) – Action-oriented details that outline how a strategic plan will be implemented.

Tagline – A short phrase that captures the essence of an advertised message.

Target market – The group of persons for whom a firm creates and markets a product.

Targeting request – An ad placed to reach a specific target audience of a website, for which a premium is usually paid.

Teardown – See Bump-out.

Telemarketing – The use of telecommunications to promote the products and services of a business; involves outbound calls (company to customer) and inbound calls (customer to company).

Telephone interview – In marketing research, the collection of information from a respondent by telephone.

Test marketing – Placing a commercial, set of commercials, or print ad campaign in one or more limited markets that are representative of the whole to observe the impact of the ads on consumers.

Testimonial – An ad in which a typical user of the product presents the message.

Text messaging – The transmission of short text-only messages via cell phone.

Timeline Chart – A chart indicating when various planning activities start and finish.

Tip-in – An insert that is glued to a page in the publication using a removable adhesive.

Trade allowance – A temporary price reduction that encourages larger purchases by distributors.

Trade promotion – An incentive offered to channel members to encourage them to provide marketing and merchandising support for a particular product.

Trade show – An event that allows a company to showcase its products to a captive audience and generate leads.

Trademark – The part of a brand that is granted legal protection so that only the owner can use it.

Transient rate – A one-time rate, or base rate, that applies to casual advertisers.

Transit poster – A transit ad in the rack above the window or near the door of a bus or subway car.

Transmission – The sending of a message through a medium such as television, radio, newspapers, magazines, outdoor advertising, Internet, and so on.

Trial close – A failed attempt at closing a sale; the buyer said "no."

Unique selling point (USP) – The primary benefit of a product or service that distinguishes it from its competitors.

Unique visitor – The number of unduplicated visitors to a website during a specified period.

Universe – See Population.

Validity (of data) – A research procedure's ability to measure what it is intended to measure.

Venue marketing (venue sponsorship) – Linking a brand name or company name to a physical site, such as a stadium, arena, or theatre.

Venue sponsorship – See Venue marketing.

Verbal skills – Comfort and ability with speaking and listening.

Vertical rotation – The placement of radio commercials based on the time of day (within various dayparts).

Video messaging – The transfer of video messages and other content (for example, television shows) via cell phones and other personal electronic devices.

Video strip – A rich-media banner ad that shows a strip of video in the banner space but, when clicked on, expands to reveal the video and audio in a full-sized panel.

Viral marketing – Online marketing that encourages the receiver of a message to pass it along to others to generate additional exposure.

Visit – A sequence of page requests made by one user at one website. A visit is also referred to as a session or browsing period.

Volume discount – A discount linked to the dollar volume purchased over an extended period; the greater the volume purchased, the higher the discount.

Wallpaper ad – A large image that replaces the web background.

Washroom advertising – A mini-poster ad located in a public or institutional washroom; usually placed above the urinal or on the back of the stall door.

Webcasting (webisodes) – The production of an extended commercial presented on the web that includes entertainment value in the communications.

Webisodes – See Webcasting.

Window ad – A rich-media ad that downloads itself immediately and plays instantly when a page is loading.

Word-of-mouth marketing – The transfer of a product message by people (often using technology) to other people.

Index